RUSSIA

SWEDEN
FINLAND

ESTONIA
LATVIA
LITH.
BELARUS
POLAND
UKRAINE
MOLDOVA
CZECH
AUSTRIA HUNGARY
YUGOSLAVIA ROMANIA
BULGARIA
ALB.
ITALY GREECE
TUNISIA
LIBYA

KAZAKHSTAN

MONGOLIA

GEORGIA AZER.
ARM.
TURKEY

UZBEKISTAN
TURKMENISTAN
KYRGYZSTAN
TAJIKISTAN

N. KOREA
S. KOREA
JAPAN

PEOPLE'S REPUBLIC OF CHINA

PACIFIC

OCEAN

SYRIA
LEBANON
ISRAEL
JORDAN
IRAQ
IRAN
AFGHANISTAN
PAKISTAN
NEPAL
BHUTAN
TAIWAN

EGYPT
SAUDI
ARABIA
KUWAIT
QUATAR
U. ARAB EMIRATES
OMAN
INDIA
MYANMAR
BANGLADESH
LAOS
HONG KONG

CHAD
SUDAN
YEMEN
YEMEN (N)
DJIBOUTI
THAILAND
VIETNAM
PHILIPPINES

CENT. AFR. REPUB
ETHIOPIA
SOMALIA
SRI LANKA
KAMPUCHEA

CAMEROON
ZAIRE
UGANDA
KENYA
MALAYSIA
SINGAPORE
INDONESIA
NEW GUINEA

CONGO
RWANDA
BURUNDI
TANZANIA
SUMATRA
PAPUA
NEW GUINEA
SOLOMON ISLANDS

ANGOLA
ZAMBIA
MALAWI
MOZAMBIQUE
JAVA

NAMIBIA
ZIMBABWE
BOTSWANA
MADAGASCAR

AUSTRALIA

SWAZILAND
SOUTH
AFRICA
LESOTHO
TRANSKEI

INDIAN OCEAN

NEW ZEALAND

UNDERSTANDING POLITICS

IDEAS, INSTITUTIONS, AND ISSUES

The ideas of economists and political philosophers, both when they are right and when they are wrong, are more powerful than is commonly understood. Indeed the world is ruled by little else. Practical men, who believe themselves to be quite exempt from any intellectual influences, are usually the slaves of some defunct economist. Madmen in authority, who hear voices in the air, are distilling their frenzy from some academic scribbler of a few years back. I am sure that the power of vested interests is vastly exaggerated compared with the gradual encroachment of ideas. Not, indeed, immediately, but after a certain interval; for in the field of economic and political philosophy there are not many who are influenced by new theories after they are twenty-five or thirty years of age, so that the ideas which civil servants and politicians and even agitators apply to current events are not likely to be the newest. But, soon or late, it is ideas, not vested interests, which are dangerous for good or evil.

John Maynard Keynes

THIRD EDITION

UNDERSTANDING POLITICS

IDEAS, INSTITUTIONS, AND ISSUES

THOMAS M. MAGSTADT
UNIVERSITY OF NEBRASKA AT KEARNEY

AND PETER M. SCHOTTEN
AUGUSTANA COLLEGE

ST. MARTIN'S PRESS
NEW YORK

Senior Editor: **Don Reisman**
Development and Project Editor: **Douglas Bell**
Editorial Assistant: **Amy Horowitz**
Production Supervisor: **Alan Fischer**
Text and Cover Design: **Sheree L. Goodman**
Map Design and Preparation: **John Johnston**
Photo Research: **Barbara Salz**
Cover Photo: **Chris Michaels/FPG International Corp.**

For information, write:
St. Martin's Press, Inc.
175 Fifth Avenue
New York, NY 10010

ISBN: 0–312–05018–6

PREFACE

The world has witnessed profound changes since 1988, when the second edition of *Understanding Politics* was published. Consider only this: the very next year, a wave of democratic revolutions in eastern Europe swept away Communist regimes that had previously been impervious to popular pressures. These revolutions were spontaneous, but they would not have occurred in the absence of the radical reforms instituted by Mikhail Gorbachev in the Soviet Union. The abortive coup against Gorbachev in August 1991 led to the breakup of the Soviet Union a few months later. Where there was one sovereign state (widely hailed as a "superpower"), there were 15 in 1992. In a region long characterized by stultifying stability, there is now pervasive instability.

Thus the end of the Cold War has been accompanied by the geopolitical transformation of Europe and Asia. Moreover, the structure of international relations has changed fundamentally as well. No longer does the East-West division make sense. The North-South conflict still has some relevance, but the emergence of the newly industrialized countries (NICs) and the high degree of economic and political differentiation among the developing nations raises doubts about the validity of this notion too.

The structure of international politics has changed, but the nature of politics *on all levels* remains essentially the same. The struggle for power and justice continues, wars and civil strife persist, and the quest for political alternatives to anarchy or tyranny is ongoing in many parts of the world. There is no notable absence of injustice, intolerance, myopia, or human misery.

In the face of these difficulties, some voices call for a "new world order" or a new agenda with new priorities. But the old patterns of political behavior persist. Traditions do not change overnight. Human nature may not change at all. Underlying realities—struggles for power, ancient animosities, gross inequalities of wealth—do not seem to change much at all. The well-known French epigram is all too appropriate: the more things change, the more they stay the same.

Just as we cannot easily change the essence of politics, neither can we escape the consequences of politics. Indeed, the study of politics is fundamental to our understanding of history, society, and human nature itself. Yet too often students approach this study with apprehension or apathy. A successful introduction to politics, then, must balance two opposing objectives: (1) to dispel anxieties associated with the very idea of political science, especially for the uninitiated, and (2) to provide the intellectual stimulation needed to challenge more advanced students.

To achieve these two objectives, we seek throughout this book to demonstrate that the science and philosophy of politics falls within the liberal arts tradition. The phrase "science and philosophy of politics" points to one of the deepest cleavages within the discipline: Analysts who approach politics from the standpoint of science often stress the importance of power, whereas those who view it through the wide-angle lens of philosophy often emphasize the importance of justice. We believe that the distinction between power and justice—like that between science and philosophy—is too often exaggerated. Moral and political questions are usually inseparable. That is, the exercise of power in itself is not what makes an action political; rather, what makes the employment of power *political* are considerations about its proper and improper use or who benefits or suffers from it. Thus whenever questions of fairness are raised in the realm of public policy (for example, concerning such issues as abortion, capital punishment, or the use of force by police), the essential ingredients of politics are present. Excessive attention to either the concept of power or to morality is likely to confound our efforts to make sense of politics. For this reason, we have attempted to balance the equation, blending an awareness of power in general with an appreciation for the power of justice in specific instances.

Similarly, the dichotomy so often drawn between facts and values is misleading. Rational judgments, in the sense of reasoned opinions about what is good and just, are sometimes more definitive (or less elusive) than facts. (The statement "Adolf Hitler established an unjust political regime in Nazi Germany" is such a judgment.) Other value-laden propositions can be stated with a high degree of probability but not absolute certainty. (For example, "In the United States, a high incidence of poverty correlates with a high crime rate"). Still other questions of this kind may be too difficult or too close to call—in the abortion controversy, for example, does the right of a woman to biological self-determination outweigh the right to life of the unborn?

It makes no sense to ignore the most important questions in life simply because the answers are not easy. Even when the right answers are not obvious, it may be possible to recognize wrong answers—in itself a moderating force.

Throughout this book we have also tried to balance a keen awareness of contemporary political issues with the recognition that more enduring questions often underlie them. The issue of who would make the best mayor, governor, or president in any given election raises underlying questions about how we are to understand and define the qualifications for these high offices. Similarly, conflicts between specific nations (Serbia and Croatia, Armenia and Azerbaijan, Ethiopia and Somalia) raise general questions about why nations fight at all. Such questions are perennial. We have made a conscious effort to underscore this point by the copious use of carefully selected examples.

Although we have minimized the use of names and dates, political ideas cannot be discussed fruitfully in a historical vacuum. Our choice of historical examples throughout the book is dictated by a particular understanding of politics. We believe that some episodes in twentieth-century history (among them the October Revolution in Russia, the rise of National Socialism in Weimar

Germany, the breakup of colonial empires after World War II, the Cold War, the civil rights movement in the United States, and the collapse of communism in Europe) are so important and raise such fundamental questions that anyone who claims to be liberally educated must come to grips with their meaning.

We make no apology for the fact that some themes and events are discussed in more than one chapter: The world of politics is more like a seamless web than a chest of drawers. In politics as in nature, a given event or phenomenon often has many meanings and is connected to other events and phenomena in ways that are not immediately apparent. Emphasizing the common threads that run through the major political ideas, institutions, and issues helps beginning students make sense of seemingly unrelated bits and pieces of the political puzzle. Seeing how the various parts fit together is a big step toward understanding politics.

Our own political understanding has been influenced strongly by the liberal arts tradition in American higher education, with which we have long been associated both as students and as teachers. Consequently, this book reflects a high regard for the attitudes and attributes liberally educated individuals ought to display. These include the spirit of moderation that grows out of respect for the thoughtful opinions of others. For this reason the pages that follow also reflect a high regard for the values and traditions of the past. In this sense, our approach is conservative. However, readers will also discover that the book is decidedly liberal in that it encourages critical thinking and presents both sides of contemporary debates over controversial issues.

The Plan of the Book   This edition of *Understanding Politics* represents a thorough revision of the book, but we have again consciously sought to preserve the essence of the original work as we did in the second edition. The five-part structure of the second edition has been replaced by three parts in the new edition. Chapter 1 ("The Study of Politics") lays the groundwork for what follows and therefore stands alone.

Part I is titled "Political Systems in Comparative Perspective." Several of its chapters required extensive revision, but none so extensive as the one on communist political systems, which for obvious reasons bears little resemblance to its predecessor.

Part II, "Politics, Participation, and Civic Order," examines the political process, using the U.S. political system as a case study throughout. Chapters in this part of the book look at citizenship and political socialization, political participation (including opinion polling and voting behavior), political organization (political parties and interest groups), leadership, political ideologies (or divergent "approaches to the public good"), and contemporary public policy issues.

Part III, "Politics, Conflict, and World Order," contains chapters on revolution, terrorism, war, and international relations (principles and concepts), the international order (the evolving structure and changing context of world politics), and international organizations. The last three chapters introduce students to key concepts in the study of international relations, explore contemporary political patterns and problems, and examine international law and organizations.

We have retained the pedagogical features that characterized the first and second editions. Each chapter again offers an outline and a summary, highlighted key terms, review questions, and an annotated list of recommended reading. Numerous maps, drawings, tables, and photographs help bring the narrative to life. Finally, students who are interested in careers in political science can be encouraged to consult the afterword.

Acknowledgments Motivation to write a textbook invariably comes from a variety of sources, not the least of which, in our case, was the stark necessity we faced many years ago to teach a course called "Introduction to Politics." We soon discovered that there were (and are) no generally accepted method, no well-defined body of materials, and no magic formula for success. The challenge of teaching, then, led to intense series of discussions in which we compared notes, exchanged ideas, and frequently argued about politics. We hope that the panoply of ideas in this book will encourage students to cultivate a greater appreciation for the importance of politics in human affairs. We hope, too, that it will persuade colleagues in political science departments at other institutions that an introductory course ought to be an essential element in every undergraduate political science curriculum.

We wish to acknowledge the help of those who assisted with previous editions of this book, including Professors George Bowles, John Bylsma, James Meader, and Richard Stevens.

Among those who offered helpful suggestions during the revision of *Understanding Politics* were William Anderson, Western Illinois University; Elizabeth Crozier, Indiana University; Ethan Fishman, University of South Alabama; Melvin Kulbicki, York College of Pennsylvania; William Mangun, East Carolina University; and Norma C. Noonan, Augsburg College. Particularly helpful for this edition were the suggestions of Professors Paul Zagorski and Joseph Dondelinger. We also gratefully appreciate the help of student assistants, especially Patricia Bonderman and Teresa Fisher, and we would like to thank Susan Hansen, who compiled the Instructor's Manual for the third edition. We would like particularly to thank Doug Bell, development and project editor at St. Martin's Press, for his patience, help, and good counsel for this edition, as well as the many talented professionals who assisted in the preparation of this edition—Amy Horowitz, Bruce Emmer, Andrew Goldwasser, and Alan Fischer.

Finally, we owe a large debt of gratitude to our families. Without the patience, support, and encouragement of our wives, Mary Jo (who died in 1990) and Bernice, and our children, David and Cheryl, it is unlikely that the idea for this book would ever have come to fruition.

Thomas M. Magstadt
Peter M. Schotten

Note to Instructors We would like to note the availability of an instructor's manual that contains approximately 600 test questions. The manual is available in both print form and in a format for IBM-compatible and Macintosh computers. For more information, please call or write St. Martin's Press, College Desk, 175 Fifth Avenue, New York, NY, 10010; or contact your local St. Martin's sales representative.

CONTENTS

UNDERSTANDING POLITICS

IDEAS, INSTITUTIONS, AND ISSUES

CHAPTER 1

THE STUDY OF POLITICS

AN INTRODUCTION

CHAPTER OUTLINE

Basic Concepts of Politics
Order • Power • Justice

Politics and Everyday Life
The Pervasiveness of Politics • The Pursuit
of Justice

How Politics Is Studied
For What Purposes? • By What
Methods? • From What Perspective?

Why Study Politics?
Self-interest • Self-improvement •
Self-knowledge

(Sepp Seitz/Woodfin Camp)

THE OTHER DAY we heard about the unhappy exploits of a student named Joe. Sitting in his introductory political science class day after day, Joe heard his professor discuss challenges facing Europe in the 1990s, the recent history of warfare and strife in the Middle East, and the division of opinion in Congress over American foreign policy in the post–Cold War era. Since Joe had never been to Europe, did not know the Middle East from the Middle West, and had always thought that the Cold War had something to do with the Ice Age, nothing about the course interested him. In fact, Joe had no interest whatsoever in politics or foreign policy. Nor did he care about state or local politics. Political science was, in a word, boring.

This particular day when Joe left class he went to his campus mailbox. Inside was a letter from the financial aid office informing him that his educational aid package for next year had been reduced by a federal government budget freeze.

Since Joe was not familiar with this legislation (or any other legislation, for that matter), he was in a quandary. Not knowing what to do, he decided to call his girlfriend. However, he could not get the pay phone to work (the state Public Utilities Commission had authorized a 10-cent increase, which Joe, of course, had failed to notice). Frustrated and angry, he trudged through the snow to his car, intending to drive to his girlfriend's apartment in search of sympathy and soothing words. Unfortunately, Joe's car was no longer where he had parked it. It had been towed away under the city's new snow emergency plan, which had been adopted the week before. You guessed it: Joe had not gotten the word.

BASIC CONCEPTS OF POLITICS

Our example is purely hypothetical, but it illustrates an important point. Our day-to-day lives are affected much more than we realize by the actions and policies of governments. To understand better the role of politics in society, we need to begin with a brief examination of three fundamental concepts: order, power, and justice.

Order

Simply stated, the study of *politics* seeks to understand how human life in the aggregate is ordered. Almost always, it begins by identifying a specific kind of social order commonly known as a community.

Community A *community* is an association of individuals who share a common identity. Usually that identity is at least partially defined by geography because people who live in close proximity often know each other, enjoy shared experiences, speak the same language, and have similar values and interests. Sometimes a new community can be created by instilling a sense of common purpose or a single political allegiance among otherwise diverse groups, but, as the breakup of the Soviet Union and Yugoslavia in the early 1990s illustrates, such an undertaking is extremely difficult. Whatever their origins, however, communities arise to fulfill a wide variety of social functions (such as physical security, economic prosperity, cultural enrichment) that cannot be met by individuals acting on their own.

Not all communities are equally self-sufficient. Some are geographic or administrative subdivisions of larger communities. Both the city of Detroit and the state of Michigan, for example, are communities, but they are also administrative subdivisions of a more comprehensive (and more self-sufficient) community, the United States of America.

Government   Every community is maintained and perpetuated by a political order, or *government,* which is why the study of politics focuses on institutions and processes associated with governance. Whenever a government successfully asserts its claim to rule (that is, to *make* the rules) within a given territory, it is said to possess *sovereignty.* Sovereign states exercise *authority,* meaning that they command the obedience of society's members. Moreover, they enjoy *legitimacy* to the extent that their claim to rule is willingly accepted. Such acceptance, of course, is most likely when the rulers uphold moral and political principles that are embraced by the ruled. The term *legitimacy* is easy enough to define; it is a much more difficult task, however, to determine whether a particular government is, in fact, legitimate.

Nation-State   The most important modern form of political organization is the *nation-state.* A *nation* is a distinct group of people who share a common background, including any or all of the following: geographic location, history, racial or ethnic characteristics, religion, language, culture, and belief in common political ideas. Geography heads this list because members of nation-states typically exhibit a strong collective sense of belonging that is associated with a particular territory or motherland for which they are willing to fight and die if necessary. Nations vary in terms of age and homogeneity (similarity among members). The older and more homogeneous a nation is, the more likely it will be to display commonalities in all or most of the elements just listed. Poland, for example, is an extremely homogeneous nation, whereas the United States—more recently formed and comprised of immigrants from all over the world—is necessarily more diverse. Both, however, are nations because the vast majority of their populations have been fully assimilated into their respective societies. By contrast, the Soviet Union and Yugoslavia have failed as nation-states, in part, because their diverse ethnic groups were not fully assimilated. Both experienced great turmoil associated with the multinational character of their populations.

The term *state* denotes the existence of a viable, sovereign government exercising authority and power in the name of society. In the language of politics, a state is usually synonymous with *country* (and, in everyday language, is used synonymously with *nation*). France, for instance, may be called either a state or a country. Yet in certain federal systems of government, a state is an administrative subdivision, such as New York, Florida, Texas, or California in the United States. Thus the concept of the modern nation-state avoids a certain amount of semantic and conceptual confusion.[1]

The nation-state is the most distinctive and largest self-sufficient political configuration in the modern world. It is also the most consequential. Its actions and reactions affect not only the welfare and destiny of its own people but also the fate of peoples in other lands.

Power

Governments cannot maintain peace, guarantee security, promote economic growth, or pursue effective policies without *power.* The effective exercise of authority involves much more, however, than the ability to use physical force. Indeed, the sources of power are many. An overwhelming election mandate, a gift for eloquent oratory, vast wealth, or a vigilant secret police all represent quite different sources of power. Of course, the more abundant the power sources (or resources), the greater the capabilities of government. Weak governments often cannot do much harm (at least not directly), but they seldom can do much good either.

Power can never be equally distributed in any society or state. Yet the need to concentrate power in the hands of a few inevitably raises questions, doubts, and sometimes suspicions among the many. Who wields power and whether power is exercised effectively are important to the common welfare. Thus the question "Who rules?" may give rise to a highly controversial political issue. Sometimes the answer is simple; one only has to look at a nation's constitution and observe the workings of its government. But it may be difficult to determine who *really* rules when the government is cloaked in secrecy or when, as is often the case, informal patterns of power deviate sharply from the formal structures of authority outlined in the nation's basic law.

In any nation-state, the number of people holding political office and exercising power is minuscule compared to the population at large. No less important than the question "Who rules?" and how effectively is the issue of whether political power is wielded justly.

Justice

The fact that the governors are always vastly outnumbered by the governed gives rise to competing—and sometimes conflicting—claims regarding the fairness of a government's policies and programs. It is often asserted that the rule of some citizens over others can be accepted only if the public interest is significantly advanced in the process. Thus the exercise of power must be tempered by the question of *justice:* Is power exercised in the interest of the ruled or merely for the sake of the rulers? For more than 2,000 years, political observers have maintained the distinction between the public-spirited exercise of political power on the one hand and self-interested rule on the other; this attests to the importance of justice in political life.

Not all states allow questions of justice to be raised; in fact, throughout history most have not. Even today, some governments brutally and systematically repress political discussion and debate because they fear that if public attention focuses on basic issues of justice and the common good, the legitimacy of the existing political order might come under attack. All too often, criticism of the *way* the government rules may call into question its moral or legal *right* to rule. This is one reason why political liberty is important. The map shown in Figure 1-1 indicates the degree of political freedom found in each country in January 1992, as measured by Freedom House.

Although questions of public morality may be suppressed, they can never be extinguished. Questions about which ruler is legitimate or what policy is desirable naturally crop up in everyday conversation. This fact seems to stem from human nature itself. The Greek philosopher Aristotle (384–322 B.C.) observed that, in contrast to animals, who can only make sounds signifying pleasure and pain, human beings use reason and language "to declare what is advantageous and what is just and unjust." Therefore, "it is the peculiarity of man, in comparison with the rest of the animal world, that he alone possess a perception of good and evil."[2] Thus the same human faculties that make moral judgment possible also make political discussion necessary.

POLITICS AND EVERYDAY LIFE

Politics, then, is all about the way human beings are governed, which involves order, power, and justice. However, as we have suggested (remember Joe?), politics is more than an abstract study. Whether or not we are aware of it, opinions and attitudes about the uses and abuses of power almost always inform our judgments regarding the government's day-to-day performance. As the following two hypothetical examples show, even the routine concerns of everyday politics cannot be divorced from their proper political context.

A man named John Doe, who has confessed to two rapes, several armed robberies and assaults, and a variety of lesser sex offenses too numerous to mention, is released from prison by a district court judge on a legal technicality. Doe, who has been undergoing psychiatric examination at a state mental facility, announces to the press that he is a changed man, that he has found religion, and that he hopes to return to his hometown of Pleasantville and resume a normal life. The same week he comes back to town several brutal rapes occur in Pleasantville. Although there is no reason whatever to believe that Doe is responsible for these crimes, local residents are up in arms. The latest rapes serve to reinforce their opinions that (1) dangerous criminals lurk in their midst; (2) it is very difficult to apprehend such criminals, no matter how boldly and frequently they strike; and (3) even when apprehended, self-confessed robbers, murderers, and rapists sometimes go free because of quirks in our system of justice. The people of Pleasantville vow to hold the judges and politicians responsible for the terror that envelops their town each night. "There is something wrong with a legal system that allows things like this to happen," they tell each other.

An old woman named Mary Smith, who just turned 90, lives alone in the house she and her husband built in a little northern Minnesota community nearly 65 years ago. Smith is still capable of caring for herself and refuses to move to a retirement home. Because her wants and needs are simple, she managed to get along quite nicely on her modest pension until the price of fuel oil (with which she heats her home) skyrocketed. Since then, her savings, like those of many senior citizens trying to take care of themselves, have dwindled with each passing year. The past two winters,

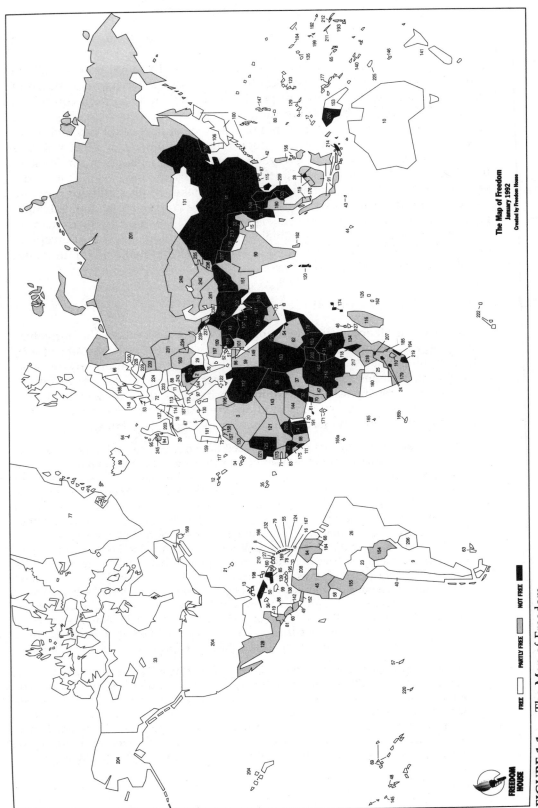

FIGURE 1-1 The Map of Freedom

SOURCE: Copyright © 1992. Freedom House, 48 East 21st Street, New York, NY 10010.

The Map of Freedom—1992

FREE STATES

9	Argentina
10	Australia
11	Austria
13	Bahamas
15	Bangladesh
16	Barbados
18	Belgium
19	Belize
20	Benin
23	Bolivia
25	Botswana
26	Brazil
29	Bulgaria
33	Canada
35	Cape Verde Isls.
40	Chile
49	Costa Rica
51	Cyprus (G)
52	Cyprus (T)
223	Czechoslovakia
53	Denmark
55	Dominica
56	Dominican Republic
58	Ecuador
230	Estonia
66	Finland
67	France
71	The Gambia
72	Germany
76	Greece
78	Grenada
86	Honduras
88	Hungary
89	Iceland
94	Ireland
96	Israel
97	Italy
99	Jamaica
100	Japan
104	Kiribati
106	Korea (S)
228	Latvia
229	Lithuania
114	Luxembourg
122	Malta
123	Marshall Islands
126	Mauritius
129	Micronesia
131	Mongolia
180	Namibia
135	Nauru
136	Nepal
137	Netherlands
141	New Zealand
148	Norway
153	Papua New Guinea
224	Poland
159	Portugal
166	St. Christopher-Nevis
167	St. Lucia
169	St. Vincent and the Grenadines
171	Sao Tome & Principe
243	Slovenia
177	Solomon Isls.
181	Spain
186	Sweden
187	Switzerland
195	Trinidad & Tobago
199	Tuvalu
203	United Kingdom
204	United States
206	Uruguay
140	Vanuatu
208	Venezuela
212	Western Samoa
217	Zambia

RELATED TERRITORIES

4	Amer. Samoa (US)
5	Andorra (Fr-Sp)
7	Anguilla (UK)
138	Aruba (Ne)
12	Azores (Port)
21	Bermuda (UK)
27	Br. Vir. Is. (UK)
34	Canary Isls. (Sp)
36	Cayman Isls. (UK)
157	Ceuta (Sp)
39	Channel Isls. (UK)
43	Christmas Is. (Austral.)
44	Cocos (Keeling Isls.) (Austral.)
48	Cook Isls. (NZ)
57	Rapanui/Easter Is. (Chile)
63	Falkland Is. (UK)
64	Faeroe Isls. (Den)
68	French Guiana (Fr)
69	French Polynesia (Fr)
222	French Southern & Antarctic Terr. (Fr.)
75	Gibraltar (UK)
77	Greenland (Den)
79	Guadeloupe (Fr)
80	Guam (US)
95	Isle of Man (UK)
113	Liechtenstein (Swz)
117	Madeira (Port)
127	Mahore (Fr)
124	Martinique (Fr)
158	Melilla (Sp)
130	Monaco (Fr.)
132	Montserrat (UK)
139	Ne. Antilles (Ne)
225	New Caledonia (Fr)
145	Niue (NZ)
146	Norfolk Is. (Austral.)
147	No. Marianas (US)
17	Belau (Palau) (US)
220	Pitcairn Islands (UK)
160	Puerto Rico (US)
162	Reunion (Fr)
165	St. Helena and Dependencies (UK)
165a	Ascencion
165b	Tristan da Cunha
168	St. Pierre-Mq. (Fr)
170	San Marino (It)
192	Tokelau (NZ)
198	Turks & Caicos. (UK)
210	Virgin Isls. (US)
211	Wallis & Futuna Isls. (Fr)

PARTLY FREE STATES

2	Albania
3	Algeria
6	Angola
8	Antigua & Barbuda
237	Armenia
238	Azerbaijan
14	Bahrain
233	Belarus
22	Bhutan
37	Central African Republic
45	Colombia
46	Comoros
47	Congo
244	Croatia
59	Egypt
60	El Salvador
62	Ethiopia
65	Fiji
70	Gabon
81	Guatemala
83	Guinea-Bissau
84	Guyana
90	India
91	Indonesia
98	Ivory Coast
101	Jordan
240	Kazakhstan
235	Kyrgystan
109	Lebanon
110	Lesotho
116	Madagascar
119	Malaysia
121	Mali
128	Mexico
234	Moldova
133	Morocco
134	Mozambique
142	Nicaragua
143	Niger
144	Nigeria
151	Pakistan
152	Panama
154	Paraguay
155	Peru
156	Philippines
163	Romania
201	Russia
173	Senegal
175	Sierra Leone
176	Singapore
179	South Africa
182	Sri Lanka
184	Suriname
185	Swaziland
42	Taiwan (China)
236	Tajikistan
190	Thailand
193	Tonga
196	Tunisia
197	Turkey
241	Turkmenistan
231	Ukraine
242	Uzbekistan
73	Yemen
218	Zimbabwe

RELATED TERRITORIES

87	Hong Kong (UK)
245	Northern Ireland
115	Macao (Port)
221	Western Sahara (Mor)

NOT FREE STATES

1	Afghanistan
28	Brunei
205	Burkina Faso
30	Burma (Myanmar)
31	Burundi
102	Cambodia
32	Cameroon
38	Chad
41	China (PRC)
50	Cuba
54	Djibouti
61	Equatorial Guinea
239	Georgia
74	Ghana
82	Guinea
85	Haiti
92	Iran
93	Iraq
103	Kenya
105	Korea (N)
107	Kuwait
108	Laos
111	Liberia
112	Libya
118	Malawi
120	Maldives
125	Mauritania
150	Oman
161	Qatar
164	Rwanda
172	Saudi Arabia
174	Seychelles
178	Somalia
183	Sudan
188	Syria
189	Tanzania
191	Togo
200	Uganda
202	United Arab Emirates
209	Vietnam
215	Yugoslavia
216	Zaire

RELATED TERRITORIES

24	Bophuthatswana (SA)
219	Ciskei (SA)
214	East Timor (Indo.)
232	Eritrea
226	Irian Jaya (Indo.)
227	Kashmir (India)
149	Occupied Territories (Isr.)
213	Tibet (China)
194	Transkei (SA)
207	Venda

This map is based on data developed by Freedom House's *Comparative Survey of Freedom*. The *Survey* analyzes factors such as the degree to which fair and competitive elections occur, individual and group freedoms are guaranteed in practice, and press freedom exists. In some countries, the category reflects active citizen opposition rather than politcal rights granted by a government. More detailed and up-to-date *Survey* information may be obtained from Freedom House.

which were severe even for northern Minnesota, have nearly wrecked Smith's personal finances. Then Smith gained new hope from a newspaper article that stated that the federal government had enacted a law providing fuel oil subsidies to the elderly. When she called the toll-free number in the telephone directory, however, she was informed that if she had any savings left in the bank, she was not eligible for a subsidy. Now Smith is desperate. "What will become of me?" she asks. "The government will not be satisfied until I am penniless and homeless. Where is the justice in this world?"

The cases of John Doe and Mary Smith illustrate how the practical problems of everyday politics, which at first glance may appear to affect only one individual, become inextricably bound up with the perpetual quest for what is fair or just in light of the public interest. In other words, issues are more or less political to the extent that the use of public power affects the lives and well-being of private citizens.

The Pervasiveness of Politics

Sometimes it is impossible in the abstract to predict the extent to which a given question will become political. Under the right circumstances, even an ordinarily mundane decision can become highly politicized. Consider the following hypothetical case:

The city council in a small midwestern town with trees stricken by Dutch elm disease must decide where to plant several hundred Marshall seedless ash trees that have just been purchased with the local taxpayers' dollars. After 12 hours of continuous deliberations that produce nothing but deadlock, the mayor, angry and exasperated, storms out of the meeting, muttering under her breath, "I wish I had never heard of ash trees."

The issue involved here (tree planting) usually would be thought of as "political" only in the sense that government must render a decision. In this particular town, however, this seemingly insignificant matter has suddenly become a source of conflict. Controversy abounds. Members of the city council may act for the best or worst reasons. They may desire to help friends and relatives beautify their streets, or they may wish to pay back political debts. They may genuinely favor a particular plan on aesthetic or other grounds, or they may want to "rehabilitate" a deteriorating neighborhood. They may even view the whole matter as a public relations sideshow.

Whatever their motives, however, the members of the city council must deal with an issue that has assumed, in the eyes of the public, communitywide significance. What course of action will do the most good for the community as a whole, both now and in the future? At the council meeting, a number of competing claims were put forward. Business representatives argued that the trees should be planted downtown or in shopping mall areas, to attract out-of-town shoppers. Residents from the town's older areas (where trees are dying off fast) made a plea for replacing their fallen elms. Still other residents contended that the trees were most badly needed in the town's new housing developments. After all, as one citizen pointed out, years ago the city had planted trees in the

Citizens of local governments are often encouraged to voice their concerns to elected or appointed government officials regarding proposed legislation and to help determine if the legislation is consistent with the general good of the community. (George Bellerose/Stock, Boston)

boulevards and parkways of the then-fashionable parts of town, and it would only be fair to do the same thing for owners in the community's new neighborhoods.

When considering these "special interests," the council has a public duty to determine which interests are most consistent with the general good of the community. No matter how trivial the issue may seem to an outsider, both the decision itself and the manner in which it is made will affect neighborhood pride, civic spirit, the mood of the taxpayers—all significant aspects of political life.

The Pursuit of Justice

The tree-planting example illustrates how an ordinary city council decision can become highly politicized. But some decisions are intrinsically political; in such cases, the exercise of public power raises important moral questions. Suppose, for example, that Congress were debating a law that would require the federal government to award contracts only to businesses that hire minority applicants at a rate of twice the minority representation in the local community or region. Whether or not a business has actually practiced race discrimination would be irrelevant under the proposed law, which is intended solely to redress the invidious treatment that some minorities have suffered for centuries in the United States. The bill would provide a combination of special training and job preference for designated minority members—at substantial cost to the taxpayers. Obviously, this effort to ensure compensatory benefits for various minorities would disadvantage white workers, who as individuals may well be totally innocent of racial prejudice or wrongdoing. Such legislation would inevitably be controversial, because it would raise a fundamental question of fairness involving the rights of some citizens and the responsibilities of others.

It is clear that a minority jobs program for the whole nation presents a far more politically significant question than tree planting in a single locality does. In the first place, the scope of the legislation is much broader in the former case than in the latter. Obviously, congressional legislation mandating job hiring would affect far more people than a small town's decision to plant or not plant a few hundred ash trees. Then, too, the individual impact of the legislation in the jobs program example is much greater; jobs are generally more critical in people's lives than trees (unless one happens to have a job planting trees). But its scope and impact alone cannot account for the great intensity of feeling that the congressional legislation would surely provoke. A spirited public debate in this case would reflect the keen interest taken by the ordinary citizen in the proposed legislation, not simply because many people would be affected by the bill but also because many of the people most directly affected would believe that they had been unequally, and therefore unfairly, treated.

Thus although considerations of justice are present in both the tree-planting and the jobs program examples, the basic question of fairness is raised in a much more significant way in the latter case. Each side in the jobs program controversy could argue with equal conviction that the idea of equal rights under the law directly supports its position. Advocates of the bill might well argue that the law would provide historically disadvantaged minorities with the long-overdue equal opportunity to obtain not only good jobs but also, ultimately, comfortable and productive lives. In rebuttal, opponents would probably contend that good and decent citizens would be denied jobs and would be treated unequally for no reason other than the accident of racial or ethnic origin, a factor over which they have no control.

The fact that practical questions in the everyday life of a community or society frequently reflect important principles such as equality and justice explains why such questions are political. Governmental decisions are therefore significant politically not only to the extent that they affect large numbers of people or that they help some and harm others but also insofar as they touch directly on fundamental questions of justice and morality.

HOW POLITICS IS STUDIED

Many regard the Greek philosopher Aristotle as the first true political scientist.[3] Not only did he write about the nature of politics, but he also described different political orders and suggested a scheme for classifying and evaluating them. For Aristotle, *political science* simply meant political investigation; thus a political scientist was one who sought, through systematic inquiry, to understand the truth about politics. In this sense, Aristotle's approach to studying politics more than 2,000 years ago has much in common with what political scientists do today. Yet the discipline has changed a great deal since Aristotle's time.

Today, there is no consensus on how politics can best be studied. The result is a fragmented discipline with different political scientists choosing different approaches, asking different kinds of questions, and addressing different audiences. The fragmentation is not necessarily bad. Rather, it reflects the diversity and vitality of the discipline, as well as the vast universe of human activity with which modern-day political science must deal. The following pages explore why and how contemporary political scientists study politics.

For What Purposes?

In one sense, the study of politics is no different from the study of biology, history, or psychology. Just as students in each discipline seek the truth about their respective subjects, so political scientists attempt to understand the truth about political things.

Besides gaining knowledge for its own sake, practical advantages accompany the disciplined study of politics. A political scientist who examines interest groups in the United States not only possesses a great deal of information about the number, composition, and influence of interest groups but is also able to advise such groups about how to become more effective. Similarly, an expert in modern-day international relations is not only aware of various treaties the United States has signed and ratified over the past 25 years but can also offer advice regarding the implications and long-term consequences of entering into new treaty arrangements.

Yet experts in any specialized field frequently disagree. In political science this disagreement goes beyond specific issues and involves such basic questions as whether or not it is possible to have a "true" science of politics. Should political scientists be able to predict or forecast events to the degree that physicists or meteorologists usually can? Sharp divisions of opinion exist within the discipline over questions like this, reflecting the divergent approaches to, perspectives on, and purposes for studying politics. To appreciate the diversity among political scientists, we will look first at what is commonly called "methodology."

By What Methods?

There are many ways of classifying political scientists. However, since this is an introductory textbook, we will focus on two broad schools in contemporary political science, *traditionalists* and *behaviorists*. Bear in mind that the categories are not mutually exclusive and that political scientists often integrate the two approaches.

The Traditional Approach   *Traditional political scientists* are interested in understanding specific political phenomena. Although mastery of the "nuts and bolts" of politics is important, traditionalists give equal emphasis to evaluation.

They want to assess how well a particular policy, process, or institution works. In considering Congress's committee system, nuclear deterrence, or the efficacy of the United Nations, they ask, "Are there better alternatives?"

The bases for such judgments are diverse. In making their assessments traditional political scientists draw on the texts of documents, political essays, philosophical writings, speeches by government officials, court cases, various essays and arguments advanced by other experts, and the like. In addition, the specific research interests and methods of traditional political scientists are often rooted in what they consider to be fundamental and enduring questions. For example, their study of the American separation of powers (into executive, legislative, and judicial branches of government) might begin with a review of the Constitution and no doubt would include James Madison's explanation in *The Federalist* (1787–1788). Such an analysis might also examine various theories of political thinkers regarding the separation of powers, a review of case studies that evaluate the workings of this system of governance, a summary of relevant Supreme Court cases, and a comparison of parliamentary systems that have no such separation of powers. Finally, traditional political scientists would also be inclined to ask whether and to what extent the separation of powers has aided the development of American democracy and even whether democracy as a form of government is (as most Americans believe) praiseworthy.

The Behavioral Approach   Generally speaking, *behavioral political scientists* place little emphasis on such abstract or normative political questions. This school of thought, which became prominent after World War II, focuses on the more concrete task of describing and predicting political behavior and the dynamics and outcomes of political processes. Unlike traditional political scientists, behaviorists generally avoid moral and philosophical judgments about politics. Because they believe that such judgments are little more than speculations and cannot be proved scientifically (and are therefore subjective), they find them irrelevant or even detrimental to the study of politics.

Behavioral political scientists shy away from studying "values," preferring instead to concentrate on facts. In so doing they follow the methodology of scientists in such fields as biology, physics, and chemistry. As a result, they tend to ask only questions that can be answered by means of scientific measurement and analysis. They often construct experiments to test hypotheses and formulate theories. For example, they might attempt to determine the relative effectiveness of various forms of political advertising by showing preselected audiences different versions of a campaign ad. Sometimes, when such experimentation is impossible, behavioral political scientists must attempt—through collection, classification, and computerized manipulation of "real-world" data—to construct a theory explaining or predicting political behavior.

An example of the behavioral approach will help to illustrate its methods. In June 1986 a study titled "The President and the Political Use of Force" was published by two political scientists in a well-known scholarly journal.[4] The study asked, "Under what circumstances is the president of the United States likely to use military force, short of outright involvement in extended hostilities, in order to advance foreign-policy objectives?" The authors were not concerned with evaluating the ultimate wisdom of using military force. Rather, as behaviorists, they were more interested in formulating a theory to explain such a decision—a theory that would allow political scientists to predict future presidential behavior.

In this study the authors identified three presidential functions that impinge on a decision to use force. First, as commander in chief, the president is bound to protect the interests of the United States in the international arena. Second, as chief executive, the president has an obligation to the people of the United States to exercise leadership on behalf of peace. Third, as a political leader, the president must be assured of continued support among party members. Thus the authors argue that the president must operate within three "environments" at once—international, domestic, and political—and that for each environment, research and intuition posit particular relationships among variables. These relationships form patterns representing the conditions under which the president would most likely use force (see Table 1-1). The authors then go on to present a method of quantifying these influences in order to build a predictive model. Throughout their study, they assume a rational (and therefore predictable) pattern of decision making, asserting that "man, viewed as a behaving system, is quite simple" and that the "apparent complexity of his behavior over time is largely a reflection of the complexity of the environment in which he finds himself."[5]

When the authors tested their model by applying it to a set of data from 1948 to 1976, it proved to be approximately 75 percent accurate in predicting whether or not the president would use force in specific situations. This study also led to several new insights. Somewhat surprisingly, for instance, the authors discovered that "the absolute and relative levels of popular support turn out to be the most important influence on the political use of force."[6]

This study, because of its thoroughness and sophistication, epitomizes the kind of methodology often employed by behavioral political scientists. Yet there is no consensus regarding the overall merits of such an approach. In fact, political scientists during the 1950s and 1960s engaged in a spirited debate over this very issue. Behaviorists dismissed the published works of traditionalists as "unscientific," and they accused traditionalists of being behind the times in failing to recognize the superiority of quantitative research techniques. Traditionalists countered by arguing that even if normative questions could not be resolved according to the standards of the physical sciences, not all "value judgments" are arbitrary or mere prejudice. Confining the study of politics only to questions with quantifiable answers, they argued, is tantamount to condemning political science to a trivial pursuit.

Some traditionalists also question the extent to which behavioral political scientists can accurately explain and predict political phenomena. They cite the difficulties of distinguishing between causality and correlation in human behavior. For instance, several studies indicate that criminals tend to be less intelligent than noncriminals. Does this mean that low intelligence is the *cause* of crime (because criminals are less capable than law-abiding citizens of comprehending

TABLE 1-1
General and Specific Factors That Influence a President's Decision to Use Military Force

General Factors	Specific Factors

I. International environment
   A. Level of international tension
	I. International contextual factors
	   A. High levels of international tension between the superpowers increase the propensity to use force.

B. Relative strategic balance	B. However, the greater the strategic dominance of the U.S., the less the likelihood that force would be used.
C. Extent of U.S. involvement in ongoing war	C. The deeper the involvement of the U.S. in a shooting war, the lower the propensity of the president to exercise force elsewhere in the international arena.

II. Domestic environment
    A. Public attitude toward risks of international involvement—international tension
	II. Domestic contextual factors
	    A. During those times when the U.S. public is concerned about the level of international tension, the propensity to use force will be reduced.

B. Public attitude toward risks of international involvement—strategic balance	B. During those times when the U.S. public is aware of the relative strategic dominance of the U.S., there will be a greater propensity for the president to use force.
C. Public aversion to war	C. In the period following involvement in a war, the propensity to use force will be affected negatively.
D. Condition of the domestic economy	D. As the state of the domestic economy worsens, there will be an increased propensity to use force.

III. Political environment
     A. Level of public support
	III. Personal and political contextual factors
	     A. The higher the president's current approval rating, the more the propensity to use force will be expected to decrease.

B. Overall political success	B. However, as the overall success rating of the president declines, this propensity will be increased.
C. Position on the electoral calendar	C. During national electoral campaigns, the propensity to use force will increase.

SOURCE: Charles W. Ostrom and Brian L. Job, "The President and the Political Use of Force," *American Political Science Review* 80 (June 1986), p. 549. Reprinted with permission.

the long-term consequences of their acts and have more difficulty understanding the value of deferred gratification)? How does lower intelligence relate to age, gender, personality, body build, child abuse, drug and alcohol addiction, and other factors? Does the concept of free will play any role?

Given the complexity of human behavior, it is no surprise that experts might argue over methodology. The dispute between traditional and behavioral political scientists has not been resolved, but it is less polemical than it was some years ago.

From What Perspective?

No matter how political science is studied, it encompasses a wide range of subject matter. Political scientists must therefore specialize in one or more areas of teaching and research. At the broadest level, the discipline of political science can be divided into at least five subfields: political theory, American government, comparative politics, international relations, and public administration. Scholarly research, although falling within these broad areas, is usually much more specialized. As we have seen, a researcher who is interested in American government may focus on the presidency and may be particularly interested in determining which factors would convince a president to use military force. To cite other examples, a political theorist may devote attention to a particular time period (for instance, classical Greece); a particular author and work (say Plato's *Republic*); or a specific problem (perhaps determining what virtues would exist in the just state). In fact, one could easily combine these concerns into a single study by examining how Plato, in comparison with other Greek thinkers, understood the requirements for political justice.

Several other more specialized areas of political science deserve mention. Generally, depending on how they are studied, these specialties fit within one or more of the subfields we listed. Constitutional law, for example, is a traditional specialty that focuses on a specific aspect of American government. Public policy (which stresses modern management techniques such as zero-based budgeting, cost accounting, and systems analysis) involves both American government and public administration. Political parties and interest groups as a special research and teaching area falls within either American government or comparative politics. And methodology, the study of behavioral and quantitative techniques, can be employed in the subfields of American government, comparative politics, international relations, and public administration. Now let's look more closely at the five subfields into which political science programs in the United States are often divided.

Political Theory   Political theory (or political philosophy, as some prefer to call it) dates back to Plato (427?–347? B.C.) and comprises the oldest form of political inquiry. It asks: What is the good life? What is good government? To what extent will good government produce the good life? Can good government actually be achieved? Political theorists try to apply the lessons of this type of inquiry to contemporary problems and issues. In so doing, however, they continue to raise timeless political questions. What are human beings really like? Is their nature good and do they cooperate easily, or is human nature basically egotistical and selfish? Is human nature easily changed? What kind of state best takes account of that nature without sacrificing the common good? Beyond order and security, is the primary end of the state to improve human beings morally, to make them equal, to ensure their freedom, or to do something else? Pursuant to these ends, should government be strong and vigilant or weak and permissive? When is revolution justified? How can political stability be safeguarded?

Political theorists believe that answers to these questions can often be discovered through reason and logic supported by the writings of political thinkers such as Aristotle, Rousseau, Locke, Mill, and countless others. Such an approach is necessarily concerned with judgments—that is, with determinations of right and wrong or good and bad. Because people who advocate change and those who oppose it both do so in the belief that they are morally right, understanding politics requires familiarity with the criteria by which policies and programs are judged good and bad.[7] Political theory undertakes the systematic study of better and worse in politics. Normative theorists contend that without knowledge of the moral ends of politics, citizens and political leaders alike will lack direction and a clear sense of purpose.

American Government   It should be no surprise that there are experts on virtually every aspect of American government, including those who study state and local government; the executive, legislative, and judicial processes; and political parties and interest groups. In addition, many professional consultants and academic experts specialize in public opinion and voting behavior.

Why do so many political scientists in the United States study their own governmental institutions? One obvious reason is proximity; we want to understand our immediate environment. But other reasons are less obvious. First of all, American government (like all of politics) is much more complex than is often imagined, and therefore it requires intensive and continuous examination. Second, because most political scientists teach politics, they perform an important role in political and civic education. Specifically, it is crucial that citizens in a democracy understand how their government works, what rights they are guaranteed by the Constitution, and so on. Finally, it is important to remind ourselves that the United States intrinsically merits study because it was the first, and continues to be, the most enduring large democratic republic established in modern times.

Comparative Politics   Comparative politics, as the term implies, is all about comparing and contrasting different governments. Comparative analysis of forms of government, stages of economic development, domestic and foreign policies, and political traditions leads political scientists to formulate meaningful generalizations about government and politics. Some comparative political scientists specialize, studying a particular region of the world or a particular nation intensively. Others focus on a particular political phenomenon such as instability or voting behavior.

All political systems share certain characteristics. Figure 1-2 depicts one famous model, first formulated by political scientist David Easton in 1965, which postulates that all political systems function within the context of political cultures, which consist of traditions, values, and common knowledge. Furthermore, citizens invariably have expectations and place demands on the political system.

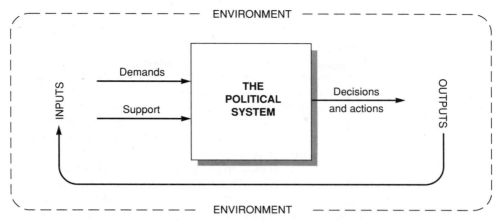

FIGURE 1-2   Simplified Model of a Political System
SOURCE: Copyright 1965, 1979 by David Easton. All rights reserved.

But they also support the system in various ways: They may participate in government, vote, or simply obey the laws of the state. Citizens' demands and support, influenced by the political culture comprising their beliefs about what is and should be happening in society, in turn influence the decision-making capacity of the political system. From this ongoing process, governmental decisions and actions emerge, usually in such forms as edicts, laws, and orders.

Nations, of course, differ in their political cultures, in citizens' demands and support, and in the policies and processes of government. Some political scientists see the differences among nations as being more significant than the similarities, and they differentiate among political systems in various ways. In this book, for example, we distinguish among democratic, authoritarian, and totalitarian states. Some political scientists are uncomfortable with the totalitarian category, and so they merely contrast democratic and nondemocratic states. Others stress the idea that politics takes place in quite different environments: in the industrialized world of the United States, Canada, western Europe, Australia, Japan, and the newly industrialized countries (NICs) of Asia (South Korea, Taiwan, Hong Kong, and Singapore); in the communist world, in 1992 confined to the People's Republic of China, Vietnam, North Korea, Cuba, and a few other Marxist-Leninist nations (Laos, Angola, and Mozambique); and in the Third World, comprising the "less developed countries" (LDCs). Still other political scientists point to the maldistribution of the world's wealth and posit a politically significant division (commonly called the "North–South conflict") between richer nations north of the equator and poorer nations to the south.

International Relations   Specialists in international relations analyze how nations interact. Why do nations sometimes live in peace and harmony but go to war at other times? What is the relative impact of diplomacy, economic interdependence, the United Nations, and nuclear deterrence on efforts to maintain peace? The advent of the nuclear age has, of course, brought new urgency to the study of international relations.

War and peace, conflict and cooperation—these are the most pressing concerns of international relations, but they are by no means the only ones. Other issues run the gamut from trade and tourism to terrorism, from foreign policy to farm policy, from economic integration to emigration. Issues in these and many other areas are valid pursuits for experts in international relations, but no individual can hope to master the intricacies of them all. Hence international relations, like the other subfields of political science, is multifaceted.

The role of morality in foreign policy continues to be a matter of lively debate. Some political scientists (generally called "realists") argue that considerations of national interest have always been paramount in international politics and always will be. Other political scientists (sometimes called "idealists") contend that a heightened concern for morality will lead to world peace and an end to the "war system," which the realists accept fatalistically. Still others suggest that the distinction between national interest and international morality is false; democracies, for example, can actively support the welfare of other democracies and by so doing serve both their own self-interest and the cause of world peace and prosperity.

Public Administration   In recent years the study of public administration has emerged in some schools not simply as a subfield of political science but as a separate discipline designed to train people seeking a career in public service. Essentially, public administration focuses on how the bureaucracy implements governmental policies. Usually the emphasis is on national government, but public administration is also concerned with state and local government and with intergovernmental relations. Students of public administration seek to understand what helps as well as what hinders the bureaucracy in carrying out its assigned functions. Bureaucratic structures, procedures, and processes are examined in an attempt to improve efficiency and reduce waste and duplication. Of particular concern are how and why bureaucracies develop their own policy interests, quite apart from the governmental policies they are established to implement.

Political scientists who study public administration frequently concentrate on case studies. They pay attention not only to the ways in which governmental power is exercised but also to whether power is exercised in a manner consistent with the public interest. In that sense, public administration shares the concerns of political science as a whole.

WHY STUDY POLITICS?

How professional political scientists study politics reveals a great deal about the discipline in general but little about the importance of political science for beginning students. We believe that a basic understanding of politics is a vital part of any undergraduate's education, for reasons spelled out in the following

In January 1990, Lithuanians protested to demand independence. If public attention focuses on basic issues of justice and the common good, the legitimacy of the existing political order might come under attack. (Victor Yurchenko: AP/Wide World Photos)

pages. To realize the benefits that can flow from the study of politics, however, students must make a sincere effort to learn.

Self-interest

Because personal happiness depends in no small degree on what government does or does not do, we all have a considerable stake in understanding how government works (or why it is not working). To college students, for example, federal work-study programs, state subsidies to public education, low-interest loans, federal grants, and court decisions designed to protect (or not protect) students' rights are political matters of great significance. Through the study of politics, we become more aware of our dependence on the political system and better equipped to determine when to favor and when to oppose change. At the same time, such study helps to reveal the limits of politics and of our ability to bring about positive change. It is sobering to consider that each of us is only one person in a nation of millions (and a world of billions), most of whom have opinions and prejudices no less firmly held than are our own.

Self-improvement

The study of politics also fosters moral and intellectual growth—that is, self-improvement—which should be an essential part of all education. As we have seen, politics is characterized by competing claims about what constitutes a wise use of political power. These claims, along with the persons who make them, should be subjected to critical examination. For this reason, political science is by nature a rigorous discipline; students of politics must learn to be skeptical of what they read and hear because both the people who make political news and those who report it are not always completely impartial or objective. Careful observers must constantly filter the truth from the overwhelming flow of information that characterizes modern democratic societies. An example will illustrate this point:

> Suppose that you turn on your television and find that the lead story on the evening news concerns the chronic problem of unemployment in the United States. After the anchorwoman announces that official Department of Labor figures indicate that the national unemployment rate has remained at 9 percent for the third straight month, the scene switches to the living room of a modest two-story home in a West Virginia town, where Mr. and Mrs. Schweigert and their four children, who range in age from 3 to 15, are waiting to be interviewed. After asking Mr. Schweigert, "How does it feel to be unemployed?" and Mrs. Schweigert, "How are you managing the family budget?" the reporter turns to the oldest daughter and asks if her family's "financial situation" has made any difference in the way her classmates treat her. Following a brief exchange, the reporter closes the story with these words: "The government's announcement of a leveling of the unemployment rate at 9 percent is a sterile statistic; the plain fact is that there are real people, like the Schweigerts, who are struggling to keep home and family together. And even though some economic indicators point to an upturn in the economy, it may not come in time to help the Schweigerts, or thousands of families like them." The reporter then gives his name and the location of his report and signs off.

What do we know from this news story? Assuming that the portrayal of this family's predicament is basically accurate, we know that such people exist and are having difficulty coping with the economic times. We know, too, that other families in the United States are experiencing similar problems. What we are *not* given in this story is the solid information we need to make an intelligent judgment about the implications of unemployment for the national economy. Consider, for example, the following set of interrelated questions that have not been answered:

1 How is unemployment defined? Does the definition include people who wish to be employed but cannot find work?

2 Is 9 percent unemployment unreasonably high for a large, advanced industrial society like the United States? What percentage of the jobless rate simply reflects sociological trends—for example, more women choosing to work outside the home? What should we make of the fact that the *absolute* number of people in the labor force (those who are gainfully employed) has never been higher?

3 Given a 9 percent overall unemployment figure, what *kinds* of unemployment exist? How many people want to work but cannot find a job? How many are changing jobs? How many are second-income earners, as opposed to sole supporters of families?

4 Who, specifically, is unemployed? Statistics by age, race, and region must be furnished before we can draw accurate political and economic implications and devise appropriate solutions.

5 What kind of governmental aid is available to the unemployed? Is it adequate? Does it provide a reasonable standard of living? Is it so high that people may be discouraged from seeking employment?

6 Is all unemployment bad? Sometimes, for example, the fact that a working wife can "afford" to be unemployed for a period of time while she carefully chooses her next job may be a sign of economic vitality.

7 In lowering the unemployment rate by a given percentage, what costs are likely to be incurred? How much must be spent in tax money to create a given number of public works jobs? What would be the effect on the inflation rate if the government were to stimulate the economy to create several million more jobs in the private sector? Is the trade-off between less unemployment and more inflation worth the effort?

8 Can unemployment ever be eliminated? If not, what level of unemployment should the government set as "acceptable"?

9 Who is to blame for unemployment? The government? Big business? Labor? Competing foreign labor? No one?

These questions by no means include all the elements needed for a full and fair evaluation of this seemingly simple news story. Thus by failing to show the complexity of an issue, a news story can be unintentionally misleading. The ability to think critically, then, is an essential attribute of responsible citizenship. In training the mind to ask the right questions, to recognize when a fact is relevant and when it is not, and to construct logical, reasoned arguments, the study of politics fosters the habit of critical thinking—a habit that more than anything else gives meaning to participatory membership in a democratic society.

Self-knowledge

In addition to self-interest and self-improvement, the study of politics also fosters self-knowledge. What could be more important than to know who we are, in terms of moral character and conduct? Indisputably, a person's moral disposition is both formed by and reflected in the kinds of everyday decisions and choices the person makes. These decisions and choices are in turn greatly influenced by the kind of political society in which the person happens (or chooses) to live.

It has been demonstrated repeatedly that people with very similar capabilities and desires can develop, over time, quite different moral dispositions. Different circumstances and the presence or absence of daily adversity account at least partly for dissimilar behaviors by similar people (or for the different consequences of similar behavior). Out of these vital differences, various personality types may develop. Thus politics, understood as the way human beings govern and are governed in established communities, can be a decisive factor in the moral development of all citizens.

A Negative Example   The Nazi regime in Germany from 1933 to 1945 illustrates the tremendous impact a political regime can have on the moral character of citizens. Headed by Adolf Hitler, the most significant and striking aspect of *Nazism* was its ideology (the public rationale for the regime's existence). Its political doctrine was explicitly grounded in racism; according to Nazi dogma, the country was obliged to maintain the purity of the so-called Aryan race, which was supposedly being threatened with contamination by "social inferiors." Policies based on this *Weltanschauung* (world view) resulted in the willful and systematic murder of millions of innocent men, women, and children. Allegedly, Jews represented the greatest threat to "Aryan purity," and approximately 6 million of them were killed in cold blood (although Nazi atrocities went beyond the extermination of Jews). So intent were the Nazis on carrying out their "final solution" to the alleged problem of racial contamination that in the closing months of World War II, the operation of extermination camps continued even at the expense of military campaigns.

The Holocaust—this gruesome spectacle of gas chambers and mass graves—forces us to ask how horrors on this scale could take place in a supposedly civilized country. How could a nation with an impressive humanistic tradition, which nurtured and lionized so many of the world's finest artists and thinkers, have permitted such a thing to happen?

In the Nazi era the German nation appears, at first glance, to have become little more than an extension of Hitler's will—in other words, that the awesome moral responsibility for the Holocaust somehow rests on the shoulders of one man. But more astute observers dispute this interpretation. Although granting that Hitler was the prime mover behind Nazism, they point out that he could not have carried out his appalling program without help. What about all those others who voted for, worked for, or conspired with him? What about those who helped to plan, coordinate, and administer his policies? According to Irving Kristol:

> When one studies the case of The Nazi there comes a sickening emptiness of the stomach and a sense of bafflement. Can this be all? The disparity between the crime and the criminal is too monstrous.
>
> We expect to find evil men, paragons of wickedness, slobbering, maniacal brutes; we are prepared to trace the lineaments of The Nazi on the face of every individual Nazi in order to define triumphantly the essential features of his character. But the Nazi leaders were not diabolists, they did not worship evil. For—greatest of ironies—the Nazis, like Adam and Eve before the fall, knew not of good and evil, and it is this cast of moral indifference that makes them appear so petty and colorless and superficial.[8]

Kristol is not alone in thinking that many Nazis were not so much morally evil as morally ignorant. Many observers have characterized Albert Speer, Hitler's minister of armaments and munitions, as just such a person.[9] Another, according to political theorist Hannah Arendt, was Adolf Eichmann, a Nazi functionary who administered much of the extermination program. In Arendt's view, Eichmann was not a particularly unusual man.[10] His most distinctive personality trait was a desire to get ahead, to be a success in life. He took special pride in his ability to do a job efficiently. Although not particularly thoughtful or reflective, he was far from stupid. Arendt also described him as somewhat insecure, but not noticeably more so than many "normal" people. Most startlingly, he claimed to have no obsessive hatred toward Jews (although, obviously, he was not sufficiently skeptical or mentally independent to resist the widespread anti-Semitism that existed in Germany at that time). In short, Eichmann was morally indifferent; in Kristol's words, he "knew not of good and evil." He also, we might add, *cared* not of good and evil.

What is most remarkable about Kristol's and Arendt's works is that they describe people who participated in terrible acts of barbarism in terms that remind us of people we all know—perhaps even of ourselves. It would not be difficult, for example, to picture an Eichmann in surroundings more familiar to us—as an ambitious up-and-coming executive in a large American corporation, perhaps, or as a young foreign service officer determined to get ahead. Such a person would most likely be a workaholic, devoted to company or country, concerned with advancement, and eager to please superiors. Not lacking decent human qualities, he or she might, for instance, be a faithful spouse and loving parent. (It was not unusual for the Nazis to display great affection for their families.) The key point is that this make-believe person is so caught up in the "real world," as defined in terms of narrow career objectives, that he or she has no time for, or interest in, "abstract" moral questions.

If it is true that many people in our midst are like Adolf Eichmann, then why are there so few Eichmanns? In large measure, the answer can be found in the un-Nazi-like character of the political regimes under which most individuals live and work and raise their families. The Nazi experience—that is, the totality of influences emanating from Hitler's rule—was a crucial factor in shaping the personality and character of Eichmann. Just as every conscientious grocery store manager knows that the goal of the job is to increase productivity and profits, so Eichmann understood that it was his job to kill people. In addition, he knew that success, like that of the grocery store manager, would be measured largely in terms of a single criterion: efficiency. What mattered to Eichmann was not what he was doing but how well he did it. Very likely he would have discharged his responsibilities with equal zeal had he been in charge of park planning or flower planting rather than mass extermination. The banality of this evildoer and the magnitude of his evil are both appalling and instructive, for they reflected the prevailing political order.

The German leadership regarded mass extermination as an irreducible necessity. It would have required a rare combination of intellectual independence and moral courage not to go along with this prevailing view. Tragically, those were precisely the qualities Eichmann so sorely lacked; indeed, they are qualities many of us lack to some extent. Consider how often our own actions and attitudes result from going along with the crowd, even when, as individuals, we may have misgivings. From this simple truth we must conclude not only that it is never difficult to find people with many of the personality traits of an Eichmann but also that in many countries—perhaps even in our own—such people may be in the majority. The crucial point, however, is that only under the most extreme political orders, such as Nazism, do common citizens degenerate into uncommonly evil individuals capable of performing the most heinous acts as part of their everyday duties.

Conclusions   The case of Adolf Eichmann invites reflection about the influences on personality structure under different political circumstances. No doubt Eichmann is an extreme case, but the phenomenon he represents does not require the existence of enormous political extremes. The relationship between citizens' morality and their political society deserves (and will receive) more attention than we can give it in this introductory chapter.

Yet it should be apparent that the political environment can make a huge difference in how we view the world and our own place in it. Whether we are aware of it or not, there is generally a strong correlation between our political values and our personal values. To understand this simple fact is to learn something very important about ourselves—namely, the extent to which we are *not* the free spirits most of us like to think we are.

We all want to "do our own thing" and make our own choices about how to live our lives. But few of us can resist social pressures to conform, especially when those pressures are reinforced by ideology and authority. To become more aware of the dangers to which this "go along with" tendency gives rise, however, can lead to new awareness of our capacity for critical thinking. In the realm of politics, making your own judgments about right and wrong, good and evil, truth and falsehood, is not only an intellectual possibility; as the case of Adolf Eichmann shows, it can also be a moral necessity.

Summary

The study of politics is based on three fundamental concepts: order, power, and justice. Understanding that human life is ordered constitutes the first recognition of political life. Specifically, political order is reflected in the communities where human beings live, which are associations of individuals who share a common identity. Communities are ordered, maintained, and perpetuated by government. The addition of government, imposing a structure on the most consequential and self-sufficient communities, has produced the modern nation-state.

Power, which has many sources, refers to government's ability to perform its required tasks. Questions of justice arise if the public interest is not advanced by the exercise of governmental power. Thus politics plays a vital and pervasive role in everyday life, for the irrepressible human pursuit of justice is intimately bound up with the exercise of public power, even though moral questions may at times be obscured from public view.

Political scientists study their discipline to discover the truth about political institutions, forces, movements, and processes. Traditional political scientists are interested in assessing the workings of government, whereas behaviorists use scientific methods to describe and predict political outcomes. Almost all political scientists specialize. The broadest subfields of the discipline are political theory (or philosophy), American government, comparative politics, international relations, and public administration.

Among the many valid reasons for studying politics, three are especially important: (1) An understanding of politics is a matter of self-interest, (2) the study of politics leads to self-improvement, and (3) by exploring politics, a person gains self-knowledge. The critical importance of self-knowledge among ordinary citizens was illustrated tragically by the rise of Nazism in Germany.

Key Terms

politics	sovereignty	nation-state	traditional political scientists
community	authority	power	behavioral political scientists
government	legitimacy	justice	Nazism

Review Questions

1. What does the study of politics entail?

2. How does one identify a political problem? Are some conflicts more political than others? Explain.

3. In what ways do political scientists differ from one another?

4. How can individuals benefit from the study of politics and government?

Recommended Reading

ARISTOTLE. *The Politics.* Edited and translated by Ernest Barker. New York: Oxford University Press, 1962. An account of the necessity and value of politics.

BETTELHEIM, BRUNO. "Remarks on the Psychological Appeal of Totalitarianism." In *Surviving and Other Essays.* New York: Knopf, 1979; Random House, 1980. Bettelheim examines the stifling effect totalitarian systems can have on people who only silently oppose them. A compelling argument regarding the relationship of politics to human well-being.

CRICK, BERNARD. *In Defense of Politics* (2nd ed.). Chicago: University of Chicago Press, 1973. An argument that politics is an important and worthy human endeavor.

DRUCKER, PETER. "The Monster and the Lamb." *Atlantic* 242 (December 1978), pp. 82–87. A short but moving account of the effect an extremist government had on several individuals.

EASTON, DAVID. *The Political System: An Inquiry into the State of Political Science* (2nd ed.). Chicago: University of Chicago Press, 1981. A pioneering book that laid the foundation for a "systems theory" approach to political analysis.

LEWIS, C. S. *The Abolition of Man.* New York: Macmillan, 1978. An elegant discussion of the necessity of moral judgments.

MILGRAM, STANLEY. *Obedience to Authority.* New York: HarperCollins, 1983. A report on a series of social science experiments that demonstrated the degree to which many individuals obey authority.

STRAUSS, LEO. "What Is Political Philosophy?" In *What Is Political Philosophy? and Other Studies.* Westport, Conn.: Greenwood Press, 1973 (reprint of 1959 edition). An extremely cogent introduction to the value and necessity of political philosophy.

Notes

1. We will use the terms *nation, state,* and *country* synonymously.

2. Aristotle, *The Politics,* trans. and ed. Ernest Barker (New York: Oxford University Press, 1962), p. 4.

3. As opposed to Plato, who is sometimes classified as the first political *philosopher.*

4. Charles W. Ostrom and Brian L. Job, "The President and the Political Use of Force," *American Political Science Review* 80 (June 1986), pp. 541–566.

5. Ibid., p. 544.

6. Ibid., p. 559.

7. See Leo Strauss, *What Is Political Philosophy? and Other Studies* (New York: Free Press, 1959), pp. 10–12.

8. Irving Kristol, "The Nature of Nazism," in *The Commentary Reader,* ed. Norman Podhoretz (New York: Atheneum, 1965), p. 16.

9. See Albert Speer, *Inside the Third Reich,* trans. R. and C. Winston (New York: Avon, 1971). Compare Stanley Haverwas and David Burrell, "Self-deception and Autobiography: Reflections on Speer's *Inside the Third Reich,*" in *Truthfulness and Tragedy: Further Investigations in Christian Ethics,* ed. Stanley Haverwas et al. (South Bend, Ind.: University of Notre Dame Press, 1977), pp. 82–97.

10. Hannah Arendt, *Eichmann in Jerusalem: A Report on the Banality of Evil* (New York: Penguin Books, 1964). Compare Gideon Hausner, *Justice in Jerusalem* (New York: Schocken Books, 1968), p. 465.

PART I

POLITICAL SYSTEMS IN COMPARATIVE PERSPECTIVE

CHAPTER 2

UTOPIAS

MODEL STATES

As CITIZENS, WE often favor (or oppose) political policies, programs, and leaders because we believe they will help us make ours a better or more just society. Behind many of our political preferences, then, is some idea of what constitutes the public good and the good society. Usually, this notion is unexamined if not unformed; that is, though we believe in a certain kind of political order, we are often unable to spell out the specific contents of this belief.[1] Yet political thinkers have long held that it is important to articulate and analyze the underlying assumptions behind our political beliefs. If we are to make meaningful comparisons between or among political systems (which is our goal in Part I), we need not only to describe those systems but also to formulate the criteria according to which we can better judge them. Thinking about utopias can help us clarify our ideas about what we desire politically and what we should expect from government, which is, by definition, imperfect.

The word *utopia* comes from the title of a book written by Sir Thomas More (1478–1535), the lord chancellor of England under King Henry VIII and an influential humanist. More coined the word from the Greek terms *ou topos*, meaning "no place," and *eutopos*, "a place where all is well." In common usage *utopia* tends to incorporate both of these meanings. Hence we might say that a **utopia** is a nonexistent place where people dwell in perfect health, harmony, and happiness.

The literature of political philosophy in the West contains a number of elaborate utopian blueprints, each of which represents its author's best attempt to formulate the complete and good (or completely good) political order. Utopian models differ in specific features, but they all serve similar purposes. Without exception, all utopia inventors have sought to pursue the logic of political life to its final conclusions. And in doing so, they have often engaged in implicit and explicit criticism of existing political, social, and economic conditions. Because of this critical function, utopian constructs can be and have been used as standards of political measurement or as criteria used in judging the performance of political systems. Then, too, abstract models of the perfect society have occasionally served as practical guides to political action. So despite its appearance of impracticality, utopian thought does serve significant purposes and has affected political activities, directly or indirectly.

Our exploration of famous utopias will begin with Plato's *Republic*, which we will contrast with three later versions of utopia—those found in Sir Francis Bacon's *New Atlantis*, in Karl Marx's writings extolling the virtues of the "classless society," and in B. F. Skinner's *Walden Two*. In focusing on these writers, we do not mean to denigrate the importance of other utopian thinkers. Thomas More's *Utopia* (1516) remains essential reading. Tommaso Campanella's *City of the Sun* and James Harrington's *Oceana* (1656) also deserve special mention, as do the writings of such French utopian socialists as Charles Fourier and the Comte de Saint-Simon. The American writer Edward Bellamy (1850–1898) incorporated a number of similar proposals in a book titled *Looking Backward* (1888). These visionaries and their followers all helped to keep the idea and the ideals of utopia alive.

PLATO'S *REPUBLIC:* PHILOSOPHY IS THE ANSWER

Plato's *Republic* is a long dialogue between Socrates and interlocutors. Socrates (469–399 B.C.), who is considered the first Western political philosopher, held that "the unexamined life is not life worth living"—an idea that has become a cornerstone of Western civilization. As preserved and elaborated on by Plato, Socrates's most brilliant student, Socratic philosophy represents a fundamental alternative to the earlier works of Homer, who praised the virtues of courage and honor, and the later teachings of Jesus, who proclaimed belief in God and moral behavior in accordance with the given Word to be the basis of the most exalted life.

Because of his penchant for relentlessly seeking answers to penetrating philosophical questions, Socrates was mistrusted by the rulers of Athens. Eventually he was accused, in court, of undermining belief in the established gods and corrupting Athenian youth. He was convicted and sentenced to death. The execution of Socrates (by a self-administered drink of hemlock) stands as a poignant reminder of the tension between intellectual freedom and the political order.

In *The Republic*, Plato has Socrates begin by inquiring into the meaning of justice and then proceed to describe the best political order as a society devoid of all tension between philosophers and rulers.[2] (In such a society, the charges

Plato (427?–347 B.C.), one of the great philosophers of ancient Greece. Through his teachings, Plato attempted to show the rational relationship between the soul, the state, and the cosmos. "Until philosophers are kings, . . . cities will never have rest from their evils." (Culver Pictures)

leveled against Socrates would have been groundless. There could be no fear of teachers making youth disloyal, for it would be possible to be *both* philosophic and patriotic.) The founding and construction of such a city would reflect nothing less than the perfection of political thought.

The Just City

Initially, Socrates is prompted to elaborate on his conception of the ultimate political good by a skeptical listener who challenges him to explain why it is better to be just than to be unjust. Is it not true, he is asked, that the successful man who gains power and possessions from unjust actions is much happier than the just man who, like Socrates, has neither power nor possessions? Because justice will be easier to identify in a city than in a person, the search for the just city begins.[3]

Socrates first proposes that political life arises from the fact that no individual can be self-sufficient. He then describes a very simple society with no government and no scarcity, whose farmers, shoemakers, and other artisans produce just enough for the perpetuation of a plain and placid way of life. In this society, which seeks to satisfy the basic needs of the body (food, drink, shelter, and so on), each person performs one specialized function.

To avoid monotony, however, adornments are required. But the creation of luxury liberates desire and gives rise to restless spirits. The city then becomes "feverish" and needs to expand. Specifically, it must acquire more land, and for that task soldiers are necessary. The soldiers, who form the second class in the republic, are initially called guardians. Their task becomes clearer as the dialogue progresses: They are to protect the *polis* as sheep dogs protect a flock of lambs.

As described in *The Republic*, the education of the guardians encompasses the entire range of human activities, including the aesthetic, intellectual, moral, and physical aspects of life. Socrates suggests that the purpose of education is to teach the truth. Therefore, censorship of untrue or dangerous ideas is required. Throughout the course of this training, strict discipline is maintained. Everything is held in common, including personal property and spouses. Love of the community is to replace ordinary human love.

At age 20, the students are divided into two groups. Some of them are designated auxiliaries and are assigned the role of defending the city; they will be the republic's soldiers. The others, who retain the name of guardian, continue their education. Other, later screenings determine the jobs eventually held by those in the guardian class. All choices are based on merit. At the end of a prolonged period of study, a guardian, by understanding the truth of things, may become a philosopher. Supreme in wisdom, philosophers alone are fit to hold the highest offices. In this manner, the republic is governed by *philosopher-kings*.

Thus Plato's republic is made up of a class of farmers and artisans, a class of warrior-auxiliaries, and a class of philosopher-guardians. (This tripartite division reflects Plato's idea that the human soul is divided into three parts: an appetitive part, which derives from physical desires; a spirited part, which produces anger and indignation when something dear is threatened; and a reasoning part, which seeks to know the truth.) Each class embodies one essential virtue. The workers and artisans, who provide for the city's physical necessities, possess moderation: Their lives are governed in an orderly and proper fashion. Although the warrior-auxiliaries also possess moderation, their particular virtue is courage, which is the perfection of the spirited part of the soul. The perfection of the reasoning part, wisdom, is reserved for the philosophers (who, of course, also possess the other two virtues). Only philosophers possess a completely excellent soul; every part of their being is perfect, as is the relationship among the parts of their soul. Because of their all-encompassing excellence, the philosophers alone understand justice, the most comprehensive virtue of all. Furthermore, since each component of the republic does its job well (growing food and making things, defending the city, or ruling), and in so doing prominently displays a particular cardinal virtue (moderation, courage, or wisdom), this imaginary city is also just.

And what a city it is! One commentator has suggested that "all of Western man's aspirations to justice and the good life are given expression and fulfillment in Socrates' proposals."[4] This is a city where

> men's faculties are not denied their exercise by poverty, birth, or sex, where the accidental attachments of family and city do not limit a man's understanding and pursuit of the good; it is a regime, finally, where wise, public-spirited men rule for the common good.[5]

All citizens perform the tasks for which they are best equipped, and they receive recognition, honors, and respect in proportion to the value of their contributions to society. This city suggests an answer to the question Socrates was asked originally. It is the philosophers who are just and yet seem to be the happiest of persons (certainly happier than the unjust), and their happiness does not depend on possession of power unjustly obtained. Of course, in the republic, philosophers are not persecuted; they are placed in charge, not put on trial.

Because philosophers rule and because they are just and wise, otherwise objectionable practices can be instituted. For example, to ensure that public servants place the public interest above their private interests, family relationships are banned among the soldier and guardian classes. The continued existence of exceptional individuals is ensured by a eugenics program that provides for nothing short of state control of human sexual relations. The guardian class is to propagate only through a system of carefully orchestrated "marriage festivals" planned for the sole purpose of collective (and selective) breeding. Nothing is to be left to chance.

The Noble Lie

Furthermore, to convince the members of the lower class of their proper status (considering that they would probably neither understand nor accept their humble station in society), the philosopher-kings are in charge of perpetuating the noble lie on which the just city depends. That is, at a certain point, all citizens except the philosophers are told that their memories about past experiences are only dreams; in reality, they are informed, they all had been under the earth together, being fashioned and trained. When they were ready, their mother, the earth, sent them up to the surface. Furthermore, during the formative process they were given souls fashioned out of gold (in the case of philosophers), silver (auxiliaries), or iron and bronze (farmers and artisans). This myth is designed to persuade the residents of the republic that they are all brothers and sisters—and to ensure popular acceptance of the class system so essential to the republic's existence.

In describing the best political society, Socrates also reveals the difficulties involved in its creation and maintenance. Not only is the republic concept impractical, but it also seems impossible to realize. Socrates clearly shows the price that would have to be paid for the creation of such a political order. As we have seen, that price includes the abolition of families, the establishment of censorship, the presence of a widespread falsehood regarding the moral basis of the regime, and the rule of people who do not desire to rule.

But if *The Republic* is not intended to be a blueprint for some future political regime, it is valuable in several other respects. Above all, it systematically and insightfully explores important political ideas such as justice, tyranny, and education. Then, too, it demonstrates one thoughtful model of the best political order while simultaneously exposing the practical impediments to its implementation. In sum, *The Republic* should be taken less as a political prescription than as a philosophical exercise. Socrates's excursion into utopia represents an attempt to perfect human thought, not a formula for the perfection of human deeds.

FRANCIS BACON'S *NEW ATLANTIS:* SCIENCE IS THE ANSWER

In *The New Atlantis,* written in 1622, Francis Bacon (1561–1626) describes the imaginary voyage of travelers who discover an island called Bensalem. They have suffered greatly during a long sojourn in the Pacific, and they need food and rest. At first the islanders warn them not to land, but after some negotiations, the travelers are allowed to disembark. As their original impression of inhospitality fades, the visitors come to see the island as a blissfully happy place.

Stability and Science

Most of the practical details of day-to-day life in Bensalem are merely sketched in by Bacon. Although its envoys have made secret expeditions to Europe, to learn about and bring back any advances in science, the island is otherwise cut off completely from other societies. This geographic isolation, conveniently enough, precludes the need for self-defense. The island is also economically self-sufficient—indeed, Bacon creates the unmistakable impression of a land endowed with an abundance of natural resources.

Bensalem is a Christian society, but one that emphasizes religious freedom. Members of various religious faiths hold important positions, and toleration is

Francis Bacon (1561–1626), English philosopher, scientist, essayist, and statesman. "Nature, to be commanded, must be obeyed." (Culver Pictures)

the norm. The religious disputes that had torn apart many European nations are absent from this utopia.

The social basis of Bensalem is the family; marriage is described as the foundation of society. During a special holiday known as the Feast of the Family, instituted and paid for by the state, the heads of particularly large families are honored and family unity and moral behavior are celebrated as the cornerstones of close-knit and stable community life. The stability of the community is underlined by the fact that it was founded some 2,000 years earlier by a benevolent ruler, Solamona, who promulgated laws so perfect that they have never required revision.

If stable, however, Bensalem is also a progressive society. The best minds of Bensalem are assembled at a great college, appropriately called Salomon's House, where the rules of science are applied, through experimentation and observation, to the discovery of "knowledge of the causes and secret motions of things; and the enlarging of the bounds of human empire, to the effecting of all things possible." In contrast to Plato's *Republic*, then, knowledge is pursued not simply for its own sake in Bensalem but rather for the conquest of nature. Greater material comfort, better health, and a more secure and prosperous way of life make up the great legacy of the academy's laboratories, experimental lakes, medicine shops, and observatories. In Bensalem, there is not the slightest doubt that science can and should be used for "the relief of man's estate."

Bacon's seventeenth-century vision seems prophetic in many respects. Through science, life expectancy on the island has been increased dramatically, as whole strains of illness have been eradicated. New fruits and flowers have been produced, some with curative powers. In fact, medical treatment has undergone a technological revolution. The Bensalemites can even predict impending natural disasters, for their science has uncovered nature's darkest secrets.

Blueprint for the Future

Although scholars disagree about Bacon's true intention, a seriousness of purpose definitely marks his work. One noted authority declared that Bacon was the "first really modern utopian" because he was the first thinker actually to expect his ideal society to come into existence.[6] Does this mean that *The New Atlantis* was meant to be a *precise* outline of the future? Not at all. Bacon was simply suggesting one possible form for a society in which scientific progress was allowed to proceed unimpeded. Bacon's vision of a technological utopia was not intended as a protest against existing society or as a Platonic ideal of political thought but rather as a grandiose blueprint for the radical improvement of the human condition.

KARL MARX'S CLASSLESS SOCIETY: ECONOMICS IS THE ANSWER

Karl Marx (1818–1883) was a utopian thinker, but in a different way from Plato or Bacon. Marx's utopian predecessors began with elaborate descriptions of their paradises; if they engaged in social criticism, most of their criticisms were implicit rather than explicit. Marx, by contrast, began with an extremely explicit criticism of existing society and sketched only the broadest outlines of his utopia. He thought of himself as a hardheaded realist, not a starry-eyed dreamer. Because he considered his world view to be the product of a correct empirical understanding of historical and socioeconomic reality, Marx would have adamantly objected to any suggestion that his ideas were rooted in visionary thinking.

Nevertheless, the utopian element in Marxism cannot be denied. Unlike earlier utopians, Marx believed that his ideal society was not merely possible but inevitable. The bitter class struggle he envisaged (see Chapter 14) can be properly understood only as the necessary prelude to a utopian life in a promised land of peace and plenty. This prophecy represented to Marx the end product of supposedly irresistible forces that were propelling human history toward its inevitable destiny, the classless society.

The Centrality of Economics

Marx's attack on economic inequality was influenced by the harsh working conditions and widespread suffering associated with capitalism in the mid-nineteenth century. The wealthy commercial and industrial elites (the "bourgeois capitalist" class) opposed reforms aimed at improving the living conditions of

Karl Marx (1818–1883), German philosopher, economist, and revolutionary. "The history of all hitherto existing society is the history of class struggle." (Granger Collection)

the impoverished working class (the "proletariat"). Marx's *Capital* is punctuated with vivid descriptions of employment practices that aroused his anger, such as the following:

> Mary Anne Walkley had worked without intermission for 26½ hours, with 60 other girls, 30 in one room, that only afforded ⅓ of the cubic feet of air required for them. . . .
>
> Mary Anne Walkley fell ill on the Friday [and] died on Sunday. . . . The doctor, Mr. Keys, called in too late to the death-bed, duly bore witness before the coroner's jury that "Mary Anne Walkley had died from long hours of work in an overcrowded workroom."[7]

To Marx, the deaths of Mary Anne Walkley and others like her were not mere accidents. He believed that economics—the production and distribution of material necessities—was the ultimate determinant of human life and that, historically, human societies rose and fell according to the inexorable dynamic of economic forces. Thus Mary Anne Walkley, having been born into the age of capitalism, was preordained to spend a brief and meager life working for subsistence wages so that the owners of the means of production—the capitalist class—could enrich themselves further. Her harsh life and premature death had been dictated by the economics of the mid-nineteenth century. But equally inevitable, according to Marx, was the downfall of the capitalist system through an apocalyptic revolution of the impoverished, alienated, and exploited working class, the proletariat.

The Dictatorship of the Proletariat

Marx referred to the stage of the revolutionary process immediately following the overthrow of capitalism as the ***dictatorship of the proletariat.*** This historical epoch, Marx asserted, will comprise the ***first stage of communism*** and will represent the advent of the socialist millennium in human history. As a temporary phenomenon, the dictatorship of the proletariat will survive only as long as there remains a need to guard against counterrevolution. During this time, revolutionary new programs will be launched, based on the principle "From each according to his abilities, to each according to his needs." These policies will include the abolition of all private ownership of property, a heavily progressive income tax, the abolition of the right of inheritance, the centralization of all credit in the state and of all means of communications and transportation, the introduction of free education for all children, the abolition of child labor, the extension "of factories and instruments of production owned by the State," and "the bringing into cultivation of waste-lands, and the improvement of the soil generally in accordance with a common plan."[8]

After completing these steps, the government will simply wither away, as (according to Marx's collaborator, Friedrich Engels) class differences and antagonisms naturally fade away, the injection of state power in social relations becomes unnecessary, and "the government of persons is replaced by the administration of things and the direction of the process of production." In the end, "The State is not 'abolished.' It dies out."[9]

In essence, then, Marx viewed the dictatorship of the proletariat, or the socialist stage of communism, as a necessary way station on the road to a classless utopia. Marx believed that human beings come into the world with a clean slate and that what is subsequently written on that slate is determined by the nature of human society rather than individual genetic inheritance. Further, Marx saw no inherent tension between the true interests of the individual and the interests of society. During the socialist era, therefore, people would naturally acquire socialist values. Unlike capitalist states, which allegedly produce competitive citizens who degrade and exploit one another, the socialist state would produce cooperative citizens who respect and support one another. Class conflict would inevitably disappear, displaced by a natural harmony of interests.

The Marxist belief in the withering away of the state was thus based on a kind of harmony-of-interest logic. Eliminate private property and the division of labor, and you eliminate social inequality. Eliminate social inequality, and you eliminate the cause of armed conflict. (Obviously, no class struggle is possible when classes no longer exist.) Finally, eliminate armed conflict, and you eliminate the need for the state. After all, past societies were nothing more than human contrivances for the perpetuation of class dominance. With the disappearance of social classes, government as we have known it will simply atrophy as a result of its own obsolescence.

The Classless Society

The natural demise of government, Marx prophesied, will usher in the *second stage of communism,* the classless society. In this communist utopia, true human fulfillment will be possible. Under capitalism, Marx wrote, "everyone has a definite, circumscribed sphere of activity, which is put upon him and from which he cannot escape. He is a hunter, a fisherman, a shepherd or a 'critical critic,' and he must remain so if he does not want to lose his means of subsistence."[10] Under communism, in contrast,

> when each one does not have a circumscribed sphere of activity but can train him-self in any branch he chooses, society by regulating the common production makes it possible for me to do this today and that tomorrow, to hunt in the morn-ing, to fish in the afternoon, to carry on cattle-breeding in the evening, also to criticize the food—just as I please—without becoming a hunter, fisherman, shep-herd or critic.[11]

Along with individual self-fulfillment, social bliss will blossom in this new order, which will be populated by "loyal, wise and incorruptible friends, devoted to one another with an absolutely unselfish benevolence."[12] Marx's class-less society resembles virtually every other utopia in this respect. One stu-dent of Marxist utopianism has observed that Marx's description of communist society shares with most other utopian works a "single ethical core" charac-terized by "cooperative rather than competitive labor, purposeful achievement for societal ends rather than self-indulgence or private hedonism, and an ethic of social responsibility for each member rather than of struggle for survival of the fittest."[13]

The picture of the future that Marx and Engels presented to the world was indeed exciting—and utopian:

> Crime would disappear, the span of life would increase, brotherhood and cooperation would inculcate a new morality, scientific progress would grow by leaps and bounds. Above all, with socialism spreading throughout the world, the greatest blight of humankind, war, and its twin brother, nationalism, would have no place. Interna-tional brotherhood would follow. . . . With the socialist revolution humanity will complete its "prehistoric" stage and enter for the first time into what might be called its own history. . . . After the revolution a united classless society will be able for the first time to decide which way to go and what to do with its resources and capabilities. For the first time we shall make our own history! It is a "leap from slavery into freedom; from darkness into light."[14]

B. F. SKINNER'S *WALDEN TWO:* BEHAVIORAL PSYCHOLOGY IS THE ANSWER

B. F. Skinner (1905–1990) has been perhaps the most influential writer on **behavioral psychology** of modern times. His experiments designed to control animal behavior (including the training of pigeons to play Ping-Pong) and his theories about the relationship of human freedom to behavior modification have been the object of both acclaim and alarm. In the fictional work *Walden Two* (1948), Skinner outlined his notion of a modern utopian society.

It is worth noting at the outset that Skinner actually believes it would be possible to create a society such as the one described in *Walden Two*—that the necessary tools have been made available by the new science of human behavior.

B. F. Skinner (1905–1990), American psychologist.
"We simply arrange *a world in which serious*
conflicts occur as seldom as possible." (Christopher
S. Johnson/Stock, Boston)

The Good Life

As described in *Walden Two*, Skinner's utopia is, first of all, a world within a
world. Its founder, a psychologist named T. E. Frazier, has managed to obtain
"for taxes" a tract of land that previously contained seven or eight run-down
farms. Bounded on one side by a river and rolling hills and on the other three
sides by densely wooded terrain, it is conveniently self-enclosed—which turns
out to symbolize that it is also largely self-sufficient.

Although concerned about the problem of creating a good society, Frazier is
no philosopher. In fact, he disdains philosophy. Difficult questions such as
"What constitutes the good life?" are dismissed as irrelevant. "We all know
what's good, until we stop to think about it," he declares.[15] For Frazier, the basic
ingredients of the good life are perfectly obvious: good health, an absolute
minimum of unpleasant labor, a chance to exercise one's talents and abilities,
and finally, true leisure (by which is meant freedom from the economic and social
pressures that, in Frazier's view, render the so-called lesiure class the least relaxed
of people). These goals are realized at Walden Two in a pleasant atmosphere of
noncompetitive social harmony.

The Science of Behavioral Engineering

Frazier sums up his view about how to produce individual happiness and group
harmony this way:

> I can't give you a rational justification for any of it. I can't reduce it to any principle
> of "the greatest good." This *is* the Good Life. We know it. It's a fact, not a theory. . . .
> We don't puzzle our little minds over the outcome of Love versus Duty. We simply

arrange a world in which serious conflicts occur as seldom as possible or, with a little luck, not at all.[16]

The key word here is *arrange*. The *kind* of world to be arranged is of only passing interest to Frazier; what commands his attention is the question of *how* to do the arranging. He is concerned not with ends but with means, not with philosophy but with scientific experimentation. He is the quintessential methodologist.

Frazier has no time for politics or politicians. Because political action has not helped build a better world, "other measures" are required. What other measures? Nothing short of a revolution in the science of behavior modification:

> Considering how long society has been at it, you'd expect a better job. But the campaigns have been badly planned and the victory has never been secure. The behavior of the individual has been shaped according to revelations of "good conduct," never as the result of experimental study. But why not experiment? The questions are simple enough. What's the best behavior for the individual so far as the group is concerned? And how can the individual be induced to behave in that way? Why not explore these questions in a scientific spirit?[17]

The Walden Two experiment represents this kind of scientific exploration. Initially, an experimental code of good behavior is developed. Everyone at Walden Two is expected to adhere to the code, under the supervision of certain behavioral scientists, such as Frazier, called managers. In the outside world, Frazier notes, behavioral technology has been misused by psychologists, educators, religious leaders, politicians, ideologues, advertisers, and salespeople, among others. At Walden Two, positive reinforcement, rather than punishment, is employed to instill behavioral patterns, and a system of finely tuned frustrations and annoyances is used to eliminate the destructive emotions of anger, fear, and lust. For example, to engender self-restraint Frazier has the schoolteachers hang lollipops around the children's necks. If a child, having been instructed not to lick the candy, fails to resist the temptation, further self-control training is administered. Such **behavioral engineering** will prove successful, Frazier asserts, not because it physically controls outward behavior but because it effectively influences "the *inclination* to behave—the motives, the desires, the wishes."[18]

To ensure proper socialization, children are placed in a scientifically controlled environment from earliest infancy. They are raised in nurseries, and at no time during childhood or adolescence do they live with their parents. (Nor do their parents live with each other.) The overriding importance of community is emphasized in other ways: Private property is abolished; meals are taken together in common dining halls; and boys and girls customarily marry and have children at age 15 or 16, according to the dictates of Walden Two's genetic plan.

The Scientist as God

Much that is familiar in the outside world is notably absent at Walden Two. Although its residents feel free, there is no freedom in this community. The idea of freedom is illusory, Frazier argues, because all behavior is conditioned. History is viewed "only as entertainment"; schoolchildren do not even study this "spurious science." Religion is not forbidden, but, like government in Marx's utopia, it has simply withered away through social obsolescence ("psychologists are our priests," Frazier asserts). Moral codes of right and wrong have given way to "experimental ethics." Politics has no value whatever: "You can't make progress toward the Good Life by political action! Not under *any* current form of government! You must operate upon another level entirely."[19]

It soon becomes apparent to the reader that life at Walden Two has been organized to create the most propitious circumstances for the managers' experiments in behavior modification. Although Frazier justifies this on the basis of increased human happiness, we are left with the gnawing sense that something significant is missing here—some sort of check on the power of the behavioral engineers who run the community.

We are told that the managers will not become corrupted by their power because the planners "are part of a noncompetitive culture in which a thirst for power is a curiosity."[20] Then, too, we are assured, the managers do not use force (nobody does at Walden Two), and the offices they hold are not permanent—in time, they will once again become everyday citizens. These reassurances have a hollow ring, however. Clearly, the love of power is not absent from Frazier's own soul. As the founder of Walden Two, he appears to view himself as a kind of messiah who has discovered the secret to a whole new way of life: "I look upon my work and, behold, it is good."[21] Another brave new world, it would seem, has arrived.

UTOPIAS EXAMINED

In every utopia we have examined, there are no conflicts, jealousies, rivalries, rancorous disputes, or individual frustrations. No deep-seated tensions divide individuals, and no great antagonisms exist between society and the state. Each of these ideal states, however, is inspired by a different vision and ordered according to a different plan.

The Inspiration for Utopia

As we have observed, political thinkers construct utopias for a variety of reasons. In *The Republic,* Plato explored the limits of human perfection; that is, he sought not only to depict his conception of the best political order but also to make clear the problems that would accompany any attempt to bring about such a political order. In contrast, Bacon wrote *The New Atlantis* not to show the limits of human achievement but rather to indicate what a society wholly predicated on modern science might achieve. Bacon was concerned with the possibilities, not the limitations, of humanity. His is a hopeful work that promises a tangible improvement in human welfare.

Marx's utopian vision also is hopeful; even more, however, it constitutes a logical and necessary part of his world view. Without the promise of a classless society at the end of the road, the violence and suffering that Marx believed would inevitably accompany the end of capitalism would seem senseless. Marx's utopia, then, provides a beacon of hope in his dark vision of revolution and struggle. Skinner's *Walden Two*, by contrast, was written as an indictment of what its author saw as the ineffective and incorrect use of behavioral engineering. Skinner sought to demonstrate how a rational and scientific approach to behavior modification could produce dramatic social improvements.

The Road to Utopia

To create a completely happy and harmonious world, a writer must postulate a breakthrough in the way society is constituted. Plato saw philosophy as the key. His republic could not exist until or unless the wisest philosophers ruled. Not so with Bacon, for whom it was not the abstract quest for human knowledge that would blaze the trail but rather technical mastery of the scientific method. His Salomons were not philosophers concerned about the intangible realm of ideas; they were scientists who analyzed, observed, classified, recorded, and verified natural phenomena in an attempt to improve the human condition. For Marx, philosophy and science were overshadowed by economics; nonexploitative economic relationships, he believed, would guarantee a peaceful and plentiful world. Finally, Skinner viewed the scientific manipulation of human behavior as the key to social and personal fulfillment.

The Practicality of Utopia

With the advent of modern science and technology, some political thinkers began to take more seriously the practical possibility of achieving utopia. Armed with increasingly sophisticated tools—a new science, a new economics, a new behavioral psychology—utopians have increasingly tended to view the possibility of heaven on earth as something more than an implausible pipe dream.

This trend is clearly reflected in the utopian works we have examined. Plato, for example, demonstrated that it would be difficult, if not impossible, to bring his utopia into being and to keep it going. Bacon, in contrast, described the kind of society that might herald a radical improvement in human welfare if only the potential of modern science were realized to the fullest possible extent. To be sure, Bacon viewed utopia only as a future possibility—but a possibility well within our power to achieve. Marx's classless society, however, was not so much a possibility as an inevitability—a ratification of and reward for the final victory of the proletariat. In the sense that Marx's utopia supposedly lies within our grasp, it resembles Skinner's Walden Two. The latter, however, was to be brought into being immediately and without violence or revolution. The techniques of behavioral engineering were well enough known, Skinner believed; all that was required to achieve Walden Two was the will to put them to use.

In sum, utopias have increasingly assumed the form of blueprints for the future. Underlying these blueprints have been certain shared assumptions about human beings and what is best for them.

Utopia and Human Nature

Almost immediately after the ideal city is described in *The Republic,* its demise is outlined. According to one interpretation of the work, Plato understood that even if a perfectly ordered human community could be brought into existence, its degeneration could not be prevented. Plato thus raised a question that has plagued all subsequent utopians: How can change be avoided? A utopia, by definition, represents the best political system; therefore, all important change within it must be change for the worse. Hence, paradoxically, change necessarily becomes the deadly enemy of these innovative societies.

To banish change from their utopias, most writers have left nothing to chance in the ideal society, especially when it comes to *human nature.* Not only human vice and maliciousness, but also human unpredictability must be eradicated, or at least rigidly controlled, if people are to live together in peace and harmony.

To accomplish this, most utopias have relied on several common features, including *eugenics* programs, compulsory education, and the abolition of private property. Both eugenics programs and compulsory education have been viewed as necessary methods of ensuring the perpetuation of the best human qualities while eliminating undesirable characteristics. In the same vein, utopian thinkers have advocated eliminating private property in order to banish egoism, greed, and avarice from human nature. Most utopians have taken the position that human selfishness is caused by socioeconomic institutions that protect, sanction, and perpetuate inequalities and that these institutions can be eliminated only by a fundamental reordering of society. In many utopias, therefore, communal activities, common residences, and public meals replace the private ownership of property, in the hope that cooperation will triumph over competition.

A specific view of human nature underlies these proposals for the radical restructuring of society. Conflicts among human beings, according to this view, grow out of badly organized or corrupt societies whose overall structure can and must be drastically improved. If negative influences can be eliminated, human behavior can be elevated. At the heart of the utopian impulse, then, is the belief that human nature, if not good, is at least malleable (and therefore *potentially* good).

Utopia and the Neglect of Politics

The utopian belief that human nature can and should be easily molded raises some serious concerns. If individuals can be influenced so profoundly by their environment, they become potential candidates not only for moral perfection but also for moral corruption. Any flaw in the construction of a utopia can therefore turn a dream into a nightmare.

In almost every utopia (including Marx's "dictatorship of the proletariat" stage), political power is centralized. Accordingly, utopian governments have at their disposal powerful tools with which to control human behavior. By themselves, these tools are neutral; everything depends on how they are used—wisely or foolishly, efficiently or wastefully, morally or immorally. Utopian thinkers tend to assume that these tools will always be used benignly. But given the power of the modern technocratic state and the malleability of human nature, this assumption seems tenuous at best. What has troubled many critics of utopian schemes is not simply the concentration of power they tend to countenance but the total absence of checks and balances in the exercise of that power.

Utopian thinkers generally display little interest in politics and government. They see no real need to reconcile the conflicting claims of power and justice. Given material abundance, public-spirited citizens, and little or no conflict between human desires and human well-being (or between socioeconomic equality and individual excellence), the achievement of social justice becomes a technical, rather than a political, problem. Hence the nuts-and-bolts workings of actual governments—mechanisms for separation of powers, checks and balances, judicial review, and so forth—holds no interest for most utopians.

Dysutopias

The dangers of unchecked political power, and the more general theme of utopia-turned-nightmare, are vividly developed in such well-known works as George Orwell's *Nineteen Eighty-four* and Aldous Huxley's *Brave New World*. Both books provide graphic descriptions of a modern *dysutopia*—a society whose creators set out to build a perfect political order only to discover that having promised the impossible, they could only remain in power by maintaining a ruthless monopoly on the means of coercion and communication. In *Nineteen Eighty-four*, the totalitarian rulers retained power by manipulating not only the people's actions and forms of behavior but also their sources and methods of thought. Thus the Ministry of Truth was established for the sole purpose of systematically lying to the citizenry; a new language ("Newspeak") was invented to purge all words, ideas, and expressions considered dangerous by the government; and a contradictory kind of logic ("double-think") was introduced to make the minds of the citizenry receptive to the opportunistic zigzags of official propaganda.

But perhaps some more modest institutions for ensuring decent government deserve greater consideration than utopians have been willing to grant. As we have seen, utopian plans are fraught with unseen dangers. Although often motivated by the best of intentions and supported by the highest of ideals, utopian schemes, as Plato recognized, are as prone to failure as most other human endeavors. And in the real world, when utopian dreams collapse, they sometimes bring whole societies crashing down with them—as has been shown by the history of twentieth-century totalitarianism, much of which originated in utopian ideals.

Summary

The term *utopia*, signifying an imaginary society of perfect harmony and happiness, was coined by Sir Thomas More in the sixteenth century. More's *Utopia* was a subtle attack on the ills of English society under Henry VIII. The first important attempt to define the perfect political order, however, was made in Plato's *Republic*.

Four works stand out as representative of utopian thought in the history of Western political philosophy. In *The Republic*, Plato sought the just society through philosophical inquiry. In the seventeenth century, Francis Bacon wrote *The New Atlantis* to demonstrate how the human condition could be elevated through modern science. Karl Marx later propounded the view that only through the radical reorganization of economic relationships within society could true justice and an end to human misery be achieved. The ultimate aim of Marx's theory of social transformation is the creation of a classless society. Finally, in B. F. Skinner's *Walden Two*, a prime example of a contemporary utopian scheme, behavioral psychology holds the key to utopia. The form and content of the just society are of less concern to the author of *Walden Two* than the methods for bringing such a society into existence.

In general, utopian thought has been inspired by idealism and impatience with social injustices. However, the presumed desirability of utopia frequently conflicts with its practical possibility. The principal obstacle to utopian society is the decided unpredictability and selfishness of human nature, which utopian thinkers commonly have sought to control through eugenics programs, compulsory education, and the abolition of private property.

Utopian visionaries often blame politics for the failure to improve society. As a result, in many utopian blueprints the role of politics in bringing about desired change is either greatly reduced or eliminated entirely. This neglect of politics leaves most utopian schemes open to the criticism that they could as easily become blueprints for totalitarianism as visions of a better life.

Key Terms

utopia	behavioral psychology
philosopher-kings	behavioral engineering
dictatorship of the proletariat	human nature
first stage of communism	eugenics
second stage of communism	dysutopia

Review Questions

1. What is the origin of the term *utopia*? What does the word mean?

2. How have utopian writers differed regarding the practicality of utopia?

3. What basic assumptions regarding human nature and society have been made by modern utopian writers?

4. What is the value of utopian thought?

Recommended Reading

BACON, FRANCIS. *The New Atlantis and the Great Instauration* (2nd ed.). Arlington Heights, Ill.: Harlan Davidson, 1989. Bacon's account of a society blessed by scientific breakthroughs seems surprisingly modern.

GILLISON, JEROME. *The Soviet Image of Utopia.* Baltimore, Md.: Johns Hopkins University Press, 1975. An insightful discussion of the idealist elements in Marxist-Leninist ideology.

HERTZLER, JOYCE. *The History of Utopian Thought.* New York: Cooper Square Publishers, 1965. A thoroughgoing discussion of utopian thinkers and their ideas throughout history.

KATEB, GEORGE. *Utopia and Its Enemies* (rev. ed.). New York: Schocken Books, 1972. A sympathetic defense of the value and contributions of utopian thought.

MORE, THOMAS. *Utopia.* Translated by Paul Turner. Baltimore: Penguin, 1965. More's imaginary society inspired many later utopian writers; the work remains a charming account of one man's paradise.

ORWELL, GEORGE. *Nineteen Eighty-four.* New York: New American Library, 1961. This novel brilliantly describes a dysutopia modeled after Stalin's Soviet Union. A classic.

PLATO. *The Republic.* Translated by Allan Bloom. New York: Basic Books, 1968. Allan Bloom's interpretive essay helps make this edition of Plato's classic work especially valuable.

POPPER, KARL. *The Open Society and Its Enemies.* Princeton, N.J.: Princeton University Press, 1966. This work argues that both Plato and Marx (among others) were advocates of totalitarian government and opponents of free, democratic societies.

Notes

1. See Leo Strauss, *What Is Political Philosophy? and Other Studies* (New York: Free Press, 1959), p. 10.

2. Allan Bloom, "Interpretive Essay," in *The Republic of Plato* (New York: Basic Books, 1968), trans. A. Bloom, pp. 308–310.

3. Plato's best political order is most accurately translated as "city." The original Greek, *polis,* implies a relatively small self-sufficient community that provides for all human relationships. Modern distinctions between, for example, society and government or church and state are quite foreign to this concept.

4. Bloom, *The Republic of Plato,* p. 410.

5. Ibid.

6. Howard White, *Peace among the Willows: The Political Philosophy of Francis Bacon* (The Hague: Martinus Nijhoff, 1968), pp. 97, 102.

7. Karl Marx, "Capital: Selections," in *The Marx-Engels Reader,* ed. Robert C. Tucker (New York: Norton, 1972), p. 259.

8.   Karl Marx and Friedrich Engels, "Manifesto of the Communist Party," in *The Marx-Engels Reader*, p. 352.

9.   Friedrich Engels, "Socialism: Utopian and Scientific," in *The Marx-Engels Reader*, p. 635.

10. Karl Marx, "Outlines of a Future Society, from 'The German Ideology,' " in *Capital, Communist Manifesto, and Other Writings*, ed. Max Eastman (New York: Modern Library, 1932), p. 1.

11. Ibid.

12. Joseph Cropsey, "Karl Marx," in *History of Political Philosophy*, ed. Leo Strauss and Joseph Cropsey (Skokie, Ill.: Rand McNally, 1969), p. 717.

13. Jerome Gillison, *The Soviet Image of Utopia* (Baltimore: The Johns Hopkins University Press, 1975), p. 110.

14. Roy Macrides, *Contemporary Political Ideologies* (Cambridge, Mass.: Winthrop, 1980), p. 180.

15. B. F. Skinner, *Walden Two* (New York: Macmillan, 1962), p. 159.

16. Ibid., p. 161.

17. Ibid., pp. 104–105.

18. Ibid., p. 262.

19. Ibid., p. 193.

20. Ibid., p. 272.

21. Ibid., p. 295.

CHAPTER 3

TOTALITARIAN STATES

FAILED UTOPIAS

(UPI/Bettmann)

UTOPIAS ARE THEORETICAL states: One can imagine but not create a utopian society. But what about real political systems? How can they be classified? Perhaps the most fundamental political distinction is between democratic and nondemocratic states. Democratic states are characterized by meaningful elections, a respect for citizens' rights, and constitutionally limited governmental powers (see Chapters 5 through 7). Nondemocratic states display none of these characteristics. Rather, this type of regime, usually termed authoritarian, is headed by a dictator or an autocrat intent on maintaining political power, often at any cost (see Chapter 4). For people who live in a democracy, it is easy to assume that democratic rule is natural and authoritarian rule is unnatural. As we shall see, however, authoritarian forms of government have historically been far more common than democratic forms. Furthermore, in the twentieth century, an extreme form of nondemocratic state has arisen repeatedly. This phenomenon is commonly known as *totalitarianism.*

Almost always grounded in a utopian vision (that is, in the idea of bringing about a radically new kind of political order), totalitarian states seek to achieve their goals through total control over every aspect of the societies they dominate. This obsession with control extends beyond the public realm into the private lives of citizens. So extensive is governmental power that the regime seeks not simply to control citizens but to transform their very nature. To the extent such efforts are successful, citizens lose both moral and political autonomy. For this reason, totalitarian states are at once pervasively political in one respect and antipolitical in another. They are pervasively political in the sense that citizens' private lives are overwhelmed by the political culture and authority imposed by the government. Every activity is considered political. The government seeks to transform the nature and meaning of work, education, social organizations, and even the family (as neighbors spy on neighbors and children are encouraged to turn in "disloyal" parents). Yet these states are also antipolitical in that dissent and diversity, as well as all appeals to conscience or justice, are ruthlessly suppressed as the government seeks to transform society according to its own ideological blueprints. In these two crucial respects, totalitarian states differ from more traditional authoritarian states, which seek to suppress only the kinds of activities directly associated with multiparty politics and political opposition (see the Appendix for a comparison of the three main forms of rule).

Totalitarian states have profoundly influenced the course of the twentieth century. Yet today it seems clear that totalitarianism is in decline. Communist states have been cited as the most frequent example of contemporary totalitarianism, yet we have recently witnessed the widespread demise of communism around the world. The following question therefore arises: Why study totalitarian states at all? At least four reasons come to mind. First, communism is not the only form of totalitarian state possible. The example of Nazi Germany stands as a reminder that totalitarianism is not a product of one ideology, regime, or ruler. Second, totalitarianism is an integral, albeit tragic, part of recent history and stands in sharp contrast to the pronouncements of politicians, professors, theologians, and a host of others who all too optimistically proclaimed a belief in human progress. Many people who suffered directly at the hands of totalitarian dictators or lost loved ones in Hitler's Holocaust, Stalin's Reign of Terror, Mao's spasmodic purges, or other, even more contemporary instances of totalitarian brutality are still living. The physical and emotional scars of the victims remain even after the tyrants who inflicted the injuries and perpetrated the injustices are long gone. A third reason for studying totalitarian regimes is that they failed as utopian experiments; they are based on a particular vision of social progress and perfection that cannot be pursued without resort to barbaric measures. Thus totalitarian states demonstrate the risks of idealism gone awry. Fourth, totalitarianism remains an ever-present political possibility. It is dangerous to assume that the world has seen the last of this political evil. The best reason, then, for civilized people to study totalitarianism is to guard against the resurgence of powerful mass movements with opportunistic leaders for whom civilization has no meaning.

THE ESSENCE OF TOTALITARIANISM

Totalitarianism differs markedly from traditional authoritarian states where power is concentrated in the hands of one or a few rulers. Most authoritarian leaders are content to exercise negative powers; that is, they aim, above all, to prevent political opposition from taking shape. In a curious way, this goal limits the aspirations and methods of traditional autocrats. For example, although authoritarian rulers seldom hesitate to use coercion, they typically target people who are perceived as a direct threat to the existing order. Key social groups and economic interests are often free to function without state interference. Independent institutions such as the church or the business community are likely to exercise considerable influence in authoritarian systems.

Given their limited goals, authoritarian governments commonly display neither the need nor the desire to mobilize the citizenry in official demonstrations, mass campaigns, or political rallies and meetings. In authoritarian states, public participation in politics is normally restricted to a low level, and political apathy is frequently tolerated or even encouraged. If a dominant political party exists, its functions tend to be limited to ritual demonstrations of loyalty to the regime and other symbolic activities. Finally, the state itself may encourage a particular public image of the government (the "macho" or paternalistic quality of the leader), but generally it will not advance a well-developed political ideology.

Within totalitarian states, in contrast, violence against political enemies may assume the form of indiscriminate, mass terror and genocide aimed at whole groups, categories, or classes of people who are labeled enemies, counterrevolutionaries, spies, and saboteurs. Even ordinary citizens are expected to demonstrate their loyalty to the regime in a variety of ways and thus are subject to tight surveillance. Mass mobilization for political and economic purposes is carried out through a highly regimented and centralized one-party system dedicated to an all-encompassing ideology. To disseminate this ideology, the state employs a propaganda and censorship apparatus far more sophisticated and effective than that typically found in authoritarian states.

In sum, totalitarian governments *aim* at nothing short of total political, social, and economic control:

> Totalitarian dictatorship involves total domination, limited neither by received laws or codes (as in traditional authoritarianism) nor even the boundaries of governmental functions (as in classical tyranny), since they obliterate the distinction between state and society. . . . Totalitarianism is limited only by the need to keep large numbers of people in a state of constant activity controlled by the elite.[1]

Complete domination of society is necessary because all totalitarian ideologies proclaim the advent of a new and infinitely better commonwealth of humankind. Historically, that commonwealth has taken various forms: the society of racially pure "Aryan" supermen envisioned by Adolf Hitler's Nazi regime in Germany; the proletarian brotherhood of oppressed and downtrodden workers promised by the Soviet leaders V. I. Lenin and Josef Stalin; the new mass society of sturdy and selfless peasants fashioned in the poetic imagery of China's Mao Zedong. But whatever the specifics, the general vision of communitarian life conjured up in totalitarian ideologies has been remarkably similar. All such totalitarian prophets "have exhibited a basic likeness . . . in their determination to engender a higher and unprecedented kind of human existence."[2]

The totalitarian leader's claim of political legitimacy can be traced directly to this self-proclaimed mandate to create a new society. In the words of one expert, "The characteristic feature of totalitarian rule is the subjugation of both state and society together under a utopian, nonpolitical claim to rule."[3] In other words, totalitarian leaders assert that because the new community can come into being solely through their (or their party's) leadership, the forcible imposition on society of a set of beliefs is justified. This set of beliefs—the official ideology—invariably comprises a "reasonably coherent body of ideas concerning practical means of how totally to change and reform a society by force, or violence, based on an all-inclusive or total criticism of what is wrong with the existing or antecedent society."[4]

The ideal societies prophesied by totalitarian movements commonly exalt values such as equality and community over values such as liberty and individuality. As another authority has put it:

> The total revolutionary's true community is perfectly comprehensive and thoroughly egalitarian: no social differences will remain; even authority and expertise, from the scientific to the artistic, cannot be tolerated. Such a radical egalitarianism must necessarily reject all individualism. The rights of the individual against the collectivity disappear, and normal constitutional rights are reinterpreted as rights to conform to the group. Claims against the group—to material goods, to restricted human relationships such as love, and to privacy—are condemned as divisive. In the name of equality, there is postulated a community of such solidarity that it can be said to have a consciousness of its own, and individual consciousness becomes at best an antisocial deviation.[5]

At the heart of this harmonious community lies the concept of a reformulated human nature. In totalitarian states, the wholesale reconstruction of the human personality becomes the nonnegotiable price of admission into the utopian society promised by the official ideology. This impulse to human perfection was reflected in Lenin's repeated references to the creation of a "new Soviet man" and in the Nazi assertion that party workers and leaders represented a new type of people or a new breed of rulers. Mao Zedong displayed a near obsession with what he termed *rectification*—the radical purging of all capitalist tendencies (such as materialism and individualism) at all levels of Chinese society. It is rather striking that all twentieth-century totalitarian movements have sought to transform not only the outward appearance of society but also the innermost character of society's individual members.

Not even the most repressive totalitarian regime, however, has managed to accomplish these transformations completely. In all totalitarian states, there have remained *"islands of separateness"*[6]—the family, the church, or some other social institution through which internal resistance to the prevailing government can survive. Not even the extraordinarily totalitarian government of the fictional state of Oceania, described by the British writer George Orwell in *Nineteen Eighty-four*, managed to master its citizens totally (although it came close enough to make for extraordinarily grim reading).

But if totalitarian states have not been especially successful in creating a "new man" or a political heaven on earth, they have had surprising success in silencing their opponents while carrying out radically new programs. Totalitarian governments have understood that no new community of fellow believers can survive in the midst of dissenters, deviants, skeptics, and enemies. To them, it has not mattered that their goals, and the means adopted to achieve those goals, often seem sharply at odds with reason and common sense. Nor has it made much difference to them that many of their activities have violated the moral precepts held by most other nations. Finally, it has not even mattered that people denounced as enemies of the state frequently were either totally uninterested in politics or formerly praised as the most loyal supporters of the regime. When the nation's political goal is not merely to eliminate political opposition but also to bring about a new, higher order of political life, are not extraordinary political measures justified? From the totalitarian point of view, these measures represent the necessary price of any attempt to bring about a utopian political order.

The clearest examples of such utopian political orders were Nazi Germany, the Soviet Union under Lenin and especially Stalin, and Maoist China. As we will see, these nations have profoundly influenced our age. Totalitarianism, however, has not been confined to these nations. The political novelty of totalitarian regimes, along with their profound impact, has led some political scientists to consider totalitarianism the most significant political development of the twentieth century.

THE REVOLUTIONARY STAGE OF TOTALITARIANISM

To understand the phenomenon of totalitarianism, we must explore both how it functions and how it comes into being. In general, totalitarian states are conceived in violence and emerge from the body politic of a regime that has collapsed and died. Almost always, the midwife is revolution. To be successful, the instigators of total revolution employ various methods and tactics—specifically, leadership, ideology, organization, propaganda, and violence.

Leadership

Perhaps the most conspicuous trait of total revolution has been a reliance on what may be termed the *cult of leadership*. Virtually every such revolution has been identified with—indeed, personified in—the image of one larger-than-life figure. The Russian Revolution had its Lenin, the Third Reich its Hitler, the Chinese Revolution its Mao, Cuba its Castro. Each of these leaders was made the object of hero worship.

Philosopher Eric Hoffer summed up the importance of leadership in modern mass movements as follows:

> Once the stage is set, the presence of an outstanding leader is indispensable. Without him there will be no movement. The ripeness of the times does not automatically produce a mass movement, nor can elections, laws and administrative bureaus hatch one. It was Lenin who forced the flow of events into the channels of the Bolshevik revolution. Had he died in Switzerland, or on his way to Russia in 1917, it is almost certain that the other prominent Bolsheviks would have joined a coalition government. The result might have been a more or less liberal republic run chiefly by the bourgeoisie. In the case of Mussolini or Hitler the evidence is even more decisive: without them there would have been neither a Fascist nor a Nazi movement.[7]

Thus although revolutions have invariably been launched in the name of the masses, the initiative has always come from above. Their leaders long have recognized that the masses alone possess the raw power to change the world but lack the will and direction. (For the Bolsheviks, the missing ingredient was "class consciousness"; for the Nazis, it was "*Volk* consciousness.") The inspiration and fanatical commitment to fuse a large number of self-interested individuals into a revolutionary mass movement cannot come from a bloodless abstraction such as "the party"; it can come only from the personal dynamism of a charismatic leader who can read the minds, capture the imagination, and win the hearts of the masses. (It is ironic, but entirely logical, that all modern mass movements have emphasized the personality of the leader while deemphasizing the individuality of the followers.) A leader such as Lenin or Mao, then, is to a mass movement what a detonator is to a bomb—no matter how lethal the explosive in a bomb might be, it remains dormant and harmless until provided with an efficient trigger.

Ideology

Whatever the quality of leadership, total revolutions depend in the final analysis on the willingness of large numbers of converts to engage in extraordinary acts of self-sacrifice in the name of the cause. Such reckless devotion cannot be inspired by appeals to the rational faculty in human beings. It must arise, rather, from a believer's blind faith in the absolute truth provided by a comprehensive political doctrine.

The Need for a Scapegoat: Reinterpreting the Past As a critique of the past, ideology generally focuses on some form of absolute evil to which all national (or worldwide) inadequacies and social injustices can be attributed. To the revolutionary ideologue, the true causes of economic recession, inflation, military defeat, official corruption, national humiliation, moral decadence, and any other perceived problem are rooted in the mysteries and plots of a rejected past.

Rarely is the absolute evil a disembodied force; almost always it assumes the form of a clearly identifiable enemy. If such an enemy does not exist, one must be invented. Usually it will be an individual or a group that is already widely feared, hated, or envied. Lenin blamed the plight of the workers on money-grubbing monopoly capitalists. Hitler blamed the German loss in World War I and the economic crises that preceded his assumption of power on Jews and communists. Mao found his enemy in the guise first of wealthy landlords and later of "capitalist-roaders." Clearly, the purpose of this ploy is to focus mass attention on a readily identifiable scapegoat, on whose shoulders all of the nation's ills can be placed.

In the words of one authority, "Mass movements can rise and spread without a belief in God, but never without a belief in a devil."[8] Hate and prejudice, rather than love and high principle, are seemingly the most effective forces in bringing people together in a common cause. The deliberate cultivation of a hate object not only serves to focus blame for the injustices of the past but also helps to mobilize the masses against the alleged cause of the miseries of the present.

Revolutionary Struggle: Explaining the Present As a guide to the present, ideology provides the true believer with keys to a "correct" analysis of the underlying forces at work in contemporary society. Concepts such as class struggle for Marxist-Leninists, *Herrenvolk* (the "master race") for the Nazis, and "contradictions" for Mao's followers are used as tools to explain and predict social reality. Yesterday the enemy was preeminent; today the enemy will be defeated.

Advocates of total revolution believe that struggle is the very essence of politics. For Marxist-Leninists, class struggle is the engine of progress in history. For Maoists, struggle is a desirable end in itself; only through the direct experience of revolutionary struggle, they believe, can the masses (and especially the young) learn the true meaning of self-sacrifice. Hitler glorified the struggle for power by proclaiming war to be the supreme test of national greatness. (Revealingly, Hitler outlined his own path to political power in a book titled *Mein Kampf,* "my struggle.")

Whether the aim is to overthrow monopoly capitalists or to purify a race, revolutionary struggle is always described in terms of good versus evil. It was not uncommon for leading Nazis to depict Jews not simply as enemies of the state but as *Untermenschen* ("subhumans") and, frequently, as insects or lice.[9] Of course, the repeated use of such degrading characterizations eventually serves to dehumanize the scapegoat group in the mass mind; it is easier to justify the extermination of insects than of human beings.

Utopia: Foretelling the Future   As a promise of the future, ideology tends to paint a radiant picture of perfect justice and perpetual peace. Marxist-Leninists envision this utopia as a classless society, one from which all social and economic inequality has been abolished. The Nazi utopia was a society from which all racial "impurities" had been removed through the extermination or enslavement of racial "inferiors." Whatever its precise character, this motivating vision invariably includes the promise of material plenty stemming from the redistribution of property from the haves to the have-nots. Marxism-Leninism promises to take from the rich (the bourgeoisie) and give to the poor (the proletariat). Interestingly, Hitler made a similar promise when he proclaimed his intention to provide *Lebensraum* ("living space") in the east; he would take land away from the land-rich but slothful Slavs and give it to the land-poor but industrious Germans.

Inherent in these visions of utopia is almost always an ironclad guarantee of success in the struggle to achieve them. Thus Marxism is based on a deterministic world view (in the sense that the success of the proletarian revolution is dictated by inflexible "laws" of history). Hitler, too, was an unabashed determinist. In *Mein Kampf*, he wrote, "Man must realize that a fundamental law of necessity reigns throughout the whole realm of Nature."[10] And throughout his public career, he spoke frequently of "the iron law of our historical development," the "march of history," and the "inner logic of events." Hitler, no less than Lenin, Stalin, or Mao, claimed that he and the German *Volk* had a world-shattering mission to accomplish and that success was inevitable. He expressed this notion in what is perhaps his most famous (or infamous) pronouncement: "I go the way that Providence dictates with the assurance of a sleepwalker."

Ideology and Truth   The past, present, and future as described by a given revolutionary ideology may seem farfetched or even ludicrous to a disinterested observer. For example, the racial theory promulgated by the Nazis utterly lacked historical, sociological, genetic, or moral foundations. By the same token, the economic facet of Hitler's ideology—the "socialism" in National Socialism—was devoid of meaningful content. So watered down was Hitler's conception of socialism that in the words of one authority, "anyone genuinely concerned about the people was in Hitler's eyes a socialist."[11]

Why would anyone take such an ideology seriously? First, it appeals to popular prejudices and makes them respectable; second, it is not the message that counts so much as the messenger—the leader's personal magnetism will attract a following whether or not the words make sense; third, certitude is far more important than rectitude. Consider all that an ideology must do for the individual follower if it is to be successful:

> It must claim scientific authority which gives the believer a conviction of having the exclusive key to all knowledge, it must promise a millennium to be brought about for the chosen race or class by the elect who holds this key; it must identify a host of

ogres and demons to be overcome before this happy state is brought about; it must enlist the dynamic of hatred, envy and fear (whether of class or race) and justify these low passions by the loftiness of its aims; every means and every crime is laudable in overcoming the adversary, and the virtues of the enemy can be turned into vices by attaching some simple label, such as "bourgeois," to them; in particular, truth is what is to the advantage of the chosen class or race, falsehood what is contrary to that interest; since this truth is scientifically demonstrable and since no two people are likely to agree about it, there must be a single interpreter, whose will is law, if the ideology is to be fully effective; as the bearer of all truth, the leader is entitled to expect from his followers religious devotion and every sacrifice and every crime that will promote his interest.[12]

In the final analysis, successful ideologues can often get away with the most absurd allegations and falsehoods if they also address real problems faced by the masses. Thus many Germans recognized the extremist nature of the Nazis' racial theories but probably believed that such absurdities would be discarded by Hitler once the work of unifying the country, reviving the economy, and restoring the nation's lost honor had been accomplished. By the same token, it is doubtful that any but the most committed Bolsheviks believed that the workers' paradise was just around the corner—but the Russian people very likely *did* believe in land reform, an end to Russia's disastrous involvement in World War I, and improvements in nutrition, medical care, and education as promised by Lenin.

Organization

Ideology in total revolutions could never be implemented without sustained organization. Cohesive structure was one of the missing ingredients in pre–twentieth-century rebellions. Most such outbreaks were spontaneous affairs that burst into flame and occasionally spread but almost always burned themselves out.

Different revolutionary leaders have stressed different methods of formal organization in their quest for political power. Although the Bolshevik party did not actually seize power in Russia until October 1917, Lenin had founded the party more than 14 years earlier. Admitting only hard-core revolutionaries into the party, Lenin reasoned that the czar could be defeated only by a long, clandestine struggle. Thus a small, tightly knit group of professional revolutionaries would be far more effective in the long run than a large, amorphous mass of unruly malcontents.

To ensure secrecy, discipline, and centralized control, Lenin organized the Bolshevik party into tiny *cells,* later called *primary party organizations*. Each cell had a leader, dubbed a secretary, who acted on orders or instructions from above. Ultimately, all important decisions on strategy, tactics, and the "party line" were made by Lenin himself (though he claimed to speak in the name of the party's Central Committee). As the Bolsheviks grew in number and established cells in cities outside their St. Petersburg headquarters, intermediate layers of authority became necessary, but the principle of strict party discipline and total subordination of lower levels to higher was never relaxed.

Having formed his own faction, Lenin eventually placed a formal ban on factionalism. Any Bolshevik who opposed the party line thereafter stood in danger of being indicated as a factionalist. Before the actual seizure of power in October 1917, the penalty for dissent was frequently expulsion from the party; after 1917, revolutionary justice was often less lenient. Factionalism could not be tolerated; party members were expected to place party interests above personal interests at all times. This spirit of self-sacrifice and total commitment to the party was given a special name—*partiinost,* a term commonly used in the former Soviet Union to denote the distinctive combination of intangible qualities (such as loyalty, self-discipline, and revolutionary élan) that every party member was expected to exhibit.

In comparison with Lenin's revolution, Mao's took more than 20 years to achieve success and involved many more people—unlike its Russian counterpart, the Chinese Revolution was primarily a rural phenomenon involving a mass of discontented peasants. Under these circumstances, Mao's most pressing organizational problem was to mold the peasants into an effective military force capable of carrying out a protracted guerrilla war. His success in turning an amorphous peasant mass into an effective fighting force seemed to offer convincing proof that once organized, the poor and downtrodden could overcome seemingly insurmountable obstacles. For this reason, Mao's theory and practice of peasant-based revolution have been regarded by many radicals (especially in developing nations) as the guiding example of revolutionary organization in a rural society.

In contrast to Mao's long, concerted struggle to achieve political power, Hitler's attempts to gain power in Germany followed an erratic course, swinging from a violent, abortive coup in the early 1920s to a successful manipulation of the country's constitutional system in the 1930s. A compliant organization in the form of the Nazi party was crucial to Hitler's ultimate success.

During his rise to power, Hitler made extensive use of brute force to intimidate his opposition, but he also created numerous party-controlled clubs and associations. The Hitler Youth, a Nazi women's league, a Nazi workers' organization, a Nazi student league, and various other academic and social organizations gave the Nazis considerable political power even before Hitler took over the reins of government (see Figure 10-2). Later, through a policy called *Gleichschaltung* ("coordination"), he destroyed virtually all preexisting social organizations and substituted Nazi associations in their place. Partly for this reason, Hitler's promises and threats carried great weight throughout German society. Like all modern revolutionaries, Hitler understood the value of a carefully constructed revolutionary organization.

Propaganda

As modern political life has extended its reach to more and more people, *propaganda* (the broad dissemination of ideas and information deliberately tailored to further a political cause) has become a potent political weapon. To be successful,

Through Nazi ideology and propaganda that was developed and implemented by Adolf Hitler, the German people came to accept the persecution of the Jews, the necessity of an eventual war, and the radical transformation of German society. (Topham/Image Works)

as Hitler pointed out, propaganda must address the masses exclusively, and hence "its effect for the most part must be aimed at the emotions and only to a very limited degree at the so-called intellect."[13]

An avid student of the science of propaganda, Hitler formulated several theorems about the subject that still hold true today. To begin with, he postulated that "all propaganda must be popular and its intellectual level must be adjusted to the most limited intelligence among those it is addressed to." Hence, "the greater the mass it is intended to reach, the lower its purely intellectual level will have to be. . . . Effective propaganda must be limited to a very few points and must harp on these in slogans until the last member of the public understands what you want him to understand." Given these premises, it follows that the "very first axiom of all propagandist activity [is] the basically subjective and one-sided attitude it must take toward every question it deals with."[14] Furthermore, the bigger the lie, the better.

Hitler argued that the success of any propaganda campaign depends in the final analysis on the propagandists' understanding of the "primitive sentiments" of the popular masses. Propaganda cannot have multiple shadings: Concepts and "facts" must be presented to the public as true or false, right or wrong, black or white. In *Mein Kampf*, Hitler heaped high praise on British propaganda efforts in World War I and expressed total contempt for German propaganda, which he faulted for *not* painting the world in stark black-and-white terms.

Long before Hitler's rise to power, Lenin developed and refined his own techniques of mass propaganda. Lenin began by making a distinction between propaganda and agitation. His explanation of the difference between the two should be considered in light of Hitler's theorems:

> A propagandist, when he discusses unemployment, must explain the capitalist nature of the crisis; he must show the reason for its inevitability in modern society; he must describe the necessity of rebuilding society on a Socialist basis, etc. In a word, he must give many ideas concentrated all together, so many that all of them will not be understood by the average person, and in their totality they will be understood by relatively few.
>
> The agitator, on the other hand, will pick out one more or less familiar and concrete aspect of the entire problem. Let us say the death of an unemployed worker as a result of starvation. His efforts will be concentrated on this fact, to impart to the masses a single idea—the idea of the senseless contradiction between the growth of wealth and the growth of poverty. He will strive to evoke among the masses discontent and revolt against this great injustice and will leave the full explanation for this contradiction to the propagandists.[15]

Unlike Hitler, who was a highly effective orator, Lenin was a master pamphleteer and polemicist who relied most heavily on the written word. In the infancy of his movement, Lenin's chief weapon was the underground newspaper. Endowed with names such as *Iskra* ("The Spark"), *Vperyod* ("Forward"), and *Proletari* ("Proletariat"), these contraband tabloids often had to be produced in some remote corner of the country, or even in a foreign country, and smuggled into St. Petersburg in false-bottom briefcases and by other ingenious methods.

Violence

The fifth and final characteristic of totalitarian revolution is the use of violence and terror as accepted instruments of political policy. For revolutionaries, violence is particularly useful in reinforcing the political effect of propaganda. One student of modern totalitarian tyranny has observed that "terror without propaganda would lose most of its psychological effect, whereas progaganda without terror does not contain its full punch."[16] And according to the Nazi theorist Eugene Hadamovsky, "Propaganda and violence are never contradictions. Use of violence can be part of the propaganda."[17]

The kind of violence commonly associated with terrorism ranges from highly selective acts such as assassinations and kidnappings to indiscriminate bombings and sabotage that result in death and injury to innocent bystanders. Sabotage is designed to disrupt production, transportation, and communications systems and thereby the political stability of the state; terror is aimed at the psychological sense of personal security that is always a precondition for social stability.

Terror in support of propaganda has played a prominent role in mass movements of both the right and the left. One of the most striking examples of this revolutionary tactic was provided by the *fasci di combattimento* ("combat groups") formed by the Italian Fascist party leader Benito Mussolini shortly after World War I. After attempts to gain power by wooing the working class away from the Socialist party had failed, Mussolini began to cultivate the middle classes and to seek financing from the wealthy industrialists and big landowners. Convinced of the impossibility of capturing control of the Italian government by legal means, in the early 1920s he turned increasingly toward terror as a means of dealing with political opponents. His followers thus substituted arson and assassination for the normal, nonviolent means of political competition. One of the more novel forms of terror devised by the Fascists was the *punitive expedition,* in which armed bands would conduct raids against unsuspecting and defenseless communities. The local police often would cooperate simply by doing nothing.

The punitive expeditions mounted by the Italian Fascists epitomized the strategy and tactics of terror as part of totalitarian revolution. Cleverly employed, terrorism can create a sense of utter defenselessness in the face of an imminent but often indistinct danger. The aim of the terrorists is threefold: (1) to create an artificial atmosphere of crisis; (2) to demonstrate that the state is no longer capable of providing law-abiding, taxpaying citizens with protection from unprovoked attacks on their persons and property; and (3) to prod an increasingly fearful, desperate, and fragmented citizenry to turn for refuge and order to the very same political movement that, unbeknown to most, has caused the deepening state of social degeneration.

Hannah Arendt has provided an especially lucid explanation of the similar use of terror by the Nazis:

> The Nazis did not strike at prominent figures as had been done in the earlier wave of political crimes in Germany (the murder of Rathenau and Erzberger); instead, by killing small socialist functionaries or influential members of opposing parties, they attempted to prove to the population the danger involved in mere membership. This kind of mass terror, which still operated on a comparatively small scale, increased steadily because neither the police nor the courts seriously prosecuted political offenders on the so-called Right. It was valuable as what a Nazi publicist has aptly called "power propaganda": it made clear to the population at large that the power of the Nazis was greater than that of the authorities and that it was safer to be a member of a Nazi paramilitary organization than a loyal Republican. This impression was greatly strengthened by the specific use the Nazis made of their political crimes. They always admitted them publicly, never apologized for "excesses of the lower ranks"—such apologies were used only by Nazi sympathizers—and impressed the population as being very different from the "idle talkers" of other parties.
>
> The similarities between this kind of terror and plain gangsterism are too obvious to be pointed out. This does not mean that Nazism was gangsterish, as has sometimes been concluded, but only that the Nazis, without admitting it, learned as much from American gangster organizations as their propaganda admittedly learned from American business publicity.[18]

THE CONSOLIDATION OF POWER

Once the old order has been overthrown or fatally discredited, the totalitarian leadership can operate from, at the very least, a solid power base within the government. The next task it faces is the elimination of any competing political parties and factions. Party officials must then be placed in charge of all governmental functions throughout the country—especially in any provinces that were not particularly supportive of the revolutionary movement during its early stages. The final step in the consolidation process is the elimination of all those within the party who pose a real or potential danger to the totalitarian leader.

Throughout this stage, the totalitarian leader, like the traditional authoritarian ruler, is primarily concerned with the acquisition and maintenance of power. At his disposal are the same tools and methods used in the revolutionary stage of the movement. Ideology and propaganda serve to justify and popularize the leader's actions. Violence may be used to intimidate and silence opponents. The party organization provides the leader with tangible proof of both his popularity (witness the group of loyal followers) and his power (as the party faithful become the eyes and ears of the omnipotent state).

Perhaps the chief tool available to would-be totalitarian rulers at this stage, however, is their own skill. A number of correct decisions must be made if they are to succeed. They must know exactly what to do and must not shrink from doing it. Careful calculation, not conscience, must be the guide. In these matters, Machiavelli's advice is especially valuable: "One ought not to say to someone whom one wants to kill, 'Give me your gun, I want to kill you with it,' but merely, 'Give me your gun,' for once you have the gun in your hand, you can satisfy your desire."[19] The relevance of such advice becomes obvious as we examine the methods used by aspiring totalitarian rulers to consolidate their power.

Eliminating Opposition Parties

The first step toward political consolidation is the elimination of all competing parties and independent factions. The ruling party must be the only legitimate political organization in the state, for two reasons. In the first place, there is the traditional concern of all absolute rulers: Any opposition group, no matter how small or ineffectual it seems, poses a potential danger to the ruler. Second, the mere existence of political opponents inhibits the wholesale changes in domestic and foreign policy mandated by the movement's ideology. So political opposition must be eradicated by any means possible.

Lenin solved the problem of rival parties, one of which (the Socialist Revolutionaries) was substantially more popular than his own (the Bolsheviks), through the brilliant use of the age-old tactic of "divide and conquer." (One observer referred to Lenin's strategy as *"salami tactics,"*[20] so called because of his extraordinary ability to eliminate opponents by slicing up small but potentially dangerous groups, piece by piece.) Thus after the new revolutionary legislature, called the Constituent Assembly, was elected, he exploited an already existing division in the dominant Socialist Revolutionary party by forming an alliance with its left wing. This alliance enabled him to move against that party's more moderate wing, as well as against other rightist parties, and gave him sufficient legislative support to close down the Constituent Assembly altogether. As was to be expected, the alliance with the left Socialist Revolutionaries was cast aside as soon as it no longer suited Lenin's purposes.

Lenin's use of this strategy was not confined to the dismemberment of opposing political parties. Another target was the Soviet Union's huge peasant population, among whom the Bolshevik leader initially had little support. The lack of peasant support became a particularly acute problem during the civil war (1918–1920), when foodstuffs and other basic necessities were extremely scarce. In response, Lenin "instituted in the villages a 'civil war within a civil war' by setting poor peasants against those who were less poor,"[21] thereby helping to undermine the political opposition.

Lenin's "salami tactics" represented only one method by which opponents and rival parties have been eliminated by totalitarian movements. Mao Zedong, in contrast, was compelled by circumstances to fight his main adversary—the *Kuomintang,* or Nationalist government, led by Chiang Kai-shek—in a protracted guerrilla war. Hitler chose still another strategy. Bolstered by his Nazi party's steadily growing popularity in the polls—a formidable following of true believers—superb oratorical skills, and a special group of shock troops known as stormtroopers, he played a waiting game. By 1933 he had maneuvered himself into the chancellorship of Germany by shrewdly preying on the fears and political limitations of the people in power. Once in office, he gradually expanded his authority, first by gaining passage of new emergency powers, then by suspending civil liberties, and, finally, by ending meaningful democracy in Germany. Only then, operating from a position of strength, did he move to shut down all opposition parties. Unlike Mao, who struggled against opposing forces militarily, Hitler used native cunning and the charade of legality to destroy his opponents politically before using the power of the state to begin destroying them physically.

Purging Real or Imagined Rivals within the Party

Purges constitute the last step on the road to total power. In conducting purges, totalitarian governments almost invariably charge perceived rivals with subversive activities detrimental to the movement and the nation. Whether the charges are accurate is immaterial: They merely provide the totalitarian ruler with a public rationale for purging individuals perceived as threats or, at the very least, political liabilities. The downfall and, in many cases, sudden death of such "oppositionists" demonstrates to would-be dissidents the high price of crossing the supreme leader.

One author's observation that Mao Zedong "never hesitated to destroy his enemies [including] rival communists, Kuomintang activists, and 'landlords' "[22] can be applied to all successful totalitarian rulers. The scope and severity of such purges, however, can differ significantly from one ruler to the next. Hitler, for example, rid himself of party rivals in a single, almost surgically precise operation. By 1934, Hitler had become worried about the attitudes and actions of some of his oldest supporters, especially Ernst Röhm. As head of the SA (*Sturmabtei-lung*, or "stormtroopers"), a group of roughnecks whose primary function had been to intimidate political opponents during Hitler's rise to power, Röhm had continued to advocate and instigate violent activities at the point when the Führer's "legal" control over the government was about to be consolidated fully. Moreover, Hitler wanted to replace the SA with the more disciplined and reliable legions of the SS (*Schutzstaffel*, "security echelon"). All attempts to persuade Röhm and his compatriots to go along with these plans failed. So Hitler turned on Röhm and other party members who had been instrumental in the Nazis' rise to power; on the Führer's orders, the Röhm faction was murdered in June 1934. Blaming the whole incident on his political enemies, Hitler used the Röhm purge to his advantage, solidifying his support within Germany and focusing on the (allegedly) grave danger facing the nation.

Lenin's purges were more widespread. In 1921, following the elimination of all competing parties, he turned his attention to the people who challenged his leadership within the movement itself. Thousands of trade unionists and sailors, formerly the backbone of the Bolsheviks' popular support, were murdered by the secret police when they demanded free trade unions and elections. Next he dealt with the so-called Workers' Opposition faction of the Bolshevik party. This faction was demanding that the party reverse its previous policy and grant the workers control of their own industries. Lenin pronounced the group guilty of "factionalism" and accused it of endangering both the party and the revolution. The members of the Workers' Opposition group were expelled from the party—but, significantly, they were not murdered.

Such relatively mild actions were not characteristic of Lenin's successor, Stalin, who as the head of the Soviet Communist party (1924–1953) did not hesitate to murder those whom he perceived to be his political enemies. Stalin's ultimate success in subduing his political enemies hinged on two key factors: First, he masterfully adapted Lenin's "salami tactics"—used by Lenin to subdue rival parties but by Stalin against rivals within his own party; and second, he showed an extraordinary talent for political infighting. He turned out to be the most active, single-minded, and iron-willed member of Lenin's inner circle, a factor that proved decisive in the succession struggle that followed Lenin's death in 1924.

Creating a Monolithic Society

Totalitarian rule requires enormous organizational control over the larger society, for it seeks a complete societal transformation. Therefore, it must gain control over the economy, the arts, the military, the schools, the government—in short, over every aspect of society. Nothing can be allowed to escape its grasp, and no method of maintaining control can be ruled out. As Nazi propaganda chief Joseph Goebbels remarked, "The revolution we have made is a total revolution . . . it is completely irrelevant what means it uses."[23] No facet of society—not political parties, not religion, not artistic expression, not education or academic free-dom—can be allowed to block the creation of the new society. In such matters, the totalitarian leader's will is supreme. In the words of another Nazi official, "If the brains of all university professors were put at one end of the scale and the brains of the Führer at the other, which end, do you think, would tip?"[24]

For this program of total control to succeed, loyal followers must be put in charge of all elements of government and society in every town and region. This process was particularly well documented in Hitler's Germany.[25] Even in small towns, officeholders who had not publicly supported the Nazis were stripped of their power. Simultaneously, numerous "enemies of the people" were "discovered" and swiftly and harshly punished by the brutal *Gestapo* (secret police). The severity of these punishments, the alleged omnipresence of the Gestapo, and purported manifestations of mass support for the Nazis were well publicized and deliberately exaggerated in the media, as well as by word of mouth. Citizens had no doubt about the fate that awaited those who opposed the Nazis. Intimidation and coercion thus contributed immensely to the Nazis' success.

The effectiveness of these terror tactics helps to explain why there was so little overt resistance to the Nazi takeover, but it does not tell the whole story. The Nazis may have been able to gain power primarily through the use of intimidation, but moral apathy and self-interest played important roles as well. This point is perhaps best illustrated by a true story told by a German refugee who had been on the faculty of the prestigious University of Frankfurt. At the time of the Nazi takeover, this university had the reputation of being an exemplary (and unusually liberal) academic institution, with a faculty that epitomized professional commitment to scholarship, freedom of conscience, and democracy.[26] It was generally believed that if the Nazis could gain control of the University of Frankfurt without major incident, they would be able to use strong-arm methods to control all of German academia. Opponents of the Nazis hoped, in particular, that the party would find it difficult to overcome the opposition of a famous biochemist-physiologist on the Frankfurt faculty whose worldwide academic reputation was matched by his humane and compassionate attitude toward life. Following the appointment of a Nazi commissar at the university, every professor and graduate assistant was summoned for an important faculty meeting:

> The new Nazi commissar wasted no time on the amenities. He immediately announced that Jews would be forbidden to enter university premises and would be dismissed without salary on March 15; this was something no one had thought possible despite the Nazi's loud anti-Semitism. Then he launched into a tirade of abuse, filth, and four-letter words such as had been heard rarely even in the barracks and never before in academia. He pointd his finger at one department chairman after another and said, "You either do what I tell you or we'll put you into a concentration camp." There was silence when he finished; everybody waited for the distinguished biochemist-physiologist. The great liberal got up, cleared his throat, and said, "Very interesting, Mr. Commissar, and in some respects very illuminating; but one point I didn't get too clearly. Will there be more money for research in Physiology?"
>
> The meeting broke up shortly thereafter with the commissar assuring the scholars that indeed there would be plenty of money for "racially pure science." A few of the professors had the courage to walk out with their Jewish colleagues, but most kept

a safe distance from these men who only a few hours earlier had been their close friends.[27]

Such human frailties—weakness of will, moral blindness, and surpassing self-interest—together with ruthless strong-arm tactics, made it comparatively easy for the Nazis to place party members in positions of political authority.

THE TRANSFORMATION OF SOCIETY

Consolidating political power represents only a prelude to the most distinctive stage in the life cycle of the totalitarian state, the attempted transformation of society along ideological lines. This stage generally coincides with the regime's assumption of control over the economy and requires active government planning and intervention.[28] In justifying the drive for a new social order, the regime usually cites the widespread social disorder that lingers in the wake of every revolution, charging that all instability is caused by counterrevolutionaries, spies, and saboteurs.

At this point, totalitarian regimes clearly manifest their salient characteristics, which inevitably reflect the revolutionary movements that gave birth to them. Karl Friedrich and Zbigniew Brzezinski, two respected students of this subject, have identified six characteristics shared by all totalitarian governments.[29] Each state posits an official *ideology*, which justifies the actions of the government in the name of some future state of happiness. Each possesses a single, hierarchial *party* that is intertwined with or superior to the government. Each relies on a *secret police* willing and able to carry out campaigns of terror against enemies of the state, and each maintains a tight grip on the *armed forces* and all other instruments of organized violence. Each also seeks to exercise a *monopoly on the means of mass communication*, which are used to spread official propaganda. Finally, every totalitarian state exercises *central control over the economy*, through which it attempts to bring about drastic social change. In essence, these characteristics of totalitarian government derive from the components of the revolutionary movement (leadership, ideology, organization, propaganda, and violence), now redirected to the state's day-to-day administration and transformation.

Generally speaking, the attempted transformation of the state follows predetermined ideological prescriptions, occasionally influenced by more pragmatic concerns. Nonetheless, totalitarian regimes put much greater stock in adhering to their ideology than in responding to practical concerns at this stage. Examples taken from the political careers of Stalin, Hitler, and Mao illustrate this point.

The Soviet Union under Stalin

In 1928, having defeated his political rivals, Stalin stood poised to launch his drive to collectivize and industrialize the Soviet economy. His first Five-Year Plan for the economy (1928–1932) marked the beginning of a cataclysmic phase in the history of the Soviet Union. Over the next ten years, millions of innocent people were killed or sent to labor camps, and a whole class of relatively well-to-do landholders, the *kulaks,* ceased to exist at all. In addition, the whole pattern of Soviet agricultural production was radically reshaped.

To understand why Stalin would deliberately visit such a cataclysm on the Soviet countryside, we must first understand the preeminent role of ideology in totalitarian government. Stalin's first Five-Year Plan, which instituted a highly centralized economic system designed to foster rapid development of the Soviet economy, was motivated by power politics to a considerable degree. But the evidence suggests that Stalin was also truly committed to the ideological goal of creating an advanced industrial society based on Marxist-Leninist principles. Realizing this goal would not only provide a Marxist showcase for the rest of the world but also protect the fledgling revolution from hostile "capitalist encirclement."

Stalin decided that the only way to accomplish this remarkable feat would be to invest massively in heavy industry while squeezing every last drop of profit out of agriculture, the traditional foundation of the Russian economy. Here, Marxist-Leninist dogma reigned supreme. Private ownership of farmland, animals, and implements would have to be eliminated and farming "collectivized." Under Stalin's *collectivization* plan, most agricultural production was lodged in large cooperative units known as *kolkhozi* (collective farms), whose members shared whatever income was left after compulsory deliveries were made to the state, or in *sovkhozi* (state farms), whose laborers received wages.

Through this strategy, Stalin believed, industrial production could be doubled or even tripled during the period of the first Five-Year Plan. In effect, Soviet agriculture was collectivized to underwrite Soviet industrialization. By sweeping away all pockets of rural resistance and herding the peasants into collective farms, the state could maximize political control and minimize obstacles to its draconian system of tax collections. "Taxes" in this case meant compulsory deliveries to the state of scarce food supplies, which were used to feed the growing army of industrial workers and to pay for imported capital goods.

Seen in this light, Stalin's collectivization drive, however costly in human terms, takes on the even more disturbing dimension of a cold, calculated plan in which moral constraints never figured. As the plan progressed, Stalin was bothered not by its high human cost but because it did not seem to be working. One reason the plan did not work was the excessive amount of indiscriminate violence and brutality Stalin employed. Not only were the kulaks murdered or exiled, but whole communities of peasants were uprooted. Stories spread through the countryside of how Stalin's agents, combating the harsh effects of the remorseless Russian winter with excessive quantities of vodka, had machine-gunned whole villages. Many Russian peasants deliberately burned their crops and killed their cattle rather than cooperate with Stalin's requisition squads. The result was predictable. Despite an all-out national effort, industrial production grew only slightly, if at all. In the meantime, a killer famine depopulated the countryside.

Nevertheless, Stalin did not admit to any personal failure. He simply ignored the hunger and deprivation brought on by his economic policies and fabricated statistics to "prove" that real progress was being made. No one dared to question these figures. In the words of one expert, "The Stalin regime was ruthlessly

Josef Stalin (1879–1953) said in 1936: "You cannot make a revolution with silk gloves." (Sovfoto)

consistent: All facts that did not agree, or were likely to disagree, with the official fiction—data on crop yields, criminality, true incidences of 'counterrevolutionary' activities . . . were treated as nonfacts."[30]

But Stalin, concerned that his policies were creating new and hidden enemies, did become increasingly paranoid. In 1934, after the first Five-Year Plan had come to an unspectacular end, the Soviet dictator declared that he had uncovered a far-reaching conspiracy, orchestrated by foreign agents and counterrevolutionaries, to resurrect capitalism in Soviet Russia. This conspiracy theory gained credibility when Sergei Kirov, the dynamic young leader of the Leningrad party organization, was assassinated in December 1934. Harsh reprisals, numerous arrests, phony trials, summary executions, and large-scale deportations followed in the immediate wake of this incident. Many of the victims were loosely identified as members of the so-called Leningrad Center.

Of course, no "Leningrad Center" had ever existed, and there had been no plot to overthrow Stalin. (Premier Nikita Khrushchev hinted in 1956 that Stalin himself may have been behind the assassination of Kirov!) But the alleged plot furnished Stalin with a golden opportunity to undertake perhaps the largest blood purge of "disloyal" subordinates in history. Prominent members of Lenin's original circle of revolutionary leaders, the so-called Old Bolsheviks, were arrested and imprisoned as the purge swiftly gained momentum. During the first phase of what came to be known as the Great Terror—January 1934 to April 1936—Communist party membership fell by nearly 800,000, or approximately 25 percent. The Soviet press denounced these excommunicants as "wreckers, spies, diversionists, and murderers sheltering behind the party card and disguised as Bolsheviks."[31]

The second phase of the Stalin purges (1936–1938) was highlighted by the infamous *show trials*, in which all the Old Bolsheviks, along with many other top-ranking party leaders, were placed on public trial and forced to make outrageous "confessions." The trials, however, represented only the tip of the iceberg. Of the nearly 2,000 delegates to the Seventeenth Party Congress in 1934, more than 1,100 (about 56 percent) would be shot between 1934 and 1938. Of the 1,827 rank-and-file delegates to that congress, only 35 percent would be present at the convening of the next congress, five years later. Seventy percent of the 139 members of the Party Central Committee elected in 1934 would be murdered by 1938. By the time the smoke finally cleared in 1939, the party apparatus had been thoroughly purged.

In the Red Army the results were much the same. The Great Terror wiped out three of the five marshals of the Soviet Union, 14 of 16 army commanders, all eight admirals, 60 of the 67 corps commanders, and more than half of the 397 brigade commanders. In addition, of 81 top-ranking political commissars, all but five were purged.

Nor were the rank-and-file workers spared. Throughout the mid- and late 1930s, Stalin carried out a policy known as the *Estafette*, whereby the Soviet labor force was collectivized through the institution of forced-draft or conscript labor. Work units were structured along military lines, and strict labor regimentation was enforced. This policy gave birth to the so-called **gulag archipelago,** the network of slave-labor camps maintained and operated by the Soviet secret police. Social and political undesirables of every description were forced to live in these desolate camps. Through the gulag system, railroads, canals, and dams were constructed in remote and inaccessible areas where workers would not go voluntarily. Aleksandr Solzhenitsyn, the celebrated dissident writer who chronicled life in the labor camps, estimated that they held as many as 12 million prisoners at any given time, perhaps half of them political prisoners. "As some departed beneath the sod," he noted, "the Machine kept bringing in replacements."[32]

At the close of 1938, Stalin stood alone at the top. Industrial development had been spurred, but the Soviet Union was anything but a worker's paradise. Terror had brought about great political changes, with many luminaries from the pages of Soviet Communist party history uncovered as traitors and placed on public trial. The list of the accused read like the honor roll of the October Revolution. The military high command had been sacked, the party rank-and-file cleansed of all political impurities, and the "toiling masses" reduced to a new level of industrial serfdom. Although he ruled until his death in 1953, Stalin (and the legacy of Stalinism) would be identified, above all, with the bloody purges of the 1930s.

Germany under Hitler

The overriding theme of National Socialist (Nazi) party ideology during the Third Reich (1933–1945) was the elimination of the Jews and other "social undesirables" and the subsequent creation of a "racially pure" Aryan community created in the image of its founder, Adolf Hitler. Racism, which had obsessed Hitler throughout his political career, prompted him to attempt a drastic reformulation of German life. The means he countenanced are by now familiar: mass indoctrination of the public in the tenets of Nazi ideology; maintenance of the Nazi party, under his tight control, as the guiding force in German life; heavy reliance on the secret police, or Gestapo, to ensure public obedience; and centralized control over the economy, the military, and the mass media.

Through Nazi ideology and propaganda, the German people came to accept the persecution of the Jews, the necessity of an eventual war, and the radical transformation of German society. Every aspect of German life became politicized both through the terror tactics of the Gestapo and the SS and through an officially sponsored "cultural revolution," which called for the purging of all artists, journalists, and academicians whose political opinions could not be trusted. New governmental agencies, including the Reich chambers for literature, press, broadcasting, theater, music, and fine arts, were created for the primary purpose of censoring or quelling potentially "dangerous" forms of written or artistic expression.

In the realm of music, German folk tunes were exalted over "decadent" modern music and classical music written by composers of Jewish lineage such as Felix Mendelssohn and Gustav Mahler. Modern art was likewise condemned, and the works of virtually every well-known contemporary artist were banned. Literature under the Nazi regime fared no better. According to Karl Dietrich Bracher, one chronicler of the Third Reich:

> Blacklists were compiled ceaselessly and literary histories were revised. . . . The "cleansing" of libraries and bookstores presented some problems, but the destruction and self-destruction of German literature was achieved within a matter of months through the substitution of second- and third-rate scribblers for first-rate writers and by inhibiting contacts with the outside.[33]

The Nazi attack on the arts was indicative of the lengths to which Hitler would go to ensure that Nazi values were propagated. But perhaps no part of German life more vividly demonstrated Hitler's commitment to a new future than the Nazi school system. As Bracher points out, "While National Socialism could substitute little more than ideology and second-rate imitators for the literature and art it expelled or destroyed, its main efforts from the very outset were directed toward the most important instruments of totalitarian policy: propaganda and education."[34]

Nazi educational policy was implemented in three principal ways. To begin with, educators and school administrators who were suspected of opposing Hitler, Nazism, or Nazi educational "reform" were promptly removed from their positions. Then all academic subjects were infused with ideological content. History became "racial history," biology was transformed into "racial biology," and so on. All subjects were revised to reflect Hitler's anti-Semitic racial theories. Day in and day out, students were bombarded with the noxious racial doctrines that justified the Nazi political order. Often these theories were intertwined with tales of military prowess; virtually every academic subject had as its moral the coming triumph of the Aryans over their racial inferiors.

Finally, the Nazis established special schools to train a future party elite, including military leaders, party officials, and government administrators. Students were assigned to these schools according to age group and career orientation. The Adolf Hitler Schools, to cite one example, taught 12- to 18-year-old students who wished to become high party functionaries. Generally speaking, all special schools taught certain basic core courses (such as racial history and biology) and emphasized military drill and training.

The Nazi educational program turned out to be all too successful. In the judgment of one authority, "Just as teachers and parents capitulated to the pressures of the regime, so on the whole did the indoctrination of the young succeed. The young, who were receptive to heroic legends and black-and-white oversimplifications, were handed over to the stupendous shows of the regime."[35] Education of the young was reinforced by carefully planned pomp and ceremony: "From earliest childhood, they were exposed to flag raisings, parades, nation-wide broadcasts in the schools, hikes, and camps."[36] Indoctrination and propaganda, not terror, became the instruments by whch the children of the Third Reich were initiated into the new order.

This program of mass indoctrination, perhaps more than anything else, made it possible for Hitler to carry out the murderous racial policies that culminated in the Holocaust. After seizing power, Hitler implemented his anti-Jewish policy in stages, each more radical than the one before.[37] First came the attempt to define who precisely was and was not a Jew. Then the regime launched a

The overriding theme of Nazi party ideology was the elimination of the Jews and other "social undesirables" and the subsequent creation of a "racially pure" Aryan community. Between 1933 and 1945, some 5 to 6 million European Jews perished in Nazi death camps. (Bettmann Archives)

systematic campaign to isolate Jews from the mainstream of German life and to expropriate their property. Next all Jews who had not fled the country between 1933 and 1938 were forcibly removed from German society and sent to the infamous concentration camps. This mass deportation presaged the fourth and final step, the liquidation of every Jewish man, woman, and child within the reach of the Third Reich.

As these anti-Jewish policies gained momentum in Germany during the 1930s, Hitler drew almost every element of German society into his murderous scheme. The bureaucracy composed anti-Jewish orders and planned the logistics of the annihilation process. German businesses benefited from the expropriation of Jewish property and from the use of forced labor in the concentration camps. As Germany conquered lands to the east, special units of the army became heavily involved in all aspects of the killing operations. Finally, the Nazi party hierarchy itself played a crucial role in planning and directing the whole annihilation program. The SS, the paramilitary arm of the party, actually supervised the killing operations in the death camps.

For Hitler, World War II represented an opportunity to spread his vision of a racially purified Aryan Germany to the whole of Europe. Unlike previous tyrants, who fought wars mainly for love of territory, power, or glory, Hitler was motivated by the dream of a radically new and revolutionary society. Thus even when Germany's military fortunes plunged and the Third Reich was on the brink of defeat, Hitler moved ahead (and even accelerated) the liquidation of the Jews. Through the final days of the war, the Third Reich pursued a relentless and unstinting policy of genocide. In the end, 5 to 6 million European Jews perished in the death camps. Previous acts of racially motivated political persecution pale beside the barbarism of the Holocaust, whose architect, Adolf Hitler, sought to create a "master race" and build a brave new world in his own grotesque image.

China under Mao

Mao Zedong's rise to power in China forms an epic example of revolutionary struggle—a true mass movement in a poor, peasant-dominated society. For more than 20 years (1927–1949), Mao waged a bitter "war of national liberation" against the Kuomintang (Nationalist party), headed by Chiang Kai-shek, as well as against the Japanese during World War II. In the mid-1930s, Mao was one of the leaders of the legendary Long March, a 6,000-mile trek, during which his ragtag band of guerrillas repeatedly evaded capture or annihilation by the numerically superior and better-equipped forces of Chiang's Nationalist army. By 1949, when he finally won the last decisive battle and assumed command of the Chinese nation, Mao Zedong had been waging "class war" in the name of the Chinese masses for more than two decades.

Mao prided himself not only on his revolutionary exploits but also on his political thought, and in time, the "thoughts of Chairman Mao" attained the status of holy scripture in Chinese society. His vision of a new, classless state and of the exemplary communist cadres and comrades who would typify this morally reeducated society inspired the radical policies that have become known collectively as Maoism.

Although Mao's world view was undoubtedly shaped by the basic tenets of Marxism, China in the 1920s was a preindustrial society with nothing resembling a true proletarian (industrial-worker) class. Neither was there a "monopoly capitalist" class of the kind Marx had described in *Capital*. The bane of China's peasant masses was not factory bosses but greedy landlords and bureaucratic officials preoccupied with the preservation of the status quo and of their own power and privilege. If the oppressed majority was to be liberated, this minority would have to be overthrown. To accomplish such a historic mission, Mao believed, violent revolution "from below" would be an unavoidable necessity. "Political power," he wrote, "grows out of the barrel of a gun."[38]

As part of his adaptation (or "Sinification") of Marxism, Mao glorified the long-suffering Chinese peasants, holding them up as models of communist virtue. The Chinese peasants, in his view, were "poor and blank." Because they had never been corrupted by "bourgeois materialism" and big-city decadence, he believed, they could be molded into model communists more easily than their more sophisticated urban cousins. In this way, Mao made the peasants the cornerstone of a utopian, classless society in which exploitation would no longer occur and the masses would live happily ever after in harmony, equality, and abundance.

Armed with this glorious vision, Mao turned China, after 1949, into a kind of social laboratory. In the postrevolutionary years, the Chinese Communist party (CCP) and the Chinese army were used to carry out grandiose experiments in behavioral and environmental engineering. The first step involved mass campaigns to remove specific evils or exterminate such undesirable social elements as landlords, counterrevolutionaries, and so-called bandits. Accompanying these "reeducation campaigns" was a sweeping land reform program that eventually culminated in the wholesale collectivization of Chinese agriculture. The often bitter pill of land reform was administered with massive doses of propaganda and a large measure of physical force. In the early 1950s, a major push to industrialize China along Stalinist lines was also initiated.

Mao's rule was marked by alternating periods of freedom and repression. In 1956, for example, he announced the beginning of the **Hundred Flowers campaign,** which promised a relaxation of strict social discipline. As a high-ranking party official put it at the time, "The Chinese Communist party advocates [that] one hundred flowers bloom for literary works and one hundred schools contend in the scientific field . . . to promote the freedom of independent thinking, freedom of debate, freedom of creation and criticism, freedom of expressing one's own opinions."[39] It appeared as though limited criticism of the party leadership would even be tolerated.

What followed must have caught Mao quite by surprise. Criticism of official policy poured in from all over the country. The spate of public protests and antiparty demonstrations was especially pronounced at Beijing University and on other campuses across China. Strikes and scattered riots ensued. Voices of

Mao Zedong (1893–1976): "When the majority of the people have clear-cut criteria to go by, . . . these criteria can be applied to people's words and actions to determine whether they are fragrant flowers or poisonous weeds." (Elliott Erwitt/Magnum)

dissent, cautious at first, grew bolder and more clamorous. Isolated physical attacks on party officials were reported.

Instead of a hundred flowers, thousands of "poisonous weeds" had grown in the Chinese garden. To root them out, a vigorous antirightist campaign was launched. The official party newspaper, *People's Daily*, offered the face-saving (albeit quite plausible) explanation that the whole Hundred Flowers campaign had been a ploy to lure the enemies of the state into the open.

In retrospect, the Hundred Flowers episode looks like a mere warm-up for Mao's *Great Leap Forward* (1957–1960). The Great Leap represented a spectacular attempt to catapult China to the stage of "full communism" by means of mass mobilization. Mao now launched a program of social transformation predicated on the belief that human willpower could triumph over objective conditions rooted in the poverty, illiteracy, and external dependency that plagued China.

According to John King Fairbank, a respected American student of China:

The development strategy of the Great Leap Forward in 1958 was the sort of thing guerrilla warriors could put together. They had learned how to mount campaigns and mobilize the populace to obtain specific social objectives, much like capturing positions in warfare—indeed military terminology was commonly used. The whole apparatus of campaign mechanisms was now directed to an economic transformation, the simultaneous development of agriculture and industry, a strategy of dualism or as Mao said, "Walking on two legs," to achieve development in the modern industrial processes. . . . The CCP effort was to take advantage of China's rural backwardness and manpower surplus by realizing the Maoist faith that ideological incentives could get economic results, that a new spirit could unlock hitherto untapped sources of human energy without the use of material incentives.[40]

The most visible and dramatic symbol of the Great Leap was the establishment of innumerable communes—relatively large, self-contained, and self-sufficient social, economic, and administrative units. Private plots were absorbed into the communal lands, and private belongings, including pots and pans, tables and chairs, and other domestic items, were pooled. In addition, Fairbank noted:

> Many peasants for a time ate in large mess halls. All labor was to be controlled. Everyone was to work twenty-eight days of the month, while children went into day nurseries. This would bring large-scale efficiency to the village and get all its labor, including its womanpower, into full employment.[41]

Why were the unprecedented measures associated with this grandiose concept instituted? In Fairbank's view, "The result, it was hoped, would be agricultural cities with the peasants proletarianized and uprooted from their own land"—with an overall view toward giving the state increased control over labor resources and changing the peasants' attitudes.[42]

The Great Leap Forward turned out to be an unmitigated disaster, both because it was ill-conceived and because nature proved to be uncooperative. In the late 1950s and early 1960s, China experienced severe food shortages and unforgiving crop failures. In 1960 alone, the country's gross national product declined by as much as one-third. For the first few years of the new decade, Mao's power and influence seemed to decline. But this short-lived period of retrenchment and reconstruction was only the lull before the next storm.

From 1966 to 1969, the ***Great Proletarian Cultural Revolution*** shook Chinese society to its very foundations. To the outside world, the Cultural Revolution still stands as one of the most bizarre events of the century. It represented Mao's most ambitious attempt to revitalize the spirit of the Chinese revolution and to eradicate all remaining vestiges of bourgeois capitalism.

The Cultural Revolution took shape in two distinct stages. The first stage was designed to wash away all that was decadent in Chinese life. To this end, Mao closed all the schools and urged his youthful followers, called the Red Guards, to storm the bastions of entrenched privilege and bureaucratic authority. The spectacle of millions of Maoist youths rampaging through the country both bewildered and bemused the outside world for many weeks. Yet by the time the smoke had cleared and the chaos and confusion had subsided, this phase of the revolution had accomplished much of what Mao intended—the Red Guards had "smashed most of the Republic's bureaucratic institutions and invalidated their authority and expertise."[43] Purges, public humiliations, executions, and orchestrated anarchy racked the nation. The party, the government, and the armed forces lay in ruins.

The second stage of the Cultural Revolution, predictably, was less successful than the first. The first stage had been largely negative—the destruction of certain undesirable features of the existing social and political order. The succeeding stage, however, called for positive action to replace the previous order with a new and better one. Unfortunately, the economy, especially in urban areas, had been severely disrupted. And the schools, having been shut down to make way for the rolling tide of Mao's new revolutionary order, would not be reopened for many months—in some cases, for years. As a result, a whole generation of young Chinese failed to acquire the knowledge and skills the country's developing economy so sorely needed.

The ultimate cost of the Cultural Revolution is inestimable. One fact, however, is clear: Mao's untiring efforts to prove that human nature is infinitely malleable—and society, therefore, infinitely perfectable—foundered on the rocky shores of political reality. His death in 1976 closed a unique chapter in the political history of the modern world.

THE HUMAN COST OF TOTALITARIANISM

Totalitarian regimes embody a stark contrast between ends and means. If the goals of such states are often presented as divine, the means used to achieve those goals—institutionalized persecution, purges, and pogroms—are nothing short of diabolical. To many observers of the contemporary scene, the concentration camps of Nazi Germany and the labor camps of Stalinist Russia stand as the true symbols of twentieth-century totalitarianism. These horrors demonstrate how the unthinkable can become possible under totalitarian dictatorship because there is nothing to prevent the government from carrying its pursuit of the impossible to the most violent and even self-destructive extremes.

The most shocking estimate of the human cost of totalitarian repression can be found in a comparative study of Hitler, Stalin, and Mao written by the political scientist C. W. Cassinelli. Professor Cassinelli contends that "about 110 million people have died in the name of the three revolutions and the amount of physical and mental suffering they have caused defies the imagination."[44] According to Cassinelli, these estimates, which include World War II casualties, may actually be low. But even if we were to cut the estimated casualties in half, the numbers would still be staggering.

In a very real sense, Hitler's expansionist foreign policy can be blamed for all the war-related deaths in the European theater during World War II. Again according to Cassinelli, the war dead numbered "about 6 million for Germany and Austria, 20 million for the Soviet Union, and about 10 million for all other European countries, for a total of about 36 million."[45] Hitler's so-called Final Solution, as noted earlier, resulted in the deaths of an estimated 5 to 6 million European Jews, not to mention an indeterminate number of non-Jews whom Hitler considered social undesirables. In addition, some senile senior citizens were killed before the war, and ordinary lawbreakers were sent to concentration camps, where some perished prematurely. All in all, perhaps 42 million people died directly or indirectly as a result of Adolf Hitler's policies.

The Russian Revolution of 1917 and its aftermath were hardly less costly in terms of human life. Between 1918 and 1923, approximately 3 million Soviet citizens died of typhus, typhoid, dysentery, and cholera, and about 9 million more disappeared, probably victims of the terrible famine that scourged the country in the early 1920s. Many of the latter perished because of a severe drought in 1920–1921, but many others died of direct or indirect political, rather than natural, causes.

In the late 1920s, during Stalin's titanic industrialization drive, the kulaks were annihilated as a class. In addition, another killer famine— this one at least partially self-inflicted—occurred in the early 1930s. When deaths associated with the early stages of collectivization are combined with deaths brought on by famine, the mortality figures for the period 1929–1934 range well into the millions.

But the worst was yet to come. After 1934, Stalin's massive purges—perhaps the bloodiest reign of terror in history—resulted in the outright murder of perhaps 1 million Soviet citizens and the premature deaths of another 2 million "class enemies" in Siberian forced-labor camps. Nor did the end of the great purges in 1938 stop the political hemorrhaging that, together with World War II, drained Soviet society of so much of its vitality. Cassinelli estimates that 12 million prison and labor camp inmates may have died as a direct result of their harsh and inhuman environments between 1938 and 1950. All in all, Stalin (and to a lesser extent, Lenin) may be held morally responsible for the demise of millions of innocent and defenseless citizens for whom "revolutionary justice" meant either the slow death of the labor camps or the sudden death of the firing squad.

The human cost of the Maoist revolution has received much less notice than that of the Nazi and Soviet revolutions, yet between 1927 and 1949, an estimated 50,000 people perished. Many of these deaths are attributable to the rather routine liquidation of landlords and rich peasants in areas that came under communist control.

From the communist takeover in 1949 until the Great Leap Forward in 1957, several mass campaigns were launched for the purpose of combating allegedly counterrevolutionary forces. According to Cassinelli:

> The land reform program of 1949 to 1952 undoubtedly cost the lives of several million "landlords" and similar types; the 1951–52 campaign against counterrevolutionaries cost another million and a half; the bandit suppression campaigns, ostensibly to eliminate remaining pockets of physical resistance, disposed of many people from 1949 to 1956; the "three anti" and "five anti" campaigns of 1951–53 and the anti-rightist campaign of 1958–59 resulted in killings and other deaths; and, finally, the collectivization of agriculture from 1953 until 1967 was accompanied by a significant number of casualties. Accurate information is not available—and often even informed guesses are lacking—on the cost of the first decade of the People's Republic. An estimate of twelve million lives is modest but reasonable.[46]

These figures do not include deaths caused by hardship and privation—notably, those traceable to the dislocations that accompanied the Great Leap Forward in the late 1950s.

By 1977, former Ethiopian ruler Mengistu Haile Mariam had ruthlessly consolidated his power as dictator. During his rule, Mariam had established close ties with the former Soviet Union and Cuba, both of which had given him military aid. (AP/Wide World Photos)

The Cultural Revolution (1966–1969) was another bloody episode in Chinese history, although firm estimates of the number of casualties are impossible to make. A much heavier toll has probably been taken by the Chinese "gulag" system—as many as 15 million may have perished as a direct result of inhumanly harsh labor camp conditions. When Cassinelli tallies the total number of politically related deaths—including "another million from miscellaneous causes"—he arrives at the astonishing figure of "about 33.5 million."[47] Though these figures can never be verified, they are consistent with the available evidence. The mere fact that they are not implausible speaks volumes.

Totalitarian regimes typically refuse to concede that any goal, no matter how visionary or perverse, is beyond political reach. The compulsion to validate this gross misconception may help to explain the pathological violence that marks totalitarian rule.

THE FACES OF TOTALITARIANISM

Stalin's Russia, Hitler's Germany, and Mao's China are the most prominent examples of totalitarian states, but there are others that deserve mention and study.

Pol Pot governed Cambodia (renamed Kampuchea) from 1975 to 1979. He and his followers sought to create a radically new society, based on the rustic and spartan life of peasant cadres. All vestiges of the old order, everything from the calendar to the family, were eradicated. Pol Pot proclaimed 1978 "year 0," grotesquely appropriate, for at the end of his brief rule, 1 to 2 million Cambodians (out of a population of 7.5 million) would be dead, the victims of purges, starvation, and persecution.

Other contemporary totalitarian rulers include Ethiopia's Mengistu Haile Mariam, who ruled from the mid-1970s until May 1991. Mengistu attempted to reorganize his nation by physically relocating his people into regimented population and refugee centers for the purpose of permitting intensive governmental surveillance as well as encouraging systematic propaganda and indoctrination. His efforts destroyed his nation's agriculture, and a killer famine resulted. Although efforts were made in the West to feed the starving children of Ethiopia, the Ethiopian government appeared curiously detached. While his people went hungry, Mengistu staged lavish military parades, sold wheat to neighboring nations, and then used the money he received to buy weapons. In May 1991, his regime under siege by a coalition of rebel forces, Mengistu fled the country.

Totalitarian rulers have come to power around the world. Fidel Castro, leader of Cuba since 1959, is one of the longest-lasting. In North Korea, the iron-fisted Kim Il-Sung is the most typical totalitarian ruler in the contemporary world. Elsewhere in Asia, both Vietnam and China also continue to be ruled by communist regimes that somewhat conform to the totalitarian model.

As was pointed out at the beginning of this chapter, totalitarian regimes assume a variety of forms. One of its most intriguing examples was that of the fanatical right-wing rule of Iran's fundamentalist Islamic leader, the Ayatollah Ruhollah Khomeini (1979–1989). Khomeini transformed Iran into a *theocracy* (a government based on religion and dominated by the clergy). Eventually, no aspect of life in Iran lay outside of governmental control. Teachers, textbooks, and all education, entertainment, the legal system—even courtship and sexual mores—were made to conform to fundamental Islamic beliefs. The regime declared war on civil servants, intellectuals, professional and entrepreneurial elements of the middle class, and all who had endorsed modern Western ways and culture. Khomeini's Iran displayed most of the elements normally associated with totalitarian rule: an attempt to transform society; a dictatorship that demanded abject loyalty, obedience, and self-sacrifice; an all-encompassing creed that rationalized, explained, and justified state actions; press censorship; and secret police, show trials, summary executions, and holy wars. The Iranian case aptly demonstrates that totalitarian regimes, like democracies and traditional dictatorships, while sharing a single essence, can assume different guises throughout the world.

EPILOGUE: THE LONGEVITY OF TOTALITARIAN REGIMES

Space does not permit a complete accounting of the atrocities and oppression associated with all twentieth-century totalitarian regimes. Yet it is important to recognize that in this most violent of all centuries, totalitarian states have been directly or indirectly responsible for an enormous amount of death and suffering stemming from their participation in revolution, warfare, and systematic state terror.

Frequently, totalitarian regimes proclaim their longevity and vitality; Hitler termed his a 1,000-year empire. Yet there is growing evidence to suggest that totalitarian regimes have been relatively short-lived. They burst on the scene with a brilliant flash, but like falling stars, they soon burn themselves out. At most, totalitarian regimes have lasted no more than several decades beyond the lifetime of their revolutionary leaders. Why might this be so?

Although ruling by coercion rather than consent can maximize political stability in the short run, over the long term it undermines the economic efficiency and moral vitality on which legitimate political power ultimately rests. Thus the collapse of communist totalitarianism in eastern Europe was precipitated by the Soviet Union's economic disintegration. In addition, fatal wars with other nations and a widespread loss of faith in revolutionary ideals have proved to be the long-term enemies of other totalitarian governments. Despite the fact that totalitarian rule lasted for some 70 years in the Soviet Union and is still largely intact in the People's Republic of China after more than four decades, these periods of time are historically brief; unfortunately, experience has shown that totalitarian dictatorships need only a little time to do a lot of damage.

Summary

Totalitarian states attempt to realize a utopian vision and create a new political order. Like authoritarian states, totalitarian states are nondemocratic. Yet these two regime types differ in several important respects. In particular, totalitarian regimes seek total control over all aspects of their citizens' lives and demand active participation rather than passive acquiescence on the part of the citizenry. Totalitarianism is now in decline.

Totalitarian states typically pass through several distinct stages of development. The first stage coincides with the period of violent revolution. The five major elements necessary for a successful revolution are capable leadership, ideology, organization, propaganda, and violence.

During the second phase, which involves the consolidation of power in the hands of the totalitarian ruler, opposition parties are eliminated, the party faithful are put in charge, and real or imagined rivals within the party are killed. The third stage attempts to bring about the total transformation of society. In the Soviet Union, Stalin launched this effort with the first Five-Year Plan in 1928. In Nazi Germany, Hitler's goal of "racial purification" provided the rationale for a totalitarian drive that culminated in World War II and the Holocaust. In Maoist China, the first attempt to transform Chinese society (the Great Leap Forward) failed miserably in the late 1950s and was followed by the Cultural Revolution in 1966–1969.

The human cost of totalitarianism has been staggering. Actual statistics often cannot be verified with any degree of precision, but even the roughest estimates suggest that the totalitarian experiments of the twentieth century have brought death or appalling hardship to many millions of people.

Finally, totalitarian regimes seem to be relatively short-lived. Even so, they can appear in many guises, and there is no guarantee that new totalitarian states will not emerge in the future.

Key Terms

totalitarianism
rectification
"islands of separateness"
cells
partiinost
Gleichschaltung
propaganda
"salami tactics"
Kuomintang

purges
Gestapo
kulaks
collectivization
gulag archipelago
Hundred Flowers campaign
Great Leap Forward
Great Proletarian Cultural Revolution
theocracy

Review Questions

1. What sets totalitarianism apart from other nondemocratic forms of rule?

2. What is required for a successful total revolution to take place?

3. How do totalitarian states consolidate power?

4. What are the basic characteristics of the totalitarian system of rule?

5. What were the primary aims of Stalin's drive to transform Soviet society in the 1930s? What methods did he use?

6. How and why did Hitler try to reshape German society?

7. What was the impetus behind the Great Leap Forward and the Cultural Revolution? What methods did the Maoists employ? What kind of a society did they envisage?

8. What have been the costs of totalitarianism, measured in human terms?

9. "Totalitarianism passed away with the deaths of Hitler, Stalin, and Mao." Comment.

Recommended Reading

ARENDT, HANNAH. *Totalitarianism.* Orlando, Fla.: Harcourt Brace Jovanovich, 1968. A theoretical analysis of Nazi Germany and Stalinist Russia that spotlights totalitarian states' emphasis on terror, persecution, and mass murder.

ARENDT, HANNAH. *On Revolution.* New York: Viking Penguin, 1977. A theoretical, insightful examination of modern revolutions, including total revolutions.

BRACHER, KARL DIETRICH. *The German Dictatorship.* New York: Holt, 1972. A definitive study of Hitler's totalitarian state.

CASSINELLI, C. W. *Total Revolution: A Comparative Study of Germany under Hitler, the Soviet Union under Stalin, and China under Mao.* Santa Barbara, Calif.: Clio Books, 1976. Cassinelli argues that these regimes are fundamentally similar.

CONQUEST, ROBERT. *The Great Terror: A Reassessment.* New York: Oxford University Press, 1991. This detailed, carefully researched book provides the definitive scholarly account of Stalin's bloodiest days.

CONQUEST, ROBERT. *The Harvest of Sorrow: Soviet Collectivization and the Terror-Famine.* New York: Oxford University Press, 1987. A chilling account of Stalin's war against the kulaks and the Ukrainians.

FRIEDRICH, KARL, AND ZBIGNIEW BRZEZINSKI. *Totalitarian Dictatorship and Autocracy.* New York: Praeger, 1965. A pioneering effort that attempts to classify and describe totalitarian states.

GOLDFARB, JERRY. *Beyond Glasnost: The Posttotalitarian Mind.* Chicago: University of Chicago Press, 1991. An interesting discussion of the present and future of totalitarianism and its influence on dissenting intellectual thought. Goldfarb emphasizes the writings of eastern European poets, writers, and political thinkers.

HOFFER, ERIC. *The True Believer: Thoughts on the Nature of Mass Movements.* New York: Harper & Row, 1951. A perceptive examination of individuals who form the nucleus of mass movements.

MENZE, ERNEST (ed.). *Totalitarianism Reconsidered.* Port Washington, N.Y.: Kennikat Press, 1981. A provocative collection of essays presenting different points of view on the usefulness of distinguishing between totalitarianism and other political orders.

MOSHER, STEVEN. *China Misperceived: American Illusions and Chinese Reality.* New York: Basic Books, 1990. This controversial book not only describes the reality of Mao's China but also analyzes academic and journalistic misperceptions of it.

ORWELL, GEORGE. *Nineteen Eighty-four.* New York: New American Library, 1961. Orwell's fictional caricature of Stalinist Russia is full of insights regarding the nature of totalitarian societies.

PONCHAUD, FRANÇOIS. *Cambodia: Year Zero.* New York: Holt, 1978. A chilling historical account of Pol Pot's rule in Kampuchea.

SELZNICK, PHILIP. *The Organizational Weapon: A Study of Bolshevik Strategy and Tactics.* New York: Free Press, 1960 (reprinted 1979, Ayer Publ.). A penetrating study of Soviet institutions under Lenin and Stalin.

SHAPIRO, LEONARD. *Totalitarianism.* New York: Praeger, 1972. An evenhanded and informative discussion of the scholarly controversy that has surrounded the concept of totalitarianism.

SOLZHENITSYN, ALEKSANDR. *One Day in the Life of Ivan Denisovich.* New York: New American Library, 1963. (New trans. Farrar, Straus, and Giroux, 1991). This description of the Soviet labor camps became a *cause célèbre* in the Soviet Union during Khrushchev's de-Stalinization program.

WIESEL, ELIE. *Night.* New York: Bantam Books, 1982. A poignant autobiographical account of the suffering of the victims of totalitarian rule—in this case, the Jews under Hitler.

Notes

1. William Kornhauser, *The Politics of Mass Society* (New York: Free Press, 1959), p. 123.

2. C. W. Cassinelli, *Total Revolution: A Comparative Study of Germany under Hitler, the Soviet Union under Stalin, and China under Mao* (Santa Barbara, Calif.: Clio Books, 1976), p. 225.

3. The definition is Hans Buchheim's, as quoted in Leonard Shapiro, *Totalitarianism* (New York: Praeger, 1972), p. 104.

4. Karl Friedrich and Zbigniew Brzezinski, *Totalitarian Dictatorship and Autocracy*, 2nd ed. (New York: Praeger, 1966), p. 88.

5. Cassinelli, *Total Revolution*, p. 231.

6. Friedrich and Brzezinski, *Totalitarian Dictatorship and Autocracy*, pp. 279–339.

7. Eric Hoffer, *The True Believer: Thoughts on the Nature of Mass Movements* (New York: Harper & Row, 1951), pp. 104–105.

8. Ibid., p. 86.

9. Raul Hilberg, *The Destruction of the European Jews* (New York: Harper & Row, 1961), p. 12.

10. Cited in Cassinelli, *Total Revolution*, p. 16.

11. Karl Dietrich Bracher, *The German Dictatorship* (New York: Holt, 1972), p. 181.

12. Maurice Latey, *Patterns of Tyranny* (New York: Atheneum, 1969), p. 172.

13. Adolf Hitler, *Mein Kampf*, trans. R. Manheim (Boston: Houghton Mifflin, 1971), pp. 179–180.

14. Ibid., p. 182.

15. Cited in D. Shub, *Lenin* (Baltimore: Pelican, 1966), p. 62.

16. E. Kohr Bramstedt, as cited in Hannah Arendt, *The Origins of Totalitarianism* (New York: Harcourt, Brace and Co., 1951), p. 333.

17. Ibid.

18. Ibid., pp. 335–336.

19. As quoted in Leo Strauss, *Thoughts on Machiavelli* (Seattle: University of Washington Press, 1968), p. 9.

20. Latey, *Patterns of Tyranny*, p. 100.

21. Cassinelli, *Total Revolution*, p. 103.

22. Ibid., p. 186.

23. Quoted in Bracher, *German Dictatorship*, p. 257.

24. Ibid., p. 272.

25. W. S. Allen, *The Nazi Seizure of Power: The Experience of a Single German Town, 1930–1935* (Chicago: Quadrangle Books, 1965).

26. Peter Drucker, "The Monster and the Lamb," *Atlantic* 242 (December 1978), p. 84.

27. Ibid.

28. Friedrich and Brzezinski, *Totalitarian Dictatorship and Autocracy*, p. 374.

29. Ibid., pp. 9–10.

30. Hannah Arendt, *Totalitarianism* (Orlando, Fla.: Harcourt Brace Jovanovich, 1968), p. xiv.

31. See Stalin, *Mastering Bolshevism*, p. 10. Cited in Merle Fainsod, *How Russia Is Ruled*, rev. ed. (Cambridge, Mass.: Harvard University Press, 1964), p. 435.

32. Aleksandr Solzhenitsyn, *The Gulag Archipelago, 1918–1956* (New York: Harper & Row, 1974), p. 595.

33. Bracher, *German Dictatorship*, p. 258.

34. Ibid., pp. 259–260.

35. Ibid., p. 262.

36. Ibid.

37. Hilberg, *Destruction of the European Jews*, p. 31.

38. Mao Zedong, *Selected Works* (Beijing: Foreign Languages Press, 1960–1965), p. 224.

39. Franz Michaels and George Taylor, *The Far East in the Modern World* (New York: Holt, 1964), p. 479.

40. John King Fairbank, *The United States and China*, 4th ed. (Cambridge, Mass.: Harvard University Press, 1979), p. 409.

41. Ibid., p. 413.

42. Ibid.

43. Cassinelli, *Total Revolution*, p. 195.

44. Ibid., p. 243.

45. Ibid., p. 46.

46. Ibid., p. 186.

47. Ibid., p. 187.

 CHAPTER 4

AUTHORITARIAN STATES

TRADITIONAL RULE

(AP/Wide World Photos)

COMPARED TO TOTALITARIAN governments, *authoritarian governments* can seem almost routine. Nonetheless, these nondemocratic regimes are important because they represent a significant political alternative and an enduring means by which human beings govern themselves. (See the Appendix for a comparison of the three main forms of government.)

AUTHORITARIAN RULERS

Every authoritarian state is governed by a single ruler or an elite ruling group. The single-head form of government is called an *autocracy,* and the elite-group form is known as an *oligarchy* (sometimes referred to as a *junta,* or ruling clique). Authoritarian rulers are the sole repositories of power and authority within the political system. Their tenure in office depends not on elections (that is, the active consent of the people) but rather on a combination of myth and might. On the one hand, the people are told that obedience to authority is their moral (or sacred) duty; on the other hand, the rulers stand ready to use brute force whenever rebellion threatens their position, which they are determined to maintain at all costs.

Traditionally, authoritarian governments have been headed by a strongman, or dictator. Among notable dictators of recent times have been Idi Amin (Uganda), Emperor Bokassa I (Central African Republic), Muammar Qaddafi (Libya), Ferdinand Marcos (the Philippines), and François "Papa Doc" Duvalier (Haiti). More and more frequently in modern times, however, the top military leaders of a nation have banded together and seized political power. Such juntas tend to govern along military lines, defending their rule in terms of the nation's alleged need for order and stability. Military juntas have appeared throughout the Third World. In Latin America the list has included, at various times, Argentina, Bolivia, Brazil, Chile, Ecuador, and Honduras. Algeria, Iraq, and Yemen in the Middle East, along with Bangladesh and Thailand in southern Asia, have also fallen into this category. In Africa over the past 30 years, more than 20 countries have been governed by military rulers.

Along with strongman and military junta regimes, a number of traditional monarchies are still extant, especially in the Middle East. Examples include Morocco, Saudi Arabia, and Jordan, as well as such Persian Gulf states as Kuwait, Oman, Bahrain, Qatar, and the United Arab Emirates.

Such authoritarian rulers generally do not respect individual rights when such rights interfere with the goals of the state. Authoritarian regimes usually place the interests of the rulers above the welfare of the rank-and-file citizenry; and given the nature of the system, there is nothing to prevent them from doing so.

Yet there are differences among authoritarian rulers. They do vary in the extent to which they enforce public conformity and suppress intellectual and artistic freedom. Furthermore, the amount of force, repression, and violence employed by authoritarian rulers can differ significantly. Some rulers exert only sufficient force to retain political power. Others, appropriately referred to as tyrants, display an enthusiasm for bloodshed, violence, and repression. Finally, whereas most authoritarian rulers focus exclusively on advancing their power, wealth, and prestige, a few have also made genuine and sustained efforts to exercise political power in order to advance the national interest (for instance, Tito of Yugoslavia and Sadat of Egypt). Ambitious national programs undertaken to industrialize, reform, or modernize nations and their economies can sometimes be viewed as evidence of a "benevolent" authoritarianism. Of course, even benevolent authoritarian rulers generally permit no organized political opposition. Nonetheless, it is their nation's well-being, and not solely self-interest, that appears to guide these actions.

These practical distinctions, even if they are sometimes difficult to perceive, nonetheless have important political implications. Authoritarian states are ruled by governments that wield unchecked power. Most of these governments are, at best, only incidentally concerned with the well-being of the citizenry; yet even in the case of authoritarian states headed by self-interested dictators, important variations must be acknowledged. For even if all tyrannies are dictatorships, not all dictators are tyrants. (See Figure 4-1.)

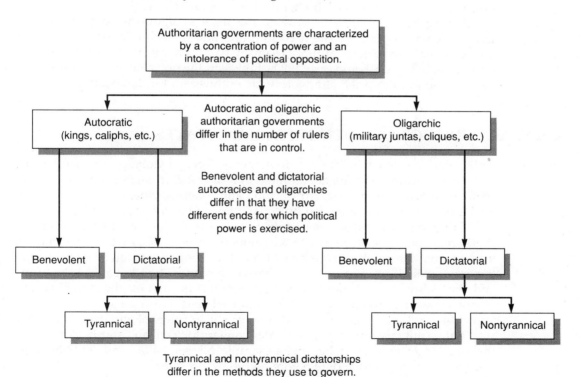

FIGURE 4-1   Types of Authoritarian Governments

THE PREVALENCE OF AUTHORITARIAN STATES

Just as there are differences among authoritarian rulers, it is difficult to make broad generalizations about authoritarian states, because of their great number and (often superficial) variety. Nonetheless, we can safely say that authoritarian rule is the oldest and has been the most common form of government known to humanity. Most primitive governments were authoritarian, and absolute monarchy was widely accepted as the only form of government in Europe from the Middle Ages until the French Revolution of 1789. In the Western world, monarchs were usually called kings or princes; in the Middle East, pharaohs, caliphs, sultans, sheiks, and emirs; in India, moguls; in China, emperors; and in Russia, czars.

Outside of a few historical periods—classical Greece and Rome, medieval and Renaissance Italy, and the contemporary age—monarchies were virtually the only form of government in existence. And even during these more "enlightened" eras, monarchy was the most prevalent form of government. In the golden age of the Greek city-state system, for example, the principal alternative to monarchy was another form of authoritarianism, oligarchy—not republican government. Perhaps because this kind of government is easiest to institute, or perhaps because it seems to provide the most straightforward and efficient governmental response to the need for order and the solution for severe social and economic problems, authoritarianism has been the rule rather than the exception. In the 1980s and early 1990s, however, the prevalence of authoritarianism declined in the wake of a worldwide enthusiasm for democracy.

CHARACTERISTICS OF AUTHORITARIAN STATES

Authoritarian rulers usually come to power by force or violence, first surprising and then overthrowing the government in a *coup d'état.* Such coups have been frequent occurrences in Asia, Africa, and Latin America, where rulers have often seized power only to be ousted by equally forceful autocrats or juntas.

Maintaining the rulers' monopoly of power is a salient characteristic of authoritarian states. To sustain such a monopoly on political power, authoritarian leaders must control the means by which political opponents can be intimidated, harassed, exiled, or even executed; that is, they must tightly control the army and the police. Such control is perhaps simpler in military dictatorships, for obvious reasons, than in civilian ones, but civilian dictators also typically maintain close ties to the military. In fact, many civilian rulers of authoritarian states start out as military strongmen and later convert to "civilian" status, largely for the sake of appearances. In Egypt, for example, Nasser, Sadat, and now Mubarak were all military commanders before becoming president.

To frustrate actual or potential political opposition, authoritarian rulers often impose strict press censorship, outlaw political parties, and exert firm control over the legal system, which is manipulated to prosecute (and persecute) political opponents. A monopoly over the mass media and the courts gives absolute rulers a highly effective means of perpetuating their rule. In itself a major source of power, this monopoly also supplies the machinery by which excesses of power can be disguised or legitimized. These measures are frequently undertaken in the name of order and stability, especially plausible in light of the problems faced by many developing nations—foreign enemies, internal ethnic and religious divisions, economic scarcity, and profound class differences.

Although some authoritarian states have actively promoted modernization and industrialization (for example, South Korea today and Turkey at various times), most are characterized by underdeveloped agrarian economies and sharp gradations between rich and poor. Authoritarian rulers tend to seek control over the economy only to a limited extent and chiefly for the purpose of collecting taxes to underwrite military and economic programs and (often lavish) personal expenditures. Such tax payments, along with occasional declarations of allegiance and passive obedience to official authority, often comprise the only demands made on ordinary citizens by autocratic regimes. Thus although an authoritarian government may exploit its citizens economically, the regime is ordinarily indifferent to the way they live their lives, so long as they stay away from politics.

To be sure, authoritarian governments rarely make the lives of their people much better—often, exactly the opposite is the case—but such governments do tend to leave ordinary citizens alone most of the time. In general, authoritarianism "does not attempt to get rid of or to transform all other groups or classes in the state, it simply reduces them to subservience."[1]

AUTHORITARIAN GOVERNMENTS AND POLITICS

Perhaps subservience is the natural result of the fact that authoritarian rulers are seldom motivated to govern for the people's benefit. This recognition caused Aristotle to contend that despite the important differences that characterize such states, they necessarily represent a perversion of good government. Asserting that "those constitutions which consider the common interest are *right* constitutions, judged by the standard of absolute justice," he argued that "those constitutions which consider only the personal interests of the rulers are all wrong constitutions, or perversions of the right forms. Such perverted forms are despotic."[2] Aristotle held, further, that the end of good government should not be the good of one individual or of a privileged few but, insofar as possible, the good of all citizens. Yet dictators and tyrants alike by definition place their own personal interests above the interests of society. Like medical quacks who become wealthy by touting fraudulent medicines as miracle cures, such rulers become powerful by promising great benefits to the people whom they most exploit.

This perversion of ends usually entails a like perversion of means. Often such rulers justify their self-serving policies on the grounds that their actions are necessary to preserve order and defend the nation from its enemies. In the worst cases, such actions can turn a society into an association of slaves or an anonymous mass of automatons.

Throughout history, authoritarian governments have been criticized for their characteristically cruel persecution of political enemies. As a rule, such states hold a negative view of politics: Either the ruler is above politics, or the sphere of politics is greatly restricted. This means that in authoritarian states, questions regarding who should rule or whether power is exercised wisely cannot be raised in public because any criticism of a ruler is considered an act of disloyalty. If such questions are tolerated at all, they are confined to a narrow circle—for instance, the palace or the court.

Right-Wing and Left-Wing Regimes

Traditionally, authoritarian states were categorized as either right-wing or left-wing in political orientation. According to some (but not all) political observers, right-wing authoritarian states were anticommunist, whereas left-wing regimes were much more open to friendly relations with communist states. Today, with the passing of the Cold War and considering the fact that not all authoritarian regimes display an explicit political orientation, there is a question as to how useful this distinction remains. But the distinction is still frequently made and therefore requires an explanation.

Right-wing dictatorships, which often are dominated by military elites, tend to resist attempts at sweeping social change. In general, they prefer to mollify entrenched elites—especially the landed aristocracy—while keeping the often impoverished and disenfranchised majority of their citizens in a state of ignorance and apathy. Vigorously pursuing order and stability as their key political goals, these dictatorships, as a rule, are highly pragmatic in their approach to economic development. Almost invariably, they prefer gradual change or no change at all to convulsive and sweeping campaigns for social and economic progress. Most such regimes rely heavily on the military or a secret police (or both) to maintain public order and eliminate actual or potential political opponents. Almost all staunchly anticommunist, right-wing dictatorships aligned themselves with the West during the Cold War era. Historical examples of this pattern include Francisco Franco's Spain, Pakistan under Ayub Khan, Iran under the Shah, the Philippines under Ferdinand Marcos, the Dominican Republic under Rafael Trujillo, Cuba under Fulgencio Batista, Argentina under Juan Perón, and Haiti under François Duvalier.

Left-wing dictatorships generally display equally salient, though somewhat different, political characteristics. Proclaiming hatred for colonialism, capitalism, and imperialism, leaders of these states commonly espouse collectivist or communal ideals and champion (but do not necessarily institute) radical programs of social change and land reform. Occasionally, these autocrats embrace a fierce nationalism which stresses independence from the control and influence of foreign powers. Specifically, they often reject a close economic relationship with capitalist countries on the grounds that it represents a kind of Trojan Horse through which former colonial powers seek to exert economic control over states that have gained political freedom (so-called *neocolonialism*). In comparison to their right-wing counterparts, left-wing dictatorships are more apt to emphasize

Saddam Hussein: Dictator

WHEN SADDAM HUSSEIN invaded Kuwait in the early morning hours of August 2, 1990, it shocked the world. But this act of aggression was not out of character for Saddam. He had, after all, attacked Iran in 1980, hoping to take advantage of Iran's revolutionary turmoil in the wake of Shah Muhammad Reza Pahlavi's overthrow by forces loyal to Islamic fundamentalist leader Ayatollah Khomeini. That bloody war had lasted eight years and ended indecisively.

Saddam remained a somewhat shadowy figure. Born in the small town of Takrit, he became president following a military coup in 1968 that brought the Baath Socialist party to power. The Baathist ideology is an odd admixture of Arab and Marxist elements combining anti-imperialism, socialism, and pan-Arab nationalism. After the death of Egypt's Gamal Abdel Nasser in 1970, Saddam aspired to become the leader of the Arab world. Saddam also ploughed resources into Iraq's nuclear weapons program. In 1983, alarmed at the prospect of a hostile nuclear power within easy striking distance of its territory, Israel attacked and destroyed Iraq's principal nuclear reactor facility.

The war with Iran was particularly barbaric. At least 500,000 Iranians died, along with an estimated 300,000 to 400,000 Iraqis. Worse still, Saddam had ordered the large-scale use of chemical weapons (poison gas) against Iranian forces, the first formal use of a chemical agent by a major combatant since World War I. The economic costs for both sides were also extremely high. Iraq's foreign debt at the end of the war totaled $40 billion—most of it for advanced weapons purchased on the international arms market.

Nor has Saddam been any less brutal in his treatment of "enemies" at home. He has persecuted Iraq's minority groups (Shiites, Persians, Kurds) and killed opposition figures without remorse. In an infamous case, he used poison gas against his own civilian population in a Kurdish

Given Iraq's crushing defeat in the 1991 Persian Gulf War, many observers questioned Saddam Hussein's ability to retain power. (Eddie Adams/Contact Press Images)

village. Saddam's justification for this action was that the Kurds have long sought to establish an independent Kurdish state, thus posing an ever-present threat to his rule.

Saddam is described as obsessed with personal security and apparently trusts only family members or fellow Takritis. Many experts and analysts characterize Saddam as irrational.

Even after Iraq's crushing defeat in the 1991 Persian Gulf War, Saddam defied the United Nations by trying to conceal Iraq's surviving missiles and continued Iraq's nuclear weapons program. When the United States threatened to take further military action if Iraq did not comply fully with all UN resolutions, Saddam backed down. Today, Iraq is no longer an immediate danger to its neighbors, but Saddam is still in power and still rules with an iron fist.

popular participation in political programs. They are also more likely to feature a ruling party that exercises sole political power. Finally, left-wing dictatorships are more likely to mask their reliance on force and violence, often by branding political opponents as "enemies of the people" and carrying out "revolutionary justice" through so-called people's courts. Examples of recent left-wing dictatorships are Libya and Algeria in North Africa, Iraq and Syria in the Middle East, and Bangladesh and Burma in Asia.

SIX MYTHS ABOUT AUTHORITARIAN STATES

Ignoring the genuine diversity among authoritarian states often leads people to generalize from extreme cases and end up with a distorted view. The understandable (and usually justified) stigma attached to authoritarianism has promoted the blanket acceptance of several myths about this form of government. We now examine those myths with a critical eye.

François "Papa Doc" Duvalier (1907–1971), former right-wing Haitian dictator, ruled from 1957 to 1971. After his reelection (with army backing) in 1961, Duvalier declared himself president for life. His long regime was a reign of terror. (Associated Press Photo)

1. All Authoritarian Regimes Are Equally Oppressive

Many observers have pointed out significant differences in the way authoritarian states wield power. Aristotle, in particular, distinguished between two different forms of authoritarianism. The more common variety, Aristotle noted, relies on such traditional methods of political control as acts of outright cruelty and repression. The purpose of such policies is clear enough: to take away the power to revolt. A second kind of authoritarian ruler seeks to deceive the people. Such a dictator gives the appearance of being concerned about the common good. He avoids displaying wealth, gives no sign of any impropriety, honors worthy citizens, erects public monuments, and so on. In short, this ruler "should appear to his subjects not as a despot, but as a steward or a King of his people."[3] Of course, the ruler's own self-interest is still supreme. He merely attempts to make a good impression in order to take away the motivation (or desire) to revolt. This kind of ruler may do the right thing, but for the wrong reasons. He is, in Aristotle's phrase, "half-good." Nevertheless, life under a "half-good" autocrat would clearly be preferable to life under a "traditional" dictator.

Thus it is not only the *extent* to which authoritarian governments affect individual lives but also the *manner* in which they do so that matters. As we have seen, some rulers imprison and murder all real or imagined political enemies, while others govern with a minimum of force. In another vein, some authoritarian governments show a marked indifference to economic development, preferring to concentrate all their energies on the preservation of political power, while others actively seek to improve economic conditions. Shah Muhammad Reza Pahlavi (1920–1980) of Iran, for example, was both an unrelenting persecutor of his political enemies and a progressive modernizer in the realm of cultural, economic, and social policy, where some measure of personal freedom existed. Similarly, the present-day governments of Taiwan and Singapore represent a curious mixture of democracy and dictatorship, yet both countries enjoy relatively high rates of economic growth and standards of living that are the envy of many Third World states.

2. All Authoritarian Regimes Are Illegitimate

Most Americans would subscribe to John Locke's view that the only legitimate governments are those based on the consent of the governed. But consent is not the only measure of legitimacy—in fact, there have been long periods in history when popular will was not even recognized as a criterion of legitimacy.

From the late Middle Ages through the eighteenth century, the prevalent form of government in Europe was monarchy, based on religion (divine right) and heredity (royal birth). Similarly, in Imperial China the dynastic principle was one source of the emperor's legitimacy, but religion also played a major role—the Chinese emperor ruled under the "mandate of Heaven." Historically, then, tradition and religion served as two of the principal sources of governmental legitimacy.

Many contemporary dictatorships have relied on a somewhat more informal and personal source of legitimacy, the popular appeal of a *charismatic leader.* Often charismatic rule is grounded in the personal magnetism, oratorical skills, or legendary feats of a national hero who has led his country to victory in war or revolution. Examples include Nasser of Egypt, Sukarno of Indonesia, and more recently, Qaddafi of Libya. Many postcolonial Third World dictatorships were based almost exclusively on hero worship of a "liberator"—a person who rallied the indigenous population in a successful struggle to win independence from European colonial rule.

Divine sanction, tradition, and charisma, then, are the historical pillars of autocratic rule. More often than not, these wellsprings of legitimacy have served effectively to sell the idea that the rulers have a *right* to rule without consulting the people. Having the right to rule does not mean the same thing as ruling rightly, of course. And unfortunately, dictators and tyrants have too often used their "rights" to commit serious wrongs.

3. All Authoritarian Regimes Are Unpopular

People living in a democracy tend naturally to believe that if given the choice, everyone would choose to live in a democracy rather than a dictatorship. Yet the evidence suggests that this belief is mistaken. Undeniably, some dictators inspire in their people not only fear—stemming from their use of force and terror to suppress political opposition—but also respect, trust, voluntary obedience, and even love. Because authoritarian leaders sometimes provide political stability and economic growth, dictators are occasionally adored. In addition, charisma is not only a source of legitimacy; it is also an extremely important source of popularity. The prototype of the charismatic "man on horseback" was Napoleon Bonaparte, who seized power in a France convulsed by revolution and threatened by foreign enemies and led the French people on a campaign of armed conquest that for a time produced a latter-day near-equivalent of the Roman Empire on the European continent. At the height of his military success, Napoleon enjoyed almost universal popularity in France. Adolf Hitler, too, received a high level of public support from the German people. (Of course, Hitler's totalitarian state exercised powers that far surpassed those of Napoleon's autocratic regime.) As one writer has pointed out:

> It is sometimes assumed that one who rules with the support of the majority cannot be a tyrant; yet both Napoleon and Hitler, two of the greatest tyrants of all time, may well have had majority support through a great part of their reigns. Napoleon, in many of his aggressive campaigns, probably had majority support among the French, but his actions . . . were nonetheless tyrannical for that. Hitler, for all we know, might have had at least tacit support of the majority of the German people in his campaign against the Jews; his action was nonetheless tyrannical for that. Let us assume—*per impossible,* one would hope—that [if] a democratically elected Prime Minister were to start on a similar campaign, he would be acting tyrannically; the probable result would be that he would be opposed by a minority so vehemently that he would have to take tyrannical measures to suppress it and thereby cease to depend on the popular vote and thus become an absolute tyrant. A tyrant, then, may

Napoleon Bonaparte (1769–1821) crowning himself emperor of France in 1804: "What is the throne?—a bit of wood gilded and covered with velvet. I am the state—I alone am here the representative of the people." (Culver Pictures)

in many of his measures have popular support, but in general his power will not depend upon it.[4]

The point of this analysis could not be sharper in its implications for the study of politics: Bad regimes will not necessarily find their evildoing impeded by good people. In this respect, modern tyrannies illustrate a truth expressed most notably by the nineteenth-century Russian author Fyodor Dostoyevsky: In an age of widespread equality, the masses, desiring security above all else, will gladly accept despotism in order to gain release from the burden of responsibility that freedom imposes on people.[5] The truth is that despotic government is often more popular than we tend to believe.

4. All Authoritarian Regimes Neglect the Public Interest

This generalization cannot survive close scrutiny. Even the worst tyrants can bring order out of political chaos and material progress out of economic stagnation. Adolf Hitler, it has been argued, should even be credited with curing Germany's economic woes. And apologists for Benito Mussolini, Hitler's contemporary and the fascist dictator of Italy, have noted that at least he made the trains run on time. Admittedly, such public policy successes by no means justified the despotic excesses of these tyrants. However, they do help to explain the domestic popularity of Hitler and Mussolini.

Perhaps the most impressive example of a despotic regime that succeeded in creating sustained social and economic progress comes not from Europe but from China. At the beginning of the modern era, the existence of a unique form of despotism in China was observed by such notable Western political observers as Baron de Montesquieu, Adam Smith, and Karl Marx.[6] And in our time, the classical Chinese system of government has been the object of much scholarly attention.[7] Particularly noteworthy, in the eyes of many Western observers, was the vast network of dikes, irrigation ditches, and waterways that crisscrossed the immense Chinese realm. This hydraulic system represented a signal achievement, exceeding in scale and scope any public works construction that governments in premodern Europe, even at the height of the Roman Empire, had undertaken. What kind of a civilization could build public works on such a stupendous scale?

One modern scholar, Karl Wittfogel, theorized that Chinese authoritarianism, which he labeled "oriental despotism," owed its distinctive features to the challenges of sustaining a huge population in a harsh and demanding environment.[8] The staple food of China has always been rice, and rice cultivation requires large amounts of water under controlled conditions. So to solve the perennial food problem, Chinese civilization first had to solve the perennial water problem. This meant building sophisticated flood control, irrigation, and drainage works. The end result was a system of *permanent agriculture,* which enabled the Chinese to cultivate the same land for centuries without stripping the soil of its nutrients.

Constructing such a system presupposes a strong central government. A project as ambitious as the transformation of the natural environment in the premodern age simply could not have been attempted without political continuity and stability, social cohesion, scientific planning, resource mobilization, labor conscription, and bureaucratic coordination on a truly extraordinary scale. Thus the technological and logistic demands of China's system of permanent agriculture gave rise to a vast bureaucracy and justified a thoroughgoing, imperial dictatorship with several unusual (by European standards) characteristics. As early European travelers and traders noted, the Chinese government was the largest landowner (in fact, private ownership of property was severely restricted). Furthermore, governmental policies and programs were designed and implemented largely by a centralized bureaucracy whose officials were dedicated to efficient administration. Admission to this class was based not on heredity, property ownership, or wealth (as would have been the case in Europe) but on a series of examinations that revealed candidates' knowledge of the Confucian classics—and, through those works, the principles of right conduct—as well as mastery of the immensely complex written language. At the apex of the power pyramid sat the emperor, who ruled under the mandate of Heaven. His power was absolute.

What about the "average" Chinese citizen under this highly centralized form of government? The individual traded food for labor and was regarded by the ruling powers primarily as a factor of production. Outside of imposing severe labor discipline on the common people, the bureaucracy pretty much left individuals alone. The government did not live in constant fear of popular revolution; Imperial China was a remarkably stable society. The fusion of religion and government, the fact that the masses were kept busy in rice cultivation and large-scale public works projects, the unavailability of modern weapons and communications technology, and the practice of rewarding the scholar-gentry class with great privileges and perquisites all combined to limit potential political opposition. This unique form of "hydraulic despotism" lasted longer than any other system of government the world has ever known.

Oriental despotism presents us with a paradox of sorts. On the one hand, it stands as an example of a political regime more despotic than most traditional forms of Western authoritarianism:

> Oriental despotism was stronger and more pervasive than either modern European autocracy of the sixteenth-to-nineteenth-century kind or Roman power at most periods. . . . Vast numbers of people were controlled and exploited by a few and on a scale far greater and with bureaucratic institutions far more elaborate than under the personal tyrannies of the city-states.[9]

On the other hand, Imperial China's economic and technical achievements, along with its art, language, and literature, were extremely impressive by any standard. Also, significant material advances accompanied China's early economic development. Although the emperors and scholar-officials were neither liberal nor politically enlightened, the Chinese system of hydraulic despotism resulted in a sufficient supply of food to support a large and growing population for centuries (albeit not without occasional famines). In view of the difficulties many Third World countries have experienced in trying to provide their people with food and shelter, the agricultural achievements of Imperial China seem even more remarkable.

A less breathtaking but similar and politically interesting modern-day phenomenon is Southeast Asia's "little dragons," especially Hong Kong, Singapore, Taiwan, and South Korea. These authoritarian regimes are far less oppressive than traditional Chinese rule; in fact, their relatively mild authoritarianism may be evolving in the direction of democracy. Singapore and Taiwan have been relatively stable; South Korea has been marked by student protests and even political assassination. Hong Kong, a British Crown Colony since 1898, is a special case. The British 99-year lease expires in 1997 and Hong Kong will then revert to the control of Communist China. Nonetheless, all four governments have brought about dramatic increases in gross domestic product and standard of living. Each nation has established an economic program of cooperation between government and private business designed to implement large-scale industrialization and to encourage manufacturing and technological developments for the purpose of dramatically increasing exports. The government safeguards native industry by adopting a variety of protectionist strategies, such as trade barriers and currency manipulation. It is not clear if these nations' economic success has been facilitated by their small size or by cultural factors (for instance, a strong work ethic), but what *is* clear is that they have managed to combine authoritarian rule with an enhanced standard of living that has significantly benefited a great number of their citizens.

5. Modern Dictators Depend on New Technology and Methods to Stay in Power

This assertion is simply not true. Technology has played only a minor role in maintaining the power of many of the world's most powerful authoritarian rulers, and there have been no great breakthroughs in the political techniques used by autocrats to retain power. The fundamental methods of consolidating and maintaining power, in fact, have been well known for centuries.

In *The Politics*, Aristotle provided an impressive catalog of the political tactics used by autocrats of ancient times, whose methods of maintaining power would be familiar to most modern-day dictators. In general, Aristotle noted, these tactics were designed to render individuals incapable of concerted political action by breaking their spirit and making them distrustful of one another. Persons who, because of their social positions, leadership qualities, or moral character, represented a political threat were eliminated. By banning common meals, cultural societies, and other communal activities, individuals were isolated from one another. Such actions fostered insecurity and distrust and thus made it difficult for dissidents to create an underground political movement. Secret police increased popular anxiety while obtaining information; spies were used for the same purposes. Poverty, heavy taxes, and hard work monopolized the subjects' time and attention. (Aristotle cited the construction of the Egyptian pyramids in this regard.) Finally, warmongering was viewed by autocratic rulers as a useful way of providing a diversion "with the object of keeping their subjects constantly occupied and continually in need of a leader."[10]

Aristotle's list of autocratic political tactics was expanded and updated by the Italian political thinker Niccolò Machiavelli (1469–1527), who literally wrote the book on gaining and maintaining political power. His book, *The Prince* (1532), can be viewed on one level as a kind of instructor's manual for the successful authoritarian ruler.

Those who would rule, Machiavelli contended, must understand the importance of *seeming* to act morally even when committing immoral acts. Successful rulers must be masters of deception. Often they will *have* to act immorally in order to survive; for this reason, they must constantly appear honest and upright, even while practicing "how not to be good."

Machiavelli also advised would-be rulers not to keep promises that are no longer in their best interest; to disguise their intentions; to inspire fear, rather than love, in their subjects; and, if possible, to cultivate the appearance of generosity while always practicing self-interest. Generosity, in his view, meant keeping one's own property and giving away that of others. When property must be confiscated or political opponents imprisoned or "traitors" executed—in other words, whenever punishment has to be inflicted—the acts should be done swiftly and simultaneously. The sooner the bloodletting was ended, Machiavelli noted, the sooner it would be forgotten. In contrast, benefits should be doled out little by little, so they can be savored and their recipients reminded of whence all good things come. Finally, Machiavelli counseled, punishment should always be severe as well as swift: Mild retribution, he argued, may arouse a spirit of rebellion; it may also make the ruler look weak and indecisive.

It is not surprising that the word *Machiavellian* has come to be associated with ruthless, immoral acts. Yet Machiavelli did not invent the methods he prescribed. He simply systematized a set of practices that were prevalent in the governmental dealings of the city-states of sixteenth-century Italy. Like Aristotle before him, he merely elaborated on the actual methods and techniques used by the autocratic rulers to maintain political power—techniques that are still used widely today.

6. Authoritarian Rule Is the Worst Kind Possible

The fallacy of this position should be readily apparent. In the first place, as we saw in Chapter 3, totalitarian states go well beyond traditional autocracies in restricting individual freedom. In the second place, as we have already noted, different kinds of authoritarian governments exploit individual citizens to greater or lesser degrees. Some aim at economic growth and social reform; others do not. Some provide the essentials of life for their citizens; others are totally indifferent to the well-being of the masses. A few may even be efficient, reform-minded, and socially progressive. Finally, authoritarian governments can become constitutional democracies, as in the cases of Portugal and Spain.

When a nation must choose between anarchy, economic collapse, or social chaos on the one hand and some kind of authoritarian government on the other, a particularly difficult dilemma arises. Under such conditions, a political despot may well offer the only hope for a workable government.

AUTHORITARIANISM UNDER SIEGE?

Despite the fact that authoritarian governments represent the most straightforward and simple solution to establishing political order, some political scientists feel that authoritarianism is currently under siege. Sometimes the collapse of communism is cited as an explanation for this phenomenon. Yet even before the collapse of communism in eastern Europe, nondemocratic governments, especially under authoritarian military rulers, were suffering severe setbacks. During the 1980s, Ecuador, Bolivia, Peru, Brazil, Uruguay, Argentina, Chile, and Paraguay replaced military rulers, opting for more democratic alternatives (Peru has since reverted to authoritarianism). Central American nations have followed the same trend. Some observers see a similar tendency developing in Africa, away from authoritarian governments and toward democracy, pointing out that in 1990 alone at least nine African countries held multiparty elections and another dozen or so adopted reforms designed to lead to such elections.[11]

The question—and it is a most important political question—is, Is there an overall trend away from authoritarian governments? Can we look forward to a future age when, for the first time in human history, nondemocratic regimes will constitute a clear minority of the world's governments? The question of whether the world is evolving politically toward an increasingly democratic future is intriguing, although still unanswerable. Certainly, the contemporary world features many successful examples of democracies and failed nondemocratic states. Furthermore, the prosperity commonly associated with democratic states encourages imitators and admirers (for an extended discussion of this point, see Chapter 9). In recent times, the democratic model has shined brightly.

And yet it is probably premature to proclaim an irreversible trend toward democracy. In some Latin American and many African nations, a modern economy has yet to be created. Gross economic and educational disparities exist among native populations (such disparities are thought to be incompatible with an enduring democracy). In many of these nations, a lack of resources and huge debt payments burden local economies. Tribal or ethnic divisions destabilize many developing societies. And even in nations where the military has relinquished power or has been removed from office, prominent generals remain, often exerting a behind-the-scene influence over civilian governments, sometimes biding their time in case those governments are unable to overcome the severe social, economic, and political challenges they face. Thus while democracy presently appears to be increasing around the world, new democratic governments remain fragile. Authoritarianism is certainly not dead; indeed, despite appearances, we cannot even be certain that it is dying.

Summary

Authoritarian states are characterized by one or more unelected rulers who exercise unchecked political power. Such states may be ruled by benevolent autocrats (who are at least somewhat concerned with advancing the public good), ordinary dictators (who are concerned solely with advancing their own interests), or tyrants (who exhibit great enthusiasm for violence and bloodletting).

Historically, authoritarian rulers have provided the most common form of government. Yet despite their prevalence, authoritarian regimes have been regarded as perversions of good government because they almost always place the ruler's interests ahead of the public good.

Misconceptions about authoritarian regimes abound. It is not true that all authoritarian states are identical, illegitimate, or unpopular with their citizens. Further, such governments can be differentiated on moral grounds: Some seek to promote the public interest; others do not. Yet another myth is that authoritarian rulers rely primarily on technology or on new techniques to maintain their political power. Nor do authoritarian regimes represent the worst possible form of government in all cases.

Finally, although there is some evidence that authoritarian government is giving way to democracy, it is too early to draw any definitive conclusions.

Key Terms

authoritarian governments
autocracy
oligarchy

junta
coup d'état
right-wing dictatorship

left-wing dictatorship
charismatic leader

Review Questions

1. What are the two basic types of nondemocratic government? Are authoritarian governments becoming less prevalent? Where are such governments found today?

2. What are the chief characteristics of authoritarian governments?

3. Are all autocrats tyrannical?

4. What kind of "advice" did Machiavelli give to rulers bent on maintaining their power?

5. There are several widespread misconceptions about authoritarian government. Describe each of the six myths that surround such governments. What are the fallacies associated with these myths?

Recommended Reading

CRICK, BERNARD. *Basic Forms of Government: A Sketch and a Model.* London: Macmillan, 1980. A short yet comprehensive outline of types of governments, which contrasts authoritarian with totalitarian and republican states.

LATEY, MAURICE. *Patterns of Tyranny.* New York: Atheneum, 1969. A study that attempts to classify and analyze various tyrannies throughout history.

LINZ, JUAN. "An Authoritarian Regime: Spain." In *Reader in Political Sociology,* edited by Frank Lindenfeld. New York: Funk & Wagnalls, 1968. A useful study of one authoritarian regime.

MACHIAVELLI, NICCOLÒ. "The Prince." In *The Prince and Other Discourses.* New York: Modern Library, 1950. This classic study describes the methods tyrants must use to maintain power.

MOORE, BARRINGTON. *Social Origins of Dictatorship and Democracy.* Boston: Beacon Press, 1966. A general discussion of the relationship between social conditions and political systems.

RUBIN, BARRY. *Modern Dictators: Third World Coup Makers, Strongmen, and Political Tyrants.* New York: McGraw-Hill, 1987. A good general discussion of various nondemocratic regimes that have held power in the post–World War II era.

WITTFOGEL, KARL. *Oriental Despotism: A Comparative Study of Total Power.* New Haven, Conn.: Yale University Press, 1957. This pioneering study offers a significant analysis of a very important non-Western political system.

Notes

1. Bernard Crick, *Basic Forms of Government: A Sketch and a Model* (London: Macmillan, 1980), p. 53.

2. Aristotle, *The Politics,* trans. and ed. Ernest Barker (New York: Oxford University Press, 1962), p. 112.

3. Ibid., p. 240.

4. Maurice Latey, *Patterns of Tyranny* (New York: Atheneum, 1969), p. 115.

5. Fyodor Dostoyevsky, *The Brothers Karamazov,* ed. Ernest Rhys (London: Dent, 1927), p. 259.

6. Crick, *Basic Forms of Government,* p. 35.

7. See Karl Wittfogel, *Oriental Despotism: A Comparative Study of Total Power* (New Haven, Conn.: Yale University Press, 1957).

8. Ibid.

9. Crick, *Basic Forms of Government,* p. 36.

10. Aristotle, *The Politics,* p. 245.

11. Robert M. Press, "Africa's Struggle for Democracy," *Christian Science Monitor,* March 21, 1991, p. 4.

CHAPTER 5

CONSTITUTIONAL DEMOCRACY

A POPULAR ALTERNATIVE

(Bettmann Archives) **103**

UNLIKE NONDEMOCRATIC TOTALITARIAN or authoritarian governments, constitutional democracies feature governments that are elected. In democracies, the people, directly or through their chosen representatives, regularly indicate their political preferences. Countries as diverse as France, Norway, Great Britain, Israel, Mexico, and India share a basic belief in the exercise of political self-determination as an overriding principle of political life. To citizens of these nations and ours, democratic government means popular government; in theory, the people are fundamentally responsible for their own political well-being. However, even though the people are the source of governmental power, they cannot simply do anything they wish. Virtually every democracy imposes limitations on majority rule. Furthermore, well-established rules and regulations usually dictate the procedures according to which government operates. Where governments are determined by meaningful elections and where such limitations are in force, the government is said to be a *constitutional democracy.* (See the Appendix for a comparison of the three main forms of government.)

DEMOCRATIC CONSTITUTIONS

All contemporary democracies have constitutions of one type or another. A nation's *constitution* delineates the basic organization and operation of government, describing both its powers and limitations. For reasons that will soon be apparent, almost all constitutions are written documents that claim to embody final authority in the political arena. A cursory examination of the constitutions of the world reveals a remarkable diversity among today's democratic systems. Constitutions vary in age and in length. Some, like those of the United States and France, are models of brevity. Others, including the Indian and Kenyan constitutions, are lengthy and detailed. India's constitution devotes no fewer than 97 items to federal control, 66 to state jurisdiction, and another 47 to joint federal-state control (or *concurrent powers*). Kenya's constitution is so explicit that in allocating authority between the central and regional governments, it even covers such subjects as animal disease control, the regulation of barbers and hairdressers, and houses occupied by disorderly residents.

It is often difficult, then, to make generalizations about democratic constitutions. For example, unlike almost all other modern constitutions, that of Great Britain essentially is unwritten. The British constitution is synonymous with the fundamental principles of the country's political culture as manifested in custom and convention. Thus rather than a written document, it is a wide-ranging compact ingrained in the public habits of the British people and entwined in the values, traditions, and institutions that animate Britain's political life.

However diverse, though, all democratic constitutions represent integral parts of political orders that are designed to advance the goals of individual security, prosperity, equality, liberty, and justice. (Chapters 14 and 15 focus on these ends of government.) Implicit in these constitutions are three concepts that, taken together, argue for the desirability of constitutional democracies. First, because such governments are democratic, they can be *responsive* to the people. Furthermore, because they are governed in accordance with fundamental rules and arrangements, they are *limited* in the goals they can pursue and the means by which they can pursue them. Finally, like all governments, constitutional democracies can be designed to govern competently, thus providing *effective* government. Inherent in the concept of constitutional democracy, then, is the ideal of a government that is—at one and the same time—responsive, limited, and effective.

DEMOCRACY AS RESPONSIVE GOVERNMENT

Constitutional democracies exercise popular control according to the principle of majority rule. Through free elections (and occasionally by means of direct participation), ordinary people play important roles in their own government. This principle of government seems so self-evident in the United States that we seldom question its validity.

Majority Rule

The validity of democracy itself, however, can indeed be questioned. As Socrates pointed out some 23 centuries ago, when one wants something done right, one goes to an expert. To recover from an illness, for example, one goes to a doctor. Why, then, if one wants good government, should one consult the people, many of whom are politically apathetic and ignorant? A contemporary commentator has pointed out that "if you visited a physician and sought advice as to whether to undergo an operation, you would be appalled if he explained that his policy in such cases was to poll a random sampling of passersby and act in accordance with the will of the majority."[1] Yet that is precisely what democracies do all the time.

Among the several possible answers to this Socratic critique of democracy, perhaps the most straightforward defense of majority rule was provided by Alexis de Tocqueville in *Democracy in America* (1835): "The moral authority of the majority is partly based upon the notion, that there is more intelligence and more wisdom in a great number of men collected together than in a single individual." Tocqueville believed that the approximate equality of human intellect was a basic assumption of democratic government. In addition, he argued, "The moral power of the majority is founded upon yet another principle, which is, that the interests of the many are to be preferred to those of the few"—a democratic precept that, in the final analysis, also rests on a belief in human equality.[2]

Whereas Socrates emphasized the great human differences in wisdom, intellect, and virtue, Tocqueville stressed human equality and contended that democracy accords moral power to the majority. Furthermore, because the majority is always changing, and today's minority can become tomorrow's majority, the principle of majority rule is appealing to all. In the United States, according to Tocqueville, "all parties are willing to recognize the rights of the majority, because they all hope to turn those rights to their own advantage at some future time."[3] The political principle of ***majority rule*** therefore finds support both in the moral

The preamble to the American Constitution in an early printing. In constitutional democracies, governments are both popular and restrained. They exist by virtue of constitutions that may differ widely in format and detail but invariably delineate the powers and boundaries of the government they create. (National Archives)

principle of individual equality and in the pragmatic calculations of self-interested citizens.

The Tyranny of the Majority

The desirability of responsible government appears obvious, but the presence of such a government is no guarantee that grave injustices will not occur. To illustrate this point, consider the jaded "wild West" scenario in which an innocent drifter is falsely accused of the coldblooded murder of one of the town's most upstanding citizens and is imprisoned. With only two exceptions, this scenario goes, everyone in town is indignant or drunk (or both), and an angry mob clamors for instant justice. Against this throng stand two solitary figures, a crotchety old deputy and the brave sheriff. The inevitable showdown takes place in the street in front of the sheriff's office. Led by the mayor and town council members (as well as by the man who actually committed the murder), a lynch mob demands that the "killer" be handed over immediately. In the end, only the heroic intervention of Matt Dillon or Wyatt Earp saves the innocent man from death at the hands of the mob.

This hackneyed plot actually represents an object lesson in political science—a vivid example of responsive government in action. The majority of townspeople have made their wishes clearly known to the sheriff (who symbolizes authority and the rule of law). The easy way out for the sheriff would be to hand over his (innocent) prisoner to the angry crowd. Could any action be more in accordance with the principle of majority rule—or less in accordance with the requirements of elementary justice?

Democratic government—when defined as the unlimited rule of the majority—*can* become synonymous with mob rule. Commonly viewed as a defense against tyranny, majority rule, ironically, can produce a new kind of tyranny, which Tocqueville called the *tyranny of the majority*.[4] For this reason, political thinkers through the ages have often rejected democracy, fearing that a majority based on one preeminent class, religion, or political persuasion would trample on the rights of minorities.

DEMOCRACY AS LIMITED GOVERNMENT

The need for limited government should be clear from our lynch mob example. Hanging a person who has not been tried and convicted is murder, and even the majority must not be allowed to get away with murder. Obviously, the notion of a morally infallible majority is nonsense—every majority consists of a collection of individuals, many or even most of whom may be misled, misguided, or misinformed on any given issue. Therefore, to prevent miscarriages of justice (such as lynchings), limitations must be placed on majority rule. These may take many forms, as can be seen in our own political system. In the United States, government is restricted as to how it can carry out public policy. Under the Constitution, it cannot, for example, pass an *ex post facto law* or a *bill of attainder* (Article 1, Sections 9 and 10). The Constitution limits governmental powers in another important respect: Various provisions of the Bill of Rights enjoin the government from jeopardizing an individual's right to freedom of speech, press, assembly, privacy, and fair trial (see Chapter 15).

Minority Rights

Constitutional restrictions on government clearly limit the principle of majority rule in the United States. If the Constitution says that a citizen has a right to a fair trial or to freedom of speech, no matter how many people want to deprive an individual of that right, and no matter how intensely they want to do so, such an action is simply not allowed. In effect, the Constitution says to members of an impassioned majority, "Cool off, settle down. Once you realize that freedom of speech or the right to a fair trial must be extended to all lest such rights be taken away from any one of you, you will be glad you did not act in haste."

For *limited government* to be anything other than a hollow concept, the government must at least be able to protect minorities against the incursions of aroused majorities. This axiom, however, is often far easier to acknowledge than to implement. First of all, the line between majority rule and minority rights in day-to-day political life is often unclear and thus open to differences of opinion. Then, too, constitutional rights are not self-defining; citizens may be entitled to speak their minds, but it is by no means always clear what "speaking one's mind" entails. In the United States, such matters are usually left to the courts to determine.

The Rule of Law

The idea that nations ought to be governed by impartial, binding laws is not new. Aristotle argued that the *rule of law* is almost always superior to the rule of unrestrained individuals. He based this argument on the concept of fairness, contending that while individuals are subject to appetites and passions for physical, material, and psychic satisfaction, the law represents (or should represent) "reason free from all passion."[5] Therefore, a government of laws is superior to one of individuals, even though individual magistrates and ministers of justice must always uphold the sanctity of the laws.

More than 2,000 years later, English philosopher John Locke (1632–1704) defended the rule of law on the basis of its important relationship to individual freedom. Locke believed that meaningful freedom could not exist outside the realm of law and politics and that, further, good government must conform to certain important rules—for instance, that taxes not be levied without the consent of the people. To Locke, these rules constituted "laws" in that they comprise fundamental maxims of political life. In other words, because they state the essence of what civil society was all about, to Locke they represented "laws above the law" that necessarily and justly placed limitations on lawmakers, no matter how large a majority such lawmakers commanded. From Locke's concept of a "higher law," the idea of constitutionalism evolved. As Locke noted (and as the inscription above the entrance to the Department of Justice building in Washington, D.C., reads), "Wherever Law ends, Tyranny begins."[6]

Locke was part of a proud English tradition that had sought since 1215 to establish fundamental legal limitations on government. In that year, rebellious barons forced King John to sign the famous **Magna Carta,** the key provision of which held that "no free man shall be taken or imprisoned, or disposed, or outlawed, or banished, or in any way destroyed . . . except by the legal judgment of his peers or by the law of the land."

During the seventeenth century, when Locke wrote, great advances were made in the limitation of government by law. The **Petition of Right** (1628), the abolition of the dreaded **Star Chamber** (1641), and the passage of the **Habeas Corpus Act** (1679) all helped to strengthen the idea that citizens of England were, by right, entitled to the protection of law. Also originating in that century was the judicial precedent that came to have enormous influence in the United States, Chief Justice Edward Coke's opinion in **Dr. Bonham's case** (1610) asserting that English common law (including the Magna Carta) should be the standard to which ordinary acts of Parliament, as well as the monarchy, had to conform. In Coke's words:

> It appears in our books, that in many cases the common law will controul Acts of Parliament, and sometimes adjudge them to be utterly void: for when an Act of Parliament is against common right or reasons, or repugnant, or impossible to be performed, the common law will controul it and adjudge it to be void.[7]

Although Locke's "higher law" theory was not adopted in England, where parliamentary supremacy became the rule, it eventually found a home in the United States, whose Constitution and Bill of Rights (largely derived from English common law) became standards against which popularly enacted laws would be judged.

Constitutionalism as Correct Procedure

Constitutionalism—synonymous with the rule of the law—may be defined as correct procedure. Along with describing how leaders are to be selected and what powers they are to exercise, a nation's constitution must also indicate what procedures are to be followed. Examples abound. For instance, procedural justice as interpreted by the U.S. Supreme Court prohibits the president of the United States, even during wartime, from seizing or nationalizing industries (such as steel mills) without congressional approval.[8] Similarly, the rule of law and fair procedure dictate that a citizen accused of a crime shall be provided with an attorney, allowed to confront witnesses, informed of the charges brought against him or her, and so on. And it is concern for the rule of law and fair procedure that compels an administrative agency to provide public notice—and an opportunity to be heard—to those who might be adversely affected by some pending decision.

In each instance, the rationale behind procedural due process is the same: No decision can be accepted as either fair or final unless it can be shown that the "rules of the game" have been strictly followed. In constitutional democracies, nothing can legitimize the results of a political contest as effectively as the public conviction that the "winner fought a fair fight"—that is, played by the rules. If anything, the U.S. government is held to a higher standard of accountability for its procedural activities than ordinary citizens because "no person is above the law."

In the end, it is not enough for a nation to *say* that it follows the rule of law; practice must coincide with proclamation. Thus, although the Constitution proclaims that all American citizens are equal before the law, blacks and other minorities were not given equal protection of the laws for many years. If the enforcement of correct procedure does not coincide with the pronouncement of political intent, all the high-minded documents in the world will not result in a free or fair society.

Federalism

Another way to limit constitutional government is through a division of powers called *federalism.* Modern examples of federal republics are the United States, Germany, Canada, India, and Mexico.

In theory, federalism represents a division of power between the national government and regional subdivisions. In the United States, there is a constitutional division of power between national and state governments. Article 1, Section 8, of the Constitution, for instance, delineates many areas in which Congress is empowered to legislate. Yet according to the Tenth Amendment, all powers not granted to the national government are reserved for the states. Traditionally, the states have been empowered to maintain internal peace and order, provide for education, and safeguard the people's health, safety, and welfare (the states' so-called *police powers*).

What is the rationale for such a division of power? In U.S. history, federalism was advocated by those who believed that the best guarantee of liberty was to ensure that government would be close to the people. Fearing that tyranny might arise from a single central government far removed from popular sentiments and local interests, some delegates at the Constitutional Convention (1787) argued successfully that the existence of states would limit the potentially tyrannical power of the new central government. In the Constitution, therefore, the separate states were given equal representation in the newly created Senate, and the federal method of electing the president (through the electoral college) was adopted. In addition, the states were to play an important role in amending the Constitution. Later, the First Congress deferred to the states in proposing the adoption of the Tenth Amendment.

The way federalism functions in the United States today differs significantly from the way it functioned during the nation's early history. Originally, great controversies flared over the question of whether a state (Virginia and Kentucky in 1798–1799, South Carolina in the 1830s) or a region (the South in 1860) could resort to states' rights federalism to justify dissent from specific policies undertaken by the national government. When questions of interest or principle (the Alien and Sedition Acts of 1798, the tariff in the 1830s, slavery in 1860) divided the nation, political wrangling centered on the constitutionality of particular

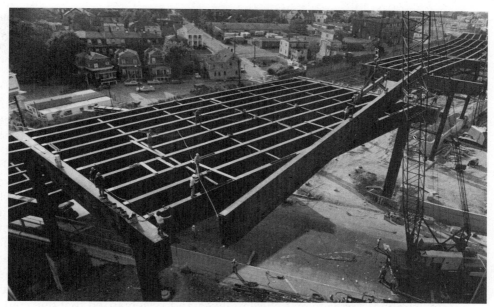

The American highway system exemplifies the cooperation that exists between the national government and the 50 states in all facets of public policy. (Spencer Grant/Stock, Boston)

governmental actions or on the question of whether state governments or the national government could legitimately exercise final authority.

Issues that the supremacy clause of the Constitution (Article 6) could not settle, the Civil War did. Although there have been some notable clashes, especially in the South over school desegregation in the late 1950s and early 1960s, the contemporary relationship between the national government and the states is characterized by cooperation rather than conflict in all facets of public policy, from the building of highways to the fighting of crime.[9] Today, the Constitution is seldom seen as a barrier to the routine intergovernmental cooperation that exists throughout the U.S. political system.

Federalism and Liberty   By guarding against the dangers of overcentralization, federalism helps to ensure that the powers of the national government remain limited. In this way, federalism helps to protect individuals against a potentially overbearing central government.[10] Like systems of *administrative decentralization* found in other nations, then, American-style federalism protects individual liberty by limiting the scope of the national government. Thus the aim of modern federalism is the same as that of political decentralization, which,

> by devolving functions to local governments, helps to limit the size of the central administrative structure and hence to make it less formidable to liberty. At the same time, decentralization draws masses of citizens into political life by multiplying and simplifying the governments accessible to them, thus activating the citizenry and habituating them to self-government. Further, these local governments become orga-

nized structures capable, in case of necessity, of resisting centralized authority or mitigating its excesses. Finally, decentralization permits government to be adapted to local needs and circumstances, and makes possible experimentation in the way problems are met. Decentralization is thus a vital safeguard to liberty and a way to educate an energetic and competent citizenry.[11]

The Alternative: Unitary Systems   A federal system such as that of the United States differs from a *unitary system* of government such as that of Great Britain, in which the central government may *choose* to turn over many affairs to local government but is not required to do so. The U.S. federal system differs even more sharply from the *centralized unitary systems* of France and Italy, which, historically, have guarded their powers and prerogatives against encroachment by local government. In the traditional French unitary system, formidable *prefects* (officials appointed by the central government) mediate between the central government in Paris and the local departments. Until reforms were instituted by the Socialist government of François Mitterrand in the early 1980s, the prefects were charged with the close supervision of local governments within their departments and had the power to veto local decisions. This system, known as *tutelage*, has long been regarded by many observers as a model of rational political administration. Tutelage was so centralized and systematized that one could supposedly tell what subject schoolchildren all over France were studying at any given time simply by glancing at a clock. To many Americans, accustomed to a multiplicity of schools, curricula, accreditation requirements, and academic standards, such government-imposed uniformity would no doubt seem curious.

DEMOCRACY AS EFFECTIVE GOVERNMENT

So far we have argued that democratic government must reflect the fundamental opinions and beliefs of its citizens but that it cannot simply mirror the momentary inclinations of the many, lest it harm the interests and rights of the few. But democratic government must be more than simply responsive and limited. It must also be effective. In other words, it must have the capacity to accomplish the purposes for which it was created.

A limited, responsive government that is capable of acting expeditiously must be based on structures that incorporate checks and balances on governmental power but do not impair the government's ability to act energetically when circumstances dictate. On this point, James Madison's incisive comment on the Constitutional Convention is apropos: "Among the difficulties encountered by the convention, a very important one must have lain, in combining the requisite stability and energy in government, with the inviolable attention due to liberty, and to the Republican form."[12] Madison argued that stability in government is essential to domestic tranquillity, national security, and public confidence, while energy is required to meet internal and external challenges. Together, he contended, stability and energy comprise the very essence of effective government.

The Need for Stability

Stability is an essential attribute of effective democratic government (or any government, for that matter). Such stability must be ensured in a variety of ways. Terms for elected representatives must be proportioned so that officeholders have sufficient time and opportunity to accomplish something worthwhile. There must be a standard way of settling political disputes that might otherwise threaten to tear the country apart. (In the United States, the Supreme Court often performs this function.) Established procedures for coping with periodic political problems, such as a change in administration, are also of utmost importance.

History and tradition, along with symbolism and ritual, reinforce the sense of continuity in governments. (Consider the pomp and circumstance surrounding the inauguration of the U.S. president every four years or the marriage of a member of the British royal family.) Citing the need for continuity, Madison opposed Thomas Jefferson's proposal for recurring constitutional conventions on the grounds that since "every appeal to the people would carry an implication of some defect in the government, frequent appeals would, in great measure, deprive the government of that veneration which time bestows on every thing, and without which perhaps the wisest and freest governments would not possess the requisite stability" and that even "the most rational government will not find it a superfluous advantage, to have the prejudices of the community on its side."[13]

The Need for Energy

To be effective, a government must also be energetic. The Founders' commitment to energetic government was clearly reflected in the Constitution they bequeathed, which not only granted the government ample powers but was also consciously designed to create a strong executive. Constitutional provisions vesting the executive power in the president and enabling Congress "to make all Laws which shall be necessary and proper for carrying into Execution the foregoing Powers" are obvious examples of the Founders' concern that the national government should be able to act decisively when necessary. To this end, Alexander Hamilton noted in *The Federalist* that "a government ought to contain in itself every power requisite to the full accomplishment of the objects committed to its care . . . free from every other control but a regard to the public good and to the sense of the people."[14]

Summary

In constitutional democracies, governments are both popular and restrained. They exist by virtue of constitutions that may differ widely in format and detail but invariably delineate the powers and boundaries of the governments they create. Inherent in the idea of constitutional democracy is the belief that a government should be popular, limited, and effective. The concept of popular control through majority rule is central to the creation of a responsive government. The rationale for majority rule holds that the wisdom and interests of the majority are preferable to the wisdom and intelligence of the minority. However, because the majority is not always correct and can sometimes be tyrannical, constitutional democracies must also place limits on the powers of the government. Protection of individual rights, the rule of law (constitutionalism), and federalism are the principal strategies used to prevent the so-called tyranny of the majority.

Democratic governments must also act effectively. One requirement of effective government is stability; another requirement is energy—the ability to act, initiate, and lead.

Key Terms

constitutional democracy	Star Chamber
constitution	Habeas Corpus Act
concurrent powers	Dr. Bonham's case
majority rule	constitutionalism
tyranny of the majority	federalism
ex post facto law	police powers
bill of attainder	administrative decentralization
limited government	unitary system
rule of law	centralized unitary systems
Magna Carta	prefects
Petition of Right	tutelage

Review Questions

1. In order to serve the public good, what general characteristics must constitutional democracies possess?

2. What is federalism? What advantages does this form of government offer?

3. Why is effective government a combination of energy and stability? How is each achieved?

4. What is constitutionalism? Why is it important?

Recommended Reading

CORWIN, EDWARD. *The "Higher Law": Background of American Constitutional Law.* Ithaca, N.Y.: Cornell University Press, 1955. This brief book traces the rise of constitutionalism from Britain across the Atlantic to the United States.

DIAMOND, MARTIN. *The Founding of the Democratic Republic.* Itasca, Ill.: Peacock, 1981. Probably the best and most readable discussion of the ideas employed by the Founders to create a responsive, limited, and effective political order.

FRIEDRICH, CARL. *Limited Government: A Comparison.* Englewood Cliffs, N.J.: Prentice Hall, 1974. A brief explanation of the relationship between constitutionalism and the idea of democracy.

GREENE, JACK (ED.). *The Reinterpretation of the American Revolution, 1763 to 1789.* Westport, Conn.: Greenwood, 1979. An outstanding collection of essays exploring American political ideas at a critical era; essays by Bailyn, Diamond, and Kenyon are especially noteworthy.

HAMILTON, ALEXANDER, JOHN JAY, AND JAMES MADISON. *The Federalist.* New York: Modern Library. The foremost exposition of the ideas underlying the American democracy by the men responsible for its creation.

MAYO, H. B. *An Introduction to Democratic Theory.* New York: Oxford University Press, 1960. A thorough discussion of the advantages, limitations, and distinctive aspects of democracy.

WHEARE, K. C. *Modern Constitutions.* New York: Oxford University Press, 1951. A general examination of constitutions and their value.

Notes

1. Stephen Cahn, *Education and the Democratic Ideal* (Chicago: Nelson-Hall, 1979), p. 3.

2. Alexis de Tocqueville, *Democracy in America* (New York: Schocken Books, 1961), vol. 1, pp. 299–300.

3. Ibid., p. 301.

4. Ibid., pp. 304–308.

5. Aristotle, *The Politics,* trans. and ed. Ernest Barker (New York: Oxford University Press, 1962), p. 146.

6. John Locke, *Second Treatise on Civil Government* (New York: New American Library, 1965), Sec. 202, p. 448.

7. 8 Co. Rep. 114a (1610).

8. See *Youngstown Sheet and Tube Company* v. *Sawyer,* 343 U.S. 579 (1952). Especially note the concurring opinion of Justice Jackson.

9. See Morton Grodzins, "The Federal System," in *Goals for Americans: The Report of the Presidential Commission on National Goals* (New York: American Assembly, Columbia University, 1960).

10. However, it does nothing to protect individuals from abuse by state or local governments, a fact that the black experience in various southern states well illustrates.

11. Martin Diamond, Winston Fisk, and Herbert Garfinkel, *The Democratic Republic: An Introduction to American National Government* (Skokie, Ill.: Rand McNally, 1970), p. 136.

12. Alexander Hamilton, John Jay, and James Madison, *The Federalist* (New York: Modern Library), No. 31, pp. 226–227.

13. Ibid., No. 49, p. 329.

14. Ibid., No. 31, p. 190.

CHAPTER 6

FORMS OF DEMOCRACY

THE UNITED STATES AND GREAT BRITAIN

(Al Stephenson/Woodfin Camp)

THE CONCEPT OF constitutionalism (the rule of law) accompanied the early growth and development of parliamentary practices in England. When the American colonists revolted, however, they rejected the British parliamentary system partly because it was British and partly because they believed it did not provide adequate safeguards against tyrannical rule.

DEMOCRATIC INSTITUTIONS: AN AMERICAN PERSPECTIVE

The Founders' efforts to combat tyranny entailed an impressive theory of institutions. In developing this theory, the Founders built on the contributions of a number of sixteenth- and seventeenth-century political philosophers, including Niccolò Machiavelli, Thomas Hobbes, John Locke, and the Baron de Montesquieu. All these thinkers had emphasized that the purpose of government was not (as Aristotle had claimed) to inculcate virtue. In their view, and that of the Founders, such a theory of government aimed too high, because people were not good by nature. Accordingly, they believed, government must recognize the political implications of humanity's moral imperfection and pursue limited goals (such as security, liberty, and prosperity), which are attainable, rather than absolute good, which is not.

A New Science of Politics

Just as the people were not presumed to be virtuous, neither were their rulers. Thus arose a troubling question: If rulers could not be made virtuous stewards, what would prevent them from becoming vicious tyrants? The Founders' answer hinged on an intricate arrangement of republican institutions. Drawing a comparison with the great advances made by Newtonian physics, the Founders not immodestly referred to this "discovery" as the *new science of politics.*

The theme of discovery is made explicit by Alexander Hamilton in *The Federalist.* Arguing that the new American Constitution would prevent "the extremes of tyranny and anarchy" that had plagued previous republics, Hamilton admonished his readers not to dwell on past examples: "The science of politics like most other sciences has received great improvement. . . . The efficacy of various principles is now well understood, which were either not known at all, or imperfectly known to the ancients." Hamilton went on to catalog the structural improvements built into the Constitution by the pioneers of this new science:

> The regular distribution of power into distinct departments; the introduction of legislative balances and checks; the institution of courts composed of judges holding their offices during good behaviour; the representation of the people in the legislature by deputies of their own election: these are either wholly new discoveries, or have made their principal progress towards perfection in modern times. They are means, and powerful means, by which the excellences of republican government may be retained and its imperfections lessened or avoided.[1]

Institutional Bulwarks against Tyranny

The Founders understood that, in James Madison's words, "enlightened statesmen will not always be at the helm."[2] In the absence of exceptional leadership, only the state itself, properly constructed, could check the ambitions of those who claimed to rule in its name. Elections provided one such check, noted Madison, but he added that "experience has taught mankind the necessity of auxiliary precautions."[3] The chief precaution taken by the Founders was the arrangement of political offices so that the ambitions of a potential tyrant would be checked by the ambitions of those whose position might be threatened should such a concentration of power occur: "The great security against a gradual concentration of the several powers in the same department, consists in giving to those who administer each department the necessary *constitutional means,* and *personal motives* to resist encroachments of the others." In short, "Ambition must be made to counteract ambition."[4]

Checks and Balances   In pursuit of this goal, the Founders attempted to make each branch of government largely independent of the other branches—as reflected in the fact that the powers of each respective branch derive from specific provisions of the Constitution (Article 1 for the legislature, Article 2 for the executive, Article 3 for the judiciary). Each branch was given constitutional authority to perform certain prescribed tasks, and each was equipped with the tools to resist any illegitimate expansion of power by the other branches. These tools, generally called *checks and balances,* ranged from the mundane (the veto power) to the extraordinary (impeachment proceedings brought by Congress against a president). Together they comprise the "necessary constitutional means" available to members of one branch of government for use against the encroachments of another.

Institutionalized Self-interest   But such tools would be useless, Madison and other Founders believed, unless the government could engage the personal motives of those who held high office. Such motives are reflected in the pride of place routinely displayed by the members of each branch of government. "The interest of the man must be connected with the constitutional rights of the place."[5] Institutionalized self-interest, the Founders felt, would infuse officeholders with a sense of the power, importance, and majesty of their particular institution and heighten their desire to maintain its prestige (and thereby advance their own careers). Thus one of the most important reasons that Congress moved to bring impeachment charges against President Nixon in 1974 was that in the wake of several alleged abuses of presidential power, the Watergate affair had damaged the prestige of Congress.

In enlisting self-interest in the pursuit of democratic goals, the Founders demonstrated a limited faith in humanity's natural goodness and in its amenability to moral improvement. According to Hamilton, "Men are ambitious, vindictive, and rapacious."[6] Madison concurred, although less bluntly:

It may be a reflection on human nature, that such devices [as check and balances] should be necessary to control the abuses of government. But what is government itself, but the greatest of all reflections on human nature? If men were angels, no government would be necessary. If angels were to govern men, neither external nor internal controls on government would be necessary.[7]

From this view of human nature Madison concluded that public officials will normally act in their own best interest. In a well-designed republic, he believed, enlightened self-interest would lead adroit politicians to the realization that in the long run they could best promote their private well-being by promoting the public well-being. If not, however, Madison's system, like Adam Smith's "invisible hand" (see Chapter 14), would automatically adjust itself to ensure that the balance of institutional power would not be upset. Thus it was not on the lofty plane of moralism or religious sentiment that the new science of politics in the United States found its justification but rather on the firmer (albeit lower) ground of institutionalized self-interest.

THE AMERICAN MODEL: THE PRESIDENTIAL SYSTEM

The governmental system of the United States, often called the *presidential system* because the chief executive is chosen by separate and direct election, grew out of the political theory of the Founders and the colonial experience in local self-government. We have already identified *separation of powers* as the chief characteristic of this system. As we have seen, the Founders believed that the concentration of power in one branch of government would lead to tyranny. Their overriding task in designing the new national government, then, was to effect a separation of the three branches, to ensure that there would always be adequate checks and balances on the power of any single branch. To this end, the government was formally organized along functional lines. Because all governments need to formulate, execute, and interpret laws, it seemed only logical to create a legislature to perform the first of these functions (rule making), an executive to carry out the second (rule implementation), and a judiciary to oversee the third (rule interpretation).

Separation of Powers

The Constitution assigns specific tasks to each branch of government. Congress, for example, is given the so-called power of the purse. The president may propose a budget, and members of the cabinet, representing the interests and concerns of their respective bureaucratic constituencies, may attempt to influence congressional appropriations, but Congress always has the final word on governmental spending.

In a few areas, power and authority are shared. Overlapping responsibilities, for example, characterize the war powers. Congress is empowered to raise and support armies (although the Constitution does limit appropriations to two years), to provide and maintain a navy, to make the rules regulating the armed forces, and to declare war. However, the Constitution makes the president the

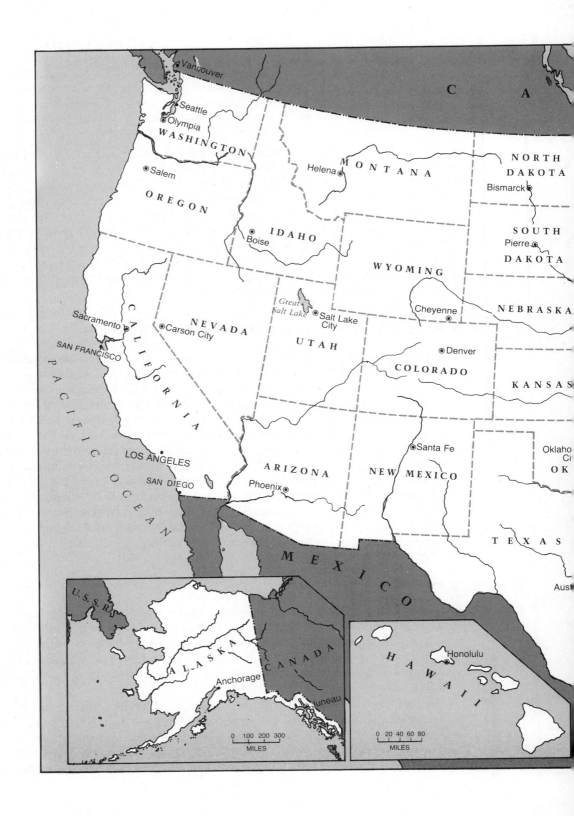

United States

0 100 200 300 400
MILES

TABLE 6-1
U.S. State Populations and Congressional Representation

State	Population	Percent of Total U.S. Population	Congressional Seats
Alabama	4,040,587	1.6	7
Alaska	550,043	.2	1
Arizona	3,665,228	1.5	6
Arkansas	2,350,725	.9	4
California	29,760,021	12.0	52
Colorado	3,294,394	1.3	6
Connecticut	3,287,116	1.3	6
Delaware	666,168	.3	1
District of Columbia	606,900	.2	—
Florida	12,937,926	5.2	23
Georgia	6,478,216	2.6	11
Hawaii	1,108,229	.4	2
Idaho	1,006,749	.4	2
Illinois	11,430,602	4.6	20
Indiana	5,544,159	2.2	10
Iowa	2,776,755	1.1	5
Kansas	2,477,574	1.0	4
Kentucky	3,685,296	1.5	6
Louisiana	4,219,973	1.7	7
Maine	1,227,928	.5	2
Maryland	4,781,468	1.9	8
Massachusetts	6,016,425	2.4	10
Michigan	9,295,297	3.7	16
Minnesota	4,375,099	1.8	8
Mississippi	2,573,216	1.0	5
Missouri	5,117,073	2.1	9
Montana	799,065	.3	1
Nebraska	1,578,385	.6	3
Nevada	1,201,833	.5	2
New Hampshire	1,109,252	.4	2
New Jersey	7,730,188	3.1	13
New Mexico	1,515,069	.6	3
New York	17,990,455	7.2	31
North Carolina	6,628,637	2.7	12
North Dakota	638,800	.3	1
Ohio	10,847,115	4.4	19
Oklahoma	3,145,585	1.3	6
Oregon	2,842,321	1.1	5
Pennsylvania	11,881,643	4.8	21
Rhode Island	1,003,464	.4	2
South Carolina	3,486,703	1.4	6
South Dakota	696,004	.3	1
Tennessee	4,877,185	2.0	9
Texas	16,986,510	6.8	30
Utah	1,722,850	.7	3
Vermont	562,758	.2	1
Virginia	6,187,358	2.5	11
Washington	4,866,692	2.0	9
West Virginia	1,793,477	.7	3
Wisconsin	4,891,769	2.0	9
Wyoming	453,588	.2	1
Total U.S. Population:	**248,709,873**		**Total Seats: 435**

SOURCE: Table based on 1990 U.S. Census data. U.S. Department of Commerce, Bureau of the Census.

commander in chief of the armed forces. Obviously, any significant military undertaking, declared or undeclared, requires the cooperation of both branches.

Besides the different tasks they perform and the different manner in which they discharge these tasks, members of the three branches serve different terms of office and different constituencies. Under the Constitution, as amended, the president must stand for election every four years and is limited to two terms of office. The president and the vice-president are the only two governmental officials in the United States who can receive a mandate from the entire national electorate. By contrast, congressional representatives serve particular districts (subdivisions of states) and are elected for two-year terms. Senators represent states as a whole and serve six-year terms in office. Supreme Court justices (and all other federal judges) are not elected at all; they are appointed by the president with the "advice and consent" of the Senate. The Founders stipulated this mode of appointment because they believed that to render impartial opinions, the judiciary must be free of the political pressures involved in winning and holding elective office.

Under the Constitution, then, no one branch possesses dominant power. Power is diffused and, to some extent, up for grabs. Given this political setup, it is not at all surprising that American politics is often characterized by policy disputes and struggles for ascendancy, particularly between the president and Congress. But just as the separation of powers creates the conditions that promote this struggle, so it helps ensure, through the countervailing forces inherent in the system of checks and balances, that no one branch of government can become too powerful.

Constraints on Majority Rule

The concentration of power in a single branch of government is one kind of tyranny that the separation of powers was intended to forestall. But, as we noted in Chapter 5, many of the Founders were equally troubled by another danger—"tyranny of the majority," the tendency of the majority in a democracy to steamroll over the rights of the minority. To some extent, *bicameralism* (the division of the legislative branch into two houses) was designed to provide a barrier against the majority steamroller. So, of course, was the separation of powers. The presidential veto, the independence of the courts, and federalism (the division of powers between the national government and the states) were additional safeguards the Founders hoped would temper the potential excesses inherent in majority rule.

A Strong Executive Branch

The Founders believed that their system not only would thwart tyranny but also would provide the best possible foundation for a strong, energetic government. To achieve this goal, they consciously sought to create a powerful and unified executive capable of resisting both the encroachments of Congress and the centrifugal pull of the states. Having created an executive whose power was checked by regular elections and the absence of the royal prerogative, they showed little fear of a tyrannical presidency.[8]

The American Agenda: A Sampler

The National Debt

American private, corporate, and government debt soared during the 1980s. Interest expenses rose more rapidly than any other federal expenditure as the cumulative federal debt rose from $909 billion to $3.2 trillion (by 1992 it had approached $4 trillion). The annual 1992–1993 budget deficit was projected to be $400 billion. Another worrisome sign: federal interest on the debt, just $74 billion in fiscal 1980, was projected to grow to $315 billion in 1993, making it the largest federal expenditure.

Free Trade and Competitiveness

The United States has run large trade deficits in the recent past. Formerly the world's largest creditor nation, the United States became the largest debtor nation in the 1980s. Heavy foreign borrowing, especially from Japan, was a concomitant of huge annual trade deficits in the late 1980s. Japan is the biggest U.S. competitor, running trade surpluses with the United States as high as $60 billion in some years. One poll found that since the collapse of communism in eastern Europe in 1989, a majority of Americans now consider Japan a bigger threat than the Soviet Union once was.

Education

A focus of growing controversy, the American educational system has been increasingly criticized for not effectively educating students. A particular concern is that the United States is not turning out workers with skills sufficient to meet the economic and technological challenges of the global marketplace.

Crime and Drug Abuse

Crime remains a serious problem in the United States. Debate continues on how the high crime rate could be most effectively combated and how American cities, in particular, can be made safer. Much of the emphasis on reducing crime has focused on a widespread educational campaign to reduce drug abuse—a practice that correlates with incidents of violent crimes, including armed burglary, mugging, murder, and rape. Even as the rate of crime remains high in the early 1990s, the government's antidrug campaign is apparently having some effect as illegal drug use has showed signs of leveling off.

Income Distribution and Health Care

The widening gap in income distribution among Americans has resulted in pockets of poverty amid middle-class affluence, particularly among the unemployed within the inner cities and among divorced women. One disturbing sign of this tendency is the existence of a homeless population, although there remains disagreement about its size and causes. Another cause for alarm—and one with important income distribution consequences—is the rapidly escalating cost of medical care. The fact that millions of Americans do not have or cannot afford adequate health insurance portends a looming health-care crisis.

For a broad discussion of American public policy, see Chapter 15.

THE BRITISH MODEL: THE PARLIAMENTARY SYSTEM

Despite a long colonial period that prepared Americans for the rigors of self-government, the American Revolution signaled the start of an important experiment in the new science of politics. As embodied in the first large republic of modern times, American constitutionalism represented a sharp break with the European monarchical tradition. That break in turn necessitated a political expla-

**Great Britain
and
Ireland**

0 20 40 60 80 100
MILES

SHETLAND
ISLANDS

ORKNEY
ISLANDS

OUTER HEBRIDES

INNER HEBRIDES

Inverness

SCOTLAND

Aberdeen

Dundee

ATLANTIC

OCEAN

Edinburgh

Glasgow

NORTH

SEA

Newcastle

NORTHERN

IRELAND

Belfast

I. OF MAN

IRISH

SEA

Liverpool

Leeds

Manchester

Hull

Sheffield

Dublin

Chester

Nottingham

IRELAND

WALES

Birmingham

Norwich

ENGLAND

Ipswich

Cork

Swansea

Cardiff

Bristol

LONDON

Bath

Southampton

Portsmouth

Calais

Plymouth

ENGLISH CHANNEL

FRANCE

Cherbourg

nation as to why the United States would succeed where earlier attempts to
establish republican governments had failed. That explanation took the form of
a political theory that sought to state the relationship between human nature
and political institutions.

In contrast, the British political tradition has not been characterized by such
a self-conscious theory of good government. Even so, a sort of home-grown

TABLE 6-2
United Kingdom: Population Distribution and Parliamentary Representation

	Population	Major City (population)	Voting Strength in Parliament*
England	47,689,400	London (6,760,700)	524
Northern Ireland	1,583,000	Belfast (296,800)	17
Scotland	5,090,700	Glasgow (695,600)	72
Wales	2,873,100	Cardiff (284,900)	38

* House of Commons = 651 total members. Data provided by the British Information Services Office and is based on April, 1992 British national elections.
SOURCE: Population data from Brian Hunter (ed.), *Statesman's Yearbook, 1991–1992,* 128th revised and updated edition. (New York: St. Martin's Press, 1991).

theory of British democracy can be found in the writings and speeches of (among others) Edmund Burke, who in the late eighteenth century celebrated the conservative forces of tradition and stability in the development of British constitutionalism. Burke detailed the decisive character of Great Britain's long unbroken chain of political development, during which, significantly, gains in economic equality have accompanied an expansion in the scope of political liberty.

A Mixed Regime

Increasingly, during the seventeenth, eighteenth, and nineteenth centuries, the British *parliamentary system* became the best-known example of what Aristotle called a *mixed regime,* the essence of which is that different classes are represented in government by different institutions. The ascendancy of Parliament over the Crown highlighted the fact that, throughout the nineteenth century, the two houses of Parliament (which wielded increasing power) reflected distinct class interests within British society. The House of Lords represented the interests of the traditional governing classes, while the House of Commons gradually came to represent the interests of the general electorate, as expressed through free elections and increasing suffrage.

Great Britain's mixed regime has historically promoted stability by providing representation for classes that, in the absence of an adequate political voice, might have become openly hostile toward one another and toward the political system as a whole. Today, this has changed; what is commonly referred to as the British welfare state is in fact an elaborate system of income redistribution aimed at the creation of a large middle class. The emergence of a broad-based middle class has rendered the traditional representation of separate and distinct economic classes largely irrelevant, although the Conservative (Tory) and Labour parties continue to represent what remains of the old upper and lower classes, respectively. This trend is mirrored in the clear ascendancy of the House of Commons over the House of Lords, which, under the Parliament Act of 1911, can be completely circumvented by the lower house. When the House of Lords in 1991 twice rejected a war crimes bill that made it impossible to prosecute aging former Nazis accused of mass murder, the government invoked the 1911 act, bypassing the House of Lords for the first time in 40 years.

Fusion of Powers

If the American presidential system is distinguished by a separation of powers, the parliamentary system is characterized by a *fusion of powers.* Our presidential system prohibits members of Congress from concurrently holding executive office. In contrast, under the British parliamentary system, the executive body, known as the *cabinet,* is made up of the leaders of the majority party within the House of Commons. After an election, the head of the victorious party names the members (ministers) of the new cabinet, the party's majority votes its approval, and a new government is formed. (Given more than two major parties, the government will normally be formed by a coalition.) The cabinet, headed by the prime minister, is responsible for formulating and initiating legislation. Although all members of Parliament, including those in the opposition party, are free to question and criticize, the majority party is virtually assured of passage of its legislative program.

Indefinite Terms of Office

U.S. presidential elections are held every four years, and all seats in the House of Representatives are contested every two years, as are one-third of those in the Senate. Under the British parliamentary system, terms of office are more indefinite: The government is required to stand for election every five years, but the prime minister can and usually does call for elections earlier if it looks as though the mood of the electorate momentarily favors the ruling party.

The authority to decide when to call new elections is an important prerogative in the British system, for it improves the ruling party's chances of remaining in power longer than five years. In 1983, for example, after serving in office for only four years, Prime Minister Margaret Thatcher capitalized on a surge of British patriotism spurred by the Falkland Islands crisis (which involved a brief war with Argentina) to renew her Conservative party's mandate to rule for another five years. In 1987 she again called for an election four years into her term and was reelected for five more years. Three years later, however, when her popularity had fallen to a low point over her support for a poll tax that many Britons considered regressive and unfair, she resigned and turned over the reins of government to a Conservative successor, John Major, who was elected on his own right in 1992 national elections. When Thatcher stepped down as prime minister, she had served continuously for over a decade—the longest uninterrupted tenure in that office in the twentieth century. The Conservatives won a narrow 20-seat majority in parliamentary elections held in April 1992, surprising even the public opinion pollsters who had predicted a Labour victory and enabling Tory government to continue as a reminder of Margaret Thatcher's deep imprint on British politics.

Other circumstances may cause a government to fall before its five-year term has expired. If the policy of the majority party becomes particularly unpopular or if the government becomes embroiled in scandal, the opposition party may call for a vote of "no confidence" in the government. Passage of a *no-confidence vote,* which usually requires the defection of disgruntled members of the majority party, forces the government to resign. As a rule, when the cabinet resigns, the prime minister asks the monarch to dissolve Parliament and call for new elections. This happens frequently in many parliamentary systems, although in Great Britain it has been rare in recent years.

A change of leadership need not always be preceded by a vote of no confidence followed by national elections. Prime Minister Neville Chamberlain resigned in 1940 despite the majority that his party still commanded in the House of Commons. So widespread was his unpopularity, and so severely had the ruling Conservative party's confidence in his leadership been shaken by his concessions to Adolf Hitler at Munich, that he was forced to step aside. No new elections were called because the Conservative party retained its large majority, and Winston Churchill, a prominent Conservative member of parliament (*MP*), was able to rally the British people behind his personal leadership.

Under the parliamentary system, a new government can emerge less directly, particularly when a very close coalition exists. One way is through the mechanism of *by-elections*, which are held when a member of the House of Commons resigns or dies. Local elections also can be important. In May 1987, Prime Minister Thatcher's Conservative party ran well in some 2,000 local elections held throughout Great Britain. This showing encouraged her to call for June elections. By contrast, the Tories made a very poor showing in the municipal elections of May 1991, which discouraged Prime Minister Major from calling early elections (under the British five-year rule, he could wait until July 1992). Thus both by-elections and local elections provide a good barometer of the changing political climate and can lead to the calling of new elections.

A unique situation occurs when the party in power is separated from the party out of power by a thin majority and the critical balance is held by a minor third party. Then the government is likely to fall whenever its "junior partner" decides to switch sides or simply to withdraw its support on a crucial vote.

Disciplined Parties

Another characteristic of the British parliamentary system is that its so-called *disciplined parties* are more inclined toward united action than their American counterparts. Thus the Conservative and Labour parties maintain coherent political platforms that represent their respective traditions—one conservative, the other socialist. Although both parties are steeped in tradition and both are deeply committed to the survival of the parliamentary system, they differ sharply in their approaches to Great Britain's political, economic, and social concerns.

British parties usually vote as a bloc in Parliament. The majority party receives a mandate to run the country, and once elected, it demands unstinting support from its members for programs it promised to put into effect. An MP who does not vote with the party on an important legislative matter runs the risk of being "purged" from the party, which means not being nominated by the party when the next election comes up. Few maverick MPs can survive failure to be nominated by their party.

Such strong party discipline does not mean that MPs never cross the aisle to vote with the opposition, however. Nor does it mean that disaffected MPs must toe the mark or take a chance of being ostracized from their own party; they can abstain in an important vote, for example. MPs who become irreconcilably opposed to their party's policies and who are joined by others who share their opposition can break away and form a new party. This rarely happens, but when it does, a major realignment of the party system can occur. In the early 1900s, the Labour party eclipsed the old Liberal (or Whig) party as the rising trade union movement transformed the British working class into a powerful political force. And in the early 1980s, disenchanted Labour MPs split with their party and formed the Social Democratic party (SDP), which then cooperated with and in the summer of 1987 merged with the old Liberal party (to form the so-called Alliance) in an attempt to capture the political center. In 1990, the rump SDP voted to disband.

What role does "Her Majesty's loyal opposition," as it is called in Great Britain, play in the parliamentary system? Because the majority party in the British system can usually enact a legislative program on its own, minority parties play a limited, though not unimportant, role. They criticize the majority's policy initiatives and are occasionally able to influence the majority's actions. Even when an opposition party has little influence, however, its criticisms are usually responsibly stated, for it "usually thinks of itself as the next government, and a wise Opposition operates within those limits which it hopes its own opponents will respect when the tables are turned."[9] No stigma whatsoever attaches to the notion of opposition in the British parliamentary tradition. As the *loyal opposition,* members of the minority believe they have a duty to criticize the government. As one expert has pointed out:

> It has become a tradition in British political life that there shall usually be a party which provides the Government, and another party which provides the Opposition and which is, in effect, an alternative Government. Organized opposition is not now considered subversive or treasonable. Indeed, since 1937, the Leader of the Opposition has been paid a special salary out of public funds, and people often talk about *"Her Majesty's* Opposition," because the existence of an Opposition is thought to be an essential part of the Queen's government.[10]

A Dual Executive

Unlike the U.S. presidency, the parliamentary executive is divided between two positions (known as a *dual executive*). In Great Britain, the nominal head of state is the reigning monarch; in nonmonarchical parliamentary systems, this role is usually filled by a separately elected president. Queen Elizabeth II, "arguably the most famous person in the world," has occupied the British throne for nearly four decades. Whether monarch or president, titular heads of state play a largely ceremonial role in parliamentary democracies. They are the center of the pomp and circumstance usually associated with national celebrations, the purveyors of protocol (for example, receiving ambassadors or other heads of state), and the national representatives at certain international events. Their key function is to

The dual executive of Great Britain: Queen Elizabeth II is a national symbol and a source of unity and stability, but the actual head of government is the prime minister, John Major. (Gavin Grilly/Impact Visuals). (Left) Flanked by Vice-President Dan Quayle and House Speaker Thomas Foley, Queen Elizabeth II addressed a joint session of the United States Congress in May 1991—a poignant reminder that the U.S. lawmaking body is an offspring of the British Parliament. (Tim Graham/Sygma)

ensure that there will be a government in case of a national emergency. The titular head of state is thus a national symbol and a source of unity and stability—standing over the government but not governing.

The actual head of the government in Great Britain, the pivot of the parliamentary system, is the prime minister, who, in close consultation with key cabinet members (often called the *inner cabinet*), sets domestic and foreign policy. Often the essence of national policy emerges from this leadership core, which then presents it to the cabinet as a whole. The support of the cabinet usually guarantees passage of any and all legislation. If a government bill is objectionable to a particular cabinet member, he or she may resign. Cabinet resignations are not uncommon; traditionally, as long as the resignation is done quietly, the dissenting cabinet member may later be asked to join another cabinet.

THE TWO SYSTEMS COMPARED

In terms of specific institutions of government, the presidential system of the United States and the parliamentary system of Great Britain share some characteristics and differ in many other respects.

The Legislature

The purpose of a legislature in any constitutional democracy is to enact laws. The specific institutional environment in which this function is performed, however, differs significantly from one type of system to another. In many respects, the

The British Agenda: A Sampler

The European Community (EC)

Under Prime Minister Margaret Thatcher's leadership, Great Britain sought to slow the momentum toward a unified economy in Europe. That policy came under attack even within her own government in 1990 when Thatcher alone among the EC leaders opposed the creation of an EC central bank. John Major, who succeeded Thatcher, adopted a conciliatory stance toward the EC. He was reelected in April 1992.

The Economy

The state of the economy has been a major political issue in Great Britain ever since World War II. The poor performance of the British economy compared to that of Germany, Italy, France, and several other west European states was a source of embarrassment and consternation. The Whigs and Tories embraced very different solutions. Labour (Whigs) favored creation of a cradle-to-the-grave welfare state, while the Conservatives (Tories) advocated less state ownership and interference, lower taxes, and greater emphasis on individualism. Under Labour leadership, Britain developed what sympathetic observers considered a model welfare state. But the sagging British economy was stricken by "staflation" (a combination of inflation and recession) in the 1970s. These economic ills helped bring Margaret Thatcher, a vigorous opponent of big government, to power in 1979. Mrs. Thatcher set about reprivatizing state-run industries in the 1980s. Although economic performance did improve

under Thatcher's free-market policies, Great Britain is still plagued by relatively high unemployment, slow growth, and a manufacturing sector that is not competitive with more technologically advanced industries found in other EC states on the continent, including Germany, France, Italy, and the Benelux countries just across the English Channel. Labour's inability to unseat Conservative John Major in the 1992 elections was taken by some experts to signal the collapse of socialism as a serious political and economic alternative within Great Britain.

Terrorism and Northern Ireland

The provisional Irish Republican Army (IRA) continues to carry out terrorist attacks in an effort to force the British to quit Northern Ireland. Some 3,000 people have died in violent acts perpetrated by both Catholic and Protestant extremists since 1969. The IRA has made bold attempts (one involving a bombing and another a mortar attack) to assassinate both Margaret Thatcher and John Major. In 1990, IRA terrorists murdered Ian Gow, a Conservative MP and Thatcher confidant. In the spring of 1991, London brokered talks between leaders of both religious communities aimed at resolving the conflict. Any such resolution will have to take account of the claims of the British-backed Protestants, who outnumber Catholics in Northern Ireland, and Catholics, who form an overwhelming majority in the Irish Republic.

British legislative branch is surprisingly unlike its American counterpart. Perhaps the most fundamental difference is one of principle. In the British tradition, Parliament is sovereign. According to Sir William Blackstone (1723–1780), the famed British jurist, Parliament can do "everything that is not naturally impossible." In the words of another authoritative writer, "This concept of parliamentary sovereignty is of great importance and distinguishes Britain from most other democratic countries. Parliament may enact any law it likes, and no other body can set the law aside on the grounds that it is unconstitutional or undesirable."[11] In contrast, the American system places the Constitution above even Congress.

Ever since the early 1800s, the U.S. Supreme Court has successfully asserted its right and duty to overturn any law passed by Congress that the Court judged to be unconstitutional.

Despite this fundamental difference, certain functions performed by the legislative branches under both systems are essentially the same. For example, either congressional or parliamentary approval is required to legitimize any new law. Also, both legislatures serve as forums in which political, economic, and social issues are debated. Finally, both Congress and Parliament represent the true arenas of representative democracy. There leaders' careers are made and unmade, conflicting claims of interest and principle are settled, and the future course of government—even the future of government itself—is shaped.

Legislative Independence   Although congressional powers are limited by the Constitution, U.S. legislators have far more latitude than their British counterparts. Parliament is nominally bicameral, but real legislative power is concentrated in the 635-member House of Commons. The prime minister and cabinet do not usually make policy without first consulting influential MPs, and cabinet domination of Parliament is supported by strict party discipline.

Congress presents an entirely different picture. Both its 435-member House and its 100-member Senate are powerful bodies whose consent is required before any measure can be enacted into law. And because representatives and senators are elected largely on the strength of their own records, Congress is really an assembly of over 500 independent spirits. Parties exercise some influence, of course, but under a presidential system they cannot enforce discipline. Besides, the two branches of Congress may be dominated by different parties (or Congress as a whole may be controlled by one party and the executive by another). Finally, representatives and senators tend to be oriented toward local rather than national constituencies. They are elected to advance local interests and have the latitude to vote accordingly. Seldom, if ever, is their first loyalty to the general program or platform of the national party.

Legislative Predictability   The greater independence allowed legislators under the presidential system makes Congress a much more unpredictable institution than its British counterpart. When a new government is elected in Great Britain, it is usually a foregone conclusion what programs will be enacted by Parliament; a party that wins a national election by a clear majority is presumed to have a popular mandate to carry out its campaign promises. Disagreements can and often do arise within the ranks of the governing party, but the general tone and direction of the government are almost always clear before Parliament sits.

U.S. elections have radically different ramifications in this respect. Even in presidential-election years—when the presidency and vice-presidency, one-third of Senate seats, and all House seats are contested—no clear national consensus may emerge. And if a national consensus does take shape, it is possible that no legislative consensus will emerge (if, for instance, the newly elected president is not skilled in dealing with Congress). Generally speaking, legislation results from a give-and-take process involving both houses of Congress as well as the

White House. The characteristically long, drawn-out budget deliberations of Congress provide a conspicuous example of the sometimes unwieldy nature of the American legislative process. Compromises depend on a variety of pressures and cross-pressures brought to bear on the officeholders as well as on perceived shifts in the mood of the people, and so it is no easy task to predict what Congress will do.

Structural Complexity   The fragmentation of authority and power in Congress makes its structure notably more complex than that of the British Parliament. Significantly, there are only six standing committees in the entire House of Commons. These committees are not specialized; their 20 to 50 members consider bills without reference to subject matter. They do not have the power to call hearings or solicit expert testimony, and they cannot table a bill; at most, they can make technical adjustments in its language. Committee work in Parliament thus tends to be unexciting and uneventful, and committees afford special interests relatively limited opportunities to lobby for their favorite causes.

How different Parliament's committee system is from that of the U.S. Congress! Both in the House and in the Senate, more than 15 specialized committees dominate the political landscape. These committees have numerous subcommittees, each of which is charged with even more specialized tasks. Moreover, committees and subcommittees have the power to hold hearings and subpoena witnesses as part of routine investigations into executive branch programs and operations. All in all, this labyrinth of committees is a powerful determinant of legislative behavior. Because U.S. legislators cannot possibly become competent in all matters covered by the wide range of congressional committees and subcommittees, they tend to specialize in various areas—agriculture, foreign affairs, labor relations, and so forth. Expertise requires time, and political scientists have long pointed to a kind of apprentice system in the two houses. Generally, the most effective legislators are those who have remained in office for some time and have become familiar with a particular aspect of public policy; when they speak on that subject, other legislators tend to listen.

The *watchdog role* of Congress takes various shapes. Policy review can occur at many points in the legislative process (during the authorization and appropriation phases of the budgetary process, for example, or by means of investigations and hearings). Program evaluation and policy review are conducted by legislators who have large professional staffs. These staffers are often powerful behind-the-scene operators on whom legislators rely heavily for advice and counsel.

In this regard, too, the British parliamentary system stands in sharp contrast. Generally, the most significant mechanism of accountability is the *question hour*, held several days a week, when individual ministers respond to questions submitted by MPs. The questions, which run the gamut from the trenchant to the trivial, are aimed at fixing governmental responsibility as well as eliciting additional information. The specialization of function that so dominates the American presidential system is largely absent from the parliamentary system of accountability.

The Executive-Legislative Nexus   Another key difference between the two political systems lies in the extent to which the legislature is involved in determining the makeup of the executive branch. As noted earlier, Parliament plays a key role in determining the composition of a new administration (the cabinet). The prime minister heads the majority party in Parliament, and the cabinet is composed of parliamentary leaders. Because the parliamentary system blurs distinctions between legislative and executive powers, it is often difficult to determine where the authority of one branch begins and that of the other leaves off.

This fusion of powers does not exist under the presidential system of government. Unlike senators and representatives, presidents are elected by *national* majorities, and the presidency derives its powers from a separate section of the Constitution. Nonetheless, Congress does have some influence over the staffing of the executive branch, because the Senate must confirm all cabinet and many other high-level appointments. And if the conduct of those in the executive branch evokes suspicion or controversy, the appropriate legislative committee, acting in its constitutional watchdog capacity, can subpoena government officials and other witnesses to testify. Thus there is constant interaction between the legislative and executive branches. Unlike the British Parliament, however, Con-

A joint session of the U.S. Congress. Just as the separation of powers creates the conditions that promote policy disputes and struggles for ascendency, so it helps ensure, through the countervailing forces inherent in the system of checks and balances, that no branch of government can become too powerful. (UPI/Bettmann)

gress does not have the power to bring down the executive. Even if Congress votes down a key program proposed by the White House, the president will remain in office for a full four years—barring extraordinary events such as impeachment, death, or resignation.

The Executive

The executive branch of government consists of the head of government and the head of state, the cabinet, and the bureaucracy. Pronounced differences, along with some important similarities, mark the executive structures of the two political systems we are examining.

Most fundamentally, the U.S. president is both the actual head of government and the titular head of the nation, whereas Britain's executive is divided between the monarch and the prime minister. The combined duties of the American presidency make that office both more influential and more prestigious than the position of prime minister. The president not only speaks both for the government and for the nation but also, unlike the British prime minister, is *personally* elected by a national majority.

The president of the United States also enjoys the security of a fixed term. As noted, only in the most extraordinary circumstances can a president be compelled to resign. The same can hardly be said for the British prime minister, whose position depends on the ability to retain the confidence of a majority in the House of Commons.

Yet another comparative advantage of the presidency is its greater autonomy in decision making. U.S. cabinet officials are basically administrators and advisers—subordinates whom the president may or may not consult before reaching a decision. By contrast, the British prime minister has traditionally been considered merely as the "first among equals" in the cabinet. Although this tradition has been eroded somewhat in modern times, prime ministers still make most executive decisions collegially. In order to retain office, they must work closely with the cabinet, especially with the powerful officials who make up the inner cabinet. In compensation, though, the concept of *ministerial responsibility* in the British system virtually guarantees that cabinet-level officials will not publicly criticize any aspect of government policy or betray an inner-cabinet confidence.

Finally, because the president's duties are clearly established by the Constitution and are largely separate from those of Congress, U.S. chief executives command greater power and prestige than British prime ministers. The president is the nation's chief diplomat—a position that is diluted in Great Britain by the existence of a divided executive. As the nation's commander in chief and chief legislator (not only because of the veto power but also because of the significant amount of legislation presidents propose), the U.S. president occupies a position whose power, authority, and prestige are unsurpassed among democratically elected chief executives. This point was illustrated once again in 1990 and 1991 when President George Bush ordered a huge military deployment into the Persian Gulf after Iraq invaded Kuwait. In early 1991, President Bush (with congressional approval) carried out the threat to remove Iraq's troops from Kuwait by force after Iraqi dictator Saddam Hussein failed to comply with a United Nations–backed ultimatum.

In one area, however, a prime minister's authority exceeds that of a president. Although U.S. presidents are seen as the natural leaders of their parties, such a responsibility is largely nominal in a system that features decentralized, loosely structured political parties. The British prime minister, however, is more than the titular head of the ruling party. Party leadership in Great Britain represents a vital duty, for success of the party's policies and programs depends on it. Only through the party can a British prime minister govern. And while American parties may exert some influence over the actions of individual representatives or senators, British parties exercise a high degree of control over the voting behavior of most MPs in the House of Commons.

The American Bureaucracy   In both the United States and Great Britain, the chief executive is the head of the *bureaucracy*—the group of nonelected officials responsible for the administration and implementation of public policy. In any nation, the bureaucracy tends to be a complex and sometimes confusing maze of bureaus, agencies, and departments. Sometimes bureaucratic systems work surprisingly well; at other times they are riddled with waste and inefficiency. The ills of bureaucracy generally result from duplication of effort, interagency rivalries, the empire-building tendencies or self-protective instincts of bureau heads, and employee apathy. Such problems are common in all large bureaucracies. But constitutional democracies face the additional problem of structuring systems of public administration that must combine maximum efficiency with maximum respect for the rule of law.

The U.S. bureaucracy employs nearly 3 million civilian workers, most of whom work outside Washington. With certain exceptions (such as the independent regulatory agencies), most bureaucratic positions fall under the executive branch. Specifically, they are apportioned among the great cabinet departments—State, Defense, Treasury, Justice, Health and Human Services, and so forth—each of which is subdivided into many components. Heading these departments are the political appointees who make up the presidential cabinet. In addition, the president directly appoints several thousand upper-level bureaucrats. In this way, new presidents can place their imprint on the management and direction of the agencies and bureaus that administer the everyday affairs of government.

Most federal workers, however, are permanent, nonpolitical *Civil Service* employees. The original purpose of the U.S. Civil Service (authorized by Congress in 1883) was to free the bureaucracy from the abuses of the *spoils system,* under which a new administration would replace almost all federal employees with faithful party workers and would fire or promote workers exclusively on the basis of political considerations. To avoid this, the Civil Service established a system under which employees are classified according to experience and performance on tests. It also set objective ground rules for the promotion, remuneration, discipline, and firing of governmental employees. In sum, the Civil

Service system was designed to insulate federal employees from political pressure and to inject a high degree of professionalism into the federal bureaucracy.

The British Bureaucracy   The U.S. Civil Service system was patterned to some extent after the British Civil Service, which has long been considered the most professional bureaucracy in the world. In Great Britain, the Civil Service extends into the top levels of government (the equivalent of an assistant cabinet secretary in the United States), and includes only about 200 political appointments. The highest-ranking career civil servants are known as permanent secretaries and provide vital links between the transient cabinets and the timeless bureaucracy. This system is all the more impressive considering that the British bureaucracy is entrusted with greater responsibilities than its U.S. counterpart because of the huge nationalized industries and wider range of social services for which the British government is responsible.

Until recently, the British bureaucracy was highly class-oriented. It was traditionally divided into upper and lower echelons on the basis of responsibility (an "administrative class" of top-level administrators and an "executive class" of middle-level administrators) and function (a professional, scientific, and technical class and a clerical class). Each class had its own separate entrance system, which resulted in little mobility across class lines. This situation was exacerbated by sharp social and educational distinctions: For example, two-thirds of the administrative class traditionally were graduates of Oxford or Cambridge.[12]

In 1971, this class-based system of administration was reorganized, unified, and integrated. Today the government consists of more than two dozen departments and ministries, each of which is staffed by career civil servants and headed by a permanent secretary. Political appointees occupy only the very top level of the bureaucracy. Ministers and two to five associates are appointed by the prime minister and are charged with overseeing their departments and instituting policy. In theory, the prime minister may demand a minister's resignation at any time, especially in the case of a scandal. Although there are exceptions, ministers usually serve in the cabinet. Generally, they are experienced members of the House of Commons or (much less frequently) the House of Lords. Thus it is possible for a minister to have legislative and executive as well as administrative responsibilities.

The Judiciary

Despite significant differences in the structures of their court systems, both the United States and Great Britain share what is generally known as the *common law* tradition. Common law is based on decisions made by judges rather than laws promulgated by legislators. The idea dates back at least as far as the twelfth century, when Henry II sought to implement a system by which judges were charged with enforcing the king's law while taking into account local customs. In the process of resolving disputes, each judge made and sent to London a record of the legal proceedings. Over the years, certain common themes and legal principles emerged from these records. As this *law by precedent* evolved over the centuries, it was enhanced by certain celebrated judicial decisions. In time, these precedents and decisions were codified by judicial commentators (the most famous of whom was William Blackstone) and carried to all corners of the globe, including the American colonies.

This shared common-law background notwithstanding, the legal systems of the United States and Great Britain differ with respect to selection of judges, organization of the judiciary, powers of judicial review, and other key structural matters.

Selection of Judges   Great Britain has two kinds of law schools. In the lower-level law schools, one studies to become a *solicitor,* a legal counsel who prepares cases for court, advises clients, and draws up contracts, wills, and other legal documents. More exclusive law schools produce *barristers,* who can do everything solicitors do but can also enter a court and plead cases. Judges are appointed only from the ranks of barristers. Furthermore, to be recommended for a judgeship (which, like federal appointments in the United States, carries a life term), a barrister must have achieved a high class rank in law school and performed several years of outstanding legal service.

American judicial selection is much more political. A judge may be appointed on the basis of high marks at a prestigious law school or years of distinguished legal practice, but that is not necessarily the case. More often, appointments to the federal bench are based on transparent political calculations—to reward an individual for favors; to appease a powerful senator, representative, or local party boss; or to achieve a certain geographic balance in the distribution of judgeships.

Federal versus Unitary Courts   The American judicial system is organized on a federal basis; that is, it comprises 51 separate court systems. The federal court system adjudicates legal questions in which either the federal government is one of the parties or a federal law is involved. The federal judiciary is subdivided into *district courts,* in which most cases originate; *appellate courts,* which review cases on appeal from district courts; and the *Supreme Court,* which acts primarily as a court of last resort, settling cases that raise particularly troublesome questions of legal interpretation or constitutional principle.

Coexisting with this national (or federal) court system are 50 state court systems, most of which also have a three-part structure. The state courts are not completely separated from the federal courts in the U.S. judicial system. The U.S. Supreme Court frequently accepts cases on appeal from the highest courts of the various states when legal questions raised in state courts have national implications.

In comparison with the American federal system, the British court system is more streamlined—reflecting Great Britain's unitary government. The absence of state courts means that many of the jurisdictional and procedural complexities that plague the American judiciary are lacking in Great Britain.

Judicial Review   Perhaps the most important *political* difference between the two judicial systems involves *judicial review,* the power of the courts to uphold or strike down legislative or executive actions. In the United States, both state and federal courts review the acts of the other branches of government—state courts on the basis of state constitutions and federal courts on the basis of the U.S. Constitution. This power of judicial review is greatly enhanced by the existence of written constitutions, which often provide a highly authoritative yardstick by which to measure ordinary (statutory) law.

To some extent, the mere existence of federalism made judicial review necessary in the United States. If state courts could decide for themselves how to interpret federal law, no national body of jurisprudence would have much meaning.[13] The need for legal uniformity and the belief that there are certain higher principles of law to which governmental action at all levels must conform lie at the core of the American concept of judicial review.

In contrast, British judges play only a limited role in governing the nation. Whereas the question of constitutionality hovers over every legislative and executive act in the United States, in Great Britain the judiciary does not possess the power to overturn an act of Parliament. Nor do British judges act as constitutional guardians of civil liberties, as American judges do whenever they assert the primacy of individual rights over legislative acts. Only rarely do British judges rule that the executive branch has overstepped its legal bounds. In the words of one authority:

> The powers of the British government are constrained in spite of rather than because of formal institutions of the laws. Englishmen voice fewer complaints about the denial of civil liberties or due process of the law than do citizens in many countries with written constitutions, bills of rights, and established procedures for judicial review.[14]

Structural Differences   One final distinction between the two systems stems from differences in their structures. These differences become particularly evident when one compares the U.S. Supreme Court to the British High Court. The Supreme Court, of course, heads a separate branch of the U.S. government, and great pains have been taken to shield it from undue political influence. Not only do its members serve for life, but any collaboration or consultation between members of Congress or the White House and Supreme Court justices is regarded as a substantial breach of political ethics and a violation of the principle of separation of powers. The Supreme Court, then, essentially is an independent body, deliberately insulated from the pressures of political life.

The parliamentary system has no such separation of powers. It often surprises Americans to learn that the British court system is headed by a member of the cabinet. This official, known as the Lord Chancellor, presides over the House of Lords and makes recommendations on judicial appointments. In fact, theoretically, the High Court of Britain *is* the House of Lords, although in actual operation it comprises only a small number of lords with distinguished legal backgrounds. The fusion of powers characteristic of the British governmental system thus involves the intermingling of legislative and judicial powers in the upper house just as it meshes the legislative and executive powers in the lower house.

Strengths and Weaknesses of the Two Systems

In the words of one American academic, "The parliamentary system is a Cadillac among governments"; the same author referred to the American presidential system as a "Model T."[15]

Admirers of the parliamentary system have credited it with being a highly responsive form of government. In parliamentary governments, parties campaign on carefully formulated platforms, and once elected, they are generally able to implement their programs. If government policies prove unpopular or impracticable or if the government falls into disrepute for any reason whatsoever, the prime minister or the ruling party can be replaced with no major shock to the political system as a whole. Finally, some observers believe that the British parliamentary system's greater party discipline makes it more efficient than the presidential system. The presidential system, critics have asserted, is too often marked by deadlocks stemming from the checks and balances built into its tripartite structure.

Defenders of the presidential system, while admitting that it is difficult to obtain a cohesive voting bloc in Congress, have pointed out that it *can* be done (consider the early legislative successes of, for example, Presidents Lyndon Johnson and Ronald Reagan). The difficulty of achieving consensus in the presidential system can also be seen as a healthy sign that the government is able to resist impassioned, unwise, or ill-considered majoritarian pressures.

Others have argued that because the presidential electoral system emphasizes local majorities and because its legislators can vote their individual preferences (or those of their constituents), it is actually more responsive to local minorities than the parliamentary system. Advocates of this position have cited presidential elections as proof of their contention. Because of the fragmented and relatively weak party system in the United States, a virtual unknown (such as Jimmy Carter) can become president by gaining sufficient support in state primaries and caucuses. Under a parliamentary system, by contrast, years of service and a record of distinguished national leadership are usually required before one can become prime minister.

Defenders of the presidential system have also argued that the legally defined term in office for presidents is by and large an asset. Although sometimes a drawback (consider how difficult it was to remove Richard Nixon, even after his abuses of power had become widely apparent), this guaranteed tenure in office often proves to be a blessing. Harry Truman, for example, who is now considered by many to have been one of the greatest U.S. presidents, was very unpopular during much of his term. Presidents have sufficient constitutional leverage to sustain effective leadership in times of national crisis, even when the public interest may require them to implement unpopular measures. This can be regarded as a clear advantage of the presidential system.

Transplanting Parliamentary Government: Limited Success Any comparison of the relative effectiveness of the parliamentary and presidential systems must take into account the experience of other democracies. Most constitutional democracies have been patterned after the parliamentary system. Both Italy and France have tried parliamentary government, with mixed results. Since World War II, Italy has struggled under a parliamentary system in which stalemate has been the salient feature. France operated within a parliamentary framework from 1876 (the beginning of the Third Republic) to 1958 (the end of the Fourth Republic). In both cases, the effectiveness of the British Parliamentary model in the main failed to survive transplantation to the Continent.

The reasons why parliamentary government has not worked as well in Italy or France as it has in Great Britain are partly political and partly contextual. Politically, the French and Italian governments came to be dominated by the legislature. The leading role of the prime minister and the cabinet, so important in the British constitutional system, was thus diminished. In contextual terms, whereas the British people tend to be tradition-bound, deferential, and pragmatic, the French and Italian electorates have deeper social divisions and have supported more extreme political parties. In both countries, intense partisanship spawned a plethora of parties and splinter groups. The commitment of many factions to preservation of the system, moreover, was (or continues to be) dubious at best. Under such circumstances, the party system became fragmented, internal party discipline broke down, and the executive branch came to depend on the whim of the legislature. Generally speaking, the more spirited and unruly the society in question, and the more numerous the factions on the political scene, the more chaotic and deadlocked the government will become. In such a society, it is essential to have a forceful and energetic executive authority—a factor missing in both France (until 1958) and Italy.

Such conditions have led to political immobilization or stalemate in both countries at different times in recent years. In France, during the entire life span of the Third and Fourth republics, no single party ever won a majority of seats in the National Assembly. During this same period, the country was ruled by no fewer than 119 governments with an average life of eight months. Sometimes weeks or even months passed between the fall of one government and the establishment of another. A similar malaise has plagued Italy, which had more than 40 prime ministers between 1945 and 1986.

Constitutions and Contexts Comparison of the relative success of parliamentary government in Great Britain with its relative failure in France and Italy serves to illustrate the important point, made most notably by Aristotle, that the study of politics can become too abstract. The statesman or legislator who wishes to improve a particular political order, Aristotle declared, must know not only what is best but also what is possible *under the prevailing circumstances*. Under a particular set of circumstances, some constitutional and some contextual, parliamentary government has worked very well in Great Britain; under different circumstances, it has not worked nearly so well in France and Italy. Aristotle's insight in this regard remains valid:

> We have not only to study the ideally best constitution. We have also to study the type of constitution which is practicable [that is, the best for a state under actual conditions]—and with it, and equally, the type which is easiest to work and most suitable to states generally. . . . The sort of constitutional system which ought to be proposed is one which men can be easily induced, and will be readily able, to graft onto the system they already have.[16]

Summary

The governments of the United States and Great Britain reflect different approaches to constitutional democracy. The American political system features a strong presidency and powers that are carefully balanced and separated. The British system is based on the principle of parliamentary supremacy, and powers are fused.

The Founders of the United States placed great emphasis on the proper construction and arrangement of political institutions. James Madison considered the theory undergirding these institutions to comprise a new science of politics. "Ambition must be made to counteract ambition" was a key concept in this theory. Accordingly, the American model of government relies for stability and effectiveness on the combined mechanisms of constitutional means and personal motives and seeks to harness and institutionalize self-interest for the benefit of the public interest. More specifically, the American presidential system is based on the concepts of separation of powers, constitutional restraints on majority rule, a strong executive, and federalism.

The British parliamentary model features a fusion of powers, indefinite terms of office, disciplined parties, and a dual executive. This model of constitutional democracy has been imitated more widely than the American model.

The American and British systems invite comparisons and offer provocative contrasts in the legislative, executive, and judicial areas. It is difficult to say which system is better in the abstract; the answer must be sought within the specific context and circumstances of each nation.

Key Terms

new science of politics	mixed regime	bureaucracy
constitutional means	fusion of powers	spoils system
personal motives	no-confidence vote	common law
checks and balances	MP	solicitor
presidential system	disciplined parties	barrister
separation of powers	loyal opposition	judicial review
bicameralism	dual executive	
parliamentary system	watchdog role	

Review Questions

1. "The new science of politics depended both on a view of the centrality of institutions and a specific understanding of human nature." Explain.

2. What are the characteristics of the presidential system? Of the parliamentary system?

3. What are the advantages of the British parliamentary system? Of the U.S. presidential system? On balance, which system works better?

4. Contrast the legislative, executive, and judicial branches under the presidential and parliamentary systems.

Recommended Reading

BAILEY, SYDNEY. *British Parliamentary Democracy* (3rd ed.). Westport, Conn.: Greenwood, 1978. This work provides a comprehensive introduction to the functioning of the British democracy.

BUTLER, DAVID, AND GARETH BUTLER (eds.). *British Political Facts: Nineteen Hundred to Nineteen Eighty-five* (6th ed.). New York: St. Martin's Press, 1986.

DIAMOND, MARTIN, WINSTON FISK, AND HERBERT GARFINKEL. *The Democratic Republic: An Introduction to American National Government*. Skokie, Ill.: Rand McNally, 1970. An introductory textbook that emphasizes the relationship between the American Founders and political institutions.

DICEY, A. V. *Introduction to the Study of the Law of the Constitution*. New York: St. Martin's Press, 1982. A classic account of the British political tradition.

DRAGNICH, ALEX, AND JORGEN RASMUSSEN. *Major European Governments*. Homewood, Ill.: Dorsey Press, 1986. The section dealing with Great Britain provides useful information on the British parliamentary system.

EHRMAN, HENRY. *Politics in France* (4th ed.). Glenview, Ill.: Scott, Foresman, 1983. A sound introduction to the government and politics of France.

ROSE, RICHARD. *Politics in England: Change and Persistence* (5th ed.). Boston: Little, Brown, 1989. An examination of the British political system and how it formulates political decisions.

Notes

1. Alexander Hamilton, John Jay, and James Madison, *The Federalist* (New York: Modern Library), No. 9, pp. 48–49.

2. Ibid., No. 10, p. 57.

3. Ibid., No. 51, p. 337.

4. Ibid.

5.   Ibid.

6.   Ibid., No. 6, p. 27.

7.   Ibid., No. 51, p. 337.

8.   Martin Diamond, Winston Fisk, and Herbert Garfinkel, *The Democratic Republic: An Introduction to American National Government* (Skokie, Ill.: Rand McNally, 1970), p. 136.

9.   Sydney Bailey, *British Parliamentary Democracy*, 3rd ed. (Westport, Conn.: Greenwood, 1978), p. 130.

10.   Ibid., p. 131.

11.   Ibid., p. 5.

12.   R. K. Kelsall, *Higher Civil Servants in Britain* (London: Routledge & Kegan Paul, 1966).

13.   See *Martin* v. *Hunter's Lessee*, 14 U.S. 304 (1816).

14.   Richard Rose, "Politics in England," in *Comparative Politics Today: A World View*, ed. Gabriel Almond (Boston: Little, Brown, 1974), p. 148.

15.   Edward Courtier, *Principles of Politics and Government* (Boston: Allyn & Bacon, 1981), p. 84.

16.   Aristotle, *The Politics*, trans. and ed. Ernest Barker (New York: Oxford University Press, 1962), pp. 155–156.

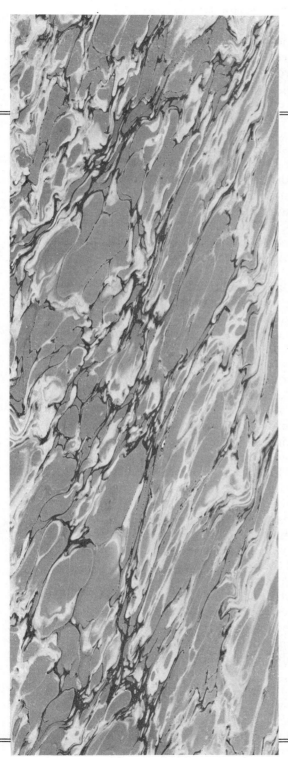

CHAPTER 7

ADAPTATIONS
OF DEMOCRACY

FRANCE, GERMANY, AND JAPAN

WINSTON CHURCHILL ONCE commented that "democracy is the worst form of government, except for all the others." This famous quotation sums up the view of many Americans, who recognize that the political system detailed in the U.S. Constitution is far from perfect but believe it is the best possible. In this chapter, we look at the varying ways in which democracy works in three countries where many astute observers once thought it impossible. Just how adaptable is democracy? The examples of France, Germany, and Japan suggest that it is far more adaptable than most theorists have imagined. This is important because democracy has become the object of ritual praise almost everywhere. Virtually every government in the world today, no matter how tyrannical, tries to give the appearance of constitutionalism and claims to be democratic. In countries where the press is state-controlled, where foreigners' movements and contacts are restricted, and where ordinary people live in fear of police reprisals, nothing prevents the government from pretending to champion democracy and liberty even as it perpetrates violence against the citizenry and suppresses all criticism.

The fact that dictatorships often claim to be democracies suggests that constitutional democracy is admired even where it is not practiced. Is it not true, then, that democracy is the best form of government for everyone? Unfortunately, the answer is not so simple. Some nations have authoritarian political traditions that make democracy seem either unnatural or undesirable. Other nations have customs and cultures that are not at all compatible with the individualism and egalitarianism inherent in the idea of democracy. Finally, for those nations engaged in a constant struggle for survival, especially those plagued by overpopulation and chronic food shortages, constitutionalism may seem a vague and meaningless abstraction. It makes little difference to people who are living on the edge of starvation whether their government is democratic or authoritarian—any government that can alleviate their poverty is, by definition, good government.

In the case of France, Germany, and Japan, however, democracy has thrived in the face of apparently insuperable cultural barriers. The extreme individualism and *incivisme* (lack of civility and civic consciousness) often cited as two facets of the French national character have long raised doubts about the feasibility of democracy in France. Nonetheless, the Fifth Republic has now survived for more than three decades—a remarkable record for a nation that has experienced numerous changes of regime over the past two centuries. Similarly, many commentators attributed the failure of Germany's Weimar Republic, established after World War I, to an allegedly ingrained antidemocratic passion for order and authority among the Germans. But the success of democracy in western Germany over the past four decades refutes that theory. By the same token, Japan had little experience with democracy before World War II; even more than Germany, Japan appeared to have far too rigid and autocratic a culture to support democracy. Yet Japan today boasts a viable (if unique) version of Western constitutionalism.

Are these nations exceptions that prove the rule? Or are generalizations about the irrelevance of democracy to many societies and cultures facile and false? We believe that the experiences of France, Germany, and Japan demonstrate clearly that constitutional democracy is a highly adaptable form of government that is potentially workable in many social, cultural, and economic contexts.

FRANCE

The presidential and parliamentary systems examined in Chapter 6 represent two basic alternatives in democratic government, but there are other possibilities as well. Under the Fifth Republic, France has fashioned a form of representative democracy that combines elements of both the presidential and parliamentary systems.

The Fifth Republic: A Hybrid System

The Fifth Republic, created in 1958, represented an attempt to remedy the defects of previous republics. It was meant to overcome what its founder and president (1959–1969), Charles de Gaulle, understood to be the great nemesis of French politics, impotent executives dominated by fractious legislatures. That prior arrangement had produced chronic governmental paralysis and popular disillusion in a degenerative process that three times ended in the downfall of parliamentary democracy in the nation. As de Gaulle was fond of pointing out, France's first three experiments in republican government all ended in dictatorship. French history from 1878 to 1958 vividly illustrated a fact that the authors of *The Federalist* understood very well: A rudderless government can become its own worst enemy.

Under the Fourth Republic (1946–1958), each new government lasted an average of six months. A profusion of political parties, some of fleeting duration, turned the French parliament, which dominated the political system, into a travesty. Furthermore, the parties at the opposite ends of the political spectrum—the Gaullists on the right and the Communists on the left—both sought to undermine the constitution of the Fourth Republic. The only thing these two parties agreed on was that the Fourth Republic was anathema. Consequently, they occasionally collaborated in bringing down governments through the exercise of what came to be known as the negative veto; that is, these two "extremist" parties had a large enough combined strength in the National Assembly to thwart initiatives and force the resignation of weak coalition governments.

Many in France hoped that the 1958 constitution would end this political instability. The new constitution was comparatively short and simple. Its provisions were guided by the political philosophy of de Gaulle, who, in one of his most famous addresses, cogently outlined its premises 12 years before its adoption:

> It is obvious that executive power should not depend on the Parliament, based on two houses and wielding legislative power, or else there will be a confusion of responsibilities in which the Government will become nothing more than a cluster of party delegations. . . . The unity, cohesion, and internal discipline of the Government of France must be sacred objects, or else the country's leadership will rapidly become impotent and invalid. How can such unity, cohesion, and discipline be preserved if the executive power emanates from another body, with which it must be balanced, and if each member of a Government which is collectively responsible before the national representative body is but the emissary of his party? The executive power should, therefore, be embodied in a Chief of State, placed above the parties, elected by a body that includes the Parliament but is larger than it. . . .

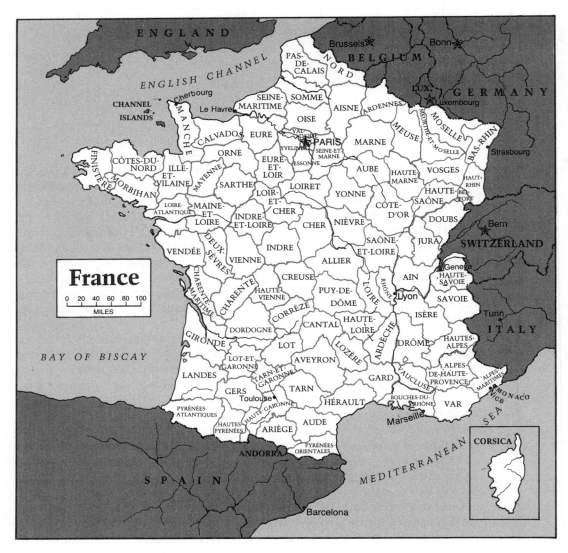

France

It is the role of the Chief of State to consider the general interest in his choice of men, while taking into account the orientation of the Parliament. It is his role to name ministers, and first of all, the Prime Minister, who will direct the policy and work of the Government. It is his role to promulgate laws and make decrees, for they obligate the citizens to the State as a whole. It is his task to preside over the Cabinet and, there, to defend the essential national continuity. It is his function to serve as an arbiter, placed above the political circumstances of the day, and to carry out this function ordinarily in the Cabinet, or, in moments of great confusion, by asking the nation to deliver its sovereign decision through elections. It is his role, should the nation ever be in danger, to assume the duty of guaranteeing national independence and the treaties agreed to by France.[1]

In sum, the centerpiece of the constitutional system, de Gaulle insisted, must be a strong executive branch to counterbalance the perennially divided parliament; the centerpiece of the executive, however, would be the chief of state (president) rather than the prime minister.

The Executive

The main outlines of de Gaulle's philosophy (*Gaullism*) are etched into nearly every provision of the 1958 constitution pertaining to the organization of public powers. In accordance with the parliamentary model, the French executive is divided. On paper, the prime minister (or premier) is the head of government, the president head of state. Unlike the British monarch, however, the French president exercises a number of important powers. In fact, the president, whose powers were originally tailored to suit the ambitions of de Gaulle himself, has become France's leading political figure. As in the American system, the French president is independent of the legislative branch, serves a fixed term in office (seven years), and possesses a wide array of powers.

The constitution positions the president as an arbitrator charged with settling differences among conflicting interests. This responsibility has led to the assumption of preeminent power in the realm of domestic and foreign policy. In addition, the president is empowered to dissolve the legislature and call for new elections, declare a state of emergency, issue decrees having the force of law, preside over cabinet meetings, and, above all, appoint and dismiss the prime minister and members of the cabinet. In addition, the president can call for a national referendum on virtually any matter he chooses. The premier and the cabinet do have a considerable voice in setting the agenda for the legislature, although in the years since 1958, the powers of the premier have steadily diminished as those of the president have grown.

The 1958 constitution originally stipulated that the president was to be chosen by an electoral college composed of local and national officials. This practice was deemed necessary in order to place the president above everyday politics. In 1962, de Gaulle imperiously placed before the French people a referendum calling for direct election of the president ("imperiously" because the constitution did not permit the president to bypass the National Assembly in the amendment process). The referendum passed overwhelmingly, and from that point on the French presidency enjoyed the enhanced authority that always accompanies the expression of a popular mandate in a democratic society. De Gaulle knew that in the modern age, no other single source of political authority is as potent as a broadly based vote of confidence, and he believed it essential to have a strong and inspirational leader (a "guide") to govern the unruly and individualistic citizenry of France.

Compared with the president, the prime minister has exercised far less power and influence. The prime minister is chosen by the president and serves at his or her pleasure. As head of the government, the prime minister presides over the cabinet and is responsible to the legislature for public policy and national defense. With the cabinet, the prime minister oversees the running of government and the bureaucracy. The unusual power and prestige of this position have made it something of a maxim of French politics to say that the prime minister and the cabinet exercise their greatest discretion over policy matters in the absence of direct presidential leadership.

The Judicial System

At its most fundamental level, the French judicial system is divided into two basic types of courts with different jurisdictions: ordinary courts and administrative courts. Despite this rather routine distinction, there are some very interesting and unusual innovations within the French legal system. For example, the High Council of the Judiciary, presided over by the president of the republic, considers issues regarding judicial promotions and discipline. Furthermore, the High Court of Justice is empowered to try the president of the republic for treason and members of the government for violations of criminal law resulting from abuses in office.

Most interesting of all is the Constitutional Council, which is composed of nine justices (three nominated by the president of the republic, three by the president of the National Assembly, and three by the president of the Senate) plus all the past presidents of the republic. Among its important tasks, the Council both supervises presidential elections and can investigate and resolve contested legislative races. Under certain conditions, it can render opinions about the constitutionality of pending legislation and make similar determinations about laws that have been enacted. Unlike American courts, the cases the Council hears are the result not of individual disputes or appeals but rather of special requests by the president of the republic, the prime minister, the two presidents of the legislature, or by a petition signed by 60 members of the National Assembly or the Senate. More often than not, the issues it considers are political and deal directly with the powers properly exercised by different branches and offices of the government.

Reduced Role of the National Assembly

If the presidency has clearly been the big political winner under the Fifth Republic, the legislature has been the loser. France's legislative branch is divided into two houses, the Senate and the National Assembly (see Figure 7-1). In 1991 the Senate, which has very limited powers, had 321 members who were indirectly elected. The *National Assembly*, with 577 members, was elected from multimember districts through a complex system of proportional representation. As the focal point of legislative power, the National Assembly must approve all proposed laws. However, the word *law* is rather narrowly defined by the 1958 constitution; many quasi-legislative decisions are left to the executive branch, which has the power to issue "decree laws."

The National Assembly is more interesting for the powers it does *not* have than for the powers it has: Its agenda is set by the executive; it has a limited number of committees; it cannot meet for more than six months each year; it has

Legislative

Executive

NATIONAL ASSEMBLY

577 members – 555 from metropolitan France and 22 from overseas territories and departments.

Mandate: Five years. Elected directly by equal and universal suffrage.

Limited Legislative Powers: Legislates on civil rights, nationality, status and legal competance of persons, penal law and procedure, taxation, electoral system, organization of national defense, administration of local government units, education, employment, unions, social security, and economic programs. Authorizes declaration of war. Can initiate constitutional revision. Can delegate above powers to cabinet – votes organic laws. Can question cabinet one day a week. Meets in regular sessions for a total that does not exceed six months. Votes budget submitted by government. If budget is not decided with Senate within 70 days, may be issued by decree. (*All other matters fall within rule-making power.*)

SENATE

321 members

Mandate: Nine years. Renewable by thirds every three years.

Elected indirectly by municipal and general councilors and members of National Assembly. Approximate size of electoral college: 110,000. Majority system, but proportional representation for seven departments with largest population.

Functions: Full legislative powers jointly with Assembly. Bills must be approved in identical terms by both houses unless prime minister, in case of discord, asks lower house to vote "definitive" text and thereby overrule Senate.

PRESIDENT OF THE REPUBLIC

Elected for seven-year term by direct popular election.

Personal Powers: Nominates prime minister; dissolves Assembly; refers bills to Constitutional Council for examination of constitutionality; calls referendums; issues decrees with force of law; nominates three of the nine members of Constitutional Council; can send messages to legislature; invokes state of emergency and rule by decree; presides over regular meetings of cabinet members – Council of Ministers; he is not responsible to Parliament.

PRIME MINISTER AND CABINET

Prime minister proposes cabinet members to president for nomination; "conducts the policies of nation"; directs actions of government and is responsible for national defense; presides over cabinet meetings; proposes referendums; has law-initiating power. Prime minister is responsible before Assembly.

ECONOMIC AND SOCIAL COUNCIL

Elected by professional organizations. Designated by government for five years as specified by "organic law."
  Composed of representatives of professional groups (approximately 195 members).
  Gives "opinion" on bills referred to it by government. "Consulted" on overall government economic plans.

CIVIL SERVICE

Judiciary

CONSTITUTIONAL COUNCIL

Composed of nine justices and all ex-presidents of Republic, Presidents of republic, Senate, and National Assembly appoint three justices each.

Functions: Supervises presidential elections and declares returns. Supervises referendums and proclaims results. Examines and decides on contested legislative elections. On request of the prime minister or the presidents of the republic, the National Assembly, or Senate, or upon request of at least 60 Senators or 60 members of the National Assembly, examines and decides on constitutionality of pending bills, and treaties and on legislative competence of Assembly. Examines all organic laws.

HIGH COURT OF JUSTICE

HIGH COUNCIL OF THE JUDICIARY

ORDINARY COURTS

ADMINISTRATIVE COURT (CONSEIL D'ETAT)

FIGURE 7-1   Major Features of the Constitution of the Fifth Republic
SOURCE: Roy C. Macridis (ed.), *Modern Political Systems: Europe*, 7th ed., © 1990, p. 80. Reprinted by permission of Prentice Hall, Englewood Cliffs, N.J.

no power to introduce financial bills, and if it fails to approve the government's budget by a certain deadline, the budget can be enacted by executive decree. Moreover, it can be compelled by the executive to cast a *package vote* on several pieces of legislation at once—either all pass or none do. Also, the government can make any particular vote a vote of confidence; in such a case, a negative vote in the National Assembly forces the resignation of the government and the dissolution of the parliament. Although this may seem to be one way in which the legislature can control the government, it is also a means by which the executive can dominate the parliament. Many legislators may well be reluctant to face new elections, especially if they have just incurred the wrath of a popular president.

De Gaulle went so far as to combine different provisions of the constitution in creative ways in order to gain even greater leverage over the parliament. Thus, for example, he was not above calling for a package vote on some part of his overall program and then making the vote itself a matter of confidence! Since de Gaulle's departure from France's political scene in 1969, the president has treated the National Assembly with greater deference.

Advising the National Assembly is the Economic and Social Council. Composed of almost 200 representatives drawn from various professions, this governmental body offers advice regarding legislation that promotes economic planning or has important economic or social impact.

Political Parties

France continues to have a variety of political parties. As is the case in most European multiparty systems, French political parties are generally classified on a left-right continuum. The two most important parties of the left (radical to liberal in orientation) are the Communist party and the Socialist party. From the conclusion of World War II until the late 1970s, the Communist party generally received at least 20 percent of the popular vote. But in recent years, there has been a steady erosion of Communist party strength, to the point that in the 1986 and 1988 elections the Communist party garnered approximately half the votes that it had traditionally received. By contrast, the Socialist party has never suffered such dramatic setbacks. In fact, in 1981 it commanded a legislative majority and its candidate, François Mitterrand, was elected president for a seven-year term. Although support for the Socialist party waned in the 1986 elections, it made a comeback in 1988 when Mitterrand was reelected. In this election, Mitterrand's Socialists gained more support than any other party. Mitterrand's popularity waned in the early 1990s and in regional elections held in March 1992, Mitterrand's Socialist party received only 19 percent of the popular vote—the lowest level of support in its history. This abysmal showing did not bode well for the ruling Socialist party in the national parliamentary elections scheduled for the spring of 1993.

On the political right (conservative to reactionary), a coalition has united under the banner of the Union of French Democracy, a right-center party that frequently stresses greater European cooperation and integration. A more conservative party is the Rally for the Republic party. In the 1988 elections, the Union

(Left) *French President François Mitterrand* (right) *meets with his prime minister, Pierre Eugène Bérégovoy, soon after his appointment.* (Bassignac-Reglain/Gamma) (Right) *Edith Cresson, France's first female prime minister, served from May 1991 until April 1992. Her appointment was controversial because women in politics are still a rarity in France, where woman suffrage was enacted as recently as 1946. Cresson's controversial comments and dwindling popularity led her into political difficulties and on April 2, 1992, she resigned.* (Reuters/Bettmann)

of French Democracy and the Rally for the Republic party cooperated in a futile attempt to unseat President Mitterrand. They came close, gaining 271 legislative seats compared to the Socialists' 276. (The legislative balance was reinforced by the Communists, who gained 27 seats.) The ultraconservative United Front party, which espouses strong nationalist, antiforeigner policies, gained only one legislative seat. So far, this party has made a lot of political noise but has not become a force in national politics.

During the 1980s, French politics exhibited a moderating tendency. The parties themselves are much closer to the political center than to the political fringes. In fact, ideological fringe parties of both the left and the right did poorly, leading some political scientists to wonder if France was heading for a two-party system. Some observers pointed out that such middle-of-the-road political inclinations could be construed as a sign of political maturity and stability. But a growing radicalization, manifested in the rising popularity of the extreme right, appeared to be the trend in the early 1990s, raising the prospect that French politics could again become highly polarized.

Constitution under Pressure: Testing the Balance

In 1964, Prime Minister Georges Pompidou (who went on to serve as president from 1969 to 1974) described the delicate institutional balance of the Fifth Republic in terms that are still relevant today:

> France has now chosen a system midway between the American presidential regime and the British parliamentary regime, where the chief of state, who formulates general

policy, has the basis of authority in universal suffrage but can only exercise his functions with a government that he may have chosen and named, but which in order to survive, must maintain the confidence of the Assembly.[2]

Without a doubt, the Fifth Republic has provided France with a significant degree of political stability. The extent to which this is attributable to the imposing presence of Charles de Gaulle and the extent to which it reflects any institutional advantages inherent in the amended 1958 constitution are open to debate. What is indisputable, however, is that de Gaulle's influence extended well beyond his presidency; his broad interpretation of presidential powers has prevailed to this day. His political policy of opposition to communism, his emphasis on resolute French independence in issues of foreign policy, his concern with increasing French prestige abroad, and his desire for economic development without nationalization—all were continued by his two presidential successors, Georges Pompidou and Valéry Giscard d'Estaing. Throughout this period, the National Assembly also broadly supported these policies.

Even after 1981 when, for the first time, the Socialist party gained a clear majority in the French legislature, it was able to utilize the many powers of the presidency on behalf of a new political agenda that included increased welfare programs and the nationalization of French industry.

About this time, structural flaws were detected in the 1958 constitution. Many political observers have argued, for example, that the president's seven-year term is too long. Ironically, while the president was seen as being too far removed from public opinion, the entire French system seemed too politicized. Since the president was elected every seven years and the national constituency was selected at least every five years, elections—and preparations for them—came to dominate French politics. Legislative and presidential elections were held in 1962, 1965, 1967, 1968, 1969, 1973, 1974, 1978, 1981, 1985, and 1988. One authority suggested that "long-range programs gave place to expediency, and party alignments obeyed the logic of electoral tactics rather than policy making."[3]

The constitution's greatest weakness was always the potential danger of a *divided executive.* What happens when the president and the prime minister are of two different parties, have two different political outlooks, and see themselves as representing different constituencies? In 1986, the Fifth Republic's intricate balance of executive power was put to its severest test when France's rightist parties emerged victorious in the national elections and Socialist President Mitterrand asked the neo-Gaullist mayor of Paris, Jacques Chirac, to form a new government. Mitterrand's choice of Chirac was influenced by his need to get along with the newly elected National Assembly. Although the Socialists drew more votes than any other single party—33 percent of the total—the main center-to-right parties received a combined vote of about 45 percent; with the support of 14 independent rightist candidates, they were able to claim a narrow majority (291 of 577 seats).

From 1986 to 1988, the problem of the divided executive led to the reality of *cohabitation*—the condition of a divided executive living uneasily together. The possibility of conflict and even deadlocked government seemed likely. Although

The French Agenda: A Sampler

Europe

Under President Mitterrand, France has promoted the European Community (EC) and backed the movement toward a single EC economy in 1992. Nonetheless, many of France's traditional industries in the north are threatened by more competitive industries in Germany and other EC countries. France also stands to lose a measure of national sovereignty if a proposed European Monetary System (EMS) becomes a reality; the Socialist government favors this measure, but the fact that French nationalism remains a powerful force in French politics could give conservative parties an issue on which to attack the Socialists in the 1993 national elections.

Immigration

The immigration issue has been taken up most strenuously by Jean-Marie Le Pen, leader of the far-right National Front. More than 3 million Arabs, mostly from former North African colonies, now live in France, plus a large number of immigrants from other former colonies in Africa and Asia. France has had a tradition of welcoming political exiles, refugees, and asylum seekers since the French Revolution in the eighteenth century. But growing domestic unemployment and urban decay, coupled with a recent influx of Third World and eastern European nationals, has forced the government to clamp down on illegal immigrants and seekers of asylum whose claims of political persecution are unfounded.

This policy reflects the fact that in France, as in other western European nations, a swing to the political right can be observed, threatening to end the political rule of the Socialists currently headed by Mitterrand.

Unemployment

France's jobless rate approached 10 percent in the early 1990s. In the French public mind, unemployment is closely linked with immigration. As foreign nationals crowd into French cities and compete for scarce jobs, the unemployment issue continues to seethe just below the surface of French politics. The fact that many university graduates are either unemployed or employed in poor-paying, menial jobs (the same jobs immigrants are often glad to have) only makes matters worse.

Education

University students in France have a history of political rebellion. In 1968, a left-wing student revolt threatened to bring down the Fifth Republic. On November 5, 1990, some 30,000 students protested in Paris, demanding more government spending on education. One week later, a demonstration by 150,000 students turned violent; cars were burned and shops looted. Faced with a mob of angry youth and no doubt recalling what had happened in 1968, the government agreed to boost the education budget.

both the president and the prime minister have stipulated responsibilities as the head of the nation and the government, respectively, the formal demarcation of authority between them was (and remains) murky in places. Most observers predicted that most likely the president would retain control of foreign affairs while the prime minister would prevail in the domestic arena. Despite the fact that this scheme had great potential for reviving political paralysis, cohabitation worked better than expected. The rapid decline in popularity of Chirac's conservative party, plus the fact that Chirac's desire to be president meant that he had little interest in reducing the power of the presidency, favored President Mitterrand throughout this period. With the 1988 elections, the divided executive and cohabitation ended. Yet there was no guarantee that France had forever seen an end to divided government, nor was it at all certain that if and when divided government reappeared, it would work out as well as it had in 1986–1988.

GERMANY

Modern Germany came into existence in the latter part of the last century. It burst onto the European scene with two impressive military victories: over Austria in 1866 and France in 1871. Following two world wars and two defeats, Germany was partitioned from 1949 until 1989, when the Berlin Wall was dismantled after the communist regime in East Germany collapsed. To understand Germany's tortuous road to democracy, it is necessary to go back to an experiment that failed.

The Weimar Republic

The point is often made that Hitler's Third Reich grew out of the *Weimar Republic*, a constitutional democracy founded in 1919. According to many experts, the problem was not so much that the Weimar Republic failed but rather that it was never allowed to succeed. From the moment of its inception, it was associated with Germany's humiliating military defeat in World War I. Furthermore, it was initially burdened by punitively high reparations payments to the victorious Allies that caused severe economic dislocations. High unemployment, widespread business failures, and rampant inflation sent periodic shock waves through the Weimar Republic. In the face of such turbulence, it was hardly surprising that German society became increasingly polarized between the extreme right and the extreme left. The emergence of extremism in turn prompted governmental crises. In the words of one expert, "Stable democratic government was in jeopardy throughout the life of the Weimar Republic. The country was governed either by unpopular minority cabinets, by internally weak Grand Coalitions, or finally, by extraparliamentary authoritarian Presidential Cabinets."[4]

Under such conditions, according to some observers, the collapse of the Weimar Republic was inevitable. Few democracies, it has been argued, could have survived such adversity. Other commentators have maintained that democracy could not have survived in post–World War I Germany even if political and economic conditions had been more favorable. After all, they have pointed out, the Germany ruled by Chancellor Otto von Bismarck (1815–1898) and William II (who reigned from 1888 to 1918) had hardly exemplified democratic values. Under those authoritarian rulers, free expression, political participation, and "party politics," all of which are essential to any democratic society, had been actively discouraged. In fact, obedience to authority was thought to be a German trademark. All the evidence seemed to suggest that Germany had been ill-prepared for democracy in 1919—a hypothesis apparently borne out by the collapse of the Weimar Republic in 1933 and the nation's subsequent embrace of the totalitarian Third Reich. Given this background, the founding of the Federal

Republic of Germany in 1949 was naturally haunted by the disturbing specter of the ill-fated Weimar experiment in democracy.

Divided Germany: Half Democracy, Half Dictatorship

It is important to understand the origins of the Federal Republic of Germany (West Germany). World War II destroyed Germany; the nation and its capital, Berlin, were subsequently divided among the Allies—the United States, Great Britain, France, and the Soviet Union. The intention was to merge the zones of occupations to prepare the way for self-government, but the Soviet Union refused to relinquish control of its portion of Germany, which declared itself the German Democratic Republic (East Germany) when the other sectors united to form West Germany. From 1949 to 1990, Germany remained a divided nation. The similarly divided Berlin became an intermittent source of tension between the United States and the Soviet Union during that time, and the very existence of a divided Germany reminded the world of the sharp political division between East and West that threatened its very future.

Although East Germany became the most prosperous Communist state in eastern Europe, its economic performance paled by comparison with that of West Germany. The West German economy was hailed as a miracle, experiencing a spectacular recovery from the devastation of the Second World War. West Germany soon became the keystone of the Common Market of the 1950s, which subsequently grew into the full-fledged European Community (EC), and the West German economy continued to be the most dynamic force within the EC.

Equally impressive, democracy took hold in West Germany, in stark contrast with both its predecessor, Adolf Hitler's Third Reich, and its Communist neighbor. The dramatic difference between the two Germanys was aptly conveyed by the Berlin Wall, erected by East German authorities, which not only divided East and West Berlin but also symbolized the political and economic differences between them.

Eventually Germany would be reunited. Pressure had long existed because East Germans, who endured far lower living standards than their western counterparts, had not been allowed to emigrate. The key spark to eventual reunification was provided by the Soviet Union's Mikhail Gorbachev, who was no longer willing or able to prop up the unpopular and insolvent European Communist regimes. Indeed, the end to East Germany came at a time when rebellion was rife in central and eastern Europe: Poland and Hungary had already taken giant steps toward dismantling Communist rule, and Czechoslovakia, Romania, and Bulgaria were not far behind.

For East German communism, the beginning of the end took the form of a mass exodus. Hundreds of thousands fled through Hungary, Poland, and Czechoslovakia (where the Communist leaders tried in vain to ride out the rising storm). At the same time, throngs of East Germans who chose to stay behind participated in gigantic demonstrations in East Berlin, Leipzig, and elsewhere. What lay ahead was even more breathtaking—the bulldozing of the Berlin Wall following the collapse of the East German regime in late 1989.

United Germany: Democracy Triumphant

Within a matter of weeks, popular pressures brought down the hard-line regime of Erich Honecker, paving the way for the merger of the two German states. This union occurred faster than most experts had expected. In the democratic elections held in the former GDR in the spring of 1990, voters overwhelmingly rejected the East German Communist party. The big winner was a conservative alliance, the Christian Democratic Union (CDU), with 41 percent of the vote. The big loser was the left-of-center Social Democratic party (SPD), which many observers expected to prevail but which garnered less than 22 percent of the popular vote. Chancellor Helmut Kohl, leader of the parent CDU party in West Germany, had campaigned actively in East Germany for both the CDU and German reunification.

In October 1990, the two Germanys entered into a formal union. Berlin was restored as the capital. Germany immediately became the dominant power in the EC—more powerful even than the Soviet Union, especially after the dissolution of the Warsaw Pact, the withdrawal of Soviet troops from eastern Europe (including East Germany), the collapse of the Soviet economy, and the disintegration of the Soviet multiethnic empire.

The cost of remaking the new Germany is high. The price for German unification is roughly $100 billion. West Germans must pay for the economic rehabilitation of East Germany in the form of a 7.5 percent income tax surcharge and higher sales taxes. German workers in the former FRG staged strikes and demonstrations in the spring of 1992 when the Kohl government resisted labor demands for a 5 percent wage increase. Labor leaders pointed to higher taxes and 4 percent annual inflation rate as proof that wage hikes were justified. Many Germans also resented the influx of immigrants from eastern Europe.

It is too soon to say what implications German unification will have for Europe and the world. Sometimes the past yields clues to the future, but in the case of Germany, history does not seem to be providing any guidelines. Rather than reverting to its totalitarian interlude under the Nazis, Germany appears to be firmly committed to representative democracy and the continued evolution of the EC. Indeed, in May 1991, Chancellor Kohl called for the creation of a United States of Europe.

Whether or not Europe eventually follows the German example, merging into one continentwide system, there is little doubt that the new Germany will be a driving force in any future economic and political arrangements in Europe. Nor is there much doubt that German democracy will continue to flourish, despite the formidable challenge of converting the former East Germany from a languishing dictatorship to a full participant in a thriving democracy and despite Helmut Kohl's planging popularity ratings in 1992.

German Federalism

Democracy is indeed thriving in Germany. Prior to 1989, the Federal Republic of Germany comprised ten states, or *Länder* (singular, *Land*), plus West Berlin. It encompassed an area about equal to that of Oregon. As noted, the merger of the

two German states in 1989 has enlarged the nation's territory and population and added six new *Länder* to the federal structure. Even so, no fewer than 25 countries the size of the new Germany would fit comfortably into the territory of the United States. The main reason for German federalism is political rather than geographic, to serve as a permanent check on the power of the center.

The actual boundary lines of the *Länder* were drawn by the Allied occupying forces after World War II, but in most cases they correspond to earlier *Länder*. Although the country's geographic compactness may suggest a lack of regional diversity, some significant differences are seen in customs, attitudes, dialects, and so forth. Some *Länder*, however, do not correspond to natural patterns of regional or local diversity. Not surprisingly, then, Germany's federal system has brought about a somewhat greater degree of standardization among the *Länder* than American federalism has.

The *Länder* are the building blocks in a system designed to ensure a high degree of political decentralization. *Land* governments have the primary responsibility to enact legislation in certain specific areas such as education and cultural affairs. They alone have the means to implement laws enacted by the federal government, to command most of the administrative personnel to accomplish this task, to exercise the police power (taking care of the health, welfare, and moral well-being of the people), to direct the educational system, and to hold sole authority to place restrictions on the press.

Impressive though the powers of the *Länder* may be, the federal government is nonetheless the main repository of political authority in the German constitutional system. The government in Berlin is given the exclusive right to legislate in foreign affairs, citizenship matters, currency and coinage, railways, postal service and telecommunications, and copyrights. In other areas, notably civil and criminal law and laws relating to the regulation of the economy, the central government and the *Länder* have concurrent (shared) powers.

TABLE 7-1
Germany's Federal System

Länder and Capital	Area (sq. mi.)	Population (1988)
Baden-Württemberg (Stuttgart)	13,803	9,332,000
Bavaria (Munich)	27,238	10,911,000
Berlin (Berlin)*	341	3,379,000
Brandenburg (Potsdam)*	15,044	3,441,000
Bremen (Bremen)	156	661,000
Hamburg (Hamburg)	291	1,606,000
Hesse (Wiesbaden)	8,151	5,515,000
Lower Saxony (Hannover)	18,311	7,147,000
Mecklenburg–West Pomerania (Schwerin)*	6,080	1,509,000
North Rhine–Westphalia (Düsseldorf)	13,149	16,778,000
Rhineland-Palatinate (Mainz)	7,658	3,646,000
Saarland (Saarbrücken)	992	1,060,000
Saxony (Dresden)*	6,839	4,989,000
Saxony-Anhalt (Halle)*	7,837	3,027,000
Schleswig-Holstein (Kiel)	6,053	2,527,000
Thuringia (Erfurt)*	5,872	1,980,000

The Federal Republic of Germany currently encompasses 16 *Länder* (states)—ten from the former West Germany and six (identified by an asterisk) from the former East Germany.

Germany is more federal than the United States; that is, its *Länder* are more powerful and receive a larger proportion of taxes than American states do. For example, individual and corporate income taxes are split between Berlin and the *Länder* in equal 40 percent shares; the cities get 20 percent. The *Länder* also receive one-third of the value-added tax, the large but hidden sales tax used throughout Europe. As a result, while some additional funds are transferred from Berlin to the *Länder* and cities, they do not have to make repeated pleas as American states and cities do in beseeching Washington for bailout money.[5]

The Executive

Germany has a parliamentary form of government with a divided executive. The most important government official is the *chancellor*, who, with parliamentary approval, appoints and dismisses those who serve in the cabinet. In case of a national emergency, the chancellor becomes commander in chief of the armed forces and is also responsible for the formulation and implementation of public policy. The president, as the titular head of state, serves a largely symbolic function, except in the event of political stalemate in parliament. Like the king or queen of Great Britain, the president alone can remain above party politics and thus represents continuity and stability. The president is chosen indirectly (by an electoral college) and serves a seven-year term. The head of the majority party in the lower house of parliament becomes the chancellor; if no one party enjoys an absolute majority, as often has been the case, a coalition government chooses the chancellor.

The Legislature

The legislative branch of the German government is divided into a lower house, known as the **Bundestag,** and an upper house, called the **Bundesrat.** In this bicameral setup, the lower house is the more important of the two legislative bodies.

The *Bundestag*   The presiding officer of the *Bundestag* is always chosen from the leadership of the majority party. Procedural matters are governed by rules inherited from the *Reichstag* (the prewar legislature). Important decisions regarding committee assignments, the scheduling of debates, and other questions of day-to-day parliamentary policy are made through the Council of Elders, which consists of the president of the *Bundestag*, the three vice-presidents (representing the two major parties and the smaller Free Democratic party), and several other members chosen by each of the parties.[6]

Bundestag deputies are democratically elected to four-year terms, although, as in other parliamentary systems, those terms may be cut short by a vote of no confidence and the subsequent resignation of the chancellor and the dissolution of the parliament. Note, however, that the **Basic Law** (constitution) of Germany, unlike most other parliamentary constitutions, requires a "positive" no-confidence vote: The chancellor must resign only if the legislature elects a new chancellor at the very same time that it votes against the old one.

The most important components of the *Bundestag* are the *Fraktionen*. To form a *Fraktion*, a political party must win at least 15 legislative seats. Under the rules and procedures of the *Bundestag*, only through this unit of parliamentary organization can deputies be assigned to committees and parties receive formal recognition. Because the most important work is done in legislative committees, it is especially vital that political parties gain enough legislative seats to form a *Fraktion*.

The *Bundesrat*   Although it is the less prominent of the two legislative houses, the *Bundesrat* must pass on any measure that would alter the balance of powers between the national government and the *Länder*. Thus the German "states" are given a powerful weapon to protect themselves against federal encroachment. As a result, the *Bundesrat* is one of the most important upper houses found anywhere in the world. Its assertive role on behalf of the *Länder* at the federal level is backed by stouthearted *Land* officials accustomed to playing a primary role in implementing federal policy as well as in helping to shape that policy in the concurrent areas designated under the Basic Law.

Political Parties   Germany's political party system was consciously designed to keep the number of parties at a reasonable level and to prevent tiny extremist groups from playing a significant role in the political life of the country. Parties must receive a minimum of 5 percent of the national vote and must win seats in a minimum of three electoral districts to gain *Bundestag* representation.

Another factor strengthening the major parties is the mode of elections to the *Bundestag*. Each voter casts two votes, one for the individual, one for a *List* determined by the party. This method of election gives the major parties a significant role in determining the future of those who aspire to careers in politics and public service, because fully half of the members of the *Bundestag* owe their office directly to their party.

Since 1949, the German Federal Republic has had just two major parties—the center-left **Social Democratic party** (SPD) and the conservative **Christian Democratic Union**/Christian Socialist Union (CDU/CSU). In addition, the relatively small **Free Democratic party** (FDP) has managed to stay afloat and, most of the time, to play a strategic role in government by striking a balance midway between the evenly matched other two parties. Because the two major parties have frequently been in almost perfect balance in the *Bundestag*, the Free Democrats often have held the decisive votes; as a result, their influence has been disproportionate to their small following, and they have enjoyed "junior partner" status in most coalition governments. In recent years, a social protest movement called the *Greens* (because of its emphasis on environmental issues) has emerged as a party of some consequence.

The Judiciary

Like Germany's other federal institutions, the court system was designed to provide a barrier against abuse of power by the central government. The regular judiciary, headed by the Federal Supreme Court, operates alongside a set of four

German Chancellor Helmut Kohl, leader of the Christian Democratic Union (CDU) party in West Germany, had campaigned actively in East Germany for both the CDU and German unification. Kohl addressed the first parliament meeting of the unified Germany in the Berlin Reichstag on October 4, 1990. (Reuters/ Bettmann)

specialized tribunals, known as the Federal Labor Court, the Federal Social Court, the Federal Finance Court, and the Federal Administrative Court. From a political standpoint, the most important judicial structure is the Federal Constitutional Court, which deals exclusively with constitutional questions and has the express power to declare unconstitutional the acts of both federal and *Land* legislatures.

In contrast to the procedures used in the selection of federal judges in the United States, Germany chooses its highest-ranking judges (those on the Federal Constitutional Court) by legislative election. Half these judges are elected by the *Bundestag* and half by the *Bundesrat*. Most judges, however, are chosen on the basis of competitive Civil Service–type examinations and are appointed for life by the minister of justice, who is assisted by nominating committees, which are in turn selected by the federal and *Land* legislatures. To move up the judicial hierarchy, a German judge must be promoted from within, much like any other government employee in the regular Civil Service. Judicial independence is ensured by the fact that judges serve indefinite terms. In general, the court system seems reasonably well equipped to act as a barrier against abuses of executive or legislative power and as a guardian of civil liberties.

The German Agenda: A Sampler

Reconstruction of the Former GDR

What was once East Germany is economically depressed relative to the former West Germany. The infrastructure is in disrepair, factories operate with obsolete equipment, workers lack essential skills, unemployment is high due to plant closings, and petty bureaucrats with little knowledge of modern management—holdovers from the Communist era—have proved difficult to dislodge from their positions. The burden for reconstruction, which will have to be borne in large part by the western Germans, is estimated at $100 billion.

Dealing with Foreign Workers and Illegal Immigrants

An increasing number of temporary workers and illegal immigrants from eastern Europe, the former Soviet Union, and the Middle East have moved to Germany in order to take advantage of its prosperity. This has led to political controversy, ethnic tensions, and even instances of xenophobic persecution by German citizens worried that their nation may be inundated with foreigners. Among the more worrisome signs is the increasing influence of the neo-fascist Republican party and increasing acts of violence against foreigners. These developments contributed to a sharp erosion of Chancellor Helmut Kohl's popularity in 1992.

Boosting the European Community

The Kohl government continues to be a staunch supporter of the European Community. Not only has it backed full unification of EC national economies, but it has also advocated a United States of Europe. One reason why Germany favors the movement toward a common Europe is that without such a legitimizing structure, the fear of a new German juggernaut like the one Hilter launched in the 1930s would likely be raised anew. Another reason is that Germany knows it will be the dominant power in a united Europe; its strong economy ensures that it will have political clout and a competitive edge over other member states.

Investing in the East

Although western Germany's primary aim is to rebuild the eastern part of the nation, the Germans are also inclined by history and geography to look to central Europe for markets, raw materials, and investment opportunities. Germany is a natural trading partner for neighboring Poland and Czechoslovakia and also has a major interest in expanding trade with the republics of the former Soviet Union.

Redefining Its Role in Europe and the World

The new Germany appears unsure exactly what course to chart for the future. Its bulk and dynamism dictate that it will play a leadership role in Europe and beyond, but the precise nature of this role is unclear. Should Germany become a bridge between the former Soviet Union and Europe? Reassess its commitment to NATO? Loosen its ties to the United States? Rid itself of existing restraints on its own military development? At a time when the Kohl government was coming under growing criticism for its handling of both foreign and domestic policy, these are some of the questions that will likely dominate the debate in Germany in the coming years.

The Basic Law and Civil Liberties

In the realm of civil liberties, as one student of German politics has declared, "the relevant historical experience was that of the Third Reich, with its oppressive flouting of all human liberties."[7] The first 19 articles of the Basic Law are devoted to a careful elaboration of the unalienable rights of every German citizen. All forms of discrimination, including religious and racial discrimination, are expressly prohibited. Freedom of speech, movement, assembly, and association are guaranteed except when they are used "to attack the free democratic order." This last proviso was clearly aimed at the two extremes of left and right, communism and Nazism, which have so afflicted German life in the present century. Doubtless it reflected most of all the postwar preoccupation with communism that prevailed throughout the Atlantic community and was particularly pervasive in Germany. However, the fear of a reawakening of neo-Nazi ultranationalism has never been far beneath the surface—as evidenced by the fact that neo-Nazi activity has generally been interpreted as constituting an "attack on the free democratic order."

A Limited Government

If we consider the cumulative effect of the constitutional provisions most fundamental to Germany (federalism, the unique organization of the legislature, the carefully structured party system, the independent judiciary, the explicit guarantees of civil liberties), it becomes apparent that one of the principal purposes behind the Basic Law was to arrange the institutional furniture in the "new Germany" to preclude a repeat performance of the "old Germany." Limited government—more than any other facet of constitutional democracy—was central to the drafters of the Basic Law, who deliberately sought to create safeguards against the concentration of power that had caused such turmoil in modern German history.

And the democratic performance of the Federal Republic in the half century since World War II has indeed been impressive. The experience of Weimar has not been repeated. Whereas the Weimar Republic was largely undone by severe economic distress, West Germany's rapid postwar recovery and sustained industrial growth after 1949 have frequently been proclaimed an economic miracle. The Federal Republic became the leading industrial nation in western Europe and the fourth-largest economic power in the world, behind the United States, the Soviet Union, and Japan. This is one reason why democracy succeeded where the Weimar Republic failed. Spurred on by a remarkable economic resurgence, the present generation of Germans has given democracy a new lease on life in a land where it was once thought to be unworkable. It was this very success, more than any other single factor, that led to the downfall of communism in East Germany.

JAPAN

Unlike Germany, Japan had virtually no experience with genuine democracy prior to 1949. In fact, its history and culture often worked against Western democratic ideas. Yet today Japan stands as a sterling example of democracy in Asia. How did this remarkable transformation come about? To answer this question, we must first sketch in the historical background.

Historical Background

Japan's feudal era lasted until the *Meiji Restoration* in 1868. At that time, under the guise of recapturing ancient glories, a new emperor was crowned, and the modernization of Japan was begun. Although some lip service was paid to democracy, Meiji Japan remained an oligarchy. For all practical purposes, a group of elder statesmen (*genro*) dominated the government. The role of the emperor was largely symbolic. Worshiped as a flesh-and-blood deity, he personified national unity.

Domestically, Japan made great progress during this period. Economic development was prompted, protected, and subsidized by a modernizing elite. Only the basic (or strategic) industries were government-owned. This program of economic modernization was modeled after that of the West. Despite periodic opposition from rural landowners, the government force-fed the economy with a program of capital development designed to promote heavy industry. Within a few decades, the leaders of the Meiji Restoration, according to one authority, "abolished feudal institutions, legalized private property in land, started a Western-style legal system, established compulsory education, organized modern departments of central and local government, and removed the legal barriers between social classes."[8]

With the conclusion of World War I and the departure of the Meiji leadership, Japan entered a new phase of political development. Nationalism, taught in the schools, became a kind of religion. Governments blossomed and withered in a rapid and bewildering succession. Attempts were made at instituting democratic reforms: In 1925, for example, economic qualifications for voting were removed, and the franchise was extended to all men over the age of 25. During the 1930s, however, such tentative democratic reforms were submerged in a wave of militarism. Arguing that politicians, with their effete democratic leanings, had kept Japan inferior, ultranationalists declared that only a strong military leadership could propel Japan to its rightful place in the world community. The militarists triumphed, but their victory led only to Japan's ignominious defeat in World War II.

The relative ease and speed with which democratic reforms were crushed in the 1930s reflected the fact that the Japanese had never really endorsed the concept of constitutional government. Sovereignty, according to popular belief, issued from the emperor-deity, not from the people. Therefore, it might be said that prewar Japan had embraced some of the form of democracy but very little of the substance.

The New Constitution

It was this state of affairs that the 1947 Japanese constitution, imposed by the United States, sought to redress. Henceforth, sovereignty would reside in the Japanese people, not in the emperor. The American influence on the new Japanese constitution is glaringly apparent, especially in its preamble:

> We, the Japanese people, acting through our duly elected representatives in the National Diet, determined that we shall secure for ourselves and our posterity the

fruits of peaceful cooperation with all nations and the blessings of liberty throughout this land, and resolved that never again shall we be visited with the horrors of war through the action of government, do proclaim that sovereign power resides with the people and do firmly establish this Constitution. . . . Government is a sacred trust of the people, the authority for which is derived from the people, the powers of which are exercised by representatives of the people, and the benefits of which are enjoyed by the people.

Like the weavers of an intricate tapestry, the framers of the 1947 constitution sought to construct an elaborate system of representative democracy. Among the fundamental rights guaranteed by the constitution were the right of citizens to an equal education and the right of workers to organize and bargain collectively. In another extraordinary feature, the Japanese constitution explicitly renounced war and pledged that "land, sea, and air forces, as well as other war potential, will never be maintained." (This provision has not, however, prevented the government from building limited "self-defense forces.")

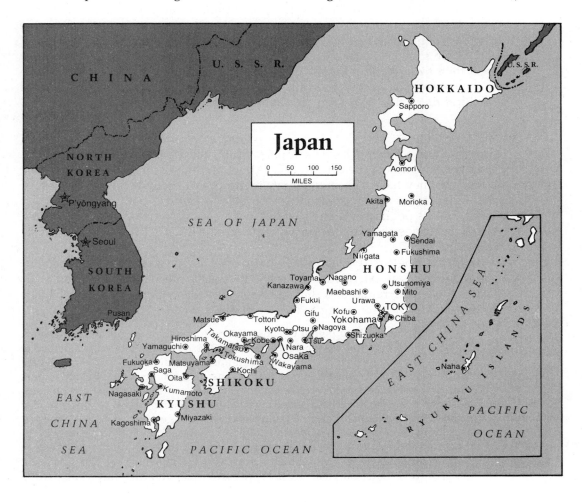

The new constitution also stipulated a parliamentary form of government. The emperor was to remain the head of state, although merely as a ceremonial figure. The head of the government was designated to be the prime minister. The authors of the constitution, however, placed the greatest amount of power in the new bicameral legislature. That body, called the *Diet*, was divided into a 491-member House of Representatives elected every four years and a 252-member House of Councillors, whose members serve six-year terms. Under the constitution, members of each house are elected by universal suffrage from multimember districts in which voters make only one selection. Smaller parties such as the Clean Government party and the Communist party have thus been able to garner a certain number of seats in the parliament because in, say, a four-member district, it is only necessary for a candidate to receive the fourth-largest share of the votes in order to win a seat.

The constitution explicitly stated that popular sovereignty was to be expressed through the Diet, the only institution of the government empowered to make laws. Whereas in the past the prime minister and the cabinet had been responsible to the emperor, they were now made responsible to the Diet, the "highest organ of state power."

As we shall see, however, the Japanese have adapted Western institutions to fit their own highly resilient cultural traditions. The result is a unique system that combines the new (democratic politics and market economics) with the old (political hierarchy, economic centralization, and social discipline).

The Party System

Essentially, the **Liberal Democratic party** (LDP) has dominated Japanese politics since the adoption of the constitution. Although numerous smaller parties have appeared, they have remained largely ineffectual. Among these minor parties, the Socialist party has occasionally been able to garner significant numbers of votes, but its political role has basically been one of parliamentary opposition. For four decades, the actual governing of the country has fallen almost exclusively to the LDP.

When a single party retains a majority of seats in a freely elected legislative assembly over an extended time span, it usually means that that party has satisfied a broad range of social interests. This description fits the relatively conservative LDP. According to two authorities:

The reasons for the long period of conservative domination are not too far to seek. In the first place, it was the conservatives who carried out the reforms and helped to see to it that there was not a complete discontinuity with the past. When independence came, they accepted the land reform. The changes they made toward a more strongly centralized system of government corrected some of the most obvious mistakes of the Occupation. The Liberal Democratic party, being in power, also controlled a considerable amount of patronage and had the advantage when seeking the support of economic and professional interest groups. With the support of the majority of the rural vote and access to the resources of the business community, the party was in a strong position. It was on intimate terms with the bureaucracy. The significant thing, however, was that close ties with the bureaucracy and with the business world

Japanese Prime Minister Kiichi Miyazawa of the Liberal Democratic party outlines his domestic and foreign policy initiatives before a plenary session of the lower house of the Japanese parliament. (Reuters/Bettmann)

and the control of patronage were not sufficient. Beginning in 1955, the Liberal Democratic party attempted to build up a national organization with mass membership. This was a surprisingly difficult thing to do in Japan where, on the local scene, groups based on personal loyalties, often around one individual, were more acceptable than branch units of a national party.[9]

The Liberal Democratic party succeeded, then, because it satisfied national aspirations and interests and because it sacrificed narrow party fervor for broad popular appeal. Today, the LDP is truly an umbrella party, made up of a loose-knit coalition of various interest groups rather than a single, cohesive voting bloc.

The makeup of the LDP becomes particularly crucial during the biennial party conferences, at which the LDP selects its president, for the person chosen as LDP president more or less automatically becomes prime minister. Choosing a prime minister at a party conference may seem to be a rather undemocratic way to form a government, yet these party conferences are anything but monolithic affairs. The outcome of the presidential vote is normally the result of intense bargaining by party factions, each of which has its own leader, its own constituencies to protect, and its own policies to promote.

In this regard, it is noteworthy that Japan has retained some elements of the patron-client system that has long characterized Japanese politics. Prior to 1947, Japan had always been ruled by powerful heads of factions and cliques who built and maintained their power bases by dispensing personal favors and rewards.

To a significant extent, this aspect of the political system has endured, although in a less pronounced form. Perhaps the most important vehicle for perpetuating Japan's patron-client democracy has been the Liberal Democratic party itself.

Because the LDP is the chief party in Japan and because it is made up of a potpourri of political interests, powerful factional leaders have emerged within the framework of the party organization. To a considerable extent, these leaders wield the power of political life and death over their followers. They feed their factions with money and influence obtained through personal support groups (*koenkai*). When the political fortunes of the party leaders rise and fall, the faction leaders act as power brokers, deciding who among them will become prime minister and which cabinet post will go to whom. By contemporary Western standards, this system may seem neither open nor democratic, but by Japanese standards, it is remarkably "Americanized." This complex and unique political setup illustrates what has been called the "paradox of Japan's being an open society made up of closed components."[10]

Decision by Consensus

The Japanese experiment in democracy remains a unique blend of native culture and imported democracy. For example, the British notion of the loyal opposition has been slow to emerge in Japan. Rather, the Japanese display a preference for arriving at decisions by consensus. According to one expert:

> This method rests on the premise that members of a group—say, a village council—should continue to talk, bargain, make concessions, and so on until finally a consensus emerges. . . . Despite the spread of democratic norms, this tradition of rule by consensus still has its appeal and sometimes leads to cries against the "tyranny of the majority"—for example, when the ruling party with its majority pushes through legislation over the strong protests of the opposition.[11]

The fact that decision by consensus is a time-honored practice in Japan helps explain why the Japanese people tend to be offended at the sight of politicians behaving in a partisan manner. On the other hand, the Diet at times presents a most undignified spectacle—in fact, a free-for-all. Here again, the requirements of constitutional democracy and native cultural influences have combined to produce quite unpredictable results. When Americans think of a legislature, stereotyped images of decorum and dignity immediately spring to mind. An unsuspecting American visitor to the Diet could be in for a rude awakening in this regard, as the following vignette makes clear:

> Every legislative body develops mores in the course of its historical development. In contrast to the British Parliament, politeness, decorum, and strict adherence to the rules of procedure do not appear to be characteristic of the [Japanese] House of Representatives. Sometimes opposition members will make so much noise with their catcalls and shouts that it will be virtually impossible to hear a prime minister's speech in the chamber. On rare occasions violence will break out; a favorite tactic is to try to prevent the speaker from getting to his seat by blocking the passageway. The government sometimes rams legislation through by devious parliamentary maneuvers like locking out the opposition. Although it is hard to prove, it seems reasonable

to assume that the behavior of the legislators has not exactly endeared them to the public at large. During demonstrations in the vicinity of the Diet, participants have been known to urinate against the main doors of the Diet building to indicate their contempt for the institution.[12]

Political Stability and Economic Prosperity

Despite such colorful and sometimes violent outbursts, Japanese democracy has proved surprisingly stable. This achievement is all the more impressive in view of the fact that Japan had virtually no prior experience with popular self-government. As in the case of Germany, economics has played a key role in sustaining democracy in Japan. Japan's economic revival after World War II was swift

---

The Japanese Agenda: A Sampler

Retaining a Competitive Edge

Japan's dominant trade position in Asia is being challenged by the so-called new industrial countries (NICs)—South Korea, Taiwan, Hong Kong, and Singapore. A second wave of rapidly developing countries led by Thailand and Malaysia could also challenge Japan at some point in the not too distant future. Japan's economy appeared to be slowing down and some analysts even proclaimed the beginning of the end of Japan's economic upsurge in 1992. Others pointed to Japan's underlying economic strength and vitality.

Maintaining Close Relations with the United States

The United States is Japan's most important ally and trading partner. As Japan's largest foreign market and favorite place to invest, the United States is vital to Japan's economic health. No less vital is the U.S. role as Japan's protector. The U.S. military presence in the western Pacific—as well as the American nuclear guarantee—has enabled Japan to concentrate on high-tech consumer industries and overseas market development while spending less than 1 percent of its GDP on defense. The post-war Japanese-American partnership has been jeopardized by a deepening dispute over trade issues prompted by a perennial U.S. trade deficit vis-a-vis Japan caused, according to many U.S. economists (and

the U.S. government) in part, by Japan's protectionist policies and insular culture.

Sustaining a High Standard of Living

Japan is an affluent society to be sure, but it is also a small country with a large population. Most of its land is mountainous and unsuitable for settlement. The problems associated with overcrowding—air and noise pollution, traffic congestion, escalating land prices—are all prevalent in Japan. Modern technology has not yet provided Japan (or any other country) with answers to these downside questions of economic overdevelopment.

Balancing Tradition and Modernity

Japanese culture still exerts a powerful force beneath the surface of Japanese society. To the casual observer, Japan appears to be the epitome of modernity. But in reality most Japanese are steeped in traditional values and attitudes. This tenacious clinging to the past and to things Japanese makes it very difficult for outsiders to gain access; it also often gives rise to frustration for those seeking to do business in Japan. There is an ongoing debate between Japanese who argue that Japan must open doors that have previously been locked to foreigners and those who fear that it has already allowed too much foreign influence and thereby jeopardized the essence of Japanese culture.

and dynamic, as bombed-out cities (symbolized, of course, by Hiroshima and Nagasaki) were turned into models of efficient and innovative industrial production. Deliberate planning by a business-minded, modernizing elite was one important factor behind Japan's resurgence; a rising volume of world trade and massive American purchases during the Korean War (1950–1953) were also crucial. Within two decades, economic management on a national scale produced huge advances in heavy industry, consumer products, and high-technology electronics, and today Japan stands as a global economic power—despite "the loss of 52 percent of Japan's prewar territories, the return of 5,000,000 persons to a country about the size of California, the loss of 80 percent of Japan's shipping, and the destruction of one-fifth of her industrial plants and many of her great cities."[13] In the mid-1980s, the success of the Japanese market economy was clearly apparent in Japan's massive multibillion-dollar trade surpluses with the United States, which had become a market for over one-third of Japan's exports. This led to much criticism of Japanese trade practices in the United States and to Japanese criticism of the shoddiness of American products. The strains between the two nations have been evident for over a decade and could be detected in the rise of right-wing nationalism within Japan and the rise of anti-Japanese, "buy American" sentiment in the United States.

Japan's rise as an economic superpower is reflected in lopsided trade balances with most of its major trading partners, including the United States. Japan has also emerged as the dominant economic force in the Asian Pacific. Three facts illustrate this point:

- Japan provides 65 percent of all investment funds now flowing into Asia and the western Pacific.
- Japan is the top aid donor to every country in Asia except Pakistan and accounts for 64 percent of all aid to the developing countries of Southeast Asia.
- Japan's total trade with Asia now surpasses that of the United States; its imports from Pacific Asia have more than doubled in recent years.[14]

In short, Japan and the United States are now both allies and economic rivals in Asia. This changing relationship is a direct consequence of Japan's successful transition from a war-devastated authoritarian state to a bastion of democracy and free enterprise. The nation's stability and prosperity made Japan's economic miracle possible.

THE ADAPTABILITY OF DEMOCRACY

It may well be that political and economic factors are more important than either cultural or historical factors in shaping the destiny of the modern nation-state. The successful development of democracy in such nations as France, Germany, and Japan indicates that self-government, adapted to suit specific national circumstances, can work in a variety of social and political contexts. Its adaptability and resilience since World War II have been striking.

Although it is commonly assumed that democracy survives best in nations with advanced economies and relatively compatible populations, it also has endured (although somewhat tenuously) in ethnically torn India, a nation of over 800 million people. In Latin America, sub-Saharan Africa, eastern Europe, the former Soviet Union, and many other nations around the world, its call beckons. Although the adoption and adaptation of democracy faces various and demanding challenges in these nations, there is good reason to believe that democracy is more adaptable than social and political scientists thought just two decades ago.

Summary

Constitutional democracy is a highly adaptable form of government. Its success in postwar France, Germany, and Japan—despite considerable cultural and other obstacles—indicates that by responding to unique circumstances, democracy can be made to work almost anywhere.

France's constitutional system is partly parliamentary and partly presidential. The current French constitution is closely associated with the leadership and political philosophy of Charles de Gaulle. As the French presidency has become the centerpiece of the Fifth Republic, the role of the National Assembly has been reduced. The chief aim of the Fifth Republic is to strike an appropriate balance between liberty and authority, given the distinctive qualities of the French national character. In 1986 a rightist coalition won the national elections; this development gave rise to a potential constitutional crisis because France's divided executive was now split between a conservative prime minister and a socialist president.

When the Federal Republic of Germany was created after World War II, the only democratic tradition in Germany's past was that of the ill-fated Weimar Republic. The German constitution strongly emphasizes federalism. The upper house of the legislature reflects the prominent role of the individual states. The judiciary is independent, and civil liberties are constitutionally safeguarded—indications of the importance attached to the preservation of limited government in Germany. Two major and one or two smaller political parties have competed for the great majority of legislative seats in the bicameral German legislature. The smaller Free Democratic party has enjoyed disproportionate influence because of its strategic location between the more or less evenly balanced Christian Democratic Union/Christian Socialist Union and the Social Democratic party.

Japan's pre–World War II political tradition was even less democratic than Germany's. Nevertheless, a democratic constitution was imposed on Japan by the United States following World War II. In the succeeding decades, Western-style democratic institutions have combined with Japanese folkways to produce a unique kind of "patron-client" democracy. In place of majority rule, the Japanese favor decision making by consensus. Although Japan has a multiparty system, the Liberal Democratic party has been in power since the mid-1950s. Japan has achieved political stability and economic prosperity under its modified form of parliamentary democracy.

Key Terms

Gaullism	*Länder*	Christian Democratic Union
National Assembly	*Bundestag*	Free Democratic party
divided executive	*Bundesrat*	Meiji Restoration
cohabitation	Basic Law	Liberal Democratic party
Weimar Republic	Social Democratic party	*koenkai*

Review Questions

1. In what ways does the French Fifth Republic represent a hybrid of the British parliamentary and American presidential systems? Why was the Fifth Republic set up this way?

2. What is the nature of France's divided executive? Under what circumstances might this arrangement lead to a constitutional crisis or political paralysis?

3. How has Germany attempted to build protections for individual liberty into its governmental structure? Why should such efforts be regarded as important?

4. What factors account for Japan's political success in creating a stable democracy? In what ways has democracy been adapted to fit the Japanese culture?

5. Compare and contrast the party systems of France, Germany, and Japan. What conclusions do you draw?

Recommended Reading

BERGER, SUZANNE. *The French Political System* (3rd ed.). New York: Random House, 1974. A well-written introduction.

CONRADT, DAVID P. *The German Polity* (3rd ed.). White Plains, N.Y.: Longman, 1986. A standard text that provides good background on Germany before reunification.

EDLINGER, LEWIS J. *West German Politics* (3rd ed.). New York: Columbia University Press, 1985. A useful overview of the West German political spectrum but, like most textbooks on the subject, now dated.

HARGRAVE, ROBERT L., JR., AND STANLEY KOCHANEK. *India: Government and Politics in a Developing Nation* (4th ed.). Orlando, Fla.: Harcourt Brace Jovanovich, 1986. A lucidly written presentation of Indian politics.

HEIDENHEIMER, ARNOLD J., AND DONALD P. KOMMERS. *The Governments of Germany* (4th ed.). New York: Crowell, 1975. A readable general introduction to the politics and government of East and West Germany.

IKE, NOBUTAKI. *Japanese Politics: Patron-Client Democracy* (2nd ed.). New York: Knopf, 1972. An extremely concise analysis of Japanese political culture and institutions. Highly recommended for its penetrating insights.

LAQUEUR, WALTER. *Germany Today.* Boston: Little, Brown, 1985. An incisive study of Germany by a leading American authority on Europe.

MACRIDIS, ROY. *Modern Political Systems: Europe* (7th ed.). Englewood Cliffs, N.J.: Prentice Hall, 1990. Section III contains a superb discussion of French politics through the 1986 election.

MAGSTADT, THOMAS M. *Nations and Governments: Comparative Politics in Regional Perspective.* New York: St. Martin's Press, 1991. A comparative study of key countries in each major region of the world, stressing political setting, institutions and processes, and contemporary problems and prospects.

MCNELLY, THEODORE. *Politics and Government in Japan* (3rd ed.). Lanham, Md.: University Press, 1985. An excellent introduction to Japanese politics.

NORTON, PHILLIP C. *The British Polity* (2nd ed.). White Plains, N.Y.: Longman, 1990. A good basic text on British politics through the late 1980s.

REISCHAUER, EDWIN O. *Japan: The Story of a Nation.* New York: Knopf, 1980. An excellent interpretive history by one of America's foremost authorities on Japan.

ROSE, RICHARD. *Politics in England: Change and Persistence* (5th ed.). Glenview, Ill.: Scott, Foresman, 1989. A solid text by a recognized authority on British politics.

SAFRAN, WILLIAM. *The French Polity* (2nd ed.). White Plains, N.Y.: Longman, 1985. A good basic text on French politics.

STEINER, JURG. *European Democracies.* White Plains, N.Y.: Longman, 1986. Well-organized and informative, this text is an ambitious attempt to compare all the democracies of Europe in the mid-1980s.

WALLACH, PETER, AND GEORGE ROMOSER. *West German Politics in the Mid-Eighties: Crisis and Continuity.* Westport, Conn.: Greenwood, 1985. A good discussion of West German politics in the years leading up to reunification.

Notes

1. Suzanne Berger, *The French Political System*, 3rd ed. (New York: Random House, 1974), p. 368.

2. Ibid.

3. Roy Macridis (ed.), *Modern Political Systems: Europe*, 6th ed. (Englewood Cliffs, N.J.: Prentice Hall, 1986), p. 120.

4. Karl Dietrich Bracher, *The German Dictatorship* (New York: Holt, 1970), p. 75.

5. Michael Roskin, *Countries and Concepts: An Introduction to Comparative Politics* (Englewood Cliffs, N.J.: Prentice Hall, 1982), p. 190.

6. Arnold J. Heidenheimer and Donald P. Kommers, *The Governments of Germany*, 4th ed. (New York: Crowell, 1975), p. 188.

7. Guido Goldman, *The German Political System* (New York: Random House, 1974), p. 56.

8. Franz Michael and George Taylor, *The Far East in the Modern World* (New York: Holt, 1964), p. 263.

9. Ibid., p. 607.

10. Robert H. Scalapino and Junnosuki Masumi, *Parties and Politics in Contemporary Japan* (Berkeley: University of California Press, 1962), p. 153.

11. Nobutaki Ike, *Japanese Politics: Patron-Client Democracy*, 2nd ed. (New York: Knopf, 1972), p. 17.

12. Ibid., p. 28.

13. Michael and Taylor, *Far East in the Modern World*, p. 603.

14. Daniel Sneider, "How Japan Became Dominant Player in Asia," *Christian Science Monitor*, November 13, 1989, p. 11.

CHAPTER 8

THE COLLAPSE OF COMMUNISM

A DEMOCRATIC FUTURE?

IN DECEMBER 1991, the Soviet Union ceased to exist. The demise of this Communist superpower was stunning and dramatic—one of the most influential and important political events of the twentieth century. Although the demise came quickly and proved shocking, important political change within the Soviet Union had been apparent for months, even years. Throughout the world, Communist governments, a fixture of the bitterly divided, post–World War II world, were collapsing of their own weight. No Communist leader was more associated with the process of the political and economic decline of most Communist states everywhere than was the last leader of the Soviet Union, Mikhail Gorbachev.

From March 1985 until August 1991, Gorbachev had instituted political and economic reforms that eroded the foundations of the Stalinist state and precipitated the downfall of communism in eastern Europe. Ever controversial, Gorbachev alienated many within the Soviet Union, including pro-democracy Russian Republic leader Boris Yeltsin (who championed free-market economic reforms, unfettered elections, a greater measure of self-determination for the national republics within the Soviet Union, and an end to the Communist party) and hard-line traditionalists (who yearned for the restoration of Communist party–led totalitarianism). During three days in August 1991, a group of eight hard-line Communist party traditionalists, primarily associated with the Soviet KGB (secret police) and the army, attempted to oust Gorbachev and seize political power. Convinced that his policies had brought the country to the brink of disaster, they were stunned when the coup attempt encountered widespread popular resistance. The hero of the day, Boris Yeltsin, remained defiant within the Russian Parliament building in Moscow, coordinating the resistance while huge crowds, frequently surpassing 100,000 people, demonstrated in the streets and vowed to fight for democracy. Yeltsin insisted that Gorbachev be restored to power; in mere days, the coup failed, and Gorbachev temporarily resumed the presidency.

In the wake of this failed coup there were breathtaking political developments, including Gorbachev's resignation from the chairmanship of the Communist party, the removal of party stalwarts from positions of power, the total collapse of the Soviet empire, the dissolution of the central government, the depolitization of the former instruments of state terror (especially the KGB and the army), and the rise to controlling political power of a new breed of political leaders (led by Boris Yeltsin) apparently dedicated to establishing democracy and a new market-based economic system. Following the formal dissolution of the Soviet Union in December 1991, Gorbachev stepped down as president and the former republics (minus the Baltic states and Georgia) formed a loose-knit *Commonwealth of Independent States (CIS)*.

The breakup of the Soviet empire was a watershed event in human history. It represented the popular (but not necessarily permanent) triumph of the democratic idea over a government's repressive force of arms and a fundamental political revolution within a once repressive state, accomplished with startling rapidity and remarkably little violence.

Not only in the Soviet Union have communism and Communist governments been defeated, in eastern Europe, communism was abandoned in the late 1980s.

Yet it is still too soon to say whether its collapse portends a permanent democratic future. The trends appear to favor democracy and market economies in such countries as Poland, Hungary, and Czechoslovakia. In Romania and Bulgaria, as well as in Albania, the movement toward democratization has been slower but not entirely absent. Yugoslavia was moving in that direction before the outbreak of civil war. And the former East Germany is a special case, having merged with West Germany in 1990, as described in Chapter 7.

In Asia, Communist regimes have been more resilient. With the exception of Afghanistan in April 1992, they have not collapsed, nor have they taken major steps toward liberalization. The People's Republic of China softened its totalitarianism after Mao's death in 1976 but has remained a despotic state, as the Tiananmen Square massacre in June 1989 vividly demonstrated. North Korea, sometimes called the "hermit kingdom," under its aging ruler Kim Il-Sung has continued to display the xenophobia, extreme secrecy, and self-imposed isolation long associated with Stalinist rule. Similarly, Vietnam has remained a monolithic state in which the Communist party tenaciously maintains its power. Cambodia and Laos, dominated by Vietnam, are two other Communist states in Asia where democratization is notably absent. Nor has communism totally lost its appeal everywhere. In the Philippines, for example, a home-grown Communist insurgency remains firmly committed to the violent overthrow of the government. In Cuba, Fidel Castro still maintains a Communist government as he clings to political power.

Nonetheless, it is clear that what was once called the "Communist world" no longer exists. The status and influence of communism declined precipitously in the decade of the 1980s. Though it may be too soon to declare communism officially dead, there is no doubt that the patient is in critical condition. Furthermore, it is important to recognize what would be entailed by the death of communism. Its possible demise raises several important questions, each of profound interest to political scientists.

For instance, will the dwindling number of Communist governments worldwide forever discredit communist ideology in present-day Communist nations and throughout the world? (For a discussion of Marxist ideology, see the discussion in Chapter 14.) That is, will Marxism and Marxist-Leninism, like the belief in the divine rights of kings, come to be regarded as antiquated and irrelevant?

Furthermore, since totalitarianism has survived longer in the form of communism than in any other form, the decline of Communist power raises the question whether totalitarian regimes can endure for more than several generations. More precisely, can regimes founded on such revolutionary principles survive for very long after the zeal associated with the original ideology has moderated and after the original leaders of the revolution (or the protégés of those leaders) have passed from the scene? Are totalitarian regimes capable of retaining their repressive form indefinitely, or are they destined to be short-lived?

A final question applies only to the former Soviet Union. As the 1990s began, it stood as the last of the world's great empires. It presided over conquered peoples and cultures, but not without great internal stresses and tensions. Can such empires endure at all in a world increasingly governed by the ideas of nationalism, egalitarianism, and a belief in self-determination? Are all such empires forever doomed?

The very existence of such important questions reflects a basic truth: The former center of that once powerful Communist world, the Soviet Union, has ceased to exist. The loss of eastern Europe, German reunification, and the dissolution of the Warsaw Pact (a military alliance that had bound the Soviet Union to its eastern European satellite nations) dealt fatal blows to Soviet power. However, these decisive events are the effects, not the causes, of the former Soviet Union's demise. As we shall see, the root causes have been internal, not external.

THE END OF THE SOVIET EMPIRE

After the failed coup in August 1991, the government of the Soviet Union broke with its own history and first sought to establish a democratic government. Then, under the leadership of Boris Yeltsin, it abolished the central government, creating a loose federation consisting of almost all of the former republics (the Commonwealth of Independent States initially included all the former Soviet republics except Georgia and the former Baltic states, and the now independent nations of Estonia, Latvia, and Lithuania). The future configurations and forms of government of the new nations that formerly comprised the Soviet Union remain to be seen. Yet, it is apparent that the independent republics today represent a dramatic departure from the former repressive, totalitarian Soviet state. Significantly, the undermining of that state began with the liberalizing policies initially undertaken by Mikhail Gorbachev.

Gorbachev's "new thinking" laid the groundwork for even more radical reforms by undercutting the moral and intellectual basis of the Stalinist state. Soviet-Style Communism had displayed all the characteristics of totalitarian rule, including central control over the armed forces, the mass media, and the economy; a dominant monopoly party; an official ideology; and a systematic program of terror against suspected political opponents and the mass murder of innocents deemed unworthy (or dangerous) by the regime. The story of how the Soviet Union emerged from totalitarianism provides the essential background for understanding the nature of Russian politics today.

Although Mikhail Gorbachev has been the most instrumental in transforming this system, he was not the first to attempt to alter the draconian regime that Lenin and Stalin carried to its logical conclusion. Nikita Khrushchev, who eventually emerged as secretary general after Stalin's death in 1953, relaxed restraints on art, literature, and even some political commentary while curtailing state terrorism, dismantling the Stalin-built gulag (prison camp) system, and ending mass purges. In a famous 1956 speech, Khrushchev stunned the delegates to the 20th Party Congress by denouncing the "crimes of Stalin" as well as Stalin's bloody purge of ranking party and state officials. Almost as if to underscore the closing of this brutal chapter in Soviet history, Khrushchev also permitted the publication of Aleksandr Solzhenitsyn's powerful novella *One Day in the Life of Ivan Denisovich*, a gripping account of life in a Stalinist labor camp. In this manner,

Khrushchev initiated the process of *de-Stalinization,* a term that has become synonymous with reduced reliance on police state methods of rule.

Despite periodic confrontations with the United States (most notably the 1962 Cuban missile crisis, in which the United States government successfully resisted Soviet efforts to place land-based intercontinental missiles 90 miles from its shores), some observers cited de-Stalinization as proof that the Soviet Union was mellowing with age. Some experts even believed that the forces of *liberalization* unleashed by Khrushchev would prove irresistible, citing gradual improvements in the standard of living and the increasing number of political dissidents as evidence that change for the better was occurring. These hopes gave rise to the so-called *convergence theory,* which held that the Soviet Union and the United States were slowly moving, from opposite directions, toward an increasingly common kind of society and government.

This thesis seemed somewhat plausible but hardly certain as the Soviet leadership displayed more propensity toward repression than relaxation for the next 30 years. After Khrushchev's ouster in 1964, de-Stalinization came to a halt with the assumption to power of Leonid Brezhnev. After a brief power struggle, Brezhnev gradually accumulated the supreme powers, honors, and titles associated with the type of personality cult that Stalin had created. Once in power, Brezhnev moved to crush the dissident movement. By the 1970s, the trend toward re-Stalinization was clearly apparent, including the especially repugnant practice of committing dissidents to psychiatric hospitals and subjecting them to various forms of "therapy." In addition, during his long tenure (1964–1982) as the Kremlin's top leader, Brezhnev became increasingly rigid in his adherence to Stalinist methods of rule and economic management. One consequence was that a stifling system of central planning remained in place despite growing evidence that Soviet economic growth was slowing to dangerously low levels. In the realm of foreign policy, Brezhnev ordered a Soviet invasion of Afghanistan in 1979, which led to a prolonged war, causing some commentators to compare it to America's travail in the Vietnam War.

Brezhnev died in 1982. There began a period of political instability, marked by the fact that the aging hierarchy of the Communist party was unwilling to relinquish its power to a new generation of leaders. Brezhnev's successor was Yuri Andropov, former head of the KGB. Sixty-eight years old when he assumed office, Andropov became ill and died in 1984 after lingering for many months. His successor, Konstantin Chernenko, was 72 years old when he took power and was virtually incapacitated from day one. He died a year later. Thus from 1982 to 1985, the Soviet Union had been led by three different rulers, all of them in ill health and all barely able (or unable) to perform their official duties. (See Table 8-1.)

THE SOVIET SYSTEM BEFORE GORBACHEV

The most important fact to keep in mind about the Soviet political and economic system before Gorbachev came to power in 1985 was that all power was centralized in the Communist party, which governed the nation. Although separate

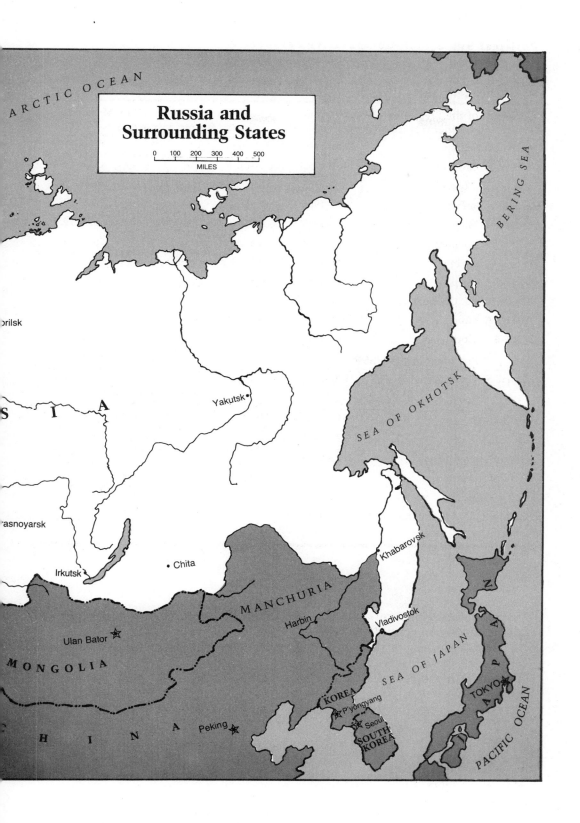

Russia and Surrounding States

0 100 200 300 400 500
MILES

ARCTIC OCEAN

BERING SEA

SEA OF OKHOTSK

rilsk

Yakutsk•

asnoyarsk

Irkutsk

• Chita

Khabarovsk

MANCHURIA

Ulan Bator ☆

Harbin

Vladivostok

MONGOLIA

SEA OF JAPAN

KOREA

P'yŏngyang

Peking ☆

Seoul

SOUTH KOREA

TOKYO

PACIFIC OCEAN

TABLE 8-1
Soviet Leaders, 1917–1991

Chairmen of the Presidium of the Supreme Soviet (Presidents)		Chairmen of the Council of Ministers (Prime Ministers)	
Mikhail I. Kalinin	1923–1946	V. I. Lenin	1917–1924
Nikolai M. Shvernik	1946–1953	Aleksei I. Rykov	1924–1930
Kliment E. Voroshilov	1953–1960	Viacheslav M. Molotov	1930–1941
Leonid I. Brezhnev	1960–1964	Josef Stalin	1941–1953
Anastas I. Mikoian	1964–1965	Georgii M. Malenkov	1953–1955
Nikolai V. Podgornyi	1965–1977	Nikolai A. Bulganin	1955–1958
Leonid I. Brezhnev	1977–1982	Nikita S. Khrushchev	1958–1964
Yuri V. Andropov	1983–1984	Aleksei N. Kosygin	1964–1980
Konstantin U. Chernenko	1984–1985	Nikolai A. Tikhonov	1980–1985
Andrei A. Gromyko	1985–1988	Nikolai I. Ryzhkov	1985–1990
Mikhail S. Gorbachev	1988–1990*	Valentin Pavlov	1991

President of the USSR

Mikhail S. Gorbachev	1990–1991

Communist Party Heads

V. I. Lenin†	1917–1924
Josef Stalin†	1922–1953
Nikita S. Khrushchev	1953–1964
Leonid I. Brezhnev	1964–1982
Yuri V. Andropov	1982–1984
Konstantin U. Chernenko	1984–1985
Mikhail S. Gorbachev	1985–1991

* In 1989, the office of chairman of the presidium of the Supreme Soviet was strengthened and renamed "chairman of the Supreme Soviet." Gorbachev was elected to this new office and served until the Congress of People's Deputies created the executive presidency in March 1990. The office of chairman of the Supreme Soviet remained, but its executive and ceremonial functions were transferred to the executive presidency.

† As chairman of the Council of People's Commissars, Lenin was the de facto head of the party and the government; although Stalin was named general secretary of the party in 1922, he was unable to assert unquestioned control over the party until after Lenin's death in 1924.

SOURCE: *The Soviet Union*, 3rd ed. (Washington, D.C.: Congressional Quarterly, 1990), p. 95; updated beyond 1990.

governmental structures and institutions existed, they were mere reflections of the fundamental control the party exercised over Soviet political life.

Furthermore, not only was the Communist party the primary repository of political power, it was also the main source of social rank, power, and privilege within the Soviet Union. The party was hierarchically organized, with sharp gradations in power and authority according to rank. All personnel matters (rank, tenure, promotion, and location), not only within the party but also in all other key Soviet institutions, were tightly controlled by the party hierarchy.

The party was headed by a *general secretary*, who was the ruler of the Soviet state. Under the general secretary was the very powerful *Politburo,* a group of fewer than 15 influential party members (including the general secretary) who met weekly and were responsible for national policy decisions. Next in importance was the *Secretariat,* an equally small group that also met weekly and exercised control over the organization of the Communist party. Communist party organizations lower down had less power, were much larger, and met less frequently. The *Central Committee,* which ratified important policies, contained just over 300 full-time members and usually met only twice a year. The *Party Congress,* of some 5,000 party representatives, met every five years, in theory to represent all party members in the USSR; in fact, this body assembled primarily for the purpose of legitimizing the party leadership and the party line.

Thus within the Communist party, power flowed downward, and the politics of the party and of the Soviet Union consisted of those powerful officials in the top posts of the party (including the general secretary) seeking to place their followers in important subsidiary positions within the party and the government. One of the most distinctive features of the Soviet party system in that regard was the *nomenklatura,* the Leninist system of personnel management (and the party members who hold those positions). Under this system, the party reserved to itself the right to make all key appointments for positions of authority in Soviet public life, including the government and the party, industry, the arts, science, and education. In this manner, a complete system of social and economic control could be effectively maintained.

Although vastly inferior in power to the party, the legislative and the executive-bureaucratic branches of the government (on paper) paralleled the Soviet party hierarchy. The legislative branch of the government consisted of the bicameral *Supreme Soviet,* headed by a steering committee known as the presidium, which was chaired in turn by the president of the Soviet Union (a largely ceremonial position). The executive-administrative branch of the government was headed by the *Council of Ministers,* composed of the chiefs of the most important government agencies. The Council of Ministers was chaired by the prime minister (known in Russia as the premier). Both in the legislative and in the executive-administrative branches of the government, the republics were represented. In theory, the USSR was classified as a federal nation-state, but its federalism was all form and little substance.

On paper the party and the government may have appeared distinct, but the day-to-day reality of Soviet political life featured a blurred relationship between the two under the party's domination. The most powerful party officials typically held several key party and governmental posts. In the early 1980s, for instance, Brezhnev was both the general secretary of the party and the chairman of the presidium of the Supreme Soviet (the president of the nation). The former Soviet Union historically has been headed by an interlocking directorate comprising a small number of powerful oligarchs, many of whom wore two or three official hats. Not surprisingly, the common denominator among this rarefied elite was membership in the prestigious party Politburo.

THE GORBACHEV REFORMATION

In 1985, Mikhail Gorbachev, at age 54, became one of the youngest general secretaries of the Communist party in Soviet history. He faced no shortage of political and economic problems. As we shall see, Gorbachev became convinced that these problems could not be surmounted without significant political and economic reforms. And since the political system was little more than a reflection of the power and influence of the Communist party, Gorbachev made a fateful and momentously important decision to reform communism and the party in order to preserve each. He therefore undertook policies that became famous in the West: *perestroika, glasnost,* and *demokratizatsiia.* Let us examine these reforms and the reasons why Gorbachev deemed them necessary.

Incentive for Reform: The Failure of Central Planning

From the time Lenin had assumed power in 1917, the Soviet Union featured a planned economy (also known as a command economy). All important economic decisions (what and how much was to be produced, and so on) were made at the uppermost level of the Communist party. Competition, the pursuit of profits, and most forms of private ownership were forbidden as inconsistent with the tenets of communism.

This system of central planning succeeded in making the Soviet Union a first-rate military power. However, by the mid-1980s, it was apparent that it had also resulted in economic stagnation that placed the Soviet Union at a competitive disadvantage with industrial, democratic nations such as the United States, Japan, and several European nations.[1] By 1985, the economic growth rate had declined to 2 percent, about half what it had been a decade earlier. One out of every nine industrial enterprises and nearly a third of state farms were losing money. Food, housing, medicine, and transportation were woefully inadequate in both quality and quantity. At the end of the 1980s, an estimated 28 percent of the Soviet population lived below the official Soviet poverty line.[2]

In the realm of agriculture, food production barely kept pace with population growth, and despite lavish investment in agriculture, the government continued to spend heavily for imported meats and grains. Meanwhile, the USSR's investment priorities in agriculture reflected terrible planning. Farm-to-market roads and facilities for storage, food processing, packaging, and retailing were woefully neglected. Soviet economists estimated that about one-fourth of all grain harvested each year was lost before it got to the market and then-President Gorbachev said that losses equaled the value of Soviet grain imports—$4 billion in 1988. As a result, meat and dairy-product consumption for the average Soviet citizen had declined 30 percent since 1970.[3]

Another critical problem was the technology gap, which widened into a gulf during the 1970s and 1980s when the computer revolution eluded the Soviets while it transformed their economic competitors. There was little encouragement for managers to invest in this new technology, and the party feared that its widespread use could empower political dissenters. The consequence was an inability to modernize Soviet industry and infrastructure.

At the root of most of these problems was central planning. It discouraged initiative because plant managers and directors of government-run farms remained tied to a central plan that imposed rigid quotas on factory and farm production. Plan fulfillment was the highest priority for all Soviet economic administrators. The Stalinist system sacrificed quality for quantity, and there was insufficient incentive or opportunity for management, operating on instructions from above, to introduce new technology. Bottlenecks due to unanticipated interruptions in the flow of essential materials and equipment frequently delayed building projects and impeded factory and farm production. Because of relentless pressures to meet overly ambitious production quotas, managers often took shortcuts and used subterfuge to avert or conceal failures.

The cynicism of the managers was matched by the low morale of the Soviet workers, who were underemployed, unhappily employed, or simply not motivated to work. The result was appallingly low productivity caused by the absence of dependable and efficient workers. Prevailing worker cynicism was commonly reflected in popular Soviet sayings such as "The party pretends to pay us, and we pretend to work." This cynicism was fed by the hypocrisy of high party officials who espoused egalitarian ideals but lived in secluded luxury while the proletariat they glorified had to stand in long lines to buy bread and other staples.

Impediment to Reform: The *Nomenklatura*

Earlier we noted that individuals who occupied positions of power and authority due to their appointed position in the Communist party comprise the *nomenklatura*. They included members of the political bureaucracy, senior economic managers, and scientific administrators. Certain writers, artists, cosmonauts, athletes, and generals who represented the Soviet state and enhanced its reputation were also included in this group, which has numbered (counting spouses and relatives) several million people.

The *nomenklatura* comprised a privileged, entrenched elite class in the former Soviet Union.[4] Its existence has proved significant for two reasons. First, the elaborate, exclusive, and largely concealed infrastructure of luxury apartments, specialty shops, vacation resorts, hospitals, clinics, health spas, and schools it used did not merely set it apart from ordinary Soviet citizens but stood in sharp contrast with the Marxist and Communist ideals of equality and justice that Soviet leaders had so frequently proclaimed. Second, the *nomenklatura*, though not always outrightly corrupt, nonetheless proved unresponsive and smug, much more concerned with perpetuating its power than with implementing official policies. In the mid-1980s, no one was more concerned about the capacity of this entrenched elite to block economic progress than the Soviet Union's new leader, Mikhail Gorbachev.

Perestroika

Initially, Gorbachev sought the reform of communism by means of *perestroika*. *Perestroika* means "restructuring," and its primary object was the reform of the economic system. Recognizing that the Soviet economic crisis was far greater than the dislocations of previous decades, Gorbachev called for "radical reforms

Former Soviet leader Mikhail Gorbachev and wife, Raisa, during an official visit to Finland in 1989. From March 1985 until August 1991, Gorbachev had instituted radical political and economic policies to reform communism and the Communist party in order to preserve both; however, his initiatives led to the erosion of the foundation of the Stalinist state and precipitated the downfall of communism throughout eastern Europe. (Markku Ulander/ Woodfin Camp)

in the economic mechanism and restructuring the entire system of economic management" in his 1987 book *Perestroika: New Thinking for Our Country and the World*. Initially, he hoped to revitalize the economy not by transforming its underlying character but rather by attacking the power, privilege, and complacency of the *nomenklatura* while simultaneously improving the efficiency of Soviet workers.

From 1985 to 1989, Gorbachev moved to enact long-term piecemeal reforms aimed at encouraging individual initiative by tying wages to job performance, restructuring the system of pricing and distribution, and limiting the power of the upper-level bureaucrats while supporting more local managerial discretion of state enterprises and encouraging worker-owned enterprises (cooperatives). Other cautious market-oriented reforms were also undertaken. None of these reforms fundamentally altered the economic system from one of state ownership of the means of production and central planning to one of private ownership and individual initiative.

By 1989, the primary story became the rapid disintegration of the Soviet economy. Although it was not certain that governmental reforms were the sole cause of the worsening situation, it was indisputable that they had not improved conditions. Shortages of consumer goods persisted and worsened, and crippling strikes by coal miners and others threatened an already fragile economy. Serious transportation problems and a deteriorating industrial infrastructure undermined the capacity to produce and carry industrial and agricultural products throughout the nation. Furthermore, inflation reduced the ability of many Soviet citizens, especially in the large cities, to pay for foodstuffs and other necessities. In 1989, the Soviet government revealed that its budget deficit was running at the extraordinarily high rate of 14 percent of GNP—approximately $200 billion. Growth rates steadily declined as the Soviet Union's recession turned into a depression (authorities estimate that by 1991 the Soviet Union's economy was contracting by at least 10 percent annually). Former competitors in western Europe and the United States airlifted food or granted large agricultural credits. Meanwhile, the Soviet government asked the West for outright economic aid and investment.

The deepening economic crisis was accompanied by political and social upheavals on a scale not witnessed since 1917. With increasing toleration of dissent in the Soviet Union, open criticism of public officials had become commonplace, and the Soviet people took to the streets. Gorbachev's popularity plummeted as anti-Gorbachev demonstrations and protest marches sprang up in Moscow. At the same time, rising demands for political independence undermined Moscow's authority in most of the 15 republics, including the Baltic states, Georgia, Moldavia, and, of course, Russia, whose president, Boris Yeltsin, challenged Gorbachev at every turn and eventually called for Gorbachev's resignation.

So what was the Soviet leadership to do? Beginning in 1990, it became clear that the top leadership was deeply divided. Radical reformers favored a sharp transition away from central planning and a command economy to a market system. Old-line conservatives (especially those associated with the military and the secret police) abhorred such revolutionary changes. A succession of incompatible economic plans was forwarded and then withdrawn as the Soviet leadership struggled to meet the mounting economic crisis.

Amid all this turmoil, Gorbachev's own economic views remained unclear. What was beyond dispute was that *perestroika*, understood as a method of revitalizing central planning and communism, was dead while revolutionary economic change (which, ironically, had been unleashed by *perestroika*) was accelerating. Throughout the Soviet Union (particularly in some of the outlying republics), revolutionary economic change had acquired a momentum of its own. Private ownership and economic incentives proliferated as events overtook governmental policy. Meanwhile, economic conditions gave no signs of improving.

Glasnost

Gorbachev's much heralded policy of **glasnost** ("openness") reinforced *perestroika*. *Glasnost* constituted the most extensive relaxation of media censorship in Soviet history. For a time, this policy won great sympathy for Gorbachev and distracted public attention from the dislocations entailed by economic reform. It also had a wide appeal beyond Soviet borders. Simultaneously, Gorbachev became the darling of the world press and topped popularity polls in many Western countries.

Despite its foreign policy advantages, *glasnost* was primarily an instrument of domestic policy. Its initial intention was to expose the official corruption and incompetence that Gorbachev blamed in part for the Soviet Union's economic malaise. Gorbachev wished to shake up the *nomenklatura*, particularly the Soviet bureaucracy. He also wished to goad the working class into working. Having neither the incentive to work nor the right to strike, Soviet workers had become complacent, lethargic, and uninspired.

Glasnost was thus linked to *perestroika:* It was a means to reinvigorate a communist society that had lost its drive and sense of purpose. A policy of political liberalization could create a climate of excitement that would energize society by permitting criticism of the old, ineffective patterns of work and governing. *Glasnost* shifted into high gear in December 1986, when Gorbachev freed Andrei Sakharov, the USSR's most famous dissident, from exile in Gorky (now called Nizhnii Novgorod). This act was the culmination of a year in which there were increasing signs of renewed de-Stalinization after more than 20 years of unremitting repression. For example, a major motion picture, *Repentance*, in the form of a parable, tried to come to terms with Stalin's terror. In another attempt to shed light on the buried past, some of the famous Old Bolsheviks who had been Lenin's comrades in arms but were later purged by Stalin and made "unpersons" now reappeared in plays and other published works without being condemned.

But 1986 was only prologue. Over the next few years, Soviet censors made available a steady stream of formerly banned books and movies. Themes that were previously taboo could now be broached. Also foreign films and books appeared in greater profusion than ever before. Even foreign newspapers and magazines could be purchased from newsstands in the shadow of the Kremlin.

Perhaps most astonishing was the transformation of the Soviet mass media from a pliable instrument of state power to gadfly and social critic. Popular new television programs exposed official corruption, abuses of power, and a wide range of social problems (crime, drugs, alcoholism, AIDS). Soviet newspapers and magazines published scorching articles challenging time-honored assumptions and policies, reopening historical questions about the 1917 Communist revolution, Stalin's role in precipitating the Cold War, the decision to invade Czechoslovakia in 1968, and many other matters.

The publication of Aleksandr Solzhenitsyn's book *The Gulag Archipelago* in 1989 signaled a major reassessment of the ideological and historical foundations of the Soviet state. Solzhenitsyn's book detailed the horrors of the Stalinist labor camps, condemned the system that gave rise to Stalin's excesses, indicted Lenin as well as Stalin, and heaped criticism on the Cheka, the forerunner of the KGB. The publication of Solzhenitsyn's book was one sign among many of the fundamental changes occurring throughout Soviet society. In 1990, the State Committee for Public Education abolished the mandatory state examination in Marxism-Leninism; in theory, every institution of higher education now had

Andrei Sakharov: Portrait of a Dissident

ONE OF THE genuine heroes of the movement for human rights and democracy in the Soviet Union was Andrei Sakharov (1921–1990). During the 1950s, he played a key role in developing the Soviet hydrogen bomb. Yet he sacrificed a lucrative and prestigious career when, in the 1960s, he began to criticize the Soviet Union for disregarding human rights and world peace. Not only did he sign petitions against the Soviet government, but he also illicitly published some of his writings in the West, where they were widely acclaimed. In the 1970s, when the Soviet government again clamped down on dissidents, Sakharov was harassed, persecuted, and eventually exiled from Moscow. A primary beneficiary of *glasnost*, he returned to Moscow in 1986 at Mikhail Gorbachev's invitation, where he participated in the 1989 Congress of People's Deputies as a vocal critic of the Communist party hierarchy. The symbolism was both moving and foretelling: A former dissident had assumed a position in the government whose reformulation he had sought. For his advocacy of human rights, Sakharov was awarded the Nobel Peace Prize in 1975—the first Soviet citizen to be so honored.

Sakharov would not live to see his vision triumph, but triumph it did.

Mikhail Gorbachev's release of Andrei Sakharov from exile in 1986 was an act that capped a year in which there were increasing signs of renewed de-Stalinization after more than 20 years of unremitting repression. (AP/Wide World Photos)

the right to replace its previously mandatory course in Marxism-Leninism with courses in philosophy, political economy, or anything else.

No doubt *glasnost* represented a stunning political change within the Soviet Union. As it assumed a life of its own and challenged the very foundations of the Soviet state, some Communist hard-liners expressed their concern and attempted to curtail it by reasserting elements of censorship (such as removing controversial television programs from state television). Yet by the end of 1991, *glasnost* had gone too far to be repealed. Its existence was welcomed by the Soviet people, although they commonly reminded Western observers of their difficult economic plight, pointing out that no matter how wonderful *glasnost* was, "you can't buy bread with it."

Demokratizatsiia

Gorbachev opened a Pandora's box in the late 1980s when he began the process of democratization. Again it appeared that he wished to shake up complacent party members while reinvigorating Soviet society.

Yet as with *perestroika*, it was not clear exactly what Gorbachev meant by his rhetorical flourishes about **demokratizatsiia.** Most likely, he intended a political system of controlled democracy that would ultimately strengthen communism and the party. In a very short time, however, democratization assumed a momentum of its own. Its effects were startling and sometimes unintended. In foreign affairs, Gorbachev's decision to support democracy abroad by not crushing the eastern European independence movement with tanks was partly justified on the grounds that political and economic reforms required that Soviet leaders pay attention to their own nation's significant domestic problems. Yet at the same time, efforts to usher in a system of controlled democracy in the USSR seemed only to hasten the precipitous decline in the authority and influence of the Communist party within the USSR. Even before the failed 1991 coup attempt, it had become clear that heading the party provided no assurance of unchallenged political authority within the Soviet Union. The reasons for this were various, but all were related to *demokratizatsiia*. They included these:

- The emergence of opposing parties and influential noncommunist and anti-communist individuals and parties
- The significant weakening of internal Communist party discipline (and a concomitant increase in acrimony and disagreement within its ranks) while its membership declined throughout the Soviet Union
- The increase in power and influence of the republics at the expense of the power and prestige of the central government
- An evolving governmental structure wherein the government, run by elected officials and headed by an executive president rather than the general secretary, would exercise actual power independent of the Communist party

How had these remarkable changes taken place? In 1988, Gorbachev unveiled a plan for partial democracy within the Soviet Union. The centerpiece of this plan was a new legislative body, the 2,250-member *Congress of People's Deputies* (CPD), which would elect a smaller, full-time Supreme Soviet. Although the elections that were held were remarkable by Soviet standards, they remained mostly controlled, with many elections featuring unopposed Communist candidates or competing candidates—all of whom were members of the party.

Despite the fact that Communist party candidates garnered 87.6 percent of the vote, and were officially committed to Gorbachev's initiatives, the election still sent a clear signal.[5] Communist party officials at all levels—including the party boss in Leningrad (now again called St. Petersburg)—suffered surprising defeats. Furthermore, although the majority of seats were set aside for the Communist party and other official organizations, the rulers had for the first time conceded the principle of free and fair elections—multicandidate contests, open nominations, secret balloting. This in turn led to a breakdown of Communist party discipline and, even more significantly, the emergence of an incipient opposition led by such mavericks as Boris Yeltsin and the late Andrei Sakharov, both of whom won seats in the new parliament. This small but extremely vocal group soon formed itself into the Interregional Group of Deputies, committed to strengthening the republics at the expense of the central government and to the cause of democratic reform at all levels. Within a year, Yeltsin, the popular president of the Russian Republic who had renounced his Communist party membership, would challenge Gorbachev's leadership and champion the cause of the republics with a tenacity that would have been unthinkable (and perhaps fatal) under Stalin or even Brezhnev. Meanwhile, internal party discipline was fragmenting in an unprecedented manner.

In February 1990, Gorbachev abandoned another fundamental principle of the Stalinist system when he persuaded the Central Committee to revoke Article 6 of the Soviet constitution, which stated that "the leading and guiding force of Soviet society and the nucleus of its political system, of state and social organizations, is the Communist party of the Soviet Union." The Marxist-Leninist concept of the party as the vanguard of the working class (and its practical corollary that the party ruled the nation) had always been sacrosanct. This step was interpreted by some observers as a prelude to the emergence of a multiparty political system. In the Baltic states and elsewhere, competing parties did spring up and often easily swept away local Communist parties. Yet no united, democratic party immediately challenged the supremacy of the Communists.

Although Gorbachev retained his position as general secretary of the Communist party, he increasingly based his power and authority on his position as president. This presidency was a reformulated, strengthened position he created in 1989 and to which he was elected by an overwhelming majority in the new Congress of People's Deputies.[6] At that time, the Soviet government assumed a parliamentary-style government that was not truly democratic because Gorbachev's election to the presidency was guaranteed by the Communist majority, which had been a foregone conclusion in the spring 1989 CPD elections.

But this form of government proved to be unstable. Ten months later, Gorbachev was elected by that same body to yet another newly formulated version of the presidency. This time, the presidency was cut loose from the legislature; its future would depend on popular (and not parliamentary) elections. Yet cynics abounded. Lack of popularity made it unlikely that Gorbachev or his party could win such an election. Furthermore, Communist party approval was also rapidly declining, a point emphasized by former foreign minister Eduard Shevardnadze's resignation from the party in July 1991. Increasingly, influential political figures throughout the Soviet Union were basing their careers on either not joining the party or opposing it. Furthermore, Communist officials in the republics had "gone local," championing local causes often in defiance of party edicts or doctrine. For all these reasons, not only Gorbachev but also the party he headed faced the prospect of eventual political defeat at the polls. Precisely because they would mean the end of Communist rule, the possibility of totally free elections was doubted by many. This whole question became moot with the disbanding of the Communist party and Gorbachev's resignation from it in August 1991. The people's anger toward the Communist party, which had ruled them oppressively for some 74 years, could no longer be denied. It seemed ironic that democratization, which along with the other Gorbachev reforms had been designed to invigorate communism and the party, played such a prominent role in its disbanding throughout the Soviet Union.

EVERYDAY LIFE: THE LEGACY OF CENTRAL PLANNING

Nowhere was the effect of the economic and political crisis affecting the Soviet Union more apparent than in the lives of its citizens. The rapid deterioration of the Soviet standard of living during Gorbachev's seven-year rule, in the face of rising expectations, created an unstable and eventual revolutionary situation. With the collapse of central political authority and the emergence of the independent republics, almost all of the economic and social problems outlined in this section have worsened significantly as these new nations attempt to achieve political and economic independence and, in a number of cases, undertake radical economic transformation by trying to achieve (almost overnight) a market economy.

Standard of Living and Scarcity

From the mid-1980s, the quality of everyday life within the former Soviet Union has declined precipitously. Despite the economic woes that were present in the mid-1980s, the standard of living for the average Soviet working-class family had increased significantly, if slowly, over the previous 40 years. Although minimal by Western standards, the improvements were plain to see, especially in the showcase cities of the European USSR that tourists typically visited. In cities such as Moscow, Leningrad, and Kiev, people generally had a guaranteed job, enough to eat, warm clothes in winter, and easy access to public transportation. Furthermore, the majority of families had their own flats with private bathrooms and kitchens. This was due to a large-scale building program that had constructed huge look-alike apartment complexes on the outskirts of Soviet cities. Although it was true that families (father and mother, children, and often at least one grandparent) frequently lived in efficiency apartments—one modest room with a small bathroom and a kitchenette—it was also true that this was an improvement for most Soviet citizens, many of whom could find shelter only with great difficulty during and after World War II.

Nonetheless, the average Soviet citizen continued to lead a relatively austere life with few of the modern conveniences Westerners take for granted. The typical Soviet family had a small refrigerator, most likely without a freezer compartment; a washing machine but no dryer; a stove but not a microwave oven. Also, the typical working-class family had a black-and-white television but no stereo, tape player, or videocassette recorder. Very few Soviet families owned a car.

Adversely affecting the average urban Soviet citizen's quality of life was the inconvenience that pervaded every aspect of daily existence. In this regard, women bore a double burden: They worked full-time and managed the household with little help from their husbands. A seemingly simple chore such as buying groceries was a constant and time-consuming hassle because the marketplace was not designed with customer convenience in mind. The Soviet Union was a society without shopping malls or supermarkets; Soviet housewives had to go from store to store, buying meat in one place, fresh fruits in another, and dairy products or baked goods in yet another.

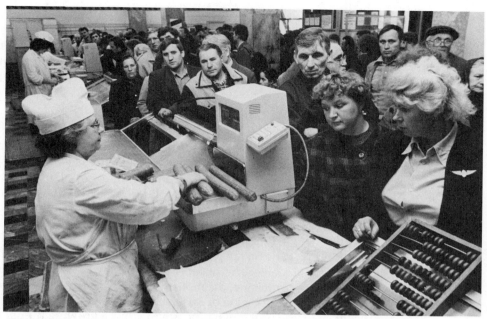

Although the system of central planning succeeded in making the Soviet Union a first-rate military superpower, the USSR's investment priorities in agriculture reflected terrible planning. The result has been long lines at stores with little foodstuffs for purchase. (Reuters/ Bettmann)

Compounding the inconvenience of going from store to store was a scarcity of consumer goods. Often stores were poorly stocked or not stocked at all. Spare parts in particular sizes sometimes simply could not be obtained. Long lines formed quickly whenever word spread that a fresh shipment of meat, fruit, vegetables, or whatever had arrived in a particular store. According to one estimate, the accepted norm was that women spent an average of two hours on line, seven days a week.[7]

These trials of daily life in the former Soviet Union have worsened since 1986 and economic conditions have collapsed since the passing of the USSR. *Perestroika,* under Gorbachev led to the first significant decline in the Soviet standard of living since World War II. The housing situation worsened as building shortfalls and large numbers of disbanded Soviet troops returning from eastern Europe combined to create a serious shortage. Although the Gorbachev government had pledged itself to increasing housing so that all Soviet families would have individual housing by the year 2000, it soon became apparent that it would be unable to meet this goal. With the central government's passing, the chance for any economic progress seems remote.

Other problems also worsened. Widespread inflation has squeezed citizens on fixed incomes. Under Gorbachev, Moscow and Leningrad had borne the brunt of recurrent food shortages, with essentials like bread being in very short supply or too expensive. As such shortages appeared, lines became even longer. With the disintegration of the Soviet empire and the collapse of the economic system (especially with the widespread inability to move and store foodstuffs), widespread hunger and even famine threaten many parts of the republics. Even airlifts of food and medicine from the West so far appear to have made little difference.

Pervasive Social Problems

Official propaganda notwithstanding, the former Soviet Union always had its share of social problems. The way these problems affected Soviet society had been influenced by a variety of factors, including a turbulent history, years of Communist rule, and the economic and political upheaval that was destabilizing the Soviet state. Despite Gorbachev's reform efforts, many of these problems continued to worsen between 1985 and 1991.

Deviant Behavior   The Soviet government struggled with three manifestations of social disorder characteristic of most modern-day states: alcoholism, drugs, and crime. Of these problems, alcoholism was and remains the most persistent and costliest: A large proportion of Russian men participate in a drinking culture, and in recent years the problem has begun to afflict a growing number of women and children. Deeply rooted in Russian culture and Soviet society, alcoholism offers an easy escape from the drudgery, drabness, and despair of everyday life.

Not surprisingly, Soviet leaders worried that this socially accepted practice adversely affects labor productivity as well as the drinker's health and family life. Furthermore, drinking was closely associated with other problems such as a disproportionately high infant mortality rate (due to drinking during pregnancy) and juvenile delinquency. According to one account:

> Eighty percent of juvenile crime is committed by persons who are drunk or who are trying to get money to buy alcoholic beverages. The job is made more complex by the fact that drinking by parents affects the home environment. . . . [A] study in Leningrad indicated that in 88 out of 100 "problem families" one or both parents had a drinking problem. [In some cases] the parents were instrumental in introducing their children to alcohol.[8]

Gorbachev had attempted to do something about alcohol abuse. In spring 1985, he launched his first major reform campaign, an antialcohol program. In the fall of 1986, the government raised the price of vodka—a move designed to reduce demand. However, this effort was soon largely abandoned for various reasons. Since alcohol sales comprised a major source of state revenue, the sales shortfall negatively affected the government's growing budget deficit. Furthermore, individuals manufactured their own (illegal) vodka and, in the opinion of some experts, this bootlegging activity gave rise to organized crime.

Increasing drug abuse also contributed to—and was, in turn, accelerated by—this rise in organized crime. Deteriorating economic conditions created fertile soil for profitable criminal activities of all kinds. As the Gorbachev reforms opened Soviet society to the outside world and reduced the role of the once ubiquitous police in the USSR, prostitution and gambling, as well as drug use and violent crime, flourished. The same kind of symbiotic relationship that exists between these two phenomena in the United States came to plague the Soviet Union. Not surprisingly, Soviet youth are the social group hardest hit by this malignant subculture. In 1986, the Soviet news media first shined the spotlight on this problem and thereafter numerous articles on drugs and drug-related crime appeared in the Soviet press.

Anyone who had ever traveled or lived in the Soviet Union knew that crime existed there, even though one usually felt safer walking on Soviet city streets after dark than in most American cities. But rising street crime was yet another sign of social disintegration during the Gorbachev era. It has hardly improved in light of continuing food shortages and political instability.

Corruption   Without widespread corruption at all levels of society, the Soviet system would probably not have survived as long as it did. The chronic absence of consumer goods and the extremely high prices that the state historically placed on products in great demand created a flourishing black market. Furthermore, so much of Soviet life was bureaucratized and required state approval—everything from individual travel to factory outputs and production schedules—that a routinized system of trading influence (*blat*) and favors had become endemic. To speed official approval or receive favored treatment, it was common for Soviet citizens to use whatever means were available.

The Embattled Consumer: A Soviet View

ALTHOUGH PUBLIC DISCUSSION of the Soviet standard of living (especially compared to the West) is now uncensored and common, the extent of consumer deprivation in the former Soviet Union was long treated as a state secret. Comparisons between the standard of living in the United States and the USSR in Soviet sources typically stressed "bourgeois" decadence and the seamy side of life in America versus the superior Soviet social benefits, including subsidized housing, cheap and efficient public transportation, and socialized medicine. Among the most prominent exploders of this myth was Soviet scholar A.S. Zaychenko. In an article published in a prestigious Soviet scholarly journal in mid-1989, he asserted that in virtually every consumer category, the United States was far ahead of the Soviet Union. Zaychenko looked at everything from nutrition and medical care to housing and transportation. For example, he calculated that "the cost of housing in our country is 41 percent higher" than in the United States and that transportation is 10 times more abundant in the United States than in the USSR. He also pointed out that the average Soviet worker toils 10 to 12 times as long as an American counterpart to buy a kilo of meat, 10 to 15 times as long to buy a dozen eggs. More daringly, Zaychenko observed that "in the last 80 years the differences in the economic accessibility of foods in the United States and the USSR have been particularly pronounced." He cited other quality-of-life indicators as well, such as the availability of desirable consumer goods; number of shopping centers, restaurants, and telephones; and government outlays for education. Zaychenko's message was unmistakable: "Let's face it, comrades, under communism the East-West gap has grown steadily." This was not exactly what Marx predicted or what Lenin promised and it helped explain popular dissatisfaction with Communist rule.

Thus corruption was an institutionalized element of the Soviet system. Gorbachev believed that corruption had caused a pervasive decline in civil morale. Yet despite renewed government campaigns to thwart these activities, they continued unabated. In fact, given the deepening post–Soviet Union economic disorder, the underground shadow economy has become more important (causing some cynics to remark that economic aid should be sent to the black market and not to the new republic governments since only the former is working).

Corruption in the former Soviet Union was by no means confined to illicit black market transactions. It included activities that ranged "from the exchange of favors among various officials to outright bribes, and from epidemic pilferage by blue-collar workers to the padding of expense accounts by their white-collar colleagues." Moreover, in a system that made everyone a state employee, "the average Soviet citizen was less likely to commit a crime against property belonging to other citizens than to take illegal advantage of opportunities offered by his or her public job."[9]

Religion   Marxism-Leninism treated religion as the "opiate" of the people, and Communist leaders historically regarded it as a subversive force from within. Thus the Soviet state long banned all religious instruction and created governmental mechanisms to control churches. Yet Soviet authorities failed to eradicate religion, despite sustained and at times brutal antireligion campaigns. No one knows precisely how many believers there were in the former Soviet Union, but estimates of the number of Russian Orthodox, by far the largest denomination, ranged from 30 million to more than 100 million. In addition, the former Soviet Union encompassed 55 million Muslims (mainly in the central Asian republics), 3 to 4 million Roman Catholics, over a million Baptists, and 850,000 Lutherans (mainly in the Baltic states). Finally, some 1.2 to 1.4 million Jews still lived in the Soviet Union in spite of the fact that Russian governments, dating back to the czarist period, had compiled a long and unenviable record of anti-Semitic pogroms—organized persecutions often condoned by the authorities.

In 1988, on the occasion of the Russian Orthodox church's celebration of the millennium of Christianity in Russia, Gorbachev's policy of *glasnost* effected a remarkable transformation in the government's official stand toward organized religion. Coexistence, not persecution, became the government's official policy. This change was most immediately manifested in the reopening of many Russian Orthodox churches that had long been closed, by the resumption of teaching at an Orthodox seminary after 30 years of prohibition, and by the revival of Russian Orthodox church schools. Several symbolic acts also signaled a major change in official policy toward religion: In 1989, Gorbachev paid an official state visit to Pope Paul II in the Vatican; then in early January 1990, during the Russian Orthodox Christmas season, the bells of St. Basil's Cathedral in Red Square rang for the first time in 70 years, and Soviet television broadcast Russian Orthodox Christmas services (also a first).

This conciliatory policy toward religion benefited all organized religious groups within the USSR. Believers of all faiths could breathe easier and practice their religious beliefs openly without fear of state reprisals. Thus Muslims, whose

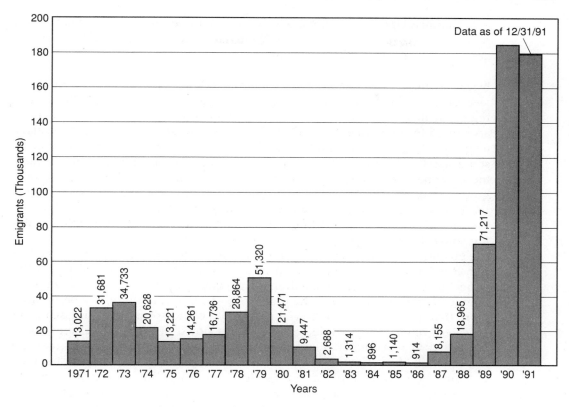

FIGURE 8-1   Jewish Emigration from the USSR

some 20,000 mosques in 1917 had declined to 700 by 1985, saw their number of mosques increase to 1,100 in 1991. Overall, registered congregations for all denominations increased to 18,600, a 50 percent increase in five years.

Circumstances still remain difficult for some groups, such as Jews and Uniate Catholics. Although Soviet Jews were allowed to emigrate en masse after 1989 (see Figure 8-1), anti-Semitism was also on the rise in Russia; this phenomenon was closely associated with a resurgence of right-wing Russian nationalism and with rapidly deteriorating economic conditions. The most notoriously anti-Semitic organization is the fascist *Pamyat* ("Memory"), a group that stresses patriotism and a return to Russian czarism, blames the Communists for the destruction of its homeland, and sees Jews as the secret power manipulators of the Soviet state and the cause of everything that has gone wrong in it. The condition of Uniate Catholics, concentrated in western Ukraine, has actually improved somewhat since the collapse of central political authority. Because Uniates recognize the spiritual authority of the pope and also because they tend to be staunch Ukrainian nationalists, Moscow had persecuted this group with a particular vengeance. In the wake of Ukrainian independence, religious persecution directed at this group has diminished.

Nationalities   As the proliferation of independence movements in various Soviet republics illustrated, the greatest source of internal instability in the Soviet regime's final days was the nationality problem. The 17 largest nationalities accounted for more than 90 percent of the Soviet population, with the Russians (slightly over 50 percent) and the Ukrainians (roughly 16 percent) accounting for some two-thirds of the total population of 294 million people in 1991. Furthermore, some 21 ethnic groups number over 1 million. Among the larger ethnic groups were the 15 nationalities for whom the union republics are named plus the Tatars, Poles, Germans, Jews, Chuvashes, Dagestanis, Bashkirs, and Mordvins. In total, more than 100 different nationalities coexisted in the USSR, speaking some 130 languages.

Historically, the Soviet government used considerable force to assimilate non-Russian groups. One of the primary instruments of state policy was the education system: All schoolchildren were required to learn Russian. As a result, bilingualism was common in the provinces, and Soviet authorities asserted that more than 80 percent of the Soviet population could speak fluent Russian. But repeated, often heavy-handed Soviet efforts aimed at instilling cultural dominance led to resentment. Reinforcing this unhappiness was the fact that the upper levels of the Communist party were dominated by ethnic Russians, who accounted for up to 70 percent of its elite leadership. The failure of the Soviet state to assimilate fully its many national minorities undermined the last great world empire.

THE TRIUMPH OF NATIONALISM OVER COMMUNISM

Moscow had good reason to fear that the "nationality question" might sooner or later be the Soviet Union's undoing. Ironically, it was Gorbachev's reforms that created the climate in which the non-Russian nationalities could dare to strive for self-determination and independence. *Glasnost*, in particular, encouraged a climate of local criticism of the central government and the Communist party. Gorbachev's fateful decision to allow the former "satellite states" (Poland, East Germany, Czechoslovakia, Hungary, Bulgaria, and Romania) to leave the Soviet fold was also crucial. The immense psychological impact of this decision was increased by the geographic proximity of many of the republics to these eastern European nations. Independence became a political idea that was catching. With the demise of the Soviet Union, independence for all of the republics became a reality.

The independence movement surged in the Baltic states first, where Lithuania, Latvia, and Estonia (which had been independent for a time before they were seized by Stalin under his infamous 1939 pact with Hitler) pushed the pace of reform farther and faster than Gorbachev intended. In 1990, Lithuania led the way. On March 11, 1990, it formally declared its independence from Moscow. For his part, Gorbachev refused to recognize the legality of the Lithuanian action. The other two Baltic states took a more cautious line but also made it clear that they too sought independence at the earliest possible date. A stalemate persisted throughout 1990; in early 1991 the tension led to a crackdown. Although surrounded, threatened, and intimidated by Soviet security forces, the government did not surrender. A similar drama was played out in Latvia. The crisis subsided and eventually the two remaining Baltic states declared their independence in August 1991.

Moldavia (formerly known as Bessarabia and now known as Moldova) was also annexed to the USSR in 1940 by Stalin in accordance with his pact with Hitler. Formerly part of Romania, the Moldavian republic joined the Baltic states in demanding great autonomy. Romania has asserted its legal right to this territory since at least the 1960s. In 1989, Moldavia asserted its cultural independence by readopting its traditional Latin alphabet. Although Moldova is hardly homogeneous (there are now many Russian and Turkic Gagauz people living in the republic), the native Moldovans have strong linguistic, ethnic, and historical ties with Romania. It remains uncertain whether the new state of Moldova will one day opt to join Romania or choose to go it alone.

The Caucasus, comprising the republics of Georgia, Armenia, and Azerbaijan, became a particularly unstable region in the late 1980s. Conflict between Armenia and Azerbaijan over the status of the Nagorno-Karabakh region—ethnically Armenian but legally part of Azerbaijan—erupted in bloody violence in February 1988 and again in January 1990. Gorbachev finally used the Soviet army to suppress the uprising, which started with turbulent popular demonstrations against Armenia only to eventually turn against Moscow. As with the Baltic unrest, Gorbachev was not able to resolve the conflict; the best he could do was contain it and buy time.

The most direct challenge to Soviet rule in the Caucasus, however, came from Georgia. In April 1989, the Georgian capital, Tbilisi, was rocked by protests calling for total independence from Moscow. The situation turned tragic when Soviet Internal Ministry troops fired poison gas pellets into a crowd, killing 20 people and injuring hundreds more. Thereafter, events moved quickly. A year later, the reconstituted Georgian legislature declared illegal the 1921 agreement under which Georgia had been incorporated into the Soviet Union. It was only a matter of months before a nationalist coalition called the Round Table, headed by Zvid Gamsakhurdia, a populist with dictatorial tendencies, ousted the Communists from power. In April 1991, two years to the day after the violent confrontation in Tbilisi, Georgia declared its independence from the Soviet Union.

But peace did not follow in Georgia. Instead, a ferocious struggle for power pitted Gamsakhurdia against opposition forces determined to overthrow him. A virtual civil war broke out in the streets of Tbilisi in late 1991, and for several days Gamsakhurdia—Georgia's elected president—was under siege in the presidential palace where he vowed to stay to the bitter end. When the smoke cleared, however, Gamsakhurdia had fled for his life. Subsequent efforts to rally his forces and restore his presidency failed.

Thus, the political future of newly independent Georgia had come under a dark cloud of uncertainty in the early 1990s. To add to the uncertainty, Georgia has its own national minorities problem. About 30 percent of the republic's population is made up of Ossetians, Abkhasians, Armenians, and Azeris, who rule autonomous provinces within Georgia. These minority groups have also expressed a desire for self-determination. But the fiercely nationalistic Georgians, despite internecine quarrels, can be expected to resist the breakup of Georgia as vigorously as they fought for independence from Moscow.

Elsewhere in the vast territories of the Soviet empire, the rumblings of national rebellion could also be detected. In Soviet central Asia, where the indigenous Muslim peoples (Kazakhs, Tadzhikis, Uzbeks, Turkmens, and others) are culturally and linguistically unrelated to the Slavic majority (Russians, Ukrainians, and Belarussians) of the European USSR, riots and other civil disturbances occurred in the late 1980s and early 1990s, but separatist sentiment was notably less evident than in Georgia, Moldavia, and the Baltic states.

Even in the heartland of the USSR—Russia, Ukraine, and Belarus—there were rising demands for a new, looser confederation to replace the highly centralized federal structure. The most notable sign of discontent took place in 1991 when coal miners and other striking workers in all three major Slavic republics pressed for greater political independence from Moscow.

In the Russian Republic, the demands for decentralization were articulated most notably by President Yeltsin. In Ukraine, where previously any signs of nationalism had been ruthlessly suppressed by Moscow, a quiet religious revival, renewed pride in Ukrainian literature and language, and open displays of anti-communism (and even Russophobia) on the streets of Kiev were among the signs of declining allegiance to the USSR. Finally, even once placid Belarus began to rebel against the deterioration in the Soviet economy, for which many Belarussians blamed Gorbachev's ineffectual, ambivalent, and incoherent reform policies.

Even before the attempted coup attempt, many observers believed that the Soviet Union was disintegrating. President Gorbachev attempted to stabilize the situation with a new **Union Treaty** that redefined the relationship between the central government and the republics. This treaty was heavily tilted in favor of the republics, so much so that some experts saw it as fundamentally transforming the very nature of the Soviet state. For instance, the treaty permitted the republics to conduct their own diplomatic and commercial relations with other countries, reserved to them the right of secession, and permitted them to suspend national law while contested laws were being litigated before a constitutional court. It was probably not coincidental that the attempt to remove Gorbachev from power took place on the eve of this treaty's signing. After the coup's failure, the treaty became moot as the floodgates were opened, and a majority of republics announced their intention to become independent (and thus ignore the treaty completely). The Baltic states of Lithuania, Latvia, and Estonia became the first republics formally to break away, and within a week of the unsuccessful coup, they were quickly recognized as sovereign states by other nations. The ethnically diverse Soviet state was grappling with the kinds of lethal disintegrative processes that have, in the past, precipitated the fall of great empires. In December 1991, the Soviet Union ceased to exist.

RUSSIA AND THE COMMONWEALTH: DEMOCRACY OR DICTATORSHIP?

The demise of the Soviet Union was the beginning of a new era of independence for the 15 republics that comprised the old USSR. Even before the USSR was formally dissolved, Russia's president, Boris Yeltsin, had engaged in talks with the leaders of the newly independent republics in search of a new set of arrangements aimed at reassociation. These negotiations proved to be highly contentious and were, at best, a limited success. The Baltic states and Georgia refused to consider entering a new association with Russia on any terms. The other eleven republics eventually agreed to join the loose-knit federation, the Commonwealth of Independent States, but reserved the right to opt out at any time. Ukraine—second only to Russia in territory, population, and wealth—has been particularly suspicious of Moscow's motives and truculent in its insistence on unimpeded freedom of action. Thus, for example, Kiev (Ukraine's capital) announced steps to raise its own army and create a currency distinct from the ruble.

Given the enormous economic, social, and political problems plaguing all the nations and regions of the former Soviet Union, what are the prospects for Russia and the new Commonwealth of Independent States (CIS)? The first set of questions revolves around the uncertain status of the CIS. As pundits were quick to point out, the Commonwealth is misnamed: A common denominator for the member states has yet to be found and there is little real wealth (despite abundant natural resources) on which to base any hopes for a prosperous future. The fact that Minsk, not Moscow, is the capital of the Commonwealth is a telltale sign of its troubled birth. The reason Minsk was chosen is its location outside the territory of either Russia or Ukraine. Minsk, of course, is also the capital of Belarus, a nation no other member state is likely to see as a threat.

Boasting 75 percent of the total land mass and about half the population of the former Soviet Union (146 million out of a total of 290 million), Russia will continue to be the dominant presence in Eurasia so long as it remains intact. But Russia, not unlike the old USSR, is a sprawling multinational empire with internal fault lines that could lead to another upheaval and perhaps even another breakup. Although this possibility remains unlikely, the danger of chronic instability in Russia (which possesses an immense nuclear arsenal second only to that of the United States) is most unsettling. It was to ameliorate this situation that the United States and other Western powers extended large-scale economic and technical aid to Russia in the early 1990s. The United States was especially concerned that the new Russian government might not be able to control the tens of thousands of nuclear weapons it had stockpiled. One nightmare scenario involved the illegal sale of nuclear weapons to terrorists or to a ruthless dictator like Saddam Hussein of Iraq. President Yeltsin gave repeated assurances that Russian nuclear arms were under tight security, and offered to cut the numbers

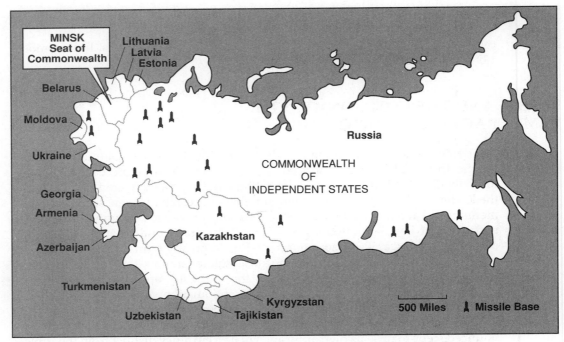

FIGURE 8-2   Soviet Disunion: The Commonwealth of Independent States
SOURCE: Courtesy of *The Star Tribune* (Minneapolis/St. Paul).

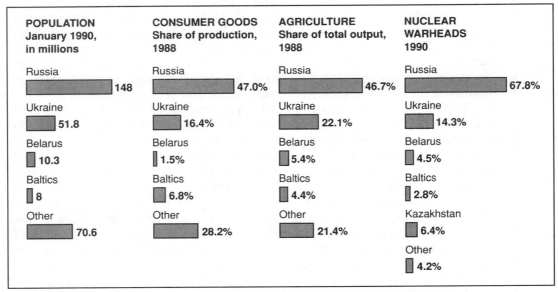

FIGURE 8-3   The Emerging Dominance of Russia and Ukraine after the Breakup of the Soviet Union
SOURCE: Courtesy of *The Star Tribune* (Minneapolis/St. Paul).

of such arms drastically if the United States would reciprocate. But the question remained: If the internal turmoil that appeared to make Russia virtually ungovernable in the early 1990s was to go on indefinitely—or worse, to give way to civil war—could anyone promise that Russia's nuclear arms would be kept under lock and key?

The problem presented by this indirect nuclear threat was compounded by the fact that when the Soviet empire broke into 15 pieces, several of the new independent states—namely, Ukraine, Kazakhstan, and Belarus—fell heir to the nuclear weapons which the former Soviet government had emplaced on their territories. As a result, the world suddenly had several new nuclear powers with which to contend. Russia sought to gather all the nuclear arms of the former Soviet state into its own arsenal, but both Ukraine and Kazakhstan initially resisted. Both new states viewed their nuclear weapons as bargaining chips and perhaps also as insurance policies in their future dealings with Moscow.

Whether Russia will be able to forge a new and lasting set of relationships with the independent republics and with the West depends, to a large extent, on the type of political system that will emerge from the ruins of the former Soviet state. Cooperation and harmony between Moscow and the various republics is likely to be achieved, if at all, in one of two ways: a stable, prosperous, and democratic Russia one day could coax the other CIS member states into a closer association or a resurgent Russian nationalism, coupled with the rise of a new authoritarian state, could lead to an attempt to restore the old czarist empire.

At its inception, economic interdependence—more precisely, the *dependence* of the other republics on Russia—was the only glue holding the unstable Commonwealth together. Soviet leaders, beginning with Stalin, had deliberately set up Soviet industry in such a way that manufacturing operations in the various republics were not self-sufficient but rather depended on raw materials and components supplied by plants in other republics. Moreover, not only the smaller republics but even Ukraine depended on Russia's abundant natural resources, in particular fossil fuels and electrical power. But this interdependence was always underwritten by Moscow through heavy subsidies in the form of extremely low prices it charged for the raw materials, power, and infrastructure Russia supplied. The economic crisis Russia faced in the early 1990s, however, compelled Moscow to charge world-market prices for its products and thus jeopardized even the economic underpinning of the fledgling CIS.

How *will* Russia and the CIS be ruled? This question becomes all the more problematical in the light of the destabilizing economic troubles afflicting Russia. One possibility, mentioned earlier, is that continuing chaos and a growing public desire for order and security may lead to the rise of a new authoritarian state reinforced by a strong Russian nationalist ideology. Such a government would not only be consonant with a centuries-old tradition of despotism and centralized rule but it would also offer the most straightforward solution to the extreme disorder that has characterized Russian society and politics in recent times.

Two other scenarios at opposite ends of the political spectrum are also possible. Some sort of totalitarianism could make a comeback, although communism has clearly lost its ideological vitality and popular appeal. Without an

Gorbachev versus Yeltsin: A Tale of Two Presidents

IN JUNE 1991, Boris Yeltsin became the first popularly elected leader in Russian history, winning a landslide victory to become president of the Russian Republic. Two months later, in August 1991, Yeltsin faced down hard-liners who ousted Mikhail Gorbachev, president of the Union of Soviet Socialist Republics (USSR), in an attempted military coup. At a dramatic moment, when the outcome was still uncertain, Yeltsin climbed onto a tank and read a now-famous manifesto declaring the coup illegal and demanding the restoration of constitutional order, including the return of President Gorbachev to power.

There was great irony in this situation. Boris Yeltsin owed his meteoric rise in Soviet politics to Mikhail Gorbachev. Yeltsin was an obscure party functionary in Sverdlovsk in the mid-1980s when Gorbachev, who had just become the top party leader, brought him to Moscow to head the local party organization. But Yeltsin soon broke with Gorbachev, charging Gorbachev with foot-dragging on real reforms and advocating more radical liberalization policies than Gorbachev was willing to countenance. Incensed at Yeltsin's sharp and highly public criticisms, Gorbachev removed the maverick Yeltsin from the Politburo in 1987.

But Yeltsin did not surrender. Instead, he built a popular following in his native Russia. With his election in 1991, Yeltsin upstaged Gorbachev, who had never been popularly elected and therefore lacked the kind of mandate Yeltsin could claim.

But it was Yeltsin's heroics in August 1991, including his key role in saving Gorbachev from an uncertain fate, that finally put Yeltsin in a dominant position vis-à-vis Gorbachev, whose credibility and prestige—and thus, his power—evaporated after the coup attempt. In the end, Gorbachev felt compelled not only to resign his chairmanship of the Communist party and to separate the party from the government, but also found it necessary to accept the dissolution of the Soviet Union. Gorbachev resigned his position as president on December 25, 1991.

Yeltsin remained in charge of the Russian government, but he faced intense opposition in the parliament due to the deepening economic crisis.

Russian Republic leader Boris Yeltsin represents a new breed of postcommunist political leaders dedicated to establishing democracy and a new market-based economic system. (Bill Burke/Impact Visuals)

ideology capable of mobilizing the masses, a full-blown totalitarian state is unlikely to reappear in Russia. If economic disaster strikes, however, one cannot rule out the possibility of a fascist movement arising. Finally, democracy may well flourish, but given the history of Russian and Soviet tyranny, the severe adjustment shocks associated with the transition from central planning to a free-market economy, and the sheer challenge of governing a country as large as Russia, this alternative, however desirable in theory, is the most difficult to realize in practice.

THE COLLAPSE OF COMMUNISM IN EASTERN EUROPE

In 1989, under popular pressure, the Communist regimes of the so-called satellite states of eastern Europe crumbled. The year began with political unrest and steps toward free elections in Poland and Hungary; it ended with the ouster of the reviled and beleaguered Communist government of Erich Honecker in East Germany, the tearing down of the Berlin Wall, and the opening of the intra-German border. In addition, by the end of the year, a groundswell had toppled the Communist regimes in Czechoslovakia, Romania, and Bulgaria. In Czechoslovakia, a soft-spoken playwright, Vaclav Havel, led the revolution and became the new president. In Romania, the Stalinist dictator Nicolae Ceauşescu was overthrown amid much civil violence; Ceauşescu and his wife were tried by an impromptu "court," sentenced to death, and summarily executed. In Bulgaria, the Communist leadership bowed to popular pressure and quietly stepped down.

The collapse of communism in eastern Europe ranks as one of the most momentous political events of the post–World War II period, not least because it signaled the end of the Cold War. This fact was underscored by Gorbachev's agreement not only to allow German reunification but also to withdraw the Soviet Union's nearly 400,000 troops from eastern Germany and to allow the reunited Germany to remain in NATO. No less significant was Moscow's acquiescence in the dissolution of the Warsaw Pact, which was formally accomplished in the spring of 1991.

The Future

The demise of communism in eastern Europe was welcomed with great enthusiasm in the West. In Poland, Czechoslovakia, and Hungary, the new popularly elected governments moved quickly to solidify democratic reforms and dismantle the failed machinery of central planning. The first task has proved easier in the short run than the second, and doing away with the old economic order has been much easier than creating a new one. For 70 years, the Soviet Union presented itself as the model for other societies seeking to make the transition from capitalism to communism, but there are no models for societies wishing to go from communism to capitalism.

Poland, Hungary, and Czechoslovakia have all chosen somewhat different paths to the marketplace. Poland's "big bang" approach (also called "shock therapy") is the most radical alternative. Some of the main elements in this transition plan are making the currency convertible, liberalizing foreign trade, allowing prices to rise sharply, closing inefficient plants, creating a stock market, allowing free enterprise, restraining wages, curtailing state subsidies, and balancing the budget. Gradually selling off state assets to private owners (*privatization*) is another important feature of the Polish plan. Incidentally, Poland was the only communist state in eastern Europe that had not collectivized agriculture on a large scale. Ironically, this "flaw" in Poland's former socialist economy in some small measure facilitated the transition back to a market-based system.

Hungary and Czechoslovakia also opted for market economies but rejected Polish-style shock therapy in favor of more cautious transition programs. All the elements of the Polish plan are present in these two countries' approaches, but the idea is to create a free-market system more slowly. The model for Hungary and Czechoslovakia seems to be closer to the social democracy of Sweden or France than the commercial democracy of the United States or Great Britain under Margaret Thatcher.

Because there is no tried-and-true formula for switching from communism to capitalism, each country is experimenting and improvising as it goes along. For example, Czechoslovakia chose to privatize the economy in two steps: First the government auctioned off small enterprises; then it converted large state-owned firms into joint-stock companies and sold shares to private investors on the open market.

Hungary had undertaken market reforms aimed at economic decentralization in the late 1960s, only to abandon the experiment in the 1970s. Under this so-called New Economic Mechanism, enterprises could make their own deals with each other, farmers could sell to state trading companies or on the open market, and small-scale private entrepreneurs operated legally. So even though the nation's economy had stagnated in the 1980s, Hungary was no stranger to the concept of market reforms. In his 1990 book *The Road to a Free Economy,* Janos Kornai, one of Hungary's leading reform economists, drew up a blueprint designed specifically for his country, arguing that the most urgent priorities were to cut state subsidies, balance the budget, and implement price reform.[10]

Romania and Bulgaria languished in a kind of limbo between the old system and the new. Central planning was discredited, but democratic institutions were slow to take root, and political uncertainties hampered progress toward economic reform.

The political future of eastern Europe is far from settled. With the exception of Czechoslovakia, no eastern European society has democratic traditions on which to draw. Nor had capitalism reached an advanced stage of development in most places. Every government in the region now faces enormous economic and social difficulties. In Czechoslovakia and Romania, for example, ethnic tensions also complicate efforts to stabilize economies damaged by decades of gross mismanagement. The possibility of a lurch to the right or even disintegration cannot be ruled out. In the 1930s, Hungary, Romania, and Bulgaria were attracted by fascist ideology and made common cause with Nazi Germany. Hence the alternative to communism in eastern Europe is not necessarily democracy. If history is any guide, dictatorship would be a more natural outcome of chaos and confusion in a region where conflict has twice in this century led to major wars.

YUGOSLAVIA: THE NIGHTMARE SCENARIO

Yugoslavia, even as it existed several years ago, is no more. Within the former Soviet Union and throughout eastern Europe, Yugoslavia's disintegration is commonly understood to comprise the nightmare scenario, the prospect of politi-

AUSTRIA

HUNGARY

SLOVENIA

Zagreb

Western
Slavonija

Eastern
Slavonija

Krajina

CROATIA

ROMANIA

VOJVODINA

* Belgrade

BOSNIA
and
HERZEGOVINA

SERBIA

BULGARIA

A D R I A T I C   S E A

MONTENEGRO

ITALY

KOSOVO

MACEDONIA

Areas for stationing
UN security forces,
February, 1992

ALBANIA

GREECE

cal collapse fueled by ethnic hatred that threatens almost all former Communist states.

By 1990, democracy and free elections had replaced communism. Accompanying the rise of democracy came the unleashing of divisive ethnic fervor and the creation of numerous native parties among Yugoslavia's many peoples. Economic collapse accompanied the uprising of nationalistic feelings as production, trade, and tourism all declined dramatically while bankruptcies and unemployment rose. By June 1991, Croatia and Slovenia, the two wealthiest, northern Yugoslav republics, declared independence. What followed was a bloody civil war which claimed an estimated 10,000 casualties. The efforts of these republics proved largely successful and by January 1992 both were widely recognized as independent nation-states. Despite the cessation of conflict, the remaining Yugoslavia (headed by a powerful Serbia) remained unstable. In the spring of 1992, intense fighting broke out in Bosnia and Herzegovina after these republics declared independence from the rump Yugoslav state. In addition, the Yugoslav republics themselves had their own internal ethnic divisions and soon declared independence. By February 1992, the United Nations voted to send a 14,000-person peace-keeping force to Yugoslavia to monitor the cease-fire and protect Croatia's Serbian minority. Yugoslavia continued to self-destruct and by April 1992, only Serbia and Montenegro remained together. The question was: How had it happened so quickly? A brief history proves useful.

Unlike the other eastern European nations, which were liberated from German occupation by Stalin's armies, Yugoslavia was liberated by the partisan forces of Marshal Josip Broz Tito. Because of his role in the Yugoslav resistance movement, Tito emerged as a national hero and eventually became the symbol of a new Yugoslav nationalism.

In the immediate postwar era, Tito refused to take orders from Moscow, and Stalin retaliated by excommunicating Yugoslavia from the socialist commonwealth. Shortly thereafter, Tito began to take definite steps to popularize his rule, first by slowing the pace of agricultural collectivization and then by totally abandoning it. Today, Yugoslavia's farm production remains predominantly in private hands.

However, Yugoslav communism has made its most distinctive mark in the realm of industrial relations. Rejecting the extreme centralization that had been practiced in the former Soviet Union, Tito proclaimed the advent of a new form of socialist economic organization based on the concept of *self-management*. This granted a large measure of regional autonomy—at least in principle—to the six republics in the Yugoslav federation. More significantly, it led to the creation of *workers' councils* in economic enterprises. Elected by factory or enterprise workers, these councils in turn elect management committees, and the management committees, meeting as regional associations, choose the directors of the various enterprises, subject to approval by the party. In 1950, workers gained the right to strike, trade unions were declared independent, and direct economic planning was replaced by "planned guidance."

In some respects, then, the Yugoslav brand of communism was designed to be more open and democratic than Soviet-style Communism. Even the party (renamed the League of Yugoslav Communists in 1952) was supposed to play a guiding rather than a directing or controlling role in society—a point emphasized by the stipulation that no party official except Tito could hold a government post. Among Yugoslavia's many unique features was its eight-member presidency, reflecting the multiethnic character of Yugoslav society. Comprised of six republics and two autonomous regions, it was the most ethnically diverse nation in eastern Europe.

Of this system, one noted writer pointed out:

> Authentic democracy exists only in areas of no political importance, such as social security and public health; and the Yugoslavs, like the Russians, like to think of "democracy" as lower-level citizen participation in administration, so-called "output"

participation, in lieu of permitting a popular input to major choices, of leadership or policies.[11]

Even the vaunted principle of workers' self-management was much diluted by party dominance in the economic enterprises; council members and delegates routinely turned out to be party members. In the past, the workers' role in management was also "considerably circumscribed by state controls upon the economy, the fixing of prices and wages, and sundry bureaucratic meddling."[12]

The 1970s saw a general tightening of controls over the Yugoslav economy and society. The prohibition against mixing party and governmental roles was eroded, and freedom of expression, previously allowed within broad limits, was constricted. Following a crackdown on dissident college professors and students, Yugoslav prisons were filled with hundreds of political detainees.

Even so, Yugoslavia was unique among Communist regimes. One scholar sketched the following picture of the nation under Tito:

> Most art and literature are apolitical, and artists and writers are free to create so long as they do not criticize sharply. There is no a priori censorship, only the possibility of subsequent ban by court order; and private publishers produce nearly as many titles as official publishing houses. Newspapers are nearly uniform, but they are very informative in comparison with those of other East European Communist states, not to speak of the Soviet Union. The foreign press is freely available. Party spokesmen denounce Western influences in the press, but magazines continue to carry sensationalism and nudes, quite contrary to Communist morality. Perhaps fifteen million persons cross the borders yearly. There is freedom of association as long as it is not anti-party. Tito has never shot and seldom jailed his opponents.[13]

During the 1980s, the power and authority of Yugoslavia's central government declined rapidly. Yugoslavia was an artificial nation composed of peoples of significantly different ethnic, cultural, and religious backgrounds—Greek Orthodox Serbs and Montenegrins, Roman Catholic Croats and Slovenes, a Muslim minority in Serbia, and mixed Bosnians, Herzegovinians, and Dalmatians. The glue that held them together was Tito's prestige and authority. When Tito died in 1980, fissures that had existed all along turned into conspicuous cracks in the structure of Yugoslav unity. The fall of communism in eastern Europe accelerated the process of disintegration. In the early 1990s, the economy was battered by heavy foreign debt ($16 billion), skyrocketing inflation (100 percent), and high unemployment (20 percent). Yugoslav society became caught up in long-simmering ethnic rivalries and animosities, and the central government was increasingly paralyzed by conflict between the republics. Politically prosperous Slovenia and Croatia were at odds with the traditionally dominant Serbs over the future of the nation. Serbia's hard-line president, Slobodan Milosevic, wanted to keep Yugoslavia's communist-led centralized federal system, while the center-right governments of Slovenia and Croatia favored a loose-knit confederation and a free-market economy. In June 1991, both Slovenia and Croatia declared their independence and a bloody civil war between Serbia and Croatia ensued. Yugoslavia, like the USSR, became a casualty of discredited communism, economic malaise, and rising nationalism and serves as a sobering reminder of the fragility of post-communist governments.

CHINA: REFORM AND RELAPSE

The path to power for Mao Zedong's Chinese Community party (CCP) differed sharply from that taken by Lenin's Bolsheviks. Because Mao's victory followed a protracted guerrilla war against the Japanese and the Chinese Nationalist government of Chiang Kai-shek, the army played a much greater role in Mao's revolutionary theory than in Lenin's. When the Chinese Communists came to power in 1949, the army and the party were fused into a single organization. Acting as a virtual government, the army was charged not only with fighting but also with administration, including maintenance of law and order, construction and public works, management of the economy, and education and indoctrination. In effect, the army became the nucleus of the People's Republic, the new government of China.

China under Mao

In the early 1950s, the People's Republic of China was heavily dependent on political, economic, and military assistance from the Soviet Union, a dependency heightened by the Korean War (1950–1953). The USSR, ruled by the aging Stalin, insisted that the fledgling Communist government in Beijing emulate the Stalinist model. Thus the political sturctures of the Chinese state, as well as the thrust of Chinese economic and foreign policies, closely resembled those of the Soviet Union. Everything from collectivization of agriculture and a lopsided emphasis on industrial investment to the Soviet educational system was borrowed almost without modification.

The turning point came when Stalin's successor, Nikita Khrushchev, made his famous speech at the 20th Party Congress in 1956, in which he denounced the crimes of Stalin and proclaimed the advent of peaceful coexistence with the West. From that point on, the CCP, under Mao's leadership, went its own erratic way.

The Great Leap Forward (see Chapter 3), launched in 1958, represented Mao's declaration of independence from the Soviet model of industrial development. In place of the Stalinist emphasis on heavy industry, especially large-scale mining and metallurgical complexes, the Great Leap stressed decentralized industrialized production to take advantage of China's greatest natural resource—human labor. The small-scale industrial enterprises known as *backyard steel furnaces* became the symbol of this labor-intensive approach.

Mao's *mass line,* holding that everything could be achieved through the inspired efforts of the peasant masses, replaced the Soviet party-state bureaucracy as the driving force behind the revolutionary transformation of society. The Great Proletarian Cultural Revolution (see Chapter 3), the Mao-inspired reaction against all bureaucracy, was the culmination of this approach. For China, the Soviet system had become a countermodel.

Changing of the Guard

The deaths of Zhou Enlai and Mao Zedong, the People's Republic's two great founders, made the year 1976 a watershed in modern Chinese history. According to one prominent China scholar, ''Mao's death marked the end of an era; what was not clear was who would lead China and in what direction in the era to come."[14]

After two years of halting reforms, the nation's post-Mao leadership under the direction of Deng Xiaoping (who had twice been purged by Mao for his alleged lack of revolutionary zeal) "mounted a major campaign to abandon ideological dogma and to adopt pragmatism—symbolized by the slogans 'practice is the sole criterion of truth' and 'seek truth from facts.'"[15] Economic development replaced class struggle, and a welcome mat replaced the "no trespassing" sign that had impeded China's trade relations with the West for nearly three decades. Banished were the mass campaigns, crash programs, hero worship, and ideological fanaticism that had been the hallmarks of Maoism.

Expanding trade, especially with the industrial democracies, became a principal aim of Beijing's diplomacy. Deng's economic reforms were implemented gradually between 1978 and 1982 as he carefully and patiently consolidated his power within the ruling Politburo. By the fall of 1982, the reform-minded Deng was in full command.

Trend toward Pragmatism

Economic reforms were at first accompanied by signs of political democratization. In 1978, a phenomenon that came to be known as the *Democracy Wall* captured worldwide attention. On this wall, located in the heart of Beijing, opinions and views at variance with the official line—including blunt criticisms of the existing system and leaders—were displayed with the tacit approval of the government. In addition to this unprecedented freedom of the "press," a newfound freedom of speech also blossomed around the Democracy Wall. But then, in 1979, the government clamped down on dissent. Subsequent arrests, show trials, and other all-too-familiar forms of political repression indicated clearly that the CCP was not about to loosen its iron grip on the levers of political power.

Nonetheless, in the fall of 1982, the leadership announced several changes in the structure of the political system—most important, the abolition of the post of chairman, which had been occupied by Mao until his death in 1976. This move formally ended an era in which the CCP had been dominated by the so-called *cult of personality.* For years, the fate of the nation had hinged on the whims of the semideified and fanatical Mao. Deng's reforms also reinforced the tendency toward increased pragmatism and stability at the top echelons of the party and the state, although they did not signal any weakening of the regime's monopoly on political power.

Bureaucratic Reshufflings

Nor were personnel changes confined to the military. Deng directed a large-scale reorganization of the convoluted (and bloated) Chinese bureaucracy—the number of ministries, commissions, and agencies directly under the State Council was slated for reduction by nearly half from about 100 to just over 50. At the same time, Deng conducted a quiet, bloodless purge. Aging cadres were replaced by younger ones at all levels, and potential leaders were sought out and placed on a "fast track" to provide them with long-denied career incentives.

This rejuvenation of China's economic and political leadership also reached the top echelons of the system: Some 60 percent of the Central Committee members chosen at the 12th Party Congress in 1982 were new. The average age of these new members was 51. Seven new members were "elected" to the 22-member Politburo as well. The process continued in 1985 when 64 more new members replaced old leaders on the Central Committee and six new Politburo members replaced ten superannuated ones. The new members were in their 50s and 60s; most of the retired members were in their 70s and 80s. In addition, Deng apparently laid the groundwork for his own succession.[16]

Market-oriented Reforms

The most far-reaching reforms, however, came in the economic sphere. Economic reforms led to a doubling of China's foreign trade during the Sixth Plan years (1981–1985). Even more dramatic was Beijing's decision to seek foreign loans and direct foreign investment, primarily in the West. This policy change—especially the solicitation of Western investment capital—would have been inconceivable in Mao's time. China's new "open door" approach to relations with the West was designed to modernize the nation's industrial sector as rapidly as possible.

Agriculture also underwent a major transformation. The watchword was "decollectivization"—a return to family-based farming. After considerable experimentation, the regime settled on a system whereby the state made contracts with individual households to purchase specified products. Peasants were guaranteed the use of their land—still formally state-owned—for at least 15 years. China's farmers obtained all the proprietary rights normally associated with ownership except the right to sell the land. Most important, they were given the freedom to dispose of their produce however they chose.

How did China's farmers respond to these new "free-market" reforms? Statistics on agricultural production under the Sixth Plan tell the story: Output of farm commodities increased, on average, more than 8 percent a year, more than double the long-term trend from 1953 to 1980.[17] With a population of well over 1 billion, China can hardly afford to ignore success on this scale. It thus seems unlikely that its leaders will reverse the direction of the agricultural reform movement.

In industry and commerce, too, China moved toward somewhat greater reliance on market forces. Direct control by central planning authorities gave way to less intrusive regulatory mechanisms. The resulting decentralization was designed to simulate market conditions in which prices and profits gradually replaced mandatory production quotas. According to China's own publicized timetable, a great majority of the enterprises should have become solely responsible for their own profit and loss by 1990.[18]

In the fall of 1986, two events underscored Deng's determination to forge ahead with economic reforms: The city government of Shenyang in northeast China announced that a debt-ridden factory had been allowed to go bankrupt (the first bankruptcy in the nation's 37-year history), and a small securities market opened in the same city at about the same time (another first for China). But politics soon derailed the train of economic reform.

Massacre in Tiananmen Square

In the late 1980s, the engines of economic reform stalled. Inflation and political unrest led to a conservative backlash, which reached its apogee in mid-1989. It was at this time that a civilian massacre and the ouster of China's leading reformer, Zhao Ziyang, dashed all hope of freedom and democracy in China, at least in the near term.

In May 1989, students and workers staged a mass march in Beijing to demand democratic reforms. The protest grew like the clouds of a summer storm; throngs of demonstrators camped in Tiananmen Square, making speeches and shouting slogans. The rest of the world watched in rapt attention as the drama unfolded before Western television cameras. The fact that Mikhail Gorbachev, the father of "reform communism," visited Beijing (the first Sino-Soviet summit in three decades) that same month only added to the sense of high drama. When the unrest spread throughout the country, Beijing declared martial law—to no avail.

Army troops entered the Chinese capital with tanks and armor on June 3; it soon became apparent that the show of force was not a bluff. The crackdown that ensued brought the democracy movement to a bloody end. Hundreds (possibly

Under the shadow of Mao's portrait, tens of thousands of striking Beijing University students and supporters demonstrated in Tiananmen Square from April 17 to June 4, 1989, in a call for democratic freedom and government reforms. Many of the protesters camped out in tents and participated in hunger strikes for the duration of the protest as a sign of devotion to their cause. The protest movement ended in a bloodbath in which an estimated 1,500 people died and as many as 10,000 were wounded. Before leaving the square, the demonstrators erected a statue to symbolize democracy and liberty, the "Goddess of Freedom," modeled after the Statue of Liberty. (Reuters/Bettmann)

thousands) of protesters were killed or injured, and many more were arrested. Subsequently, security forces rounded up thousands of dissenters, and at least 31 were tried and executed. The atrocities against unarmed civilians in the *Tiananmen Square massacre* proved clearly that China was still at its core a totalitarian state.

China's dismal human rights record gave rise to domestic pressures on the Bush administration (pressures that were resisted by President Bush) to deny China "most favored nation" (MFN) treatment, which would allow Chinese exports to the United States to enjoy the same relatively low tariffs available to America's "most favored" trading partners. Beijing's arms sales to the Third World have also been an issue. For example, China reportedly sold a nuclear reactor to Algeria and was considering the sale of offensive missiles to Pakistan. Yet, with top leaders in China in their 80s, the United States has downplayed potential conflict between the two nations, perhaps hoping that a younger generation of Chinese leaders will loosen their political grip and pursue reform. This low level of tension between the two nations provides a partial explanation of why the People's Republic did not use its veto power in the United Nations to block a key resolution authorizing the use of force against Iraq to remove Iraqi forces from Kuwait in early 1991.

OTHER COMMUNIST STATES

The collapse of communism in Europe did not spread to Asia. On the contrary, the Communist regimes and parties in the Asian Pacific region clung tenaciously to Marxist-Leninist ideology and Stalinist institutions despite declining Soviet support and increasing economic difficulties.

Asian Communism

North Korea, Vietnam, Laos, and Cambodia, are Communist states that were once securely within the Soviet camp. All these governments owed a considerable economic and political debt to the USSR. All emulated Soviet (or in some instances Chinese) political institutions and practices to a striking degree. All supported Soviet foreign policy positions in international forums such as the United Nations.

But if the Asian communist states borrowed much from the Soviet model, they were by no means carbon copies of the USSR. For example, North Korea has evolved a personality cult built on the semimythical achievements of Kim Il-Sung, the absolute dictator of the country since the end of World War II. This personal-style dictatorship resembles the Soviet system under Stalin; in some respects, however, North Korea's brand of communism is more reminiscent of Maoism than of Stalinism. Vietnam has been a particularly active totalitarian state whose revolutionary zeal has remained largely intact.[19] Each state has adapted an alien ideology to its own peculiar history and culture.

Castro's Cuba

Fidel Castro came to power in Cuba in 1959, after the triumph of his rebels over the government of Fulgencio Batista. At first he was not considered a Communist leader. But when Cuba's relations with the United States became acerbic, Castro suddenly proclaimed himself a Marxist-Leninist and turned to the Soviet Union. After some hesitation, Moscow accepted Cuba into the fraternity of Soviet-led socialist states in the early 1960s. Subsequently, Castro grew more radical than his Soviet patrons in both domestic and foreign policy. The cult of personality surrounding Castro resembles that of Stalin, although it has stopped short of the hero worship of Kim Il-Sung in North Korea.

The party has played a relatively minor role in Cuban politics, which is dominated by Castro's personal leadership and the well-trained Cuban army. As of the late 1980s, perhaps 80 percent of the party leaders had military or guerrilla backgrounds. Accordingly, much of Cuban society and economic activity is organized along military lines, with economic production (especially agriculture) actually supervised and directed by the army. Even the educational system is permeated with military symbols, slogans, songs, and themes.

Anti-Americanism has been a cornerstone of Castro's ideology ever since the late 1950s. During the first decade of his rule, Cuba supported revolution in Latin America much more militantly than the USSR—a posture that caused considerable difficulties for Moscow in its dealings with Latin American governments. When the Soviet Union invaded Czechoslovakia in 1968, however, Castro counted himself among Moscow's staunchest defenders. In the years that followed, Cuba became more and more closely linked to the Soviet Union, in part because of Havana's growing economic dependency on trade with and subsidies from Moscow. In the 1970s, Castro took steps to organize the Cuban government and society along Soviet lines. In foreign policy, Cuba acted as Moscow's proxy in two military interventions on the African continent, in Angola and Ethiopia. All in all, while Castro's brand of communism has not been identical to that found in the Soviet Union before 1985, the similarities greatly overshadowed the differences.

Nevertheless, the Cuban Revolution has fascinated many foreign observers. In part, this fascination can be traced to the romantic aura surrounding the revolution and its charismatic leaders. Furthermore, the Castro government has probably improved the lot of the ordinary Cuban in several respects. There are now more schools, clinics, and public facilities than there were under the prerevolutionary regime, and once-private beaches and expensive hotels have been opened to the general public. Class privileges seem to have been muted and submerged, though not altogether obliterated. Still, the Cuban people have paid a high price for these benefits, as widespread prosperity has remained an elusive goal and individual freedom has been sacrificed in the name of social duty.

Jacobo Timerman, an Argentine journalist who had firsthand knowledge of life in Castro's Cuba going back to the beginning of 1959, wrote that "the collapse

The End of History?

IN 1989, FRANCIS FUKUYAMA published an article entitled "The End of History?" in which he declared not only the end of the Cold War and the triumph of the West over Soviet Communism but also the "unabashed victory of economic and political liberalism." Published several months before the collapse of communism in eastern Europe and more than two years before the dissolution of the Soviet Union, this article asserted that "what we may be witnessing is . . . the end point of mankind's ideological evolution and the universalization of Western liberal democracy as the final form of human government."

Fukuyama pointed to the trend away from socialist economic principles and collectivist ideologies in Europe, Asia (including China), and elsewhere, but argued "it is developments in the Soviet Union—the original 'homeland of the world proletariat'—that have put the final nail in the coffin of the Marxist–Leninist alternative to liberal democracy." Now that the Soviet Union has ceased to exist, Fukuyama's article appears prophetic.

A careful reading of the article reveals that Fukuyama did not expect the Soviet Union to break up, nor communism to wither away, so quickly. Rather, what he suggested was that liberalism is now so widely accepted around the world as the best ideology that it will, in time, lead to the emergence of a universal homogeneous state.

History's end point turns out to be pale and uninspiring (by Fukuyama's own admission): "a liberal democracy in the political sphere combined with easy access to VCRs and stereos in the economic." Not surprisingly, the Fukuyama thesis has many critics as well as admirers. Does the breakup of the USSR portend the triumph of liberal democracy and free-market economies, or does it reveal deep-seated ethnic, religious, and nationality rivalries so powerful that they threaten the very basis of the modern nation-state? In any case, it is much easier to imagine the former Soviet Union at some point in the future as a collection of societies with "easy access to VCRs and stereos" than as functioning liberal democracies.

For Fukuyama's complete article, see Francis Fukuyama, "The End of History?" *The National Interest* (Summer 1989), pp. 3–18.

---

of the Castro Revolution [will] suddenly, inevitably occur in Cuba." What Timerman could not predict is precisely how the end would come:

> Will it break at the top? Will it explode from the bottom? What sort of hidden movements are going on in the Cuban spirit—what hidden anxiety which isn't yet erupting within the inner geography of the regime? What is going on deep inside the Cubans who decide to take a stand on a few small things while postponing all the rest, as they patiently survive by standing in lines and take refuge in music and dance, in sensuality, in the warm weather, in the sea?[20]

If Timerman is correct, the fate of Castro's Cuba has already been decided. The question is not whether Cuban communism will fall but rather when and how.

Summary

Communism, and many Communist governments, have collapsed. The demise of the USSR and the passing of Communist states from eastern Europe provide the most dramatic evidence for this. Nonetheless, communism manages to hang on in a few, scattered nations.

Traditionally, the Soviet system was totalitarian, created in the image of

Stalin. Before Gorbachev, only Nikita Khrushchev attempted to soften it. In the Soviet system, the Communist party ruled, and position in the party reflected a political figure's power. When Mikhail Gorbachev rose to head the Communist party in 1985, he faced both acute economic problems caused by the failure of central planning and opposition from the Soviet elite, the *nomenklatura*. In attempting to reform the system, Gorbachev undertook economic reforms (*perestroika*), political liberalizations (*glasnost*), and systemic political reforms (*demokratizatsiia*). Each of these measures took on a life of its own and exceeded Gorbachev's intentions and expectations.

Meanwhile everyday life within the former Soviet Union was declining rapidly. Food and housing shortages became worse under Gorbachev and reached crisis proportions after the passing of the Soviet Union. Crime, alcoholism, and corruption, too, continue to pose critical challenges. The nationalities problem helped bring down the Soviet Union and continues to be a source of political instability. With the passing of the Soviet Union and the creation of the Commonwealth of Independent States, fundamental political and economic problems remain unsolved and the future of democracy remains unclear.

The collapse of communism in eastern Europe proved remarkable, although democracy was not assured. Yugoslavia, after Tito's death, was threatened with disintegration, and China continued its oppressive political ways while experimenting with elements of a market economy. In Asia and Cuba, communism continued unabated, the last hangers-on to a failed political system.

Key Terms

Commonwealth of Independent States (CIS)	*demokratizatsiia*
de-Stalinization	Congress of People's Deputies
liberalization	*blat*
convergence theory	*Pamyat*
Politburo	Union Treaty
Secretariat	privatization
Central Committee	workers' councils
Party Congress	backyard steel furnaces
nomenklatura	mass line
Supreme Soviet	Democracy Wall
Council of Ministers	cult of personality
perestroika	Tiananmen Square massacre
glasnost	

Review Questions

1. What problems faced the Soviet Union in 1985?

2. How did President Gorbachev respond to those problems? How successful was he? Explain.

3. Have the former eastern European Communist states "gone democratic"? Explain your answer.

4.   What changes have taken place in China since Mao's death?

5.   Besides China, where are other Communist states found?

Recommended Reading

CLEMENS, WALTER C. *Can Russia Change? The USSR Confronts Global Interdependence.* Boston: Unwin Hyman, 1989. A penetrating look at the challenges the Soviet Union faced in trying to break out of its self-induced isolation.

DODER, DUSKO, AND LOUISE BRANSON. *Gorbachev: Heretic in the Kremlin.* New York: Viking Penguin, 1990. A look at the Soviet reform movement, focusing on the man who initiated it.

DRAPER, THEODORE. *Castroism: Theory and Practice.* New York: Praeger, 1965. An incisive study of the ideology and institutions that sprang from the Cuban Revolution.

FISCHER-GALATI, STEPHEN (ed.). *Eastern Europe in the 1980s.* Boulder, Colo.: Westview Press, 1981. A provocative collection of essays on eastern Europe, edited by one of the leading American authorities on the subject.

GOLDMAN, MARSHALL. *Gorbachev's Challenge: Economic Reform in the Age of High Technology.* New York: Norton, 1987. A solid and illuminating analysis of the prospects and perils of *perestroika.*

GORBACHEV, MIKHAIL. *Perestroika: New Thinking for Our Country and the World.* New York: HarperCollins, 1987. The theoretical underpinnings of the Soviet reform movement in Gorbachev's own words.

HOUGH, JERRY. *Russia and the West: Gorbachev and the Politics of Reform.* New York: Simon & Schuster Trade, 1990. An incisive analysis of the historical and political dimensions of *perestroika* by a highly respected Sovietologist.

KLOSE, KEVIN. *Russia and the Russians: Inside the Closed Society.* New York: Norton, 1986. A dated but superlative and insightful account of the rigors and oppressions of life in the Soviet Union, based on personal experience.

LAQUEUR, WALTER. *The Long Road to Freedom: Russia and Glasnost.* London: Unwin Hyman, 1989. Penetrating insights from a thoughtful student of Soviet affairs.

MEDISH, VADIM. *The Soviet Union* (4th ed.). Englewood Cliffs, N.J.: Prentice Hall, 1990. A comprehensive, insightful, and detailed introduction to the Soviet Union.

PYE, LUCIAN W. *China: An Introduction* (3rd ed.). Boston: Little, Brown, 1983. A penetrating introduction to Chinese politics.

ROBERTS, PAUL CRAIG, AND KAREN LA FOLLETTE. *Meltdown: Inside the Soviet Economy.* Washington, D.C.: Cato Institute, 1990. The final days of the woebegone Soviet economy and the outmoded Communist system.

ROTHSCHILD, JOSEPH. *Return to Diversity: A Political History of East Central Europe since World War II.* A good background study of a long-neglected region now in transition.

SMITH, HEDRICK. *The Russians.* New York: Times Books, 1983 (paper, Ballantine, 1984). A best-seller when it appeared, this book is an entertaining and extremely informative look at the reality behind the Soviet Union's pre-Gorbachev utopian façade.

SMITH, HEDRICK. *The New Russians.* New York: Random House, 1990. A revealing, updated examination of life in the USSR.

VOSLENSKY, MICHAEL. *Nomenklatura: The Soviet Ruling Class.* Garden City, N.Y.: Doubleday, 1984. A biting description and analysis of the Soviet elite.

Notes

1. Thomas M. Magstadt, *Nations and Governments* (New York: St. Martin's Press, 1991), pp. 206–207.

2. See Susan Dentzer, Jeff Trimble, and Bruce Auster, "The Soviet Economy in Shambles," *US News and World Report,* November 20, 1989, pp. 25–29, 32, 35–37, and 39.

3. Ibid., pp. 25 and 36.

4. See Milovan Djilas, *The New Class* (New York: Praeger, 1957), and Hedrick Smith, *The Russians* (New York: Times Books, 1978), pp. 30–67.

5. Some delegates who were elected as mainstream Communists, however, acted far more independently than anyone had predicted.

6. As such, it differed significantly from the old position of president, which was the chairman of the Supreme Soviet.

7. Smith, *The Russians,* p. 83.

8. Donald D. Barry and Carol Barner Barry, *Contemporary Soviet Politics: An Introduction,* 3rd ed. (Englewood Cliffs, N.J.: Prentice Hall, 1987), p. 274.

9. Vadim Medish, *The Soviet Union,* 2nd ed. (Englewood Cliffs, N.J.: Prentice Hall, 1985), p. 161.

10. Janos Kornai, *The Road to a Free Economy: Shifting from a Socialist System: The Example of Hungary* (New York: Norton, 1990).

11. Robert G. Wesson, *Communism and Communist Systems* (Englewood Cliffs, N.J.: Prentice Hall, 1978), p. 170.

12. Ibid., p. 171.

13. Ibid., pp. 172–173.

14. A. Doak Barnett, "Ten Years after Mao," *Foreign Affairs,* Summer 1986, p. 38.

15. Ibid., p. 39.

16. Ibid., p. 48.

17. Ibid., p. 57.

18. Ibid., p. 49.

19. Stephen J. Morris, "Vietnam under Communism," *Commentary,* September 1982, pp. 39–47.

20. Jacobo Timerman, "Reflections: A Summer in the Revolution, 1987," *The New Yorker,* August 13, 1990, pp. 62–81 (translated from Spanish by Tony Talbot).

CHAPTER 9

DEVELOPING COUNTRIES

DEMOCRACY OR DICTATORSHIP?

(Sygma)

IT TOOK UNTIL the twentieth century for the United States to emerge both as a modern nation-state and a great power. Geographic isolation and a vast frontier allowed for its development; wise founders and good fortune contributed to its eventual ascent to world leadership. Today, many African, Asian, and Latin American nations aspire to the level of prosperity and stability now enjoyed by the economically advanced countries of the European Community and the Pacific Rim (Australia, New Zealand, and Japan), as well as the United States and Canada. These so-called developing nations face great obstacles on the often perilous path to political, economic, and social change. To better understand the nature of the challenges they face, we need take a closer look at the circumstances in which these nations typically find themselves.

DEVELOPING COUNTRIES: THE THIRD WORLD

Developing countries are located in Africa, Asia, Latin America, the Caribbean Sea, and the Pacific Ocean. Taken together, they are sometimes simply called the *Third World,* as distinct from the *First World* (the advanced industrial democracies including western Europe, Japan, Australia, and New Zealand), and the *Second World* (the communist nations, including the former Soviet Union, China, North Korea, Vietnam, Laos, Afghanistan, Angola, and Cuba).

All three categories are problematic now. The Second World no longer includes the Soviet Union, not to mention its former satellite states of central and eastern Europe since these countries (Poland, Czechoslovakia, Hungary, Romania, and Bulgaria) abolished communism and broke away from the Soviet Union in 1989. (East Germany is now part of the First World, having merged with the Federal Republic of Germany.) But they are still not advanced industrial democracies either, although several (notably Poland, Czechoslovakia, and Hungary) are moving rapidly from central planning to a market-based economy. Several countries in this region—Romania, Bulgaria, and Albania—might even be lumped into the Third World.

In fact, many countries belong to more than one category. For example, Cuba, Vietnam, China, Cambodia, Afghanistan, and Angola all belong to the Second World because they officially embrace communist ideology and the Third World because they are still in a relatively early stage of economic development. Brazil, which became a democratic state in the mid-1980s, exhibits both First World and Third World characteristics: It is industrially developed in some respects and underdeveloped in others (for example, rural poverty, life expectancy, infant mortality, and literacy rates below those of western Europe, the United States, and Japan; great disparities between rich and poor; high unemployment and underemployment).

Another classification problem is posed by Asia's "four little dragons" (South Korea, Taiwan, Hong Kong, and Singapore) that are so-called *newly industrialized countries (NICs)* with free-market economies but political systems that fall somewhere between democratic and authoritarian on the spectrum. It now appears as though Thailand and Malaysia will soon join this select group, possibly followed by Indonesia and others. Some economists would also classify Brazil and India as NICs. All these countries exhibit some (or even many) First World characteristics, but in the early 1990s none had yet gone far enough down both roads—market-based economic development and political democratization—to justify a reclassification.

Old classification schemes, then, are becoming increasingly outmoded. There is no perfect way to categorize countries that comprise approximately five-eighths of the world's population (see Figure 9–1).[1] By most counts, over 100 of the roughly 160 nations on the globe can be classified as developing; almost 40 percent are in sub-Saharan Africa, slightly under 25 percent in Latin America, and the rest divided almost equally between the Asian Pacific and the Arab world (the Middle East and North Africa).

Although we will discuss the problem of political development in this chapter and speculate about its relationship to constitutional democracy, there are bound to be exceptions to any generalizations about developing countries. In fact, perhaps the most striking single characteristic of this grouping is its *diversity*. Some Third World states are huge—Brazil has a territory of 3 million square miles (larger than the continental United States) and a population of 150 million; India's territory of 1 million square miles supports a population of some 925 million. Contrast these giants with such tiny island states as Barbados (territory, 166 square miles; population, 252,000) in the Caribbean and Kiribati (territory,

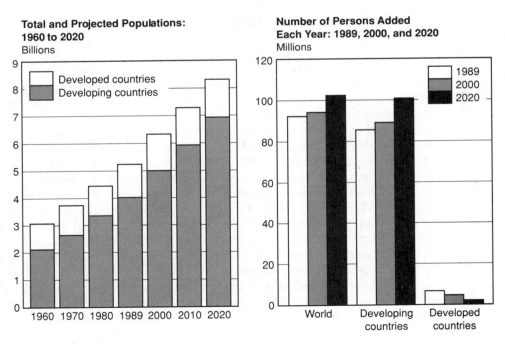

FIGURE 9-1   World Population, by Development Category
SOURCE: U.S. Bureau of the Census.

266 square miles; population, 61,000) in the Pacific. The Pacific island of Nauru may win the "pygmy" prize: It has 8,000 people living on 8 square miles of land. Nauru may be small, but it is not poor: Phosphate exports push annual per capita income above $21,000!

Diversity in size is only one indication of the contrasts marking the Third World; there are many others. Generalizations are possible, but they invariably require qualification. For example, a common characteristic of Third World nations is grinding poverty. Yet as we have seen, tiny Nauru (and other nations as well) are exceptions to this rule. Most Third World countries became independent after World War II when European power diminished and colonialism retreated; but this, too, is not true of all these states. Most Latin American nations have been independent for a century or more. The populations of almost all developing nations are nonwhite, yet the racial and ethnic differences among nations, and sometimes even within the same nation, can be profound. Although some Third World nations exhibit elements of Western culture, seldom are those elements dominant. But here again, diversity precludes absolute generalization.

Nor are foolproof generalizations about Third World economics or population possible. For instance, most states located south of the equator can be classified as developing nations; but there are notable exceptions, including Australia and New Zealand. To take another example, most developing economies depend primarily on agriculture. Yet a few, like the oil-rich states of the Persian Gulf (such as Kuwait, Qatar, and the United Arab Emirates), rely almost exclusively on mineral resources. Similarly, misconceptions abound concerning the Third World "population explosion." The developing countries account for about half the total area of the globe and slightly more than half the total population. Asia, the most densely populated part of the developing countries, has 56 percent of the world's population but only 14 percent of its area. Yet apart from Asia (and a few exceptions, such as Egypt, whose population is clustered around the Nile River), population density in the developing countries is relatively low. Africa, with about 33 percent of developing countries' land area, supports less than 10 percent of the population, while Latin America, with about 31 percent of the area, is home to only 8 percent of the population. Africa's average population density is only 16 per square kilometer, as opposed to India's 225. Although such figures do not take into account what part of the land area is habitable or the distribution of population over the land area, it is worth noting that Africa also has more arable land per capita than any other developing region.[2]

Of course, the developing nations are not the only places where social, economic, and political *development* is occurring. Development is taking place all over the world, even in more industrially advanced nations that continue to respond to ever-changing domestic and foreign pressures. Furthermore, development takes place unequally; some nations, such as Afghanistan, Bangladesh, Laos, Chad, Sierra Leone, and Uganda, are all very poor and seem to be virtually incapable of successful modernization. Yet despite these differences, it is among these nations that the struggle for development is most dramatic and arguably most important. In a very real sense, the political lives of many of these nations, and the day-to-day lives of many of their citizens, depend on the ultimate success of their efforts.

DEMOCRACY IN DEVELOPING COUNTRIES

Given these significant differences among developing nations, are meaningful political generalizations possible? In order to understand the plight and prospects of developing nations, it is important to find out to what extent such countries are currently democratic or what prospect they have of becoming democratic.

The governments of most developing countries are neither democratically elected nor avid protectors of their citizens' civil liberties. Over half of these nations are governed or controlled by the military; most of the remaining civilian governments are nondemocratic. In addition, analysis of developing nations' propensity toward democracy is clouded by the fact that they are constantly in flux. For example, in recent years, democracy seemed to be making progress in Chile, Turkey, South Korea, and Mexico while being endangered in nations like India and the Philippines. Such flux is normal and expected (and will vary significantly from time to time). Arguably, the most important political question regarding developing nations is whether these nations have a generally democratic future. Are we on the verge of a great worldwide democratic awakening, or is democracy in developing nations little more than a distant hope?

Perhaps the best way to understand how close such nations are to achieving democracy and to determine what policies and programs ought to be pursued in order to help encourage it is to focus on the existence of *democratic correlates.* These are conditions or circumstances that coincide with democracy and are therefore believed to correlate with it. Although it is impossible to say that these correlates beget democracy, political scientists do believe that the more they are present, the greater the likelihood that democracy can exist and will endure.[3]

It is usually thought that the most important democratic correlates are economic. Generally, they include the following:

- *National wealth.* For a long time, it has been thought that a measure of prosperity correlates with democracy. Conversely, poverty and democracy are believed to be in tension with each other; it would seem that democracy is a luxury that nations mired in poverty usually cannot afford.

- *A market or mixed economy.* Such an economy can feature both public and private ownership of the means of production and distribution, and it permits the combining of elements of a market economy with some amount of governmental intervention. What is important here is what such economies disallow: Economic decisions, especially those involving the production and distribution of products and services, cannot be planned exclusively by the government but must be left primarily to individuals. Such an economy permits welfare payments and other government-funded services; it simply precludes large-scale centralized state planning of the economy.

- *A middle class.* This correlate stresses not the amount of wealth that exists within a nation but its distribution. Sharp class differences are thought to be incompatible with the existence of a stable, enduring democracy.

Some political scientists stress the existence of political factors, even over economic correlates. These are cited most often:

- *Freedom of communication.* The fact that democracy requires the open airing of different points of view means that the protection of free press and media and the relative openness of information comprise an important political correlate of democracy.

- *A stable party system.* This political correlate stresses the need for a steadfast method of representing the political opinions of individuals and groups. Such a system usually implies the existence of more than one party, each of which is open and representative.

- *Political control over the military.* Since the military frequently desires political power in developing nations and would rule undemocratically if empowered, it requires regulating if democracy is to be achieved.

- *A strong, independent judiciary.* Essential to the effective functioning of any democracy is the protection of minority rights. It is doubtful if civil liberties can be meaningfully secured without the existence of an independent judiciary.

- *Political and social pluralism.* Although sharp social or political divisions within a country may actually inhibit or endanger democracy, nonetheless it is often thought that the existence of a variety of such groups and voluntary associations (unions; business and trade associations; intellectual, educational, and religious institutions; cooperatives; citizen groups committed to popular civic education and government accountability)[4] must be regarded as legitimate, thus requiring their representation for the necessary give-and-take of representative democratic politics to take place.

Important attitudinal political correlates include these:

- *A belief in toleration for others, respect for the individual, and a political culture marked by moderation (as opposed to fanaticism).* In that democracy requires acceptance of the right of others to hold different political opinions and judgments and even requires from time to time that such people govern, acceptance of and respect for political, social, and religious differences becomes an important correlate of a nation's ability to adopt and maintain democratic government.

- *A pervasive belief in democracy.* A portion of the people and a significant segment of leaders need to believe in the idea of democracy if it is to take root and develop.

Another set of factors are historical, or circumstantial, as can be seen in the following correlates:

- *A democratic history.* Some nations (Chile, Ecuador, and Uruguay are examples) have had democratic histories interrupted by bouts of authoritarian government. It is thought that such circumstances increase the likelihood that democracy will take root again.

- *The existence of democratic neighbors.* During times of political upheaval, the type of government ultimately adopted may be decisively influenced by the successful working of governments in neighboring states. Former authoritarian nations Spain and Portugal are frequently cited as examples whose political future was influenced by the presence of flourishing democracies on the continent.

Lately, another, more comprehensive theory of democratic correlates has been advocated:[5]

> *The distribution of power resources.* This index encompasses six specific correlates intended to measure the *distribution* of economic and intellectual (educational) resources within any nation (the assumption being that the greater this distribution, the more likely democracy will be). Measuring economic distribution of resources within any nation-state are the percentage of urban population and the percentage of nonagricultural population (the higher each is, the more varied economic interests are and the more widely economic resources are distributed). The percentage of family farms is positively associated with the diverse distribution of economic resources; a more complicated measure serves to gauge the decentralization of the nonagricultural sector of the economy. Finally, the distribution of intellectual resources can be determined by the number of students per capita and the percentage of literate population.

DEMOCRATIC STRATEGIES

The correlates just listed make clear that establishing democracy in developing nations is no easy task. Time and patience are usually required to bring about the economic, political, social, and attitudinal circumstances that nuture democracy and help to ensure its success. Sometimes, during times of national upheaval, political changes are forced on nations. In such circumstances, the fate of democracy will depend on the condition of local leadership, the willingness of outside nations to support democratic (or nondemocratic) leadership, and a variety of other considerations.

What strategy should a nation lacking democratic traditions pursue when it desires to establish a democracy? This concern has not been confined to developing nations; it recurred in the former Soviet Union and many of its former satellite nations in eastern Europe. Specifically, should emphasis be placed on liberalizing political reforms to be followed by economic restructuring to a greater market economy (the so-called *glasnost-first model*), or should the economic reforms come first (as the *perestroika-first model* suggests)?[6] The extreme economic and social difficulties encountered by the former Soviet Union, which pursued the strategy of instituting fundamental political changes first, and the relative successes of nations such as Chile, South Korea, Mexico, and Taiwan would seem to argue for the primacy of economic change. The reasons for this tentative conclusion are twofold. First, meeting basic economic needs is a more fundamental obligation of government than ensuring any form of government; therefore, economic well-being needs securing first. In addition, it is likely that an open economic system, more than changes in political structures, will have the greatest immediate impact on the distribution of economic resources and educational opportunity within any nation (factors that may in turn be essential for the establishment and health of democracies anywhere).

DEVELOPMENT AND DEMOCRACY: AN OVERVIEW

The democratic correlates that have been enumerated make clear that democracy is positively tied to the idea of national development or *modernization.* It appears that both political development and democracy are enhanced by such national characteristics as a relative level of prosperity, established and stable political institutions, public attitudes accepting of social pluralism, and a broad distribution of economic and intellectual resources. Although nations occasionally seek democracy for its own sake (Poland, for example), it is also true that most nations seek development. Since there appears to be a clear correlation between the two, the following question emerges: What causes nations to pursue the goals of development, which is frequently capable of leading to democracy?

This is a particularly important question because modernization is a painful and often turbulent process. Traditional bonds among people are undermined; people are uprooted; culture is changed, often irreversibly. Food shortages and social discontent frequently accompany the industrialization process. Given these facts, it is important to understand why leaders of developing nations are often willing to accept the political risks associated with this process. Consider the alternatives. A government could choose *autarky*—a go-it-alone policy that aims at economic self-sufficiency and political isolation—but few, if any, developing (or even developed) countries have the natural, human, or technological resources to implement this strategy successfully. Indeed, most developing countries face the opposite problem—excessive dependence on foreign trade, aid, and investment (including loans from foreign banks and governments).

Motives for Development

Developing countries, then, often have little choice but to modernize. Very few are as fortunate as, say, Qatar (on the Arabian peninsula), which has an abundance of oil and a small population. Venezuela, too, has been blessed with large oil deposits. But to capitalize on these natural resources, even Venezuela and Qatar have had to drill wells, build roads, train petroleum engineers, construct refineries and storage facilities, lay pipelines, establish a banking system, and develop export markets. In other words, they have had to modernize.

For less fortunate developing countries, economic development offers the only hope of escaping pervasive poverty. Most of these nations are poor; the poorest—sometimes called the "least developed countries"—have an average yearly per capita income of less than $250. Even nations that are comparatively prosperous suffer from widespread poverty. Thus in the late 1980s, few countries in Africa and Asia had surpassed the $700 mark in annual per capita income. In a sad irony, while many developing nations must pursue modernization, their extreme poverty often stands in the way of successful development programs. (See Figure 9-2.)

Another incentive for development is the belief that development holds the key to attaining national wealth, creating modern armed forces, and fulfilling a nation's destiny. In this regard, it is noteworthy that nearly all the wars of the past four decades have been fought in the Third World.[7] Aside from recurrent Arab-Israeli conflicts, examples of major Third World rivalries are those between Iran and Iraq, Pakistan and India, Vietnam and China, Libya and Chad, and Ethiopia and Somalia. Many Latin American countries, too, have long-standing disputes with their neighbors. Chile, for example, has engaged in military clashes with all three adjacent states: Argentina, Bolivia, and Peru. In addition, Peru has a smoldering border dispute with Ecuador. Relations between Colombia and Venezuela have also been tense at times because of questions over an unresolved border. Of course, warfare can interrupt—and even defeat—a nation's development efforts, especially when it saps all the government's energies. But continuing, low-intensity conflict can also spur development, especially when states are concerned with safeguarding their national interest from potential rivals.

The very existence of First and Second World countries provides a final incentive for development. Modern global communications, transportation systems, and an increasingly interdependent world make the power and wealth of the First and Second Worlds more conspicuous. Thus the success of many First

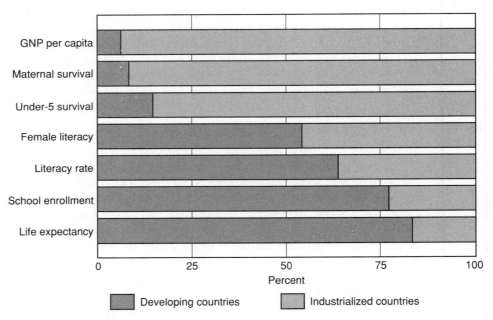

FIGURE 9-2   Disparities between Developing and Industrialized Countries (former as a percentage of latter)
SOURCE: UN Chronicle 27, no. 3 (September 1990), p. 46.

and Second World nations has given rise to what is commonly called the *revolution of rising expectations* within the Third World, a revolution whose goals can only be achieved through development.

THE DEVELOPMENT PUZZLE

Precisely what problems must nations resolve to undertake development successfully on a large scale? We divide our discussion into four parts, addressing the social, psychological, economic, and political challenges to successful development. Furthermore, though we recognize that modernization and political development are ongoing processes, taking place in nation-states throughout the world, we have chosen to emphasize nations where these concerns are central—namely, Third World nations.

Social Barriers to Development

Many developing countries were carved out of former colonial holdings with little concern for the geography or history of the area or indigenous ethnic, religious, tribal, or linguistic patterns. As a result, cultural diversity is a salient feature in many Third World countries. Sometimes this diversity has been subsumed into a new "national" political culture; more often, it has led to internecine strife and even civil war.

In every case, development poses significant problems. With fragmented populations, what drops out of the concept of the nation-state is the idea of a nation; one key element in successful development lies in forging a single national identity and the sense of a shared political destiny. Furthermore, some militant groups or movements may be hostile to social integration and peaceful modernization. For example, because Islam celebrates the idea of *jihad* (a holy war against infidels), this religion is sometimes thought to be an impediment to modernization. Finally, in the face of pronounced ethnic, religious, tribal, or linguistic differences, it is unlikely that a significant majority of the people in a given developing country will view the existing government as legitimate.

Specific examples best illustrate the practical problems associated with diverse populations. Nigeria and India are both developing countries with significant diversity problems. Nigeria comprises several distinct tribes that predominate in different parts of the country. In addition, there are many smaller tribes, and a multitude of tongues are spoken (at last count, Nigerians spoke no fewer than 395 mutually unintelligible languages).[8] Regional animosities, no doubt exacerbated by tribal and linguistic differences, erupted in a bloody civil war in 1967 when eastern Nigeria seceded as the independent state of Biafra. The war, which lasted about three years and ended in defeat for the Biafrans, claimed at least 600,000 lives.

India, too, encompasses numerous distinct ethnic groups that speak many different languages—the Indian constitution recognizes 16 languages, but census data indicate that there are over 1,500, including dialects. Until recently, three official languages were recognized in India—English, Hindi, and Urdu (Hindi is now the official language). English is the elite language, spoken by all university-educated Indians. Hindi, the most widely used of India's languages, is spoken by the Hindu plurality. (Even so, fewer than one-third of all Indians speak Hindi.) Urdu is the language of Indian Muslims, the nation's largest minority group.

Besides distinct ethnic and linguistic groups, Indian society is deeply divided by religion. Hinduism is the religion of India's majority, but there is also a large Muslim population (about 11 percent of the total) as well as other significant religious minorities (Sikhs, Jains, Parsees, Buddhists, and Christians). Since Indian independence in 1947, "communal" clashes—in some instances, massacres—have been committed by one religious group against another. Sometimes these encounters have pitted Hindus and Muslims against each other; sometimes Hindus and Sikhs. At times, other religious groups have been involved. These local conflicts have often had significant nationwide consequences, none more so than in 1984 when Indian Prime Minister Indira Gandhi was assassinated by Sikh guards and again in 1991 when Indira's son and former Prime Minister Rajiv Gandhi was assassinated while campaigning to regain office. Always these clashes have been bloody and merciless, leaving a legacy of bitter feelings that complicate official moves toward political and social integration.

In India's case, the traditional caste system created another barrier to development. Under this system, everyone is born into a particular socioreligious caste (or class) and remains in that caste for life. Obviously, this rigid framework greatly impedes social mobility—the very mobility needed to transform a traditional society into a modern one.

At least one more feature of India's diverse society is noteworthy: Societal divisions tend to be reinforcing rather than crosscutting. Thus not only do Indian Muslims practice their own distinct religion, but they also live in their own insular areas, have a distinct ethnic heritage, and speak their own language. Much the same can be said of Sikhs, Jains, and other groups. As a result, a multitude of factors conspire to make India's social groups acutely aware of their communal separateness while undermining the central government's efforts to create a sense of national unity. Sometimes these divisions can even lead to calls for separatism, much in the way the Sikhs have called for an independent state in northwestern India (where they are concentrated).

Although we have focused on India and Nigeria, many other developing countries face similar problems. Sri Lanka, for example, is split between the majority Sinhalese (74 percent), who are mostly Buddhist, and the Tamils (18 percent), who are mostly Hindu and predominate in the northern and eastern parts of the country. (Moors, Europeans, and Veddah aborigines constitute the remaining 8 percent of the population.) Militant Tamil groups seeking to secede have carried out terrorist acts and conducted guerrilla warfare against the central government since 1983, when an outbreak of communal riots left at least 2,000 Tamils dead.[9] Thus Sri Lanka, like India, displays a pattern of cultural diversity characterized by reinforcing societal divisions.

In fact, most countries in Africa and many countries in Asia and Latin America reveal a startling degree of sociocultural diversity. One survey of 132 nations found that the population was divided into more than five major groups in 53 of them (40 percent of the cases).[10] With few exceptions, these *mosaic societies* are found in the Third World. And frequently, their population diversity poses significant social barriers to development.

Psychological Barriers to Development

One's relationship with one's social group and that social group's relationship to other facets of society play important roles in determining personal identity. These relationships also help to determine whether a person will sufficiently identify with the national government as to acknowledge its right to rule (its legitimacy). A person's attitudes and beliefs, which are usually grounded in the immediate culture, also play a key part in this process. Interestingly, the attitudes and outlooks of individuals in most Third World nations must undergo important changes if development is to succeed. Let us see why.

Most of us, for better or worse, are thoroughly modern in our attitudes toward ourselves, our work, our education, and the world around us. As a result, it is often difficult for us to understand people from other cultures, especially those living in developing nations. For example, people in *traditional societies*, by definition, depend heavily on tradition for guidance in everyday living—much more so than modern people, who tend to scoff at tradition.

A traditional person is ill-disposed toward change because familiar ways are safer and more reliable, whereas new and untested ways are often feared. This tendency to avoid uncertainty—and the concomitant fear of the unknown—is understandable when so much about the environment is uncertain and the environment itself is uncontrollable and fraught with danger. Traditional people approach nature with awe and reverence because of its power over their lives; not surprisingly, their attitude toward nature's whims is one of resignation.

Traditional people tend not to trust strangers. Of course, they seldom have to deal with strangers: Generally speaking, social interaction is confined to family, clan, or at most, village members. Fear of the unfamiliar, fatalism in the face of nature's accidents, and a low sense of personal efficacy combine to make traditional peasants and villagers loath to take risks. It takes little imagination to see how such attitudes would stand in the way of modernization. Individuals who are cautious and conservative are unlikely to try new things, whether it means planting a new crop or learning about a new agricultural technology. Frequently, they experience great adjustment and identity problems if the development process dictates that they move from villages, where they and their ancestors spent their whole lives, to cities.

Other traditional attitudes can impede development as well. Traditional people are less conscious of time, less likely to plan ahead, and less inclined to believe that they can shape their own destinies than people living in modern states. The concepts of individual achievement, personal rewards and satisfactions, and "moving up the ladder" are alien to those bound by traditional values and folkways. This attitude reflects the fact that traditional societies tend to be *ascriptive societies* (the Indian caste system mentioned earlier is an extreme

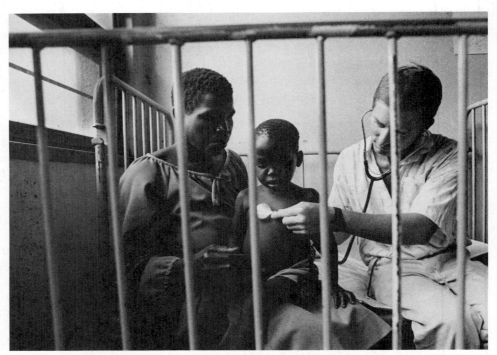

Traditional people tend not to trust strangers. Their fear of the unfamiliar, fatalism in the face of nature's accidents, and low sense of personal efficacy are attitudes that stand in the way of modernization. (Eugene Richards/Magnum)

example)—that is, status and position are ascribed by society on the basis of religion, age, and the like. Status and position are also largely determined by gender; male social and political dominance is much more evident in most developing nations where a low level of applied technology (ranging from a lack of heavy machinery to an absence of birth control devices) combines with high infant mortality rates to reinforce traditional gender roles and attitudes. Thus in developing nations, the notions of personal freedom and individual aspiration are often precluded by the customary and communal nature of most traditional societies.

Obstacles to Economic Development

Most developing nations are poor. As we have seen, this factor, more than anything else, motivates them to undertake development. Contributing to the poverty in most of these nations are unfavorable terms of trade, rising foreign debt, a rapidly increasing population, a low level of technology, an entrenched land tenure problem, illness and malnourishment, a low level of education, and an unforgiving environment. Again, exceptions exist, but the fact remains that these problems are endemic in much of the Third World. As such, they both cause national poverty and impede economic development that could ameliorate that poverty.

Most Third World economies still rely largely on agriculture, despite rapid (and accelerating) migrations of rural poor to the cities. Agricultural commodities and raw materials (minerals) are the economic mainstays of the typical developing country. Nor is it obvious that such economies are improving (see Figures 9-3 and 9-4).

But severe problems accompany excessive dependence on agriculture and mining. Some developing countries raise only one major crop (a practice called *monoculture*). Bangladesh, for example, produces nothing but jute for export. When the price of jute declines, Bangladesh—one of the poorest of the poor—has nothing to fall back on.

Though most developing countries have more than one crop or mineral resource, few are diversified enough to have a healthy mix of agriculture and industry. To modernize, developing countries must import industrial goods; to pay for manufactures, they must export food, fiber, and minerals. But the *terms of trade* work against them: The price of industrial goods is high, while the price of agricultural products and raw materials is often low. Furthermore, the prices of commodities on the world market fluctuate wildly, creating terrible uncertainties and mounting foreign debt. (In 1987, Third World countries, taken together, owed the industrial democracies roughly $1 trillion!)

Some developing countries also face a serious population problem. The industrial democracies have population growth rates of less than 1 percent—several western European countries reached zero population growth (ZPG) in the 1980s. By contrast, most developing countries have growth rates of 2 to 3 percent.

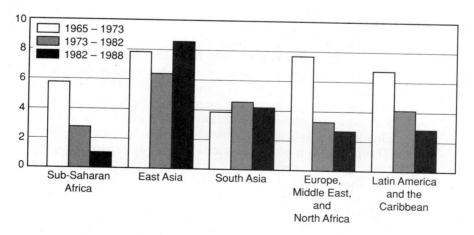

FIGURE 9-3   Growth of Real GNP in Developing Countries by Region, 1965–1988 (average percentage change)
SOURCE: International Bank for Reconstruction and Development, *World Development Report, 1989* (Oxford: Oxford University Press, 1989), fig. 1.1.

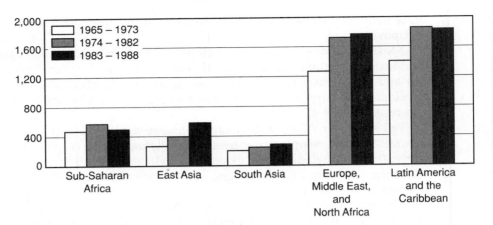

FIGURE 9-4 Real GNP Per Capita in Developing Countries by Region, 1965–1988 (period average in 1980 dollars)
SOURCE: International Bank for Reconstruction and Development, *World Development Report, 1989* (Oxford: Oxford University Press, 1989), fig. 1.2.

Thus while most of the economic growth is occurring in the First and Second Worlds, most of the population growth is taking place in the Third World.

Under such circumstances, it becomes increasingly difficult, even under optimal climatic and economic conditions, for farmers in developing countries to expand food production fast enough to keep pace with population growth, despite the *green revolution*—the dramatic rise in output that has occurred in a number of countries (including India, Mexico, Taiwan, and the Philippines) when high-yield strains of wheat, rice, and corn are combined with modern irrigation systems and synthetic fertilizers.[11]

Typically, population pressures have the greatest impact in urban areas. Rural poverty and governmental policy often encourage people to migrate to cities. In Africa, the rate of urban growth between 1950 and 1980 was 7 percent, meaning that Africa's cities have been doubling in size every ten years. Latin America's cities are growing even faster. Cities like Rio de Janeiro (Brazil), Santiago (Chile), and Caracas (Venezuela) are growing at a rate of 4 to 5 percent a year. The population of Peru's capital, Lima, is expanding even faster: In the mid-1980s, 6 million people were living in Lima (many in squalid slums on the fringes of the city). About one-third of Peru's total population now lives in and around the capital. The population of greater Mexico City was about 15 million in the mid-1980s; if current trends continue, it will have a population of more than 30 million by the year 2000.[12] Rapid urbanization is particularly nettlesome in light of the fact that developing nations do not have the resources to support public services and create new schools, hospitals, housing complexes, and, most important, jobs.

In addition to unfavorable terms of trade, rising foreign debt, and a population explosion, developing countries face three other key obstacles to successful development: a low level of technology, a significant land tenure problem, and an unforgiving environment. The green revolution mentioned is possible only where advanced agricultural technology—including improved seeds, pesticides, herbicides, synthetic fertilizers, irrigation, animal husbandry, farm-to-market roads, and storage facilities—are available. This in turn presupposes access to investment capital and foreign reserves, both of which are typically in short supply.

Land tenure also poses a significant problem in many developing countries. Land ownership patterns vary from one country (and region) to another, but few Third World nations have dealt effectively with their own particular land tenure problems. Because tradition is most resistant in rural settings, established patterns and practices there are slowest to change. The most basic problem centers on the inappropriate or economically unsuitable size of landholdings. In some areas, land ownership (and local power) is highly concentrated; in others, land is fragmented into parcels too small to be profitable. In Latin America these two problems exist side by side—huge estates (known as *latifundia*) coexist with tiny parcels (or *minifundia*). Egypt has a similar problem. Moreover, in many developing countries, it is all too common for peasants to be landless tenant-farmers subject to the whims of absentee landlords.

In Africa, communal ownership of rural land is widespread. Here a different set of problems arises. Villagers are assigned parcels of land and share the fruits, most of which are consumed rather than sold. Commercial plantations are now encroaching on village land; increasingly, cash crops are replacing traditional food crops. Worse still, young men are forced to leave their villages in a futile search for jobs; many become migrant farm workers and sink deeper and deeper into poverty and hopelessness. In Asia, the patterns are somewhat different, but the land tenure problems have the same effect: They impede government efforts to spur overall growth by revitalizing and modernizing the still predominantly rural economy.

Finally, the environment frequently makes for the most devastating obstacle to economic development in the Third World. Often the worst tragedies combine natural disasters with human folly. Thus a terrible drought across much of Africa's midsection in the 1980s was exacerbated by overgrazing. Similarly, floods in some Third World nations have been caused at least in part by upstream deforestation, prompted by a search for wood used in cooking and heating. The most common result of such disasters is pervasive and debilitating hunger. Even without these environmental tragedies and the epidemics that frequently accompany them, undernourishment continues to afflict hundreds of millions of people in developing countries, especially in Africa. People who subsist on severely limited diets do not have the energy to be productive. Thus many Third World nations are caught in a vicious cycle: They are so poor because they are not productive enough, and they are not productive enough because they are so poor.

Challenges to Political Development

Typically, Third World governments both respond to the pressures for development from within their nations and oversee the development process. Because the development process is intrinsically unsettling, the governments of many developing countries are chronically unstable, especially during rapid periods of transition. These governments are frequently coup-prone and beset by political crises. Perhaps this partially explains why most developing countries are ruled by nondemocratic, authoritarian governments.[13] Some of these governments are civilian; others are military. In some, a civilian or military strongman rules. In all developing nations, however, governments face four fundamental political challenges: nation-building, state-building, participation, and distribution.[14]

The most basic of these challenges is *nation-building,* the process by which all the inhabitants of a given territory—irrespective of their ethnic, tribal, religious, or linguistic differences—come to identify with the symbols and institutions of their nation-state. Once individuals identify with the new nation (and hence with each other), nation-building calls for them eventually to become citizens who regard their nation's government as legitimate. As we observed previously, many of the developing countries of Africa and Asia have faced enormous obstacles to nation-building because of the diversity of their populations. Some developing countries have not been able to meet this challenge and as a result have experienced wrenching civil wars and even dismemberment: Examples of the latter include Pakistan (what is now Bangladesh was East Pakistan prior to 1971) and the Congo (most of which is now called Zaire).

Political leaders have frequently addressed the challenge of nation-building by denouncing "colonialism" and "imperialism" as common enemies of the people; often the struggle for independence is itself exploited as a way to unite the new nation in a common cause. Of course, flags, celebrations, and even a national airline (which may consist of only one or two passenger jets with the country's name and colors emblazoned on the sides) help to instill identity and to impart legitimacy. Threats—real or imagined—from a neighboring state can also be useful. Finally, the presence of a *charismatic* national leader appears to be one of the most important variables of all. Notable examples from the past include Egypt's Gamal Abdel Nasser (who ruled from 1954 to 1970), Kenya's Jomo Kenyatta (1963–1978), India's Jawaharlal Nehru (1947–1964), and Indonesia's Achmed Sukarno (1949–1965). Libya's Muammar Qaddafi, a contemporary charismatic leader, uses all the means just mentioned to unite and mobilize the Libyan people.

Also critical to the development process is *state-building,* the creation of political institutions—in particular, a central government—capable of exercising authority and allocating resources all across the land. Such *political penetration* promotes economic development by encouraging and carrying out the construction of the roads, bridges, telephone lines, and other structures necessary for an integrated national economy. Similarly, to finance the creation of this type of infrastructure, the government must, at a minimum, be able to collect taxes and to govern effectively.

In the face of pronounced ethnic, religious, tribal, or linguistic differences, it is unlikely that a significant majority of the people in a given developing country will view the existing government as legitimate. (Nik Wheeler/Sygma)

A third challenge facing the political development of Third World countries is *participation*. For new societies to prosper and grow economically, their members must be actively engaged in the development process. Apart from the perplexing question, "What development strategy should we follow?" developing countries need to mobilize their populations—literally to move the popular mass in some direction. But this creates a political dilemma: As people become more aware of their social worth (the value of their labor to the state) and as they feel the effects of governmental penetration into their lives, they begin to demand a greater voice in determining who governs, how, and for what purposes. Yet if popular demands for participation outstrip the development of institutions and resources for responding creatively to those demands, the government will be faced with a serious and possibly chronic problem of instability. Hence the challenge of participation: how to harness popular energies without setting in motion the forces of political disintegration or revolution.

On the path from no political participation to the establishment of a truly national political party (or parties) and (possibly) the creation of meaningful interest groups lies the critical element of political organization. Frequently, the early patterns of popular participation in agrarian societies undergoing development often take the form of *patron-client relations.* Within the rigidly structured social systems of such states, patrons are influential figures who use their status, wealth, and connections at the national and provincial levels to secure material benefits (food, financial aid, jobs, educational opportunities, and the like) for clients at the local (village) level. In return, clients provide patrons with, among other things, support, votes, payoffs, and a power base. Since the social system is hierarchical, patrons at one level become clients at another. What develops is an intricate network of interrelated personal loyalties based on kinship and cultural or geographic ties. Exclusive in-groups are created through which political demands, instructions, and decisions can be transmitted both vertically and horizontally. Actually, because of the exclusive and particularistic character of patron-client relationships, a system of networks develops in which each network forms a political "machine" of sorts. Out of these intricate structures a truly national prototype of a modern political system may be born.

The fourth major development challenge for Third World governments involves *distribution*—how to ensure against the overconcentration of wealth, property, and power that often characterizes transitional societies. This overconcentration of resources can lead to a pervasive sense of injustice (and, in turn, to mass revolt—see Chapter 16). This sense of injustice is often rooted in a feeling that the fruits of society are not being apportioned fairly; that, as a Marxist might put it, the poor are being exploited by the rich; and that revolution is the only way to bring about real change. Initially, governments often address the challenge of distribution through land reform. Later they readjust tax burdens and may even enact social welfare legislation.

DEMOCRACY IN DEVELOPING NATIONS: TREND OR ILLUSION?

As we have seen in Chapter 3, in the 1980s, democracy replaced dictatorship in many countries from Latin America to eastern Europe. In Latin America, one military dictatorship after another gave way to popularly elected governments and multiparty democracy. Notable examples include Brazil, Argentina, and Chile. Even in Nicaragua, where the Marxist government of Daniel Ortega had turned to the Soviet Union and Cuba for economic and military aid following a revolutionary takeover in 1979, free elections have now resulted in the installation of a civilian president committed to democratic rule. In Panama, too, the Noriega military dictatorship has now been replaced by an elected civilian government (following armed intervention by the United States in 1989).

Yet it is too early to proclaim the final triumph of democracy in Latin America or throughout the world. The democratic governments of Latin America still face a struggle if they are to survive. Despite economic advances, economic and political instability still plague virtually all the governments of this region. In addition to heavy foreign debts, the developing country syndrome that includes high unemployment, periodic hyperinflation, vulnerability to natural disasters, and other woes combine to make the position of almost any government in this part of the world uncertain. In 1992, an unsuccessful coup attempt in Venezuela, and the presidential suspension of democracy in Peru, illustrates this uncertainty. Even Colombia, with a longer democratic tradition than most other Latin American states, faces major uncertainties due to the power of its drug kingpins and continued attacks by left-wing guerrilla groups.

History is also cause for some caution about the future of Latin American democracies. The military has always played a dominant role throughout the region; until recently, few Latin American countries had ever experienced genuine democracy. More often, popular elections have taken the form of plebiscites in which a *caudillo* (strongman) seeks a mandate to rule autocratically. Another familiar pattern involves a military coup d'état in which the military simply cancels the results of an election or seizes control of the government because the previous leaders—be they military or civilian—are unable to stabilize the economy, suppress an insurgency, or calm a society in revolt.

Even in sub-Saharan Africa, a democratic trend among developing nations was proclaimed by some observers in the early 1990s.[15] In 1990 and 1991, at least nine sub-Saharan African countries, including Benin, Cape Verde, and Gabon in West Africa, held free elections—most for the first time ever. In March 1991, Benin's president, Brigadier General Mathieu Kerekou, became the first African leader on the mainland to be voted out of office. Other states in the region—among them Mozambique, Zaire, and Congo—have adopted reforms designed to usher in democratic government. In several countries, including Ivory Coast, Gabon, Niger, and Zambia, rulers approved the introduction of a multiparty system only after pressures in the form of public demonstrations, strikes, and riots became overwhelming. In Nigeria, sub-Saharan Africa's biggest country, the military government has allowed two political parties to operate in a tightly controlled transition from dictatorship to democracy.

None of these changes constitutes a final victory for democracy in sub-Saharan Africa. History and economics make it unlikely that democracy will triumph in this part of the world in the near future. More likely, democratic tendencies there are a reflection of the sweeping changes in eastern Europe and South Africa in the late 1980s and early 1990s. The real test will be whether democratizing forces can keep the momentum going after the excitement over the emancipation of the eastern European nations from communist domination is replaced by disillusionment with the problems they now face and the slow pace of progress in finding solutions.

DEMOCRACY AND DEVELOPMENT: A BIASED DISCUSSION?

It can be argued that the preceding analysis of the relationship between democracy and development has a built-in Western bias. When examining whether democracy and development go together (and finding that there does seem to be some correlation), it has been generally assumed that each is desirable. Not only is democracy generally believed to be the most praiseworthy form of government, economic development is commonly assumed to be desirable. The language of political science reveals as much. Implicit in the language of even the most technical discussions of development is the unstated assumption that it is better to be developed than something—but what? Consider the antonyms: *underdeveloped, less developed, developing, traditional, primitive,* and even *backward.* Sometimes, in an effort to avoid rendering moral judgments, political scientists use the euphemism *premodern* to describe societies that are in an early stage of development.

Development theory thus assumes that development is good. Perhaps one reason is that the least developed countries—and, by definition, the least modern—are also usually the poorest. And of course, everyone prefers abundance to scarcity and wealth to poverty. Sometimes, too, as we have seen, economic development and social modernization are associated with political democracy.

Is it necessarily true, however, that modern-day citizens in an industrially developed nation-state are happier than members of an African tribe who lead a simple life, whose needs are supplied by the tribe (their immediate community), and whose religious and metaphysical questions are answered by a clear-cut set of beliefs passed down from one generation to the next? To sophisticated Westerners, such an existence is primitive and backward. According to this view, superstition, mythology, and the "dead hand of the past" block the development of both individuals and society.

But some critics point out that discussions of development often amount to little more than the praising of Western-style development and imply that Western experts on the subject are guilty of ethnocentrism.[16] Actually, Western philosophers have long struggled with this problem. In 1750, the French philosopher Jean-Jacques Rousseau argued that "our souls have been corrupted in proportion to the advancement of our sciences and arts towards perfection."[17] Indeed, much of Rousseau's political philosophy is rooted in the notion that modern civilization has eroded rather than enhanced our humanity. Undoubtedly, many people in developing countries who have been forced to forsake their villages for the vicissitudes of city life (often in squalid slums) would agree.

Summary

Although generalizations about developing countries are possible (for instance, that they are poor or that they feature agricultural economies), there will inevitably be exceptions. In fact, developing countries are marked by diversity of every kind, making such generalizations difficult.

Democracy in developing countries correlates with the existence and distribution of a number of economic, political, social, and attitudinal variables. It is assumed that to the extent that these variables are present, the opportunities for democracy in a particular nation will be enhanced. Nations wishing to institute far-reaching democratic reforms may begin by undertaking either political or economic reforms, with the latter providing the more likely prospect for success.

Democracy correlates with development. Although development occurs in many nations, it is most conspicuous and most critical in Third World countries. Third World nations are induced to undertake development programs by economic hardships, political rivalries, and rising expectations; however, in the process, they encounter significant barriers. Socially, populations are often fragmented. Psychologically, individuals are heavily dependent on tradition and frequently oppose change. Economic problems range from unfavorable terms of trade and rising foreign debt to rapidly increasing populations, a low level of technology, entrenched land tenure problems, and environmental difficulties. Politically, governments unify their people (through nation-building), provide for governmental institutions that respond to their people's needs (through state-building), encourage citizens' participation, and ensure an adequate distribution of wealth, power, and property.

Contemporary discussion of democracy in developing nation-states tends to assume the desirability of both democracy and development. These assumptions can, however, be controversial.

Key Terms

Third World	mosaic societies
First World	traditional societies
Second World	ascriptive societies
newly industrialized countries (NICs)	terms of trade
development	green revolution
democratic correlates	nation-building
glasnost-first model	state-building
perestroika-first model	political penetration
modernization	patron-client relations
autarky	
revolution of rising expectations	

Review Questions

1. What are the dominant characteristics of the Third World? How do these relate to the development process?

2. What nation-state characteristics correlate with democratic government?

3. Explain the strategies for democratization and incentives for modernization.

4. Is development always taking place? Why or why not?

5. What are the barriers to development? If the development process is so difficult, why do nations undertake it?

6. What is the fundamental assumption of development theory?

Recommended Reading

APTER, DAVID. *The Politics of Modernization*. Chicago: University of Chicago Press, 1965. Focuses on how regimes gain and hold political power—by striking a balance between coercion and information. The author identifies several different types of political systems: "mobilization" (too much coercion, too little information), "reconciliation" (improved information flow accompanied by erosion of central authority), and "neomercantilist" (in Apter's view, an optimal mixture of control and communication).

BINDER, LEONARD. "The Crises of Political Development," in *Crisis and Sequences in Political Development*, ed. Leonard Binder et al. Princeton, N.J.: Princeton University Press, 1971. A groundbreaking analysis that identifies five "crises of development": identity, legitimacy, participation, distribution, and penetration. The book is seventh in a series titled "Studies in Political Development."

BLACK, CYRIL. *The Dynamics of Modernization*. New York: Harper & Row, 1966. Provides a brief but incisive historical perspective on the modernization process.

GAMER, ROBERT E. *Developing Nations: A Comparative Perspective* (2nd ed.). Dubuque, Iowa: William C. Brown, 1982. Perhaps the best undergraduate textbook on political development currently available. Synthesizes much of the literature and provides an especially lucid, informative discussion of the patron-client networks so fundamental to the political processes of many developing countries.

GRINDLE, MERILEE S. *Politics and Policy Implementation in the Third World*. Princeton, N.J.: Princeton University Press, 1980. A comparative exploration of the political, economic, and ideological foundations of the major national policies for economic and social development in the Third World.

HEEGER, GERALD A. *The Politics of Underdevelopment*. New York: St. Martin's Press, 1974. A concise treatment of the basic problems facing developing countries, including the search for order, nationalism and its legacies, the quest for political stability, the symptoms and sources of instability, and the military threat to civilian democratic rule.

HOROWITZ, LOUIS IRVING. *Three Worlds of Development: The Theory and Practice of International Stratification* (2nd ed.). New York: Oxford University Press, 1972. A sharp distinction is drawn between modernization and development. The latter involves improvements in the general standard of living; the former can occur without such improvements. When improvements do occur, however, they are invariably the result of modernization because "development implies a new technology which makes available consumer goods."

HUNTINGTON, SAMUEL P. *Political Order in Changing Societies*. New Haven, Conn.: Yale University Press, 1969. Stresses the need to balance mass mobilization and governmental institutionalization in order to bring progress without upheaval in the Third World.

HUNTINGTON, SAMUEL P. "Will More Countries Become Democratic?" *Political Science Quarterly* 99 (1984), pp. 193–218. Articulates the economic, cultural, and social factors Huntington believes to be associated with democracy.

JAGUARIBE, HELIO. *Political Development: A General Theory and a Latin American Case Study.* New York: Harper & Row, 1973. A penetrating study of political development by a Brazilian scholar with a Third World perspective.

LIPSET, SEYMOUR. *Political Man: The Social Bases of Democracy* (expanded and updated edition). Garden City, N.Y.: Doubleday, 1983. A wide-ranging discussion of politics and nation-states that argues compellingly that national wealth is the most reliable predictor of democracy.

MEIER, GERALD M. *Emerging from Poverty: The Economics That Really Matter.* New York: Oxford University Press, 1984. An excellent survey of the basic issues of development economics. The author argues that one cause of persistent poverty is "the underdevelopment of economics itself."

REYNOLDS, LLOYD G. *Economic Growth in the Third World, 1850–1980.* New Haven, Conn.: Yale University Press, 1986. Traces the growth and development of 41 larger developing countries and examines the economic impact of colonialism, the persistence of poverty with growth, the gains from exporting (and the resulting dependency), and the proper functions of government in promoting growth.

ROSTOW, WALT WHITMAN. *The Stages of Economic Growth: A Non-Communist Manifesto* (3rd ed.). Cambridge: Cambridge University Press, 1991. A provocative study that posits that all developing economies go through basically the same stages, beginning as traditional societies and progressing through self-sustaining growth to the age of mass consumption. The theory suggests that eventually all societies will become industrialized, capitalist, and democratic.

VANHANEN, TATU. *The Process of Democratization: A Comparative Study of 147 States, 1980–1988.* New York: Taylor & Francis, 1990. A carefully researched study that argues that the widespread distribution of economic and educational resources within a developing nation-state holds the key to its ultimate democratization.

Notes

1. This is true according to almost any classification system, although whether China is considered as a developing nation does significantly affect the precise numbers. Our figures include it.

2. Djibril Diallo, "Overpopulation and Other Myths about Africa," *Christian Science Monitor,* April 22, 1986, p. 15.

3. See Seymour Lipset, *Political Man: The Social Bases of Democracy* (Garden City, N.Y.: Doubleday, 1983); Tatu Vanhanen, *The Process of Democratization: A Comparative Study of 147 States, 1980–1988* (New York: Taylor & Francis, 1990); and Samuel P. Huntington, "Will More Countries Become Democratic?" *Political Science Quarterly* 99 (1984), pp. 193–218. Also of interest is Thomas Scanton, "Democracy's Fragile Flower Spreads Its Roots," *Time,* July 13, 1987, pp. 10–11. An optimistic outlook for democracy, based on such correlates, is offered by Carl Gershman, "Democracy as the Wave of the Future: A World Revolution," *Current,* May 1989, pp. 18–23. See also Morton Kondracke, "Freedom Bummer," *New Republic,* November 26, 1990, pp. 21–24.

4. Gershman, "Democracy as the Wave of the Future," p. 23.

5. Vanhanen, *Process of Democratization*, pp. 51–65.

6. See Kondracke, "Freedom Bummer," p. 23.

7. Usually by Third World nations. A recent important exception was the war between U.S.-led United Nations forces and Iraq, fought in early 1991.

8. Jean Herskovits, "Nigeria: Power and Democracy in Africa," *Headline Series*, No. 527, January-February 1982, p. 8.

9. Vyvyan Tenorio, "Sri Lanka Peace Process at Delicate Point," *Christian Science Monitor*, September 2, 1986, p. 11.

10. Robert E. Gamer, *Developing Nations: A Comparative Perspective* (2nd ed.) (Dubuque, Iowa: William C. Brown, 1982), pp. 312–314.

11. Helio Jaguaribe, "The Dynamics of Brazilian Nationalism," in *Obstacles to Change in Latin America*, ed. Claudio Veliz (London: Oxford University Press, 1965), p. 68.

12. Charles W. Kegley, Jr., and Eugene R. Wittkopf, *World Politics: Trend and Transformation*, 2nd ed. (New York: St. Martin's Press, 1985), p. 270.

13. Developing countries colonized by England are something of an exception to this rule. India, Kenya, and Jamaica are now democratic developing nations, and Canada, Australia, New Zealand, and the United States—although not developing countries anymore—are former British colonies that became democracies.

14. These points are generally emphasized in the literature. See James A. Bill and Robert L. Hardgrave, Jr., *Comparative Politics: The Quest for Theory* (Westerville, Ohio: Merrill, 1973), pp. 70–71.

15. See, for example, Robert M. Press, "Africa's Struggle for Democracy," *Christian Science Monitor*, March 21, 1991, p. 4, and Kenneth B. Noble, "Despots Dwindle as Reform Alters Face of Africa," *New York Times*, April 13, 1991, p. 1.

16. See, for instance, Bill and Hardgrave, *Comparative Politics*, pp. 58–59.

17. Jean-Jacques Rousseau, "The First Discourse," in *The First and Second Discourses*, ed. Roger D. Masters (New York: St. Martin's Press, 1964), p. 39.

PART II

POLITICS, PARTICIPATION, AND CIVIC ORDER

POLITICAL SOCIALIZATION

BECOMING A CITIZEN

(Donna Binder/Impact Visuals)

THE YEAR IS 1932. The Soviet Union suffers a severe shortage of food, and millions go hungry. Josef Stalin, leader of the Communist party and head of the Soviet government, has undertaken a vast reordering of Soviet agriculture that involves the elimination of a whole class of landholders (the kulaks) and the collectivization of all farmland—henceforth, every farm and all farm products belong to the state. To deter theft of what is now considered state property, the Soviet government enacts a law prohibiting individual farmers from appropriating any grain for their own private use. Acting under this law, a young boy reports his father to the authorities for concealing grain. The father is shot for stealing state property. Soon after, the boy is killed by a group of peasants, led by his uncle, who are outraged that he would betray his own father. The government, taking a radically different view of the affair, extols the boy as a patriotic martyr.

THE GOOD CITIZEN

What are we to make of the historical incident described in the preceding paragraph? The excellence of citizens, declares Aristotle in *The Politics*, is relative to the political order under which they live.[1] In other words, different political regimes define the requirements of good citizenship in different ways. Thus a good citizen in Soviet Russia in the 1930s would have been a person whose first loyalty was to the Communist party. Such a person would willingly and happily blend into the crowd. The true test of good citizenship would be the capacity to subordinate all personal convictions and even family loyalties to the dictates of political authority. This definition of good *citizenship*, which is a common one under totalitarian regimes, stands in marked contrast to the usual standards of citizenship characteristic of constitutional democracies. Unlike their totalitarian counterparts, democratic nations generally prize and safeguard an individual's freedom of conscience, as well as the right of citizens to express personal opinions.

Throughout history, people of diverse moral character have laid claim to the title of good citizen. The obvious relationship between citizens' moral character and different forms of government underscores Aristotle's observation that the true measure of a political system is the kind of citizen it produces. According to this view, a good state is one whose good citizens are good people; a bad state is one whose good citizens are bad people. Simple though this formulation sounds, it offers a striking insight into the relationship between governments and citizens and points up that civic virtue cannot be divorced from questions of moral character in general.

Contrasting Definitions

Little wonder, then, that different political states embrace different definitions of citizenship. In many authoritarian states, people can be classified as citizens only in the narrowest sense of the word—that is, they reside within the territory of a certain state and are subject to its laws. Their relationship with the government is a one-way street: They pay taxes and bribe corrupt officials. As ordinary citizens, they have no voice in deciding who rules or how. Generally, the government leaves them alone as long as they acquiesce in the system.

By contrast, in totalitarian states, where the government seeks to transform society and create a new kind of citizen, people are compelled to participate in the political system. From the standpoint of citizenship, however, this kind of participation is meaningless because it is not voluntary and stresses duties without corresponding rights. Loyalty and zealotry form the core of good citizenship under such regimes, and citizens may be forced to carry out orders that contradict their personal beliefs.

In democratic societies like the United States, people view citizenship in different ways. Elementary schoolteachers consider a good citizen a pupil who causes a minimum of trouble, sets a good example, respects others, and studies diligently. Newscasters and political scientists commonly attribute good citizenship to adults who take their civic obligations seriously by obeying the laws, paying taxes, and voting regularly. Many individuals, including civil libertarians, emphasize that the essence of citizenship lies in the rights that individuals may exercise within society.

It is worth noting that the formal requirements of citizenship in the United States are minimal, even though the rewards are envied by people the world over (hence the steady flow of immigrants into the United States compared to the trickle of U.S. citizens emigrating to other countries). According to the Fourteenth Amendment, "All persons born or naturalized in the United States, and subject to the jurisdiction thereof, are citizens of the United States, and of the State in which they reside." Note that in the United States citizenship is constitutionally defined. Note, too, that citizens of the United States are distinguished from noncitizens not on the basis of how they act or what they have done but simply by their place of birth. The underlying presumption here is that once a citizen, always a citizen, barring some extraordinary misdeed (such as treason) or a voluntary renunication of citizenship. In the United States, in peacetime, the demands of citizenship are usually quite limited.

A Classical View

The minimal view of citizenship in the United States may provide a convenient way of distinguishing "insiders" from "outsiders," but it obscures the true significance of a concept that has long enjoyed a place of honor in Western civilization. To the ancient Greeks, the concept of citizenship was only partly related to accidents of birth and political geography; instead, responsible and selfless participation in the public affairs of the community formed the vital core of citizenship. Aristotle held that a citizen is a person "who shares in the administration of justice and in the holding of office."[2] Aristotle's Athens was a small political society—a city-state—according a proportionately large number of citizens significant decision-making power in the community at any given time. Citizenship was the exalted vehicle through which public-spirited and properly educated free men could rule over, and in turn be ruled by, other free men and thus preserve and advance civic virtue, public order, and the common good.

In eighteenth-century Europe, the Greek ideal reemerged in a modified form. *Citizen* now became a term applicable to those who claimed the right to petition or sue the government. Citizens were distinguished from slaves, who had no claims or rights and were regarded as chattels (property). Citizens also differed from subjects, whose first and foremost legal obligation was to show loyalty to and obey the sovereign. According to the German philosopher Immanuel Kant (1724–1804), citizens, as opposed to slaves or subjects, possessed constitutional freedom, that is, the right to obey only laws to which they had given their consent. Kant also contended that citizens possessed a civil equality, which meant that they should not be bound by law or custom to recognize any superior among themselves, and political independence, which meant that a person's political status stemmed from fundamental rights, rather than from the will of another.[3]

Clearly inherent in this evolving conception of citizenship was the idea of individual dignity. Citizens were to be treated as free and equal individuals, capable of determining their own best interests. No longer were they to be ruled arbitrarily by others; as intelligent human beings, they deserved to be treated with respect. Republican government came the closest to this ideal of citizenship. In the final analysis, as Kant and other eighteenth-century thinkers recognized, the freedom and dignity inherent in citizenship could flourish only under a republican government, and such a government could function only if its rank-and-file members understood and discharged the responsibilities of citizenship.

In modern times, many more people can legally claim the title of citizen, not only in the world as a whole but also within particular countries. In the United States, for example, racial minorities, women, and people without property can no longer be excluded by law from the full exercise of their civil rights. This expansion of meaningful citizenship has not been without pitfalls. As the number of citizens (and of people generally) has risen, effective political participation for individuals has become more difficult, and governments have been hard-pressed to provide the civic education and social environments needed to ensure that all citizens exercise their rights in a responsible manner. In ancient Athens, any citizen could hold public office and play an active role in formulating laws and policies because of the city's relatively small size and smaller number of citizens (slaves and women were excluded). In sprawling nations with millions of inhabitants, in which almost all adults are classified as citizens, meaningful and effective participation for all individuals can be an elusive ideal.

POLITICAL SOCIALIZATION

Though the proper definition of citizenship may be disputed, almost everyone agrees that good citizens are made, not born. Children grow up to be responsible citizens through the interplay of various influences and institutions—including the family, schools, peer groups, the mass media, and the law—that help to shape the individual's sense of civic duty and political self-confidence. The process of being conditioned to think and behave in a socially acceptable manner is called socialization. *Political socialization* is the process whereby citizens develop the values, attitudes, beliefs, and opinions that enable them to relate to the political system.[4]

Every self-sustaining society inculcates in its citizens certain basic values. Unquestionably, shared beliefs are the necessary building blocks of any state. Even so staunch an individualist as the British philosopher John Stuart Mill (1806–1873) acknowledged that the sense of citizen loyalty or allegiance

> may vary in its objects and is not confined to any particular form of government; but whether in a democracy or in a monarchy, its essence is always the same, viz. that there be in the constitution of the state something which is settled, something permanent, and not to be called into question; something which, by general agreement, has a right to be where it is, and to be secure against disturbance, whatever else may change.[5]

It follows that no government, however legitimate, can afford to ignore the way in which its citizens develop their political beliefs. This process begins in the family.

The Family

The family exerts the first and most important influence on the formation of individual values. Different political regimes view the family in different ways. Some governments support and nurture the family; others choose to be indifferent to it; a few seek to undermine it, regarding the love and loyalty that flow from family ties as subversive to the state. Despite these varying reactions, however, no government would deny the importance of the family in the socialization process.

In the family, children first learn what they should (or should not) do; rewards and punishments reinforce daily behavior. In this manner, children's obligations to the family are made clear. Slowly, they become citizens of the family, often with clearly defined responsibilities and occasionally with rights or privileges. Moral ground rules are emphasized even if the reason for them is sometimes not specified ("Do it because I said so"). Trust, cooperation, and self-esteem, which are generally rooted in family relations, all bear on the behavioral and moral development of individuals. These factors also help to determine the direction children's ultimate political socialization takes and how easily that socialization is accepted.

Children usually derive their initial political orientation from their parents. Often, specific party affiliation also derives from the family, especially when both parents belong to the same party. In addition, the family exerts a powerful influence on religious persuasion, which tends to correlate highly with party affiliation as well as with certain political opinions (Catholics tend to oppose abortion; Jews tend to support Israel; and so on).[6]

Of course, parental influence has its limits. In the United States, for example, only about 70 percent of children whose parents have the same party affiliation tend to affiliate with their parents' party.[7] In other words, even in circumstances highly favorable to political influence, a significant number of children do not follow in their parents' political footsteps. Similarly, studies have indicated that when it comes to opinions about more abstract political issues, parents' influence over their children is quite limited.[8] So although children are influenced by their parents' values, in no sense are their opinions predetermined by their upbringing.

Social Class and Minority Status   Several studies have indicated that patterns of political socialization vary with the social class of the parents, though not to a great extent.[9] Middle- and upper-class children are more likely to become actively involved in politics than lower-class children; observers account for this by citing statistics showing that a family's interest in politics increases as its social standing improves. Children from lower-class families, by contrast, tend to be badly informed about politics[10] and consequently to participate less in political activities.

Within families, minority status can also play a significant role in political socialization. For example, researchers have found that in the United States, black children tend to place less trust in government than white children. Black children tend also to be less confident of their ability to influence government and more deferential toward authority.[11] Not surprisingly, such attitudes correlate with political opinions; thus it is not unexpected that American blacks (holding class differences constant) tend to be more politically liberal than whites on

Just as religion can influence a young person's developing political opinions, so can politics decisively shape the role of religion within the family and the place it ultimately occupies within the larger political order. (Joel Gordon Photography)

most issues. It similarly makes sense that Asian-Americans, given their deference for authority and traditional family structure, tend to resemble white ethnic groups more closely than black ones, particularly on domestic social issues. Hispanic-Americans tend to fall between blacks and whites, although the effects of family socialization and the transmission of political beliefs have exerted an influence on Cuban-Americans, who as a group tend to be more hard-line conservative (especially on foreign policy questions) than other Hispanic-American groups, including Mexicans and Puerto Ricans. One reason is that after large numbers of Cubans fled to the United States at the time of the Cuban Revolution, Cuban leader Fidel Castro confiscated their property and persecuted the family members they left behind.

Gender   In American politics, the sexes seem to view government and politics in different ways. Like class and race, gender differences are important independent correlates of political behavior and opinions. Yet here too, the family plays an important role. Thus, some experts believe that gender differences are rooted in early family experiences and expectations; others contend that there are innate differences in the way men and women develop moral and political awareness. Both explanations have merit. Thus it has been postulated that due to some combination of socialization and biology, women—as mothers and the primary caregivers for children—tend to develop a moral and political perspective that emphasizes compassion and the protection of human life.[12]

Perhaps this helps to explain the surprising fact that differences in political attitudes between men and women do not focus primarily on gender-related issues (for example, public opinion surveys have not revealed differences between men and women regarding affirmative action programs or issues of equal rights). Rather, the primary political differences between the sexes tend to revolve around the government's use of force. Generally, women tend to be more reluctant to support war, remain more opposed to capital punishment, and are more inclined to favor gun control. Women also remain favorably disposed to issues of compassion and thus disproportionately champion many social welfare programs intended to help the disadvantaged. This *gender gap* benefits different candidates and parties at different times, depending on their stand on the issues. In recent years, the Democratic party has probably benefited the most from this gender gap.

Contemporary Trends   The family provides a stable foundation for the larger society, exerting the primary influence on the moral development of society's future citizens. When the family fails, too often the children grow into alienated and antisocial adults.

In recent years, the family as an institution in American society has been undergoing profound changes. Most significantly, the number of one-parent families doubled in the 1970s, and it is becoming increasingly common for American children to spend a considerable amount of time with only one parent. According to many observers, statistics show that the American family is in crisis. Alarmingly high divorce rates, a meteoric rise in the number of working mothers, the breakup of the nuclear family brought on by increasing mobility, and the pervasive influence of television are often cited as both causes and effects of the decline of the family. This is particularly true within American inner cities, which over the past two decades have experienced sharp increases in violence, drug use, and poverty.

Some critics believe that the government is at least partly to blame. Liberals cite the lack of comprehensive domestic legislation targeted at inner-city problems. Conservative critics also fault the government, but they concentrate their attention elsewhere. Often, they cite past Supreme Court decisions on abortion, which, by emphasizing a woman's right of free choice, have allegedly reduced reverence for human life (one foundation of the family) and weakened the bonds between husbands and wives. Other targets include the teaching of sex education and condom distribution in the public schools, which is seen as the usurpation of a traditional area of family authority, and laws exempting homosexuals from legal penalties, which are viewed as evidence that government has become nonjudgmental in matters of sexual orientation. Because of these governmental attitudes and actions, conservative critics charge, the parenting of children no longer occupies the special place it once did in American society.

Of course, there is another side to this debate.[13] The issues of abortion and homosexuality, for example, involve complex and important human-rights considerations. And as for sex education, many teachers and counselors argue that such classes are necessary precisely because the influence of the family has declined. They cite the rising incidence of teenage pregnancies as proof of the need for sex education. Our task here is not to resolve these questions but merely to emphasize that the current debate about the vitality of the American family constitutes an important public policy issue.

Religion

Either the church or the state may present itself as the true source of moral authority, which makes religion particularly important in the socialization process. And just as religion can influence a young person's developing political opinions, so can politics decisively shape the role of religion within the family and the place it ultimately occupies within the larger political order.

Sometimes religion can legitimize existing practices and lend stability to a society in transition. Hinduism in India, for instance, has proved compatible with changing political institutions. Described by one expert as "a multilayered complexity allowing for the existence of many gods, many incarnations, many layers of truth,"[14] Hinduism has tended, historically, to support the status quo. Even when the status quo involved systematic discrimination against a lower, "untouchable" class, Hinduism counseled patience and perseverence in anticipation of future lives to come.

In other parts of the world, religious doctrine has ignited aggressive policies. In Libya and Iran, for instance, Islamic fundamentalism helped fuel belligerent foreign policies and contributed to a periodic fervor for war.

Sometimes religion and politics conflict. In Nazi Germany, for example, government simply steamrolled over the Lutheran and Catholic churches. Until recently in what was the Soviet Union, the regime allowed the historically entrenched Russian Orthodox church to continue functioning but restricted and monitored its activities. The state treated believers as second-class citizens, frequently harassing and persecuting them.[15] In states where political and religious doctrines conflict and where they cannot be reconciled easily, the process of political socialization is fragmented. Tensions and uncertainties are created that have to be resolved by the individual, often later in life.

In the United States, religion and politics reinforce each other at a number of levels. Although the Supreme Court has interpreted the Constitution to prohibit government from directly supporting religion, the First Amendment also clearly prohibits government from denying an individual's free exercise of religion. Within this friendly environment, the practice of religion in the United States continues to flourish. "More than 90 percent of all Americans identify with some religious faith, and on any given Sunday morning more than 40 percent are to be found in church." Furthermore, by "most measurable indices the United States is a more religious country than any European nation except Ireland and Poland."[16] Although one might argue that religion in the United States has become a less important part of citizens' lives, its influence has remained pervasive over time (see Figure 10-1).

In this country, one general Judeo-Christian tradition holds sway, yet there is significant diversity within that tradition. Mainstream Protestant denominations constitute about 30 percent of the population; Roman Catholics, 25 percent; white evangelical Protestant churches, 20 percent; black Protestant churches, 8 percent; and Jews, 3 percent.

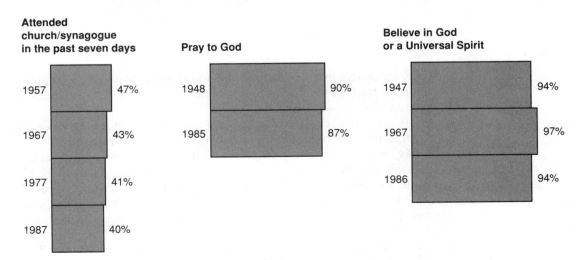

Attended church/synagogue in the past seven days

1957	47%
1967	43%
1977	41%
1987	40%

Pray to God

1948	90%
1985	87%

Believe in God or a Universal Spirit

1947	94%
1967	97%
1986	94%

FIGURE 10-1   Religious Practices of Americans

SOURCE: Reprinted with the permission of The American Enterprise Institute for Public Policy Research, Washington, D.C.

Some important political differences correlate with these differences in religious orientation, even arising from the religious doctrines themselves. Thus Quakers and Mennonites tend to be pacifists, while, as previously mentioned, Catholics tend to oppose abortion and Jews generally favor Israel. By the same token, members of black Protestant churches are more politically liberal than Protestants who affiliate with mainstream churches, and members of mainstream churches are in turn more politically liberal than their evangelical Protestant counterparts. More generally, on a scale measuring political conservatism and liberalism, Protestants are somewhat more conservative than Catholics and much more conservative than Jews. Therefore, Jews and Catholics have historically identified more with the Democratic party while Protestants have leaned toward the Republican party, although the correlation between religion and party affiliation appears to be weakening.

It is sometimes argued that religion has intrinsic political value in the United States. In this view, religion is seen as benefiting public life by providing, in George Washington's words, an "indispensible support" for representative government. When religion teaches that everyone is equal in the eyes of God and that all human beings possess dignity and deserve respect, it advocates a private morality that can elevate public life.

Sometimes political leaders can draw on religious imagery to unite citizens in a common understanding of the present or point them toward a more noble vision of the future.[17] For example, the famous American clergyman and civil rights leader Martin Luther King, Jr., inspired the nation with his dream of a day "when all of God's children, black men and white men, Jews and Gentiles, Protestants and Catholics, will join hands and sing in unison the old Negro spiritual 'Free at last! Free at last! Thank God Almighty, we are free at last.'" The tragic assassination of King, like the assassination of Abraham Lincoln a century earlier, helped to rally the American people to the cause of racial equality.

Schools

The schools play a vital role in transmitting *civic education* to the young. Through public education, states seek to influence young people before their moral character is fully formed.

All countries use schools as a means of political socialization. Some governments merely prescribe one or two courses in civics or history, require students to salute the flag, and hang a few pictures of national heroes on school walls, whereas others dictate the entire school curriculum, indoctrinate the children with slogans and shibboleths, heavily censor textbooks and library acquisitions, and subject teachers to loyalty tests. Furthermore, whereas all states attempt to perpetuate their core values, the substance of these values, as well as the methods used to instill them, may vary enormously. Different regimes inculcate different values. Under some regimes (for example, the Soviet Union in the 1930s), blind obedience to authority is the norm. In others, patriotism is encouraged, but so is the habit of critical and independent thinking.

Socialization studies have revealed much about the way children learn politically relevant values in American public schools.[18] During the elementary school years, American children tend to develop positive emotional attachments to key political concepts such as liberty and democracy. Also, small children typically think of the government in terms of an authority figure—a police officer, the president, and so on.

As children mature, they begin to react less emotionally and more cognitively; they grasp the subtleties of abstract concepts such as democracy, for instance. During adolescence and early adulthood, students' attitudes toward government often change radically. As they outgrow their dependence on parents, children cease to obey authority without question. Increasingly, they want to control their own destinies—a sentiment that is readily transferable to the political realm. With the passage of time, young people often begin to view their roles in the political system with far less complacency, coming to see themselves less as passive subjects and more as active participants.

While some consider the typical high school civics class the most important formal training ground for good citizenship, a number of studies have indicated that civics classes are less important than the total context of the student's educational experience.[19] Influential factors include teachers' attitudes toward democracy; the focus of textbooks in presenting lessons about the nation's history, culture, economic system, and so on; the overall curriculum; and formal rituals like reciting the Pledge of Allegiance and singing patriotic songs. Extracurricular activities such as music and sports can convey the importance of responsible participation and working toward a common goal. Work on the school newspaper can highlight the role of the media in public affairs. Debating clubs can familiarize students with political, social, and economic issues and teach them that there are at least two sides to every issue. Finally, participation in student government can introduce students to the fundamental rules of the political process.

In general, the higher the level of education, the greater a student's interest in keeping informed about and participating in politics. To be more precise, a positive correlation usually exists between the amount of education and a student's awareness of the impact of government on the individual, interest in following the news, overall knowledge and range of opinions about politics, and desire to discuss politics and to do so with a great number and variety of people. Finally, a higher level of education is associated with a stronger tendency to believe that one can influence government and stronger feelings of personal self-confidence and trust in others.[20]

The Impact of Higher Education   It is difficult to determine how much impact higher education has on citizen self-development. In the United States, higher education often represents a blend of vocational training and liberal arts, the latter (which includes literature, philosophy, science, history, and linguistics) placing great emphasis on the development of critical thinking.[21] To supporters of *liberal education,* critical skills can be promoted, especially at the college or university level, when students are challenged to think clearly, write precisely, and speak correctly; when they are exposed to enduring questions and great ideas in the arts and sciences; and when they are encouraged to reexamine the moral and material values that comprise the conventional wisdom of the day. Proponents of this view argue that liberal arts students gain the intellectual tools they need to assume the responsibilities of democratic citizenship. As philosopher Stephen Cahn has pointed out, "A Democratic Citizen who cannot spot a fallacious argument or recognize relevant evidence for a hypothesis is defenseless against those who can twist facts to suit their own purposes."[22]

In nondemocratic regimes, in which the preeminent civic virtue is unquestioning obedience to political authority, citizens may fail to develop participatory skills. Democratic education, in contrast, deliberately aims at producing citizens who possess such skills, especially those based on critical thinking. A good citizen in a democratic society praises the government when it deserves praise and criticizes it when it warrants criticism. Only in democratic societies, therefore, are independent thinking and public dissent not considered subversive.

The Necessity of Civic Education   "We are a most busy, inquisitive, and one might say, meddlesome people in all public affairs," wrote U.S. Supreme Court Justice Joseph Story more than 150 years ago. "We discuss them; we form opinions; we vote in masses at the polls; we insist upon a voice in all matters; and we are quick to act, and slow to doubt upon any measure, which concerns the Republic."[23] As long as the United States remains a democratic society, there will be ample reason for concern about the wisdom of the voting public. In the words of one observer:

> The crucial question is: how can the members of a democracy be provided with the necessary understanding and capability to reap the greatest possible benefits from the democratic process while at the same time protecting that process from those who would seek its destruction? The answer is to be found in the enterprise of education.[24]

Peer Groups

Most people acknowledge that peer groups exert considerable influence over one's political activities and beliefs, but at least two points must be clarified. First, there is an inherent ambiguity in the meaning of the term; a *peer group* can refer either to a group of people who are friends or to people of similar age and characteristics. In either case, the term focuses on "the tendency for individuals to identify with groups of people like themselves."[25]

A second, more serious, difficulty is that few systematic studies of this phenomenon have been conducted and fewer generalizable conclusions have been reached. For example, a 1930s study of the effect of peer-group pressure on the political attitudes of women enrolled at Bennington College concluded that the group's influence caused its members to become more liberal. In another example, a 1965 study of high school students compared peer-group and parental influences on different kinds of political issues and found that parental influence was higher on specific political issues—for instance, what party to identify with and whom to vote for in the presidential election. These studies, interesting though they may be, raise as many questions as they answer.[26]

Another unclear area regarding the influence of peer groups relates to gender. We know that young boys tend to associate with other young boys and young girls with other young girls, and we suspect that there are political differences between such groups. For example, third- to eighth-grade boys are thought to have a more mature and less idealistic concept of the presidency than girls of similar age; yet this general area of peer-group influence remains largely unexplored.[27]

The relationship between the development of antisocial attitudes by adolescent male lawbreakers and their association with like-minded peer groups (and gangs) is especially interesting in that it points to the difficulty of determining exactly what influence peer groups exert on individual attitudes and beliefs. Here, too, there have been relatively few studies.[28] And although it might seem that the concept of peer groups and gangs is especially important in understanding teenage crime, it is still not clear whether "good" boys join the "wrong crowd" and become corrupted by antisocial attitudes among their peers or whether youth gangs primarily attract criminal types who harbor antisocial attitudes when they join.

What is clear, however, is that a close peer-group association, and especially membership in a gang, increases the frequency with which the average teenage male commits crimes. It is not difficult to understand why: Peers and gangs "can affect the value a person assigns to the rewards of crime (by adding the approval of colleagues to the perceived value of the loot or the direct gratification of the act)."[29]

Psychologically, peer groups fulfill a member's need for approval; this need for approval affects the formation of political attitudes and beliefs. Generally speaking, peer groups are formed voluntarily and informally. Yet if we expand the peer-group concept to encompass such organizations as the Girl Scouts, the Young Democrats, or a high school journalism club—and think of similar organizations that operate in other political contexts—we make an important discovery. In totalitarian states, where governments attempt to transform the political order by radically reshaping people's attitudes and beliefs, peer groups in the form of social and professional organizations can be created for both young citizens and adults. These involuntary associations are designed to spread the party's (or government's) message and to educate or reeducate citizens. This phenomenon is illustrated in Figure 10-2, which shows how the hierarchy of the Nazi party (designated as PO) was able to direct a large-scale social movement whose ultimate aim was to transfigure German society. Under the National Socialist (NS) party, German life was organized through an elaborate network of centrally controlled "peer groups" to ensure that every German would, in time, adopt "correct" political attitudes and be properly socialized into the new Nazi state.

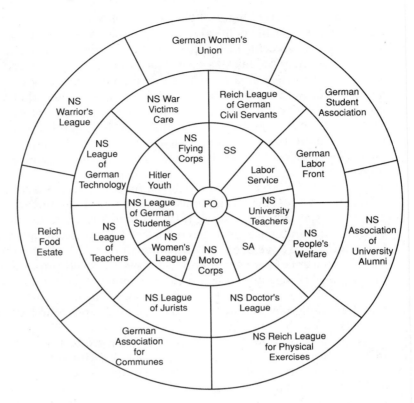

FIGURE 10-2   Organizations in the Nazi Movement
SOURCE: Mark N. Hagopian, *Regimes, Movements, and Ideologies* (2nd ed.). Copyright © 1984 Longman Inc. All rights reserved.

The Mass Media

The mass media also play a significant role in the political socialization (and continuing education) of citizens. In nondemocratic states, the mass media (television, radio, newspapers, and large-circulation magazines) are almost always owned or controlled by the state. Even some democratic governments monopolize radio and television broadcasting (as in Denmark) or own and operate television networks (as in Great Britain). In such cases, the principal difference between nondemocratic and democratic states is that democratic states pass laws or adopt procedures designed to ensure the fairness and objectivity of the media. And in the United States, where almost all television and radio networks and most individual stations are privately owned, the Federal Communications Commission, a regulatory agency charged with determining policy for the national licensing of radio and television stations, has from time to time promulgated regulations to guarantee evenhandedness in political broadcasting. Rules designed to discourage undesirable or unhealthy behavior have been promulgated as well.

Thus television stations in the United States are not permitted to broadcast commercials for cigarettes or hard liquor.

In highly industrialized nations over the past several decades, the so-called electronic media (radio and television) have gained prominence. A controversy has been brewing for some time in the United States over the growing influence of television. One troublesome area involves the use of mass media in political advertising. Television campaign advertising in particular has become increasingly important as Americans read fewer newspapers and attend fewer political party functions.[30] The high cost of such advertising, the number of challengers discouraged by it, its seeming effectiveness, and the extent to which its content is determined by media considerations and media consultants are important issues because they can affect the quality not only of the campaigns but also of the candidates.

Equally worrisome is the content of the commercials themselves. Since the mid-1970s, American political campaigns have become increasingly dominated by short, emotional advertisements (as opposed to the documentary-style ads more prominent earlier); almost always they are simple, symbolic, and personalized. Frequently, they feature dark colors, foreboding music, deep voices, and negatively perceived individual or group symbols. In this respect, an infamous advertisement run during the 1988 presidential election by the George Bush campaign against Democratic challenger Michael Dukakis, showing a furloughed murderer, Willie Horton, who had been released during Dukakis's tenure as governor of Massachusetts, proved both typical and influential. It is also revealing that the ad itself temporarily eclipsed the presidential campaign and became part of it as the candidates and their supporters debated its fairness.

Another area of concern is the way news is presented, particularly on television. Some critics contend that television news reflects a politically biased point of view, while others charge that it is superficial, that it frequently conveys the biases of newscasters and commentators to a mesmerized viewing audience, and that it has spawned cynicism toward government. Although it is certainly true that newscasters, reporters, editors, and television producers have a political viewpoint and that news specials sometimes reflect a political bias, most of the time television news informs viewers of the day's major events without undue editorializing.

A more incisive criticism is that because network television is a business whose profits depend on maintaining high audience ratings, television news tends to emphasize entertainment and drama at the expense of substance. For instance, it is not uncommon for the evening news to show a spirited exchange between a key witness and a Senate committee chairman while glossing over the substance of the testimony. This is a conscious corporate decision. Network executives know that conflict and confrontation are entertaining and that as a rule, bad news makes good ratings. For this reason also, television networks almost always emphasize the "horse race" aspect of presidential elections, dwelling on who is ahead, who gained, and who lost because of this gaffe or that new development. They compete vigorously to call the election minutes ahead of the other networks. For many citizens, therefore, the race itself now takes center

The mass media's coverage of the AIDS epidemic and the public debate concerning the ethics of condom distribution in public high schools raises questions that relate to all elements of political socialization: familial, religious, and peer-group attitudes, public education, and the influence of the media. (J. Stettenheim/Saba).

stage in presidential campaigns and elections, rather than the issues. In-depth analysis, critics say, is a casualty of Madison Avenue marketing techniques and the Nielsen ratings.

Though such criticism has some merit, it needs to be tempered. Network television is a highly competitive industry profoundly influenced by consumer tastes and preferences. Thus the news is entertaining because the people who watch it want it to be entertaining. And because the average viewer has a very short attention span, television news directors spotlight the razzle-dazzle of video technology, fast-paced interviews, and rapidly changing stories, locations, and camera angles. Network executives understand that TV viewers prefer their news in predigested snippets. After a hard day, the last thing most viewers want when they turn on the TV is a philosophical discussion of complex political issues. Unfortunately, political issues tend to be complex.

The media's tendency to focus on "negative" news—opposition party leaders attacking the administration's programs and decisions, mudslinging exchanges by rival candidates for elective office, mass rallies to protest some aspect of administration policy—at least serves as a reminder that freedom of speech and criticism of the government are protected rights in liberal democracies. The contents of newspapers and the radio and television news broadcast in a given country usually indicate how much freedom exists there. Where criticism of the government is allowed, freedom is usually the norm. Where only good news is permitted, good people are probably in prison. In the final analysis, the mass media in democratic states are both gauge and guarantor of individual freedom.

The Law

Although the law in some societies reflects citizens' values and attitudes, it often helps to form them as well. Of course, not all laws are identical. Some laws simply promote public order (driving on the right side of the street, for example). Other laws, however, prohibit behavior that society regards as inherently evil, for instance, laws against murder, false advertising, theft, and racial discrimination. The passage and enforcement of such statutes sends a message to society (and especially to its youngest members, whose moral sensibilities are shaped by such rules), that murder, false advertising, theft, and racial discrimination are considered wrong and will be punished. To the extent that this message is received, understood, and acted on, it influences a citizen's political socialization.

Key Political Values

A nation's political culture is composed of the fundamental values its people hold dear. These values need not be entirely consistent and they may even conflict at times. In addition, individuals' day-to-day political beliefs and actions need not always conform to the standard (in fact, we know that often they do not).[31] However, a coherent political culture requires that political values exist, that they be widely recognized, and that they serve as a yardstick for measuring the politics and policies of government. By their mere existence, shared values are infused into the socialization of prospective citizens, just as the aggregate socialization process itself, over time, reinforces or modifies the nation's basic political values in light of changing political circumstances. Above all, commonly held values are the best insurance a society has against chronic (or even episodic) instability.

In the United States, private values correlate highly with key public (or civic) values.[32] Americans profess a strong belief in such fundamental liberal values as personal freedom, political equality, the right to own private property, and religious tolerance, for instance. Not only are these values expressed in the nation's fundamental documents and writings, including the Declaration of Independence, the Constitution, and *The Federalist*, but they are also instilled in America's youth by a variety of socialization strategies.

WHEN POLITICAL SOCIALIZATION FAILS

When a nation fails to socialize large numbers of citizens, the consequences are far-reaching. These people will not be successfully integrated into the political system, and they will not share the norms, rules, and laws of the society. A breakdown of this kind can threaten the very survival of the state. The frequency of student protests around the world in recent decades suggests that the socialization of young people may not be as effective in many societies today as it once was. For example, students in South Korea since 1987 have staged massive demonstrations that have imperiled the government. Many of these students apparently reject the entire system and not just particular policies. In the United States, racial riots centering in Los Angeles in April and May, 1992 conveyed a similar message of alienation and mistrust toward the U.S. government.

Some people may never be completely socialized. They may remain angry, cynical, or embittered; they may even become criminals. Suppose that John's father believes the government is run by crooks. During his teenage years, John's two closest friends share this opinion. John develops an attitude of cynicism and antipathy toward government. He may well disavow the "rules of the game," believing them to emanate from a corrupt government.

John's beliefs are bound to influence his behavior. If, rejecting the law against auto theft, he steals cars for a living, he would be labeled a criminal by any reasonable standard. But suppose John steals only government cars. Suppose further that he gives the money he earns from stealing and selling these vehicles to various radical groups and to the poor. This behavior would still be considered criminal by the state, notwithstanding John's "Robin Hood" tendencies.

John's defenders might not call him a criminal; rather, he might be labeled a revolutionary (or at the very least a political dissident acting on principle). Furthermore, if the government he acts against is tyrannical, some moral philosophers would no doubt assert that his "crimes" are just actions taken against an unjust government. Thus whereas the failure of political socialization always bodes ill for the government in power, evaluating the moral and political implications of that failure proves to be a more difficult matter.

Summary

The concept of citizenship is defined differently by different governments. Almost all states espouse a minimal definition of citizenship that encompasses simple adherence to the rules and birth in, or naturalization into, the political order. In democratic states, the ideal of citizenship is also tied to the ideas of equality and liberty, as well as to the notion of meaningful participation in political affairs. This ideal of democratic citizenship dates back to the ancient Greek city-states, which were small enough to permit meaningful participation by a substantial proportion of citizens.

How are citizens formed? Political socialization is the process whereby citizens develop the values, attitudes, beliefs, and opinions that enable them to relate to and function within the political system. Specific influences on the developing citizen include the family, religion, public education, the mass media, the law, peer groups, and key political values. Political socialization is of paramount importance because if a nation fails to socialize its citizenry on a large-scale basis, the nation's political stability can be endangered.

Key Terms

citizenship	gender gap	liberal education
political socialization	civic education	peer group

Review Questions

1. Why has the concept of citizenship been of central importance to Aristotle and other political thinkers?

2. In what contrasting ways can citizenship be defined? Which definition comes the closest to the way you understand citizenship? Explain your answer.

3. It is sometimes said that true citizenship can be found only in a democracy. What is the meaning of this statement?

4. What factors influence the socialization of citizens?

Recommended Reading

ALMOND, GABRIEL, AND SIDNEY VERBA. *The Civic Culture: Political Attitudes and Democracy in Five Nations.* Princeton, N.J.: Princeton University Press, 1963. A comparative study of politics and political culture in the United States, Great Britain, former West Germany, Italy, and Mexico.

BENNETT, LANCE W. *News: The Politics of Illusion* (2nd ed.). White Plains, N.Y.: Longman, 1988. An intriguing analysis of television news that argues that everyday viewers tend to be more trusting and hence more frequently misled than less frequent and consequently more skeptical viewers.

CAHN, STEVEN M. *Education and the Democratic Ideal.* Chicago: Nelson-Hall, 1979. This simple, straightforward book argues that there is an important relationship between higher, liberal education and meaningful democratic citizenship.

EPSTEIN, EDWARD JAY. *News from Nowhere: Television and the News.* New York: Random House, 1974. A dated but nonetheless provocative and convincing study of how television presents the news.

HOLLOWAY, HARRY, AND JOHN GEORGE. *Public Opinion* (2nd ed.). New York: St. Martin's Press, 1985. A thoughtful general introduction to the American political culture.

JAROS, DEAN. *Socialization to Politics.* New York: Praeger, 1973. A short description of the process of political socialization.

KERN, MONTAGUE. *30-Second Politics: Political Advertising in the Eighties.* New York: Praeger, 1989. A detailed and disturbing analysis of contemporary political advertising on television.

REICHLEY, A. JAMES. *Religion in American Public Life.* Washington, D.C.: Brookings Institution, 1985. The best discussion available of religion's influence in the United States.

ROELOFS, H. MARK. *The Tension of Citizenship: Private Man and Public Duty.* New York: Rinehart, 1957. A discussion of the development and different conceptions of citizenship.

WALZER, MICHAEL. *Obligations: Essays on Disobedience, War, and Citizenship.* Cambridge, Mass.: Harvard University Press, 1970. A collection of philosophical essays dealing with the meaning of citizenship, written by one of the United States' leading socialist thinkers.

YERIC, JERRY L., AND JOHN R. TODD. *Public Opinion: The Visible Politics.* Itasca, Ill.: Peacock, 1983. A clearly written summary of recent research.

Notes

1. Aristotle, *The Politics*, trans. and ed. Ernest Barker (New York: Oxford University Press, 1962), p. 101.

2. Ibid., p. 93.

3. Immanuel Kant, *The Science of Right* (Chicago: Encyclopaedia Britannica, 1952), vol. 42, p. 436.

4. The modern study of political socialization is closely tied to the Greek concern for character formation. One key difference between the two is that whereas behavioral political science focuses primarily on the process by which political opinions are formed, the Greeks placed greater emphasis on the traits of character all good citizens should display.

5. John Stuart Mill, *A System of Logic, Ratiocinative and Deductive* (London: Longmans, Green, 1879), vol. 2, p. 518.

6. Harry Holloway and John George, *Public Opinion*, 2nd ed. (New York: St. Martin's Press, 1985), pp. 73–77.

7. Herbert Winter and Thomas Bellows, *People and Politics* (New York: Wiley, 1977), p. 120.

8. Dean Jaros, *Socialization to Politics* (New York: Praeger, 1973), pp. 87–88.

9. Ibid., p. 83.

10. See M. Margaret Conway and Frank Fergert, *Political Analysis: An Introduction* (Boston: Allyn & Bacon, 1972), p. 106.

11. Holloway and George, *Public Opinion*, p. 79.

12. See M. Kent Jennings, "Preface"; Henry Kenst, "The Gender Factor in a Changing Electorate"; and Arthur Miller, "Gender and the Vote," in *The Politics of the Gender Gap: The Social Construction of Political Influence*, ed. Carol Mueller (Newbury Park, Calif.: Sage, 1987). Much of the political literature presumes the existence of scholarship in the field of developmental psychology; see Carol Gilligan, *In a Different Voice* (Cambridge, Mass.: Harvard University Press, 1982), and M. Belenky, B. Clinchy, W. Goldberger, and J. Tarule, *Women's Ways of Knowing: The Development of Self, Voice, and Mind* (New York: Basic Books, 1986).

13. Holloway and George, *Public Opinion*, pp. 71–73.

14. Ralph Buuljens, "India: Religion, Political Legitimacy, and the Secular State," *Annals of Political and Social Sciences* 483 (January 1986), p. 107.

15. Philip Walters, "The Russian Orthodox Church and the Soviet State," *Annals of Political and Social Sciences* 483 (January 1986), pp. 143–145.

16. A. James Reichley, *Religion in American Public Life* (Washington, D.C.: Brookings Institution, 1985), p. 2.

17. This is not to deny, of course, that religion can be exploited by unscrupulous leaders for ignoble purposes.

18. This discussion builds on William Flanigan and Nancy Zingale, *Political Behavior of the American Electorate* (Boston: Allyn & Bacon, 1979), pp. 184–187.

19. Kenneth Langton and M. Kent Jennings, "Political Socialization and the High School Civics Curriculum," *American Political Science Review* (September 1968), p. 851.

20. Conway and Fergert, *Political Analysis*, p. 110.

21. Or so it would seem. But it is important to determine not only what is studied but also how it is studied. See Albert Speer's comments on German education in Albert Speer, *Inside the Third Reich*, trans. R. and C. Winston (New York: Avon, 1971), p. 35.

22. Stephen Cahn, "The Content of Liberal Education," in *The Idea of a Modern University*, ed. S. Hook, P. Kurtz, and M. Tudorovich (Buffalo: Prometheus Books, 1974), p. 101.

23. Joseph Story, "Statesmen: Their Rareness and Importance," *New England Magazine*, August 1834; reprinted in James McClellan, *Joseph Story and the American Constitution* (Norman: University of Oklahoma Press, 1971), p. 373.

24. Steven M. Cahn, *Education and the Democratic Ideal* (Chicago: Nelson-Hall, 1979), p. 6.

25. Jerry L. Yeric and John R. Todd, *Public Opinion: The Visible Politics* (Itasca, Ill.: Peacock, 1983), p. 49.

26. Ibid., pp. 49–50.

27. Richard Dawson et al., *Political Socialization*, 2nd ed. (Boston: Little, Brown, 1977), pp. 62–63.

28. James Q. Wilson and Richard Hernstein, *Crime and Human Nature* (New York: Simon & Schuster, 1985), p. 293.

29. Ibid., p. 311.

30. This section builds on the analysis offered in Montague Kern, *30-Second Politics: Political Advertising in the Eighties* (New York: Praeger, 1989).

31. Hence the author of one famous behavioral study concluded that "the principles of freedom and democracy are less widely favored and enthusiastically favored when they are confronted in their specific or applied forms." See Herbert McCloskey, "Consensus and Ideology in American Democracy," *American Political Science Review* 58 (June 1964), pp. 361–384.

32. Donald Devine, *The Political Culture of the United States* (Boston: Little, Brown, 1972), pp. 187–230.

CHAPTER 11

POLITICAL PARTICIPATION

CITIZENSHIP IN ACTION

(Bruce Davidson/Magnum)

CHAPTER 10 ARGUED that although citizenship is defined in different ways by different political regimes, true citizenship involves meaningful participation in politics. To be meaningful, political participation must satisfy at least two criteria: It must be voluntary, and there must be a reasonable possibility that the participants' actions, whether undertaken individually or collectively, will have the intended effect on policy or policymakers.

Although political participation might appear rather straightforward, a closer look reveals some ironies. For example, participation is sometimes most extensive in totalitarian societies, where it is least meaningful for the participants. Ironically, political participation can be quite low in the most open Western societies, those with the fewest barriers to citizen participation and with the most long-standing democratic traditions.

Such a result can be surprising because many Americans hold certain unexamined assumptions about democracy and political participation. Not only do we believe that a sign of democratic well-being can be measured by the level of citizen participation, but we often also assume that such participation is *natural* (that is, that citizens want to participate), is *knowledgeable* (that the participants know and understand the political choices they make), and is *influential* (that the system generally responds to citizens' opinions). These assumptions are worth analyzing, and we will do so after examining the various ways in which citizens participate in the political process.

FORMS OF PARTICIPATION

Under any form of government, citizens wishing to participate in politics have two alternatives—they can engage in legal or illegal activities. Most citizens choose to participate legally or not at all.

Legal Forms

Legal participation can assume a variety of forms, which we shall categorize and examine.

Conventional Participation *Conventional participation* encompasses the most familiar methods of political activity—those accepted as appropriate by the dominant political culture. Most citizens participate in politics in largely symbolic, passive, or ritualistic ways—for example, attending a political rally, responding to a political poll, watching a candidate on television, or putting a bumper sticker on the car.

Voting constitutes the most visible form of conventional participation. However, the effectiveness of voting as a measure of active citizen participation depends on a number of factors: the extent to which votes are counted fairly, the size of the electorate (the larger the number of voters, the less impact each individual vote has), and the availability of meaningful choices. Voting that offers no choice and does not make a difference may be considered merely symbolic. But even when the act of voting is classified as symbolic—when an individual's vote seems minuscule compared to all votes cast—the fact that so many people vote may be significant. Sometimes voting can convey an important message; it can even be a powerful form of peaceful protest. In 1959, for example, the citizens of São Paulo, Brazil, elected a rhinoceros in the local zoo to the city council![1] Similarly, the past two decades have witnessed a proliferation of issue-oriented initiatives and referendums; during that time, state voters have judged the wisdom (or folly) of issues as divergent as reducing property taxes, urging the U.S. government to initiate a nuclear freeze, and requiring the use of seat belts and motorcycle helmets.

Organizational (Institutional) Participation   In the United States, a relatively small number of citizens play an active role in organized politics. Studies of *institutional participation* have estimated that between 25 and 30 percent of the adult population participates actively in politics, although this figure seems high.[2] Many of these political activists contribute time and money to the political party of their choice, belong to public interest groups such as the American Civil Liberties Union, Common Cause, or the Sierra Club, and do volunteer campaign work for their favorite candidates (see Chapter 12).

In another example of organizational participation, this one much more nonpartisan, many citizens serve on governmental bodies, especially at the state and local level. Often these citizens are paid only a nominal fee or nothing at all for their efforts. However, this form of participation can serve as a school for future political professionals, providing valuable firsthand experience in the procedures, norms, and practices of governing.

Professional Participation   Political activists are fairly rare in the United States, but those who seek full-time careers—that is, *professional participation*—in politics are even rarer. This group includes people who exercise authority through paid political positions or elective office (party officials, lobbyists, political appointees, legislators, and the like).

Of course, not all public officials start out as professionals. Indeed, one anomaly of political participation in democratic societies—especially in the United States—is that the highest-ranking officials are sometimes the least experienced. Fred Grandy, a former Hollywood actor on the television show *The Love Boat*, was elected to Congress by Iowa in 1986. Such elections exemplify the amateurism that sometimes characterizes political life in societies where anyone can participate. A well-known aphorism makes this point succinctly: "Politics is the only profession for which no previous experience is thought to be necessary."

Unconventional Participation   *Unconventional participation* refers to forms of political action that are legal but nonetheless considered inappropriate by a majority of citizens. Of course, acceptable political behavior depends on the prevailing political culture and varies widely from one country to another.

In the United States, where most citizens place a high value on law and order, the majority has traditionally disapproved of protests and demonstrations. This pattern changed somewhat during the turbulent 1960s and early 1970s,

Among the legal but unconventional forms of political participation, only three—signing petitions, engaging in lawful demonstrations, and supporting boycotts—are considered appropriate by the majority of Americans. (Janet Fries/Black Star)

a period of upheaval marked by racial strife (the civil rights movement) and widespread student protests (against the Vietnam War). However, even after the Watergate revelations reached their peak in 1974—when President Nixon resigned to avoid impeachment and popular confidence in government had sunk to a very low point—only 8 percent of the public endorsed such actions as sit-ins, mass meetings, and demonstrations to obstruct government activity.[3]

In that same year, a study found that out of ten forms of unconventional political action, a majority of U.S. citizens approved of only three: signing petitions, engaging in lawful demonstrations, and supporting boycotts (such as not buying lettuce to show solidarity with underpaid migrant workers).[4] Only 2 percent of those surveyed believed that violence was justified to achieve political aims. During the past quarter century, support for relatively innocuous forms of unconventional participation has increased substantially in the United States and several European nations.[5] However, this support falls off sharply as the action in question approaches the line between legality and illegality.

Illegal Forms

Political regimes differ widely in what actions they classify as *illegal participation* and in how severely they punish such behavior. Nondemocratic governments normally outlaw a great many more political activities than democratic ones. For example, under democratic rule, few, if any, political parties are declared illegal, and citizens usually can affiliate with any party they choose. Under totalitarian rule, all parties except one are illegal. Moreover, nondemocratic governments often define "political crimes" more broadly and punish the perpetrators of such crimes more harshly than their democratic counterparts.

Some illegal acts—in particular, those classified as *civil disobedience*—are intended to stir a nation's conscience (and therefore prove to be far more effective in some nations than in others). Civil disobedience involves breaking specific laws to demonstrate their injustice. Mahatma Gandhi used civil disobedience in the struggle for India's independence from Great Britain; similarly, Martin Luther King, Jr., advocated nonviolent protest in the push for racial equality in the United States. Human rights activists in the Soviet Union also engaged in civil disobedience in the 1970s, although strict press censorship and neo-Stalinist repression (culminating in the show trial of Jewish dissident Anatoly Shcharansky) abruptly ended this practice.

Civil disobedience stresses nonviolence and encourages participants to accept their punishment as legitimate. At the other end of the spectrum stand political *terrorism*, using violence or threats of violence to demoralize, intimidate, and subjugate opponents; *subversion*, attempting to undermine a government, often with outside assistance; and *sedition*, inciting rebellious, antigovernmental acts. All are revolutionary actions. Depending on the regime, however, subversion or sedition can be defined as anything from attending an illegal meeting or joining an outlawed political party to publishing a pamphlet critical of the government or merely holding opinions at odds with official policy or ideology. In many nondemocratic nations, "antigovernmental agitation" is an elastic concept that can be stretched to include an action as innocuous as writing a letter to a friend that includes implicit criticism of the regime in power.

Premeditated terrorist acts against the government are always revolutionary; such acts are illegal even in countries ruled by self-styled revolutionary regimes. Indeed, "revolutionary" states generally deal more harshly with their own revolutionaries (whom they call counterrevolutionaries) than democratic or more traditional authoritarian states.

PUBLIC OPINION AS PARTICIPATION

Motivating these diverse modes of political participation is the simple fact that many citizens believe that their opinions can make a difference. The aggregate total of political participation helps produce a national *public opinion* that can have profound effects on a nation's leaders and their policies and even the nation's continued existence. So important is public opinion that no government can afford to ignore it. This generalization is most broadly true in democracies, where public opinion can usually be easily determined and freely expressed. In such states, public opinion is always consequential, but it becomes perceptibly more important when elections are close at hand. Apart from its direct relationship to elections in democracies, the influence of public opinion in any nation depends on the number of citizens actively expressing an opinion on any particular issue, the distribution of opinion (whether it is lopsided or evenly balanced on a given issue), and the intensity with which beliefs and opinions on particular issues are held and expressed.

Polling

All governments make some effort to assess and analyze public opinion. In democratic states, public opinion on a variety of issues is gauged and discussed freely, and efforts to identify the majority opinion on any particular issue are undertaken not only by public agencies but also by political parties and candidates, the media, various private organizations and research institutes, and inquiring scholars. To determine how the public stands on a given issue, organizations rely on *public opinion polling* (canvassing citizens for their opinions), which has become the most popular and accurate means of defining and charting changes in public opinion.

The *Literary Digest* Poll: What Went Wrong?

MODERN POLLING TECHNIQUES are highly sophisticated and usually quite accurate. Few if any politicians doubt the value of polling. But David Holmstrom, a writer for *The Christian Science Monitor*, cautions his readers not to forget the 1936 presidential election and the infamous poll of *Literary Digest* magazine, the poll that changed professional polling techniques forever.

Polling was in its infancy in 1936. Using a sample drawn mainly from automobile registrations and owners of telephones around the country, *Literary Digest*, one of the most popular magazines of the day, mailed out more than 10 million straw vote ballots (as part of a promotion campaign).

The final tally of responses just before election day gave Republican Alf Landon 1,293,699 votes (55 percent), Democratic candidate Franklin D. Roosevelt 972,897 votes (41 percent), and the rest for a third candidate.

Of course on election day Roosevelt won by a landslide with 61 percent of the vote to Landon's 37 percent. The electoral vote was a staggering 523 to 8. *Literary Digest* had previously conducted polls on each presidential election since 1920 and had predicted the winners.

What went wrong? First, the sample was biased (not everyone who could vote owned a car or had a telephone in the 1930s). Second, not everyone sampled chose to respond (many voters most likely to prefer Roosevelt had little education or money and possibly could ill-afford a five-cent stamp at that time). Third, even within the middle-class ranks (i.e., voters with cars and telephones) there was a split: upscale Republicans comprised the largest response group.

Holmstrom concludes:

What this 1936 poll did was put an end to the assumption among professional pollsters that the quantity of respondents in polling was the road to accuracy. More proved not to be better. From then on the art of polling became more sophisticated. It turned to cautious random sampling as a better indicator of attitudes and preferences, and therefore enhanced the ability to forecast the results with some degree of accuracy.

SOURCE: David Holmstrom, "Election-Year Polls Saturate the Public," *The Christian Science Monitor* (March 13, 1992), p. 13. Reprinted with permission from *The Christian Science Monitor* © 1992, The Christian Science Publishing Society. All rights reserved.

Over the past few decades, public opinion polling has grown increasingly sophisticated. Through so-called scientific polling, researchers predict the actions of a large population based on the answers given by a relatively small number of respondents. In the preferred method of polling, a *random sampling* of citizens is taken from among the entire population (or "universe") being polled. (Statisticians have determined that 1,500 is an ideal number of respondents for polls involving large numbers of people.) In such surveys, differences in age, race, religion, political orientation, education, and other factors within the sample polled closely approximate those differences within the larger population. Because it is not always possible to conduct hundreds of separate interviews, pollsters sometimes use smaller, preselected samples based on such key characteristics as age, religion, income, and party affiliation. This method of polling is known as *stratified sampling*. Exit polling, which permits the television networks to predict political winners as the polls close, illustrates two levels of stratified polling. First, pollsters identify precincts that statistically approximate the larger political entity (a congressional district, a state, or the nation). Then those who conduct the exit interviews try to select a sample that reflects the overall characteristics of the precinct. *Tracking polls*, conducted by candidates for public office, are a particularly important type of private polling. In these polls, the same voters are sampled repeatedly in the course of a campaign. Such polls seek to determine shifts in voter sentiment and correlate them with media strategy, changing issues, candidates' gaffes, and so forth. These polls are designed to inform candidates about which strategies are working (and which are not) in any particular campaign.

Polls are usually quite accurate, but they are hardly infallible; even the best polls may contain errors. Generally, they have a margin of error of 3 percent at the .05 level of confidence, which means that 95 out of 100 times the error is no more than 3 percent in either direction. Public opinion polls are less than perfectly accurate for several reasons, including limitations in the design of the survey questionnaire or in the representativeness of the sample of people interviewed. The exact wording of a given instrument is particularly important on issues where most people do not have well-formed opinions; given a choice between two policies (for example, "Should the government see to it that all people have housing, or should individuals provide for their own housing?"), some respondents can be so influenced by the order in which the policies are mentioned that a 30 percent variance between the two choices may result, depending solely on which policy alternative is given first in the question.[6] Furthermore, asking this same question in a way so that only one side of the issue is mentioned (for example, "Should the federal government see to it that all people have adequate housing?") is likely to produce a significantly greater level of agreement with the policy and the question than phrasing it to include policy alternatives. These results demonstrate that polls cannot be any clearer or more precise than the opinion they are designed to measure, and where that opinion is fragile or ill-formed, polling results are apt to be misleading. Furthermore, from this example we can see how polls can be used not only to *measure* public opinion but also to *influence* it. Candidates, corporations, and organizations of all kinds who wish to demonstrate the popularity of their position or product can often obtain the results they want through careful phrasing of the questions. Unfortunately, stacking the deck in this way is a common practice in both the public and private sectors.

Another reason why polls can be inaccurate relates to a lack of candor on the part of some respondents (for example, even though they are promised anonymity, voters may not always respond truthfully about how they intend to vote, especially if they believe their choice may be perceived as unpopular or irresponsible). In any case, it is important to remember that polls conducted during election campaigns (or at any time about any issue in politics) are mere snapshots of public opinion; they are not perfect representations of that opinion or perfect predictors of elections or voter preferences. And not all polls are equal or equally accurate, as demonstrated in Figure 11-1, which reveals the significantly different predictions of various polls taken during the 1984 presidential race between candidates Ronald Reagan and Walter Mondale.

Some polls conducted between elections can rival in importance polls conducted during election campaigns. For example, a president's popularity, as measured in public opinion polls, helps to determine how much political influence the chief executive can wield on a wide range of political issues. The same holds true for relations between the president and Congress, especially when the latter is controlled by the opposition party.

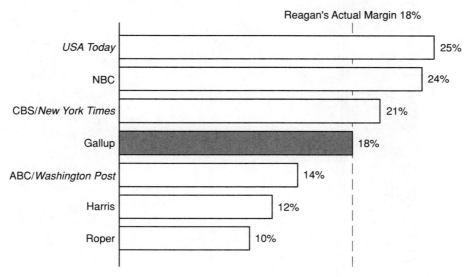

FIGURE 11-1   Predictions and Actual Results of 1984 Election
SOURCE: *U.S. News & World Report,* November 19, 1984, p. 15.

Elections

Meaningful elections give polling its most important political justifications and uses. In fact, without elections, the political uses of polls would be far more limited.

Importance of Elections   Elections serve different functions in different political systems. Under most military dictatorships, for example, regular elections simply do not take place—a reflection of the minimal, or nonexistent, citizen participation in such regimes. In totalitarian states, elections take on the aura of a stylized political ritual, whereby the rulers certify and legitimize their authority. In constitutional democracies, by contrast, elections act as the principal means by which citizens determine who will govern and, indirectly, what policies will be pursued.

Free elections are tied to the concept of representation. Representatives, acting on behalf of voting citizens, make the legislative and executive decisions that voters in the aggregate could not possibly make for themselves, considering the sheer numbers of people involved. In Chapter 13 we will explore how elected representatives should act—whether they should simply echo every majority opinion of their constituents or rather exercise personal judgment and attempt to reshape public opinion accordingly. At this point, we need only note that

French voters cast ballots in the March 1992 French regional elections. Political representation is implicit in the very idea of modern constitutional government, and elections are essential to the functioning of a truly representative system. (Karim Daher/Gamma)

political representation is implicit in the very idea of modern constitutional government and that elections are essential to the functioning of a truly representative system.

Limitations of Elections   Ideally, elections should enable a democratic society to translate the preferences of its citizens into wise policies adopted by competent political leaders. In reality, however, elections do not always produce such happy results. Among the inherent limitations of elections as vehicles of public choice are the following:

1 If public opinion on the most important issues of the day is ill-defined or badly divided, newly elected officials may receive no clear mandate from the voters. And even if such a mandate is given, an elected official may regard public opinion on a particular issue to be misguided and either ignore it or try to change it.

2 The great expenditure of time and money required to run for public office may either discourage capable candidates from seeking office or give an unfair advantage to incumbents.

3 To attract as many voters or interest groups as possible, candidates for public office may waffle on an issue. This studied ambiguity can pose difficulties for conscientious voters interested in making an intelligent choice.

4 Candidates may find that they cannot carry out their promises once elected to office. Certain pledges prove impossible to implement, either because candidates deliberately overstated what could be accomplished or because they simply underestimated the forces of resistance. In the United States, political change becomes difficult when a president's policies differ from those espoused by one or both houses of Congress, when Congress is hampered by an unwieldy budget process, or when both branches seek to implement policies that run counter to the interests of the entrenched federal bureaucracy.

5 After being elected to office, a candidate may simply have a change of heart about the desirability or feasibility of a particular policy. The influence of new interest groups, exposure to more and better information, or the realization of the intricate relationships among various domestic and foreign policies can have a profound impact on a newly elected official.

Despite these limitations, elections work better than any other method of translating citizen sentiment into public policy, especially in a large and diverse society. In fact, there is good reason to believe that political promises are kept far more often than they are broken.[7] From time to time, elected officials may turn out to be disappointments, but they are seldom surprises. Voters usually have a fairly good idea of what to expect when they elect a particular candidate.

In sum, without free elections, the vast majority of citizens would have no meaningful say in setting the national agenda, defining policy alternatives, and determining who will rule. In nondemocratic states, elections have far more to do with the appearance than with the reality of grass-roots participation. Rigged elections may be a charade, but they also constitute a form of flattery, and the old adage about flattery—that it is the tribute vice pays to virtue—might also be applied to staged elections.

Electoral Systems

Winner-Take-All Systems   U.S. representatives are elected by plurality vote in single-member districts; that is, in our *winner-take-all system,* only one representative is elected from each electoral district, and the candidate who gets the most votes in the general election wins the seat. Furthermore, because a state's two senators are elected in different years, entire states function as single-member districts as well. Finally, the 50 states are each single-member districts in the presidential race, for *all* the electoral votes in any state are awarded to the electors of the presidential candidate who receives the most votes in that particular state.

The practical political implications of such a system are wide-ranging. In any election within a single-member district, if only two candidates are seeking office, one of them necessarily will receive a *simple majority*—defined as the largest bloc of votes. If three or more candidates are vying for a seat, however, the one who receives a plurality of the votes is elected: In a five-way race, for example, a candidate might win with 25 percent (or less) of the votes. As we shall see, this method of election strongly favors the emergence of a two-party system.

The effects of a winner-take-all electoral political system are graphically illustrated by the hypothetical United States congressional race depicted in Table 11-1. Notice that this system has at least one important advantage: It produces clear winners. Here a simple majority decides who will represent the district. In the example cited in the table, Liberal is the clear winner.

But note the complications: 57 percent of the electorate did not vote for Liberal. For all it mattered, they might as well have stayed home. Furthermore (given our hypothetical example), it is likely not only that the differing views espoused by candidates Conservative and Noparty will not be represented in this congressional district but that a majority political perspective may have been rejected (Conservative and Noparty, after all, might have shared positions on many more issues than either would have shared with Liberal).

Furthermore, the winner-take-all electoral system can also produce *national* political distortions. In our hypothetical race, Liberal won only 43 percent of the popular vote in his district, but he gained 100 percent of its representation. His candidacy (and Conservative's candidacy as well) was no doubt aided by the

TABLE 11-1
A Hypothetical Political Race

Party	Candidate	Votes Received	Percent of Vote
Democratic	John Liberal	25,800	43
Republican	Jane Conservative	24,600	41
Independent	Joe Noparty	9,600	16

superior organization, finances, and perceived electoral advantages of their affiliation with one of the two major American political parties. Inevitably, the losers are minor-party candidates. This means, in practice, that major parties gain representation disproportionate to the actual popular vote they receive. Hence a major party receiving 40 to 45 percent of the popular vote may win a clear majority of legislative seats. Sometimes this type of distortion is so pronounced that a major party turns a less than absolute majority vote into an electoral landslide.

In this way, the American (and, to a lesser extent, the British) electoral system encourages the emergence of two major political parties and hampers the growth of smaller political parties and splinter groups. This makes for greater political stability than can be found in many multiparty systems. In the view of some critics, however, such stability is achieved at the expense of political responsiveness. Because the winner-take-all system does not represent the total spectrum of voter opinions and interests, they point out, it tends to magnify the legislative power of the major party (or parties) and stultify the attempts of minor parties to secure a legislative toehold.

Proportional Representation Systems   The alternative to winner-take-all is an electoral system based on *proportional representation,* which is designed to ensure that the representation of parties in the legislature approximates party support in the electorate. Usually, under this type of system, the nation is divided into electoral districts (and into more comprehensive electoral regions). These are usually *multimember* districts, meaning that several representatives are elected from each. Among the countries that have adopted this system are Israel, Belgium, Norway, and Ireland.

Generally, candidates in a district win office if they receive at least a specified number of votes. The minimum number of votes required is determined by dividing the number of votes cast by the number of seats allocated per district. For example, let us assume in Table 11-1 that a proportional representation system is in place, that the district in question has been allocated three votes, and that a total of 60,000 votes have been cast. Under those circumstances, a representative will be elected for every 20,000 votes a party receives. According to this formula, candidate Liberal and candidate Conservative would each be elected because each received more than 20,000 votes. The district's third representative would be determined by a regional distribution, which works like this: 5,800 Democratic votes, 4,600 Republican votes, and 9,600 Independent votes would be forwarded to the region, where they would be combined with other districts' votes and reallocated (where regional distributions fail to seat a candidate, a final, national distribution may be necessary). In this manner, a proportional representation system attempts to ensure that everyone's vote counts equally.

However, some countries have modified their proportional representation systems to prevent a proliferation of small, fringe parties. In these countries, minor parties must receive a certain minimum of the national vote to qualify at all for district representation. In Germany, this figure is 5 percent; in other nations, it can be 15 percent or even higher.

The *list system* is by far the most common method of proportional representation in use. Under this system, a party may run as many candidates as it wishes in any particular electoral district, but it must rank its candidates on the ballot. If the party receives enough votes in the district to win only one seat, the candidate ranked first on the list gets that seat; if the party garners enough votes to elect two delegates from that district, the candidate ranked second also gets a seat; and so on. The list system strengthens political parties significantly, because citizens vote primarily for the party (as opposed to the candidate) and because the party controls the ordering of the candidates on the ballot.

The other method of proportional representation, known as the *Hare plan,* is based on a single, transferable vote and emphasizes individual candidates (or personalities) rather than parties. Candidates compete freely for a given number of elective offices. A quota is set in advance, and all candidates who receive a stipulated number of votes are declared elected. But this system offers an unusual twist: Each voter indicates both a first and a second choice, and if there are any seats left unfilled after the first-choice votes have been counted, surplus votes are transferred to the remaining candidates on the basis of the voters' second-choice preferences.

Strengths and Weaknesses of Electoral Systems   Both the list system and the Hare plan have certain advantages over the winner-take-all method of representation. Fewer votes are "wasted," in the sense that a broader spectrum of views can be represented and more parties gain seats in the legislature. Furthermore, these systems appear to be fairer and more equitable than our own because the available seats are apportioned according to the vote totals that each party actually receives.

However, proportional representation, especially under the list system, has several by-products, including a pronounced tendency toward party centralization, the emergence of single-issue splinter parties, more intense parliamentary factionalism, increased difficulty in forming a national consensus, and a de-emphasis on individual candidates in favor of political parties as the main vehicles of political choice. Some of these side effects may be desirable; on balance, however, it seems likely that most Americans would not want to trade their present system, whatever its defects, for a new system with a new set of problems.

Direct Democracy

In some democracies, such as Switzerland and Australia, as well as a number of American states (see Figure 11-2), citizens can bypass (or supersede) their elected representatives by voting directly on specific questions of public policy. Generally, such elections are called *plebiscites.* In the United States, these direct democratic elections take three specific forms. A *referendum* occurs when the state legislature or constitution refers a question of public policy to its voters. In some

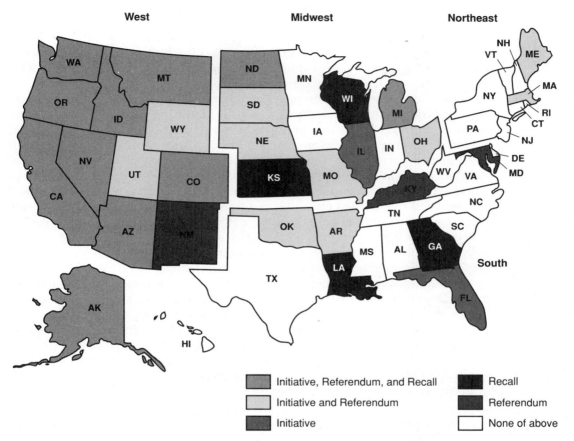

FIGURE 11-2   Citizen-initiated Initiative, Referendum, and Recall at the State Level

SOURCE: Reprinted by permission of the publishers from *Direct Democracy: The Politics of Initiative, Referendum, and Recall* by Thomas E. Cronin, (Cambridge, Mass.: Harvard University Press). Copyright © 1989 by the Twentieth Century Fund, Inc.

instances, citizens by their vote merely advise their representatives regarding their policy preferences; in other cases, voter approval is required before the contested statute can be enacted into law. An *initiative* is put on the ballot by the voters themselves, who file petitions containing a stipulated number of valid signatures. The *recall* is a political device intended to remove an elected official from office. It works much like an initiative and is also placed on the ballot by obtaining the signatures of a predetermined number of citizens.

Notable instances of important political issues decided by this kind of direct vote have occurred in many democracies. In 1962, French President Charles de Gaulle used a referendum to amend the French constitution to provide for the direct election of the president (de Gaulle himself). In 1973, Great Britain held the first referendum in its history to decide whether or not the nation should join the Common Market. (A narrow majority voted in favor of joining.) The modern era of direct democracy in the United States can be traced to 1978 and California's passage of the famous Proposition 13, which not only cut property taxes by at least half but also spurred a large number and variety of initiatives and referendums throughout the nation.

Direct democracy measures have been championed as a means of strengthening democracy.[8] They are seen as a way of increasing government's responsiveness and accountability, improving voter participation, and addressing elected representatives who are corrupt, inept, or unresponsive. Opponents of direct democracy fear that money and special interests may play a disproportionately larger role in these special elections than they do in the ordinary legislative process. They also contend that initiatives and referendums are often so complex and technical that the issues cannot be understood by the average voter. However, this last concern is not shared by a foremost student of these processes, who contends that experience "in the states suggests that on most issues, especially well-publicized ones, voters do grasp the meaning of the issues on which they are asked to vote, and that they act competently."[9]

Hence negative evaluations of direct democracy measures have been overstated. Does this mean that there is no reason for concern regarding the proliferation of initiatives and referendums? Not necessarily. The problems is to strike the right balance. Such measures often enhance self-government at the local level. But once these measures become too numerous, and the issues they involve so complex, the opportunity for special interests grows and the possibility of competent voter review diminishes. Ultimately, direct democracy is best viewed as a supplement to, not a substitute for, representative democracy.

ASSESSING PARTICIPATION: WHY DON'T CITIZENS VOTE?

Underlying the debate over direct democracy is the assumption that citizen participation is natural—that citizens want to participate in their democratic government but can sometimes be shut out of the process. Such a belief is certainly plausible. Ordinary men and women have struggled to win the franchise in nations around the world because they prize free elections and voting rights so highly. Yet often rights that were so hard to gain for earlier generations are taken for granted by later ones. This is particularly true in the United States. The question is why.

Voting in the United States

The two important facts to understand about voting in the United States is that voting rates are low and that they are declining. In 1960, in the Kennedy-Nixon election, nearly 63 percent of the adult population voted. By 1988, the percentage had declined to 50.2 percent. An even better measure of voting participation is midterm elections (when there is no presidential race). In 1962, that rate was 46.3

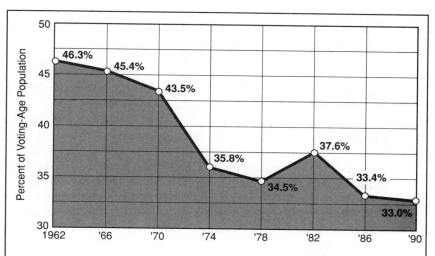

The voter turnout rate in midterm elections has been declining since 1962. It fell abruptly after the voting age was lowered to 18 in 1971 and has continued downward since (the lone exception was the recession year of 1982). In 1990, turnout for House contests reached the lowest point since the wartime election of 1942: less than one-third of the nation's voting-age population (33.0 percent) cast ballots.

In Tennessee, Mississippi, and Louisiana (where only one district was decided in November), the turnout rate did not reach 20 percent. In only four states did a majority of the voting-age population participate in voting for the House: Maine (55.6 percent), Minnesota (54.8 percent), Montana (54.6 percent), and Alaska (52.5 percent).

FIGURE 11-3   U.S. Midterm Election Turnout, 1962–1990, Based on House Votes Cast (percentage of voting-age population)
SOURCE: *Congressional Quarterly Weekly Report,* February 23, 1991, p. 484.

percent; by 1990, it had declined to 33 percent (see Figure 11-3). Compared to other democracies (in Italy, Austria, Belgium, Sweden, Greece, the Netherlands, Australia, Denmark, and Norway, for instance, an average of over 80 percent of the electorate participates in presidential elections or their equivalent), voter turnout in the United States seems embarrassingly low.[10]

What is intriguing about these low and declining rates of voter participation is their unexpectedness. In fact, as two experts have pointed out:

> During the period of declining turnout much happened that should have increased participation. For one thing, there were the changes over time in the law. Provisions designed to burden voter access to the ballot, such as poll taxes, literacy tests, and lengthy residence requirements, were largely done away with. The voting age was lowered to 18. In effect, the nation created legally the potential for a huge mass electorate consisting of virtually all adults, with only minor exceptions.[11]

Moreover, "broad changes in the population have boosted levels of education, income, and occupation, all associated with enhanced rates of turnout."[12]

Patterns of Participation

It has long been established that only a minority of American citizens actively participate in politics. A pioneering study done in 1950 by Julian L. Woodward and Elmo Roper revealed that about 70 percent of the adult population was politically inactive.[13] A later study found that approximately 26 percent of the American population could be classified as activists and that the rest of the population limited participation to voting or avoided politics altogether.[14] Active participants can be readily identified: Percentagewise, more middle-aged citizens than younger or older people vote, more white-collar workers than blue-collar workers, more married people than singles, and more whites than blacks. When differences in family income, formal education, socioeconomic background, and self-esteem are taken into account, it becomes evident why some people are more highly motivated politically than others: Those who take an active role in political life have a greater belief that they can make a difference. Not surprisingly, this sense of *political efficacy* often reflects a mixture of innate ability, individual conditioning, and social circumstances.

Yet the question remains, given the fact that a small minority of Americans actively participates in politics, why do so many not even vote, and why has that rate decreased so dramatically in the past three decades? Explanations abound. Some observers cite the lowering of the voting age to 18 in 1971, pointing out the relatively low rate of voting among citizens 18 to 21 years old. Others point to increased citizen mobility and the accompanying sense of alienation generated by moving from community to community and suggest that this has also had a negative effect on voting participation. Still other observers cite attitudinal factors, especially the falling rate of party identification and a growing feeling that individual actions are ineffectual or that politics has become boring or superficial. A different attitudinal explanation notes that most people vote because they feel that they ought to and then goes on to suggest that there is currently in the United States a decreasing sense of both voter and general citizen responsibility. Finally, many believe that the increasingly lengthy political campaigns (especially for president) and a repetitious number of distasteful television advertisements may well sour some potential voters on the whole process.

Individualism and Public Participation

Such factors may well explain the decline in voter participation. But what accounts for the fundamentally low level of voter turnout? Some social scientists have argued that the relatively low level of political participation in the United States proves that widespread *alienation* exists in American society. Although some Americans feel politically impotent or unimportant, and a small percentage of Americans are thoroughly alienated from the system, it is also true that most Americans do not consider themselves either alienated or disaffected. On the contrary, most Americans are satisfied with their circumstances most of the time.[15] We must look elsewhere to explain the high level of nonparticipation in American political life.

As a rule, Americans who take little or no interest in politics simply do not care sufficiently about politics. Roughly 160 years ago, French writer Alexis de Tocqueville (1805–1859) observed that wherever a widespread belief in equality exists, as in the United States, individuals tend to rely primarily on themselves for guidance as to how to lead their lives. The established sources of instruction in such matters—religion, family, monarchy, tradition, even government—simply do not carry the weight they do in other societies.

Tocqueville regarded this social characteristic, which he called *individualism,* as the moral equivalent of selfishness. "Individualism," he wrote,

> is a mature and calm feeling, which disposes each member of the community to sever himself from the mass of his fellow creatures; and to draw apart with his family and friends; so that, after he has thus formed a little circle of his own, he willingly leaves the society at large to itself.[16]

Tocqueville thought that Americans were so concerned about their own private worlds that concern for the common good was in danger of extinction. To him, the will to succeed in a society in which success is defined as "keeping up with the Joneses" condemned Americans to constant agitation arising from private ambitions. Thus he noted that "in America the passion for physical well-being . . . is felt by all" and that "the desire of acquiring the good things of this world is the prevailing passion of the American people."[17]

Tocqueville's observations about the American character have held up amazingly well. Many of the same points were made recently by the political scientists Harry Holloway and John George. In *Public Opinion,* Holloway and George observed that "Americans strive hard to succeed and tend to keep savings low and to consume heavily" and that "the continuous extension of work and educational effort, the low savings, the optimism, and the innovative consumer demand are all of a piece with . . . rising expectations." After noting that these signs suggest "American individualism and self-reliance . . . are not unreal," they concluded:

> This American motivation for economic success and the consumerism that accompanies it is illuminating. Much American striving is oriented not toward politics but toward economic betterment perceived in rather private terms as advancement for oneself and one's family, and most American families do a good deal more to prepare their children for success economically than for success in the political arena. We can see now why Americans tend to stress personal concerns, including the economic, and divorce the private from the public sector.[18]

As Tocqueville understood long ago, Americans are often too caught up in their private lives to take an active interest in public life.

Political Apathy: An American Pathology?

Of course, the United States is not entirely free of political disaffection. Many Americans express a pervasive distrust of politicians—a sentiment reinforced by scandals such as congressional checking improprieties and the Iran-Contra affair.[19] But voter apathy in the United States does not always arise from a general belief that most elected officials are corrupt or that the political system has broken down and is beyond repair. Quite the opposite is true. The main reason most Americans are so nonchalant about politics is that they do not usually feel threatened, oppressed, egregiously overtaxed, or otherwise victimized by their government. Seen in this light, *political apathy* is a kind of luxury that many citizens apparently feel they can afford because the government is doing a good enough job without their input. Only in an affluent and relatively well-governed society are people apt to be so preoccupied with their own private affairs that they forget to vote on election day!

Furthermore, the common observation that widespread political apathy is a sign of political decay is not necessarily valid. To the contrary, American democracy has managed to work quite well in spite of high levels of political nonparticipation. When people who are normally apathetic suddenly begin to express high anxiety about politics, usually all is not well. Shortly before the Civil War, for example, political apathy almost disappeared amid the controversy over slavery and states' rights, yet the country was on the verge of disintegration. When there is a division of opinion so sharp that no compromise appears possible and when the issue involved is so important that large numbers of citizens are vitally affected, participation and instability tend to increase in tandem.

It would be wrong to conclude, however, that because American democracy can function in spite of apathy and because instability is often associated with increased participation, apathy is good and participation is bad. On the one hand, apathy that grows out of a deep sense of alienation is cause for serious concern; on the other, high levels of participation stemming from a genuine commitment to the public good represent the best antidote to excessive individualism. Finally, although high levels of participation are not necessary in a democracy, a minimal level of voter interest is essential if representative government is to work effectively.

ASSESSING PARTICIPATION: ARE VOTERS KNOWLEDGEABLE AND THOUGHTFUL?

In the United States, voters are a select group. They care somewhat about politics. They bother to register and vote. But do they vote intelligently? Occasionally, the media carry stories of voter gullibility. Frequently, these stories are predictable, although they are almost always amusing. Dead candidates are elected to state offices; accused felons, running for public office on a lark, get thousands of votes. Political consultants point out that in many races (particularly city and county races with long ballots), having one's name at the head of the ballot can be worth hundreds or thousands of votes. What does it say about the competence of voters and about democracy in general when candidate Aaron can gain significant advantage over candidate Zuba simply because of the spelling of a name (or because of some other equally arbitrary way of determining the order of candidates' names on a ballot)?

Therefore, even though voters are more highly motivated and better informed than ordinary citizens, this turns out to be a modest claim indeed. It appears that a great number of adult Americans cannot identify the names of governmental leaders, are unfamiliar with election issues, and often display a general ignorance of politics. Such a conclusion has been documented in numerous academic studies. For instance, fewer than 15 percent of adult Americans can identify the chief justice of the United States; under 40 percent can name both of their state's U.S. senators; and less than half the voters can identify the two major-party candidates for the House of Representatives from their district.[20] A foremost student of American government, James Q. Wilson, provides a generally accepted conclusion when he observes that "public opinion on many matters suffers from ignorance, instability and sensitivity to the way the question is worded." Wilson puts the best possible face on this observation, implying that something like individualism is the root cause of voter unawareness, for it is not "that the American people are ignorant, unstable or gullible, only that most Americans do not find it worth their while to spend the amount of time thinking about politics that they spend on their jobs, families and friends."[21]

But it is not only the lack of factual information that accounts for concern regarding voter competence. Consider the following facts: Before the 1990 midterm elections, pollsters repeatedly found only one-third or less of the American people had any real confidence in Congress, while two-thirds favored replacing incumbents. Furthermore, many Americans exhibited a healthy distrust of congressional representatives in general. To improve Congress, Americans favored limiting terms of House representatives to 12 years. Yet at the same time, these voters liked their own elected representative (and senators), and when it came time to vote, they overwhelmingly reelected them—as usual—often to terms in excess of 12 years (see Figure 11-4). How can we reconcile these peculiar voter attitudes and behaviors?[22] Surely, voters cannot be right that their elected representatives alone are above average and therefore entitled to long terms. Furthermore, what district and state voters often liked about their representatives (that they successfully looked after local interests and helped to solve individual problems) was exactly what was disliked by the vast majority of out-of-state and out-of-district voters, who saw such acts as the mere protection of narrow, special interests.

Thus it would appear that most American voters not only lack political knowledge but also are not especially thoughtful. This pattern is worrisome, not least because a successful democracy requires an informed and intelligent citizenry. The picture of an electorate that is neither well informed nor thoughtful is hardly comforting.

But this concern is also probably exaggerated. First, democracy can endure a great deal of voter ignorance and survive. Furthermore, many elections are complicated and feature numerous obscure state and local candidates and issues. Frequently, many candidates have no clear political stance; others who do take positions try deliberately to obfuscate them. Then too, in most instances, voter choice is quite understandable and defensible. It is probably fair to say, for example, that citizens devote to voting the same amount of study, impulse,

1970	'72	'74	'76	'78	'80	'82	'84	'86	'88	'90

Congressional incumbents who retired

33	46	50	55	59	39	43	26	44	29	30

Congressional incumbents who sought reelection

432	417	418	409	407	427	423	438	421	435	438
1970	'72	'74	'76	'78	'80	'82	'84	'86	'88	'90

Incumbents defeated in primary

11	14	10	3	8	10	10	3	2	1	1

Incumbents defeated in election

18	18	42	22	34	40	31	19	13	10	16

Percentage of incumbents reelected

93.3	92.3	87.6	93.9	91.6	88.3	90.3	95.0	96.4	97.7	96.3
1970	'72	'74	'76	'78	'80	'82	'84	'86	'88	'90

FIGURE 11-4   The Advantage of Incumbency
Although the 1992 elections proved particularly challenging for incumbents (due to redistricting, a high level of voter discontent during difficult economic times, and several prominent political scandals), the political advantage enjoyed by incumbents has been, as this chart illustrates, a powerful trend in American politics for over two decades.
SOURCE: Copyright 1992, *USA Today*. Reprinted with permission.

information, and rationality as they devote to buying a car. Patently unwise election choices and foolish car purchases can result, but in general they are the exceptions rather than the rule. For the most part, both cars that sell well and political representatives who are popularly elected reflect reasonable decisions.

Finally, we need to explain why citizens vote for individual congressional representatives while distrusting Congress as an institution. This may well be little more than a case of voters trying to maximize their immediate economic and political interests by electing representatives who are committed to safeguarding those interests (against the threats posed by representatives from other states). This may not be the most worthy or enlightened approach to electing officials, but it is wholly rational. Furthermore, the American political system was designed to take account of individual self-interest (see Chapter 6). All in all, though the American voter may not be perfect, the picture is not quite so gloomy as commonly portrayed.

Blind Ballots?   33,004 Vote for Candidate Who's in Jail

IT APPEARS THAT some Minnesotans haven't the slightest clue of who they're voting for when they step into the voting booth.

Consider that 33,004 Minnesotans cast ballots Tuesday for Leonard J. Richards, a state treasurer candidate who never actively campaigned: He is in Hennepin County jail, awaiting his second trial for first-degree murder. He's the one whose mug shot appeared in the newspaper voters guide—the one who had 300 S. 4th St. #36 (the county jail) listed as his address.

"It's impossible for the voters to know a lot about all the candidates," theorized Secretary of State Joan Growe, the state's official vote counter. "You have to remember that the primary is just one step along the way. That's one of the reasons we have all these steps, so we don't have these kinds of things, hopefully. It's not a perfect system, but it's understandable. It's the nature of what happens in a real, open democracy."

Richards, 48, finished third in a field of three candidates vying for the DFL nomination for treasurer. Still, he got more votes than each of Mark Dayton's challengers for state auditor, save one.

Richards, who ran for the U.S. House in 1974 and the U.S. Senate in 1978, was unavailable for comment yesterday. He spent the morning making a brief court appearance on a pretrial procedural matter.

Richards was convicted in the 1987 shooting and stabbing death of his tax attorney, Robert Stratton, but was granted a new trial by the Minnesota Supreme Court because he was not allowed to be his own attorney. That enabled him to file for office, since technically, it obliterated his only felony conviction.

Richards also has been indicted on murder charges in the 1982 death of his half-sister, May Wilson, whose throat was slashed in a crime allegedly motivated by a large insurance award. He has not gone to trial on that case but a civil jury blamed him for the murder when it denied him the insurance.

"I have no theory about why anybody would vote for him," said incumbent Michael McGarth, who won the DFL nomination for treasurer with 148,617 votes. But neither McGrath nor runner-up Bob Johnson exactly ran their campaigns against Richards, either. Said McGrath: "I only said nice things about him."

SOURCE: Kevin Diaz, "Blind Ballots? 33,004 Voted for Candidate Who's in Jail," *The Star Tribune,* Minneapolis/St. Paul (September 13, 1990; pp. 1A and 17A). Used with the permission of *The Star Tribune.*

ASSESSING PARTICIPATION: UNDERMINED BY A POWER ELITE?

Sometimes it is suggested that even if rank-and-file citizens took an active and informed part in government, it is by no means certain that their efforts would make a difference. Because of the complexity and size of modern states and because only a few can govern at any one time, utopian expectations about the political influence of the ordinary citizen seem remote.

But what about groups of highly placed citizens acting in coalition? Several influential political theorists have argued that "power elites" control the political process from top to bottom. The most popular version of this theory holds that ordinary citizens never exercise much influence, elections and public opinion polls notwithstanding. The political system, according to this view, is manipulated from above rather than from below. The manipulators are the power elite, a small group of individuals who float back and forth between the commanding heights of industry and the rarefied echelons of government, exercising enormous power over the political destiny of the nation. The status, wealth, and power of this self-perpetuating political class ensure that access to the levers of government is generally denied to most citizens. The power elites run the country to benefit their own private good, not to aid or advance the public good.

Elitist Theories

One of the best known of the *elitist theories of democracy* applied to the United States was propounded most influentially in the 1950s by the sociologist C. Wright Mills.[23] Mills's views are quite compatible with those embodied in Robert Michels's pioneering theory of elitism, known as the *Iron Law of Oligarchy.* But whereas Mills's studies dealt exclusively with what he believed to be the ruling class in the United States, Michels's theory applied to all modern bureaucratic organizations. The latter's views were distilled from an intensive study of the German Social Democratic party (SDP), which before the outbreak of World War I was the largest socialist party in the world. Michels reasoned that because the SDP favored equality in wealth and status, it should be sufficiently committed to democratic principles to internalize them in its own modes of operation. He found, instead, that the SDP was run by elite groups who derived their power and authority from well-honed organizational skills.

Michels postulated that all large organizations, including governments, are run in the same fashion. He believed that however democratic they may seem, they become increasingly oligarchic as their leaders gain more information, greater control of communications, and sharper organizational skills, while the great mass of members (or citizens) remain politically unsophisticated, preoccupied with private affairs, and bewildered by the complexity of larger issues. According to this view, the people, for whose benefit democratic institutions were originally conceived, are inevitably shut out of the political or organizational process as corporate officers or bureaucratic officials govern in the name of the rank-and-file shareholder or citizen.

In theories such as those of Mills and Michels, democracy is seen as a sham or a myth: It does not matter what the people think, say, or do because they have no real influence over public policy anyway. If most people believe that public opinion matters, it is only because they have been duped by the ruling class.

Although elitists generally agree that the dominance of elites and the contrasting quiescence of the masses make democracy a myth, they disagree on whether or not such dominance is a bad thing. Most believe that "democracy for the few" violates the very essence of government by consent as promoting the public good, the true end of government, becomes submerged in the self-interested policies and decisions of the ruling elites. A few theorists have argued that the American political system is dominated by the privileged few and that we are all much better off for it. According to this view, those who control the levers of power are the fittest to rule; in contrast, the people as a whole are unfit to govern themselves. In the words of one pair of authorities, the "masses are authoritarian, intolerant, anti-intellectual, atavistic, alienated, hateful, and violent."[24] From this perspective the "irony of democracy" is clear: Allowing the people real power, permitting them to rule, will only result in the expression of antidemocratic preferences and policies.

Pluralists versus Elitists

The chief opponents of the elitist school of thought are known as *pluralists.* Pluralists and elitists alike accept certain obvious axioms: principally, that in any society there are gradations of power and certain groups of individuals exercise disproportionate influence over particular policies. The main point of disagreement between pluralists and elitists involves their perceptions of the fundamental nature of the political system itself. According to the pluralists, the American political system is intricate and decentralized. They concede that various organized interest groups, by concentrating all their energies, resources, and attention on one issue (or issue area), can and do exert disproportionate influence in that specific policy area. They also admit that from time to time, certain disadvantaged or unpopular groups may not be adequately represented. Nonetheless, no single individual or group could exercise total power over the whole gamut of public policy. The political system is too wide open, freewheeling, and institutionally fragmented to allow for any such accumulation of power. In the opinion of one prominent pluralist:

> The most important obstacle to social change in the United States, then, is not the concentration of power but its diffusion. . . . If power was concentrated sufficiently, those of us who wish for change would merely have to negotiate with those who hold the power and, if necessary, put pressure on them. But power is so widely diffused that, in many instances, there is no one to negotiate with and no one on whom to put pressure.[25]

Of course, the fact that there are millions of Americans and only a small number of public offices does place some constraints on direct political participation. But because power is so diffused and there are so many opportunities to exert political pressure at the local, state, and national levels, pluralists argue that the public interest—defined as the aggregation of private interests—is generally better served under constitutional democracy than under any other system.

The pluralists do not deny that those who hold the highest positions in government and business tend to have similar backgrounds and characteristics: Without a doubt, a clear majority are males from well-to-do WASP (white Anglo-Saxon Protestant) families who have had Ivy League or similar-caliber educations. But in the eyes of the pluralists, the mere fact that wealth, status, and education correlate closely with political participation does not prove that the system is closed and public policy predetermined, nor does it demonstrate that democratic citizenship is a sham.

When assessing the debate between pluralists and elitists, it is important to realize that elitist theory is almost impossible to disprove formally: Too much of

Demonstrators from ACT-UP (AIDS Coalition to Unleash Power) stage a "die-in" in front of the New York Stock Exchange to protest the high cost of AZT and to call for a boycott of all products by Burroughs Wellcome, the manufacturer of the drug. As a result of this and other demonstrations, Burroughs Wellcome reduced the cost of AZT. (AP/Wide World Photo)

the argument rests on the elites' motives, which are hardly open to critical examination. The elitist argument rests to a large extent on what cannot be seen (or proved). Successful political manipulation is most effective when it seems implausible and perhaps impossible.

Accepting the elitist critique is, then, to some extent a matter of faith. What is not a matter of faith is the fact that decisive political decisions and changes in political policy *have* been effected at times by public opinion. Widespread and steadily growing popular sentiment against the Vietnam War, for example, was instrumental in pressuring America to withdraw from that conflict. Similarly, large-scale disenchantment with government regulation, high taxes, and a feeling of American meekness and inferiority played a decisive role in the 1980 election of Ronald Reagan. Public opinion in the United States may often be fragmented or ill-formed, but this does not mean that it does not exist at all or is irrelevant.

EXPANDING PARTICIPATION: THREE CONTROVERSIAL REFORMS

Political participation is frequently championed as a means to citizen self-actualization as well as a way to invigorate democratic government. If voters are not sufficiently involved or informed, perhaps it is not because they do not want to be but rather because the political system discourages their active participation. What can be done to make American politics more interesting and individual citizen participation more important? The following reforms have been presented as means to these ends.

Limit House and Senate Terms

We have already noted that congressional representatives get reelected easily (see Figure 11-4). What is wrong with the fact that voters generally approve of the job performance of their House and Senate representatives? Many observers argue that this approval is itself the function of an unequal political system that unfairly rewards incumbents by allowing them to promote their name recognition as well as their oft-proclaimed concern for local voters. Only incumbents have huge staffs to service constituent problems. Campaign finance laws (about which more will be said later) also favor incumbents because contributors, loath to alienate the politicians in power (who will most likely be reelected), pledge disproportionately large amounts to incumbents. Then there is the free franking (mailing) privilege that legislators enjoy. Originally envisioned as a means for keeping citizens informed, this practice has proved a useful way of aiding incumbents; for example, in 1990, a year in which he stood for reelection, Senator Larry Pressler of South Dakota mailed more than 2.8 million pieces of mail, the equivalent of ten items per household![26]

Reformers suggest a variety of term limitation proposals, the most frequent suggestion being to limit representatives and senators to 12 years in their respective legislative branch. They hope that this reform will increase competitiveness in congressional elections and thereby promote more active citizen participation. Not everyone agrees. Critics of this proposal suggest that term limitations deprive the nation of necessary legislative experience. They also assert that such proposals are undemocratic, contending that citizens ought to be able to elect whomever they wish to Congress.

Reform Campaign Financing

Reforming campaign financing laws is also favored as a means of increasing electoral competitiveness and thereby promoting citizen participation. Presently, incumbents enjoy a significant advantage (see Table 11-2). Advocates point out that election contributions from organized interests during the 1988 election favored incumbents by a 7-to-1 ratio; they also explain that congressional incumbents ended the 1988 elections with $63 million while challengers were able to raise only $39 million in total. This disparity is particularly troubling because of the skyrocketing costs of elections (a successful run for the Senate in New York and California in 1986 cost incumbents $13 million, approximately what it cost John Kennedy to be elected president in 1960. It is estimated that senators must raise $3,000 a day—every working day—for six years, in order to run for reelection).[27] To even the playing field, a variety of campaign reforms are championed. These include increased or total public financing of election cam-

TABLE 11-2
Financial Advantage of Incumbents (in millions of dollars)

	Incumbents Seeking Reelection	Challengers
Senate		
Campaign contributions, 1985–1990	129.3	38.5
Free mailings, fiscal 1990	15.0	0.0
House of Representatives		
Campaign contributions, 1985–1990	146.0	24.0
Free mailings, fiscal 1990	75.0*	0.0

* Estimated

SOURCE: Data from Jeffrey Birnbaum, "Stacked Deck: Despite Voter's Ire, Most Incumbents Have Powerful Advantages," *Wall Street Journal*, November 6, 1990, p. A9.

paigns, free or subsidized television access (especially for advertisements), and campaign contribution and spending limitations.

These proposals are controversial and raise complex issues that we can only touch on here. Limiting campaign contributions and requiring subsidized or free television access may well raise constitutional problems, centering on the question of whether the government can restrict freedom of speech and expression by dictating how money is to be spent and how television time is to be allocated in regard to political candidates and issues.[28] Another fundamental question asks if the public ought to undertake financing for private candidates to run for elected office. A related concern questions whether the United States can presently afford the expensive task of underwriting all congressional campaigns. A final problem posed by campaign spending reforms is that they may further weaken political parties while encouraging a significantly greater number of candidates to pursue congressional office. In the latter event, the cost of political races might escalate; at the very least, it would require controversial and difficult restrictions regarding who exactly would be entitled to receive the benefits of public financing.

Adopt a National Referendum or Initiative

Although proposed less frequently, a national referendum or initiative might well offer a method for enhancing citizen participation in the political process.[29] Such a reform might assume a number of formats. For instance, a national referendum could require a countrywide election in the event Congress and the president are deadlocked regarding an important domestic issue. Or a national initiative might permit a similar election after some predetermined number of nationwide signatures were received and verified. Although most proposals assume that such elections would be binding, they need not be; an *advisory referendum* or advisory initiatives might simply recommend national policies but not require their adoption.

A national referendum or initiative is sometimes pictured as a means of revitalizing democracy. Citizens would be encouraged to become more informed about politics. Furthermore, they would have a greater opportunity to become involved in important political decisions. Not only voter indifference but alienation would be counteracted by direct citizen involvement.

Criticism of this political reform is twofold. First, critics suggest that the political system is already sufficiently democratic. For instance, House representatives are elected every two years. Therefore, there exists ample opportunity for the people to make their opinions known. A more frequent criticism is that adopting a national referendum or initiative would undermine legislative competence. Even more than at present, difficult decisions would be postponed as increasing use of the national direct-election process would be made. Furthermore, critics contend that legislative competence would be compromised by the weakening of legislative power and representative government. Realizing that their decisions can be appealed, the deliberation and compromise so much a part of a legislative process that promotes political moderation would be undercut, producing a process that could promote sharp national divisions.

Summary

In modern societies, citizens can participate in the political system in a variety of legal ways: conventionally, by voting and taking part in public opinion polls; organizationally, by joining political parties or interest groups; or professionally, by working full-time for such organizations. Some types of political participation are unconventional, such as engaging in protests or economic boycotts. Illegal participation goes beyond unconventional means—from deliberately nonviolent actions (civil disobedience) to extremely violent acts (terrorism).

To influence government, citizens in constitutional democracies must be able to aggregate their opinions and interests. Public opinion can be expressed through polls, which have great influence in the political process. Elections, despite their inherent limitations, represent the best means of translating public preferences into public policy. In democratic republics, which can be structured on a winner-take-all or proportional representation basis, voters elect representatives who are responsible for formulating, implementing, and explaining public policy. Representative democracy can be supplemented by direct democracy measures, which include referendums, initiatives, and recalls, intended to allow citizens to participate directly in the formulation of public policy.

It is generally assumed that citizens want to participate in politics. Yet voting rates are low in the United States and are declining. Explanations for this limited level of participation abound; perhaps the most important are strong feelings of individualism among American citizens.

It is also commonly assumed by advocates of citizen participation that voters are knowledgeable and thoughtful. Yet there is good reason to question this belief.

Participation theory also assumes that individuals can make a political difference. Yet some observers have argued that political participation by the masses is more illusionary than real and that power is actually concentrated in the hands of a small, elite group of influential people. This elitist theory is disputed by the advocates of pluralism, who argue that in a democratic society, power is diffused rather than concentrated and that political phenomena are too complex to be reduced to the simplistic terms of elitist theory.

It is sometimes assumed that the political system discourages political participation. Three controversial reforms that could increase citizen participation would limit House and Senate terms, reform campaign financing, and adopt the process of holding national referendums or initiatives.

Key Terms

conventional participation	proportional representation
institutional participation	list system
professional participation	Hare plan
unconventional participation	plebiscite
illegal participation	referendum
civil disobedience	initiative
terrorism	recall
subversion	political efficacy
sedition	alienation
public opinion	individualism
public opinion polling	political apathy
random sampling	elitist theories of democracy
stratified sampling	Iron Law of Oligarchy
tracking polls	pluralists
winner-take-all system	advisory referendum
simple majority	

Review Questions

1. In what ways can citizens participate in the political process?

2. Describe the different forms of electoral systems. Contrast their advantages and disadvantages.

3. Is apathy the enemy of the meaningful practice of citizenship in democratic nations? Explain.

4. How do the elitist theories of democracy differ from the pluralist model? What political implications follow from the elitist theories?

5. What assumptions are generally made about political participation in democracies? Are they correct?

6. How can political participation be enhanced? Should the measures you cited be adopted? Why or why not?

Recommended Reading

BARBER, BENJAMIN. *Strong Democracy: Participatory Politics for a New Age.* Berkeley: University of California Press, 1984. An examination of the meaning of democracy and citizenship by one of the foremost advocates of citizen participation.

CAMPBELL, BRUCE. *The American Electorate.* Fort Worth, Texas: Holt, Rinehart and Winston, 1979. A good introduction to the political behavior of Americans.

CONWAY, M. MARGARET. *Political Participation in the United States* (2nd ed.). Washington, D.C.: Congressional Quarterly Press, 1991. A good summary of the literature.

CRONIN, THOMAS. *Direct Democracy: The Politics of Initiative, Referendum, and Recall.* Cambridge, Mass.: Harvard University Press, 1989. A measured examination of the history, advantages, and disadvantages of direct democracy measures.

DAHL, ROBERT. *Democracy in the United States* (4th ed.). Boston: Houghton Mifflin, 1981. An introduction to American government that emphasizes a pluralist approach.

KLEPPNER, PAUL. *Who Voted? The Contours of Electoral Turnout, 1970–1980.* Westport, Conn.: Greenwood, 1981. A historical analysis based on statistics and surveys.

MICHELS, ROBERT. *Political Parties,* trans. E. and P. Paul. New York: Free Press, 1966. The original study that produced the Iron Law of Oligarchy.

MILLS, C. WRIGHT. *The Power Elite.* New York: Oxford University Press, 1956. The original formulation of the power elite thesis.

NIEMI, RICHARD G., AND HERBERT F. WEISBERG. *Controversies in Voting Behavior* (2nd ed.). Washington, D.C.: Congressional Quarterly Press, 1984. The first section analyzes the controversy regarding voter participation in American elections.

POMPER, GERALD M., WITH SUSAN LEDERMAN. *Elections in America: Control and Influence in Democratic Politics* (2nd ed.). New York: Dodd, Mead, 1980. A persuasive argument that elections serve an important purpose in the American political system.

ROSE, ARNOLD. *The Power Structure: Political Process in American Society.* London: Oxford University Press, 1967. A pluralist refutation of Mills's power elite thesis.

ROSE, RICHARD. *Electoral Behavior: A Comparative Handbook.* New York: Free Press, 1974. An examination of political participation in 12 Western nations.

TOCQUEVILLE, ALEXIS DE. *Democracy in America.* New York: Schocken Books, 1961. The classic theoretical account of the role of the American citizen in a democratic age.

Notes

1. M. Margaret Conway, *Political Participation in the United States* (Washington, D.C.: Congressional Quarterly Press, 1987), p. 10.

2. Later in the chapter we will look more closely at voting patterns in the United States.

3. Conway, *Political Participation,* pp. 52–53.

4. Ibid.

5. See Max Kaase and Alan Marsh, "Political Action Repertory: Change over Time and a New Typology," in *Political Action*, ed. Samuel H. Barnes and Max Kaase (Newbury Park, Calif.: Sage, 1979), chap. 5.

6. Howard Schuman and Stanley Presser, *Questions and Answers in Attitude Surveys* (Orlando, Fla.: Academic Press, 1981), pp. 70–71. This study is illustrated in James Q. Wilson, *American Government*, 4th ed. (Lexington, Mass.: Heath, 1989), p. 99.

7. One study found that almost two-thirds of the promises made in major-party platforms were kept; see Gerald M. Pomper with Susan Lederman, *Elections in America: Control and Influence in Democratic Politics*, 2nd ed. (New York: Dodd, Mead, 1980), p. 161.

8. This discussion is indebted to Thomas Cronin, *Direct Democracy: The Politics of Initiative, Referendum, and Recall* (Cambridge, Mass.: Harvard University Press, 1989).

9. Ibid., p. 87.

10. The fact that voters in many democracies do not need to register is often cited as a reason why their participation rate is higher. In several democracies (including Australia and Belgium), citizens who do not vote are subject to a fine.

11. Harry Holloway and John George, *Public Opinion: Coalitions, Elites, and Masses*, 2nd ed. (New York: St. Martin's Press, 1986), p. 161.

12. Ibid., pp. 162–163.

13. See Julian L. Woodward and Elmo Roper, "Political Activity of American Citizens," *American Political Science Review* 44 (1950), pp. 822–885.

14. Sidney Verba and Norman Nie, *Participation in America* (New York: Harper & Row, 1972), pp. 79–80.

15. See Holloway and George, *Public Opinion*, pp. 157–166.

16. Alexis de Tocqueville, *Democracy in America* (New York: Schocken Books, 1961), vol. 2, p. 18.

17. Ibid., pp. 153, 159.

18. Holloway and George, *Public Opinion*, p. 78.

19. The Iran-Contra affair was a scandal in the mid-1980s in which the Reagan administration made a secret arrangement to provide funds to anticommunist rebels (Contras) in Nicaragua from profits gained by a sale of arms to Iran.

20. Studies demonstrating lack of citizen and voter knowledge are numerous and are frequently summarized even in introductory textbooks, including Wilson, *American Government*, p. 99; Thomas Patterson, *The American Democracy* (New York: McGraw-Hill, 1990), pp. 177, 223; and W. Phillips Shively, *Power and Choice*, 2nd ed. (New York: McGraw-Hill, 1991), p. 117.

21. Wilson, *American Government*, p. 100.

22. The belief that incumbents' inherent advantages cause voters to be more favorably disposed toward them is examined later in the chapter.

23. C. Wright Mills, *The Power Elite* (New York: Oxford University Press, 1956).

24. Thomas Dye and L. Harmon Ziegler, *The Irony of Democracy: An Uncommon Introduction to American Government*, 4th ed. (North Scituate, Mass.: Duxbury Press, 1978), p. 374.

25. Andrew Greeley, "Power Is Diffused throughout Society," in *Taking Sides: Clashing Views on Controversial Political Issues*, ed. George McKenna and Stanley Feingad (Guilford, Conn.: Dushkin, 1983), p. 23. Also see Arnold Rose, *The Power Structure: Political Process in American Society* (London: Oxford University Press, 1967), pp. 483–493.

26. See "Lawmakers for Life," *Wall Street Journal*, April 18, 1990, p. A20.

27. See Mark Green, "Take the Money and Reform," *New Republic*, May 14, 1990, pp. 27–29.

28. The leading case that held that limitations on campaign expenditures violate the First Amendment is *Buckley* v. *Valeo*, 424 U.S. 1 (1976).

29. See Cronin, *Direct Democracy*, pp. 157–195.

CHAPTER 12

POLITICAL ORGANIZATION

PARTIES AND INTEREST GROUPS

(AP/Wide World Photos)

ORDINARY CITIZENS WHO seek to influence governmental policy face a formidable barrier: In modern societies, the voice of one individual is usually too weak to affect the course of government. To be noticed by society, the voice of any one person must be magnified many times. For this reason, the most effective forms of citizen participation involve the aggregation of individual interests and opinions into collective expressions of public sentiment. Political parties and interest groups represent two structural ways in which, under favorable circumstances, citizens may influence government. The availability or effectiveness of these structures in a particular society depends in large part on the extent to which the government protects political and civil rights and is responsive to the political judgments of its citizens.

In constitutional democracies, the emergence of political parties and interest groups is inevitable. Moreover, political parties aggregate a variety of special interests. Yet in recent years, an important trend has been evident in both the United States and Europe: As the power of political parties has declined, the influence of interest groups has increased. We now examine the reasons for this development and its implications for democratic government.

POLITICAL PARTIES

In the United States, political parties are now permanent fixtures, but they were not part of the Founders' original plan. In fact, the emergence of a two-party system was a seminal development in U.S. political history.

Historical Background

The Constitution does not mention political parties, and many of the Founders abhorred them. George Washington sought to avoid partisanship by forming a cabinet composed of the best available talent, including Thomas Jefferson as secretary of state and Alexander Hamilton as secretary of the treasury. The appointment of these two gifted but philosophically opposed individuals reflected Washington's belief that the public would best be served by calling on the nation's wisest and most public-spirited citizens to work together for the common good.

Unfortunately, Washington's noble attempt to avoid partisan politics ultimately failed. Personal animosities developed between Jefferson and Hamilton, in large part because of conflicting understandings of government and public policy, and the two became fierce rivals. In the late 1790s, Jefferson and his followers founded a loosely organized Republican party to oppose the strong anti-French policies of Federalists such as John Adams and Alexander Hamilton. Yet in 1789, Jefferson himself had written, "If I could not go to heaven but with a party, I would not go there at all."[1]

Why did many statesmen of Jefferson's generation distrust political parties? In Jefferson's case, dislike of parties stemmed from a peculiarly American brand of individualism that has survived to this day. "I never submitted the whole system of my opinions to the creed of any party of men whatever, in religion, in philosophy, in politics, or in anything else, where I was capable of thinking for myself," he observed, concluding that "such an addiction is the last degradation of a free and moral agent."[2]

Other Americans of Jefferson's generation, like some of their English counterparts, believed that political parties fostered narrow self-interest at the expense of the general or public interest. In this sense, political parties often were seen as the public extension of private selfishness.

Only gradually did partisanship lose this stigma. In England, the idea that parties embodying different political philosophies could be beneficial (for example, by providing policy alternatives) rather than subversive had begun to take hold by the late seventeenth century. The experience of the leading American statesmen a century later led to a similar, albeit grudging, recognition of the vital importance of political parties in the democratic process.

General Aims

Political parties typically strive to gain (or retain) political power; in practical terms, this means capturing control of the government. Since the right to rule in a constitutional democracy is determined by elections, political parties in democratic states concentrate above all on winning elections. They seek to build a broad-based consensus for their party platform, which is designed to offer an appealing alternative to the other party or parties.

Typically, the successful *political party* fashions a national consensus out of myriad economic, social, ethnic, and cultural interests. The party must appeal to various voter interests while reconciling and forging them into a workable majority. Even if a party has no hope of gaining a majority following, its influence and legislative strength usually depend on the size and distribution of its vote total, which in turn reflects its success in attracting voters across a relatively wide spectrum.

Candidates frequently appeal for votes by promising to be more responsive and energetic than their opponents in addressing the rank-and-file voter's everyday concerns—the so-called bread-and-butter issues. Sometimes, however, candidates and parties stress ideological issues or advance controversial domestic and foreign policy initiatives. Using these strategies, parties create political alternatives, frequently between liberal policies of the left and conservative policies of the right. This is especially true in Great Britain and in the continental European parliamentary (and quasi-parliamentary) democracies, where a number of parties often vie for votes and each can formulate distinctive national and international policy alternatives. In such systems, the political platforms of the major parties are much more important than the personal popularity of individual candidates because parties in a parliamentary system seek to capture and maintain a majority of seats in the parliament. Thus the party that controls the parliament controls the government. As a result, political parties in a parliamentary system tend to be not only more disciplined, hierarchical, and centralized but also more policy-oriented and ideologically distinct than their American counterparts.

In the United States, where the legislative and executive branches are sepa-

An Important American Party Vote

ALTHOUGH AMERICAN POLITICAL parties are not unusually hierarchical or disciplined, key political votes nevertheless often follow party lines. In addition to political party, geographic region and the political orientation of representatives' districts mattered most. Interestingly, nearly all Democratic candidates mentioned as party nominees for the 1992 election voted against authorizing the use of force, thus establishing their credentials as war opponents should the war have gone badly.

How Members of Congress Voted on Authorizing the Use of Force against Iraq, January 12, 1991

	House		Senate			House		Senate	
	Yes	No	Yes	No		Yes	No	Yes	No
Total vote	250	183	52	47	**Total vote**	250	183	52	47
Party					*Race*				
Democrats	86	179	10	45	White	246	150	52	45
Southern	53	32	7	10	Black	1	23		
Northern	33	147	3	35	Hispanic	3	7		
Republicans	164	3	42	2	Asian	0	3	0	2
Independents	0	1			*Sex*				
					Men	239	166	51	46
					Women	11	17	1	1

SOURCE: Rhodes Cook and Ronald Elving, "Even Votes of Conscience Follow Party Lines," *Congressional Quarterly Weekly Report*, January 19, 1991, pp. 190–195.

rated and candidates for national office are often selected on the basis of personal rather than political attributes, parties seldom present sharply defined policy alternatives. As a rule, the presidential candidate who is widely perceived to be closest to the political center is elected.[3] Of course, Republican candidates do tend to be more conservative and Democratic candidates more liberal. However, most presidential campaigns are waged within the relatively narrow confines of a preexisting consensus about the most important issues of public policy. Usually, the two major-party candidates for president embrace similar policies and goals, differing only on specific prescriptions, not on general principles. The contrast of personalities is at least as important as the clash of political views. According to its admirers, the American two-party system produces stability and politically moderate candidates while discouraging strident ideology and political polarization. Critics—especially those who admire the way parties function under the British parliamentary system—dismiss American presidential elections as mere popularity contests. Nonetheless, all parties in constitutional democracies seek to build consensus and provide alternatives by carrying out certain essential tasks: selecting or encouraging candidates, raising money, and launching media campaigns—including newsworthy public appearances and paid political advertising. In the party's platform and in more private negotiations, proposals and policies must be formulated that will win the favor of key interest group leaders.

Between elections, parties perform other important functions. The winning party (or coalition) organizes the government in a British-style parliamentary system; in a nonparliamentary republic like ours in the United States, where the executive and legislative branches are separated, political parties help to coordinate the actions of the two branches, especially when the same party dominates both. Furthermore, just as the winning party plays a prominent role in setting the nation's political agenda and facilitating governmental action, so the losing party performs a vital function by opposing and criticizing the current government and offering an alternative in the next election. The very legitimacy of this opposition allows defeated parties to accept their loss routinely (and peacefully); they know there will always be another election day. Seldom can a party in power satisfy the electorate indefinitely; when inflation soars or unemployment climbs to an unacceptable level, the voters will seek new leadership and new policies.

Depending on the prevailing rules of the game, however, political parties play different roles in different nations. To determine how political parties operate, we must first take note of whether a particular system permits only one legitimate party (a one-party system), two major parties (a two-party system), or an indefinite number of parties (a multiparty system).

One-Party Systems

Our focus to this point has been on constitutional democracies, where parties are called on to shape a national consensus and offer political alternatives in order to win elections. Political parties can also be found, however, in countries that do not hold free elections. These nondemocratic nations may be authoritarian or totalitarian. They are invariably one-party systems.

In authoritarian states, the party exists as much to discourage political alternatives as it does to build a popular consensus. A mere tool of the ruling regime, it serves to enhance state power and suppress political opposition.

In totalitarian states, the party performs a wide range of functions, including political recruitment, indoctrination, mobilization, and surveillance. In Nazi Germany, as in many communist countries, the party became the government. As these states evolved, all vital functions of government came to be performed either by the party directly or by bureaucratic officials operating under the constant supervision of party leaders. The concept of the party as a vehicle for the expression of popular will was thus turned upside down as parties became instruments of centralized social control fully capable of suppressing all attempts at individual self-expression. As was pointed out in Chapter 11, mass participation under these circumstances is little more than a charade designed to mask the antidemocratic nature of the regime.

Although most one-party systems are found in nondemocratic states, some are embedded in more or less democratic political orders. Ordinarily, this situation comes about when a single party, for specific historical and cultural reasons, manages to win the sympathy and trust of a vast majority of the people, who repeatedly vote to extend its tenure in office. Although other parties are permitted, the dominant party encompasses a variety of interests and viewpoints, and meaningful national politics takes place *within* the party. For many years, this has been the case with Mexico's Institutional Revolutionary party. In India, political power in the immediate postindependence period rested almost exclusively with the Indian Congress party. And for more than a quarter of a century, the Liberal Democratic party has enjoyed an unbroken string of national election victories in Japan. Even in the United States, which is not noted for its one-party tendencies, the Democratic party dominated the South for nearly a century after the Civil War. In none of these cases did the dominant party achieve its position primarily by intimidation or fraud; rather, its advantage grew out of specific circumstances unique to the country or area involved.

Nonauthoritarian one-party systems are relatively rare. Political orders of this type occasionally stay intact for extended periods, but in general, they change as the particular circumstances that brought them into being change. The experience of Mexico, Japan, and to a lesser extent India notwithstanding, such systems tend to evolve into either democratic multiparty sytems or authoritarian one-party systems.

Two-Party Systems

In contrast to one-party systems, which abound in every part of the world except North America and western Europe, two-party systems are quite rare (those in Great Britain, New Zealand, and the United States being prime examples). Under a two-party system, the vast majority of voters support one major party or the other, only major-party candidates for office stand much chance of being elected, and the opposition party is constitutionally protected from undue interference or intimidation by the government. Not surprisingly, such a system of legitimate dissent is difficult to institutionalize.

One key advantage of two-party systems is their tendency to produce relatively stable government. They often thrive in social environments where the majority shares fundamental political beliefs and is culturally and ethnically homogeneous (a condition that often is absent in developing countries). To some extent, continuity is assured by the system itself because the two major parties keep to the middle of the road to appeal to a broad range of interests. At the same time, a basic advantage of a two-party system is the ever-present availability of a qualified and experienced opposition ready and able to take over the government.

Two-party systems are not legally or constitutionally limited to two parties. Minor parties can and do exist, although in the United States such organizations have rarely endured for very long. Commonly, a minor party comes into being through the efforts of a single political figure who has broken with one or both major parties (for example, Teddy Roosevelt's Bull Moose party in 1912). In

Germany, whose political setup is basically two-party, the small Free Democratic party has enjoyed power and influence greatly disproportionate to its size.

Multiparty Systems

A multiparty system prevails when more than two influential, well-established parties gain sufficient strength to guarantee that no one party can maintain a permanent majority. Unlike their U.S. counterparts, individual parties in a multiparty system tend to eschew compromise during elections and to run on specific issues or programs. Only after the precise legislative strength of each party has been determined by the voters do compromises take place, as the strongest party attempts to form a *coalition government.* Once a coalition has been forged, it governs until a new election is called or mandated or until the coalition falls apart.

The multiparty system offers as its chief advantage many choices for the voter. The major disadvantage is that this system can be unstable, especially in the face of serious social and economic disruptions. As stresses grow more pronounced, parliamentary majorities become more and more difficult to maintain, and governments may come and go very quickly. Furthermore, this process can feed on itself: Stresses bring about factious quarrels both within the government and without, the general disarray at the political center leads to a "crisis of confidence," and that crisis in turn causes more stress. At various times in the postwar era, the governments of France and Italy have exemplified this hazard of multiparty systems.

Useful Generalizations

What determines the number of political parties in a particular nation? First, the form of government is crucial. Totalitarian and authoritarian states typically permit only one party because such governments do not tolerate political opposition, and as we have seen, the main function of parties out of power is to oppose the government. Thus although constitutional democracies exhibit a variety of party systems, authoritarian or totalitarian regimes are incompatible with more than a single, state-controlled party.

Second, a nation's party system, as well as its basic form of government, is often prescribed by its constitution. Constitutions differ on how they treat political parties; some, like the U.S. Constitution, do not address the subject, whereas others refer to them explicitly or implicitly.

Third, tradition influences a nation's form of government and the party system it adopts. Since most developing nations have authoritarian regimes and lack a democratic tradition, it is not surprising that single-party systems are quite common in the Third World. Two notable exceptions in Latin America are Venezuela and Colombia, both of which have developed impressive democratic traditions since World War II. Both these governments have been highly stable; in Colombia, even a long-standing insurgency has not seriously threatened the system's survival.

Fourth, where deep social, economic, cultural, or religious splits exist, political life is likely to be polarized, infused with emotion, and ideologically charged. Such circumstances favor the development of multiparty rather than two-party systems. (Table 12-1 shows a sample of the number and variety of parties in selected democratic nations.)

Concerning the kind (as opposed to the number) of parties likely to develop in any particular nation, several generalizations are possible. Parties in totalitarian states exert the most power and the most all-pervasive influence anywhere. The hierarchy of the party in totalitarian states often becomes interlaced with, and indistinguishable from, the structures of the government, consolidating all power in the party itself. Parties in totalitarian states also attempt to influence, direct, and supervise virtually every aspect of social, cultural, and political life through sweeping, all-pervasive programs. By contrast, the scope of authoritarian parties is narrower. These parties implement the ruler's edicts and policies but do not launch mass mobilization campaigns, grandiose construction projects, or "revolution from above" designed to transform or purify society. Although both totalitarian and authoritarian parties are usually centralized and regimented, they are not necessarily efficient. Nondemocratic parties are by no means exempt from the waste, stultification, and conflicting interests that can be found in large bureaucracies everywhere.

Democratic parties are comparatively less powerful and more limited in scope. American parties are typical in this respect. Between elections, they are managed by a small group of professionals. Party ranks may swell during election campaigns as volunteers turn out to support the candidates of their choice, but these additional activists join parties to get candidates elected, not to administer the government. In most democracies, there is a clear distinction between the party, which helps to organize politics and government, and the bureaucracy, which is charged with administering the government.

Parties vary significantly from one democracy to another. In some, authority is highly structured and power is concentrated at the top. For instance, British political parties are more disciplined and centralized than the major parties in the United States. Party centralization is important in a parliamentary system because, with the fusing of both legislative powers, legislators must either "follow the party line" or risk bringing the opposition to power. A centralized party can best exert the political pressure necessary to enforce party discipline. Furthermore, because the party program, and not the personalities of individual candidates, counts most in a parliamentary system, planning, organizing, and financing campaigns at the national level works best.

Another important consideration is whether the political system is centralized or decentralized. In nations with federal systems, parties structure their national organization to mirror the federal structure of the government. A practical example illustrates this point. In the United States, vote totals in presidential elections are determined nationally but counted (and weighted) by states. The winner in each state receives all that state's electoral votes. Therefore, the Democratic and Republican party organizations must be strong in nearly every state.

TABLE 12-1
Samples of Political Parties in Selected Democratic Nations

Country	Radical Left	Communism	Environmentalism	Democratic Socialism	Liberalism	Christian Democracy	Conservatism	Reactionary Right
Canada*				New Democratic party	Liberal Party of Canada		Progressive Conservative party	
France	United Socialist party (PSU)	French Communist party (PCF)	The Greens	•Social Democratic party •Socialist party (PS)	Radical party	Union of the Center	•Union of French Democracy (UDR) •Gaullists (RPR)	National Front (FN)
Germany		German Communist party (DKP)	The Greens	Social Democratic party (SPD)	Free Democratic party (FDP)	Christian Democratic Union (CDU)	Christian Social Union (CSU)	National Democratic party (NPD)
Italy	Proletarian Democracy (DP)	Italian Communist party (PCI)	National Federation for the Green List	•Italian Socialist party (PSI) •Social Democratic party (PSDI)	Republican party (PRI)	Christian Democratic party (DC)	Liberal party (PLI)	Italian Social Movement (MSI)
Sweden	Communist Workers' party	Left party	The Green Ecological party	Social Democratic Labor party	•Peoples' party •Center party	Christian Democratic Community party	Moderate Coalition party	
United Kingdom			The Greens	Labour party	Liberal party		Conservative party	
United States					Democratic party		Republican party	

* Canada has a major separatist movement in Quebec headed by the *Parti Quebecois.*

SOURCE: Adapted from David M. Wood, *Power and Policy in Western European Democracies*, 3rd ed. (New York: Macmillan, 1986), p. 78.

To gain this strength, parties and their candidates must respond to local issues; in such a political environment, a decentralized political structure is indispensable. Strong state-level party organizations help elect senators, representatives, and state and local officials in the United States. A similar system operates in other federal systems.

Thus compared to many other political parties, American parties are weak. But this weakness stems from their place within a decentralized democracy, performing particular functions that revolve around periodic elections. But perhaps the main reason American political parties are not more powerful is that they do not need to be. The United States is largely a middle-class society with a broad consensus on first principles in politics. This means that neither major party is dogmatic in its ideology or narrow in its appeal; each is more like a loose coalition of diverse groups and interests than a monolithic body of like-minded adherents. Above all, in the United States, presidents are even more important than political parties in directing and coordinating the operations of government.

Prospects: Eclipse of Political Parties?

Many experts believe that the power and prestige of political parties in the United States and western Europe is waning. They cite opinion polls that show an erosion of public respect: Parties are perceived as being unable to keep elected officials responsive to the electorate, voters are not identifying themselves as party members as they once did, and ticket splitting has become commonplace. Political parties are perceived as increasingly ineffectual, as the 1992 *independent* presidential campaign of business executive Ross Perot initially revealed.

What accounts for this turn of fortune? Some observers contend that contributors are choosing not to dilute their influence by giving money through political parties, preferring instead to make more direct contributions. Others suggest that many voters place unrealistic expectations on parties or that parties were the outgrowth of a class struggle between labor and business that has faded in importance.[4] Still others see them as part of a failed political process.

In the United States, the very idea of party politics has come into conflict with the ideal of democracy in recent years. At both the state and national levels, Democrats and Republicans alike have tried to reduce the influence of party professionals in the candidate selection process. The none-too-pleasant image of party bosses in smoke-filled rooms deciding who will run for what office goes counter to our concept of democracy. Real or imagined, this image has clearly helped to spur election reform.

Over the past quarter century, significant efforts have been made to democratize party affairs in general and the nomination process in particular. State primary elections, once the exception, have become the rule. States now compete to hold the earliest primaries. (The elections themselves have become a bonanza for some states, attracting revenue and wide media attention.) Other states hold party caucuses, where rank-and-file party members choose delegates who later attend state conventions where they in turn select delegates pledged to support particular candidates at the party's national convention.

Such reforms make the average citizen more a part of the party's nominating process. They also diminish the power of both state party regulars and national party leaders. More and more, delegates to national nominating conventions are pledged to one candidate or another in advance (and are therefore, at least initially, far less susceptible to arm-twisting on the convention floor).

In addition, a greater number and variety of candidates have stepped forward to run for office, since gaining nomination depends more on winning state primaries than on being acceptable to party bosses. At the same time, with more states holding primaries, American presidential campaigns have grown more arduous, costly, and prolonged; the presidential nomination and election process can last for well over a year. (British parliamentary elections often last less than a month and cost a tiny fraction of what American elections cost.) Furthermore, unannounced fund-raising and organization planning efforts generally precede the formal elections themselves. Not only presidential elections but senatorial and House races as well require extensive candidate planning efforts, prompting cynics to remark that in the United States, elections have become nonstop events.

In many constitutional democracies like the United States, parties still help their candidates get elected, but they cannot come close to providing the level of funding now required. How is this gap filled? Where do candidates turn for financial backing? As we are about to see, interest groups have rushed in to fill the breach, but not without raising new questions about the implications for the nation's democratic ideals.

INTEREST GROUPS

Interest groups are formal or informal associations that magnify group influence over public policy. Unlike political parties, their primary purpose is to influence public policy rather than recruit, nominate, and elect public officials. Thus interest groups do not seek direct control over government. Instead, they concentrate on shaping legislation and government programs in specific issue areas of particular interest to their members—farm subsidies, federal aid to education, or wildlife conservation, for example. We begin our discussion by examining the different types of interest groups.

Types of Interest Groups

The most commonly used classification scheme for interest groups was developed by Professor Gabriel Almond, who distinguishes among four basic types.[5] First are *associational interest groups*, the most familiar kind, which typically have a distinctive name, national headquarters, professional staff, and the like. Examples include the National Association of Manufacturers (NAM), the National Rifle Association (NRA), and the United Auto Workers (UAW).

Second are *nonassociational interest groups*, which do not have a name and lack formal structures but reflect largely unarticulated social, ethnic, cultural, or religious interests capable of coalescing into potent political forces under the right set of circumstances. Such groups can be found in all societies—for example,

Jesse Jackson represents this type of interest group in the United States. Nonetheless, nonassociational interest groups are more prevalent in the economically and politically less developed countries of the Third World.

Unlike the two types already mentioned, *institutional interest groups,* the third type, exist *within* the government. Normally one sees government as being the object rather than the initiator of interest group activity, but the various departments and agencies of government develop their own vested interests in certain policies and programs for which they lobby from the inside—often out of public view. Thus the Pentagon joins defense contractors in promoting weapons programs like the Strategic Defense Initiative, and departments such as Labor, Agriculture, and Education are frequently accused of being captives of the special interests most directly affected by the programs they administer.

Fourth, *anomic interest groups* sometimes develop spontaneously when many individuals strongly oppose specific policies. The nationwide student demonstrations against the Vietnam War in the late 1960s and early 1970s serve as an excellent historical example of this phenomenon. Professor Almond suggests that street riots and even some assassinations can also be placed in this category.

Besides the different types of interest groups, significant differences also exist among interest groups of the same type. For example, associational interest groups differ in at least four important respects: in their specific reason for being, in the focus of their activities, in their organizational assets and attributes, and in the tactics they employ.

In the United States, an astonishing number of interest groups champion an equally astonishing number of causes. And their diversity is equally impressive: One group seeks to advance the rights of a particular ethnic minority while another advocates favorable treatment of small businesses (or big businesses or start-up businesses). Still other groups favor increased expenditures on higher (or primary and secondary) education, fight for the abolition of capital punishment, or (in the case of competing interest groups) call for stiffer sentencing of criminals or a crackdown on drunk drivers. There are even interest groups opposed in principle to "special interests"; these seek instead to represent the public interest. Common Cause, an organization founded by a former secretary of Health, Education and Welfare, with a membership now of more than 300,000, exemplifies this type of interest group.

Not only do interest groups differ in the issues they emphasize, but they also differ in focus. All interest groups are motivated by self-interest, but the focus of that self varies considerably. A fairly narrow focus characterizes most ethnic groups (the Italian-American Foundation, for example), religious groups (the American Jewish Congress), occupational groups (the American Association of University Professors), age-defined groups (the American Association of Retired People), and a variety of groups that cannot be easily categorized (such as the Disabled American Veterans). In each case, these ***private interest groups*** primarily seek to advance the self-interest of their members.

The focus of ***public interest groups*** is broader. They promote causes that they believe will benefit society as a whole. One example of such an organization, the Sierra Club, lobbies for strict environmental protection and comprehensive conservation policies. Although not everyone agrees with the Sierra Club's goals, no one can accuse its members of pursuing narrow self-interest; indeed, all citizens benefit from clean air and pure water. Nonetheless, a word of caution is in order here—interest groups typically argue that adopting policies they favor will benefit the nation as a whole. Thoughtful citizens examine such claims very closely and critically.

Associational interest groups differ greatly in their assets and attributes. The key differences relate to the size of their membership, the amount of money they can raise, and the size and competence of their professional staffs. In addition, interest groups differ greatly in the tactics they use to maximize their influence, including face-to-face lobbying with government officials, political contributions, mass mailings, sponsoring lawsuits, organizing rallies and demonstrations, and funding studies of key issues.

Effectiveness of Interest Groups

Organizations representing a large and distinct group of citizens, who are acutely aware of their common identity or interests, have a clear advantage over more heterogeneous organizations. This edge is especially sharp if the issues involved are specific and keenly felt and there are no competing or countervailing interest groups stressing the same issues. The National Rifle Association is a prime example of an entrenched lobby with a large number of like-minded members and an issue monopoly (gun control), which opposing organizations have seldom been able to challenge successfully. In contrast, family farmers in the United States are represented by a variety of competing organizations; the result has been a historically fragmented agricultural lobby in Washington. Many observers believe the continuing "farm crisis" derives, at least in part, from this legacy of fragmentation. Thus strong member identification with the relevant issues, specificity of purpose (gun control versus the farm program), and the absence of multiple groups that dissipate or offset efforts to exert concerted pressure on the government—these factors spell success for interest groups.

Of course, money also helps to determine success and can, under some circumstances, make up for the absence of a large following. Even relatively small groups whose members are affluent can sometimes exert influence dispro-portionate to their size by launching expensive media campaigns or contributing large sums to political campaigns. In addition, the members of such groups are likely to have personal networks and political contacts that can also be crucial in influencing how a representative or a senator votes on a particular issue.

Interest groups can sometimes gain advantage from close ties to a political party, especially outside the United States. In western Europe, for instance, the giant trade unions maintain close ties to working-class political parties (for instance, the British Labour party and Trade Union Congress, which have the support of some 85 percent of organized labor in Great Britain). In the United States, by contrast, interest groups increasingly bypass political parties entirely, providing direct financial support to their favorite candidates. In some cases, interest groups hedge their bets by contributing to both candidates in the same race!

As in all political activity, capable leadership is essential to interest group success. In addition to ensuring sound management, dynamic leadership translates into political influence: Soliciting funds through computerized direct-mail appeals is one important way in which interest groups gain that influence. Finally, leaders of interest groups orchestrate and often personally spearhead lobbying efforts, attempting to persuade legislators or decision makers to support or oppose a particular measure in one-on-one meetings. How successfully interest groups operate often depends on the strength of the individual lobbyist's personality and reputation. With that in mind, interest groups frequently vie for former presidential advisers (and pay them handsomely) as special-interest representatives in Washington.

The Interest Group Explosion

A few statistics about associations in the United States illustrate why some observers are alarmed at the proliferation and rapid growth of interest groups in recent years. In the early 1980s, one estimate indicated that there were nearly 15,000 national nonprofit organizations, an increase of 40 percent over 1968.[6] According to another study, in the nine-year period between 1976 and 1985, the number of registered *lobbyists* in Washington increased from 3,320 to 8,800. Some experts, however, estimated that there were as many as 20,000 lobbyists in Washington in the late 1980s! In 1976, some 2,100 associations were located in the nation's capital. By 1986, that number had increased almost 50 percent, to 3,100.[7] According to one observer, associations today are the third largest industry in Washington, behind only government and tourism, with 87,000 employees involved in lobbying Congress.[8]

Several reasons for this interest group explosion have already been suggested. The dramatic increase in governmental benefits accompanying the rise of the welfare state has promoted the growth of new associations designed to protect and extend those benefits. The declining influence of political parties has encouraged interest groups to lobby directly. Furthermore, the increasing complexity and diversity of American society has given rise to a variety of single-issue interest groups, such as the National Rifle Association and right-to-life groups, as well as organizations advocating a much broader political agenda, running the gamut from Common Cause to the League of Women Voters. Furthermore, mass mailings and computer technology make founding such organizations relatively easy. Higher levels of education have increased individuals' interest in such associations, and relative prosperity has made them more able to pay dues. Also noteworthy are congressional reforms enacted during the 1970s that opened committee, subcommittee, and conference committee meetings to the public. This change has enhanced lobbyists' effectiveness by providing not only easier access but also simpler monitoring of legislative behavior.

In the early 1970s, a new kind of interest group known as *political action committees (PACs)* came into their own. Congress had attempted to curb election abuses by prohibiting corporations and labor unions from contributing directly to political campaigns. However, the law (as finally passed by Congress and interpreted by the courts) did not prohibit special interests from spending money indirectly through specially created committees. From that time forward, the growth of PACs was "exponential."[9] In the period from 1974 to 1981, PACs grew in number from approximately 600 to 2,900.[10] Today there are well over 4,000 such organizations, nearly half of which represent corporations. The money raised by these groups accounts for an ever-larger share of campaign funds; most of these funds tend to flow into the war chests of incumbents seen as likely winners. In both 1986 and 1988, PACs spent more than $125 million on congressional races.

The rise of interest groups in the democratic states of western Europe has, in its own way, been no less impressive.[11] In a number of European nations, interest groups have been officially recognized by the government and have achieved quasi-governmental status. For instance, in Sweden and Norway, a ministry considering an administrative action is obliged to consult affected groups, thus directly involving interest groups in policies of the government. Furthermore, interest groups are represented on many governmental boards and agencies. In France, a national system of consultation between government and the private sector encompasses some 500 councils, 200 committees, and 300 commissions. Serving on each of these governmental bodies are representatives of both government and interest groups.

For better or worse, as interest groups in the United States and western Europe have gained the ascendancy, their image has also improved. To be sure, Americans still refer to "special interests" in an often derogatory manner, meaning groups that oppose interests or policies favored by the majority of citizens. But on the whole, interest groups today are generally accepted by Americans as a fact of life. Two decades ago, such groups were careful to couch their policy preferences in the form of high-minded arguments designed to demonstrate that what was good for them was good for the entire nation. Today, one hears a far franker political language spoken. Leaders of various private interest groups (representing middle-class taxpayers, apartment house owners, Hispanic-Americans, the elderly, and the like) unabashedly protest that their respective constituencies have not received their fair share of the public goods. Talk of the public interest is far less common now; more and more, American politics is viewed as a contest, with the winners—usually influential interest groups—claiming their shares of the government's bounty. And along with the growing power of interest groups has come an increased public acceptance of selfish interest as a key motivating factor in political life.

Interest Groups in Democracies

Although ordinary citizens (who tend to believe that politics ought to be above crass self-interest) often display an almost reflexive aversion to the term *special interests*, pressure groups are endemic to democracies. There are at least three reasons why.

First and foremost, constitutional governments protect individual freedoms, including the freedom of expression and the freedom of association. Thus interest groups can be considered both an essential part and an inevitable consequence of a free society. As James Madison, perhaps the preeminent political theorist among the Founders, pointed out in *The Federalist*, liberty is to factions (interest groups) as air is to fire: Factions can be suppressed, but to do so, liberty would have to be extinguished.[12]

A second reason why interest groups are natural concomitants of constitutionalism is that democratic societies tend to be more politically and economically complex than nondemocratic ones. In democracies, not only are individuals free to express and act on their opinions and interests, but the interests themselves proliferate *because* of political freedom. For this reason, democracies characteristically generate a multiplicity of political, economic, and social interests.

An example from economics illustrates this point. Western economies can be broken down into "such diverse business organizations as giant corporations, small businesses, heavy industries, service firms, unionized industries, nonunionized industries, agricultural firms, multinational corporations, and nationalized or state-owned industries—all having unique political needs and interests."[13] But this classification scheme only hints at the many potential patterns of competition and cooperation within each of these economic sectors. And the fact that a distinct economic interest can be identified does not necessarily mean that it is represented by only one interest group. For example, farm interests in the United States are promoted by the American Farm Bureau Federation, the National Grange, the National Farmers Organization, the Farmers Union, the National 4-H Club Foundation, the Future Farmers of America, and many other groups. These organizations represent different aspects of a single sector of the economy, underscoring the relationship between the complexity of free societies and their affinity for interest groups.

But diversity of opinions is by no means confined to economic issues. To cite one more example, in the 1980s, vociferous animal rights advocates appeared on the political scene. Even this small movement harbors a significant number of organizations, including the Animal Liberation Front, People for Ethical Treatment of Animals (PETA), the Animal Rights Network (ARN), the Progressive Animal Welfare Society (PAWS), and the Committee to Abolish Sport Fishing and Hunting (CASH).

A final reason why interest groups prosper in constitutional democracies is that these governments regularly distribute benefits, often through cradle-to-grave social programs. In the annual "battle of the budget," the allocation of these benefits is up for grabs. Interest groups, vying for their share of these benefits, have proliferated with the rise of the welfare state in Western democracies. A profusion of benefits for young and old alike, ranging from subsidized Medicare payments to food stamps and school hot-lunch programs, have helped to incubate new interest groups. Furthermore, it is not only the beneficiaries of these programs who lobby for their continued existence. Government agencies and corporate participants—all the providers of the program—have a vested interest in its continuation.

Organized interest groups, by concentrating all their energies, resources, and attention on one issue or issue area, can and do exert disproportionate influence in that specific policy area. Interest groups often recruit celebrities to further their cause; here, television game show host Bob Barker marches with animal rights activists. (AP/Wide World Photos)

Eclipse of the Public Interest?

Critics of interest groups believe that their growth and acceptance in the United States and western Europe imposes a particular hardship on the most disadvantaged segments of society.

The least wealthy and influential sectors of society, they argue, are poorly organized and underrepresented by interest groups in the political arena. By contrast, well-funded and highly organized interests battle to retain their influence and power. In short, the ascendancy of interest groups in democracies, according to this view, has produced a system that promotes the most powerful interests in society at the expense of weaker and economically disadvantaged interests.

Critics also contend that as competition between interest groups has grown more intense, propriety has been sacrificed in the relationship between lobbyists and governmental officials. Of particular concern are the number of governmental officials who have left high positions to work for companies with whom they previously had contacts (such as Pentagon officials working for defense contractors) or former presidential advisers who have become lobbyists and parlayed their access and connections into high-salaried positions. Congress has taken action to limit some of these less than wholesome practices. In 1978, it banned high-ranking officials from any contact with their former agencies for a year and prohibited them from attempting to influence the government on matters related to their "official responsibility" for two years. Despite these laws, however, loopholes remain, prompting some critics to charge that United States politics is more riddled with "influence peddling" today than it has been in many years.

Despite these problems, some political scientists suggest that the worst problems of improper ethics can be solved by improved legislation. In addition, they stress that interest groups perform a valuable function in a democratic society. Lobbyists advocate a wide variety of policy alternatives and viewpoints. As paid professional agents for specific clients in the political arena, they offer valuable information to elected representatives. In that respect, they facilitate rather than obstruct the legislative process.

Furthermore, though not all individuals and organizations are represented equally by interest groups, defenders suggest that the vast majority of citizens *are* adequately represented. The profusion of groups can create a system of countervailing power that tends to keep them all in check. This theory can be traced back to James Madison, who believed that a constitutional democracy that featured a "multiplicity of sects and factions" would be quite unlikely to become tyrannical. Madison thought that the inevitable compromises required to create majorities in a nation where different interests proliferated would make compromise necessary and foster a spirit of moderation. Fanaticism would thus be averted. A number of contemporary political scientists agree, believing that interest groups represent a healthy and thriving pluralism. In this view, diversity is the best guarantee of democracy.

Interest Groups in Nondemocratic States

Interest groups do not flourish in nondemocratic states because opposition is generally discouraged. Since many authoritarian states are in the early stages of economic development, individual interests are often expressed through basic identity groups, which may be tribes or clans. Generally, the military wields considerable influence, even when it is not in charge, because its support is essential for the government to retain power. In some Latin American nations, the Roman Catholic church sometimes exerts limited influence over the government. In countries marked by some industrialization and urbanization, the beginnings of an organized labor movement can often be detected. However, where unions exist, there is "a fundamental difference between a political party in a Western country seeking a labor union's support and a political party in a Third World country seeking such support": In "Western countries the labor unions maintain their independent identities and support parties of their choice; in the Third World the labor unions often become a part of political parties and become subordinate to them."[14]

Thus oblique comparisons can be drawn between formal associations in nondemocratic states and their counterparts in democratic countries. The most significant lobbies in nondemocratic systems often are not interest groups representing citizens but bureaucratic cliques and intraparty factions that compete for priority treatment in the centralized allocation of limited budgetary resources.[15] These are not interest groups in the normal sense, but they do introduce an element of pluralism into political regimes not otherwise tolerant of opposition.

Summary

To influence government, citizens in modern states must combine their efforts. In democratic states, the structures through which citizens attempt to influence public affairs are parties and interest groups. In nondemocratic states, parties are tools of the government rather than instruments for the expression of the popular will. Interest groups, to the extent that they exist in such nations, play a much more limited role than they do in democratic states.

In the United States, political parties were originally regarded as divisive and dangerous. Today they are generally understood to perform key functions in democratic states. They help to organize governments by building a national consensus and offering alternatives, especially during the election process. Political parties may operate in the context of one-party, two-party, or multiparty systems. The scope and organization of parties can be influenced by a variety of factors within a nation, including its traditions, its constitution, and its cultural and economic diversity. Recently, political parties have declined in power.

Interest groups can be classified in several ways; one method is to distinguish private interest groups from public interest groups. A number of factors determine the effectiveness of these groups, including their size, the intensity of political opinions held by their members, their financing, and their leadership. In recent years, these associations have become more numerous and powerful. Some observers fear that they have become too influential, but others believe that their great number and diversity help to promote political stability and ensure the survival of free institutions.

Key Terms

political party	public interest groups
coalition government	lobbyists
interest groups	political action committees (PACs)
private interest groups	

Review Questions

1. Contrast the various party systems and discuss their implications.

2. To what extent does the functioning of interest groups depend on the political system in which they operate?

3. Why has the power of interest groups increased while the power of political parties has decreased? To what extent are these phenomena interrelated?

4. "Not all interest groups are created equal." Explain.

Recommended Reading

BEST, PAUL, KUL RAI, AND DAVID WALSH. *Politics in Three Worlds: An Introduction to Political Science*. New York: Wiley, 1986. Chaps. 8 and 9 contain an excellent cross-cultural study of political parties and interest groups around the world.

GOLDWIN, ROBERT (ed.). *Parties U.S.A.* Skokie, Ill.: Rand McNally, 1964. A stimulating collection of essays that presents important and contrasting interpretations regarding the theory and practice of American political parties.

GOLDWIN, ROBERT (ed.). *Political Parties in the Eighties*. Washington, D.C.: American Enterprise Institute, 1980. A contemporary collection of essays that examines the health and status of American parties.

HOFSTADTER, RICHARD. *The Idea of a Party System: The Rise of Legitimate Opposition in the United States, 1780–1840*. Berkeley: University of California Press, 1969. A historical examination of the origins of the American party system.

LIPPMANN, WALTER. *Public Opinion*. New York: Free Press, 1965 (paperback, Transaction Books, 1990). This book, written by a man often considered the greatest American journalist of the twentieth century, explores the relationship between public opinion and democracy.

MILBRATH, LESTER. *The Washington Lobbyists*. Westport, Conn.: Greenwood, 1976 (reprint of 1963 ed.). An often-cited study of the methods and value of American interest groups.

ROTH, DAVID, AND FRANK WILSON. *The Comparative Study of Politics*. Englewood Cliffs, N.J.: Prentice Hall, 1980. A comprehensive examination of comparative politics that covers in greater depth many of the topics discussed in chaps. 11 and 12.

SKILLING, GORDON, AND FRANKLYN GRIFFITHS (eds.). *Interest Groups in Soviet Politics*. Princeton, N.J.: Princeton University Press, 1971. This major study of Soviet politics uses the pluralistic model as its framework of analysis.

Notes

1. Thomas Jefferson to Francis Hopkinson, March 13, 1789, *The Political Writings of Thomas Jefferson*, ed. Edward Dumbauld (Indianapolis: Bobbs-Merrill, 1955), p. 46.

2. Ibid.

3. A theory to explain why this is so is presented in Harry Jaffa, *Equality and Liberty: Theory and Practice in American Politics* (New York: Oxford University Press, 1965), pp. 3–32.

4. Paul Best, Kul Rai, and David Walsh, *Politics in Three Worlds: An Introduction to Political Science* (New York: Wiley, 1986), pp. 271–272.

5. Gabriel Almond and G. Bingham Powell, *Comparative Politics: A Developmental Approach* (Boston: Little, Brown, 1966), chap. 4.

6. Robert H. Salisbury, "Interest Groups: Toward a New Understanding," in *Interest Group Politics*, ed. A. J. Cigler and B. A. Loomis (Washington, D.C.: Congressional Quarterly Press, 1983), pp. 356–357.

7.   Fred Barnes, "The Parasite Culture of Washington," *New Republic*, July 20, 1986, p. 19. But figures vary. According to the *Wall Street Journal*, in 1991 there were just under 6,000 registered lobbyists and some 80,000 people working for associations whose purpose is to lobby Congress. See Jeffrey Birnbaum, "Overhaul of Lobbying Laws Unlikely to Succeed Thanks to Opposition of Lobbyists Themselves," *Wall Street Journal*, May 30, 1991, p. A20.

8.   Barnes (ibid.) attributes this comment to R. William Taylor, president of the American Society of Association Executives.

9.   Harry Halloway and John George, *Public Opinion: Coalitions, Elites, and Masses*, 2nd ed. (New York: St. Martin's Press, 1986), p. 227.

10. Ibid.

11. This paragraph is based on the discussion in Best et al., *Politics in Three Worlds*, pp. 228–229.

12. Alexander Hamilton, James Madison, and John Jay, *The Federalist* (New York: Modern Library, n.d.), No. 10, p. 55.

13. Best et al., *Politics in Three Worlds*, p. 220.

14. Ibid., p. 240.

15. Gordon Skilling and Franklyn Griffiths, eds., *Interest Groups in Soviet Politics* (Princeton, N.J.: Princeton University Press, 1971).

CHAPTER 13

POLITICAL LEADERSHIP

WISE LEADERS, ORDINARY POLITICIANS, DEMAGOGUES, AND CITIZEN-LEADERS

(AP/Wide World Photos)

MORE THAN ANY other group in contemporary life—more than sports personalities, physicians, business leaders, or even entertainers—politicians tend to be lumped together, stereotyped, and subjected to invidious generalizations. Nonetheless, whenever we make a campaign contribution or cast a ballot in an election, we express a preference for one candidate over another and thus betray an underlying belief that it *does* make a difference which candidate is elected. According to one eminent scholar, "Politics in essence is leadership or attempted leadership of whatever is the prevailing form of political community."[1] Just as airline passengers cannot afford to be indifferent to the skill of the flight crew, so the average citizen can ill afford to be unconcerned with the judgment, character, experience, and abilities of those occupying or seeking positions of political leadership.

The well-being of nations often depends on the capacity of leaders to choose wisely and act prudently. President Richard M. Nixon's Watergate actions, for example, had a significant and profoundly unsettling impact on the nation. Even more, President Lyndon B. Johnson's decision to escalate the war in Vietnam and commit over 500,000 American troops there had substantial consequences for the United States and the world. And after World War II, President Harry Truman made a series of historic decisions—to rebuild Europe by means of the Marshall Plan, to create new military alliances such as the North Atlantic Treaty Organization (NATO), and to confront the Soviet Union's perceived expansionism with a firm policy of containment. In all likelihood, Woodrow Wilson, Warren Harding, or Jimmy Carter would not have adopted those strategies. Clearly, leadership really does matter.

This chapter examines four types of leaders—wise leaders, ordinary politicians, demagogues, and citizen-leaders—who are often differentiated according to character, ability, methods, and purposes. *Wise leaders*, through the exercise of uncommon political prudence and skill, lead their countries successfully through times of national stress. In contrast, *ordinary politicians*, who make up the majority of elected officials in a democracy, concentrate on getting reelected and thus merely represent their constituents. Not all politicians who gain leadership positions are wise, of course; *misguided leaders* are those who govern unwisely or even foolishly; most often, they are remembered principally for their lack of political judgment. *Demagogues* use their political skills to deceive and manipulate the people for malign or illicit ends. Often these distinctions are easier to draw in theory than to apply in practice. Observers differ in their assessments of the quality and qualities of specific leaders. For example, one person may view Franklin Delano Roosevelt as a great leader, while others may view him as an ordinary politician, a misguided leader, or even a demagogue. (Or as a representative of all four types—obviously, the same leader may fit into different categories at various times in a career in public life.) But the difficulty of making such distinctions does not diminish their importance, nor should it obscure the fact that some leaders clearly fall into one category or another. It is generally (although not universally) agreed, for instance, that Adolf Hitler was a demagogue and Winston Churchill a wise leader. And even individuals who disagree over this specific classification most likely would agree that in the period immediately preceding the outbreak of World War II, Hitler was not a wise ruler,

Churchill was not a demagogue—and neither was an ordinary politician. Finally, *citizen-leaders* are able to exert a significant influence over government even though they hold no official position. Usually they oppose governmental policy or established practice by the force of their personality or the moral force of their position, and they succeed by attracting a following of political consequence.

WISE LEADERS: FOUNDERS AND PRESERVERS

The idea of wise leadership (traditionally called *statesmanship*) has occupied a rich and enduring place in Western political history. Plato and Aristotle both examined the idea (Plato's *Socrates* was depicted partaking in a dialogue by that name). During this century, the title of statesman has (rightly or wrongly) been bestowed on a variety of world leaders, ranging from Josip Tito, the founder and first leader of Yugoslavia, to Golda Meir, the former Milwaukee, Wisconsin, schoolteacher who, in 1969, became Israel's fourth prime minister.

Wise leaders are men and women of rare quality who display an overriding concern for the public good, possess a variety of political skills, and exhibit practical wisdom. In addition, in times of crisis, these men and women provide crucial leadership that makes an important difference for the well-being of society—a task in which good fortune usually plays a large role. For this reason, these individuals sometimes come to be seen as the preservers or saviors of society, to whose prudent and courageous leadership the very survival of society may be ascribed.

Finally, such leaders may assume the role of founders of nations, without whose vision, wisdom, and inspirational leadership a particular nation or government might never have existed at all. An especially exalted place has been reserved for leaders of this type in the tradition of Western political thought.

The Ingredients of Wise Leadership

Defining practical wisdom is no easy task. As we have noted, at its core lie certain intangible qualities that are difficult to express in concrete terms. In *A Preface to Morals*, the astute political observer Walter Lippmann attempted to isolate these qualities by contrasting wise rulers with run-of-the-mill politicians. Lippmann suggested that most politicians only work "for a partial interest." Examples include politicians who feather their own nests or slavishly follow the party line. Statesmanship, in contrast, "connotes a man whose mind is elevated sufficiently above the conflict of contending parties to enable him to adopt a course of action which takes into account a great number of interests in the perspective of a longer period of time."[2]

Lippmann recognized that the line between politician and wise leader is by no means clear. Even they cannot ignore special interests—in a democracy, all leaders must sometimes act like politicians. Nonetheless, a political leader begins to act wisely

> whenever he stops trying merely to satisfy or to obfuscate the momentary wishes of the constituents, and sets out to make them realize and assent to those hidden

interests of theirs which are permanent because they fit the facts and can be harmonized with the interests of their neighbors.

Concern for the Public Good The wise leader is motivated neither by crass self-interest nor by narrow partisanship but instead by considerations of the nonpartisan public good or the general welfare. By choosing what "the people will in the end find to be good against what the people happen ardently to desire," such a leader eschews immediate popularity. By refusing to promise the politically impossible, they choose honesty and moderation over flattery. Such a decision, according to Lippmann, requires the "courage which is possible only in a mind that is detached from the agitations of the moment," as well as the "insight which comes from an objective and discerning knowledge of the facts, and a high and imperturbable disinterestedness."

Although this concept of concern for the public good can be described in terms of moderation, detachment, insight, and honesty, it does not lend itself to neat generalizations. For instance, concern for the public good usually entails honest dealings with the public, but there are exceptions. When the issue is of crucial importance, when something less than full honesty is essential to accomplish the leader's intended purposes, and when those purposes are in the best interests of the nation, the statesman may legitimately withhold the truth from the public or even tell an outright lie. Extreme political circumstances occasionally compel them to be less than fully candid with their constituents. For example, both before and during the Civil War, Abraham Lincoln consistently downplayed the slavery issue, preferring to keep the political spotlight on the overriding importance of preserving the Union. Lincoln understood that explicit mention of the slavery issue would alienate members of the precarious coalition on whose support his political popularity rested, ultimately harming the cause of both black emancipation and the Union.[3]

Practical Wisdom Outstanding leaders must also possess a quality Aristotle called prudence or practical wisdom: They must have a compelling vision of the public good and of the best means for achieving that good. Such breadth of vision comes from an objective and discerning knowledge of the facts, combined with the flexibility to identify the public good in a given set of circumstances. They must understand the relationship between immediate actions and ultimate consequences and must correctly anticipate the reactions of friend and foe alike. Finally, exceptional leaders must be able to distinguish between what is fundamental and what is superficial and between what is truly possible and what is foolishly unrealistic or utopian. In sum, such statecraft requires rare insight regarding the political health of society and the steps needed to preserve or restore a basically healthy social condition. In this sense, wise leaders bear a significant resemblance to physicians, whose success is ultimately measured not in dollars and cents but in the health of their patients.

Leadership Skills A third requirement is overall political competence—the capacity to translate farsighted policies into political realities. It is not sufficient that a president, for example, have the national interest at heart; the chief executive must also have the ability to turn good intentions into good programs. Furthermore, such a political leader must be able to gain public support for proposed programs and policies. In a democracy, wise policies (and in the case of elections, the leaders themselves) must generally gain popular consent to be successful. For the wise democratic leader, then, reconciling wisdom and consent in the often turbulent public arena commands primary attention.

In the everyday political world, such a leader must also be able to manage a vast bureaucracy and direct a large personal staff, work with the legislature to ensure a majority for the passage of the administration's programs, and rally public opinion behind the administration's policies. The wise leader must display skill in organization, persuasion, and other political abilities.

This aspect of political wisdom presupposes that the requisite leadership skills are put to good and proper use; political adroitness is commendable only when a political leader's abilities are directed toward the public good. If those abilities are used primarily to advance the career or line the pockets of the officeholder, then his or her success represents a failure of the democratic system. By the same token, even if the political leader's goals are praiseworthy, the methods used to achieve them may be repugnant. Political leaders who seek to remove obstacles to needed social reforms by ruining, jailing, or killing their opponents can hardly be praised for their actions, no matter how beneficial their policies might be.

Extraordinary Opportunities   Historians have frequently observed that great times make great leaders. To become a true leader, a person must live at a time when the actions and decisions taken can make a crucial difference in the history of society and perhaps the world. Such a leader may be genuinely concerned about the public good, have extraordinary political skills, and possess enormous practical wisdom, yet fail to make a great or lasting impact. During times of politics as usual, even the most capable leaders lack the opportunity to exercise their special talents.

Is it, then, the individual or the times that make for political greatness? Here an analogy with medicine is again appropriate. The doctor who receives the greatest acclaim is not the one who gives competent day-to-day health-care advice but the one with a reputation for pulling patients through life-threatening illnesses or traumas. Like individuals, nations go through crises that may threaten their very existence. At such times, moral inspiration and political expertise are essential if the nation is to endure; such a situation is tailor-made for the exercise of statecraft.

Good Fortune   The final prerequisite for wise political leadership is good luck. No political leader can be successful without a certain amount of good fortune. A turn in the tide of a single battle, a message thought about but not sent (or sent too late), or any number of other seemingly unimportant incidents or actions may prove decisive. Great leadership can never be attributed entirely to good luck, but considering the complex environment in which such leaders operate, good luck often makes the difference between success and failure.

The Lure of Fame

Often political leaders (or aspiring leaders) assume positions of public responsibility at significant cost to themselves. They must endure long separations from family, relinquishment of more lucrative careers, and constant public criticism. The question inevitably arises, Why would men and women of outstanding ability devote the best years of their productive lives to the pursuit of political excellence? What would inspire such individuals to work for the public good, often at the expense of more obvious and immediate self-interests?

According to historian Douglass Adair, the Founders of the United States were motivated primarily by the idea of fame. For individuals such as George Washington, James Madison, Alexander Hamilton, and Benjamin Franklin, narrow self-interest, defined in terms of personal power or wealth, was not an overriding concern. Nor was individual honor, which Adair defined as a "pattern of behavior calculated to win praises from [one's] contemporaries who are [one's] social equals or superiors."[4] Rather, the Founders' great motivating force was a desire for fame—a concept that, according to Adair, has been deeply embedded in the Western philosophical and literary tradition since the classical era. Applying his interpretation to the U.S. Founders, Adair wrote:

> Of course they were patriots, of course they were proud to serve their country in her need, but Washington, Adams, Jefferson, and Madison were not entirely disinterested. The pursuit of fame, they had been taught, was a way of transforming egotism and self-aggrandizing impulses into public service; they had been taught that public service nobly (and selflessly) performed was the surest way to build "lasting monuments" and earn the perpetual remembrance of posterity.[5]

Just as not all (or even most) political leaders are wise, so not all wise leaders are motivated by the desire for fame. Sometimes the simple desire to do a good job or to win public approval provides sufficient incentive. But it seems likely that the greatest leaders have been motivated principally by a desire for fame. Alexander Hamilton observed that a love of fame is "the ruling passion of the noblest minds."[6] In studying such leaders, one should not discount their desire for earthly immortality.

Four Model Leaders

Great leaders have appeared at many times and in many places throughout history. As the following political biographies of four world-famous leaders demonstrate, the backgrounds, qualities, and motives of leaders who have risen to the first rank of leader display both remarkable similarities and wide disparities.

Rómulo Betancourt (1908–1981)   In 1830, Venezuela became a nation. From then until 1959, when Rómulo Betancourt assumed the elected presidency of Venezuela, no democratic ruler had survived in office for even two years. Betancourt not only survived, battling seemingly insurmountable obstacles, but his public career prospered, giving life to his country's fledgling democracy. Although he acted as a strong president, Betancourt made very clear the difference between democratic leadership and dictatorial abuse of power. Thus he encouraged a politics of moderation, compromise, and toleration; he heeded the rightful powers of the other branches of government, followed the constitution, respected the rights of his citizens, and almost obsessively avoided using his power for material advantage (or permitting anyone under him to do the same).[7] And when his five-year term expired, Betancourt did what no Venezuelan had ever done before; as the constitution written during his term of office required, he turned over his office to his democratically elected successor.

For these reasons, Rómulo Betancourt can justly be considered the founder of democracy in Venezuela. As a founder, he differs markedly from other twentieth-century founders such as Pol Pot and Fidel Castro, who zealously undertook to establish and then exercise unlimited political power with insufficient regard (and even with utter contempt) for individual suffering. Furthermore, the evidence is clear: Betancourt sought power not for its own end but rather for the public good that it might accomplish. For that reason, he was able to relinquish it willingly, understanding that great lesson of political leadership: Wise leaders deliberately make themselves dispensable by preparing the people to govern in their absence.[8]

Who was this extraordinary individual? Betancourt's political career began when he was still a university student. Venezuela was ruled from 1908 to 1935 by Juan Vicente Gómez, a military dictator (called a *caudillo* in the Latin American tradition). In 1928, at the age of 20, Betancourt became a student leader in a failed revolution, eventually ending up in jail.

After his release from jail, Betancourt went into exile in Costa Rica for eight years, returning shortly after the death of the dictator. After that, he became an active and increasingly recognizable political figure in his native Venezuela. Yet from the mid-1930s until his resumption of the presidency in 1959, Betancourt was frequently a political figure in opposition. Often he was on the run and active in the underground, sometimes living in exile as he continued his opposition to the nondemocratic governments that ruled his land. During his early opposition years, his views were communist, although they moderated with time to favor democracy and socialistic gradualism. Betancourt's most notable achievement during this time consisted of laying the groundwork for what would become Venezuela's leading party, Acción Democrática. Throughout most of his opposition years, both Betancourt and his party consistently championed widespread democratic participation for all citizens, agrarian reform, mass education, broad improvements in health, and economic diversification beyond oil.

Betancourt's most controversial action was to join (and, according to some versions, head) a group of military reformers in a coup overthrowing Venezuela's military government in October 1945. Betancourt ended up as president, championing a foreign policy in which Venezuela refused to extend diplomatic recognition to dictatorships and urged other governments in the region to follow suit. Domestically, Betancourt decreed that the large oil companies in Venezuela turn over half of their income, enabling the government to undertake a far-reaching program to establish schools, hospitals, public water and sanitation facilities, and low-cost housing developments. Betancourt sponsored a new constitution in 1947, promoted elections, and declared that he would not be a candidate for office. The candidate who was elected to succeed Betancourt lasted only nine months before being ousted by a military coup. It would not be until 1959 and Rómulo Betancourt's election to the presidency that democracy would return to Venezuela.

During this five-year term as president, Betancourt continued most of the progressive policies he had originally undertaken. Particularly notable was the fact that he worked to encourage foreign investment and made concerted efforts to improve urban housing. Betancourt also undertook a program of land reform. His economic and political achievements were all the more remarkable because when he took office, his nation was facing an economic crisis, the military did not support his rule, and coup attempts from both the left and the right punctuated this term in office (Betancourt survived more than one assassination attempt).

In the end, Betancourt not only accomplished much but also became beloved by his people. What accounted for his great success? Significantly, he possessed many of the attributes of a model leader:

> Rómulo Betancourt's political capacity was unique—expertise in maneuver, ability to judge the motives and probable behavior of others, almost unerring judgment as to when it was best to strike hard and when to compromise; capacity to listen to advice but to rely on his own assessment of a situation; an ability to make difficult decisions; a vast degree of self-control; great and widely recognized personal valor, both moral and physical. He combined all these qualities with a high degree of practical idealism—a clear vision of what he wanted to accomplish for his country, and commitment to values which (together with ambition) had for several decades motivated him in national politics.[9]

Rómulo Betancourt was Venezuela's indispensable political leader. He succeeded against long odds. One of his foremost biographers, Robert J. Alexander, has observed that "no other Venezuelan political leader of his time could have succeeded under all these circumstances,"[10] The historian John Fagg has written, "If moral authority and high principles counted, Rómulo Betancourt loomed as a titan in the history of Venezuela."[11] It seems only appropriate that the historic founder of Venezuela's democracy has not been forgotten by history.

Winston Churchill (1874–1965)   Unlike Betancourt, Winston Churchill was no founder; Great Britain had had a representative government long before he became its prime minister in May 1940. Until that moment, he had had a checkered public career. A colorful personality, Churchill was brilliant, charming, witty, controversial, cantankerous, and courageous. His public career reflected a steadfast devotion to the cause of political liberty. Furthermore, he was *right* at a very important time when freedom was threatened. Almost alone among the major political figures of the 1930s, he recognized and consistently pointed out the grave dangers posed by Nazi Germany. In discerning these dangers long before they became apparent to most of his contemporaries, he proved himself to be the most perceptive political observer of his day.

Winston Churchill, who never confused what his nation wanted to hear with what it needed to hear: "We shall not flag or fail. We shall go on to the end. . . . We shall never surrender." In 1953, Churchill was awarded the Nobel Prize in literature for his writing and his oratory. (UPI/Bettmann)

Winston Churchill was born into a prominent English family that traced its lineage directly back to John Churchill, the first duke of Marlborough. Winston's father had been a distinguished member of Parliament and cabinet minister; his mother was an American. He himself was elected to Parliament at the tender age of 25 and almost immediately acquired a reputation as an eloquent and outspoken maverick. In 1911, he was appointed First Lord of the Admiralty, a high office he held through the first year of World War I. He was forced to resign in 1915, after the dismal failure of an amphibious attack on Turkey, by way of the Dardanelles, which he had sponsored. Churchill's political prestige then fell to an all-time low, although he managed to recoup sufficiently to be appointed minister of munitions in 1917.

Churchill remained a Conservative MP throughout most of the 1920s and even held the prestigious position of chancellor of the exchequer (comparable to the U.S. secretary of the treasury) for an extended period. Despite a solid record of public service, he entered the 1930s as something of a political outcast, having alienated the leadership of his party. Even though the Conservatives held power, he was excluded from the government, and he found himself increasingly isolated in Parliament. At the age of 56, he seemed to be facing a premature end to his political career.

He was not one to remain silent about dangers to the nation, however. From the time of Hitler's ascent to power, Churchill sought to alert the Western democracies to the danger from Berlin. He repeatedly pointed to the German rearmament program and publicly decried the comparative weakness of Britain's military forces—especially its air power. Not only did his warnings go unheeded, but he was also criticized and even ridiculed by many mainstream politicians and commentators. In the words of his foremost biographer, Churchill's was a voice in the wilderness.[12]

As the 1930s progressed and Churchill's alarms began to arouse the nation, there still was no place for him in his party's cabinet. Only after Britain entered World War II was he asked to return to the government, initially in his former post as First Lord of the Admiralty and subsequently as the prime minister. His inspiring leadership proved decisive as Britain for a time stood alone against the Axis powers. In Churchill's own words, "Alone, but upborne by every generous heartbeat of mankind, we had defied the tyrant in his hour of triumph."[13]

Churchill had rare leadership qualities. He understood the darker side of human nature and thus grasped the great danger to civilization posed by Adolf Hitler. He had the courage of his convictions, never yielding to the pressures of public opinion—even if it meant being ostracized by his own party. His rhetoric inspired a nation. Above all, he was proved right about the urgent need for military preparedness. Although his message (that another terrible war was coming unless Britain did something to prevent it) was one his compatriots did not want to hear, he never confused what the nation wanted to hear with what it *needed* to hear. It is no exaggeration to say that Winston Churchill's statesmanship helped to save his country from foreign domination.

Abraham Lincoln (1809–1865)   Winston Churchill's leadership helped to protect his nation from foreign enemies; Abraham Lincoln's political genius helped to save his nation from itself.

The central political question in Lincoln's time was slavery. Churchill conceivably could have changed British public opinion before World War II, but Lincoln had no chance of persuading the majority of his fellow citizens that slavery should be abolished. The South's economic dependence on slavery, along with the persistence of racial prejudice in the North, guaranteed that no political figure who favored the immediate abolition of slavery could serve as president of a truly united nation. This was the context in which Abraham Lincoln decided to run for president, a decision that culminated in his election to the nation's highest office in 1860.

Lincoln's politics were guided by a basic moral precept and a profoundly practical judgment. The moral precept, which he repeatedly voiced in his debates with Stephen Douglas during his 1858 campaign for the Senate, was that slavery was wrong in principle, everywhere and without exception. In declaring slavery to be unjust and immoral, Lincoln did not resort to abstract philosophy; rather, he based his judgment squarely on the Declaration of Independence, which states that "all men are created equal." Thus for Lincoln, slavery violated the most basic principle of the American political order.

Lincoln exercised profound practical judgment in evaluating the conditions under which slavery might be eradicated in the United States. He believed above all that it was necessary to maintain the Union as a geographic entity, as well as preserve its integrity as a constitutional democracy. Only through a single central government for North and South alike could slavery be ended (although this

Model leaders provide crucial leadership for the well-being of society. As Abraham Lincoln put it, "The occasion is piled high with difficulty, and we must rise with the occasion." (Granger Collection)

was by no means inevitable). Conversely, any breakup of the Union would mean the indefinite extension of slavery, at least in the South.

Lincoln's belief in political equality and his conviction that such equality could only be achieved by preserving the Union help to explain the pre–Civil War stands he avoided taking, as well as the ones he adopted. Although he believed that slavery was morally wrong, he did not propose its immediate abolition; he knew that such a proposal would prompt the South to secede and ensure the survival of slavery in that region. Nor did he support Northern abolitionists who sought to disassociate themselves from the Union so long as it continued to countenance slavery. Here again, Lincoln recognized that such a policy would only entrench the very institution it was designed to eliminate. Finally, he opposed Stephen Douglas's formula of "popular sovereignty," under which each new state would be allowed to declare itself for or against slavery. The question of slavery, Lincoln believed, was too fundamental to be submitted to the vagaries of the political marketplace.

Rather than pursue any of these policies, Lincoln favored an end to the extension of slavery into the territories so that from then on, only free states would be admitted to the Union. To Lincoln's mind, this was the strongest antislavery policy that had any chance of gaining popular acceptance. The keys to his strategy were patience and perseverance. Adoption of his plan would ultimately bring about an end to slavery in the whole United States, as the relative weight and legislative strength of the slaveholding states diminished with the passage of time and the admission of new nonslaveholding states.

When it became evident that his policy would not win the day, Lincoln accepted the Civil War as inevitable. Yet during the course of this conflict, his approach to the slavery question varied according to the circumstances of the war. As we noted earlier, when the tide of battle ran against the Union and victory seemed to depend on not alienating several of the slaveholding border states, Lincoln went out of his way to soft-pedal the slavery issue. The North needed military victories, not pious pronouncements, if the Union was to endure. It could not endure, he believed, so long as it remained "half slave and half free." In the final analysis, the reason Lincoln was willing to countenance civil war was, paradoxically, to preserve the kind of Union the Founders had intended.

Both before and during the Civil War, Lincoln's policies were aimed at achieving the maximum amount of good possible within the confines of popular consent. As commander in chief, he pushed his constitutional authority up to (if not beyond) its legal limits. But just as his ultimate political purposes were not underminded by the compromises he undertook to save the Union in time of peace, so his moral integrity was not corrupted by the dictatorial powers he wielded in time of war. For his ability to combine the exercise of power with an overriding concern for justice and political principle, Abraham Lincoln stands as a monument of wise political leadership.

Anwar el-Sadat (1918–1981) Anwar el-Sadat became president of Egypt in 1970 and held that position until his assassination in 1981. He succeeded Gamal Abdel Nasser, the acknowledged leader of the Arab world and a prime mover in the post–World War II anticolonialist movement. Nasser was an autocratic ruler who governed Egypt with an iron fist and staunchly opposed the existence of the state of Israel. When Nasser died in 1970, he was succeeded automatically by Sadat, who as vice-president was Nasser's handpicked successor. Under Egypt's constitution, Sadat was to hold office on an interim basis for only 60 days, during which the National Assembly was required to choose a permanent successor. Ironically, this legislative body eventually endorsed Sadat only because it was thought that he would be noncontroversial and would adhere tightly to his predecessor's policies.

There was little reason to expect anything else from Sadat, whose early political life was devoted to securing Egyptian independence from Great Britain. His anti-British activities during World War II included contacts with Germans aimed at collaboration against the British imperialists. For these efforts, Sadat spent two years in a detention camp. Later he would spend three more years (1946–1949) in prison, charged with attempting to assassinate a British official. In their pursuit of a pronationalist, anti-British strategy, Sadat and Nasser cooperated closely. It was Sadat who publicly announced the overthrow of the Egyptian monarchy and the establishment of the new, independent republic of Egypt, under Nasser's leadership, in July 1952.

Given this history, it seemed inevitable that as president, Sadat would continue Nasser's policies. Events seemed to bear out this expectation. In 1971, he was instrumental in forging the Federation of Arab Republics, an alliance of Egypt, Libya, and Syria motivated by Nasser's policy of uniting the Arab world. The federation ultimately failed, but not for want of trying on Sadat's part.

In 1973, Sadat led Egypt in a war against Israel. Although Egypt was defeated,

Sadat stressed that the Egyptian army had won a major battle at the outset of the war; this victory, he maintained, restored Egypt's national honor.

In the aftermath of the war, a new emphasis on peace marked Sadat's policies. The transformation of Sadat from belligerent Arab nationalist to committed advocate of peaceful coexistence was capped by his precedent-shattering state visit to Israel, where he delivered a memorable speech before the Israeli Knesset (parliament) on November 20, 1977. More important than the speech itself was the symbolic significance of his official presence in the Israeli seat of government: Egypt had become the first Arab country to recognize Israel as a sovereign state.

This dramatic act of conciliation by Sadat paved the way for the Camp David accords between Egypt and Israel the following year. The Egyptian-Israeli agreement at Camp David, Maryland, which set the stage for Israel's withdrawal from the Sinai peninsula, caught foreign observers by surprise and stunned the Arab world. Sadat was bitterly attacked by many of his fellow Arab rulers as a traitor to the Palestinian cause. To the Arabs, and to many of the most astute observers as well, Sadat's bold step toward a lasting Arab-Israeli peace was as unexpected as it was unprecedented.

Why did Sadat take this extraordinary step? Some experts have suggested that Sadat recognized that given the serious economic problems facing his impoverished, densely populated nation, Egypt simply could not afford a perennial cycle of war with Israel. Others have pointed to the fact that Israel had furnished Egypt with valuable intelligence about the activities of its increasingly hostile neighbor, Libya. Finally, it has been argued that Sadat was a pragmatist who concluded that the only way Egypt was ever going to regain the Sinai, which Israel had occupied since 1967, was by signing a peace treaty.

Although all of these factors may have figured into Sadat's calculations, they do not explain the intensity of his peace efforts or the magnitude of the personal and political risks he was willing to take. He knew that his actions would alienate most of the Arab world (including many of his fellow citizens). It seems likely that just as the young Sadat was moved by the ideal of a free and independent Egypt (which he helped to bring about), so an older Sadat was inspired by an even more noble vision. As he himself expressed it on the occasion of the signing of the Camp David accords:

> Let there be no more wars or bloodshed between Arabs and Israelis. Let there be no more suffering or denial of rights. Let there be no more despair or loss of faith. Let no mother lament the loss of her child. Let no young man waste his life on a conflict from which no one benefits. Let us work together until the day comes when they beat their swords into plowshares and their spears into pruning hooks.[14]

The eradication of hatred, religious bigotry, and incessant warfare from a region where they had been a way of life (and death) for as long as anyone could remember would indeed be a great act of statesmanship. The attempt to bring peace to the Middle East may well have been Sadat's own personal bid for immortality. He may not have been aware of Hamilton's views on the subject of leadership, but through his actions Sadat bore out the truth of Hamilton's observation that love of fame is the "ruling passion" of history's most exceptional leaders. Should Sadat's efforts to achieve peace ever bear fruit, he will be long remembered—not only by his fellow Egyptians, but also by future generations the world over.

The Eclipse of Political Wisdom?

It may seem strange to devote such a large part of a chapter on political leadership to a discussion of wise political leadership. After all, a well-known aphorism of American politics holds that a statesman is nothing but a politician who has been dead for a while. Like the proverbial prophet who is not honored in his own country, wise leaders often are not honored in their own time.

Full appreciation of such rulers, of course, may come only after enough time has passed for the practical results of farsighted leadership to become widely apparent. But there is another, peculiarly modern reason why this kind of leadership is held in such low esteem in American political life: Its existence—if not its very possibility—has been cast into doubt. Just as American citizens tend to be highly suspicious of the public pronouncements of any elected official (frequently looking for deeper personal or political motives—which, in fact, often lie beneath the surface), so we have come to believe that wise leaders, too, are little more than clever and successful politicians of the past. Significantly, whereas the 1934 edition of the *Encyclopedia of the Social Sciences* included a brief but incisive essay on statesmanship by a celebrated British scholar, a more recent edition has omitted all mention of statesmanship as a category of political thought.

In addition, discounting the idea of political wisdom also reflects how little value is assigned to excellence in an egalitarian age.[15] As modern democratic societies more and more emphasize that everyone is equal, it becomes less and less fashionable to recognize that anyone excels at anything—a tendency that is especially pronounced where the political profession is concerned.

From this frame of mind comes the modern propensity to debunk the very concepts of wise rule and political wisdom. To the debunkers, vague historical determinants or narrow self-interest, not free will, are the true motive forces in history, and it is naive to believe that some leaders really do care about the public good. This cynical view leads to a drastically reduced opinion of outstanding leaders in world history. It is as if "the old histories full of kings and generals whom our ancestors foolishly mistook for heroes are, we suppose, to be replaced by a kind of hall of fame of clever operators."[16]

The most serious consequence of this increasing reluctance to recognize political achievement is that it makes political life less attractive to capable and conscientious individuals who might choose to distinguish themselves by serving public rather than private interests. By denying public officials the respect they are due, a democratic society can do itself considerable harm. A pervasive belief that corrupt and mediocre politicians are everywhere can become a self-fulfilling prophecy by causing only the corrupt or mediocre to seek public office.

ORDINARY POLITICIANS

Citizens in democratic states frequently make disparaging remarks about politicians without realizing how rare such people really are. As a distinctive type of political leader, ordinary politicians are, in fact, extraordinary, for they are found only in democratic states, which comprise a distinct minority among the world's governments. Nondemocratic states have rulers and officials but not politicians.

Most politicians, like most lawyers, teachers, and doctors, have neither great vision nor outstanding abilities. On a day-to-day basis, they do what they must to maintain their authority and reputation. Much of the time, they want to do the right thing, although they may have no comprehensive or profound idea of what that entails, especially when complex moral and political questions arise. Generally they are not corrupt, but under certain circumstances they are corruptible. In short, they act as most of us might act in their position—they are, in this respect, quite ordinary.

In democracies, citizens frequently place contradictory expectations on their political leaders: Politicians are expected to be ordinary, identifying with the common citizen, yet at the same time they are expected to display uncommon dedication and ability in discharging their public duties. The would-be leader in a democratic society must face the perennial question of whether to act as the voters' delegate, carrying out their (presumed) wishes, or as their trustee, exercising independent judgment in the discharge of political responsibilities.

Nearly every democratic state is a *representative* democracy—that is, the leaders have an obligation to represent the views, opinions, and attitudes of their constituents. The political system itself seems to require leaders to be responsive if they wish to be reelected. But leaders must lead as well as represent—and there lies the politician's dilemma.

Legislators as Delegates

The ideal democracy has been described as a nation in which each citizen takes an active part in government. Such a goal is clearly impossible in a nation of 240 million people (or 2 million people, for that matter). Where each individual cannot personally represent his or her own interests, it has been argued, democratic governments should at least reflect the configuration of interests and opinions within the larger society. Of particular importance in this scheme is the national legislature, because it is usually the most representative branch of government. According to the **delegate theory of representation**, a legislature "is representative when it contains within itself the same elements, in the same proportion, as are found in the *body politic* at large. It is typical of us; we are all in it in microcosm."[17]

If this model of democratic government is valid, elected representatives should act like instructed delegates. Since the legislature exists to pass laws that the people want, the representative should translate diverse popular desires into unified (and uniform) public policy. The representative, according to this theory, is a receptacle of public opinion; in effect, the voters hire somebody at each election to do their bidding in the legislature.

Underlying the instructed-delegate theory of political representation is a fundamental belief in the wisdom, intelligence, and decency of the people. One prominent advocate of this theory, believing that there is a "relative equality of capacity and wisdom between representatives and constituents," argued that it would be "arbitrary and unjustifiable for representatives to ignore the opinions and wishes of the people" and that the more often political issues involve "irrational commitment or personal preference, choice rather than deliberation, the more necessary . . . that the representative consult with the people's preferences and pursue their choice."[18]

As a corollary benefit, according to its advocates, this concept mitigates the effects of corruption. Although elected officials may initially be very much like the people they are elected to represent, this argument goes, once in office they can easily be corrupted by the exercise of power. A requirement that they vote their constituents' beliefs, then, imposes a necessary constraint on the potential abuse of power.

Legislators as Trustees

The instructed-delegate theory of representation does not enjoy universal support. Its detractors have contended that it requires elected officials to be too passive—in effect, to be followers rather than leaders. The foremost critic of the instructed-delegate theory was Edmund Burke (1729–1797), the eighteenth-century British writer and legislator. Burke did not suggest that legislators could or should ignore the feelings and opinions of their constituents. But while representatives must pay careful attention to public opinion, he argued, they must also maintain their independence of thought and action. Specifically, according to Burke, the elected representative must isolate specific complaints about real problems from the grumblings that characterize a sometimes irascible (and even irrational) electorate. He contended that the politician as legislator must listen to the complaints of constituents but not give all complaints equal weight: Competent legislators distinguish between complaints that arise from defects in human nature (and cannot be remedied) and those that "are symptoms of a particular distemperature" of the day.[19] Understood in this fashion, popular opinion becomes a valuable barometer. If legislators wish to get a reading on popular sentiment or whether a storm is brewing on a particular issue, they must first consult public opinion.

Given this relationship between public opinion and political representation, what role did Burke assign to the legislator? To put it bluntly, he believed that a natural aristocracy, made up of the best and the brightest, should govern and that elected officials should act as trustees for their constituents, not as mere mouthpieces or puppets. As Burke declared in a famous speech to his own constituents, "Your representative owes you not his industry only, but his judgment; and he betrays, instead of serving you, if he sacrifices it to your opinion."[20]

Burke's *trustee theory of representation* fits perfectly into his larger philosophy of government. Good government, he argued, was a matter not simply of will but also of "virtue and wisdom." To be workable, in other words, representative government must be based on upright behavior and careful deliberation, with an eye toward discovering and carrying out the true public good. Burke characterized his own Parliament as "a *deliberative* assembly of *one* nation, with *one* interest, that of the whole—where not local purposes, not local prejudices, ought to guide, but the general good, resulting from the general reason of the whole."[21]

Unlike instructed-delegate proponents, Burke believed that a wide gulf of ability did and should separate members of the legislature from ordinary constituents. He believed that in a sound republic, representatives should be wiser and better informed than constituents and hence should be able, after careful deliberation, to solve most of the political problems that beset a nation. Finally, he argued that the welfare of the whole nation (the public or national interest) should take precedence over the welfare of any of its parts (local or special interests). For these reasons, Burke stressed the importance of the legislator as leader rather than follower.

Politicos

In recent years, some American political scientists have used the term *politico* to describe American legislators who have successfully reconciled the functions of delegate and trustee. Specifically, politicos are political representatives who fight for approval of the bread-and-butter legislation favored by their constituents while taking forceful, independent stands on issues that do not directly engage the "pocketbook" interests of those constituents. Although politicos generally champion the special economic interests of their district or state, the positions they take can be issue-oriented. Thus it is not surprising to see liberal senators from rural states oppose gun control legislation, a position that reflects the opinions of a majority of their most politically active constituents.

William Fulbright, while serving as senator from Arkansas, gave a speech at the University of Chicago shortly after the conclusion of World War II in which he articulated the politico's approach to the problem of democratic leadership.

> The average legislator early in his career discovers that there are certain interests, or prejudices, of his constituents which are dangerous to trifle with. Some of these prejudices may not be of fundamental importance to the welfare of the nation, in which case he is justified in humoring them, even though he may disapprove. The difficult case is where the prejudice concerns fundamental policy affecting the national welfare. A sound sense of values, the ability to discriminate between that which is of fundamental importance and that which is only superficial, is an indispensable qualification of a good legislator. As an example of what I mean, let us take the poll-tax issue and isolationism. Regardless of how persuasive my colleagues or the national press may be about the evils of the poll tax, I do not see its fundamental importance, and I shall follow the views of the people of my state. Although it may be symbolic of conditions which many deplore, it is exceedingly doubtful that its abolition will cure any of our major problems. On the other hand, regardless of how strongly opposed my constituents may prove to be to the creation of, and participation in, an

ever stronger United Nations organization, I could not follow such a policy in that field unless it becomes clearly hopeless.[22]

Fulbright's own career in the Senate (1945–1975) would seem to provide an example of the politico in action. Often he voted against legislation, especially civil rights measures, that in all likelihood he personally favored. He realized that because his constituents' racial views, at that time, were sharply opposed to his own, he could not remain in office without deferring to the deep-seated prejudices of the Arkansas majority on this subject. Fulbright sometimes justified this approach on the ground that many civil rights issues were not of fundamental importance.

Fulbright's deference to his home state's majority opinion on the question of race relations gave him great latitude in the area of foreign policy, an area in which the Arkansas voters had little interest. In time, he became the chairman of the powerful Senate Foreign Relations Committee and was acknowledged widely as a leading spokesman for liberal causes in the realm of foreign policy—even though he represented a state that, by all accounts, was among the nation's most conservative!

Misguided Leaders

Everyday politicians who are genuinely concerned with the public good, who relentlessly pursue their political objectives, and who are able to "get things done" are usually praised. When their vision of the public good is clouded, however, they can be fairly labeled as misguided leaders. Misguided leaders form an interesting subset of ordinary politicians because of the wide chasm between the actions they intend and the results they achieve. What they believe to be the public interest and what is actually good for the nation turn out to be two very different things. Thus if they win, the country loses.

Perhaps the clearest example of such a leader was Neville Chamberlain, prime minister of Great Britain from 1937 until 1940. In retrospect, it is clear that during this pre–World War II period, Germany was rapidly rearming. But Chamberlain earnestly believed in the futility and waste of military armaments and warfare, and he was equally convinced that negotiation and compromise could and should form the basis of all politics, including international politics. As late as October 1938, Chamberlain contended in the House of Commons that "fresh opportunities of approaching this subject of disarmament are opening up before us, and I believe that they are at least as hopeful today as they have been at any previous time" and asserted that

> to such tasks—the winning back of confidence, the gradual removal of hostility between nations until they feel that they can safely discard their weapons, one by one, . . . I would wish to devote what energy and time may be left to me before I hand over my office to younger men.[23]

Many of Britain's "younger men," however, were soon to die on the battlefield, thanks to Hitler's uncompromising militarism. Chamberlain's analysis of international politics was not without vision or sincerity; it was merely mistaken.

DEMAGOGUES

The difference between Chamberlain and Hitler was the difference between a sincere but mistaken leader of high moral principles and an opportunistic leader with a total lack of scruples. The most dangerous species of politician, of which Hitler was a prime example, is the demagogue. Originally, in ancient Greece, a demagogue was a leader who championed the cause of the common people. Today the term *demagogue* is applied to a leader who exploits popular prejudices, distorts the truth, and makes empty promises to gain political power. Generally, demagogues combine unbridled personal ambition, unscrupulous methods, and great popular appeal. Demagogues are not always embraced by the voters; they may manage to capture absolute power by other means, fair or foul—quite often the latter.

If wise leaders are the best kind of leaders, demagogues are the worst. Demagoguery, in fact, might be seen as the perversion of leadership. Statesmen genuinely care about justice and the public good; demagogues only pretend to care about such things to win a public position they can exploit for their own advantage.

Demagogues come to power primarily in democratic societies, where leaders must gain popular approval to hold office. Unlike great democratic leaders, however, demagogues are rarely remembered after they leave power. Occasionally, they leave an indelible mark. When this happens, they achieve infamy, not fame.

American political history is punctuated with the rise and fall of demagogues. Some had a purely local impact; others affected the entire nation. All are remembered chiefly with scorn.

Theodore Bilbo (1877–1947)   As governor and senator, Bilbo dominated Mississippi politics from the 1920s through the 1940s. He campaigned equally hard against blacks and his political opponents, linking them whenever possible. His campaign rhetoric was colorful and outrageous. In the heat of one political campaign, he denounced his opponent as a "cross between a hyena and a mongrel . . . begotten in a [racial slur deleted] graveyard at midnight, suckled by a sow, and educated by a fool."[24] Although Bilbo's white supremacy politics and down-home language endeared him to a great many Mississippians, not everyone was impressed. Even political allies viewed him as a self-serving political operator. According to one writer, Bilbo was "pronounced by the state Senate in 1911 'as unfit to sit with honest upright men in a respectable legislative body,' and described more pungently by his admirers as 'a slick little bastard.' "[25] And in the eyes of the editor of the *Jackson Daily News*, Bilbo stood "for nothing that is high or constructive, . . . nothing save passion, prejudice and hatred, . . . nothing that is worthy."[26]

Huey Long (1893–1935)   While Theodore Bilbo has mercifully escaped the attention of most American historians, Huey Long, a politician from the neighboring state of Louisiana, has not. Known to his Cajun constituents as the Kingfish, Long was far more ambitious than Bilbo. Of humble origins, he completed the three-year law program at Tulane University, passed a special examination from the Louisiana Supreme Court, and became a licensed attorney at the age of 21. In his own words, he "came out of that courtroom running for office."[27] A mere three years later, he was elected state railroad commissioner, and in 1928 he gained the Louisiana governorship.

Huey Long ruled Louisiana with an iron hand during his four-year reign (1928–1932) and his subsequent term as U.S. senator, which was cut short by an assassin's bullet in 1935. As governor, Long controlled every aspect of the state's political life. Surrounded by bodyguards and aided by a formidable political machine, he used state police and militia to intimidate voters, handed out patronage and political favors like candy, created a state printing board to put unfriendly newspapers out of business, ordered a kidnapping on the eve of a crucial election vote to avoid personal political embarrassment, and generally acted more like a despotic ruler than a democratically elected governor. Under his autocratic rule,

> men could be—and were—arrested by unidentified men, the members of his secret police, held incommunicado, tried, and found guilty on trumped-up charges. A majority of the State Supreme Court became unabashedly his. . . . A thug, making a premeditated skull-crushing attack upon a Long opponent, could draw from his pocket in court a pre-signed pardon.[28]

Despite these excesses and a penchant for luxury, he always took care to picture himself as "just plain folks." The true villains in American society, he said, were rich corporations such as Standard Oil, which consigned ordinary people to lives of poverty while enriching a few corporate officers.

To counteract this alleged thievery by big business, and to create a popular platform for the upcoming presidential race in 1936, Long developed an unworkable (but popular) "Share the Wealth" program, tailor-made to appeal to people suffering through the Great Depression. Long's proposal included restrictions on maximum wealth, mandated minimum and maximum incomes, so-called homestead grants for all families, free education through college, bonuses for veterans, and pensions for the aged—as well as the promise of radios, automobiles, and subsidized food through government purchases. However implausible and impracticable this program seems, it should be remembered that the people to whom Huey Long was appealing were not inclined to quibble or question. They needed someone to believe in.

Huey Long, like many other demagogues, gained power by promising hope to the hopeless. Demagogues generally vow to defeat the forces of evil that, according to them, are solely responsible for the people's plight. Of course, those forces—blacks in the case of Bilbo, corporations for Long—invariably do not exercise anything like the controlling influence attributed to them. Nonetheless, once accepted as the champion of the little people against enemies they themselves have conjured up, demagogues often have been able to manipulate the unsuspecting populace for their own illicit ends.

Joseph McCarthy (1906–1957)   Such was the case with an obscure politician from Wisconsin named Joseph McCarthy, who, during the 1950s, identified a demon that greatly alarmed the American people and then claimed to find evidence of this malignant force in all areas of public life.

While serving as a Republican senator from Wisconsin, McCarthy attracted national attention by making the shocking "revelation" that the U.S. Department of State was infiltrated by communists. For approximately four years, he leveled charges of treason against a wide array of public officials, college professors, and even Hollywood stars. Using his position as chairman of the Senate Committee on Investigations, McCarthy badgered, intimidated, and defamed countless people in and out of government. As his accusations helped to create a national climate of fear, his power grew, and those who opposed him did so at their own risk.

In 1954, McCarthy accused the secretary of the army of concealing foreign espionage operations. That accusation, along with innuendos aimed at General George C. Marshall—next to President Dwight D. Eisenhower, perhaps the most respected public servant in America—marked a turning point. McCarthy had gone one step too far. Ironically, his unscrupulous methods were exposed in the Senate investigations that resulted from his own irresponsible accusations. The hearings received national radio and television coverage and made front-page headlines in every major newspaper in the country. In the end, McCarthy was cast into ignominious obscurity as rapidly as he had been catapulted into national prominence.

CITIZEN-LEADERS

Occasionally, an individual can decisively influence the course of political events without holding an official position in the government. An individual's unique dedication to a cause, personal magnetism, or even outright courage can garner quite a political following. Such a person is called a *citizen-leader.* In the following section, we look at four examples of such grassroots leadership.

Vaclav Havel   In the mid-1960s, before he had turned 30, Vaclav Havel had gained worldwide acclaim for his satiric absurdist plays, including *The Garden Party* (1964) and *The Memorandum* (1965). In the summer of 1968, Havel and thirty other Czech cultural figures signed a statement calling for the revival of the outlawed Social Democratic party in Czechoslovakia. In August of that same summer, the increasing but cautious trend toward liberalization within Czechoslovakia that had begun in 1963 was swiftly and successfully thwarted when the Soviet Union invaded the country to reassert hard-line Soviet control. During the conflict, Havel played a key role in putting the Free Czech Radio on the airways and used this underground radio broadcast to direct daily commentary to Western intellectuals as a plea for assistance.

Over the next two decades, Havel became Czechoslovakia's most famous playwright. His plays often contained biting satire aimed at the communists who ruled in Prague. But his writings were not the only reason for his increasing notoriety. He also became Czechoslovakia's foremost dissident and human-rights champion. In 1977, he coauthored the Charter '77 manifesto that denounced Czechoslovakia's communist rulers for failing to abide by Basket Three of the 1975 Helsinki Accords in which all signatories promised to respect civil and political rights. For such acts of political defiance, Havel was jailed repeatedly, serving sentences that often included hard labor. Despite these punishments, he would not be silenced.

In December 1989, after Czechoslovakia's communist regime collapsed under the crushing weight of popular civilian discontent, Havel became president by consensus. The fact that Havel had been in prison at the beginning of 1989 made his sudden ascent to power all the more remarkable. But then no other public figure in Czechoslovakia could come close to matching the moral authority Havel had accumulated during three decades of courageous citizen-leadership.

Martin Luther King, Jr. (1929–1968)   An outstanding citizen-leader was the renowned black civil rights champion Martin Luther King, Jr. From the moment he became president of the newly formed Southern Christian Leadership Conference in 1957, King's national prominence grew. King led sit-ins, marches, demonstrations, and rallies throughout the South, all aimed at ending segregation and overcoming discrimination in jobs and housing. Practicing nonviolent civil disobedience, protesters under King's leadership would openly break the law (which sanctioned segregated lunch counters, required parade permits, forced blacks to sit at the back of buses, and so on), and would then accept punishment for their action.

King intended to stir the conscience of the nation by reaching legislators and judges and, in the end, the American people. As he stated in his famous 1963 letter from Birmingham jail (King had gone to Birmingham to lead an economic boycott aimed at desegregating public facilities and was jailed for organizing an unlicensed parade):

> I submit that an individual who breaks a law that conscience tells him is unjust, and willingly accepts the penalty by staying in jail to arouse the conscience of the community over its injustice, is in reality expressing the very highest respect for law.[29]

King's hope was clear: "We must see the need of having nonviolent gadflies to create the kind of tension in society that will help men to rise from the dark depths of prejudice and racism to the majestic heights of understanding and brotherhood."[30]

The influence of Martin Luther King and other black leaders on civil rights policy has been decisive. Although extremely controversial at the time, their courageous efforts proved crucial to the passage of the landmark 1964 Civil Rights Act, which banned discrimination in public accommodations and employment. Later, other civil rights legislation was passed, further ensuring equal treatment under the law for all citizens. In 1964, King was awarded the Nobel Peace Prize for his efforts. Four years later he lay dead, the victim of an assassin's bullet. He had not yet turned 40.

Martin Luther King, Jr., who intended to stir the conscience of the American people: "Injustice anywhere is a threat to justice everywhere." King was awarded the Nobel Peace Prize in 1964—four years before his assassination. (Leonard Freed/Magnum)

Ralph Nader   Occasionally, an individual emerges as a citizen-leader from unlikely circumstances. Consider the case of consumer activist Ralph Nader, a Harvard-trained lawyer, an average speaker, a good but hardly exceptional writer, an individual described by the press as colorless and eccentric. Fresh out of law school, he spent seven years battling big government and big business on behalf of the public interest. Undaunted, he took on one of America's largest corporations, General Motors. His 1965 book *Unsafe at Any Speed* exposed the Chevrolet Corvair as a car that, shockingly, failed to meet the most minimal safety standards. In the end, Nader's efforts almost single-handedly ensured the passage of the 1966 National Traffic and Motor Vehicle Safety Act. Through his public interest crusade, Ralph Nader helped to launch a national campaign to make U.S. automobiles and highways safer. It is impossible to say how many traffic deaths have been averted because of the direct and indirect effects of Nader's efforts, but he has certainly earned a respected place as one of America's important citizen-leaders.

Rosa Parks   Rosa Parks pricked the conscience of a nation—remarkably, with a single act of courage. On December 1, 1955, she left work after spending a long day as a tailor's assistant at a Montgomery, Alabama, department store. Boarding a bus that would take her home, she found a seat. Soon, however, she (along with three other black passengers) was asked to stand up to make room for a white man who had no seat (Montgomery's customary practice required that all four blacks would have to stand in order to allow one white man to sit, since no black person was allowed to sit parallel with a white person).[31] Parks stayed put:

> I was thinking that the only way to let them know I felt I was being mistreated was to do just what I did—resist the order. . . . I had not thought about it and I had taken no previous resolution until it happened, and then I simply decided that I would not get up. I was tired, but I was usually tired at the end of the day, and I was not feeling well, but then there had been many days when I had not felt well. I had felt for a long time, that if I was ever told to get up so a white person could sit, that I would refuse to do so.[32]

The bus driver had her arrested.

Many historians date the origin of the American civil rights movement to the Montgomery bus boycott, conducted in the wake of Rosa Parks's arrest. Her single act of symbolic defiance is remembered today as an act of political valor that drew attention to racial injustice and led to a chain of events that eventually changed the nation forever.

Summary

Political leaders who occupy governmental positions can be classified as wise leaders, ordinary politicians, and demagogues. Citizen-leaders, even though they hold no official office, can also exert significant political influence.

Wise leaders display an overriding concern for the public good, superior leadership skills, and keen practical wisdom in extraordinary situations in which the well-being (or the very existence) of a nation is at stake. Historically, they have been motivated largely by the lure of fame. Modern neglect of the concept of statecraft has led some observers to view it as a dying art.

Wise leaders are relatively rare. Most prevalent in representative democracies are ordinary politicians. All elected officials must decide whether to exercise positive leadership or merely represent the views of their constituents. According to the delegate theory of democratic representation, politicians should act primarily as conduits for the expressed wishes of the electorate; the trustee theory, by contrast, stresses the importance of independent judgment in political office. Politicians who seek to combine these two concepts of representation are known as politicos. Some ordinary politicians can be classified as misguided leaders—well-meaning but naive or incompetent public servants whose errors in judgment may lead to disaster.

More sinister is the demagogue, who combines reckless personal ambition, unscrupulous methods, and charismatic appeal. Demagogues are most prevalent in democracies, and their fall is often as sudden and spectacular as their rise to power.

Citizen-leaders combine dedication to a cause, personal ability or magnetism, and opposition to governmental policy (or established practice). They inspire others and attract a sympathetic following, frequently on a worldwide scale. Their power is a function of the moral force generated by the cause they come to personify.

Key Terms

wise leaders
delegate theory of representation
trustee theory of representation

politico
demagogue
citizen-leader

Review Questions

1. How can political leaders be classified? Explain the differences between the various categories.

2. Why is the study of political leadership an important aspect of the overall study of politics?

3. Why are wise leaders rare?

4. What theories explain the duty of representatives in a democracy? Which theory do you believe is more effective? Why?

5. Why can it be said that demagoguery is the perversion of wise leadership?

6. "Only political leaders can exert leadership." Comment.

Recommended Reading

ADAIR, DOUGLASS. "Fame and the Founding Fathers." In *Fame and the Founding Fathers: Essays by Douglass Adair*. New York: Norton, 1974. Adair's essay on the relationship between fame and statesmanship in the founding of the United States is a classic.

ALEXANDER, ROBERT J. *Rómulo Betancourt and the Transformation of Venezuela*. New Brunswick, N.J.: Transaction Books, 1982. An admiring biography of Venezuela's leading democratic statesman.

BURNS, JAMES MACGREGOR. *Leadership*. New York: HarperCollins, 1982. An exhaustive study of all facets of the leadership phenomenon.

FRISCH, MORTON, AND RICHARD STEVENS (eds.). *American Political Thought: The Philosophic Dimension of American Statesmanship* (2nd ed.). Itasca, Ill.: Peacock, 1983. A collection of essays on American statesmen that features a brief but outstanding introduction.

GARROW, DAVID J. *Bearing the Cross: Martin Luther King, Jr., and the Southern Christian Leadership Conference 1955–1968*. New York: Morrow, 1986. An exhaustive in-depth examination of the life and accomplishments of America's greatest twentieth-century citizen-leader.

GILBERT, MARTIN. *Winston S. Churchill: The Prophet of Truth*. Boston: Houghton Mifflin, 1977. Vol. 5, 1922–1939. This 1,115-page volume comprehensively documents Churchill's statesmanship during the most trying times.

JAFFA, HARRY. *Crisis in the House Divided*. Chicago: University of Chicago Press, 1982. Jaffa documents the political wisdom that characterized Abraham Lincoln's statesmanship.

LONG, HUEY. *My First Days in the White House.* New York: Da Capo Press, 1972. A fanciful and amusing piece of propaganda written by one of America's foremost demagogues.

PITKIN, HANNAH (ed.). *Representation.* New York: Atherton Press, 1969. A rich collection of essays with a straightforward and enlightening introduction by the editor.

TUCKER, ROBERT C. *Politics as Leadership.* Columbia: University of Missouri Press, 1981. A thought-provoking essay on the central importance of leadership in political life.

WILDAVSKY, AARON. *The Nursing Father: Moses as a Political Leader.* Tuscaloosa: University of Alabama Press, 1984. A thoughtful analysis of political leadership in a biblical context.

Notes

1. Robert C. Tucker, *Politics as Leadership* (Columbia: University of Missouri Press, 1981), p. iii.

2. Walter Lippmann, *A Preface to Morals* (Boston: Beacon Press, 1960), p. 280. The quotations that follow are from pp. 279–283.

3. See Harry Jaffa, "The Emancipation Proclamation," in *100 Years of Emancipation,* ed. Robert Goldwin (Skokie, Ill.: Rand McNally, 1964), pp. 1–24.

4. Douglass Adair, "Fame and the Founding Fathers," in *Fame and the Founding Fathers: Essays by Douglass Adair* (New York: Norton, 1974), p. 10.

5. Ibid., p. 8.

6. Alexander Hamilton, John Jay, and James Madison, *The Federalist* (New York: Modern Library, n.d.), p. 470.

7. Robert J. Alexander, *Rómulo Betancourt and the Transformation of Venezuela* (New Brunswick, N.J.: Transaction Books, 1982), p. 435.

8. Aaron Wildavsky, *The Nursing Father: Moses as a Political Leader* (Tuscaloosa: University of Alabama Press, 1984).

9. Alexander, *Rómulo Betancourt,* p. 436.

10. Ibid.

11. John Edwin Fagg, *Latin America: A General History,* 2nd ed. (New York: Macmillan, 1969), p. 627.

12. Martin Gilbert, *Churchill* (Garden City, N.Y.: Doubleday, 1980), pp. 100–126.

13. Ibid., p. 127.

14. U.S. Department of State, *Selected Documents,* April 1979.

15. Alexis de Tocqueville, *Democracy in America* (New York: Schocken Books, 1961), vol. 2, pp. 102–106.

16. Morton Frisch and Richard Stevens, "Introduction," in *American Political Thought: The Philosophic Dimension of American Statesmanship,* ed. Morton Frisch and Richard Stevens (Dubuque, Iowa: Kendall/Hunt, 1976), p. 5.

17. The quotation is by Joseph Tussman, as cited in Marie Collins Swaley, "A Quantitative View," in *Representation,* ed. Hannah Pitkin (New York: Atherton Press, 1969), p. 83.

18. Hannah Pitkin, "The Concept of Representation," in *Representation,* ed. Hannah Pitkin, p. 21.

19. Quoted in Harvey Mansfield, Jr., *Statesmanship and Party Government: A Study of Burke and Bolingbroke* (Chicago: University of Chicago Press, 1965), p. 23.

20. Edmund Burke, "The English Constitutional System," in *Representation,* ed. Hannah Pitkin, p. 175.

21. Ibid.

22. Cited in Malcolm Jewell and Samuel Patterson, *The Legislative Process in the United States* (New York: Random House, 1966), p. 32.

23. Martin Gilbert, *Winston S. Churchill: The Prophet of Truth* (Boston: Houghton Mifflin, 1977), vol. 5, p. 993.

24. The quotation appears in Roman J. Zorn, "Theodore G. Bilbo: Shibboleths for Statesmanship," reprinted in *A Treasury of Southern Folklore: Stories, Ballads, Traditions, and Folkways of the People of the South,* ed. B. A. Brotkin (New York: Crown, 1949), p. 304.

25. James W. Silver, *Mississippi: The Closed Society* (Orlando, Fla.: Harcourt Brace Jovanovich, 1964), p. 19.

26. Ibid.

27. Hodding Carter, "Huey Long: American Dictator," in *The Aspirin Age: 1919–1941,* ed. Isabel Leighton (New York: Simon & Schuster, 1949), p. 347.

28. Ibid., p. 361.

29. Martin Luther King, Jr., "Letter from Birmingham City Jail," in *Civil Disobedience: Theory and Practice* (New York: Pegasus, 1969), pp. 78–79.

30. Ibid., p. 75.

31. David J. Garrow, *Bearing the Cross: Martin Luther King, Jr., and the Southern Christian Leadership Conference 1955–1968* (New York: Morrow, 1986), p. 11.

32. Ibid., p. 12.

CHAPTER 14

APPROACHES TO THE PUBLIC GOOD

IDEOLOGIES AND PERSPECTIVES

(AP/Wide World Photos)

AT ONE POINT in Lewis Carroll's delightful *Alice's Adventures in Wonderland,* Alice becomes lost, only to encounter the Cheshire Cat, sitting on a tree branch. "Would you tell me, please, which way I ought to go from here?" asks Alice. "That depends a good deal on where you want to get to," replies the Cat. "I don't much care where," says Alice. "Then it doesn't matter which way you go," muses the Cat.

Like Alice lost in the forest, nations and their governments frequently find themselves unsure of where they want to go, not knowing which road to take. Political leadership can be woefully deficient or hopelessly divided. But intelligent discussion of programs and policies, as Alice's encounter with the Cheshire Cat illustrates, can take place only if decision makers have definite goals.

POLITICAL ENDS AND MEANS

In politics, ends and means are inextricably intertwined. Debates over what particular new policy is desirable almost always assume that *something* must correspond to the **public good** or be in the public interest—that is, that there are common goals that require a common effort (and at times, uncommon exertions). For example, politicians may disagree over whether a tax cut at a particular time will help to promote national prosperity (by encouraging saving and investment, balancing the national budget, reducing the rate of inflation, and so on), but arguments of this kind concern ways and means rather than purposes or ends. Although they may disagree emphatically about the best monetary and fiscal strategies, both sides would agree that the national government should promote economic growth and stability.

Every political community is built on a substructure of basic, widely shared beliefs and values. In most cases, these underpinnings of society encompass the goals of public policy. When factions and parties disagree emphatically on such goals, which constitute the first principles of political life, the very foundations of the political community are undermined.

Every government attempts to achieve certain political goals. In some nondemocratic nations, however, the overriding aims of government may have little to do with the populace's well-being; rather, they may be limited to the consolidation, perpetuation, and expansion of the power of a dictator or a ruling oligarchy. Although such governments can be understood only in terms of their obsession with the monopolization of power, it would be absurd to claim that such a goal had anything in common with the actual good of the public. As Aristotle pointed out, the lust for personal power as an end in itself is inimical to the pursuit of the public interest—and, accordingly, of good government.[1]

Whatever the particular form of government, the public good is generally associated with the fullest possible attainment of security, prosperity, equality, liberty, and justice. These goals represent the political buoys by which the ship of state is kept on course. Arguments about whether the ship should tack this way or that, given the prevailing political currents and crosswinds, comprise the essence of most public policy debates. How closely the government comes to

Whatever the particular form of government, the public good is generally associated with the fullest possible attainment of security, prosperity, equality, liberty, and justice.
(A. Tannenbaum/Sygma)

reaching its desired destinations is the ultimate test of the leadership's performance. In other words, the closer a government comes to realizing the stated goals of political life, the higher the marks that can be awarded to that system, as well as to the leaders responsible for its design, its preservation, and its adaptation to constantly changing circumstances.

IDEOLOGIES AND THE PUBLIC INTEREST

When political leaders and citizens hold fixed ideas about how to serve the public good, those ideas are said to constitute an *ideology. Ideology,* as used here, refers to "any organized set of ideas about the good life and the institutional framework for their realization."[2] As Max Mark, the author of this definition, has pointed out, "Usage has increasingly become less strict so that any combination of socio-political values having a connecting rationale is referred to as ideology."[3] Under such a diluted definition, even the political and economic views of the National Association of Manufacturers or the AFL-CIO could be considered ideological, insofar as they grow out of a certain "combination of socio-political values having a connecting rationale." If such views are to be labeled "ideological," however, they must also be considered in an entirely different light from the all-embracing world views espoused by, for instance, neo-Nazis or Communists.

The classification of political viewpoints as ideologies is a semantic convenience that allows us to discuss *kinds* of political orientations and sets of political preferences without having to specify where an individual who embraces a particular kind of orientation or set of preferences stands on each and every issue. An American conservative, for example, will generally favor a strong national defense, limiting social welfare programs underwritten by the federal government, deregulation of business and industry, and similar programs. An American liberal, by contrast, will tend to favor public assistance programs, reductions in military spending, and governmental regulation in such areas as the food and drug industry, occupational safety and health, housing, transportation, and energy.

Although most people in the United States favor either the liberal or the conservative ideology, very few Americans are ideologues. To be an *ideologue,* one must adhere strictly to an ideology, or "party line"; in addition, ideologues hold their convictions with great intensity. Individuals who are inclined to think for themselves or who are politically apathetic (the great majority of Americans) obviously do not fit this description.

Ideologies may be categorized in a number of ways. Here we have grouped them under three headings: antigovernment ideologies, right-wing ideologies, and left-wing ideologies. The terms *left* and *right* have their origins in the European parliamentary practice of seating parties that favor social and political change to the left of the presiding officer and those opposing change (or favoring a return to a previous form of government) to the right. Of course, not every political viewpoint fits neatly into these categories. This is especially true of crackpot ideologies. For instance, the ideas and programs of onetime political activist Lyndon LaRouche defy political classification (including his often-stated belief that the key to understanding international relations is recognizing that there exists a giant conspiracy to sell and distribute drugs, headed by the queen of England).

Antigovernment Ideologies

People who oppose any form of government, no matter how limited, are called *anarchists.* The development of an anarchist ideology is often credited to the Russian revolutionary Mikhail Bakunin (1814–1876), who unabashedly proclaimed the "joy of destruction" and called for violent uprisings by society's beggars and criminals. *Anarchism* bears a close relationship to nihilism, which holds that the total destruction of all existing social and political institutions is a desirable end in itself. This extremely negative ideology has had little historical impact outside of prerevolutionary Russia (and possibly Spain), although some contemporary terrorist groups appear to embrace a kind of anarchistic or nihilistic world view.

Libertarians are somewhat less hostile to the idea of formal government, although they believe that government must be kept to a bare minimum. (For this reason, they are sometimes called minimalists.) Proponents of *libertarianism* emphasize the overriding importance of individual freedom. Libertarians generally oppose public policies that limit self-reliance and free choice—even those aimed at such seemingly unarguable goals as citizen safety or income security for the elderly. In their view, the invisible hand of the marketplace can regulate the interplay of social and economic forces better than the intrusive hand of the government, and the individual's right to privacy should encompass a very wide range of economic and moral choices. For example, libertarians defend the right of a citizen to print and distribute pornographic materials, no matter how obscene or repugnant those materials might be to the majority (including most libertarians). By the same token, they generally oppose the military draft, on the ground that joining the armed forces ought to be a matter of personal choice.

Right-Wing Ideologies

At the opposite end of the political spectrum from anarchism and libertarianism are ideologies that stress the paramount importance of a central authority and political order. It may seem strange, but just a century ago, monarchy was a prevalent form of government throughout the world. Whether they are called kings or emperors, czars or sultans, sheiks or shahs, monarchs have ruled in all ages and all places. Those who have held fast to the crown in the face of revolutionary challenges and popular demands for democratic reform are known as royalists or monarchists. And lest we dismiss *monarchism* too lightly, let us recall that Aristotle regarded monarchy—rule by a wise king—as the best form of government (although he recognized that wise kings, as opposed to tyrants, were very rare). It is also important to remember that several powerful countries are still ruled by monarchs—Jordan, Morocco, Saudi Arabia, and the oil-rich Persian Gulf states, to name a few.

Fascism   As the principal ideology of the extreme right, however, monarchism was superseded in the twentieth century by *fascism*.

Fascism exerted a powerful influence in Europe and South America from the 1920s to the 1940s. Most commonly studied, of course, are the principal Axis Powers (Germany, Italy, and Japan) in World War II. But there were other important instances of fascism as well—for example, in Spain, Hungary, and Argentina. Despite its elitist character, fascism enjoyed genuine mass appeal, in part due to its ultranationalistic coloration. In addition to this heavy stress on the concept of nation (and, in Hitler's case, race), fascism had varied ideological roots including romanticism, xenophobia, populism, and even, oddly enough, a hierarchical, nonegalitarian, and particularistic form of socialism. (Nazi Germany, an example of a right-wing ideology put into practice, was discussed in greater detail in Chapter 3.)

One of the distinguishing features of many extreme right-wing ideologies is a blatant appeal to popular prejudices and hatred.[4] Such an appeal often strikes a responsive chord when large numbers of people, who are part of the racial or ethnic majority, have either not shared fully in the benefits of their society or have recently seen an erosion in their socioeconomic position. People in this situation, especially if they lack formal education and political discernment, may well be predisposed to believe a demagogue's explanation for their plight. Generally, scapegoats are blamed—a racial, ethnic, or religious minority group; an opposing political party; a foreign country; and the like.

The present-day *American Nazi party* and the **Ku Klux Klan (KKK),** for example, hold fast to the doctrine of white supremacy, which supplies the premise for a whole range of extremist policies dealing with immigration (foreigners must be kept out), civil rights (blacks, Jews, and other minorities are genetically inferior and do not deserve the same constitutional protections as whites), and foreign policy (threats to white America, especially by "godless communism," must be met with irresistible force). Both groups are organized along paramilitary lines, and both advocate violence against their "enemies." Although the KKK's strength is estimated in the range of 8,000 to 10,000 members, its long history of bigotry and violence toward blacks (symbolized by the white sheets worn by its members and crosses set ablaze at rallies) makes it a group whose strength is carefully monitored both by the government and by concerned citizens.

The New Right   The new right is no longer new, and it is debatable whether it remains an identifiable political movement or ideology. Nonetheless, its effect on American politics has been noteworthy, and on that account alone it merits discussion.

The emergence of the new right can be traced to 1980. The election of a conservative Republican, Ronald Reagan, as president both coincided with and accelerated efforts to create a new right-wing political coalition in the United States. As it took shape, this coalition combined the modern political techniques of mass mailings, extensive political fund-raising, and the repeated use of the mass media (especially television) with a call for the restoration of traditional values, including an end to abortion, the reinstatement of prayer in the public schools, a campaign against pornography, the recognition of the family as the basis of American life, and a drive to oppose communism relentlessly on every front. This emerging conservative movement (alternately called the new right, the new religious right, or the new Christian right) soon became identified with fundamentalist Christianity, especially with the political preachings of television evangelist Jerry Falwell and his Moral Majority movement. Throughout the 1980s, political observers disagreed about the size of the new religious right's political following and the extent to which it functioned within the mainstream of American public life. Critics labeled the new right extremist and dangerous. Others suggested that although it was quite conservative, it was not the danger its detractors made it out to be.

A setback for the new right's political strength occurred when evangelical minister Pat Robertson failed to win the Republican party's nomination for the presidency in 1988. Robertson had gained national recognition as the host of a Christian television talk show, *The 700 Club.* He was the first (and possibly the last) candidate clearly identified with the new right, for as the 1990s progressed, it seemed increasingly apparent that the movement was becoming assimilated into the mainstream of the Republican party. Although many of its members became more open to compromise, a few hard-line conservatives have been unrelenting. For example, new-right columnist and television personality Patrick Buchanan challenged President Bush in the 1992 presidential campaign charging that the president had departed from true conservative principles. This attempt to revitalize right-wing politics failed to arouse the electorate. Thus the new right has retained its conservative credentials but seems to have lost its identity as a distinct branch of conservatism.

Left-Wing Ideologies

Left-wing ideologies posit a view of human beings living together cooperatively, freed from demeaning and invidious social distinctions. In the realm of economics, these ideologies are rooted in the principle of *collectivism,* which holds that the public good is best served by common (as opposed to individual) ownership and administration of the political community's means of production and distribution. Collectivism is thus fundamentally opposed to the theory of *capitalism,* which contends that individual ownership of the means of production, in the form of private wealth (capital), offers the most efficient and most equitable way of enriching the community as a whole. In modern times, the collectivist principle has been expressed most often in the form of *socialism,* which can be defined as "an ideology that rejects individualism, private ownership, and private profits in favor of a system based on economic collectivism, governmental, societal, or industrial-group ownership of the means of production and distribution of goods, and social responsibility."[5]

Socialism, as it is understood today, was formulated originally by the French revolutionary François Noël Babeuf (1760–1797), who proposed that economic equality and common ownership of land should be attained by force, if necessary. Babeuf's ideas were adapted and moderated by the so-called *utopian socialists,* including the Comte de Saint-Simon (1760–1825) and Charles Fourier (1772–1837), who envisioned an ideal (utopian) society based on collectivism, cooperation, and benevolence. Louis Blanc (1811–1882) advocated a considerably more down-to-earth approach to the implementation of socialist ideas, including the establishment of worker-controlled councils and workshops, and took an active role in worker uprisings in 1848. From these and other thinkers and revolutionaries of the late eighteenth and early nineteenth centuries have evolved the theories and methods espoused by most left-wing ideologies of the twentieth century, from revolutionary communism to democratic socialism.

Revolutionary Communism   The extreme left-wing ideology loosely described as *revolutionary communism* or revolutionary socialism evolved principally from the writings of Karl Marx (1818–1883) and his associate, Friedrich Engels (1820–1895). Marx broke with the utopian socialists by asserting that the collectivist ideal could be attained only by open class conflict and that the outcome of that conflict was preordained by scientific "laws" of history. This emphasis on the inevitability of and the necessity for revolution by the *proletariat* (working class) distinguishes Marxism, or communism, from other forms of socialism.

Marx (and Engels) opened the *Communist Manifesto* (1848) with the bold

New-right columnist and 1992 Republican presidential candidate Patrick Buchanan charged that incumbent George Bush had departed from true conservative principles. His attempt to revitalize right-wing politics ultimately failed to arouse the electorate. (AP/Wide World Photos)

assertion, "All history is the history of class struggle." This statement is based on two premises: that economic, or material, forces are behind all human activities and that in history, change and progress are produced by a constant clash of conflicting economic forces—or, to use the term borrowed from the German philosopher G. W. F. Hegel (1770–1831), by the dialectic process. All societies, Marx contended, evolve through the same historical stages, each of which represents a dominant economic pattern (the thesis) that contains the seeds of a new and conflicting pattern (the antithesis). Out of the inevitable clash between thesis and antithesis comes a synthesis, or new economic stage. What we now call the Industrial Revolution was, according to Marx, the capitalist stage of history, which succeeded the feudal stage when the **bourgeoisie** (urban artisans and merchants) wrested political and economic power from the feudal landlords. The laws of **dialectical materialism**, as Marx termed this view of history, made the rise of capitalism inevitable. Equally inevitable, according to those same laws, was conflict between capitalists and the proletariat, which would result in victory for the workers and the advent of a stable and classless society. (This Marxist utopia is discussed in Chapter 2.)

Marxist theory holds that the main feature of modern industrial capitalism is the streamlining of society into two antagonistic classes—the capitalists, who own the means of production, and the proletariat, who have no choice but to work long hours for subsistence wages. The difference between those wages and the value of the products created through the workers' labor is *surplus value* (excessive profits), which the capitalists pocket. In this way, capitalists systematically exploit the workers and unwittingly lay the groundwork for a proletarian revolution.

This revolution, according to Marx and his adherents, will come about in the following way. Under the so-called *law of capitalist accumulation*, capitalists must expand at the expense of their competitors or be driven from the marketplace. As the stronger capitalists expand, they eliminate the weaker ones and capture an ever-increasing share of the market. Eventually, the most successful competitors in this dog-eat-dog contest force all the others out, thus ushering in the era of monopoly capitalism, which immediately precedes the downfall of the whole capitalist system. Why should capitalism be overthrown at this stage, when it appears that the monopoly capitalists have taken the reins of power? Because at the same time that the rich have been getting richer, the poor have been getting poorer. As human labor is replaced by machine labor, in an effort to gain a competitive edge, unemployment grows, purchasing power dwindles, and domestic markets shrink. This built-in tendency toward business recession and depression in turn gives rise to still more unemployment, even lower wages, and so forth. Countless human beings become "surplus labor"—jobless, penniless, and hopeless. Thus the human tragedy of capitalism is inescapable, as dictated by what is known to Marxists as the *law of pauperization*. For orthodox Marxists, this "crisis of capitalism" and the resulting proletarian revolution are equally inevitable. Because capitalists will not relinquish their power, privilege, or property without a struggle, the overthrow of capitalism can occur only through violent revolution.

The belief that violent mass action is necessary to bring about radical change was central to the theories of Marx's follower V. I. Lenin, the founder of the Communist party of the Soviet Union and the foremost leader of the Russian Revolution of 1917. Marxist-Leninists, as they sometimes are called, argue that parliamentary democracy and "bourgeois legality" are mere superstructures designed to mask the underlying reality of capitalist exploitation. As a result, these revolutionary communists held no special brief for the kind of representative institutions prevalent in the United States and western Europe.

With the fall of communism in the Soviet Union and eastern Europe, Marxism has lost a great deal of its luster. Even so, this doctrine retains some appeal among the poor and downtrodden, primarily due to its crusading spirit and its promise of deliverance. In many ways, revolutionary Marxism resembles a militant fundamentalist religion, not unlike Islam in recent times and Christianity in the early Middle Ages. The British philosopher Bertrand Russell illustrated the parallels between Marxism and Christianity with a rather striking comparison.[6]

> To understand Marx psychologically, one should use the following dictionary:
>
> Yahweh (God) = Dialectical Materialism
> The Messiah = Marx
> The Elect = The Proletariat
> The Church = The Communist Party
> The Second Coming = The Revolution
> Hell = Punishment of the Capitalists
> The Millennium = The Communist Commonwealth

According to Russell, the terms on the left give the emotional content of those on the right, and this analogy helps to explain Marxism's great emotional appeal.

Communism and Democracy   There has never been a strong Communist party in the United States, and relatively few American citizens would ever had admitted to having any sympathy whatever with communism. Yet in many other parts of the world, Communist parties have, until recently, flourished. In the former Soviet Union, eastern Europe, China, North Korea, Vietnam, Cuba, and several other Third World countries, Communist parties have dominated under the banner of Marxism (in most cases, Marxism-Leninism).

Although communism has suffered a rapid worldwide collapse of influence, it is important to remember that for over forty years after the conclusion of World War II, Communists and Communist parties played important political roles in some countries where they are not in power. Especially in the Third World, Communists or Marxists spearheaded "national wars of liberation" aimed at the overthrow of existing governments. In many other countries, most notably in western Europe, nonruling Communist parties achieved democratic respectability. The Communist parties of France, Italy, and Spain, to cite but three examples, were legally recognized and popularly accepted participants in national elections and, occasionally, in coalition governments. For the most part, these parties played by the political rules and earned a considerable measure of public trust, although they have never come close to winning the majority vote needed to gain control of the national government. In the 1970s, Communist party leaders in Italy and Spain initiated a movement called *Eurocommunism*, which was subscribed to by several other western European Communist organizations. The Eurocommunists renounced a number of time-honored tenets of Marxism-Leninism, including advocacy of violent revolution, belief in the dictatorship of the proletariat, and dogmatic attachment to the principle of democratic centralism (which demands strict obedience to the party line and forbids dissent).

Democratic Socialism   In contrast to revolutionary communism, *democratic socialism*, the other main branch of socialist ideology, embraces collectivist ends (and hence rejects capitalism) but is committed to democratic means. Adherents of this evolutionary (as opposed to revolutionary) credo pursue a strategy of winning popular elections and bringing about social change through legislative action. Unlike orthodox Marxists, democratic socialists believe in *gradualism*—the concept that reform, not revolution, is the key to improving the human condition.

In general, democratic socialists favor a greatly expanded role for government and a highly constricted role for the marketplace. Most socialist parties advocate the nationalization of the "commanding heights" of the economy—transportation, communications, public utilities, banking and finance, insurance, and such basic industries as automobile manufacturing, iron and steel processing, mining, and energy. They also champion the modern-day *welfare state*, in which the government assumes broad responsibility for the health, education, and welfare of its citizens. The goal of the welfare state is to alleviate social insecurity and enhance economic equality through large-scale income redistribution. Sometimes described as a cradle-to-grave system, the welfare state usually features free university education, free (or heavily subsidized) medical care, generous public assistance (family allowances), pension plans, and a variety of other free or subsidized services. To finance these programs and services, socialists advocate heavy taxation, including steeply progressive income taxes and stiff inheritance taxes designed to close the gap between rich and poor. Such a policy is required by socialist ideology, which tends to equate social justice with economic equality.

Democratic socialism has had a major impact in western Europe and a number of Third World countries. Examples of the welfare state can be found in Scandinavia and in Great Britain (though to a lesser degree now than before the Thatcher era); beginning in the 1930s and 1940s, the Social Democratic party introduced the welfare state in Sweden, and the Labour party spearheaded the same effort in Great Britain. Germany's Social Democratic party has played a major role in shaping public policy in that country, in recent years primarily as the opposition to the center-right Christian Democrats. François Mitterrand, a Socialist, was elected president of France in 1981, and in national elections held shortly thereafter, his party won enough legislative seats to form the first left-wing government in the history of the Fifth Republic (which dates from 1958).

It is important to note that most European Socialists, Mitterrand included, have not dogmatically rejected private enterprise. They avoid blanket indictments of capitalism and display considerable tolerance for artisans, shopkeepers, farmers, and others engaged in classically middle-class occupations. To return to a distinction made earlier, democratic socialists may be guided by more or less fixed ideological precepts, but they are not necessarily ideologues.

In contrast to western Europe, democratic socialism as an organized political force has not had much impact on postwar U.S. politics. In the 1930s, Norman Thomas did manage to attract considerable support in his campaign for president on the Socialist party ticket; earlier, in 1912 and 1920, the Socialists had polled over 900,000 votes in national elections. These achievements, however, represented the high-water marks of organized socialism in the United States. Why has this been the case?

In the first place, Americans tend to be individualistic and distrustful of "big government." Then, too, especially after World War II, they have identified socialism with communism and rejected it out of hand on that basis. Nonetheless, many public programs that are now widely accepted and firmly entrenched closely resemble measures long advocated by democratic socialists the world over. Examples include social security, Medicare, family assistance, unemployment compensation, and federally subsidized housing. Welfare state measures, in other words, have fared much better in the United States than the socialist ideology that spawned them.

Radical Egalitarianism   This is not a straightforward ideology in the sense that it owes its existence to the writings of a single individual or consists of one or two overarching and clearly defined principles, nor is it universally recognized; nevertheless, radical egalitarianism does represent a clearly identifiable approach to the public good. Radical egalitarians champion a world of complete equality. They hold that most conventional, everyday distinctions accepted by society (who succeeds, what is read and studied, and so on) have resulted primarily from bias or ethnocentrism. Radical egalitarians feel strongly that racial minorities, women, homosexuals, handicapped individuals, and others outside the mainstream have suffered and continue to suffer from social discrimination, and now every effort must be made to ensure their advancement, success, and full equality. These groups have been neglected for too long (in favor of privileged white males); they must therefore be made both the object and the source of study, and works written about them and by them must be read as part of any college curriculum. Finally, the argument goes, these groups have not been examined adequately because of systemic discrimination and bias endemic in Western civilization; therefore, other societies and civilizations must be explored and perhaps emulated as alternatives.

The radical egalitarian analysis of American higher education, society, and civilization is, of course, highly controversial. Conservative critics have objected to the radical egalitarians' characterization of American society and Western civilization, bemoaned their lack of concern with excellence and achievement, and bristled when their critique was rejected as racist, sexist, homophobic, or otherwise biased. These critics have suggested that radical egalitarians have created an emotionally charged climate where only "politically correct" thought is accorded respect. By the early 1990s, the *political correctness controversy* was raging on American college campuses, often as a kind of semantic shorthand for debate on the desirability of a world view governed by radical egalitarian assumptions.

AMERICAN-STYLE LIBERALISM AND CONSERVATIVISM

American politics is essentially a tug-of-war between "liberals" and "conservatives." Because these terms often generate confusion, and because it is difficult to understand the central issues in American politics apart from the liberal/conservative distinction, we must analyze at length these two uniquely American approaches to the public good.

The Problem of Definition

Most of us have a general idea of what it means to be a liberal or a conservative, but the problem of definition becomes surprisingly difficult when we move from generalities to specifics. There are at least three reasons why it is hard to define precisely what *liberalism* and *conservatism* mean in the context of U.S. politics.

To begin with, the role of ideology is strictly limited in the United States by a political culture in which everyday politics involves a struggle among opposing interests rather than a conflict over irreconcilable ideas or principles. Usually, the public stands taken by elected officials are shaped to reflect local economic interests, to coincide with the shifting social or economic moods of the national electorate, or to confront a particularly pressing problem. Therefore, although American politics theoretically has its share of liberals and conservatives, in practice American politicians tend to be pragmatic rather than dogmatic. Even watered-down center-right and center-left ideologies can be too confining for the nonideological politicians who typically win election to public office in the United States.

In a related problem, though liberals or conservatives as a group may share many orientations and opinions, many individuals in both categories do not fit any one mold. For example, it is generally true that conservatives favor laws against pornography whereas liberals oppose such statutes. (Hence it is sometimes said, with tongue in cheek, that liberals buy the books that conservatives want to ban, whereas conservatives form censorship committees and read the books as a group.) Nonetheless, certain so-called minimalist conservatives, or libertarians, oppose all restrictions on the sale, display, distribution, or ownership of any kind of reading material. And certain liberal—even radical—advocates of women's rights would join conservatives in banning such books, arguing that pornography exploits and degrades all females for the gratification of a few perverted (or profiteering) males.

Finally, conservatism and liberalism are creatures of time and place. A half century ago, for example, liberals tended to be interventionists in foreign affairs, arguing in favor of active American leadership in the world; conservatives, for the most part, were isolationists. Today the reverse is more nearly the case. Sometimes, too, positions defended by liberals or conservatives simply become irrelevant. Conservatives once defended the power and privilege of aristocracy, but in the United States all formal titles of nobility were outlawed by the Constitution more than two centuries ago. In Europe, where hereditary titles were previously the key to wealth and power, they are now an anomalous throwback to the past, a quaint reminder of their former preeminence. Although conservatives, more than liberals, still tend to represent the interests of the rich, no serious political figure in this country would dare to suggest the resurrection of a formal aristocracy.

Table 14-1 presents the ratings that six senators received from various liberal and conservative interest groups before the 1988 election.

Common Themes

At one time, the terms *liberalism* and *conservatism* may have reflected coherent and clearly defined alternatives. In contemporary American political life, however, it would be a mistake to think of them as distinct and completely formed ideologies, like communism or fascism.

In the United States, both liberalism and conservatism have developed from, and represent variations on, a fundamental set of political principles.[7] This American creed owes much to the political writings of John Locke. As summed up in the Declaration of Independence, it holds that all human beings are created equal; that they are endowed with certain unalienable rights, including the rights of life, liberty, and the pursuit of happiness (Jefferson's expansion of Locke's

TABLE 14-1
Ratings of Six Senators before the 1988 Election

Senator	ADA	ACLU	COPE	CFA	LCV	ACU	NTLC	NSI	COC	CEI
D'Amato (R—New York)	15	28	46	50	40	80	40	100	64	31
Kassebaum (R—Kansas)	30	39	21	42	40	61	63	80	71	52
Kennedy (D—Massachusetts)	95	88	93	100	70	0	5	0	27	14
Mikulski (D—Maryland)	95	77	100	100	70	0	5	0	29	10
Nunn (D—Georgia)	40	44	41	83	20	42	22	100	50	29
Simpson (R—Wyoming)	15	40	7	58	20	92	80	100	86	55

ADA   Americans for Democratic Action (liberal)
ACLU   American Civil Liberties Union (pro–individual liberties)
COPE   Committee on Political Education of the AFL-CIO (liberal-labor)
CFA   Consumer Federation of America (proconsumer)
LCV   League of Conservator Voters (environmental)
ACU   American Conservative Union (conservative)
NTLC   National Tax-Limitation Committee (pro–tax limitation)
NSI   National Security Index of the American Security Council (pro–strong defense)
COC   Chamber of Commerce of the United States (probusiness)
CEI   Competitive Enterprise Institute (pro–free enterprise)

SOURCE: Adapted from Michael Barone and Grant Ujifusa, *The Almanac of American Politics 1990* (Washington, D.C.: National Journal, Inc., 1989), fig. 14-1. Copyright 1989 by National Journal, Inc. All rights reserved. Reprinted with permission.

"right to property"); and that government exists to protect those rights and acquires legitimacy by ruling according to the consent of the governed. The Declaration also states that when government becomes unmindful of the reasons for which it was created, the people have the right to alter or abolish it.

Note that the Declaration, in very general terms, specifies those ends of government to which we referred at the beginning of this chapter. *Liberty* is explicitly mentioned, as is the individual's right to life, or *security*. *Prosperity* is alluded to in the form of government's obligation to safeguard a person's right to pursue happiness (after all, how can the pursuit of happiness exclude the pursuit of wealth in a commercial society?). *Equality* is taken to be a fundamental human condition, and American citizens are guaranteed, among other things, equal liberty. Finally, it is assumed that a government that does not adequately protect or respect the individual's right to life, liberty, and the pursuit of happiness is not worthy of its good name; such a government, the Declaration implies, violates the principle of *justice* and can be altered or abolished. In the U.S. Constitution, whose avowed purpose was to "establish Justice, insure domestic Tranquility, provide for the common defence, promote the general Welfare and secure the Blessings of Liberty," these basic ends of government are spelled out even more clearly.

Conservatives and Economic Rights

Conservatives in the United States generally stress the primacy of economics and economic rights. In so doing, they echo and expand on arguments first propounded by certain seventeenth- and eighteenth-century political philosophers and economists. Although these now-famous thinkers did not necessarily regard themselves as conservatives, their concepts underlie much of contemporary conservative thought.

John Locke (1632–1704)   Although he is recognized primarily as a political philosopher, Locke also contributed greatly to the idea of the *commercial republic*, an economic concept that forms the core of modern conservatism. Locke declared clearly and emphatically that individuals have a *right* to property—especially property they acquire through their own exertions—and that one of the primary purposes of government should be the protection of private property. He thus provided the political rationale for property rights, legal liabilities, and contractual obligations—the foundations of the commercial state. In addition, he gave the acquisitive instinct a newfound respectability in intellectual discourse. Many earlier philosophers, from Aristotle to Thomas Aquinas (1224–1274), had cautioned *against* excessive concern for worldly possessions. Locke, in contrast, envisioned a society in which individuals would constantly endeavor to improve their lot, the spirit of enterprise and invention would flourish, and money would serve as the universal medium of exchange. Wealth could then be accumulated, reinvested, and expanded. Society would prosper—and a prosperous society, Locke reasoned, would be a happy one.

Baron de Montesquieu (1689–1755)   If Locke developed the general theory of the commercial republic, it was the French political philosopher Montesquieu, in his famous *Spirit of the Laws* (1748), who identified a number of specific advantages associated with business and commerce. In Montesquieu's view, nations that trade extensively with other nations would be predisposed toward peace because war disrupts international commerce. He also asserted that commerce would help to produce more just political orders by opening up new avenues for individual self-advancement; in other words, through hard work and perseverance, even those born into poverty could become wealthy. In addition, an emphasis on commerce would inoculate a society against religious fanaticism, as a preoccupation with creature comforts and "keeping up with the Joneses" would replace the fanatical zeal that leads to religious strife. A final advantage of a commercial order would be its positive effect on individual morality. A commercial democracy, Montesquieu believed, would foster certain modest bourgeois virtues, including "frugality, economy, moderation, labor, prudence, tranquility, order, and rule."[8]

Adam Smith (1723–1790)   After Locke had laid the political foundations for the commercial state and Montesquieu had pointed out the advantages of such a state, the Scottish economist Adam Smith explained its operating principles.

Smith was persuaded that both individual happiness and social harmony are closely tied to ways in which goods and services are produced. In his enormously influential *Inquiry into the Nature and Causes of the Wealth of Nations* (1776), he set out to delineate how a commercial society can function in an orderly and prosperous fashion without central government regulation or planning of economic affairs. More than any other work, this book provided the rationale for modern capitalism.

Like Locke before him, Smith was impressed with the central role of self-interest in human activity. In the economic marketplace, he argued, self-interest not only spurs individuals to work but also prompts them to select occupations that correspond to specific social needs:

> It is not from the benevolence of the butcher, the brewer, or the baker, that we expect our dinner, but from their regard to their own self-interest. We address ourselves, not to their humanity but to their self-love, and never talk to them of our own necessities but of their advantages.[9]

Interacting with individual self-interest in the commercial state, according to Smith, is the "invisible hand" of the marketplace, as expressed in the *law of supply and demand*. This law, he argued, determines market value. Where supply is large and demand is small, the market value (or price) of the item in question will be driven down until only the most efficient producers remain. Conversely, where demand is great and supply is low, the market value of a given item will be driven up. Eventually, prices will decline as competition intensifies, again leaving only the most efficient producers in a position to retain or expand their share of the market. In this way, the market automatically seeks supply-and-demand equilibrium.

Smith believed that self-interest and market forces would combine to sustain economic competition, which would in turn keep prices from ranging very far from the actual cost of production (if they did, producers would be undercut by eager competitors). In this view, self-interest and market conditions make prices self-adjusting—high prices provide an incentive for increased competition and low prices lead to increased demand and hence increased production. Finally, Smith's *free-enterprise theory* holds that individuals voluntarily enter precisely those professions and occupations that society considers most valuable because the monetary rewards often are irresistible even if the work itself is not particularly glamorous.[10] Taken as a whole, these concepts define what has come to be known as *laissez-faire* ("let the people do as they wish") *capitalism*—the idea that the marketplace, unfettered by central state planning, is the best regulator of the economic life of a society.

Modern Conservatism   Building on the writings of Locke, Montesquieu, and Smith, contemporary conservatives usually stress the right of people to pursue happiness in their own individual ways, emphasizing particularly the Lockean right to hold, accumulate, and dispose of property without governmental interference. They also tend to defend the interests of business and corporate industry, arguing along the lines of Adam Smith that the private pursuit of wealth will ultimately lead to public prosperity. Finally, conservatives generally decry state intervention in the marketplace (such as social welfare programs that redistribute wealth) and bureaucratic "meddling" in business affairs (for example, federal regulations mandating minimum environmental standards).

At the heart of the conservative public philosophy is a commonsense assumption concerning the source of human happiness: Conservatives define the good as that which produces pleasure or reduces pain and further stress that the private pursuit of wealth is, by logical extension, good because it fulfills the individual's desire for physical gratification. In addition, the quest for individual affluence brings with it certain collective benefits, including a shared belief in the work ethic, a love of order and stability, and an enforced attitude of self-restraint on the part of government. These collective "goods" are most likely to result from a political system that assures the best possible conditions for the pursuit of personal gain. It may be that Montesquieu's "frugality, economy, moderation, labor, prudence, tranquility, order, and rule" do not comprise the highest of all possible virtues, but to the conservative mind, they provide the best available insurance for a decent and stable political order.

Liberals and Civil Rights

Like conservatives, liberals stress that individuals are endowed with certain rights. But the rights most dear to liberals are *civil rights*. Thus they tend to be vigorous defenders of individuals or groups who have allegedly been denied their civil rights or discriminated against, such as racial minorities, the poor, and other disadvantaged people. Liberals generally espouse vigorous governmental action to promote equal liberty. When it comes to the individual's substantive rights and liberties, however, they argue that government must take a hands-off position. They tend to oppose, for example, most governmental restrictions on freedom of expression as well as other governmental efforts to "legislate morality" for the purpose of upholding community standards and traditions.

Behind this emphasis on personal liberties lies a fundamental belief in the virtue of individuality. Protection of and respect for the uniqueness and dignity of each person in the society should be the overriding goal of government, in this view. The case for *individualism* was eloquently stated in John Stuart Mill's *On Liberty* (1859):

He who lets the world, or his own portion of it, choose his plan of life for him, has no need of any other faculty than the ape-like one of imitation. He who chooses his plan for himself, employs all his faculties. He must use observation to see, reasoning and judgement to foresee, activity to gather materials for decision, discrimination to decide, and when he has decided, firmness and self-control to hold to his deliberate decisions. And these qualities he requires and exercises exactly in proportion as the part of his conduct which he determines according to his own judgement and feelings is a large one. It is possible that he might be guided in some good path, and kept out of harm's way, without any of these things. But what will be his comparative worth as a human being? It really is of importance, not only what men do, but also what manner of men they are that do it. Among the works of man, which human life is rightly employed in perfecting and beautifying, the first in importance surely is man himself. . . . Human nature is not a machine to be built after a model, and set to do exactly the work prescribed for it, but a tree, which requires to grow and develop on all sides, according to the tendency of the inward forces which make it a living thing.[11]

Mill goes on to make the point that individuality is constantly threatened by the stifling conformity of mass opinion. Precisely for this reason, liberals argue, individuality requires protection against governments founded on majority rule. A democratic society, they point out, tends to confuse quantity and quality of opinion, to equate numerical superiority with political truth; and in the process, dissenters are often frowned on or even persecuted.

In the eyes of Mill and his intellectual heirs, individualism is good for society, as well as for individuals; for it is from the creativity, dynamism, and inventiveness of individuals that social progress springs. Following this line of logic, liberals often argue that by granting citizens the full range of freedom to develop their talents and disseminate their ideas, government can set up a symbiotic relationship in which both the individual and society will prosper and grow.

Essential Differences

At the root of the differences between liberals and conservatives lie contrasting opinions about human nature. Liberals believe in the essential goodness of human beings. Even though they would not deny that some individuals act in an antisocial manner, they tend to view such miscreants as victims of their environment. Most present-day American liberals would say, for instance, that to reduce crime, society must alleviate the conditions of poverty, racism, and despair that breed antisocial behavior. In other words, human beings are equal in dignity and deserve to be treated as such both by their government and by their fellow citizens.

Conservatives hold a somewhat harsher view of human nature. They consider human beings to be inherently selfish and often unruly. Individuals seek to advance themselves ahead of others, but they differ in motivation, ability, moral character, and luck. Such differences, conservatives argue, are beyond the ability of any government to minimize. Consequently, they have fewer qualms than their liberal compatriots about disparities in wealth or privilege within society. In addition, they are generally less inclined to attribute antisocial behavior to environmental factors, contending instead that there will always be some "bad apples" in society.

An additional difference between the two political types is that liberals, unlike conservatives, view themselves as part of an evolving historical process through which the human condition has improved and will continue to do so. In other words, they take a progressive view of history, believing that the average human being is better off now than a generation ago or a century or two ago. This belief leads to the conviction that future social arrangements, both at home and abroad, can be constructed to bring out the best in all human beings. Hence liberals tend to be forward-looking and optimistic about the long-term possibilities for making society and the world a better place.

Conservatives, by contrast, look to the past for guidance in meeting the challenges of the present and dispute the notion that change can be equated with progress. To them, a political community is a fragile organism held together by shared beliefs and common values. Custom and convention, established institutions (such as the family, church, and government), and deeply ingrained social reflexes provide the only sound basis for a stable social order. Like society itself, traditions should never be changed (or exchanged) too rapidly. Most conservatives, in sum, would subscribe wholeheartedly to Edmund Burke's admonition that when change is not needed, there is no need to change.

Conservatives, Liberals, and Public Policy

From these differing views of human rights, human nature, and human history stem the differing public policy orientations of liberals and conservatives. A devotion to property rights, along with a belief that prosperity is the essence of human happiness, generally leads conservatives to favor unregulated commerce and industry and to oppose governmental interference in the marketplace. For the same reasons, they tend to oppose social programs that involve large-scale redistribution of wealth, heavy or progressive taxation, governmentally funded health insurance programs, and the like. On another level, a somewhat harsh view of human nature predisposes conservatives to be tougher than liberals in dealing with perceived threats to personal safety, public order, and national security. They do not share the liberal concern with protecting provocative speech—especially where those involved are perceived as "radicals"—and they typically favor stiffer sentences for criminals and firmer, more wary foreign policy. Finally, in the realm of equality, conservatives generally believe that an excessive concern with economic equality will undermine the incentive system that, in their view, has made the United States such a prosperous society. (For example, governmental attempts to secure economic equality through such devices as job quotas are thought to stifle individual initiative and sever the link between personal achievement and pecuniary reward.)

Because liberals tend to picture the world as a more benign place and because they see more inherent good in human beings, they are also apt to see opportunities for cooperation, accommodation, and remedial action where conservatives see challenges, threats, and dangers that must be met with firmness and (when necessary) force. Thus in foreign affairs, liberals tend to favor reduced defense spending (whereas conservatives tend to follow the old adage, "Fear God and keep your powder dry"). And in domestic affairs, they generally believe that society as a whole will benefit from wholesale governmental intervention to provide disadvantaged or unfortunate persons with better housing, jobs, health insurance, and so on. No matter what the level of prosperity in the society at large, they argue, gross inequalities in the distribution of wealth must be readjusted by public policy, for if all humans are truly created equal, then no one should have to suffer the indignities of grinding poverty in a society in which others live in the lap of luxury. Moreover, believing that the perpetrators of crime are also victims (of economic and social injustice) and recognizing that the poor have the most difficult encounters with the criminal justice system, they demand maximum legal protection for the rights of the accused. Finally, for the contemporary American liberal, individuality can best be protected by prohibiting government from interfering with any exercise of the constitutional rights of free speech, press, religion, assembly, association, and privacy.

Summary

All governments seek to attain certain social and economic goals in accordance with their view of the public good. How they implement these goals depends on the ideologies, or organized sets of beliefs about the public good, they embrace.

Ideologies can be classified as antigovernment (anarchism, libertarianism), right-wing (monarchism, fascism), or left-wing (revolutionary communism, democratic socialism, radical egalitarianism) in orientation. United States politics is dominated by two other quasi-ideologies: liberalism and conservatism. It is surprisingly difficult to differentiate clearly between these two viewpoints, principally because liberalism and conservatism in the United States share many fundamental values and assumptions. Conservatives stress economic rights; liberals tend to be more concerned about civil rights. Liberals believe in the basic goodness of human beings; conservatives take a less charitable view of human nature. Liberals look to the future, believing that progress will ensure a better life for all; conservatives look to the past for guidance in dealing with the problems of the present. These differences are reflected in the divergent public policy aims espoused by the two camps.

Key Terms

public good
ideology
anarchism
libertarianism
monarchism
fascism
Ku Klux Klan (KKK)
collectivism
capitalism
socialism
utopian socialists
revolutionary communism
proletariat

bourgeoisie
dialectical materialism
law of capitalist accumulation
law of pauperization
Eurocommunism
democratic socialism
gradualism
welfare state
political correctness controversy
liberalism
conservatism
laissez-faire capitalism

Review Questions

1. Constitutional governments might define the public good in terms of attaining what goals?

2. Why might it be said that the performance of a government depends essentially on its ability to help to realize the public good?

3. Explain *ideology*. Is this a scientific term that would be easy to apply in a political analysis? Why or why not?

4. Contrast revolutionary communism with democratic socialism. On which political questions do the two movements agree? On which do they disagree?

5. How can one distinguish a liberal from a conservative in the United States? Are there any fundamental assumptions that separate these two schools of thought?

Recommended Reading

BERNSTEIN, EDWARD. *Evolutionary Socialism: A Criticism and Affirmation*. Translated by E. C. Harvey. New York: Schocken Books, 1961. A classic work espousing the cause of evolutionary socialism.

D'SOUZA, DINESH. *Illiberal Education: The Politics of Race and Sex on Campus*. New York: Free Press, 1991. A controversial and influential attack on political correctness as practiced on American campuses.

FALWELL, JERRY. *Listen America!* Garden City, N.Y.: Doubleday, 1980. States clearly the basic program and rationale of the new religious right as advocated by one of its chief proponents.

FRIEDMAN, MILTON. *Capitalism and Freedom*. Chicago: University of Chicago Press, 1981. A vigorous argument for minimal governmental participation in the private sector.

GALBRAITH, JOHN KENNETH. *The New Industrial State* (4th ed.). Boston: Houghton Mifflin, 1985. An argument that concentrated economic power requires a powerful, active government.

HAYEK, FRIEDRICH. *The Road to Serfdom*. Chicago: University of Chicago Press, 1956. A classic attack on the welfare state.

MACRIDIS, ROY. *Contemporary Political Ideologies, Movements and Regimes* (4th ed.). Glenview, Ill.: Scott, Foresman, 1989. A summary of the characteristics and relative importance of the ideologies that have shaped our world.

MARK, MAX. *Modern Ideologies*. New York: St. Martin's Press, 1973. A careful and comprehensive survey of contemporary ideology.

MILL, JOHN STUART. *On Liberty*. Lake Bluff, Ill.: Regnery/Gateway, 1955. A profoundly important work whose discussion of individualism is vital to an understanding of the root assumptions of liberalism.

Tucker, Robert (ed.). *The Marx-Engels Reader* (2nd ed.). New York: Norton, 1978. Marx's writings, including the *Manifesto,* must be read if one is to understand modern revolutionary communism; this book contains a good selection of those writings.

Notes

1. Aristotle, *The Politics,* ed. and trans. Ernest Barker (New York: Oxford University Press, 1962), p. 5.

2. Max Mark, *Modern Ideologies* (New York: St. Martin's Press, 1973), p. 247.

3. Ibid.

4. The Anti-Defamation League of B'nai B'rith, *Hate Groups in America: A Record of Bigotry and Violence* (New York, n.d.), p. 11.

5. Jack C. Plano and Roy Olton, *The International Relations Dictionary* (Santa Barbara, Calif.: ABC, 1982), p. 81.

6. Bertrand Russell, *A History of Western Philosophy* (New York: Simon & Schuster, 1965), p. 364.

7. Martin Diamond, Winston Fisk, and Herbert Garfinkel, *The Democratic Republic: An Introduction to American Government* (Skokie, Ill.: Rand McNally, 1971), pp. 4–5.

8. Baron de Montesquieu, *The Spirit of the Laws,* trans. Thomas Nugent (New York: Hafner Press, 1949), bk. 5, chap. 6, p. 46.

9. Adam Smith, *An Inquiry into the Nature and Causes of the Wealth of Nations* (New York: Modern Library, 1965), p. 14.

10. As is pointed out by Robert Heilbroner in *The Worldly Philosophers: The Lives, Times and Ideas of the Great Economic Thinkers* (New York: Modern Library, 1965), p. 14.

11. John Stuart Mill, *On Liberty* (Lake Bluff, Ill.: Regnery/Gateway, 1955), p. 85.

CHAPTER 15

ISSUES IN PUBLIC POLICY

PRINCIPLES INTO PRACTICE

(Martine Franck/Magnum)

In Chapter 14, we noted that the public good in democratic countries typically encompasses the goals of security, prosperity, equality, liberty, and justice. But precisely how should these goals be realized? In democracies, the search for answers to this question is expressed in ongoing debates over the changing issues of public policy.

Because a comprehensive, comparative study of public policy issues is beyond the scope of this text, our discussion of these issues will focus exclusively on the United States. It should be recognized, however, that many of the policy problems addressed in this chapter arise in somewhat different forms in all democracies.

THE PURSUIT OF SECURITY

The first goal of almost every political society is to provide a reasonable amount of security for its citizens. With some notable exceptions, such as tyrannies that deliberately implant suspicion and fear among their citizens, governments tend to view individual and group security as important in its own right and as a prerequisite for the achievement of all other worthwhile ends. Among influential political philosophers, Thomas Hobbes argued most strenuously that safety from harm constituted the chief justification for a government's existence. Hobbes was not alone in this contention, however: The venerable Aristotle may have stressed other, higher aims of politics, but he also understood clearly that the first goal of political life was the protection of life itself.[1]

Security from Foreign Enemies

National security became a commonplace expression in the post–World War II vocabulary of American politics. Protecting the United States from foreign (and domestic) enemies has been the highest national priority, a fact that was reflected in soaring defense spending and, in the 1980s, gaping budget deficits. But with the fading of the Cold War, the question arises: Has the world changed so fundamentally now so as to drastically alter America's priority and greatly diminish the importance of military preparedness?

From 1945 until the late 1980s, the most important national security dispute within the United States focused on the Soviet threat. Those who saw the Soviet Union as powerful but nonthreatening questioned high levels of arms expenditures and favored collaborative efforts (above all, strategic arms reductions) between the two superpowers. Other observers who believed the Soviet Union to be a dangerous expansionist power bent on world domination championed high defense budgets and favored concerted efforts to develop new high-tech weapons systems. This continuing American national security debate was basically a disagreement about the motives of the Soviet leaders and the character of the Soviet system.

With the collapse of the Soviet Union at the beginning of the 1990s, high levels of American defense spending (as high as $291 billion a year) became increasingly difficult to justify to American taxpayers. But skeptics point out that the world had not suddenly become a completely safe place even if many Americans *felt* safer. Economic and strategic threats to American interests were always possible (witness Iraq's invasion of Kuwait in 1990), and the persistence of regional or local conflicts, coupled with the proliferation of mass-destruction weapons (ballistic missiles, as well as nuclear, chemical, and biological weapons), meant that new dangers were appearing on the horizon.

Yet as the decade of the nineties began, it did appear that the danger of a major war on the scale of World War II had receded. Little wonder, then, that politicians in both major American political parties advocated sizable force reductions and cuts in weapons development and acquisition programs. Liberals and conservatives alike, citing budgetary constraints and pressing domestic needs, welcomed this prospect. Not only Congress but even a normally cautious President Bush jumped on the bandwagon in hopes of realizing a so-called peace dividend. In his 1992 State of the Union message, the president called for a 30 percent overall cut in defense spending "and no more." The caveat was directed at critics in Congress, the media, and society at large who were demanding much deeper cuts. (The Bush administration had earlier ordered the elimination of all ground-launched tactical nuclear weapons in Europe and the removal of all such weapons from American submarines and surface ships as well.) Even President Bush's announced plans to halt production of the MX and Midgetman ballistic missile systems, sharply curtail the B-2 (Stealth) bomber and Seawolf submarine acquisitions, and continue to draw down American troop levels stationed abroad did not placate Democrats and others who wanted nothing short of a radical re-allocation of federal budgetary resources.

Security from Fellow Citizens

Another important security-related goal of government is protection of the life and property of individual citizens against the depredations of their fellow citizens. Today, this second security goal provokes even more controversy than national security issues. Disagreements occur over what causes crime, what American society ought to do about crime, and whether acts currently classified as crimes should continue to be punished.

Although most people would agree that the U.S. crime rate is too high, they disagree susbstantially on the reasons why. According to some experts, crime is essentially a social phenomenon—a reflection of personal frustration or alienation caused by poverty and neglect, racial discrimination, and unequal economic opportunity. Why else, they ask, would the crime rate be highest in urban slums, where median incomes and living standards are the lowest? In their opinion, crime is a product of governmental neglect and social indifference.

Critics of this theory do not even concede that there is a direct correlation between crime and economic deprivation. They point out that in the United States during the 1960s, both prosperity and the crime rate increased. Clearly, factors other than economics have a bearing on the crime rate. Of course, to a person born into poverty and facing a bleak economic future, the benefits of crime may seem more attractive (and the costs of being caught less unattractive).

But with increasing prosperity, the opportunities for crime also increase, suggesting at least one reason why the crime rate might rise during peak economic times. Finally, even if poverty does relate to crime, the precise nature of this relationship is far from clear: Sometimes poverty leads to crime; sometimes crime (some forms of which can pay poorly) results in poverty, according to this school of thought. So what does this all mean? These critics contend that individuals, not social conditions, cause crimes; that individuals must be held accountable for their actions; and that crime is a continuous problem whose harmful effects cannot be eradicated but can perhaps be contained.

Such sharply conflicting views reflect the difficulty of determining the causes of crime. Not surprisingly, the supporters of these two schools of thought differ radically in their approaches to reducing the crime rate. Those who see antisocial behavior primarily as a function of social environment believe that crime could be significantly reduced by adopting more generous or better-designed public assistance programs. By contrast, those who favor a "get tough" approach tend to believe that swift and certain punishment (through limitations on the discretion of judges, prosecuting attorneys, and parole boards) would both deter would-be criminals and keep hard-core felons in prison (and thus off the streets) longer.

One problem with the tough law-and-order approach is that many state and federal prisons are already overcrowded. Reducing sentences (or actual time served), reserving prison space only for the most serious offenders, and building more prisons are viable policy alternatives, although each has its costs. One approach toward reducing pressures on prisons (and on the whole criminal justice system) involves decriminalization of certain illegal acts. Thus some people argue strenuously for decriminalization of so-called victimless crimes. The justification for such a position is not simply practical—that it would reduce police, prosecutorial, and prison time and costs—but philosophical as well. Acts as different as prostitution and vagrancy share a common focus: Each is undertaken freely by an individual or among individuals, and no specific member of society is harmed.

In recent years, the decriminalization debate has focused on drug legalization. Originally advocated on behalf of marijuana, the argument has been extended lately to include cocaine as well. Advocates of decriminalization argue that the undesirable social aspects of drug addiction occur primarily because many addicts rob and steal to support a habit made expensive by the government's declaring it to be illegal. Legalize drugs, and the price will drop significantly and the associated crime rate decrease (as will the profits made by organized crime). Opponents of legalization dispute this claim. Although they agree that legalization may truly lessen the cost to society imposed by presently addicted individuals, legalization would also inevitably increase the number of addicts, thus harming society by creating an unproductive, self-destructive, and growing number of drug-addicted citizens. In the end, the main argument against legalized drug addiction proves to be the same as that made against legalizing victimless crimes—that society ultimately bears the final cost, whether it be in a drug-addicted citizenry or in neighborhoods frequented by prostitutes and vagrants, whose very presence often threatens the security and stability of these neighborhoods.

Security from Natural and Environmental Enemies

Another aspect of personal security has to do with humanity's natural enemies, such as hunger, illness, and infant mortality, as well as floods, hurricanes, fires, and other acts of God. What is government's proper role in helping individuals combat these perennial threats to life and health? Food stamps, farm subsidies, social security, Medicare and Medicaid, and other social welfare programs are widely accepted governmental attempts to ensure a decent standard of living for all. Governments also assume responsibility for flood prevention, fire protection, disaster relief, and low-cost loan programs for reconstruction. The public policy questions these programs raise usually center on what level of support the government should provide. For instance, as the AIDS epidemic continues into its second decade, some question whether the government has undertaken enough research into its causes and done enough to help combat its lethal effects. Is this, and are other government-sponsored social welfare programs, underfunded? If so, how should additional monies be raised? Or is there widespread abuse of government and social welfare programs that could and should be eliminated by cracking down on waste, fraud, and mismanagement?

An issue that is certain to animate American politics for years to come involves the spiraling cost of health care in the United States. The facts here are obvious and relatively undisputed. The American population is aging and requires ever-increasing levels of medical care; the cost of that care is increasing at unparalleled rates far exceeding inflation (15 percent a year, according to some estimates); and both private and public employers, who have footed most of the health care bills, are finding it increasingly difficult to do so. Furthermore, many Americans are not covered by health plans and cannot afford to pay directly for health insurance (and, in some cases, because of congenital health problems, may not even be eligible to purchase such insurance). Thus illness (and to some extent, infirmities associated with old-age care) threatens to bankrupt even middle-class Americans who, in increasing numbers, cannot afford to pay the sharply increasing costs associated with health insurance and health care. Although the governmental cost will be significant, it is probable that the federal government, on its own or working cooperatively with private insurance companies, will soon act. The main question once again will be the level of governmental involvement. For instance, will the federal government use its power to try to limit price increases while helping to fund the cost of catastrophic illnesses, or will it undertake a wholesale reform of the health industry, perhaps bringing much of it directly under the control of the federal government?

No doubt, the costs of treating illness in a modern industrial society are considerable. Yet human-caused hazards can also endanger the health and safety of the public. Thus the government tests new medicines before they are placed on the market and sets minimum safety standards for public transportation. Particularly noteworthy are governmental efforts to protect the environment from human destructiveness. Mandatory clean air standards, required environmental impact statements imposed before funding new public projects, increasingly stringent waste disposal requirements, and vigorous recycling efforts all aim at preserving the environment from damage caused by human neglect or indifference. Government conservation efforts also aim at protecting endangered species of wildlife. In recent years, there has been increasing public support for many of these environmental programs. Critics sometimes complain, however, that the government's efforts hamper industrial development and economic growth and that the cost in terms of needless delays and red tape is too high.

Security from One's Own Actions

Occasionally, the government acts to protect individuals from doing themselves physical harm. For example, some states have adopted laws requiring motorcyclists to wear safety helmets or banning the sale of harmful drugs. Governmental intervention in personal affairs may also extend to questions of morality. The Eighteenth Amendment, which established Prohibition, was the most conspicuous example of national legislation aimed at preventing citizens from harming themselves morally as well as physically. Other examples include the various local, state, and federal laws banning the sale or distribution of pornography and those outlawing prostitution.

Defenders of moralistic legislation assert that no community can ignore the moral character of its citizens, especially when violating certain norms of behavior has adverse social consequences. Opponents of such statutes reply that governmental action of this type unduly restricts personal liberty. They also point out that people voluntarily participate in the prohibited actions and that each person ought to be able to determine his or her best interest.

THE PURSUIT OF PROSPERITY

Observers frequently characterize the United States as a commercial nation in which citizens are forever in search of financial security and the consumer is king. A century and a half ago, Alexis de Tocqueville noted that Americans were prey to constant agitation caused by their relentless pursuit of individual affluence. The condition has always been a salient characteristic of American society. In fact, the Founders envisaged a society of hardworking citizens dedicated to the entrepreneurial principles of self-reliance, upward mobility, and the profit motive. In the words of one scholar, James Madison's Constitution was intended to lead to Madison Avenue.[2]

In establishing a commercial republic, the Founders consciously launched a political experiment that had been championed by philosophers and economists (including Locke and Montesquieu) for over 100 years. In their view, a political order that encouraged the growth of commerce and trade would provide the best means of ensuring a robust national economy. Such a society, where success was based on hard work and natural ability rather than accidents of birth, would enable citizens to achieve and acquire as much wealth as they desired or needed.

During the nineteenth century, the increasing influence of Adam Smith's free-market rationale, the rise of the business corporation, and the increasing influence of technology transformed the commercial state into the capitalist state. By definition, *capitalism* means the private (and usually unregulated) ownership, manufacture, and distribution of goods and services. By the beginning of the twentieth century, however, the federal government had begun to enforce regulations designed to protect citizens from monopolies, abusive business practices, and other perceived economic injustices. This trend in public policy was strengthened enormously during the Great Depression of the 1930s, when, under the initiative of President Franklin Roosevelt, the government instituted a number of programs designed to ensure the economic well-being of ordinary citizens. These early programs, such as unemployment compensation and social security, were supplemented by other, more wide-ranging programs of the 1960s and 1970s, including Medicare, special training and jobs programs, and expanded welfare and food stamp benefits.

By the 1980s, federal intervention in the economy had become so pronounced that many economists referred to a **mixed economy**, containing elements of both private enterprise and welfare socialism. Former president Ronald Reagan and others of like mind suggested that government had gone too far in its efforts to ensure individual economic prosperity and security. Were these critics correct in charging that the United States could no longer afford increasing levels of expenditures for such programs? Or were the perceived shortcomings of social welfare programs a sign that wealth must be redistributed even more radically, through special programs, progressive taxation, and government grants?

The National Debt

The federal government expends the astounding total of $1.5 trillion a year. Conservatively speaking (accounting makes all the difference here), it spends approximately $400 billion more than it takes in. The difference is known as the *budget deficit*. Aggregated over time, these deficits become the *national debt*. According to some economists, the trend line and magnitude of the national debt has important long-term implications for the economic health and well-being of the United States.

Less than 25 years ago, many conservative Republicans advocated a balanced federal budget while liberal Democrats countered that occasional budget deficits made little difference. Perhaps no policy debate in the United States has changed more radically in recent years than this one. In 1981, when President Reagan assumed office, the national debt totaled less than $1 trillion. In 1988, at the end of President Reagan's term in office, it had surpassed $2.5 trillion (and by 1992 approached $4 trillion). The Reagan budgets (approved by a Democratic Congress) established important budgetary givens that dominate current American politics. First, continuing budget deficits are a given. Any discussion of a balanced federal budget by a major political figure today would be regarded as irresponsible, if not absurdly unrealistic. Second, the size of the national debt is increasing at an alarming rate: A national debt that had taken almost 200 years to accumulate, in the decade of the 1980s increased more than 150 percent (in current dollars). Nor is there any relief in sight, as budget deficits of over $300 billion became common during the early 1990s.

Why does this matter? When government spends more than it receives, it has to borrow the difference. According to Figure 15-1, the federal government in fiscal 1992 borrowed some 19 percent of its budget (up from 11 percent five years earlier). Economic slowdowns have only increased the deficit by decreasing collected revenues (taxes). Furthermore, during nonrecessionary, normal economic times, when there exists a demand for funds throughout the economy, such a dramatic increase in borrowing has the effect of increasing real interest rates (how much the interest rate exceeds the rate of inflation) because the government's great financial need requires it to pay attractive interest to entice investors. At the same time, private corporations, whose investments are not as safe as government debt, find themselves competing with the government in the debt market, and it becomes more expensive (and sometimes impossible) to obtain funds. Since this is precisely the money businesses need to start up, modernize, grow, and expand—and in each instance to hire or retain employees—the effects of unnecessarily high interest rates are detrimental to economic growth.

Furthermore, artificially high real interest rates mean that the government must pay out more to bondholders to whom they owe debt. As Figure 15-1 indicates, some 14 percent of the budget goes to pay interest on the national debt. If this figure continues to grow faster than the economy, it compounds, causing the taxes citizens pay to government to be increasingly used, not to fund necessary public services or to pay for important national priorities, but merely to service past debt. No wonder the economic and political consequences of the United States' debt-related problem were being hotly debated in the early 1990s.

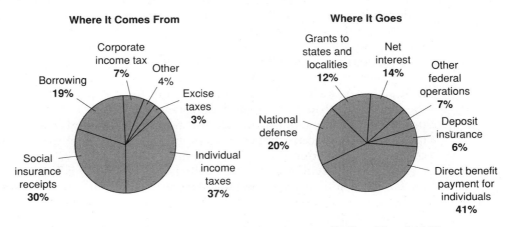

FIGURE 15-1   The Federal Government Dollar, Fiscal 1992
SOURCE: Congressional Quarterly Weekly Report, February 9, 1991, p. 333.

But if the rapidly spiraling national debt poses such a problem for the economic and political well-being of the United States, why don't the nation's elected representatives do something about it? The answer is obvious but nonetheless painful: The two most likely solutions, reducing governmental programs or raising taxes, are disliked by voters (who, it is sometimes said cynically, want both more public services and lower taxes). Therefore, representatives who wish to be reelected usually find supporting deficit budgets preferable to curtailing expenditures or raising taxes. Elected officials realize that (short of a crisis atmosphere) budget cuts are easier to make in the abstract than in concrete categories. Interest payments cannot be adjusted; defense cuts often create a local backlash when large defense contractors or military bases are threatened; some programs, like social security transfer payments (some 20 percent of the government's expenditures), are politically untouchable. Thus even modest proposals to adjust the social security cost-of-living formula have met with resounding opposition. Other programs—for instance, veterans' benefits and federal employees' salary levels—are also supported by very strong constituencies.

In recent years, the budget deficit crisis has led to political gridlock as elected officials have uniformly declared the need to solve this problem while vehemently disagreeing about how it should be solved. In the meantime, heavy state government indebtedness or budget crisis (engulfing well over half the states in the Union), increased corporate and private debt (which made the financing of public debt more precarious), a savings and loan crisis (most of the cost of which did not turn up on the formal federal budget and was estimated at $200 billion—or $1.4 trillion if financed over a 40-year period),[3] and increasingly precarious banking and insurance industries all imperceptibly yet fundamentally threatened the future prosperity of the United States.

Educational Malaise

It may seem peculiar to discuss American education as a facet of the quest for national prosperity, but this approach is peculiarly American. Americans tend to measure the value of education primarily in terms of its practical benefits.[4] Frequently, students are urged to remain in high school and attend college because this schooling will presumably aid them in obtaining better jobs, careers, and higher status. Furthermore, national as well as personal economic well-being is at stake: A literate, skilled, and able work force is particularly important if the United States is to compete with foreign nations in the realms of product production and innovation. In fact, it is frequently asserted that the best single measure of American competitiveness in the international marketplace is the competence and education of its work force.

Thus when evidence of a national crisis in education is highlighted by the media, it is commonly assumed that American economic competitiveness (especially vis-à-vis Japan) is threatened. The signs of such a crisis have been reported for years. Declining college entrance examination scores, cross-cultural comparisons revealing that American students score worse on mathematical tests than comparable European and Asian students, high failure rates on elementary-level literacy tests given by large American corporations—all have been cited as examples of a failure of American primary and secondary education (see Figure 15-2). American business spends $25 billion a year training students in skills that they should have learned in school. That accounts for the widespread suspicion that American students are receiving greater rewards and recognition for learning less. If this is the case, what is to be done?

Proposals for educational reform abound. Some stress accountability; one proposal (backed by the Bush administration) urges the implementation of national school testing. Such a system of testing promises to identify strong and weak schools and teachers and would therefore prove to be a catalyst for improvement. Other proposals champion parent and student choice, arguing that encouraging competition within education would also encourage more thorough teaching and learning. One method of encouraging such choice would be the adoption of a voucher system, in which government transfer payments would partly offset the cost of attending private and parochial schools that meet state accreditation standards.[5] Since many reformers believe that most of these schools already tend to perform better (Catholic schools are frequently singled out in this respect), they reason that the public schools would be compelled to deliver improved instruction to their students.

U.S. students trail the global pack

in science		in math		but not spending	
Avg. pct. of correct answers by 13-year-olds				Pct. of GNP on education	
South Korea	78%	South Korea	73%	Israel	10.2%
Taiwan	76%	Taiwan	73%	United States	7.5%
Switzerland	74%	Switzerland	71%	Canada	7.4%
Hungary	73%	Soviet Union*	70%	Jordan	7.1%
Soviet Union*	71%	Hungary	68%	Soviet Union*	7.0%
Slovenia	70%	France	64%	Ireland	6.7%
Italy	70%	Italy	64%	France	6.1%
Israel	70%	Israel	63%	Hungary	5.7%
Canada	69%	Canada	62%	Scotland	5.2%
France	69%	Scotland	61%	Switz.	4.8%
Scotland	68%	Ireland	61%	S. Korea	4.5%
Spain	68%	Slovenia	57%	Italy	4.0%
United States	67%	Spain	55%	Taiwan	3.6%
Ireland	63%	United States	55%	Slovenia	3.4%
Jordan	57%	Jordan	40%	Spain	3.2%

*Russian-speaking schools in 14 republics.

FIGURE 15-2   U.S. Students Trail the Global Pack
SOURCE: The Associated Press. Used with permission.

SOURCE: Mike Peters. Reprinted with permission of UFS, Inc.

Public school administrators and teachers have generally dissented from such reform proposals. They have expressed doubts about the capacity of standardized tests to measure educational achievement. Furthermore, they have suggested that a voucher system would undercut the public schools by encouraging the most able and motivated students to abandon them, leaving behind their least motivated and most poorly behaved or most disadvantaged peers. Finally, they argue that many of the worst problems faced by the public schools merely reflect larger social problems, including crime, breakdown of the family, drug use, and lack of interest in education. These difficulties are beyond the ability of the public schools to solve. One thing nearly everyone agrees on, however, is that an improved system of education is essential to the economic health and welfare of the nation.

Income Distribution

A final economic issue focuses on the distribution of wealth in the United States. This issue raises both economic and moral questions. Economically, individuals must be able to make enough money to afford the goods and services that society produces. If they do not, and if those goods and services cannot be exported, the economy will suffer. From a moral standpoint, glaring economic inequalities are difficult to justify in a society steeped in democratic traditions. If all human beings are created equal, how far can the extremes of rich and poor be allowed to go?

There are many ways of gauging income inequality. Of concern is the economic distance between the best-off and worst-off in society. Of equal importance is the concentration of wealth. In that regard, it is noteworthy that for over 50 years, the top 1 percent of the population has retained about as much after-tax income as the bottom 20 percent, and the top fifth has had about as much after-tax income as the bottom three-fifths.[6] Furthermore, this trend appears to be worsening. In the 1980s, wealth became even more concentrated in the hands of the affluent. Finally, it is worth noting specifically who is disadvantaged. One observer has pointed out that even though during the 1980s "the strong, the well-educated, the well-married and the well-off *within* these groups made gains above the national average," nonetheless "a disproportionate number of women, young people, blacks and Hispanics were among the decade's casualties." Of particular concern were those who lived in the inner city as well as a "growing underclass of high school dropouts, unwed mothers, female heads of households, unemployable young black males and homeless persons of all races," whose growing existence "was beginning to provoke worried questions about the nation's future."[7] Urban riots, most notably in Los Angeles in the spring of 1992, seemed to emphasize this point.

Yet, some observers believe that concerns about income distribution have been exaggerated. They point out that the United States has had a remarkably large middle class since its founding. They also argue that attempts to redistribute income to the economically disadvantaged (by increasing governmental benefits or by altering the tax structure) can do as much harm as good.[8] They argue that the government encourages prosperity by adopting policies that improve the business climate and reward people who take the greatest economic risks, work the hardest, invest wisely, and provide the goods and services that people want and need. Such policies may leave Americans with unequal pieces of the American economic pie, but all the pieces will be larger, they assert, if society's efforts are concentrated not on income redistribution but rather on encouraging economic growth.

THE PURSUIT OF EQUALITY

Equality is a bedrock principle of American political life. The assertion in the Declaration of Independence that "all men are created equal" reflects the principle that American citizens should enjoy equal rights to "life, liberty, and the pursuit of happiness." A century before the Declaration of Independence was written, John Locke had enshrined the universal rights of "life, liberty and property." Despite the small difference in emphasis, it is clear that the ideal of *equal* rights has deep roots in the Anglo-American political tradition.

Racial Discrimination

In at least one respect, however, American practice has not lived up to the original goal of equal rights for all. Discrimination against black Americans has been an indisputable fact of political life in the United States. Until the 1860s, the institution of slavery made a mockery of American ideals. So profound was this gulf between American principle and American practice that a devastating civil war had to be fought before the issue could be settled.

But if the outcome of the Civil War meant an end to slavery, it did not ensure equality under the law. Nor did enactment of the Fourteenth Amendment, which, among other things, guaranteed that no person shall be denied "the equal protection of the laws." Significantly, it was the Supreme Court that largely nullified the egalitarian intent of this amendment in two landmark decisions made in the closing decades of the nineteenth century. Through the decisions handed down in the *Civil Rights Cases* (1883) and *Plessy* v. *Ferguson* (1896), the Court not only sanctioned strict racial segregation in the South but also helped to legitimize a social system in which blacks were discriminated against, brutalized, and even murdered.

Two Landmark Cases   In the *Civil Rights Cases*,[9] the Court ruled than an act of Congress prohibiting racial discrimination in public accommodations (restaurants, amusement parks, and the like) was unconstitutional. The equal-protection clause of the Fourteenth Amendment, the justices held, was intended to prohibit only *state* discrimination, not private discrimination. Discriminatory acts committed by individuals having no official connection with a state agency, in other words, were beyond the range of the federal government and, therefore, of the federal courts. If, for example, a restaurant owner turned away blacks from his establishment, he would merely be exercising his rights as a private individual, and no public remedy would be called for.

Thirteen years later, in *Plessy* v. *Ferguson*,[10] the Court went even further. In upholding the constitutionality of a state law mandating racially segregated railway carriages, the Court in *Plessy* devised the now-notorious *separate-but-equal doctrine*. Plessy (described by the Court as of "seven-eighths Caucasian and one-eighth African blood") had taken a seat in the white section of a train, only to be told that he was required to move to the "colored" section. A nearly unanimous Court rejected Plessy's claim that the segregation law violated his right to equal protection of the law, arguing that the law was neutral on its face; that is, it provided equal accommodations for persons of both races. The Court majority went so far as to suggest that if "the enforced separation of the two races stamps the colored race with a badge of inferiority," that "is not by reason of anything found in the act, but solely because the colored race chooses to put that construction upon it."

In both the *Civil Rights Cases* and *Plessy* v. *Ferguson*, only Justice John M. Harlan dissented. On each occasion, he argued that the Court's decision had the effect of defeating the egalitarian purpose behind the Fourteenth Amendment, which, he declared, had "removed the race line from our government systems." Because he believed that no government, at any level, possessed the constitutional power to pass laws based on racial distinctions, he viewed the Constitution as "color-blind." Harlan's dissenting opinion in *Plessy* would not become the law of the land for another 68 years.

Two landmark Supreme Court cases at the turn of the twentieth century sanctioned strict racial segregation in the South, and Justice Harlan's dissenting opinion that the Constitution is "color-blind" did not become law for almost 70 years. (Bettmann Archive)

Racial Equality: Changing Laws, Changing Attitudes   Legally protected or dictated racial segregation was the norm throughout the South (and in many parts of the North, as well) into this century. Beginning in the late 1940s, however, the Supreme Court began to reinterpret the old legal formulas, with a view toward promoting racial equality. For example, in *Shelley* v. *Kraemer* (1948),[11] it held that judicial enforcement of discriminatory private contracts was unconstitutional. Legal enforcement of such agreements, the Court ruled, amounted to "state action" for the purpose of discrimination, which was prohibited by the Fourteenth Amendment. Also, although it declined to outlaw them outright, the Court began to insist that segregated state facilities be *truly* equal. Thus in *Sweatt* v. *Painter* (1950),[12] it held that the University of Texas law school had to be integrated because the state could not provide a black law school of equal quality and reputation.

Not until 1954, in *Brown* v. *Board of Education of Topeka*,[13] did the Court actually overturn the separate-but-equal doctrine. In that case, the justices declared that segregated schools were unconstitutional because "separate educational facilities are inherently unequal." This decision sparked a heated political debate over the meaning of "equality" in the United States. Despite an initial howl of protest, a national consensus gradually emerged. Ten years later, Congress passed the Civil Rights Act of 1964, the first of a series of national measures designed to help to ensure racial equality. (Interestingly, the 1964 act contained an equal-accommodations section very similar to the one ruled unconstitutional in the *Civil Rights Cases*.)[14] By the late 1960s, after a decade of intense civil rights activities and the most serious civil disorders since the Civil War, the government was fully committed to the goal of ensuring equal rights under the law for all citizens. The public policy battle between advocates of racial equality and of white supremacy thus gave way to an increasingly complex and heated debate over the appropriate means to the goal of equality.

The Busing Controversy   The question of how far the government could and should go to promote equal rights was crystallized in the school busing controversy of the 1970s and 1980s, which grew out of an ambiguity in *Brown* v. *Board of Education*. In that case, as we have seen, the Court ruled that legal segregation in education was unconstitutional. In accepting the view that black children tend to learn more in integrated schools, however, the Court seemed to imply that merely ending legal (*de jure*) segregation might not be sufficient. There still remained the problem of *de facto* segregation resulting from the socioeconomic effects of black poverty—that is, from the concentration of much of the black population in inner-city slums.

But how could segregated residential patterns be broken down for the purpose of integrating schools? One obvious possibility was to integrate school districts by transporting schoolchildren across district lines. Not only did busing offer the most straightforward way of integrating urban schools, but it also served to demonstrate in clear and unequivocal terms the nation's firm commitment to "equal opportunity." The onset of school busing put every locality in the nation on notice that henceforth racially homogeneous schools would not pass the constitutional test of "equal protection of the laws."

Critics attacked school busing on several grounds. Some of the opposition came from parents who harbored prejudice toward blacks, but much more came from parents who believed that local schools best served their children's educational needs. Other critics argued that the schools should not be turned into "social laboratories." School administrators feared that parental interest and participation would decrease as the physical distance between home and school increased. Finally, unhappiness with busing coincided with a national "crisis of confidence" in the public schools.[15] Declining student test scores, drug and discipline problems, lax academic standards, and presentiments of future funding problems provided unmistakable signs that all was not well with the public schools.

Has the time and money spent on busing been justified? Authorities still disagree on this question. Busing often had the effect of simply redistributing minorities from one part of the city to another. Some localities did attempt to bus children between the predominantly black inner city and the predominantly white suburbs, but the Supreme Court generally invalidated such plans unless it could be shown that the outlying school districts had practiced some form of governmentally imposed discrimination for which busing provided an appropriate remedy.[16]

Affirmative Action or Reverse Discrimination?

As controversial as the busing question proved to be, it was overshadowed in the late 1970s by another public policy question involving equality—namely, *affirmative action,* or "reverse discrimination," as its critics have come to call it. At issue here were governmental programs and regulations that accorded special preference to minorities in job hiring and promotion, admission to colleges and professional schools, and similar situations. The oft-declared purpose of such programs was to remedy the persistent effects of past and present discrimination against minorities. Like busing, these programs were established in the name of equality. But, many people asked, were such programs really fair? Were they even constitutional?

The second question was answered in part when the Supreme Court in 1978 handed down a ruling in a suit brought by Allan Bakke, a white student who had unsuccessfully sought admission to the medical school of the University of California at Davis.[17] Bakke contended that the medical school's special-admissions program (which set aside certain places for minority students, several of whom had significantly lower grade point averages and standardized test scores than Bakke did) had unfairly undercut his chances of acceptance simply because of his race. In a close (and rather unclear) decision, the Court agreed with Bakke that rigid affirmative action quotas were unconstitutional and ordered that he be admitted to the medical school. It also indicated, however, that preference for minorities could be maintained under certain circumstances. In later decisions, the Supreme Court has generally upheld broadly based affirmative action hiring programs as practiced by government and business (drawing the line at plans that provided minorities with preferential protection against layoffs). It has also upheld the use of affirmative action in the employment of women, arguing that they may be preferred over better-qualified men in order to improve the balance in the work force.[18]

Although recent Supreme Court decisions in this area have been confusing and perhaps even contradictory (with the justices actively disagreeing among themselves), two generalizations about the current status of the law are still possible. First, the Supreme Court has suggested that the Constitution gives Congress much more latitude than state and local governments to remedy the past effects of discrimination. Second, state and local governments' color-conscious affirmative action programs intended to advantage minorities are most likely to be upheld when there exists the clearest evidence of specific (and not general social) discrimination against them.[19]

While the courts attempt to resolve disputes about the constitutionality of affirmative action programs, private and public employers have used a variety of strategies to bolster minority employment opportunities. Among the most controversial of them has been the Department of Labor's policy of *race norming* and the State Department's practice of *gender norming.* These procedures aim at increasing the hiring of designated groups by using percentile scores derived from standardized employment test scores normed according to race or gender. Applicants are thus ranked against each other initially according to their race or

"Sorry, Mr. Spock, but we're long on pointy-eared Vulcans, and short on left-handed bisexual Andromedans . . . Next!"

When liberal cartoonists attacked conservatives on the busing issue, conservative cartoonists responded with criticisms of affirmative action efforts by the liberals. (Reprinted with the permission of M. G. Lord and Carl Moore) gender. For instance, a raw score of 63 earned by a woman in a gender-normed test would be ranked against all other women (and a 63 score earned by a man would similarly be ranked against all other men), each producing a normed percentile that would guarantee that an equal number of men and women would be hired.

Such programs have proved controversial, and not surprisingly, the debate over affirmative action programs and guidelines continues to swirl. Advocates of strong programs of affirmative action generally couch their arguments in terms of social justice and equality of result. Accordingly, they contend that such programs are justified because minorities have suffered systematic discrimination for generations. Moreover, the argument continues, minorities such as blacks have remained relatively disadvantaged because of social circumstances arising from past instances of discrimination. Thus "while blacks comprise 11.5% of the population, they constitute only 1.2% of the lawyers and judges, 2.0% of physicians, 2.3% of engineers, 2.6% of college and university professors."[20] In other words, they have been poorer, held lower-paying jobs, lived in worse housing, and had more difficulty achieving economic security, political influence, and social mobility than their white counterparts.

Opponents of affirmative action focus not on the person or group being helped but on the individuals harmed by such policies. The problem with any form of institutionalized discrimination, critics point out, is that it unfairly punishes people for attributes that have nothing to do with merit. In their view, what ought to govern the allocation of scarce resources—job promotions, financial aid, professional school admissions, and the like—is a fair evaluation of who deserves what according to relevant criteria applied in an equitable manner. Opponents of affirmative action also argued that society is punished when the most competent individuals are not allowed to succeed. According to this view, true justice does not demand a society in which each race is represented proportionally in each profession; it requires only equality of opportunity. Such equality demands, as Justice Harlan asserted, that the Constitution be color-blind—nothing less and nothing more.

Implementing Equality: Unresolved Issues

The centurylong battle over equal rights for blacks has sent a number of shock waves through American society. The resulting questions of public policy have proved complex and difficult to decide. For example, should other minorities be considered eligible for preferential treatment? Native Americans have also been discriminated against. Do they, too, merit preferential treatment under the law? What about Hispanic-Americans? Chinese-Americans have suffered because of their race—yet they are overrepresented in such prestigious fields as mathematics and computer science. Does such overrepresentation negate any claim to preferential treatment?

The question of sex-based discrimination has raised even thornier issues. From the early 1970s through the 1980s, this debate centered on the ill-fated Equal Rights Amendment, which would have ensured that "equality of rights under the law should not be denied or abridged by the United States or by any State on account of sex." As we have already seen, another, related question was whether (and to what extent) women were entitled to preferential treatment to remedy the effects of past sex discrimination. Controversy also has arisen over how it should be determined when or whether such discrimination occurs and who is most disadvantaged by it. For instance, federal law requires only males to register for the military draft.[21] Does this law recognize only the natural physical differences between the sexes? Does it favor men by treating women as second-class citizens incapable of fully carrying out their civic duties? Or does it favor women by exempting them from an unpleasant obligation? The same controversies have embroiled a number of other statutes, including statutory rape laws that make it illegal for males to have sexual relations with underage females but not for females to have sex with underage males.[22]

The poor and disadvantaged comprise yet another group often thought to deserve preferential treatment. They could particularly be seen among the working poor, among the homeless (whose numbers and causes were hotly disputed but whose existence was undeniable), and within the inner cities. Numerous governmental programs designed to ensure a minimum standard of living (welfare, food stamps) and to induce upward social mobility (job training programs) have been enacted in the past half century. To a great degree, the very existence of poverty is viewed as posing a persistent challenge to a nation that prides itself on its commitment to equal opportunity.

There is sharp disagreement, however, over the extent of this problem in the United States. In part, this controversy stems from differing definitions of poverty. Is it present only when people are teetering on the brink of starvation? Or does it encompass deprivation in any degree? If the latter, how is this condition defined for purposes of public policy? Obviously, such questions are extremely difficult to answer. Some experts classify as poor a certain percentage of the population at the lowest end of the income scale. But this method of identifying who is and is not poor begs the question of what level of income is consonant with a decent standard of living in an affluent, egalitarian society.

And to what extent are the poor, however defined, responsible for their own economic condition? Opponents of social welfare programs maintain that poor people often live in squalor because they will not change the habits and attitudes that led to their wretched condition in the first place; therefore, they argue, government can do little to alleviate such self-induced poverty. In response, some experts contend that many poor people are merely the victims of an indifferent society and an impersonal economic system, and thus the government can and should use its powers to advance the cause of economic and social equality.

Finally, there is the issue of whether other groups, defined not by color, ethnic background, or gender, have nonetheless been the object of past discrimination and are therefore entitled to special consideration in the competition for jobs, schooling, and social benefits. For instance, what about the handicapped? Homosexual men and women? Have these individuals been disadvantaged by discrimination, and if so, are they entitled to be included in affirmative action programs? These questions raise the issue of what a truly representative society would look like and further demonstrate the practical problems inherent in bringing such a society into existence.

THE PURSUIT OF LIBERTY

As surely as equality is a primary goal of contemporary political life, so too is liberty. Slogans extolling the virtue of political freedom respond throughout the history of the American republic. "Give me liberty or give me death," declared Patrick Henry in a phrase that has been enshrined as a national motto.

The Value of Liberty

Political liberty in the Western world has long been understood as freedom from governmental restraint. Such freedom has commonly been seen as a valuable political asset, for four principal reasons.

1 Life is robbed of its meaning if an individual cannot freely choose how to lead it. Because such freedom of choice is a distinctly human trait, liberty means the opportunity to act in a distinctly human way. Also, freedom is a prerequisite for human dignity. Because most adult citizens are capable of assuming moral responsibility for their own actions, the absence of freedom deprives individuals of the opportunity for self-realization and keeps them in a permanent state of arrested development. In other words, the absence of freedom reduces adults to the status of children.

2 Liberty is based on the assumption that individuals know and generally pursue their own best interests. Human happiness, according to this view, can be achieved only when individuals control their own lives and when they (rather than the government) decide how best to spend their time, energy, and money.

3 Liberty is necessary for the meaningful exchange of ideas, as well as for social progress. Only in a free society can the full range of human ideas, inventions, and opinions be explored and exploited for the benefit of society and the advancement of human understanding. Freedom of expression, therefore, advances the truth and helps to promote a healthy diversity of behavior and values that leads to social improvements within society and to the overall advancement of the community.

4 The absence of liberty frequently results in abuses of power. For example, we might all agree that a certain type of behavior is desirable—say, bathing at least once a week—and further that freedom in this particular instance would be difficult to defend (a constitutional right to practice poor hygiene?). Yet we would probably not want the government to pass a law requiring baths or showers, for such legislation would be very difficult to enforce and would set a dangerous precedent. If government can invade one's privacy in a matter as personal as bathing, the argument goes, what is to prevent it from interfering in more significant personal matters?

Liberty and the First Amendment

In the United States, legal questions that involve individual freedom are often decided by judicial interpretation of the First Amendment, which provides that

Congress shall make no law respecting an establishment of religion, or prohibiting the free exercise thereof; or abridging the freedom of speech, or the press; or the right of the people peaceably to assemble, and to petition the government for a redress of grievances.

Thus the First Amendment protects four important aspects of citizen liberty: freedom of speech, freedom of the press, freedom of religion, and freedom of peaceable assembly. Because the language of the First Amendment is brief and general, the first three rights in particular have required an unusual amount of judicial interpretation.

Freedom of Speech   Most authorities agree that the overriding purpose behind the First Amendment was the protection of political speech. In a republic, open debate between political opponents is vital to the effective functioning of the political system. Most of the time, the *exercise* of free speech is not controversial, even though the speech itself might be.

However, freedom of speech can become a hotly contested issue when it is exercised by individuals who represent unpopular causes or who challenge the integrity or legitimacy of the political system. Extremists often arouse strong passions. Nazi speakers understandably arouse a particularly high level of revulsion among Jews, and Ku Klux Klan spokesmen have the same effect on blacks. During the early days of the Vietnam War, youthful protesters were frequently regarded as unpatriotic and disloyal by their more conservative elders. Several years later, after the war had become more unpopular, defenders of the U.S. role in Vietnam were booed and shouted down when they spoke on college campuses. The First Amendment, however, safeguards the right of all citizens to express political opinions, no matter how repugnant or unpopular, subject only to a few limitations (that the speech not be part and parcel of an illegal act, that it not foment riot, that it not constitute a direct personal provocation—so-called "fighting words"—and so on).

Of course, the protections offered by the freedom-of-speech clause are not confined to political speech alone. The Supreme Court has placed a very broad interpretation on *speech,* defining it as synonymous with *expression.* Artistic expression, symbolic statements (such as black armbands), and advertising are among the areas that, according to the Court, are protected by the First Amendment. Once it is determined that an activity comprises symbolic free speech, its content or message makes no difference. Thus flag burning has been upheld as a protected form of symbolic free speech.[23] Of course, as with pure speech cases, the context of symbolic free speech is almost always constitutionally more important than its content. The Ku Klux Klan's burning of a cross in an isolated field may be an objectionable act, but it is nonetheless a constitutionally protected form of symbolic expression.[24] Burning a cross in front of a black church or on a black person's lawn is a more difficult legal question, for it may well be regarded as an incitement, an insult, or a threat beyond the scope of First Amendment protection.[25]

Freedom of the Press   This freedom guarantees public access to news and information by protecting publishers from almost all forms of official censorship. In other words, newspapers and periodicals can publish what they wish, including criticisms and indictments of the government. The same holds true for the broadcast media. A diverse and unhampered press, the Founders believed, is crucial to self-government because in a democracy, every citizen is an important decision maker (in the voting booth) and because even popularly elected officials need someone (or something) to keep them honest.

The Supreme Court has consistently reaffirmed that under the Constitution, the press cannot be subject to *prior restraint.* This means that except in times of war or grave national emergency, the government does not have the power to prevent a newspaper or a periodical from publishing material of any sort—even papers classified as secret by the government or information that a trial judge may later rule as constituting prejudicial pretrial publicity.[26]

Freedom of Religion   By prohibiting the establishment of a state-sponsored religion, the First Amendment requires the government to be neutral in religious matters—neither to help nor to hinder any religion. This requirement complements the clause that guarantees citizens the free exercise of religion. Taken together, these two clauses (the *establishment* and *free exercise clauses*) ensure that citizens may practice any religion in any manner they like, within reasonable limits.

When religious practices pose a threat to society, however, government has the power to outlaw them. No court in the land, for instance, would uphold ritual murder on the ground that the free exercise of religion was guaranteed by the Constitution. Even certain religious practices that do not present any obvious danger to society, such as polygamy, are not constitutionally protected.[27] These examples, however, are isolated exceptions to the rule. In general, the courts have allowed wide latitude in the exercise of religion, upholding the right of conscientious objectors to refuse induction into the armed services, the right of certain Amish children to be exempted from public education requirements, and the right of Jehovah's Witness schoolchildren to refrain from saluting the flag (on the ground that such a practice would constitute, under their religion, worship of a graven image).

A more controversial matter has been school prayer. In a number of decisions, the Supreme Court has held that prayer (even if nondenominational) and Bible reading in public schools violates the establishment clause of the First Amendment.[28] The Supreme Court has gone so far as to disallow a moment of silence in the public schools if a teacher suggests that it might be used for prayer.[29] Observing that public schools, teachers, and school boards are creatures of state government and that student enrollment in the public schools is mandated by state compulsory education laws, the justices have consistently ruled that school prayer unconstitutionally involves the state in the establishment of religion.

Some Court critics argue that these decisions should be reversed. School prayer, they contend, helps keep alive the religious traditions that made this country great and that alone can stem moral decadence among the country's youth. In rebuttal, defenders of the Court's decisions emphasize that daily prayer and Bible-reading sessions in the schools adversely affect the religious liberty of students who do not hold religious values. The cause of religious freedom, they maintain, is best served by an absolute minimum of governmental interference in matters of faith.

The establishment clause has also been invoked in the public debate over governmental assistance to parents whose children attend private schools, particularly church-related or denominational schools. The argument has often been made that parents should have a maximum amount of choice in determining where their children go to school. All parents, as citizens, pay taxes to support the public schools, but sometimes they prefer to send their children to private or religiously sponsored schools for religious, social, or educational reasons. Because these parents must also pay private school tuition, policymakers question whether the government should aid parents who choose to send their children to such schools by granting them tax credits or some other financial assistance. With this sort of financial relief in mind, various "voucher" plans have been drafted in Congress over the past few years.

The Right to Privacy

The freedoms we have examined so far are protected by the First Amendment to the U.S. Constitution. There are, however, other important liberties not explicitly protected by that amendment (or by any single article or amendment).

Primary among such liberties is the so-called right to privacy, or right of choice, which generally means the right of adult citizens to decide issues of fundamental importance to their own well-being. Citing this right to privacy, the Supreme Court has ruled that women have a substantial, though not unlimited, right to choose an abortion. Initially, the Supreme Court took particular care to eliminate roadblocks to the exercise of that right. Recently, however, the Court (whose decisions reflected its changing composition) has become a less enthusiastic supporter of this right. It has ruled that the existence of a woman's right to an abortion did not require that public funds be spent to reimburse poorer women for the cost of abortions, nor was the government required to pay public employees for performing or assisting in abortions, nor did it even require federally funded family planning clinics to counsel patients regarding abortion.[30]

Objections to the Supreme Court's initial decision affirming a woman's right to an abortion have come largely from "right to life" groups, whose members believe that human life begins at conception and that abortion therefore amounts to legalized murder. A human embryo or fetus, they argue, possesses constitutional rights, including a right to life, that in all but a few cases (such as when the mother's life would be threatened by pregnancy or childbirth) outweigh the mother's right to privacy. Such reasoning influenced several states to adopt stringent anti-abortion statutes that, on their face, seemed to violate the Supreme

Since the 1973 Supreme Court's ruling in Roe v. Wade *affirming a woman's right to an abortion, pro-choice and anti-abortion activists in the United States have demonstrated vocally (and sometimes violently). International debates also abound, including challenges in 1992 to strict anti-abortion laws in Ireland.* (Hazel Hankin/Stock, Boston)

Court's original proabortion decision. There is little doubt that the abortion question will remain a heated issue both in the courts and in state legislatures. Many constitutional experts wonder aloud if the Supreme Court will soon overturn its original abortion decision (*Roe* v. *Wade*).

THE PURSUIT OF JUSTICE

Besides security, prosperity, equality, and liberty, justice is an important goal of constitutional democracies. In the following discussion, the term *justice* is narrowly defined as a particular end of government, achieved through the courts and the criminal justice system. A just society in this sense is one in which civil and criminal rules are applied fairly and the punishment fits the crime.

Crime and Punishment

No society can afford to let seriously antisocial or criminal behavior go unpunished. By punishing people who violate its rules, a society makes clear that such behavior will not be tolerated. The severity of the punishment demonstrates exactly how undesirable a particular behavior is.

There are four rationales behind the punishment of antisocial behavior.

First, the protection of society is advanced when *incarceration* is imposed upon criminals. Second, punishment of one criminal may dissuade other individuals from committing a similar crime (*deterrence*). Third, punishment is an essential precondition for reeducating criminals, so that they can eventually resume normal and productive lives (*rehabilitation*). Finally, punishment compensates the innocent victim of crime, who deserves the satisfaction of seeing the perpetrator punished (*retribution*).

Justice as Fair Procedure

An old legal cliché holds that 90 percent of fairness in the law is fair procedure. This saying recognizes the vital need for procedural safeguards to prevent the innocent from being falsely accused and the accused from being falsely convicted. These safeguards, which comprise what is known as *due process of law,* are outlined in the Bill of Rights of the Constitution, particularly in Amendments 4, 5, and 6. Under the Constitution, citizens have the legal right (1) not to be subjected to unreasonable searches and seizures by the government, (2) not to be tried twice for the same offense, (3) not to incriminate themselves, (4) to receive a speedy and public trial by an impartial jury, (5) to be informed of the nature of the charge made against them, (6) to be confronted by any witnesses against them, (7) to obtain witnesses in their favor, and (8) to have legal counsel.

Of course, each of these constitutional guarantees is subject to judicial interpretation. Taken as a group, however, they represent the heart of our system of justice. In the words of one observer:

> When a man is brought into court and is accused of having committed a grave offense against society, all the machinery of the state is set in motion to bring him to justice. The public prosecutor or the district attorney often has a veritable army at his disposal, all trained to ferret out information that may be relevant to the crime, all paid by the state to spend their working hours questioning witnesses, examining evidence, and building a case that will presumably lead to conviction of the accused. The latter, on the other hand, usually has very limited means at his disposal. More often than not, a defendant is fortunate if he has enough assets to pay the fees of an attorney. Few men can hire teams of private investigators who can devote their time, skills, and resources exclusively to the search for evidence and the building of a defense. No private citizen can match the modern state when the latter brings all its forces into play after he has been accused of having violated the law.[31]

Thus procedural guarantees are essential to the protection of defendants from miscarriages of justice.

The Limits of Legal Protection

Despite these important safeguards, the criminal justice system does not always produce justice. The poor, for example, have always received a substantially lower level of legal aid. And historically, the greatest injustices in this country have stemmed from racial prejudice. For a long time, this was particularly true in the South, where the imposition and severity of punishment correlated more closely with race than with any other consideration. Blacks who were convicted (often falsely) of raping white women were commonly sentenced to death or life in prison, whereas whites who were accused of similar crimes against black women were often not even brought to trial.

Whenever such blatant injustices occur, legal procedures have failed. But if shortcomings are sometimes easy to recognize, the best ways to correct defects in the system usually are not. Virtually every due-process guarantee has been the object of bitter controversy. For example, the Constitution clearly states that a defendant has the right to an attorney. This seems straightforward enough. But what if the accused cannot afford to hire an attorney? Does the state have an obligation to provide an attorney for an indigent person accused of a felony? What about an indigent accused of a misdemeanor? And what about appeals? Must the state provide legal counsel for a defendant who, after having been convicted of a crime, wishes to appeal the case? If so, must counsel be provided for every appeal the defendant wishes to make or for only the first appeal?[32]

The definition and application of procedural protections for the accused, then, often raise complex questions. Few people would disagree with the assertion that certain protections are necessary if justice is to be served. To the contrary, it has often been argued, quite plausibly, that the rights themselves must be *broadened* in application to afford meaningful protection for the accused. Obviously, however, there are limits to the scope of these legal safeguards. Were they to be applied as broadly as is theoretically possible, the monetary cost could become prohibitively high, or it could become next to impossible to convict anyone accused of anything, or the judicial process could become so sluggish that justice itself would be impeded or undermined. In the end the proper scope of procedural safeguards must be determined by balancing the rights of the accused against the obligation of government to punish those who are truly guilty of violating the law.

The Exclusionary Rule   No due-process issue has raised the question of fairness more sharply than the so-called *exclusionary rule*. Essentially, the exclusionary rule holds that when evidence has been illegally obtained, it cannot be entered in a court of law. The Supreme Court, in promulgating this rule, argued that the Fourth Amendment's prohibition against illegal searches and seizures would be meaningless if illegal police behavior were not discouraged by the certain knowledge that any evidence obtained in violation of the Constitution would be excluded from the courts.[33] In the view of the Court, then, the exclusionary rule provides an indispensable barrier to deliberate abuse of police powers.

Critics of this rule (including several Supreme Court justices)[34] focus their arguments on the serious problems it causes police officers, whose searches and seizures must conform to very complex guidelines handed down by the courts. Few searches and seizures, they point out, conform to textbook cases; most of the time, the police officer on the spot is compelled to make a spur-of-the-moment decision. To penalize the police for making a faulty on-the-spot decision—a determination often made several years later in the serenity of a courtroom—is to penalize the public on the basis of a questionable technicality.

At the heart of the dispute over the exclusionary rule lie several important differences of opinion. Advocates tend to view most law enforcement officers as overzealous, while critics see them as well-intentioned victims of convoluted and confusing laws. In addition, advocates of the rule see it as a valuable guarantee of justice, whereas its opponents see it as an impediment to law enforcement. The Supreme Court has tried to strike a balance between these two poles by allowing the admission of illegally obtained evidence when the error was unintentional by the police and when they had demonstrated a good-faith effort to comply with the law.[35] This "harmless error" exception to the exclusionary rule attempts to balance the rights of the accused and the safety of the public.

Judicial Discretion   Until recently, the prevailing legal theory has been that wide discretion should be accorded to prosecutors (to prosecute, plea-bargain, or not prosecute), judges (to pronounce indeterminate sentences), and parole boards (to determine how much actual time a convicted criminal should serve). The rationale behind judicial and administrative discretion in this realm is that individuals accused or convicted of similar crimes differ significantly in background, motivation, exposure to crime, prospect for rehabilitation, and other factors. With discretionary authority, magistrates and other officials can take such individual circumstances into account when determining charges or the severity of sentences. Such discretion was considered even more important as the number of crimes rose and the number of prison cells remained almost static; in such a situation, many judges expressed reluctance to send all but the most hardened criminals to overcrowded and understaffed prisons.

This aspect of the judicial system has been attacked by many critics as arbitrary and open to all sorts of subtle abuses. They assert that prosecutors may make decisions based on political considerations or individual whim, that judges may sentence according to pet theories of the law, and that parole officers may be taken in by convicts whom they really do not know or understand. These loopholes and uncertainties in the judicial system, it is alleged, severely dilute the deterrent effect of punishment. Even worse, critics charge, an individual's punishment depends too much on circumstances that ought to be irrelevant in judicial matters, such as which judge happens to try which case. The force of these arguments has led a number of states to adopt such legal reforms as the reduction or elimination of indeterminate sentences.

Capital Punishment   The public debate over the propriety of capital punishment has been waged on at least two separate levels. In practical terms, experts differ radically over the question of whether capital punishment actually deters future murders. The evidence has been so fragmentary and the interpretations have been so diverse that a definitive answer seems unlikely. On another level, there has been agonized disagreement over whether capital punishment is morally defensible. Interestingly, both sides emphasize the sanctity of human life. Defenders of capital punishment contend that justice demands the imposition of the death penalty precisely because justice places such a high value on human life—because, in other words, society is morally obligated to condemn the murder of innocent persons in no uncertain terms.

SOME CONCLUSIONS

In the United States, most people do not maintain hard and fast convictions about politics, if only because determining how the public good is to be attained in modern society is no simple task. Certainly, the five aims of government examined in this chapter—security, prosperity, equality, liberty, and justice—are not easy to realize. As we have seen, controversial and complex issues arise within each category, and the best way of pursuing the various ends of public policy is rarely obvious.

Many times, the goals themselves conflict. For example, one important end of government is liberty. But during times of war, the government often restricts individual liberty (by imposing curfews, limiting profits, restricting the job mobility of certain workers, prohibiting protests, establishing "relocation" camps, and so on) in the name of national security. Judges sometimes limit freedom of the press to ensure justice for a defendant in a highly publicized trial. Governmental rules, formulated in the name of equality, may compel employers to pay minimum wages or meet safety standards, thus interfering with their pursuit of prosperity (as well as their liberty). A myriad of examples can be cited. The point to remember is that conflicts among the legitimate ends of government can make the full realization of those ends impossible.

And how does one evaluate the performance of government in terms of public policy goals? Alexis de Tocqueville made the incisive observation, in *Democracy in America* (1831), that the more nearly equal people become, the more glaring even the slightest departure from equality appears to be. In other words, the closer a political system comes to fulfilling the goal of equality, the more it appears to fail when it has not fully reached that goal. Much the same can be said with respect to the other chief ends of government. And because conflicts among goals always prevent the full realization of any one goal, there is always the danger in a democracy that citizens and leaders alike will lose sight of the need to hold all these worthy goals in proper balance.

Recognizing both the complexity of public policy issues and the difficulty of achieving (or even adequately defining) the public good leads reflective citizens to appreciate the vital importance of political moderation. Such moderation inoculates citizens against unreasonable political expectations. It also guards against single-minded efforts to achieve one end of government at the expense of other essential ends. Discussions of public policy in a democracy can be inflamed by the zealotry and fanaticism of those who obsessively pursue singular and unattainable goals. Shrill cries may then drown out the quieter voices of those who understand that without patience and moderation, democracy will inevitably fail to strike the delicate balances that are the essence of good government.

Summary

Public policy issues revolve around five universal goals of democratic government: security, prosperity, equality, liberty, and justice.

Security is the most fundamental goal of government because other values cannot be pursued or preserved without it. In pursuing security, government attempts to protect citizens from foreign enemies, from fellow citizens, from natural enemies, and even, in some instances, from themselves.

In the United States, the goal of prosperity has historically been associated with a free-enterprise economy based on the idea of the commercial republic. In the twentieth century, however, government has attempted to ensure the economic well-being of individuals through social welfare and other programs. These programs have sparked heated debate over the proper role of government in economic matters, especially as the budget deficit has worsened. Problems in the educational system endangered American competitiveness in the international economy. The income distribution of Americans also made for a lively topic of national debate.

The question of equality in the United States has been closely identified with the effort to end racial discrimination. Two landmark Supreme Court cases in the post–Civil War period helped to perpetuate state laws and public attitudes upholding established patterns of racial inequality. In modern times, the case of *Brown* v. *Board of Education* (1954) spearheaded the civil rights movement, which culminated in legislative, judicial, and administrative measures aimed at bringing about genuine racial equality. These civil rights gains were followed by new controversies over the issue of mandatory school busing to achieve racial integration and so-called affirmative action guidelines designed to rectify past inequalities. Other major public policy issues related to equality have involved the rights of various ethnic groups, women, and the poor and disadvantaged.

The pursuit of liberty is a core value of American society. Among the personal liberties protected explicitly by the First Amendment are freedom of speech, freedom of the press, and freedom of religion. The right to privacy, or freedom of choice, is another significant aspect of personal liberty in the United States.

The pursuit of justice as a goal of government can be narrowly defined as the attempt to ensure equitable and efficient operation of the criminal justice system. The true test of justice, then, is whether or not the courts fairly and impartially apply the laws of the land. All societies punish antisocial or criminal behavior through criminal justice systems. In the United States, this system strives to uphold a commitment to due process, or fair procedure. Due-process safeguards, as enumerated in the Constitution and interpreted by the courts, pose several difficult problems in modern society. The controversial exclusionary rule attempts to balance the defendant's right to due process against society's right to be protected against criminals. Questions of judicial discretion and capital punishment also involve balancing defendants' and society's rights.

Conflicts among these five goals always prevent any one of them from being fully realized. In evaluating the relative importance of each goal in public policy issues, therefore, citizens must assume a moderate and rational point of view.

Key Terms

national security	gender norming	incarceration	due process of law
mixed economy	prior restraint	deterrence	exclusionary rule
affirmative action	establishment clause	rehabilitation	
race norming	free exercise clause	retribution	

Review Questions

1. Public policy questions involving security arise in many contexts in American public life. Identify some political issues that involve security concerns.

2. What economic problems face the United States?

3. Contrast the ideal and practice of equality in the United States throughout history.

4. Why is liberty valuable? How is it protected in the United States?

5. What issues currently plague the American criminal justice system? Why are they important?

6. What is the relationship between the public good and moderation?

Recommended Reading

Because public policy questions are forever changing, exposure to information and thoughtful opinion is vital. Appropriate reading would include highly respected newspapers (such as the *New York Times* and the *Washington Post*), weekly news magazines (such as *Time* and *Newsweek*), magazines of opinion (including *The Nation, The New Republic, Atlantic, Harper's, Commentary,* and *National Review*), and certain scholarly journals that specialize in public policy questions (such as *The Public Interest*).

Notes

1. Aristotle, *The Politics,* ed. and trans. Ernest Barker (New York: Oxford University Press, 1962), p. 5.

2. Martin Diamond, personal communication.

3. Michael M. Thomas, "The Greatest American Shambles," *New York Review of Books,* January 31, 1991, p. 30.

4. As Tocqueville pointed out; see Alexis de Tocqueville, *Democracy in America,* ed. and trans. J. P. Mayer (Garden City, N.Y.: Doubleday, 1966), pp. 302, 459–468.

5. Of course, this raises First Amendment establishment clause questions.

6. Arthur Okun, *Equality and Efficiency: The Big Trade-off* (Washington, D.C.: Brookings Institution, 1965), pp. 68–69.

7. Kevin Phillips, *The Politics of Rich and Poor* (New York: Random House, 1990), p. 202.

8. Okun, *Equality and Efficiency*, pp. 68–69.

9. *Civil Rights Cases*, 109 U.S. 3 (1883).

10. *Plessy* v. *Ferguson*, 163 U.S. 537 (1896).

11. *Shelley* v. *Kraemer*, 334 U.S. 1 (1948).

12. *Sweatt* v. *Painter*, 339 U.S. 629 (1950).

13. *Brown* v. *Board of Education of Topeka*, 347 U.S. 483 (1954).

14. And it was upheld as a legitimate exercise of the government's commerce power; see *Heart of Atlanta Motel* v. *United States*, 379 U.S. 241 (1964), and *Katzenbach* v. *McClung*, 379 U.S. 294 (1964).

15. See Peter Schotten, "The Establishment Clause and Excessive Governmental-Religious Entanglement: The Constitutional Status of Aid to Non-public and Secondary Schools," *Wake Forest Law Review* 15 (1979), pp. 240–244.

16. *Milliken* v. *Bradley*, 418 U.S. 717 (1974).

17. *Regents of the University of California* v. *Bakke*, 438 U.S. 265 (1978).

18. See *Wyant* v. *Jackson Board of Education*, 106 S.Ed. 1842 (1986), and *Johnson* v. *Transportation Agency, Santa Clara County*, 107 S.Ct. 1442 (1987).

19. See, for instance, *United States* v. *Paradise*, 480 U.S. 149 (1987); *City of Richmond* v. *J. A. Croson Co.*, 488 U.S. 469 (1989); and *Metro Broadcasting, Inc.* v. *Federal Communications Commission*, 110 S.Ct. 2997 (1990).

20. John C. Livingston, *Fair Game? Inequality and Affirmative Action* (New York: Freeman, 1979), p. 10.

21. *Rostker* v. *Goldberg*, 453 U.S. 57 (1981).

22. *Michael M.* v. *Superior Court*, 450 U.S. 464 (1981).

23. *Texas* v. *Johnson*, 105 L.Ed. 2d 342 (1989).

24. *Brandenberg* v. *Ohio*, 395 U.S. 444 (1969).

25. This issue is one question among several raised by the pending Superior Court case of *R.A.V.* v. *St. Paul*. A white 18-year-old male burned a cross on the lawn of the only black family living in a St. Paul, Minnesota, neighborhood. Although he might have been arrested for trespassing or disturbing the peace, he was charged under a local hate crime ordinance that made it illegal to place "on private or public property, a symbol, object or graffiti, including but not limited to a burning cross or Nazi swastika, which one knows or has reasonable grounds to know arouses anger, alarm or resentment in others on the basis of race, color, creed, religion or gender." A first, obvious question is, Does the statute violate the First Amendment?

26. See *New York Times Co.* v. *United States*, 403 U.S. 713 (1971), and *Nebraska Press Association* v. *Stuart*, 427 U.S. 539 (1976).

27. *Wallace* v. *Jaffree*, 472 U.S. 38 (1985).

28. *Reynolds* v. *United States*, 98 U.S. 145 (1879).

29. Most notably in *Abington School District* v. *Schempp*, 374 U.S. 203 (1963), and *Engle* v. *Vitale*, 370 U.S. 421 (1963).

30. The original case declaring a woman's right to an abortion is *Roe* v. *Wade*, 410 U.S. 113 (1973). Recent confining cases include *Webster* v. *Reproductive Health Services*, 106 L.Ed. 2d 410 (1989), and *Rust* v. *Sullivan*, 10011 S.Ct. 1759 (1991).

31. Burton Leiser, *Liberty, Justice, and Morals: Contemporary Value Conflicts* (New York: Macmillan, 1973), p. 192.

32. The answer provided by the Supreme Court is that the state must provide effective assistance of counsel through the first appeal. See *Evitts* v. *Lucey*, 469 U.S. 387 (1985).

33. *Mapp* v. *Ohio*, 367 U.S. 643 (1961).

34. See, for instance, Chief Justice Burger's dissent in *Bivens* v. *Six Unknown Agents of the Federal Bureau of Narcotics*, 403 U.S. 388, 411 (1970).

35. *United States* v. *Leon*, 468 U.S. 897 (1984).

PART III

POLITICS, CONFLICT, AND WORLD ORDER

CHAPTER 16

REVOLUTION

IN THE NAME
OF JUSTICE

(Sophie Elbaz/Sygma)

FEW WORDS ARE used as loosely as *revolution* or *revolutionary*. Television commercials abound with descriptions of "revolutionary" new shaving creams and household appliances or automobiles that will bring about a "revolution" in transportation. Of more importance to us, governments can also be revolutionary. But what exactly constitutes a revolution or a revolutionary government?

Fundamentally, the adjective *revolutionary* denotes great change. Thus a revolutionary shaving cream, appliance, or automobile would be a new product that represents a dramatic transformation of past shaving creams, appliances, or automobiles. The word *revolution* is frequently used in this manner: The so-called Industrial Revolution, for example, represented a fundamental change in the mode of production, one that altered the way national economies operated and societies were structured.

In a political context, a **revolution** is a phenomenon that brings about a significant change in an existing government and society. But not just any political change constitutes a revolution. If a *coup d'état* brings to power one set of leaders whose policies mirror those they replace and the country or society is affected little by that action, no revolution has occurred, and the resulting government cannot properly be called a revolutionary government.

THE PERSISTENCE OF REVOLUTION

Revolutions have occurred throughout human history, particularly during times of strong population expansion and rapid economic change.[1] Significant changes in governmental structure took place in many Greek city-states in the seventh and sixth centuries B.C., in Rome in the first century B.C., in the Islamic world in the eighth century, and in Europe, particularly from 1500 to 1650 and from 1750 to 1850.

In the twentieth century, revolutions have occurred more frequently than ever. In a sense, this is part of a surge in national violence that has marked most of the century. In the 1930s, the renowned Harvard sociologist Pitirim Sorokin made an impressive study of "internal disturbances" in 11 political communities. In western Europe alone, he was able to identify no fewer than 1,622 such disturbances in the post–World War I era, of which fully 70 percent "involved violence and bloodshed on a considerable scale."[2] Moreover, he found that in every country studied, for every five years of relative peace there was one year of "significant social disturbance." Overall, Sorokin came to the conclusion that the twentieth century was the bloodiest and most turbulent period in history—and that judgment was made before World War II!

Subsequent events have borne out this judgment. For example, in the period from 1945 to 1970, fully 40 of the approximately 100 developing countries witnessed at least one military takeover. And in the period from 1943 to 1962, attempts to overthrow an existing government occurred in virtually every country in Latin America, in two-thirds of the countries of Asia, and in half the African countries that had gained independence.[3] Between 1946 and 1959, the *New York Times* reported 1,200 separate instances of "internal war," including "civil wars, guerrilla wars, localized rioting, widely dispersed turmoil, organized and apparently unorganized terrorism, mutinies, and *coups d'état.*"[4] Recent times have seen no decrease in revolutions and civil disturbances. If violence, organized and unorganized, has always been an integral part of political life, it has in the twentieth century become both better organized and more prevalent.

No other single historical change has held more profound implications for contemporary politics than the unprecedented frequency, scope, and intensity of change itself. And revolutions have become a significant cause of such change.

MODERN REVOLUTIONS: TWO TRADITIONS

Any study of modern revolutions must begin with an analysis of two pivotal eighteenth-century revolutions, separated by a mere 13 years, that have provided a wealth of raw material for generations of social scientists. The American Revolution of 1776 and the French Revolution of 1789 represent two of the great political events of the modern age. But if both influenced the destiny of generations to come, they also differed dramatically from one another. In the words of one authority:

> It is certainly indisputable that the world, when it contemplates the events of 1776 and after, is inclined to see the American Revolution as a French Revolution that never quite came off, whereas the Founding Fathers thought they had cause to regard the French Revolution as an American Revolution that had failed. Indeed, differing estimates of these two revolutions are definitive of one's political philosophy in the modern world: there are two conflicting conceptions of politics, in relation to the human condition, which are symbolized by these two revolutions. There is no question that the French Revolution is, in some crucial sense, the more "modern" of the two. There is a question, however, as to whether this is a good or bad thing.[5]

The American Revolution: Sober Expectations

There is no doubt that the American Founders considered the war for independence fought against George III to be a legitimate revolution. In waging a war against the mother country in the 1770s, the American colonists became the instigators of the modern world's first successful anticolonial revolution. Their break with Great Britain in time became complete and irreparable. For that reason, it is tempting to say that the American Revolutionary War created a model for what we have come to know as wars of national liberation. On the other hand, as will soon become apparent, the American Revolution differed decisively from almost all twentieth-century revolutionary upheavals.

Historical Significance   To understand the historical significance of the American Revolution, we must first examine the political opinions of its leaders. It is noteworthy that the American freedom fighters saw the Revolutionary War as a special and unique experience. "From the very beginning," according to one authority, it was believed by those who participated in it—on the western side of the Atlantic—to be quite a remarkable event, not merely because it was their revolution, but because it seemed to them to introduce a new phase in the political evolution of mankind, and therefore to be touched with universal significance.[6]

This claim is all the more impressive for being made by an uncommonly erudite and enlightened group of political leaders. In addition to the more popular political treatises of their day, the Founders were well acquainted with world history and with the writings of the great political philosophers, including Montesquieu, Locke, Rousseau, Hume, and Voltaire.[7] With their great respect for the political classics, they were not inclined to overestimate the value of new or experimental approaches to politics.

The revolutionaries of 1776 believed their rebellion to be of decisive worldwide significance because they thought that the language of liberty expressed in the Declaration of Independence was of fundamental importance and that the deeds associated with their struggle were unprecedented. In other words, the Founders perceived an intimate relationship between the political words they employed (which reflected their innermost thoughts about politics and government) and the deeds they performed.[8] Thus if we want to discover what was truly revolutionary about the American Revolution, it is necessary first to uncover what these American leaders wrote about government and then to observe what they did about it.

Justification   The clearest exposition of the American revolutionary credo can be found in the Declaration of Independence. In addition to proclaiming separation from Great Britain, the Declaration enunciated the reasons for that separation. The British government, it asserted, had grievously violated the principles of good government. Following John Locke's lead, Thomas Jefferson (the chief author) argued that those principles were twofold: that government must conform to the will of the majority (according to the Declaration's precise language, such a government must be based on "the consent of the governed") and must protect the unalienable rights of all individuals to "life, liberty, and the pursuit of happiness." These principles, in Jefferson's view, established the criteria by which the legitimacy of all governments in all times and places should be measured. A good (or legitimate) government, in other words, draws its authority from the consent of the governed and acts to ensure the unalienable rights of all its citizens. By making human rights the philosophical basis of good government, the Declaration departed significantly from past precedent. Formerly, governments had come into existence to guarantee order, to build empires, to punish impiety, or to enforce obedience. Now, for the first time in history, a political regime dedicated itself unequivocally to the principle of promoting popular rights and liberties.

It followed from the Declaration's principles that governments that repeatedly jeopardized rather than protected those rights forfeited their claim to rule. Having stated this conclusion in the Declaration, the colonists continued to wage their war for independence. Although initially they had desired only to be treated as equal British subjects, with the drafting of the Declaration they insisted on nothing less than complete self-government. Nor would just any government do; they wished ultimately to create a government consistent with the self-evident truths they had pronounced in the Declaration. And these truths, they believed, were applicable far beyond the boundaries of the 13 colonies. Jefferson found *universal* meaning in the enduring words of the document he had drafted:

> May it be to the world, what I believe it will be (to some parts sooner, to others later, but finally to all), the signal of arousing men to burst the chains under which monkish ignorance and superstition had persuaded them to bind themselves and to assume the blessings and security of self-government.[9]

Social and Political Changes   Jefferson's sentiments were expressed in language that ranks with the best revolutionary rhetoric of his or any other time—certainly, it stirred citizens to fight and die for the cause. Even so, it would be a serious mistake to view the American Revolution solely in the context of the fighting that ensued. While the historic battles raged, great social, economic, and religious changes took place. Restrictive inheritance laws such as primogeniture and entail were abolished; large British estates were confiscated and redistributed in smaller holdings; royal restrictions on land settlements were repealed; important steps to secure religious equality and separation of church and state were taken; and old families lost power, their places "taken by new leaders drawn from younger men, from the common people, and from the middle classes."[10] Significantly, all these changes tended to advance the cause of equal liberty.

Important political changes also occurred, as every colony wrote a new constitution. Drafted in the heat of war, these constitutions perpetuated preexisting systems of local self-government (especially in terms of the executive branch) while protecting individual liberties. The concepts and principles incorporated in these documents were then reflected in the Articles of Confederation and, eventually, in the U.S. Constitution. The importance of this preoccupation with the rule of law, or legality, and procedural correctness cannot be overemphasized. What we might call the *constitutional process* culminated in the creation of popular government (government by majority rule) at a time when the people of Europe were still largely subject to the autocratic rule of monarchs. Moreover, the colonists' steadfast concern for constitutionality was instrumental in defusing or preventing conspiracies and cabals that could ultimately have divided the new nation into many feuding political subdivisions.

A Moderate Revolution   In retrospect, the moderation with which the American Revolution was fought seems truly remarkable (so remarkable, in fact, that some political scientists do not classify it as a true revolution). The conflict was marked by a "rare economy of violence when compared to other revolutions."[11] In comparison with later revolutionary conflicts (such as the French Revolution, the Russian Revolution, and the Spanish Civil War), civilian reprisals between insurrectionists and loyalists were mild. Also, the leaders of the American Revolution were never purged or murdered, as so many instigators of later revolutions

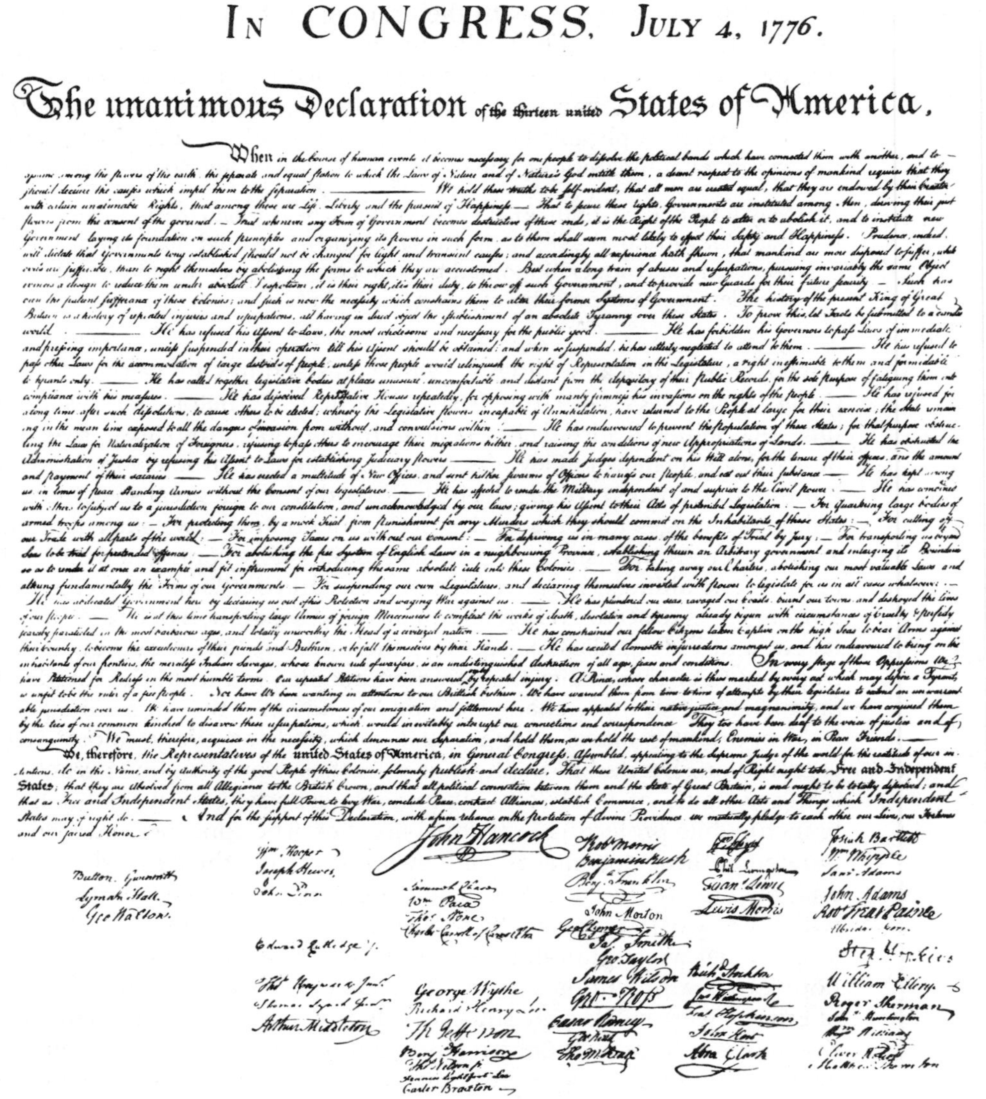
IN CONGRESS, JULY 4, 1776.

The unanimous Declaration of the thirteen united States of America,

When in the Course of human events, it becomes necessary for one people to dissolve the political bands which have connected them with another, and to assume among the powers of the earth, the separate and equal station to which the Laws of Nature and of Nature's God entitle them, a decent respect to the opinions of mankind requires that they should declare the causes which impel them to the separation. — We hold these truths to be self-evident, that all men are created equal, that they are endowed by their Creator with certain unalienable Rights, that among these are Life, Liberty and the pursuit of Happiness. — That to secure these rights, Governments are instituted among Men, deriving their just powers from the consent of the governed, — That whenever any Form of Government becomes destructive of these ends, it is the Right of the People to alter or to abolish it, and to institute new Government, laying its foundation on such principles and organizing its powers in such form, as to them shall seem most likely to effect their Safety and Happiness. Prudence, indeed, will dictate that Governments long established should not be changed for light and transient causes; and accordingly all experience hath shewn, that mankind are more disposed to suffer, while evils are sufferable, than to right themselves by abolishing the forms to which they are accustomed. But when a long train of abuses and usurpations, pursuing invariably the same Object evinces a design to reduce them under absolute Despotism, it is their right, it is their duty, to throw off such Government, and to provide new Guards for their future security. — Such has been the patient sufferance of these Colonies; and such is now the necessity which constrains them to alter their former Systems of Government. The history of the present King of Great Britain is a history of repeated injuries and usurpations, all having in direct object the establishment of an absolute Tyranny over these States. To prove this, let Facts be submitted to a candid world. — He has refused his Assent to Laws, the most wholesome and necessary for the public good. — He has forbidden his Governors to pass Laws of immediate and pressing importance, unless suspended in their operation till his Assent should be obtained; and when so suspended, he has utterly neglected to attend to them. — He has refused to pass other Laws for the accommodation of large districts of people, unless those people would relinquish the right of Representation in the Legislature, a right inestimable to them and formidable to tyrants only. — He has called together legislative bodies at places unusual, uncomfortable, and distant from the depository of their Public Records, for the sole purpose of fatiguing them into compliance with his measures. — He has dissolved Representative Houses repeatedly, for opposing with manly firmness his invasions on the rights of the people. — He has refused for a long time, after such dissolutions, to cause others to be elected; whereby the Legislative powers, incapable of Annihilation, have returned to the People at large for their exercise; the State remaining in the mean time exposed to all the dangers of invasion from without, and convulsions within. — He has endeavoured to prevent the population of these States; for that purpose obstructing the Laws for Naturalization of Foreigners; refusing to pass others to encourage their migrations hither, and raising the conditions of new Appropriations of Lands. — He has obstructed the Administration of Justice, by refusing his Assent to Laws for establishing Judiciary powers. — He has made Judges dependent on his Will alone, for the tenure of their offices, and the amount and payment of their salaries. — He has erected a multitude of New Offices, and sent hither swarms of Officers to harrass our people, and eat out their substance. — He has kept among us, in times of peace, Standing Armies without the Consent of our legislatures. — He has affected to render the Military independent of and superior to the Civil power. — He has combined with others to subject us to a jurisdiction foreign to our constitution, and unacknowledged by our laws; giving his Assent to their Acts of pretended Legislation: — For Quartering large bodies of armed troops among us: — For protecting them, by a mock Trial, from punishment for any Murders which they should commit on the Inhabitants of these States: — For cutting off our Trade with all parts of the world: — For imposing Taxes on us without our Consent: — For depriving us in many cases, of the benefits of Trial by Jury: — For transporting us beyond Seas to be tried for pretended offences: — For abolishing the free System of English Laws in a neighbouring Province, establishing therein an Arbitrary government, and enlarging its Boundaries so as to render it at once an example and fit instrument for introducing the same absolute rule into these Colonies: — For taking away our Charters, abolishing our most valuable Laws, and altering fundamentally the Forms of our Governments: — For suspending our own Legislatures, and declaring themselves invested with power to legislate for us in all cases whatsoever. — He has abdicated Government here, by declaring us out of his Protection and waging War against us. — He has plundered our seas, ravaged our Coasts, burnt our towns, and destroyed the lives of our people. — He is at this time transporting large Armies of foreign Mercenaries to compleat the works of death, desolation and tyranny, already begun with circumstances of Cruelty & perfidy scarcely paralleled in the most barbarous ages, and totally unworthy the Head of a civilized nation. — He has constrained our fellow Citizens taken Captive on the high Seas to bear Arms against their Country, to become the executioners of their friends and Brethren, or to fall themselves by their Hands. — He has excited domestic insurrections amongst us, and has endeavoured to bring on the inhabitants of our frontiers, the merciless Indian Savages, whose known rule of warfare, is an undistinguished destruction of all ages, sexes and conditions. In every stage of these Oppressions We have Petitioned for Redress in the most humble terms: Our repeated Petitions have been answered only by repeated injury. A Prince, whose character is thus marked by every act which may define a Tyrant, is unfit to be the ruler of a free people. Nor have We been wanting in attentions to our British brethren. We have warned them from time to time of attempts by their legislature to extend an unwarrantable jurisdiction over us. We have reminded them of the circumstances of our emigration and settlement here. We have appealed to their native justice and magnanimity, and we have conjured them by the ties of our common kindred to disavow these usurpations, which, would inevitably interrupt our connections and correspondence. They too have been deaf to the voice of justice and of consanguinity. We must, therefore, acquiesce in the necessity, which denounces our Separation, and hold them, as we hold the rest of mankind, Enemies in War, in Peace Friends.

We, therefore, the Representatives of the united States of America, in General Congress, Assembled, appealing to the Supreme Judge of the world for the rectitude of our intentions, do, in the Name, and by Authority of the good People of these Colonies, solemnly publish and declare, That these United Colonies are, and of Right ought to be Free and Independent States; that they are Absolved from all Allegiance to the British Crown, and that all political connection between them and the State of Great Britain, is and ought to be totally dissolved; and that as Free and Independent States, they have full Power to levy War, conclude Peace, contract Alliances, establish Commerce, and to do all other Acts and Things which Independent States may of right do. — And for the support of this Declaration, with a firm reliance on the protection of divine Providence, we mutually pledge to each other our Lives, our Fortunes and our sacred Honor.

John Hancock

Button Gwinnett, Lyman Hall, Geo Walton, Wm Hooper, Joseph Hewes, John Penn, Edward Rutledge, Thos Heyward Junr, Thomas Lynch Junr, Arthur Middleton, Samuel Chase, Wm Paca, Thos Stone, Charles Carroll of Carrollton, George Wythe, Richard Henry Lee, Th Jefferson, Benja Harrison, Thos Nelson jr, Francis Lightfoot Lee, Carter Braxton, Robt Morris, Benjamin Rush, Benja Franklin, John Morton, Geo Clymer, Jas Smith, Geo Taylor, James Wilson, Geo Ross, Caesar Rodney, Geo Read, Tho M:Kean, Wm Floyd, Phil Livingston, Frans Lewis, Lewis Morris, Richd Stockton, Jno Witherspoon, Fras Hopkinson, John Hart, Abra Clark, Josiah Bartlett, Wm Whipple, Saml Adams, John Adams, Robt Treat Paine, Elbridge Gerry, Step Hopkins, William Ellery, Roger Sherman, Saml Huntington, Wm Williams, Oliver Wolcott, Matthew Thornton

July 4, 1776: The American credo put forth in the Declaration of Independence upheld two principles—that government must be based on "the consent of the governed" and that it must protect the rights of all individuals to "life, liberty, and the pursuit of happiness."

would be. To the contrary: "The military chief [Washington] became the first president of the Republic and retired at his own choice; the author of the Revolutionary Manifesto [Jefferson] was its first Secretary of State."[12]

What accounted for the unique orderliness of this revolution? Most important, the colonial leaders combined a Lockean attitude toward revolution with the pursuit of realistic, down-to-earth political goals. By "Lockean attitude," to which we will return later, we mean that, with few exceptions, the Founders regarded the revolution as a necessary evil. It was necessary because they knew of no other way of achieving independence from Great Britain, but it was an evil insofar as it caused suffering, bloodshed, and devastation. The American Revolution remains unique precisely because it was not led by fanatics and zealots who embraced an inflexible ideology or who thought that any means were appropriate to achieve their political ends. Rather, its leaders were contemplative individuals who continually questioned themselves (and one another) about the correctness of what they were doing. Although there was no lack of enthusiasm on the part of the revolutionary leadership, "this enthusiasm was tempered by doubt, introspection, anxiety, and scepticism."[13] In short, the American Revolution never took its own goodness for granted.

These tempered revolutionary values were placed in the service of sober and clear-eyed goals. Essentially, what the colonial leaders wanted from the revolution was separation from the mother country and the formation of a system of government founded on consent and respect for the rights and liberties of the people. Significantly, both these goals fell within the realm of human possibility. The Revolutionary War itself was far from an impossible dream, as the eventual American victory amply demonstrated. And the intertwined concepts of self-government and the protection of citizens' rights, far from being unattainable, had been evolving in the colonies at both the state and township levels well in advance of the revolutionary conflict. But if progressive, incremental changes in government were sought, wholesale changes in the government's form or configuration were avoided. Unlike later revolutionaries, the colonial leaders did not attempt to institute something radically new and different. Understanding the dangers inherent in quixotic or utopian idealism, they knew all too well that "the political pursuit of impossible dreams leads to terror and tyranny in the vain effort to actualize what cannot be."[14]

Far from being an event marked by such terror and tyranny, the American Revolution was, in the words of one authority, "a revolution of sober expectations."[15] Sobriety, moderation, and prudence were the watchwords of this revolution and the chief characteristics of the "well ordered union" the Constitution would later ordain.

The French Revolution: Infinite Expectations

The French Revolution was quite a different affair. For years, France had experienced growing political instability and popular dissatisfaction. Seeking to preserve the sharp class distinctions that marked French society, the aristocracy had repeatedly frustrated attempts at economic and political reform. Furthermore, the government had demonstrated a clear inability to cope with changing circumstances. Even a skilled and intelligent monarch (which Louis XVI certainly was not) would have found it difficult to overcome the liability of governmental institutions that were decentralized and difficult to coordinate. In addition, by the late 1780s, the government was facing increasing difficulties in raising taxes to pay off the massive debt left from earlier wars. And then, just at the wrong time (from the point of view of those in power), economic reversals occurred. Although the economy had been growing, the fruits of that growth were terribly maldistributed. Particularly hard hit were the urban poor and the peasants, many of whom faced the probability of crushing material deprivation rather than the promise of continued economic development.

By 1789, eddies of discontent had swelled into a sea of dissension. Middle- and upper-class reformers demanded both political and social changes. In their most moderate form, these demands included restrictions on class privileges and reform of the system of taxation. Some leaders wanted more radical changes, including the creation of a political order governed by the principles of popular sovereignty. All these demands were put forward at the May 1789 meeting of the *Estates-General*, a giant parliament elected by broad male suffrage and divided into three estates, or houses, representing the clergy, the nobility, and the commoners. After considerable debate (and a good deal of turmoil), a majority of the delegates, led by the numerically preponderant Third (commoner) Estate, formed a popular National Assembly. In addition to asserting the right to approve or reject all taxation, the members of this body demanded an end to aristocratic privileges.

These actions constituted a direct attack on the monarchy. Louis XVI responded with predictable ineptitude, applying just enough force to incense his opponents. When he marshaled his troops in an effort to bar the National Assembly from meeting, the delegates promptly repaired to a nearby indoor tennis court, where they resolved to meet continuously until they succeeded in drafting a constitution. Wavering somewhat, the king made concessions in the area of tax reform several days later but refused to abolish the privileges of the aristocracy. At the same time, he deployed troops in strategic positions. Both these measures proved inadequate. The concessions were too little too late, and the threat of force proved inconsequential. Sporadic outbursts of violence, including the storming of the Bastille, followed swiftly, and as violent activity directed against the king's power became a prominent feature of French political life, Louis XVI was forced to accede to demands for a constitution.

The New Constitution   In the two years it took to draft the French constitution of 1791, an egalitarian spirit swept the land. Aristocratic privileges were abolished, and church land was appropriated. A political document of fundamental importance, the Declaration of the Rights of Man, enshrined a slogan epitomizing the egalitarian spirit of the times: "liberty, equality, fraternity."

The new constitution created a constitutional monarchy. No longer would Louis XVI rule autocratically according to divine right. Although the constitution placed the king at the head of the armed forces and charged him with responsibility for foreign affairs, it assigned most legislative powers to the National Constituent Assembly, which was given the power of the purse as well as the power to declare war. A new elective administration was also created, and voting laws were liberalized.

Thus a stunning democratization of French political and social life was achieved in an amazingly brief period. The king's power, hitherto almost unlim-

July 14, 1789: The storming of the Bastille constituted a direct attack against the monarchy. Louis XVI conceded too little too late, and "liberty, equality, and fraternity" swept France. (Bettmann Archive)

ited, had been undermined, apparently forever, and radical social reforms had been effected.

Political Instability   The constitutional monarchy set up by the 1791 constitution lasted less than one year, during which time the nation floundered without effective political leadership. Naturally, the king despised the new government, which had been imposed on him. (At one point, Louis XVI even tried to flee the country to join opponents of the new government, but he was caught and returned to Paris.) The legislature was staffed by inexperienced legislators because the constitution barred former members of the Constituent Assembly from serving in the new legislature. Additional problems arose when the newly elected local administration failed to perform efficiently and when interests that had lost power under the new reforms (especially the Catholic church and the aristocracy) began to oppose the new regime. A war with Austria and Prussia exacerbated existing difficulties, and the expected economic improvements were not forthcoming. Persistent rumors of the king's imminent return to absolute power swirled through Paris, inspiring a widespread fear of counterrevolution that undermined the political optimism brought on by the reforms.

The Rise of Radicalism   In the chaotic political and social environment of the early 1790s, events moved swiftly. Louis XVI was convicted of treason, deposed, and then beheaded in June 1793. A committee of political radicals, called *Jacobins*, thereupon took over the reins of government. The first priority of the Jacobin leader, Maximilien Robespierre, was to win the war against Austria and Prussia. This aim required military conscription and strict discipline on the battlefield, as well as national unity on the home front. In the ensuing atmosphere of external emergency, all political opposition was considered treasonous. This situation, though perhaps deplorable, was not unexpected—then as now, political repression during times of war was a common phenomenon. But Robespierre was not satisfied simply to enforce national unity. In addition, he wished to create a regime of virtue—to rebuild French society from the ground up, so to speak, by remaking the French citizenry in the image of moral perfection. According to one authority:

> Robespierre wanted a France where there should be neither rich nor poor, where men should not gamble, or get drunk, or commit adultery, cheat, or rob, or kill—where, in short, there would be neither petty nor grand vices—a France ruled by upright and intelligent men elected by the universal suffrage of the people, men wholly without greed or love of office, and delightedly stepping down at yearly intervals to give place to their successors, a France at peace with herself and the world.[16]

However grandiose, Robespierre's utopian idealism was not meant merely as a statement of what *ought* to be; for him, it represented a manifesto to be carried out with ardor and thoroughness. Determined to create a "new citizen," Robespierre could not countenance the goal of individual freedom or the individual pursuit of happiness, as the American revolutionaries had. How could such latitude for individual choice exist in a world divided between absolute good and absolute evil? Robespierre was committed not to the creation of a free country but rather, in his own words, to the establishment of a "despotism of liberty."

The institutionalization of virtue, however, comprised only one aspect of the idealism of the French Revolution. The other aspect was a compassionate revulsion toward the persistent problems of hunger and poverty. Emancipation from economic want—and even the promise of permanent abundance—became an important goal of Robespierre's revolution, which was waged in the name of the oppressed against the selfish interests of the oppressors.[17] Only through such a policy, Robespierre believed, could the development of a virtuous and contented citizenry be ensured.

The New Agenda   To advance virtue and end poverty in the shortest possible time, Robespierre proposed a sweeping reformulation of French life. Governmental institutions, legal arrangements, social practices—everything was to be changed. Even a new calendar was proposed, as a symbol of the belief that a new era of history had dawned. The spirit of change was total—heaven on earth was the ultimate goal. One observer has noted that the reigning spirit was that of "undiluted, enthusiastic, free floating messianism . . . satisfied with nothing less than a radical transformation of the human condition."[18]

The problem with messianism, however, is that only God (or God's messenger) can fulfill its great promises. Robespierre possessed no such divine qualifications. Problems began to surface when he and his colleagues discovered that to proclaim a new order was one thing, but to govern a nation was quite another. Disagreements over policy emerged as bitter disappointments confronted unlimited expectations. Ominously, active opposition to the new rulers began to spread.

The Reign of Terror   Robespierre's response to the growth of opposition and the seemingly intractable difficulties involved in day-to-day government was to reinforce the regime of virtue with the *Reign of Terror*, carried out by the all-powerful Committee of Public Safety. Executions by guillotine became commonplace, particularly in Paris. Originally aimed at the active opponents of the regime, governmental violence soon moved forward with a momentum of its own. It came to include people who shared Robespierre's vision but disagreed with his methods. Later, those who were merely *suspected* of dissenting became victims of the guillotine. Deep distrust enveloped those in power, as the survivors feared for their own safety. Eventually, this collective fear led to the overthrow (and execution) of Robespierre himself. During his yearlong rule, some 40,000 people had been summarily executed.

Consequences of the Revolution   The results of the French Revolution are not easy to evaluate. Clearly, it did not achieve its desired ends. After Robespierre's fall, a corrupt and incompetent government known as the Directory assumed power. In 1799, that regime gave way to the dictatorship of Napoleon Bonaparte, who managed to restore order and stability. Under Napoleon, France tried to conquer all of Europe in a series of ambitious wars that ultimately led to the country's defeat and Napoleon's downfall.

Thus no popular government followed on the heels of the French Revolution. After Napoleon's deposition, in fact, the monarchy was reinstituted. Many worthwhile and long-lasting changes did come about, however. For instance, the monarchy installed in power in 1815 was significantly more limited in its powers than the prerevolutionary regime had been. Moreover, important social and political reforms stemming from the revolutionary era were retained, and the government was now more centralized and more efficient. Despite these changes, however, the restored monarchy stood in sharp contrast to the egalitarian vision of a new society that had inspired Robespierre and his followers.

The Two Revolutions Compared

If the American Revolution can be characterized as a revolution of sober goals, the French Revolution might be described as one of infinite expectations. In the beginning, the French revolutionaries believed that nothing was impossible for the pure of heart. Their goals were basically utopian, and to realize their utopian goals, they were forced to use extraordinary methods, including terror. Revealingly, America's best-known radical, Thomas Paine, found himself in a French prison during the revolution because his politics were not sufficiently extreme! In the 13 colonies, most of the revolutionaries were political moderates. In France, moderates were executed or imprisoned.

The French Revolution fell short of its American counterpart only in terms of political results gained. The American Revolution, with its more modest aims, managed to produce the first great example of republican government in the modern age. France had no such luck. Yet subsequent revolutionary movements have been influenced more by the French than the American example.[19]

It is entirely understandable why the French Revolution—with its concern for the eradication of poverty and suffering and its compassion for the oppressed—has fired the imagination of revolutionaries everywhere. But if concrete and lasting results are to be achieved, political ends must be realistic and must be capable of being accomplished by humane means; otherwise, the impossible dreams of utopian idealists can turn into nightmares. Revolutions cannot be evaluated according to their original intentions; rather, they must be judged by their ultimate consequences. The terror that grew out of the French Revolution bears witness to the eventual failure of almost all revolutions motivated by utopian goals.

THE DESIRABILITY OF REVOLUTION: BURKE, PAINE, AND LOCKE

Insofar as such generalizations are possible, we might ask whether revolution is likely to lead to a happier and healthier state of individual or collective well-being. More than 200 years ago, British conservative Edmund Burke and American revolutionary Thomas Paine carried on a memorable debate over this question. Much of this debate coincided with the early phase of the French Revolution, and the crux of their dispute centered on whether that revolution was ultimately in the interest of the French people, in whose name it was being waged. From disagreement over this question, they moved inevitably to the more abstract political question of whether revolutions were generally useful or detrimental to society.

Burke's Position

The French Revolution inspired Edmund Burke to write perhaps the most famous critique of revolution ever written in the English language, *Reflections on the Revolution in France* (1790). Burke did not believe that the French Revolution resulted from deep-seated economic and social forces. To his mind, the real revolutionaries had been the philosophers who had expounded the subversive doctrine of rationalism and worshiped the god of science. By teaching that government existed to fulfill certain simple goals (for example, to secure the rights of man), he argued, they had created misleading impressions—most important, that radical change almost always brought great improvements. This way of thinking undercut what Burke believed to be two of the most important foundations of political society: religion and tradition.

Burke argued that dangerous political abstractions were at the heart of the French Revolution. By grossly oversimplifying politics and engendering unwarranted expectations at odds with French history and tradition, simplistic concepts such as "liberty, equality, fraternity" endangered the public order, on which all other political values and virtues ultimately rested. Good order, he noted, is the foundation of all good things.

The science of good government—how to run it, maintain it, or reform it—could not be mastered through philosophical speculations, Burke contended. He saw government as an "experimental science" whose practitioners must have the wisdom and insight born of experience. And experience, by its very nature, cannot be acquired overnight; it must be accumulated, nurtured, cherished, and, above all, transmitted from generation to generation. Burke's view implied a veneration of the past as well as a respect for age and achievement. Society, to his mind, was an intricate tapestry of laboriously handcrafted institutions possessing an inner logic and perpetuated by the force of habit, custom, and convention.

This sober view of government, and of human capacities and limitations, led Burke to stress the importance of pragmatism and prudence in politics. Prudence, he said, was the "first of all virtues." And as for pragmatism, he maintained that given the complexity of humanity and society, no simple, all-embracing political formula could work the kind of profound changes promised by the French theorists.

Finally, Burke criticized the extreme impatience of those who glorify revolution. Arguing in favor of gradual and deliberate reform, he warned that unless political change occurred slowly and circumspectly, the main mass of the population would end up in worse straits than ever: "Time is required to produce that union of minds which alone can produce all the good we aim at. Our patience will achieve more than our force."[20]

By promising more than any political order can ever deliver and by raising unrealistic expectations for some immediate utopian breakthrough, the masses may be dazzled by visions of a bountiful (but unattainable) future and blinded to the wisdom of the past. In short, though politics can be understood as the "art of the possible," in the distorted mirror of revolution it becomes the science of the impossible.

Paine's Rebuttal

Thomas Paine attempted to refute the Burkean view of revolution in his *Rights of Man*, written in two parts in February 1792 and addressed specifically to Burke. In defining the legitimacy of popular revolution, Paine stressed the many injustices perpetrated by the British monarchy on the American colonists.

For Paine, in fact, tyranny was equated with monarchy. The motivating force behind all monarchies, he declared, was ignorance,[21] and therefore monarchy was wrong in principle.

All hereditary government is in its nature tyranny. An heritable crown, or an heritable throne, or by what other fanciful name such things may be called, have no other significant explanation than that mankind are heritable property. To inherit a government, is to inherit the people, as if they were flocks and herds.[22]

In another passage, he wrote:

When we survey the wretched condition of man under the monarchical and hereditary systems of government, dragged from his home by one power, or drived by another, and impoverished by taxes more than by enemies, it becomes evident that those systems are bad, and that a general revolution in the principle and construction of government is necessary.[23]

In support of these generalizations, Paine cited numerous examples of monarchical injustice and corruption. The greatest injustice, he believed, was the denial of the people's right to choose their own government. It seemed obvious to him that the people should in no way be bound by their ancestors' decisions. "Every age and generation must be free to act for itself, in all cases, as the ages and generations which preceded it. . . . The vanity and presumption of governing beyond the grave, is the most ridiculous and insolent of all tyrannies."[24]

Needless to say, Paine saw revolution in France as emphatically just. In seeking to overthrow the monarchy, he contended, the French people were merely exercising a fundamental right (which grew out of their equal, natural right to liberty). Paine possessed an almost religious faith in the essential goodness and wisdom of the people. This faith pushed him to the conclusion that when the French Revolution is compared with that of other countries, it becomes apparent "that *principles* and not *persons*, were the meditated objects of destruction."[25]

The Lockean View

While Burke abhorred popular revolution, Paine glorified it.[26] Roughly a century earlier, John Locke had taken something of a middle ground between these two extremes in his *Second Treatise on Government*. Locke began with the premise that to escape the inconveniences of anarchy in the state of nature, human beings consent to be governed. For Locke, then, consent formed the basis for both civil society and formal government, and the latter existed chiefly to protect the rights deemed essential to human life. He then raised the question, What happens if the government, contrary to its *raison d'être*, endangers the life, liberty, and property of its citizens? In such a case, he concluded, the government has exercised "force without right," and the people have the right to resist. In his words:

The end of Government is the good of Mankind, and which is *best for Mankind*, that the People should be always expos'd to the boundless will of Tyranny, or that the Rulers should be sometimes liable to be oppos'd, when they grow exorbitant in the use of their power, and imploy it for the destruction, and not the preservation of the Properties of their People?[27]

Locke was no glorifier of revolution. He admonished that popular rebellion should not be launched on a mere impulse. The people will accept individual errors and instances of misrule, he asserted; what they will not accept is "a long train of Abuses, Prevarications and Artifices."[28] Locke even suggested that his doctrine of revolution could serve as a deterrent to revolution: Awareness of the people's right to rebellion, he pointed out, would cause governments to think twice before engaging in repressive actions. Finally, he noted that cognizance of the *right* of the people to revolt against an oppressive government amounts to little more than the recognition that under sufficiently oppressive conditions, the people *will* revolt. Whether or not such a right is acknowledged by the government, in other words, in the end is unimportant:

> If the majority of the people are persuaded in their Consciences, that the Laws, and with them their Estates, Liberties, and Lives are in danger, and perhaps their Religion, too, how they will be hindered from resisting illegal force used against them, I cannot tell. This is an Inconvenience, I confess that attends all Governments.[29]

So in solemnly proclaiming the **right to revolution,** Locke seemingly did little more than endorse what he saw as an inevitability of political life. That point, however, does not diminish the importance of Locke's theory. His clear assertion of the people's right to revolt was itself revolutionary in the late seventeenth century. Even in England, where a few decades earlier King Charles I had been beheaded, the question of whether or not dynastic rulers had a divine right to wield the scepter and command the sword was still being debated. In most other European nation-states, monarchs took the doctrine of divine right for granted. Not surprisingly, these kings did not trifle with anything so mundane as the will of the people, for they believed that their authority stemmed from the will of God.

Locke's theory of revolution helped to sound the death knell for the doctrine of divine right. Revolution, Locke claimed, becomes necessary when government acts contrary to its reason for being. Does revolution ensure good government? Not necessarily—it may lead only to anarchy or more tyranny. Does revolution create the *possibility* of better government? Definitely. Often, Locke declared, only by revolting can the people replace tyranny and seize the opportunity to create a new and better government, one that will protect their rights to life, liberty, and property.

Thus Locke made no utopian claims about the relationship between revolution and political revitalization. As he saw it, revolutions may stem from the desire for better government, but they cannot guarantee that happy result. New governments, he argued, are invariably new only in the sense that they supersede previous governments. Like Aristotle before him, Locke assumed the existence of a finite number of governmental forms. So revolutions could not be considered as quests for new forms of government. Rather, they should be understood quite literally as revolutions (*revolvings*) from one enduring form of government (tyranny) to another.[30]

Revolution, thus defined, hardly seemed a romantic endeavor. In Locke's view, it involved the exchange of one imperfect form of government for another, perhaps less imperfect form; it invariably encompassed great changes in the larger society; and it implied in almost every case the use of political force and violence. The tendency of revolutions toward anarchy and upheaval meant that the process was to be feared, even if the goal was eminently desirable.

THE CAUSES OF REVOLUTION

Locke held that revolutions are necessary and proper when citizens simply cannot endure any more. But what specifically is it they "cannot endure"? What, in other words, causes citizens to discard ingrained political habits and support revolution?

The Traditional Explanation

To many observers, both history and common sense suggest that injustices perpetrated by government over a prolonged period foster the conditions in which the seeds of revolution can germinate. This traditional explanation of the cause of revolution originated with Aristotle, who observed in the fourth century B.C. that although sedition may spring from small occasions, it ordinarily does not turn on small issues. The spark that ignites a revolution, in other words, should not be confused with the underlying causes of revolt. In most cases, Aristotle postulated, revolutions are caused by the administration of unequal justice. Under every political order, he argued, competition for honors and wealth may give rise to the popular belief that one or both have not been fairly distributed. Revolution, then, may grow out of the tension created between the numerous poor (democrats), who want equality, and the wealthy few (oligarchs), who wish to preserve their power and riches.

Aristotle's concern over the perennial tension between rich and poor in political life established a theme in Western political thought that has gained importance with the passage of time. James Madison, for example, declared in *The Federalist*, No. 10, that the "most common and durable source of faction is the various and unequal distribution of property" and then set out to develop a theory of government under which this common source of political tension might be lessened. A half century later, Karl Marx declared inequality in wealth to be the ultimate cause of all revolutions. Revolution, according to Marx, was synonymous with class warfare and invariably stemmed from pervasive injustice. As the economic distance between the wealthy capitalists and the impoverished workers increased, he believed, so did the possibility of revolution.

Modern Theories

To say that revolution grows out of injustice is to describe revolutions in philosophical terms. This view emphasizes the importance of a sense of injustice as the cause of action: The *idea* that the government has acted unfairly or ineffectively is seen as a principal cause of revolution. Modern-day social scientists, however, generally prefer psychological, sociological, or political explanations to philosophical ones. At the same time, they try to explain the revolutionary process itself in terms more precise than those used by earlier political philosophers.[31]

Many social scientists seek to identify particular conditions capable of producing social stress and individual unrest. The social and political pressures brought on by modernization, war, rapid population increase, significant technological change, inflation, economic collapse, and the introduction of a new ideology have all been cited as possible preconditions for revolution. As a next step, researchers try to isolate some key variable that is particularly affected by the new condition. Some researchers view the frustration of certain individuals in society as such a key variable, theorizing that *psychological* dislocations among members of particular groups or subgroups within society are the principal sparks for revolutions. Other social scientists argue that the ability of the social system to adapt to changing conditions ordinarily dictates whether or not revolution will break out. Theirs is a *sociological* explanation of revolution. Yet other researchers cite as the crucial factor in revolutions the conflicts among important political leaders and groups that often occur under changing conditions. The argument that revolutions stem from the attempt of one individual or group to gain political power and oust competitors furnishes a *political* explanation of revolution.

There is a great deal of truth in each of these explanations of the causes of revolution. When rapidly changing conditions rock a society, people are apt to become distressed, the social system is likely to be disrupted, and competition among political leaders is bound to intensify. In such situations, the probability of revolution naturally increases as the questions of who should rule and for what purposes come to the fore. Throughout history, people have demonstrated a willingness to fight and die for what they believed to be the proper answers to these questions.

The Social Psychology of Revolution

What is it that persuades an ordinary individual to disregard the strong social pressure for conformity and participate in a revolutionary movement? Karl Marx held that desperation caused by poverty and social alienation was the chief psychological spur to revolutionary action, and his explanation has been widely accepted in modern times. A few years before Marx outlined this position in *The Communist Manifesto* (1848), however, Alexis de Tocqueville had offered an alternative view. In studying the French Revolution, Tocqueville observed that "it was precisely in those parts of France where there had been the most improvement that popular discontent ran the highest. There, economic and social improvement had taken place, and political pressure had lessened, but still there existed the greatest amount of unrest."[32]

From this observation, he concluded that economic improvement led to revolution because once the people saw that some improvement was possible, they inevitably yearned for more. No longer were they willing to put up with inconveniences and annoyances—only *real* improvement, *immediate* improvement, would satisfy them. Thus is the incentive to revolution born, Tocqueville argued.

The positions of Marx and Tocqueville seem incompatible, but in 1962, James

The Patterns of Revolution

BY THE 1930s, scholarly students of revolutions had identified a common pattern of events in the development of revolutions. The pattern has held up remarkably well, although the American Revolution proved to be something of an exception.

1. Intellectuals (writers, lawyers, teachers, clergy) oppose the regime and demand reforms.

2. Just before the regime falls, the old government attempts to meet criticism by adopting reforms.

3. The actual fall of the regime begins with an acute political crisis brought on by the government's inability to deal with some economic, military, or political problem.

4. After the old government falls, and after a period of brief euphoria, the revolutionary opposition fragments and becomes disunited.

5. The first group to seize power consists of moderate reformers.

6. The moderates (and their policies) create more radical opponents.

7. The great changes in organization and ruling ideology occur when the radicals gain political power and replace the more moderate rulers.

8. Prevailing social disorder and the implementation of radical control significantly increase coercion and state-authorized violence.

9. The struggle between radicals and moderates (and between defenders and opponents of the revolution) frequently allows military leaders to move into leadership positions.

10. The radical phase of the revolution eventually gives way to pragmatism and a more moderate pursuit of progress.

Despite its usefulness, this discovery of a pattern does not answer the fundamental question of why revolutions occur.

SOURCE: Adapted from Jack A. Goldstone, "The Comparative and Historical Study of Revolutions," in *Revolution: Theoretical, Comparative, and Historical Studies*, ed. Jack A. Goldstone (Orlando, Fla.: Harcourt Brace Jovanovich, 1986), pp. 2–5.

C. Davies wrote a celebrated article in which he suggested that "both ideas have explanatory and possibly predictive value, if they are juxtaposed and put in the proper time sequence."[33] Davies came to this provocative conclusion after making a careful study of Dorr's Rebellion of 1842, the Russian Revolution of 1917, and the Egyptian Revolution of 1952. After discerning in these events a remarkably similar pattern of revolutionary development, he concluded that revolutions are most likely to erupt when conditions have been getting better for a prolonged period of time and then suddenly take a sharp turn for the worse. Elaborating on Davies's thesis, Raymond Tanter and Manus Midlarsky subsequently argued that the *rates* of earlier economic growth (and the speed of any economic decline) are especially significant factors in this regard. The higher the growth rate in per capita gross national product prior to a revolutionary upheaval and "the sharper the reversal immediately prior to the revolution," they declared, "the greater the duration and violence of the revolution."[34] In other words, revolutions stem not so much from terrible suffering as from crushing disappointment. Intense discontent, bred by the failure to acquire the goods and experience the conditions of life to which people believe they are rightfully entitled, induces them to revolt.[35]

New Insights into the Causes of Revolution

Several more recent studies have shed new light on the causes of revolution. The overall aim of these studies is to discover why conditions that cause economic dislocations, political polarization, and psychological stress sometimes produce revolutions and sometimes lead to less dramatic manifestations of social tension. In general, the theories advanced to explain this phenomenon grow out of case studies of particular revolutions. Although they offer no comprehensive explanation of the causes of revolution, they help to illuminate the origins of at least some revolutions.

Revolution: When and Where?   Not every society, it seems, runs the same risk of revolution during times of stress; certain kinds of states apparently run a much greater risk of revolution than others. Particularly revolution-prone, it has been argued, are *agrarian-bureaucratic states,* "societies in which a more or less centralized bureaucracy, with the aid of locally powerful landlords, subsists on the surplus of a predominantly agricultural economy."[36] Such societies tend to suffer from certain structural or institutional weaknesses. Government elites and landlords may clash over the division of the agricultural surplus (profits versus taxes). The peasants may clash with both groups if, as is often the case, land is maldistributed. Finally, the primary source of the nation's wealth—agriculture—cannot easily be increased in times of war or domestic upheaval and is especially sensitive to the vagaries of nature. These potential economic and political trouble spots can become causes of revolution under the right circumstances.

The Importance of Structural Features   To identify the specific type of agrarian society most prone to revolution, researchers have subjected the social, economic, and political structures of such societies to systematic scrutiny. Often, the evidence has been inconclusive and the findings contradictory. For example, are landless peasants or peasants with modest holdings more likely to join revolutionary movements? Similarly, is the pattern of land ownership the key variable, or do the degree and type of peasant organization matter most? Researchers have disagreed widely on the answers to these questions.[37]

These disagreements aside, recent studies provide a number of valuable insights into the structural causes of revolution. For instance, it has been argued convincingly that where the governmental bureaucracy includes officials drawn from the rich, landholding class, the landed interests are often able to block reforms designed to defuse a serious—and potentially revolutionary—domestic crisis.[38] By pointing to a particular set of structures (such as an entrenched bureaucracy with strong ties to the landholding elite) in the context of a particular kind of society (agrarian-bureaucratic), this type of analysis helps to explain why, in the face of social, economic, or political dislocations, some nations undergo the ordeal of revolution but others do not.

Foreign Influence   Studies also indicate that nations suffering from internal disorders are particularly prone to revolution if they are simultaneously affected by certain important outside influences.[39] These influences can be categorized as follows.

War   Nations involved in major wars, especially if they come out on the losing side, appear to be prone to outbreaks of revolutionary activity. Historically, many revolutions have been preceded by military setbacks. The list includes the seventeenth-century Puritan revolution in England, the Paris Commune of 1870, both Russian revolutions (1905 and 1917), the fascist seizure of power in Italy after World War I, the National Socialist (Nazi) revolution in Germany, and the Chinese Revolution of the early twentieth century.[40] One investigator counted no fewer than 19 revolutions following wartime defeats in Europe alone between 1204 and 1919.[41]

Nations that have waged costly wars run a greater risk of revolution for two principal reasons. In material terms, a country is usually much worse off after a long war. As one expert points out, "The general dislocation caused by war, the material losses and human sacrifices create a climate conducive to radical change"; moreover, "a large section of the population has been armed; human life seems considerably less valuable than in peacetime."[42] And from a psychological standpoint, military defeats have often paved the way for revolution. Gamal Abdel Nasser's rise to power in Egypt in the early 1950s, for instance, was made possible largely by the popular sentiment that inferior leadership had led to the country's defeat in the 1948–1949 war with Israel. Then, too, Adolf Hitler's rise to power in Germany in the early 1930s was aided in part by the widespread feeling that Germany had been betrayed by internal enemies in World War I.

Foreign Economic Penetration   Economic challenges can also be highly destabilizing, especially to nations at a comparatively low level of industrial development. An influx of foreign capital in such countries can induce changes in state and landlord behavior that may in turn lead to popular revolt. For example, landlords may decide to mechanize agricultural production, or the state may adopt policies aimed at encouraging the production of crops for export rather than for local consumption in order to earn the foreign exchange necessary to launch an industrialization drive. In either case, landless or land-poor peasants may be forced to move from their traditional rural homes to the unfamiliar surroundings of the city in search of jobs. Social disruption and rapid, ill-planned urbanization often result from this migratory pattern. Adequate housing, sanitation, medical, educational, and other facilities are usually lacking in the cities. In many Third World nations today, this process is starkly evident in the squalor of suburban slums that ring many major cities. To cite one example, it has been estimated that at current rates of growth, the population of Mexico City may reach 32 million by the year 2000.[43] It is not difficult to understand how mass discontent can reach dangerous levels under such conditions.

Instability in Neighboring States   Revolutions sometimes seem to spread from one society to another. The French Revolution touched off political instability in Germany, Belgium, and Ireland; the revolutionary disturbances that rocked Paris in July 1830 ignited insurrections in Poland, Belgium, Italy, Switzerland, Germany, Spain, and Portugal; and the years 1848 and 1918–1919 were marked by widespread European political unrest. The most spectacular example of this phenomenon, however, occurred in the quarter century following World War II, when anticolonialist movements spread swiftly and inexorably through Africa and Asia.

Two major explanations have been advanced for this phenomenon. First, whenever revolutions begin to take shape, popular expectations and past promises are constantly pushed to the forefront of social consciousness, and such expectations and promises often cut across national boundaries. Visions of national independence, economic security, or greater freedom may stir hearts and raise hopes everywhere. In addition, the dangers of economic and social dislocation may seem less threatening to ordinary citizens as revolutions occur politically and geographically closer to home.

Governmental Weakness   Signs of rising popular discontent—the desertion of elites, increasing criticism from intellectuals, coup plotting within the mili-

In December 1989, the wave of revolutions rolling across eastern Europe struck Romania where, for over two decades, the nepotistic dictatorship of President Nicolae Ceauşescu had victimized the society and wrecked the economy. Ceauşescu and his wife, Elena, were caught trying to flee the country, given a mock trial, and executed. Romania's revolution was especially violent and so far has failed to bring any improvements in the plight of the Romanian people. (Eric Gaillard/Bettmann)

tary—can all cause fear and insecurity among the rulers. Beleaguered governments react to perceived internal threats in different ways. Sometimes they become more repressive; sometimes they ease up. Surprisingly, the latter course is the more dangerous, for it gives the impression of governmental weakness.

In his study of the French Revolution, Alexis de Tocqueville noted that French citizens took up arms against the government precisely when the government began easing its crackdown. He concluded that "generally speaking, the most perilous moment for a bad government is one when it seeks to mend its ways."[44] Tocqueville believed that underlying this paradox (as well as his contention that reform, not repression, is the great accomplice of revolution) is a psychological truth:

> Patiently endured so long as it seemed beyond redress, a grievance comes to appear intolerable once the possibility of removing it crosses men's minds. . . . For the mere fact that certain abuses have been remedied draws attention to the others and now appears more galling; people may suffer less, but their sensibility is exacerbated.[45]

In sum, tyrants cannot afford to institute reforms because to do so would be to admit past injustices and to activate "the rancor and cupidity of the populace."[46]

Modern studies have provided some support for Tocqueville's observations. In a major analysis of the role of the armed forces in revolutionary episodes, one writer argued that revolution never succeeds where the armed forces remain loyal to the government and are effectively employed.[47] Where internal security measures are applied too late, too haphazardly, or as the last resort of a desperate government, there is a good chance that official acts of repression may only make matters worse. Apparently, governments that shrink from the systematic use of physical force in revolutionary situations run the greatest risk of being overthrown.

Toward a Comprehensive Theory of Revolution?   If we put all the factors together, we come up with a reasonably good idea of the kind of nation that is susceptible to revolution. When great economic or political stress affects an agricultural-bureaucratic state, when that nation displays certain structural attributes (such as peasants who live in highly organized communities), when the nation is also significantly affected by foreign influences such as instability in neighboring nations or a past war, and if the government, at the critical moment, loses its nerve and refuses to resort to force to preserve its power, the nation in question is a good candidate for revolution. This does not mean that revolution is certain in such cases. Neither does it mean that nations possessing only some of these characteristics might not have a revolution. The new insights on the causes of revolution are only hints: They help social scientists to determine where revolutions are likely, not where they are inevitable.

Summary

In political terms, a revolution involves a significant change in the form of a nation's government. Such changes have become increasingly common in many parts of the world during the modern era.

There are two basic revolutionary traditions, the American and the French. The American Revolution was a limited revolution with limited aims. The French revolutionary leaders, unlike their more pragmatic American counterparts, sought nothing less than a radical and complete change in the social, political, and moral fabric of their country.

The question of whether revolution is desirable has been fiercely debated since the late eighteenth century, when Edmund Burke stressed the many dangers associated with revolution and Thomas Paine emphasized its many benefits. Earlier, John Locke had taken a more moderate position; to Locke, revolution was necessary and justified when a government became oppressive.

The precise causes of revolution are difficult to isolate. Aristotle argued that injustice lay at the root of popular rebellion. Modern social scientists have stressed the psychological, sociological, and political causes of revolution. There has also been disagreement over what convinces the ordinary citizen to participate in a revolution. Karl Marx contended that worsening economic and social conditions led to participation in revolutions; Alexis de Tocqueville asserted that improving conditions were to blame, for they caused individual hopes to outrun social reality. A modern view was put forth by James C. Davies, who combined Marx's and Tocqueville's positions in arguing that revolutions are most likely to erupt when sharp economic or social reversals follow a period of rising expectations and moderate improvements in conditions. More recent studies on the causes of revolution emphasize the structural weakness in societies where traditional values, institutions, and economic and social relationships come under outside pressures.

Key Terms

revolution	Jacobins	right to revolution
Estates-General	Reign of Terror	agrarian-bureaucratic states

Review Questions

1. What is the meaning of the word *revolution*? Have revolutions become more or less prevalent in the twentieth century in comparison with previous eras?

2. Compare the American Revolution with the French Revolution. In what important respects did they differ?

3. In the debate over the desirability of revolution between Edmund Burke and Thomas Paine, what position did each take? What were Burke's chief arguments? How did Paine respond?

4. What was John Locke's view of revolution? Why did he assert the right of citizens to overthrow their government? In what sense does Locke occupy a middle ground between Paine and Burke?

5. According to Aristotle, what is the principal cause of revolution? How have modern social scientists sought to go beyond Aristotle's philosophical insights into revolution?

6. Has contemporary research shed any new light on the causes of revolution? If so, have any common elements arisen from recent theoretical research, or are the findings hopelessly contradictory?

7. At the level of a society as a whole, how do revolutions typically develop?

8. What theories have been advanced to explain how and why individuals become sufficiently disenchanted to join a revolutionary movement?

Recommended Reading

BRINTON, CRANE. *The Anatomy of Revolution* (rev. ed.). New York: Vintage Books, 1965. A classic study of revolution that contains valuable historical insights into the causes and signs of revolution.

DAVIES, JAMES C. "Toward a Theory of Revolution." *American Sociological Review*, February 1962, pp. 5–18. An influential essay that contends that sudden economic reversals, not oppression, cause revolutions.

GLADSTONE, JACK A. (ed.). *Revolutions: Theoretical, Comparative, and Historical Studies*. Orlando, Fla.: Harcourt Brace Jovanovich, 1986. A fine collection of readings, many of which examine specific revolutions.

GREENE, THOMAS. *Comparative Revolutionary Movements* (3rd ed.). Englewood Cliffs, N.J.: Prentice Hall, 1990. A wide-ranging discussion of revolution and the extent and limits of our knowledge of this phenomenon.

GURR, TED. *Why Men Rebel*. Princeton, N.J.: Princeton University Press, 1970. Gurr argues that citizens' perceptions of relative deprivation cause revolution.

SKOCPOL, THEDA. *States and Social Revolutions: A Comparative Analysis of France, Russia, and China*. Cambridge: Cambridge University Press, 1979. A thorough examination of why revolutions occur that emphasizes the importance of community structure and international pressure.

Notes

1. Jack A. Goldstone, "Revolutions in World History," in *Revolutions: Theoretical, Comparative, and Historical Studies*, ed. Jack A. Goldstone (Orlando, Fla.: Harcourt Brace Jovanovich, 1986), p. 320.

2. Quoted in Thomas Greene, *Comparative Revolutionary Movements* (Englewood Cliffs, N.J.: Prentice Hall, 1974), p. 5.

3. Ibid., p. 5.

4. Ibid., p. 6.

5. Irving Kristol, "The American Revolution as a Successful Revolution," in *Readings in American Democracy*, ed. Paul Peterson (Dubuque, Iowa: Kendall/Hunt, 1979), pp. 52–53.

6. Cecilia Kenyon, "Republicanism and Radicalism in the American Revolution: An Old-fashioned Interpretation," in *The Reinterpretation of the American Revolution, 1763–1789*, ed. J. Greene (New York: Harper & Row, 1968), p. 291.

7. See, for instance, Bernard Bailyn, "Political Experience and Enlightenment in Eighteenth-Century America," in *Reinterpretation of the American Revolution*, ed. J. Greene, pp. 282–283.

8. Martin Diamond, "The Revolution of Sober Expectations," in *Readings in American Democracy*, ed. Paul Peterson, p. 66.

9. Jefferson to Roger C. Weightman, June 24, 1826, in *The Political Writings of Thomas Jefferson: Representative Samples*, ed. Edward Dumbauld (Indianapolis: Bobbs-Merrill, 1965), p. 9.

10. Benjamin Wright, *Consensus and Continuity, 1776–1787* (New York: Norton, 1967), p. 3. Wright here relies on the work of J. Franklin Jameson.

11. Ibid., p. 1.

12. Ibid.

13. Kristol, "The American Revolution," p. 53.

14. Diamond, "The Revolution of Sober Expectations," p. 73.

15. Ibid., p. 65.

16. Crane Brinton, *The Anatomy of Revolution* (New York: Vintage Books, 1965), pp. 122–123.

17. Hannah Arendt, *On Revolution* (New York: Penguin, 1976), p. 60.

18. Kristol, "The American Revolution," p. 6.

19. Ibid., p. 61.

20. Edmund Burke, *Reflections on the Revolution in France* (Indianapolis: Library of Liberal Arts, 1955), p. 197.

21. Thomas Paine, "The Rights of Man," in *Thomas Paine: Representative Selections*, ed. H. Clark (New York: Hill and Wang, 1967), p. 159.

22. Ibid., pp. 184–185.

23. Ibid., p. 162.

24. Ibid., p. 61.

25. Ibid., p. 70.

26. Nonetheless, Burke became something of a supporter of the American cause in the Revolutionary War, urging his nation to recognize the legitimacy of the Americans' grievances.

27. John Locke, "An Essay Concerning the True Original Extent and End of Civil Government," in *Two Treatises on Government* (New York: New American Library, 1963), p. 466.

28. Ibid., p. 463.

29. Ibid., pp. 452–453.

30. See Joseph Cropsey, *Political Philosophy and the Issues of Politics* (Chicago: University of Chicago Press, 1977), pp. 157–162.

31. As has been pointed out by Jack A. Goldstone in "Theories of Revolution: The Third Revolution," *World Politics,* April 1980, pp. 425–453.

32. Alexis de Tocqueville, *The Old Regime and the French Revolution* (Garden City, N.Y.: Doubleday, 1955), p. 176.

33. James C. Davies, "Toward a Theory of Revolution," *American Sociological Review,* February 1962, p. 6.

34. Raymond Tanter and Manus Midlarsky, "A Theory of Revolution," *Journal of Conflict Resolution* 11, no. 3 (1967), p. 272 and tab. 6.

35. Ted Gurr, *Why Men Rebel* (Princeton, N.J.: Princeton University Press, 1970), pp. 3–21.

36. Ibid., p. 440. See also Theda Skocpol, *States and Social Revolution: A Comparative Analysis of France, Russia, and China* (Cambridge: Cambridge University Press, 1979).

37. Goldstone, "Theories of Revolution," p. 452.

38. For instance, Skocpol, *States and Social Revolution,* p. 249.

39. Goldstone, "Theories of Revolution," p. 435.

40. Walter Lacqueur, "Revolution," in *International Encyclopedia of the Social Sciences* (New York: Macmillan/Free Press, 1968), p. 501.

41. Robert Hunter, *Revolution: Why? How? When?* (New York: Harper & Row, 1940), p. 126.

42. Lacqueur, "Revolution," p. 501.

43. Charles Kegley, Jr., and Eugene Wittkopf, *World Politics: Trend and Transformation* (New York: St. Martin's Press, 1985), p. 270.

44. Tocqueville, *The Old Regime,* p. 176.

45. Ibid.

46. Ibid., p. 187.

47. D. E. H. Russell, *Rebellion, Revolution and Armed Forces: A Comparative Study of Fifteen Countries with Special Emphasis on Cuba and South Africa* (Orlando, Fla.: Academic Press, 1974).

CHAPTER 17

TERRORISM

WEAPON OF THE WEAK

(Philippe Ledru/Sygma)

ON JULY 24, 1986, some 31 innocent people were killed and 33 more wounded when a parcel exploded on a packed bus in northern Sri Lanka. It was the second bus bombing there in three days. Far away, in the West Bank city of Jericho, 13 Israeli youths on a bicycle outing were injured when someone threw a hand grenade at them from a rooftop. On the same day, police shot and killed Roberto Porfili at the pope's summer villa in Italy after Porfili, brandishing an ax, threw a bag of garbage at them. " 'This package is for you and the pope,' Porfili shouted as the police guards, *fearing a terrorist bomb attack,* ducked for safety," according to the United Press International wire story.[1] It was a typical day around the world.

None of these stories made the headlines in most American newspapers because by the mid-1980s, terrorism had become an everyday occurrence. The three incidents were unrelated; they happened in three different parts of the world and appeared to have little in common. Two were clearly terrorists acts; the other may have been a criminal act perpetrated by a madman—like John Hinckley's attempt to assassinate President Reagan. The security guards at the pope's villa did not shoot Porfili for throwing a bag of garbage: They assumed he was a terrorist. Why? Italian society has been particularly hard hit by terrorist violence since the 1970s. Five years earlier, in May 1981, a Turkish terrorist, Mehmet Ali Agca, shot and seriously wounded Pope John Paul II in St. Peter's Square in the Vatican. Three years before that, Italy's Red Brigades had kidnapped and eventually murdered former Christian Democratic Prime Minister Aldo Moro. Typically, terrorists strike swiftly and without warning. Security forces in societies afflicted by terrorism have learned a terrible lesson: Sometimes, they who hesitate die.

Nor is there reason to believe that terrorism has abated since the mid-1980s. In 1991, the Provisional Irish Republican Army (IRA) launched a mortar attack on 10 Downing Street in an attempt to kill British Prime Minister John Major (the IRA had also attempted to assassinate Major's predecessor, Margaret Thatcher). In May 1991, former Indian Prime Minister Rajiv Gandhi was killed by a bomb as he campaigned in national elections. Several weeks later, in June, Sikh separatists in India raked two trains with gunfire, ruthlessly killing as many as 110 passengers. There seemed no end to terrorist violence.

The foregoing discussion offers a glimpse of the scope and persistence of the problem. Political terrorism has existed for many centuries. What distinguishes today's terrorism is the disturbing frequency and variety of terrorist acts, the expanded opportunities (and means) available to would-be terrorists, and the unparalleled publicity terrorism and terrorists sometimes receive (due, in large part, to television's worldwide reach). Unfortunately, none of these conditions is apt to change. Nor can we expect the ethnic, religious, ideological, or nationalistic fervor on which terrorism feeds to disappear anytime in the very near future.

When and how did modern terrorism get its start? Let us examine this question briefly.

THE ORIGINS OF MODERN TERRORISM

Experts generally agree that modern terrorism sprouted from seeds planted in the 1960s; some are even more specific, citing 1968 as the year of inception. The confluence of turbulent and unsettling events in the late 1960s included racial strife in the United States, an escalating conflict in Vietnam, and the Arab-Israeli Six-Day War of 1967. The year 1968 brought these glimpses of things to come:

- Three Palestinian terrorists seized an Israeli El Al airliner and forced it to fly to Algeria, one of the first of many acts of air piracy.
- The Baader-Meinhof gang announced its presence in West Germany by torching a Frankfurt department store.
- Yasir Arafat, an advocate of armed struggle against Israel, became the leader of the Palestine Liberation Organization (PLO).
- The assassination of Martin Luther King, Jr., precipitated an outbreak of domestic violence in the United States by groups such as the Black Panthers and the Weathermen.[2]

In addition, at least three longer-term historical forces helped to create a climate conducive to terrorism. First, direct military confrontations and conflicts had become infinitely more dangerous in the nuclear age; even a conventional war might escalate out of control. Therefore, nations whose interests coincided with certain terrorist objectives sometimes provided moral, financial, or military support to these groups. In this manner, terrorism became a kind of proxy for violence between nations. Second, European colonialism had drawn to a close, leaving many newly formed nations to work out a host of unresolved territorial, national, and religious disputes. The result was a variety of low-intensity wars, many punctuated by terrorist activity, within and between these nations. Third, a reverence for life and a concern for the individual common to democratic societies combined with dramatic "up-close-and-personal" worldwide television news coverage to make terrorist incidents major media events. Thus the impact of such incidents—the publicity "payoff" from the terrorist's point of view—has been greatly magnified since the 1960s.

But it was in the 1970s that terrorism and *counterterrorism* became major growth industries. According to one estimate, the number of terrorist incidents multiplied tenfold between 1971 and 1985.[3] The level of terrorism remained high throughout the 1980s (see Figure 17-1). Precise figures vary widely, however, reflecting, among other things, differences in how terrorism is defined. Risks International, for example, put the total number of terrorist incidents in 1985 at slightly over 3,000, while the U.S. government conservatively counted one-fourth that many.[4]

Whatever the exact figures, they bear out the fact that terrorism has increased significantly since the 1960s and remains all too prevalent. Its causes are complex and controversial. Furthermore, there is good reason to believe that terrorism

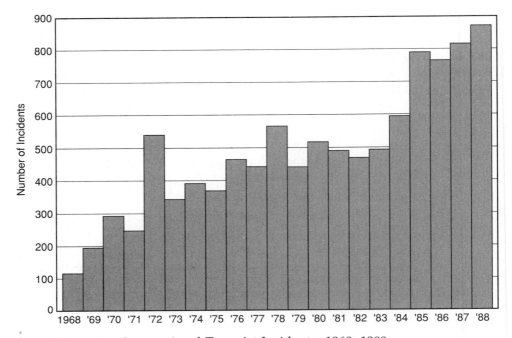

FIGURE 17-1   International Terrorist Incidents, 1968–1988

SOURCE: Charles W. Kegley, Jr., ed., *International Terrorism: Characteristics, Causes, Controls* (New York: St. Martin's Press, 1990), p. 15. U.S. State Department data.

will continue to plague many societies—especially democratic ones, as we shall see. What is terrorism? How is it different from other illegal acts? Do terrorist groups and terrorists exhibit certain common characteristics? We turn to these questions next.

WHAT IS TERRORISM?

Despite its growth and worldwide spread, terrorism remains an elusive concept. *Webster's New World Dictionary* gives the following definition: Terrorism is "the use of force or threats to demoralize, intimidate, and subjugate, especially such use as a political weapon or policy." A simpler definition views terrorism as "the deliberate attack on innocent civilians for political purposes."[5] Another analytically useful definition of terrorism breaks it down into four basic components:

- Terrorism is a method of combat or a strategy to achieve certain goals.

- To achieve these goals, terrorism aims to induce a state of fear in its potential victims and a proclivity toward repressive actions by the government.

- Terrorism is by nature ruthless and does not conform to commonly accepted standards of decency or humanitarian norms.
- Publicity is an essential factor in terrorist strategy.[6]

As this breakdown suggests, any adequate understanding must come to grips with the nature of terrorism (that is, how does it differ from ordinary criminal or subversive behavior?), the strategies and tactics terrorists use, and the characteristics of terrorist groups. We now consider each of these questions.

Classifying Terrorists: Criminals, Guerrillas, or Revolutionaries?

What gives terrorism its distinctive characteristics? There is general agreement that terrorism is fanaticism in the service of political ends. But how is such fanaticism best understood? The United States government has continuously viewed terrorism as a *political* problem and associated terrorists with subversives whose purpose is to disrupt and ultimately to overthrow democracratic governments. The American approach has stressed the illegitimacy of fanatical terrorism and advocated combating its unfortunate effects with swift punishment and steadfast deterrence. By contrast, several European governments—especially those ruled by socialists or social democrats—have viewed terrorism as primarily a *social* problem. Although these governments have not been averse to punishing terrorists, they have pictured them as victims of injustice and have argued for compassion on the ground that terrorism will disappear only when the underlying causes of injustice, despair, and hopelessness are also eradicated.

Given this disagreement on how best to understand terrorism, is there anything we can say for certain? The answer is yes—there is good agreement on what terrorists are and are not. First, terrorists are criminals, though by no means ordinary, run-of-the mill criminals. Rather, they are *political* zealots who routinely commit violent, antisocial crimes against innocent and unarmed civilians. Of course, killing and kidnapping, robbing banks, and hijacking airplanes are heinous crimes no matter who perpetrates them or why; they become terrorist acts because of their *political motivation*. When serial murderers go on a killing spree, innocent people die and whole communities can be terrorized. Their aims, however, are not political: They are mass murderers first and "terrorists" only incidentally. Occasionally, terrorists cooperate with criminals or criminals adopt terrorist tactics, but such circumstances are relatively rare and are usually confined to "narcoterrorists"—individuals in nations such as Colombia and Panama associated with powerful drug lords who have a vested interest in undermining legitimate governmental authority.

If terrorists are not ordinary criminals, neither are they best understood as "guerrillas" or "freedom fighters," as they sometimes claim. Guerrillas are the armed wing of a revolutionary movement or party—Mao's Red Army is perhaps the most famous example. Guerrilla forces are trained to engage enemy forces—other combatants—in battle. No one would claim that guerrilla forces never commit atrocities; indeed, some guerrilla movements have used terrorism as a major instrument in dealing with recalcitrant peasants as well as with the police, the military, and the government (for example, Peru's Shining Path). Here the line becomes blurred at times, but the key point is that most insurgent violence is directed at the security forces and the government. By contrast, terrorists direct most of their violence at civilians and noncombatants.

Nor are terrorists simply "ordinary" revolutionaries. Certainly, revolutionaries in the twentieth century have at times resorted to terror—both before and after taking power. But revolutionaries concentrate primarily on overthrowing the government. To that end, they attempt to build a subversive party; infiltrate the government, the police, and the military; spread propaganda; agitate among trade unions; recruit and indoctrinate the young; and incite strikes, riots, and street demonstrations.

Thus terrorism, though used by revolutionaries, is not their primary tactic. By contrast, terrorists typically concern themselves almost exclusively with planning and carrying out acts of terrorism. Also, most revolutionaries target their victims; most terrorists, by contrast, though occasionally bent on assassinating political leaders, are ordinarily less discriminating, sharing the view of Emile Henry, a Frenchman who, when charged with throwing a bomb in a café in 1894, replied, "*Il n'y a pas d'innocents*" (No one is innocent).

Thus although terrorists violate the law, they are not ordinary criminals; neither are they guerrillas, as that term has been generally used. In the sense that they seek to undermine existing political institutions, they are revolutionaries, but not in the more complete sense that they undertake a strategy by which they intend to exercise political power. Furthermore, it is important to recognize that while all terrorists are revolutionary opponents of existing governments, not all revolutionaries are terrorists in that not all undertake indiscriminate violence on behalf of their cause.[7]

The Logic of Terrorist Strategies

At the very least, terrorists commit acts of violence to make an emphatic political statement, to protest a particular government or policy, or to call attention to their radically dissenting viewpoints. Often terrorists push to accomplish more; their actions are designed to undermine support and confidence in the existing government by creating a climate of fear or collapse. Thus terrorists use violence in a program of psychological warfare on behalf of their cause, whether that cause is to advance some distinct national identity or to promote some political, religious, or social doctrine.

Terrorists are emphatically anti–status quo. They undertake programs in the hope of bringing about immediate change and outright chaos. But the results of their actions are often unpredictable. For example, in Uruguay, the Tupamaros, once Latin America's most notorious urban guerrilla movement, achieved a major objective when an elected civilian president turned over effective control of his government to the military in 1973 amid continuing political violence. Three

Types of Terrorism

GRASPING THE CONCEPT of terrorism is complicated by the many forms it assumes. Classification schemes vary widely, depending on the basis for comparison. For example, some experts, stressing the scope of the incidents, classify acts of terrorism as national, subnational, or international. Some would add transnational terrorism—the kind involving links between terrorist groups in different countries. The most important distinction, however, is between state terrorism and subversive terrorism. (State terrorism is often—but not exclusively—associated with totalitarian regimes and is discussed in Chapter 3.)

State terrorism is carried out by government security forces to intimidate and coerce their own people. Nazi Germany and Stalinist Russia are perhaps the best-known examples.

Subversive terrorism originates within society and is directed against the state. It is discussed in this chapter. It takes two main forms:

• *Nationalist-separatist terrorism* is carried out by Basques in Spain, Irish Republicans, Palestinians, Tamils in Sri Lanka, Sikhs in India, and others seeking their own homelands. Also called *subnational terrorism,* such separatist violence has a long history.

• *Indigenous **ideological terrorism*** is often anarchic, religious, or militantly Marxist; it seeks to destabilize society and dates from about 1968 in its modern form. Examples include the Red Army Faction in Germany, the Red Brigades in Italy, Direct Action in France, and Fighting Communist Cells in Belgium. Largely self-sufficient, such terrorist groups acquire money and arms by robbing banks, extorting ransom payments for kidnappings, and buying or stealing weapons. They train their own members close to home.

---

years later, the military staged a coup, took complete control, and eventually did in the Tupamaros (civilian government was not restored in Uruguay until 1985).[8]

Initially, the Tupamaros did not despair when Uruguay's democratic government turned over power to the military. It may seem odd that radical leftists would exhibit such an attitude toward the empowerment of right-wing military generals. But terrorists and terrorist organizations who believe that the present government and society are intolerable or who share a fervent belief in the future trust that any political change will ultimately be a change for the better. Thus frequently the terrorists aim not to bring on an immediate revolution but to turn popular governments into repressive governments, thereby preparing the way for a later revolution and a better future.

What is that future? Perhaps it is some ill-defined Communist utopia. Perhaps it is a national homeland. Perhaps it is anarchy. But no matter what the future holds, terrorists believe that they must protest and combat the corruption and injustice of the existing political order largely through acts of random violence. Significantly, such terrorism does not occur where governments are most unjust but rather where they are the weakest. Indeed, one expert on terrorism notes that "societies with the least political participation and the most injustice have been the most free from terrorism in our time."[9] Terrorists seize the opportunity to attack where they sense weakness and vulnerability.

Terrorist Tactics

Terrorism has often been described as the weapon of the weak, groups small in numbers and lacking in resources, because it is readily available to individuals and tiny cells, its targets are infinite and often defenseless, it requires little money and can be "funded" by actions normally associated with common crime (such as armed robbery), and its preferred instruments are often crude and cheap (for example, small arms and dynamite).

Terrorist tactics, although varied, have become all too common (see Figure 17-2). Planting bombs at crowded train terminals, kidnapping wealthy business executives, and blowing up airliners no longer seem extraordinary or even unusual. The relationship between such tactics and terrorist objectives is revealed in the Brazilian terrorist Carlos Marighella's chilling and incisive *Mini-manual for Urban Guerrillas.* This is a 48-page do-it-yourself manual for aspiring terrorists

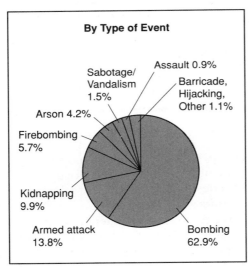

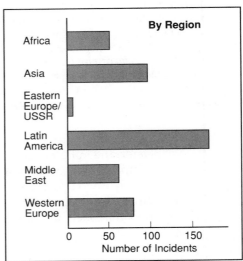

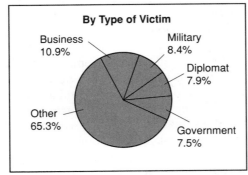

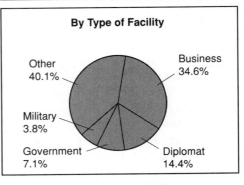

FIGURE 17-2   International Terrorists Incidents, 1990
SOURCE: U.S. Department of State.

and revolutionaries of all stripes. It spells out how to blow up bridges, raise money through kidnappings and bank robberies, and plan the "physical liquidation" of enemies. The handbook offers a range of practical advice: Learn to drive a car, pilot a plane, sail a boat; be a mechanic or radio technician; keep physically fit; learn photography and chemistry; acquire "a perfect knowledge of calligraphy"; study pharmacology, nursing, or medicine. It also stresses the need to "shoot first" and aim straight: "Shooting and aiming are to the urban guerrilla what air and water are to human beings."[10]

Obviously, all these skills are to be put to bad use—after all, the terrorist's job is to terrorize. Terrorism succeeds when strategies and tactics come together. Thus Marighella writes:

> The government has no alternative except to intensify repression. The police round-ups, house searches, arrests of innocent people, make life in the city unbearable. [The government appears] unjust, incapable of solving problems. . . . The political situation is transformed into a military situation, in which the militarists appear more and more responsible for errors and violence. . . . Pacifists and right-wing opportunists . . . join hands and beg the hangmen for elections.
>
> Rejecting the "so-called political solution," the urban guerrilla must become more aggressive and violent, resorting without letup to sabotage, terrorism, expropriations, assaults, kidnappings and executions, heightening the disastrous situation in which the government must act.[11]

Characteristics of Terrorist Groups

Having distinguished the essence of terrorism and the strategies and tactics it employs, it is important to note a few common characteristics of terrorist groups. This is made especially difficult by the fact that more than 600 such groups exist worldwide.[12] But generalizations about them are still possible. They tend to be small—seldom numbering more than 100 members and usually less than several dozen. Most are tight-knit, radical organizations that espouse anarchy, like Direct Action in France and the Red Army Faction in Germany. And because they are ethnically and politically homogeneous—often all close friends or even relatives of one another—terrorist cells are extremely difficult for intelligence agents to penetrate.

In addition, the life span of most terrorist groups is short—five to ten years (the Red Army Faction, successor to the Baader-Meinhof gang in Germany, is an exception, as are national separatist movements)—and their leaders do not hold power for more than a few years (although again there are exceptions, the most notorious being Abu Nidal, the shadowy figure behind the hijacking of the cruise ship *Achille Lauro* and bombings of the Rome and Vienna airports). Finally, terrorist groups seldom operate from a fixed location, and most terrorist cells have relatively little training, use unsophisticated equipment, and frequently acquire the tools of their trade—much of which could be purchased at any hardware store—by theft.

Notable exceptions are a number of highly nationalistic, separatist, or irredentist movements like the Basques in Spain, the IRA in Northern Ireland, and the PLO in the Middle East. Terrorist groups have been far more active in Europe than in the United States, although the February 1993 bombing of the World Trade Center in New York City proved all too well that American soil is not immune to terrorism. The Middle East, which has become a spawning ground for many diverse and competing terrorist groups, has been particularly hard hit. Terrorism is also a pervasive problem throughout the Third World, where it often grows out of protracted insurgency. In Latin America, for example, terrorist groups can be found in such countries as El Salvador, Colombia, Ecuador, Peru, and Chile.

WHO ARE TERRORISTS?

Not all terrorists are poor or come from urban backgrounds. Some grow up in the midst of urban poverty; others merely react against it. Yet any comprehensive explanation of modern terrorism must take account of the social and cultural context where terrorism breeds, including urban poverty and decay, the breakdown of the family structure, high rates of youth unemployment, and the dehumanizing effects—the sense of alienation and anomie—arising from the everyday struggle to survive in a fast-paced, overcrowded, and often impersonal city. People unable to cope with or accept these stresses react in different ways: Some turn to crime; others, to alcohol or drugs; and some drop out. Only a tiny fraction become terrorists. Of that fraction, most are male and single. Surprisingly, many are better educated and wealthier than average; to a surprising extent, they are individuals who have merely observed severe injustice or have experienced it vicariously. They are disproportionately young.[13]

Terrorism and Youth

The Shiite suicide bomber who drove her explosive-packed Peugeot into an Israeli Army convoy in southern Lebanon in 1985 was 16 years old. The Jordanian who tried to assassinate a United Arab Emirates diplomat in Rome in 1984 was 22. Of the four *Achille Lauro* hijackers, the oldest was 23; the youngest, 19. Research puts the median age of terrorists at 22.5 years. A German psychologist who interviewed captured members of the Red Army Faction notes elements of an "adolescent crisis" among terrorists, while an expert on the Provisional Irish Republican Army sees a "terrorist tradition" at work in some countries where "whole families pass on to their children that [terrorism] is the way you struggle for your rights."[14]

Eric Hoffer touches on the susceptibility of certain youths to fanatical causes in *The True Believer*. He places them in a group he calls "misfits," a category he further breaks down into temporary and permanent. Hoffer writes: "Adolescent youth, unemployed college graduates, veterans, new immigrants and the like are of this category. They are dissatisfied and haunted by the fear that their best years will be wasted before they reach their goal."[15] At the same time, although they tend to be "receptive to the preaching of a proselytizing movement," he argues that they "do not always make staunch converts." Indeed, student activists in Japan, Europe, and the United States—including American students who gained prominence as anti-Vietnam protest leaders—have rather quickly taken their place in the work force. Unlike past and present "antiestablishment" youths, however, terrorists typically commit capital crimes and, in so doing, cut off all avenues of reentry into civil society.

The Psychology of Terrorism

According to an expert on the psychology of terrorism, "terrorists with a cause" are the most dangerous to democratic society.[16] Who are these crusaders? What motivates them?

Numerous experts agree that certain key characteristics mark a majority of terrorists. Considering the young age of most terrorists, it is hardly surprising that these traits are often associated with adolescence:[17]

- *Oversimplification of issues:* Terrorists see complex issues in black-and-white terms; they have no interest in debate; they often live out a "fantasy war" imagining that the people overwhelmingly support their cause.

- *Frustration:* Terrorists feel that society has cheated them, that life is unfair, and that they deserve far more; they are unwilling to wait or work for something better and believe that the only way to get is to take.

- *Orientation toward risk taking:* Many terrorists seek situations involving adventure and are easily bored.

- *Self-righteousness:* Terrorists display belligerent assertiveness, dogmatism, and intolerance of opposing views.

- *Utopianism:* They harbor an unexamined belief that heaven on earth is just over the horizon—the only thing standing in the way is the corrupt and oppressive existing order.

- *Social isolation:* Terrorists, one expert notes, are often "people who are really lonely." For some, a terrorist cell may be the only "family" they have.

- *A need to be noticed:* Terrorists share a need to feel important, a desire to make a personal imprint by getting newsprint.

- *A taste for blood:* Interviews with captured terrorists, testimony by relatives and acquaintances, and eyewitness accounts by former hostages point to a final, startling characteristic: Some terrorists kill without an ounce of remorse. Recall that terrorists often oversimplify reality; thus they may see victims as mere objects—a habit of mind observed among Nazi guards at extermination camps during the Holocaust.[18]

Is there such a thing as a terrorist mindset? Once again, Hoffer's discussion of fanatics in *The True Believer* proves apropos. Fanaticism (excessive, blind devotion), whether political or religious, is almost always based on hatred, according to Hoffer. In this view, the fanatic places hatred in the service of a cause or a vision. Hatred is in turn a unifying force for like-minded fanatics (whereas love is divisive). Thus hatred provides a reason for living, often appealing to individuals who are insecure, have little sense of self-worth, or lack meaning in their lives.

Hoffer's characterization of the fanatical state of mind merits attention:

> The fanatic is perpetually incomplete and insecure. He cannot generate self-assurance out of his individual resources—out of his rejected self—but finds it only by clinging passionately to whatever support he happens to embrace. This passionate attachment is the essence of his blind devotion and religiosity, and he sees in it the source of all virtue and strength. Though his single-minded dedication is a holding on for dear life, he easily sees himself as the supporter and defender of the cause to which he clings. And he is ready to sacrifice his life to demonstrate to himself and others that such indeed is his role. He sacrifices his life to prove his worth.[19]

Nor are fanatics necessarily motivated by an excellent cause:

> The fanatic is not really a stickler for principle. He embraces a cause not primarily because of its justness and holiness but because of his desperate need for something to hold on to. Often, indeed, it is his need for passionate attachment which turns every cause he embraces into a holy cause.[20]

Thus the *specific* cause may not matter very much to some fanatics—any cause will do. This insight helps to explain how individuals seemingly motivated by lofty idealism can commit barbarous acts that violate the most elementary standards of morality. It also suggests that terrorism is not necessarily—or even primarily—a reflection of social injustice.

TERRORISM AND DEMOCRACY

It is striking that in Europe, terrorism during the Cold War era afflicted primarily democratic societies and that Communist states were nearly immune. The U.S. State Department reported that only one terrorist incident occurred in eastern Europe during all of 1985 (compared with 175 to 200 in western Europe during the same period). And although only four attacks occurred in North America that year, U.S. targets overseas were involved in 25 percent of the cases. However, the causality rate from terrorist attacks against American citizens fell quite sharply in 1989 through 1990 following the collapse of communism in eastern Europe and the end of the Cold War (see Figure 17-3).

Staunch Opponents: Democracy and Terrorism

Ideological terrorist organizations that are fanatically Marxist, anarchic, or religious are often the proclaimed enemies of democratic governments. Sometimes, as in the case of the IRA and the government of Great Britain, particular democratic governments may be targeted. When such organizations break the law or harm citizens, democratic governments in turn proclaim terrorist groups to be an abiding menace and a grave threat to democracy.[22]

Although terrorist groups can threaten any kind of government, a particular tension exists between terrorism and democracy. Democracy depends for its long-term survival on respect for the right of the majority to rule and the minority

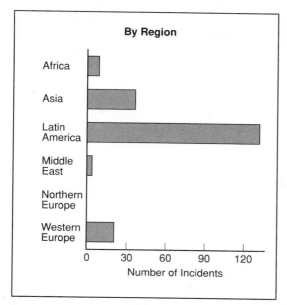

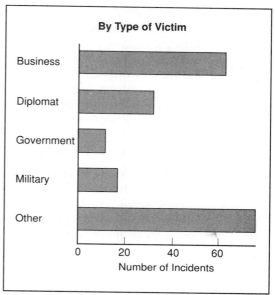

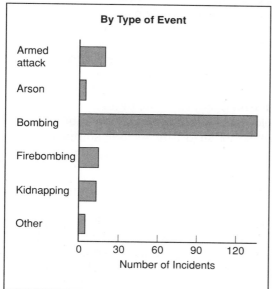

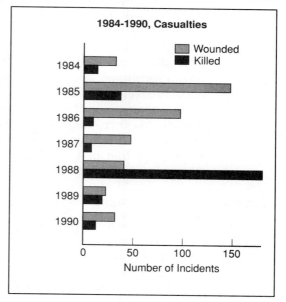

FIGURE 17-3   Anti-U.S. Terrorist Attacks, 1990
SOURCE: U.S. Department of State.

to oppose. In other words, democracy values the right of each individual to hold an opinion. The validity of individual political, economic, or religious opinions may be questionable, but there is no doubt that all individuals are deserving of respect because they are citizens and human beings capable of formulating and holding such opinions.

It is precisely this respect for others that fanatical terrorists deny. So certain are they of their truths that they are willing to kill not only political opponents but innocents as well. By acting in this way, the very existence of terrorists reminds us of an important lesson that the American Founders well understood: that zealotry remains the implacable enemy of democracy.

The Vulnerability of Democratic Societies

Open societies are particularly vulnerable to terrorism, sometimes in ways that are rather obvious and sometimes in ways that are more subtle. Freedom has always been synonymous with opportunity; yet in the hands of the wrong people, freedom can become deadly. In a democracy, for example, people can move about freely; associate with whomever they please; change addresses and jobs at will; drive a car or truck almost anywhere without being stopped by the police; purchase chemicals, weapons, and communications equipment; and so forth. The same constitutional guarantees that protect law-abiding citizens from arbitrary arrest or unwarranted searches and seizures shield terrorists. In addition, a society that stresses respect for personal privacy makes it relatively easy to avoid normal social contact without arousing suspicions.

Democracies are also vulnerable in less obvious ways. Democratic nations generally place a high value on the individual—the senseless death of a single citizen sometimes causes whole societies to grieve. As a consequence, terrorists have discovered that by taking hostages, killing one or two, and threatening to kill the others unless their demands are met, they can sometimes gain concessions that would otherwise be unattainable. Thus the Reagan administration, despite its hard-line policy against state-sponsored terrorism, secretly shipped arms to Khomeini's Iran in 1986. But this concession did not prevent terrorists from taking several more hostages.

Terrorism and Tourism

In addition, terrorism has been given an unintentional boost by changing patterns of international travel and tourism. Terrorists discovered in the late 1960s that the tourist industry is one of the "weakest links" in Western economies and can provide an unlimited forum for publicity. The age of air travel afforded new opportunities in this regard. Before 1968, there were only 16 successful hijackings of scheduled U.S. aircraft on record; in 1969 alone, there were 33.[23]

The terrorist assault on Western tourism was intensified in October 1985 when Palestinian terrorists hijacked the Italian cruise ship *Achille Lauro* and murdered an American passenger, Leon Klinghoffer. Two months later, terrorists, again Palestinians, carried out back-to-back massacres in the Rome and Vienna airports; among those who died in the resulting carnage were five Americans. As a result, many U.S. citizens canceled trips to Europe and other overseas destinations. By mid-1986, travel agents in the United States were reporting a 20 to 30 percent reduction in their transatlantic tourist trade, and U.S. carriers handling European routes were retrenching. Another serious worldwide decline in tourism occurred in 1991 during the Persian Gulf War when the threat of terrorism intimidated large numbers of potential tourists. These events dramatized the terrorists' potential for gaining publicity as well as for inflicting significant, if limited, economic damage—especially in the West, where many industries, including a number directly and indirectly affected by tourism, could be forced into decline, at least temporarily.

Terrorism and the Media

There is little disagreement on one point: Terrorists seek publicity. In their view, the more attention they can get, the better. Why? Because media coverage—especially television—permits terrorists to draw worldwide attention to themselves and their cause. Not only is this coverage politically useful, but it is also personally gratifying—it makes otherwise obscure and nondescript individuals feel important. Moreover, the prime-time exposure terrorists often get on network news shows is free. And of course, the most daring, deadly, or otherwise sensational terrorist acts receive the most extensive media attention.

In light of terrorists' reactions to publicity, many political analysts outside the journalism profession blame the rapid rise of terrorism in part on the media—television, in particular. After all, bad news makes for better headlines and better copy than good news, and bad news that is also shocking garners even more attention. In this sense, at least, terrorism is tailor-made for television.

In a market economy, simply reporting the news is not enough; the news industry must also sell the news. The share of the television audience—the news market—that chooses to watch the evening news determines how much companies will pay to advertise their products during this peak viewing time each day. Thus the producers of network evening news shows are loath to pass up a good story, even if it means playing into the hands of the terrorists.

In defense of the media, is there any doubt that, say, an airplane hijacking involving hundreds of innocent people is newsworthy? Is it not true, especially in a democracy, that the media have a "constitutional" responsibility to keep people informed? And even if one network decided not to cover a particular terrorist incident or pay only slight attention to it, would the others ignore it too?

In the final analysis, collusion and censorship are the only "solution"—but the cure, in this instance, would undoubtedly be worse than the disease. If democratic governments were to violate their own constitutions in response to terrorist acts, the perpetrators of terrorism would have won a major moral victory. Futhermore, protests and demonstrations that would likely result from censorship might actually destabilize a society—and imperil democratic institutions—more than terrorism itself.

Only a partial remedy—media self-restraint—is left. Realistically, the news industry is not likely to cut back significantly on its reporting of terrorism until public opinion turns against such reports. As consumers of news, we would do well to remember that the media mirror, as well as shape, consumer preferences. This observation does not remedy the problem, but it does put the media's role in perspective.

STATE-SPONSORED TERRORISM

Acts of terrorism usually seem spontaneous, and they generally are. But sometimes terrorism assumes an important international component. Former Central Intelligence Agency (CIA) Director William Casey asserted that much terrorism was "inconceivable apart from the financial support, military training, and sanctuary provided to terrorists by certain states."[24] Casey was referring to *international terrorism* (also known as *state-sponsored terrorism*), which occurs when its purveyors are knowingly supported or sent by the government of one country to attack the citizens, interests, or assets of another country on foreign soil, often in a third country. Examples of international terrorism have been numerous over the past two decades, although there is some reason to believe it is currently in decline.

The December 1985 attacks on the Rome and Vienna airports provide a good example of state-sponsored terrorism. The operation was reportedly masterminded by the leader of a Palestinian terrorist group bearing his name, Abu Nidal, who was thought to be living in Libya at the time. (Libya called the attacks "heroic.") The attackers had several Tunisian passports evidently supplied by Libya's Muammar Qaddafi. (The Libyan government had confiscated the passports from Tunisian workers banished earlier in the year.) According to Italian authorities, the terrorists were trained in Iran and had traveled to Europe via Syria. Again, this is only one incident among many in which the largely invisible hand of state sponsorship—international support for terrorism provided through clandestine channels—played a key role.[25]

In 1988, the U.S. Department of State identified a number of nations sponsoring international terrorism, including Cuba, Iran, Libya, North Korea, Syria, and South Yemen. Frequently, blame for specific incidents was difficult to affix with certainty, but there remained strong suspicions that state-sponsored terrorism was at work. For instance, the bombing of a Marine barracks in Beirut and the hijacking of TWA flight 847 in the 1980s, for example, were both perpetrated by Shiite extremists—probably aided and abetted by Iran. Syria, another major "exporter," has maintained terrorist training camps in Lebanon and has supplied arms to some of the Middle East's bloodiest Palestinian groups, including Abu Nidal. Libya's Colonel Qaddafi has also encouraged terrorist strikes against Western and Israeli targets and has supplied money and arms to a variety of terrorist training camps. In addition, he has used Libya's diplomatic missions in foreign capitals as conduits and command posts for terrorist activities. Significantly, a number of European nations (especially certain Scandinavian nations) that have officially condemned such acts of terrorism have sometimes provided tacit or passive support to such activities, primarily out of fear that a more adversarial policy might invite retaliation.[26]

There is no doubt that a significant number of terrorist acts have involved varying degrees of state sponsorship. During the Cold War, many Western observers (including former CIA director Casey) believed that the former Soviet Union headed a terrorist conspiracy; they charged that it nurtured an invisible network of client states and terrorist leaders through which information, instructions, money, and weapons for terrorists flowed.[27] Did such a conspiracy really exist? Much circumstantial evidence implicated the Soviet Union in global terrorism from the late 1960s until the mid-1980s. In view of the long-standing Soviet geopolitical strategy of destabilizing Western democracies, it would be surprising if the Soviet Union did not sometimes support and even sponsor terrorism. Still, there is an enormous difference between supporting terrorism and orchestrating it. Considering the diversity of terrorist groups and their disparate causes, motives, and objectives, it is difficult to imagine how any government, no matter how practiced in international conspiracy, could have organized, directed, and controlled terrorism worldwide.

Since 1987, with the steady decline and ultimate collapse of American–Soviet hostility, there has been a decline of state-sponsored terrorism throughout the world. With the decline of hostility between these nations has come the "deideologization" of politics throughout the world, with the result that dogma and fanaticism play less important roles in world politics. Furthermore, "much of today's terrorism is based on ethnic, national and religious causes far removed from the Cold War, and even the left-wing insurgency movements are driven by local social, economic and political inequities far more than by Marxist ideology."[28] These local factors are the givens of worldwide terrorism and exist whether or not there is a Cold War. State-sponsored terrorism still exists (it was never confined to a single nation), but it is important to recognize that most terrorism can and does occur without the help of state sponsors.

COUNTERING TERRORISM

The question facing democratic societies is not "How can terrorism be stopped?" but rather "How can terrorism be stopped without curtailing freedom?" To solve the problem of terrorism by infringing on the civil rights that make democracy worth defending would be tantamount to admitting defeat: Destroying democracy is terrorism's most immediate objective. But if there is danger in overreacting, there is equal danger in doing too little too late.

Cooperation among Democratic States

When President Reagan ordered the bombing of Libya in April 1986, it was a first in two ways: That action represented the first time that the United States had used conventional forces against state-sponsored terrorism and the first time that the NATO alliance was tested as a framework for fighting terrorism. Initially, only the British supported the U.S. strike against Libya; the French government, fearing terrorist reprisals, refused to allow U.S. warplanes based in the United Kingdom to fly over French territory. Soon after, however, fragmentary signs of a newly emerging multinational consensus began to appear.

On April 21, 1986, the European Community voted to impose economic sanctions against Libya. The following month, the heads of the seven leading industrial nations, meeting in Tokyo, agreed to take the following steps:

- Ban arms sales to terrorist-sponsoring nations
- Deny entry to suspected terrorists
- Expedite extradition procedures
- Impose tougher immigration and visa requirements
- Improve cooperation among security organizations
- Cut back the diplomatic staffs of known state sponsors

In the summer of 1986, Libyans were expelled from Britain, West Germany, France, Italy, Spain, Denmark, Belgium, the Netherlands, and Luxembourg. It was a modest but auspicious beginning.

The bombing of Libya helped to unify the Western alliance, but the "military option" is not feasible in most cases. Thus as a complement to joint efforts, democratic societies must turn to less dramatic forms of self-help.

Unilateral Counterterrorist Measures

The concept of deterrence applies to terrorism as well as war. More precisely, deterrence against terrorism requires, at a minimum, a steadfast refusal to negotiate concessions to terrorists—especially if they are holding hostages. To do so is tantamount to rewarding evil. Such a strategy is also self-defeating: It virtually ensures future hostage-taking.

It seems likely that the demonstrated will and ability to take military or paramilitary countermeasures is also necessary to deter terrorism effectively. The daring raid by Israeli commandos at Uganda's Entebbe Airport in July 1976 proved that terrorists are not invincible even after they have taken hostages and secured their position. Success in hostage rescue operations, in addition to luck, requires highly skilled, quick-hitting *commando units* like Germany's GSG-9 (which freed hostages from a Lufthansa airliner hijacked to Mogadishu, Somalia, in 1977), Britain's Special Air Services (SAS), and the U.S. Delta Force.[29]

Local police agencies are not equipped or trained to deal with terrorism, as Kenneth Goddard's novel *Balefire* graphically illustrated.[30] Another expert in counterterrorism, addressing the same point, wrote:

> When you are operating with the S.A.S. on the ground in an area like South Armagh [in Northern Ireland], you very quickly realize that you are fighting a war, not taking part in a police operation. Night after night . . . I.R.A. active-service units [infiltrate] from the safety of the South or [move] about freely in areas they have made safe for themselves by murder, torture, kneecappings and other intimidation. They are using sophisticated weapons, [including] heavy machine-guns, rocket launchers, land-

Counterterrorism in Italy: A Success Story

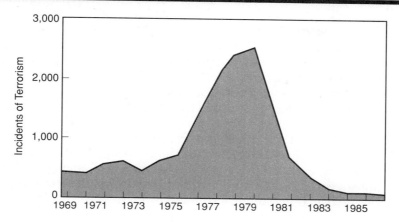

IN THE 1970s, Italy was the most terror-ridden country in the West. The extreme left-wing Red Brigades kidnapped and killed hundreds of judges, industrialists, and politicians—symbols of capitalism and the establishment. From 1969 to 1983, more than 14,000 acts of terrorist violence were recorded, 409 people were killed, and 1,366 were injured.

In 1978, the Red Brigades kidnapped Aldo Moro, a former prime minister and one of Italy's leading politicians. When the government refused to negotiate with Moro's abductors, he was murdered. In the end, however, it was the terrorists who lost. Shocked and outraged, the public demanded a tough counterterrorist program. Thereafter, the Red Brigades went into sharp decline.

How did Italy do it? First, the police infiltrated Red Brigades terror cells and subsequently arrested hundreds of members. Second, reduced prison sentences were offered to repentant terrorists who supplied information about the activities and whereabouts of other terrorists. Third, the police concentrated on a limited and manageable number of terrorist targets such as airports, harbors, and border crossings. Yet they disrupted society as little as possible and, for the most part, followed normal police procedures (even though, as we have seen, terrorists are not "normal" criminals).

Deprived of publicity and of sympathy for their causes, Italy's terrorists were isolated, and today they pose little threat to the country's stability.

mines and massive quantities of explosives. Through audio surveillance, you listen to the planning sessions at which the orders are given for acts of sabotage that will involve indiscriminate civilian casualties.

Civilian police procedures cannot deal with this kind of threat. If you locate a team of men who are in the process of organizing an attack on a shopping center with milk churns packed with high explosives and nails, you send a fighting patrol to attack it, you don't call the local bobby.[31]

However, the availability of special counterterrorist units like the British SAS is not enough: Governments must be willing to use them. As one expert has put it, the central objective of counterterrorist policy is "to establish an unmistakable pattern of failure and retribution."[32] Debacles such as the 1980 U.S.

attempt to free the hostages in Iran and Egypt's 1985 attempt to recapture an Egyptian airliner hijacked to Malta are bound to occur—sometimes with tragic consequences. But the long-term consequences of not acting decisively can be even more tragic.

Other steps that governments can take include controlling arms and explosives and, perhaps most important (and most difficult), developing better intelligence-gathering capabilities against terrorism. Only by getting information on terrorists' hideouts and whereabouts can attacks be prevented; only by knowing in advance when and where terrorists plan to strike can most targets be defended.

Obviously, the nature of democratic societies and the constitutional framework in which police and investigatory agencies function create justifiable obstacles. Citizens, quite properly, are unaccustomed to spying on their neighbors, and intelligence gathering is divided among several agencies, in part to prevent any one of them from gaining too much power. (In the United States, for example, the CIA is forbidden by law from engaging in domestic spy operations against U.S. citizens or groups.)

Private Measures

Finally, private citizens and firms have developed strategies to protect themselves.[33] Just as many governments were "hardening" their embassies and other overseas facilities in the mid-1980s, private companies were spending an estimated $21 billion annually on security services and hardware in the United States alone. One Rand Corporation expert believed that this figure could triple by the end of the century.[34] Of course, most private citizens cannot afford to hire their own security guards. Public awareness, however, can make the terrorist's job a great deal more difficult. In Israel, for example, where terrorism is a constant threat and everyone is acutely aware of it, officials claim that 80 percent of bombs in public places are disarmed because suspicious objects are usually noticed and reported in time.[35]

In sum, there is no single solution to the problem of terrorism. The variety of solutions that various experts propose reflects the difficulty of devising an all-encompassing theory of terrorism. The bottom line is that there is little agreement on the root causes of this phenomenon and consequently little agreement on the best remedies.

CAN TERRORISM BE CONTAINED?

Terrorism as a political instrument is not likely to disappear even if governments steadily improve their capabilities for and better coordinate their approaches to dealing with this problem. Nonetheless, as we have seen, there are ways of limiting the opportunities available to terrorists, discouraging some of them and punishing the misdeeds of those who are captured. Unfortunately, even one terrorist can be too many; indeed, one well-trained terrorist with a small support system—a few friends, safehouses, suppliers—can inflict enormous damage.

To date, no political system has been destroyed by terrorism alone. Governments are often embarrassed and occasionally undermined by subversive groups using terrorism as a tactic—again, Italian fascists in the early 1920s and Uruguayan Tupamaros in the early 1970s are two examples. Statistically speaking, even though terrorism escalated sharply in the 1970s, international terrorism recently has leveled off, apparently in response to tighter governmental and private sector security measures, heightened public awareness, and changes in the international political system. Thus despite the fact that terrorist incidents continue to garner publicity, most observers remain optimistic that democratic governments can contain terrorism even though they cannot eradicate it altogether.

Summary

Terrorism has become an everyday occurrence in the contemporary world. Although not a new phenomenon, terrorism has grown enormously in scope and significance since the late 1960s. Although terrorism is difficult to define, it is clear that terrorists are not criminals, guerrillas, or ordinary revolutionaries. A terrorist is a kind of revolutionary who does not seek to otain political power but primarily wishes to protest and combat the injustice of the existing political order through random acts of violence. Terrorists seek to create a climate of collapse—to increase political instability in the hope that these tactics will advance their preferred political future. Terrorists invariably form groups that are close-knit, homogeneous, small, and short-lived. Individually, terrorists tend to be young and share a variety of important psychological characteristics, including fanaticism and hatred.

Democracy and terrorism are implacable enemies. Democracy depends for its existence on citizens' willingness to compromise and respect other people's opinions, while terrorists are zealots who are willing to undertake any action for the sake of their cause. Furthermore, democratic societies are by nature open and vulnerable to terrorist attacks. This vulnerability is both physical and psychological.

An important support for terrorism in recent years has been state sponsorship. Yet in light of the demise of the Cold War and the profoundly local influences that affect terrorism around the world, the phenomenon of state sponsorship is in decline.

The problems that democracies face in countering terrorism are complicated by the need to preserve individual freedom while protecting collective security. Although constitutional governments afflicted by terrorism have been slow to react, recent steps—taken both unilaterally and jointly—give renewed cause for optimism.

Key Terms

counterterrorism
state terrorism
subversive terrorism
ideological terrorism

international terrorism
state-sponsored terrorism
commando units

Review Questions

1. How is terrorism different from common crime? From guerrilla warfare?

2. What tactics do terrorists typically employ, and how are their ends and means related?

3. Discuss the psychological roots of terrorism and the characteristics of the typical terrorist.

4. Assess the terrorist threat to constitutional democracies. Why are democracies vulnerable?

5. What is state-sponsored terrorism? Is it increasing or decreasing?

6. What obstacles stand in the way of an effective counterterrorist policy?

7. What steps have constitutional democracies taken to protect themselves from terrorism? What more, if anything, can be done?

Recommended Reading

ASCENCIO, DIEGO, AND NANCY ASCENCIO. *Our Man Is Inside*. Boston: Little, Brown, 1983. Gripping account of a hostage situation in Bogotá, Colombia, in which 15 ambassadors, including the U.S. ambassador to Colombia, were held captive by Marxist terrorists for 61 days.

CLARK, RICHARD C. *Technological Terrorism*. Old Greenwich, Conn.: Devin-Adair, 1980. Deals with the danger that fissionable or fusionable materials may be diverted into the hands of terrorists; also examines chemical and biological weapons, Andromeda strains, and so on; makes policy suggestions.

CLUTTERBUCK, RICHARD. *Protest and the Urban Guerrilla*. New York: Abelard-Shuman, 1974. Examines the roots of protest and violence in Britain and Northern Ireland; surveys the rise of urban guerrilla movements worldwide; ponders the implications of terrorism for the future of democratic societies.

GODDARD, KENNETH. *Balefire*. New York: Bantam, 1984. A gripping work of fiction showing how a single well-trained terrorist could paralyze a local police department and wreak havoc in a community unaccustomed to living under the menacing cloud of terrorism. The author is an expert in forensic science and criminal justice and has composed a thriller with a very serious point.

HACKER, FREDERICK J. *Crusaders, Criminals, Crazies: Terror and Terrorism in Our Time.* New York: Norton, 1976. A probing, essential study of the psychology of the terrorist.

JENKINS, BRIAN (ed.). *Terrorism and Personal Protection.* Boston: Butterworth, 1985. The best and most comprehensive book on the subject by an impressive collection of experts.

KEGLEY, CHARLES W., JR. (ed.). *International Terrorism: Characteristics, Causes, Controls.* New York: St. Martin's Press, 1990. A good collection of essays with well-crafted introductions by the editor to each of the book's three parts (characteristics, causes, controls).

KIDDER, RUSHWORTH M. "Unmasking Terrorism," five-part series in the *Christian Science Monitor,* May 13–21, 1986. Examines the origins and development of terrorism since the late 1960s, the problem of state-sponsored terrorism, the terrorist mentality, the manipulation of the media, and recent efforts to curb terrorism.

LACQUEUR, WALTER. *Terrorism.* Boston: Little, Brown, 1977. A penetrating study of the origins, ideology, and sociology of terrorism by a leading scholar and writer. Lacqueur also examines various theories and surveys the modern history of terrorism.

LONG, DAVID E. *The Anatomy of Terrorism.* New York: Free Press, 1990. A balanced, thoughtful analysis of contemporary terrorism. A useful appendix lists and describes specific terrorist groups.

RIVERS, GAYLE. *The Specialist: Revelations of a Counterterrorist.* New York: Charter Books, 1985. Ostensibly a true story about the underworld of terrorism and counterterrorism written under a pseudonym by a mercenary who specializes in carrying out antiterrorist operations under contract to Western (and other) governments; reads like a James Bond thriller.

WEINBERG, LEONARD, AND PAUL DAVIS. *Introduction to Political Terrorism.* New York: McGraw-Hill, 1989. A helpful overview of terrorism.

Notes

1. *Washington Post,* July 25, 1986, p. A22. Emphasis added.

2. Rushworth M. Kidder, "Unmasking Terrorism," *Christian Science Monitor,* May 13, 1986, p. 19. (Five-part series)

3. Ibid., p. 20.

4. Ibid.; see Figure 17-1.

5. "Nihilism and Terror," *New Republic,* September 29, 1986, p. 11.

6. Walter Lacqueur, "The Futility of Terrorism," *Harper's,* March 1976, p. 4. The author asserts that "the media are the terrorist's best friend. The terrorist's act by itself is nothing, publicity is all."

7. Terror is associated with revolutions recalling the French much more than the American tradition; see Chapter 16.

8. Richard Clutterbuck, *Protest and the Urban Guerrilla* (New York: Abelard-Shuman, 1974), pp. 250–254.

9. Walter Lacqueur, *Terrorism* (Boston: Little, Brown, 1977), p. 220.

10. Clutterbuck, *Protest and the Urban Guerrilla*, pp. 239–267.

11. Claire Sterling, *The Terror Network: The Secret War of International Terrorism* (New York: Holt, 1981), pp. 21–22.

12. Statistics from David E. Long, *The Anatomy of Terrorism* (New York: Free Press, 1990), p. 165.

13. Ibid., p. 17.

14. Kidder, "Unmasking Terrorism," May 15, 1986, p. 18.

15. Eric Hoffer, *The True Believer* (New York: Harper & Row, 1951), p. 49.

16. See Frederick J. Hacker, *Crusaders, Criminals, Crazies: Terror and Terrorism in Our Time* (New York: Norton, 1976).

17. Kidder, "Unmasking Terrorism," May 15, 1986, p. 19.

18. Regarding the lack of remorse, see Long, *Anatomy of Terrorism*, p. 19.

19. Hoffer, *True Believer*, p. 80.

20. Ibid., p. 81.

21. Kidder, "Unmasking Terrorism," May 13, 1986, p. 18.

22. Although during the heyday of the Cold War, it was often charged that the United States and other democratic regimes supported insurgent anticommunist groups that employed terrorist tactics.

23. Kidder, "Unmasking Terrorism," May 15, 1986, p. 20. Not surprisingly, the Middle East had the highest incidence of terrorism (nearly half the total); Latin America, where most countries had returned to democratic rule by the mid-1980s, also continued to be hard hit.

24. Ibid., May 14, 1986, p. 18.

25. Ibid., p. 17.

26. Long, *Anatomy of Terrorism*, p. 9.

27. For support of this position, see Ray S. Cline and Yonah Alexander, *Terrorism: The Soviet Connection* (New York: Crane Russak, 1984); Christopher Dobson and Ronald Payne, *Counterattack: The West's Battle against the Terrorists* (New York: Facts on File, 1982); Sterling, *The Terror Network*; and Angelo M. Codevilla, "The Terrorist Mosaic" (review of the book *Hydra of Carnage*, ed. Uri Ra'anan et al.), *Commentary*, August 1986, p. 54.

28. Long, *Anatomy of Terrorism*, p. 164. It is precisely for these reasons that the Soviet Union was increasingly the victim of terrorism. In 1990, no airline was hijacked more often than Aeroflot.

29. See Dobson and Payne, *Counterattack*, and Gayle Rivers, *The Specialist: Revelations of a Counterterrorist* (New York: Charter Books, 1985).

30.   Kenneth Goddard, *Balefire* (New York: Bantam, 1984).

31.   Rivers, *The Specialist*, p. 40.

32.   Clutterbuck, *Protest and the Urban Guerrilla*, p. 287.

33.   See Brian Jenkins, ed., *Terrorism and Personal Protection* (Boston: Butterworth, 1985).

34.   Kidder, "Unmasking Terrorism," May 21, 1986, p. 16.

35.   Ibid., p. 17.

WAR

CAUSES AND CLASSIFICATION

(AP/Wide World Photos)

PERHAPS 35 MILLION people, 25 million of them civilians, have perished as a result of warfare in the twentieth century.[1] This serves as a grim reminder that in this century and throughout history, war has been the central problem in international politics. Indeed, the most glaring defect of the international system has been its inability to eradicate or even minimize armed conflict between nations. In terms of sheer cost, war represents by far the most wasteful and destructive of human activities. This point was made most emphatically by General William Tecumseh Sherman—certainly no paragon of pacifistic sentiment—in a speech delivered 15 years after the U.S. Civil War. "There is many a boy," General Sherman declared, "who looks on war as all glory, but, boys, it is all hell."

ATTITUDES TOWARD WAR

Unfortunately, not everyone has viewed war in General Sherman's terms. Some of history's most illustrious (or infamous) personalities, in fact, have reveled in the "glory" of war. Others, while not condoning bloodshed, have acknowledged war's perverse attractions. In the eighth century B.C., the Greek poet Homer noted that men grow tired of sleep, love, singing, and dancing sooner than they do of war. And in his poetry, he celebrated the self-sacrifice and courage that war demanded. The Greek philosopher Aristotle, writing some 500 years later, listed courage as a fundamental (although not the foremost) human virtue. To Aristotle, courage in battle ennobled human beings because it represented the morally correct response to fear in the face of mortal danger.

This emphasis on the benefits of war was not confined to the ancient Greeks, or even to ancient writers as a group. Perhaps no writer in modern times typified the tendency to rationalize war better than the German philosopher G. W. F. Hegel (1770–1831), who argued that "if states disagree and their particular wills cannot be harmonized, the matter can only be settled by war." There is nothing particularly shocking about this statement, although it does seem rather pessimistic. Hegel went on to argue, however, that war is actually salutary because "corruption in nations would be the product of prolonged, let alone 'perpetual' peace." During times of peace, Hegel reasoned, society becomes flabby and factious. "As a result of war, nations are strengthened, but peoples involved in civil strife also acquire peace at home through making war abroad."[2]

Hegel contended that "world history is the world court." In other words, for Hegel the ultimate test of validity or worth was not some abstract moral standard but success. And because success in world politics is measured, above all, in terms of power and size, this means that *might* and *right* are often synonymous. This theme was revived with a vengeance a century later by the warlike dictators Adolf Hitler and Benito Mussolini. Mussolini, like Hegel, scoffed at pacifism. According to the father of Italian fascism, "War alone brings up to their highest tension all human energies and puts the stamp of nobility upon the peoples who have the courage to meet it."[3]

Today, in an age of mass destruction, most reasonable human beings would readily agree that, all things being equal, peace is better than war. But is world-

Hiroshima, Japan, October 1945: Two months and one mile from where the bomb fell. In our age of mass destruction, only the symptoms and severity of the disease have changed. (DAVA)

wide peace a realistic possibility, considering the harsh nature of international politics? Throughout the ages, many political thinkers (not to mention utopian dreamers) have maintained that reason or God or history would sooner or later deliver the world from the agonies of war. But even among these optimists there has been little agreement about the root causes of war. And if war is ever to be eradicated, it would seem necessary, above all, to determine its causes.

CAUSES OF WAR

To some degree, the causes of war have differed from one era to another. For example, any detached observer living in Europe or the Middle East in the twelfth century A.D. would probably have attributed the frequency and ferocity of war at that time to religious zealotry. The Crusades, which began at the end of the eleventh century and continued for 200 years, were marked by the kind of unmerciful slaughter that, paradoxically, has often accompanied the conviction that "God is on our side."

But the lethal potential of religious or moral arrogance, as demonstrated in the Crusades, has played little or no role in the wars of this century. In no sense was religious fanaticism the cause of World War I, for instance. Many observers attribute the outbreak of that conflict to nationalism, a phenomenon that was virtually unknown in the twelfth century. Others stress the arms race conducted by European nations, arguing that the momentum of military preparations carried Europe inexorably into war. Still others blame imperialism: The scramble for colonial territories in the second half of the nineteenth century led to war, they contend, when there were no longer any "unclaimed" colonial lands left in Asia and Africa.

On the surface, then, the causes of World War I differed radically from those of the Crusades. But on a deeper level, it can be argued that whatever their immediate causes (religious zealotry, nationalism), every war represents merely another outbreak of the same disease and that through the ages, only the symptoms and the severity of the malady have changed. The exact nature of this disease has been hotly disputed by historians, philosophers, and politicians. Essentially, however, three schools of thought regarding the ultimate causes of war have emerged: that wars stem from a defect in human nature, that they are caused by some defect in the makeup of some or all nation-states, and that they arise from imperfections (or perceived imperfections) inherent in nature.

Human Nature

Those who attribute war to a flaw in human nature advance a variety of explanations for humankind's unfortunate behavior. One of the most profound influences on Western political thought in this regard has been the Christian tradition. From their understanding of the Old Testament, early Christian thinkers surmised that the human race was irreparably flawed by original sin—that is, by Adam and Eve's violation of God's law in the Garden of Eden. The story of the Fall as recorded in the book of Genesis recounts the frailty of human nature in the face of temptation. According to Saint Augustine (A.D. 354–430), the influential early Christian theologian, war is simply one of the burdens humanity must bear because of the corruption inherent in human nature.

Many secular thinkers display a similar pessimism regarding human nature, without citing original sin as the cause. The Greek philosopher Plato, who often celebrated humanity's highest attributes, also on occasion reminded humanity of its basest characteristics. In *The Republic*, for instance, he attributed wars at least partly to the feverish human passion for worldly possessions and creature comforts. The sixteenth-century Italian thinker Niccolò Machiavelli painted an equally depressing picture of the interaction between human nature and politics. In *The Prince*, Machiavelli observed that political success and moral rectitude are often inversely related: Rulers tend to prosper in direct proportion to their willingness to commit immoral acts for the sake of political ends.

If some have looked to religion and others to philosophy for an explanation of humanity's aggressive tendencies, others have turned to psychology. Sigmund Freud (1856–1939), the founder of psychoanalysis, believed that humans are born with a "death wish"—innate self-destructive tendencies—that they somehow manage to sublimate (redirect into other activities) most of the time. But during times of conflict, Freud theorized, human beings direct these destructive tendencies against others. In this view, wars serve an important psychotherapeutic function: They offer an outlet for otherwise self-destructive impulses. Other psychologists have argued that aggression is an innate human drive constantly seeking an outlet, that aggression is a normal human response to frustration, or that human beings exhibit the same sort of "territorial imperative" that supposedly accounts for the aggressive behavior of many of the lower species of the animal kingdom. According to the territorial imperative theory, latent aggressions are lodged deep in human nature, and threats to a person's territory (property, loved ones, and so on) are especially apt to trigger aggressive action.

Still other observers have contended that the ultimate cause of war can be found not in a hopelessly debased human nature or in deeply rooted psychological instincts but in deficiencies of the human intellect. In the words of a prominent pacifist writing between World Wars I and II,

> The obstacle in our path . . . is not in the moral sphere, but in the intellectual. . . . It is not because men are ill-disposed that they cannot be educated into a world social consciousness. It is because they—let us be honest and say "we"—are beings of conservative temper and limited intelligence.[4]

Finally, many political thinkers have linked war with moral defects in human nature. The preeminent spokesman for this point of view was Thomas Hobbes, the seventeenth-century English political philosopher. Hobbes was, above all, a realist who sought to understand human nature as it is, not as it ought to be. To discern humanity's *true* nature, he believed, one must analyze human behavior outside the distorting environment of civil society—that is, in the state of nature. The conclusions he drew from this analysis have exerted a profound influence on how we view human nature in general and the human proclivity for conflict in particular.

Hobbes on War   According to Hobbes, human beings in the state of nature were governed by a keen instinct for self-preservation. They feared death above all and especially shrank from the prospect of sudden, violent death. This fear of death, however, did not result in meekness or passivity; on the contrary, humans were driven by their passions toward aggressive and violent behavior.

> So that in the nature of man, we find three principall causes of quarrell. First, Competition; Secondly, Diffidence; Thirdly, Glory. The first maketh man invade for Gain; the second, for Safety; and the third, for Reputation. The first cause [men to turn to] Violence to make themselves Masters of other mens persons, wives, children, and cattell; and the second, to defend them; the third, for trifles, at a word, a smile, a different opinion, and other signe of undervalue. . . .
>
> Hereby it is manifest, that during a time men live without a common Power to keep them all in awe, they are in that condition which is called war; and such a war, as is of every man, against every man.[5]

Hence, the state of nature, for Hobbes, was a state of war.

Hobbes went on to argue that the realm of international relations also reflects a state of war. Just as individuals in the state of nature were governed by base motives and drives, he declared, nations are governed by leaders who are moved by those same motives and drives. And just as the state of nature lacked a sovereign power to enforce laws restraining destructive human passions, so the international system lacks a sovereign power over nations. In both cases, Hobbes contended, the ultimate cause of conflict lies in human nature.

Appropriately enough, Hobbes found that three kinds of disputes corresponded to the three defects he discerned in human nature: *aggressive wars*, caused by competitive instincts; *defensive wars*, caused by fears; and *agonistic wars*, caused by pride and vanity. Through this compact theory he sought to explain not only how human beings would act outside the civilizing influence of society and government (human beings would constantly be at each other's throats were it not for the civilizing effect of government-imposed law and order) but also why nations often seem to go to war over seemingly frivolous issues.

The Hobbesian Legacy   Variations on the Hobbesian theme of human depravity can be found in the writings of many of the most influential thinkers of our age. Arnold Toynbee, the British historian, explains European instability during the Ethiopian crisis of the mid-1930s in precisely these terms.[6] He accuses the Italians (who had invaded Ethiopia) of "positive, strong-willed, aggressive egotism," the British and French of "negative, weak-willed, cowardly egotism," Western Christendom as a whole of the "sordid" crime of failing to come to the defense of Ethiopia, and the League of Nations for its overall "covetousness" and "cowardice." The Americans, seen as "captious and perverse," hardly fare much better than the Europeans in Toynbee's bill of particulars. Toynbee's characterizations may seem intemperate, but his underlying premise, that the activities of nations reflect individual human behavior, has been embraced by many political thinkers.

More recently, the eminent political scientist Hans Morgenthau has argued forcefully that human nature is fundamentally flawed. According to Morgenthau, "Human nature, in which the laws of politics have their roots, has not changed since the classical philosophies of China, India, and Greece endeavored to discover these laws," and "politics, like society in general, is governed by objective laws that have their roots in human nature."[7] The key to understanding the operation of these laws is the "concept of interest defined as power." Conceptualizing politics in this way means that human beings are motivated by self-interest, which predisposes human behavior toward an eternal "struggle for power." Morgenthau makes this point particularly clear when he states that "international politics, like all politics, is a struggle for power. Whatever the ultimate aims of international politics, power is always the immediate aim." Like Hobbes before him, Morgenthau rejects the mistaken (idealist) view that "assumes the essential goodness and infinite malleability of human nature." Instead, he embraces the "realist" view "that the world, imperfect as it is from the rational point of view, is the result of forces inherent in human nature."[8]

According to Morgenthau and like-minded political theorists, then, human nature and the drive for self-aggrandizement is a leading (if not *the* leading) cause of war. Such an analysis hardly presents a cheerful picture of humankind—or of humanity's prospects for banishing war. For if wars derive from defects in human nature and if human nature is a constant (in the sense that it is by definition unchangeable), then within the context of the nation-state system, we will never see an age without warfare. As we are about to see, this view of the human condition, however compelling, is not the only plausible explanation of why wars are fought.

Society

Not all political thinkers have found the causes of war lurking in the human psyche or in human nature. Some blame political society, while still other theorists believe that *particular* kinds of political states pose disproportionate dangers to peace. In this section, we examine the different approaches of political theorists and leaders who have blamed society (or certain political societies) for war's destructiveness.

Rousseau: Property Is to Blame   "Man is born free, and everywhere he is in chains." With this attack on the modern nation-state, the French philosopher Jean-Jacques Rousseau began the first chapter of his classic *Social Contract* (1762), in which he directly challenged Hobbes's assertion that human beings were naturally cunning and violent. Rousseau started from the premise that human beings were naturally "stupid but peaceful" creatures, quite capable of feeling pity for those who are suffering. Accordingly, he went on, Hobbes erred in attributing innate characteristics such as ambition, fear, and pride to human beings in the state of nature. To Rousseau, these traits represented attributes of *social* humanity and sure signs of human corruption—that is, he saw them as inherent in society rather than in human nature: "It is clear that . . . to society, must be attributed the assassinations, poisonings, highway robberies, and even the punishments of these crimes."[9]

Rousseau believed that society was the cause of almost every human failing, including war. Specifically, he blamed the institution of private property—a cornerstone of all eighteenth-century European societies—for the miseries that had beset the human race since it abandoned its natural innocence for the false pleasures of civilization. Property divided human beings, he argued, by creating unnecessary inequalities in wealth, status, and power among citizens within particular nations and, eventually, among nations.

> The first person who, having fenced off a plot of ground, took it into his head to say *this is mine* and found people simple enough to believe him, was the true founder of civil society. What crimes, wars, murders, what miseries and horrors would the human race have been spared by someone who, uprooting the stakes or filling in the ditch, had shouted to his fellow-men: Beware of listening to this imposter, you are lost if you forget that the fruits belong to all and the earth to no one.[10]

Specifically, Rousseau postulated that just as the creation of private property led to the founding of the first political society, the original founding mandated the creation of additional nation-states. And because each of these nations remained in a *"state of nature"* vis-à-vis the others, there arose great tensions that eventually led to the "national wars, battles, murders, and reprisals which make nature tremble and shock reason."[11] With the "division of the human race into different societies," Rousseau concluded, the most decent men learned to consider it one of their duties to murder their fellow men; at length men were seen to massacre each other by the thousands without knowing why; more murders were committed on a single day of fighting and more horrors in the capture of a single city than were committed in the state of nature during whole centuries over the entire race of the earth.[12]

Rousseau's view that private property is the root of all evil exerted a profound influence on modern intellectual history. Even among political thinkers who reject Rousseau's specific diagnosis of the corruption of the nation-state, there has been widespread acceptance of his general theory that "man is good but men are bad." Several twentieth-century variations on this theme have appeared. As we shall see, each differs in substantial ways from the others, but all share the assumption that the fatal flaw leading to war resides in society rather than in human nature.

Nationalism Is to Blame   Many modern thinkers hold that war is inherent in most or all societies by virtue of their very existence as separate and sovereign political communities. The principal manifestations of these potent separatist tendencies, it usually is argued, is nationalism (sometimes referred to, in its most extreme forms, as "jingoism" or "chauvinism"). Nationalism commonly denotes the patriotic sentiments felt by the citizens of a given country toward their homeland. According to one authority,

> Each nation has its own rose-colored mirror. It is the particular quality of such mirrors to reflect images flatteringly: the harsh lines are removed but the character and beauty shine through! To each nation none is so fair as itself. . . . Each nation considers (to itself or proclaims aloud, depending upon its temperament and inclination) that it is "God's chosen people" and dwells in "God's country."[13]

Small wonder that nationalism has been called an idolatrous religion. Although nationalism may foster unity and a spirit of self-sacrifice within a society, between societies it has led, directly or indirectly, to militarism, xenophobia, and mutual distrust.

Nationalism can be manipulated in support of a war policy, and warfare can in turn be used to intensify nationalism. The chemistry between nationalism and war is sufficiently volatile to have caused many *internationalists* (theorists favoring peace and cooperation among nations through the active participation of all governments in some sort of world organization) to single out nationalism as the main obstacle to achieving peace and harmony among the sundry peoples of the world.

The most important implication of this analysis is that to the extent that nationalism is an artificial passion (one that is socially conditioned rather than inborn), political society is to blame for war. Not surprisingly, some advocates of this view suggest a radically (critics would say "deceptively") simple formula for eliminating war: Do away with the nation-state and you do away with nationalism; do away with nationalism and you do away with war.

Wilson and Kant: Tyranny Is to Blame   Although many observers identify nationalism as the major cause of this century's worldwide conflicts, most twentieth-century Western statesmen blame despotism for the calamitous world wars. This belief was perhaps best enunciated by Woodrow Wilson, president of the United States from 1913 to 1921. At the end of World War I, Wilson sought to secure lasting European peace through a treaty based on his so-called *Fourteen Points*—principles of international political behavior on which, he hoped, a stable and peaceful international order could be founded. The cornerstone of this proposed system was to have been **national self-determination,** or the right of people everywhere to choose the government they wished to live under. Self-determination, Wilson believed, would lead to the creation of democracies, which he viewed as naturally more peace-loving than dictatorships.

But why should democracies inherently be more peace-loving than dictatorships? The eighteenth-century Germany philosopher Immanuel Kant had provided a plausible explanation. (So germane are Kant's writings to Wilson's ideas that at least one authority has suggested that "Woodrow Wilson's Fourteen Points were a faithful transcription of both the letter and spirit of Kant's *Perpetual Peace.*")[14] In his political philosophy, Kant postulated that to remain strong, nations had to promote education, commerce, and civic freedom. Education, he theorized, would lead to popular enlightenment, and commerce would produce

President Wilson, honored in Britain at the end of World War I, had hoped to make the world "safe for democracy," but democracies have not been notably more successful than dictatorships at avoiding war. (Bettmann Archive)

worldwide economic interdependence, each of which would advance the cause of peace. Most important, through expanded political freedom, individual citizens would become more competent in public affairs. And because liberty is most pronounced in republican regimes, such governments would be the most peace-loving *by nature*. The reason for this is simple: In republics—unlike monarchies or aristocracies—the citizens who decide if wars are to be fought are the same citizens who must then do the fighting:

> A republican constitution does offer the prospect of [peace-loving behavior], and the reason is as follows: If . . . the consent of the citizens is required in order to decide whether there should be war or not, nothing is more natural than that those who would have to decide to undergo all the deprivations of war will very much hesitate to start such an evil game. . . . By contrast, under a constitution where the subject is not a citizen and which is therefore not republican, it is the easiest thing in the world to start a war . . . as a kind of amusement on very insignificant grounds.[15]

Kant envisioned an evolutionary process whereby steady, if imperceptible, progress would be made toward a peaceful world order as governments everywhere became increasingly responsive to popular majorities. Eventually, he felt, war would become little more than a historical curiosity.

Kant's linking of republicanism and peacefulness became Wilson's political credo. Both Kant and Wilson looked to the reconstruction of the nation-state as the key to a world without war. More specifically, both called for the global extension of democracy, education, and free trade to promote peace. Wilson, in particular, placed enormous faith in the morality and common sense of the ordinary person; he became convinced that the ideal of national self-determination was the key to humanity's political salvation. He also believed that if the peoples of the world were given an opportunity to make a conscious choice among alternative forms of government, they would universally choose liberal democracy and peace. Finally, Wilson felt that if all nations were governed by democratic institutions, the moral force of both domestic and world public opinion would serve as a powerful deterrent to armed aggression.

Lenin: Capitalism Is to Blame   Among those who did not agree that world peace hinged on the creation of more democracies and the elimination of dictatorships was an equally famous contemporary of Wilson's, the leader of the Russian Revolution and the first ruler of the former Soviet Union, V. I. Lenin. Lenin was as violently opposed to bourgeois democracy as Wilson was enthusiastic about it. Although both extolled the virtues of national self-determination, the term meant very different things to them. Wilson assumed that given the choice between democracy and some other system, any nation would choose democracy. Lenin assumed that any nation given a choice between capitalism and communism should choose communism. For Wilson, the primacy of politics was self-evident. For Lenin, as a follower of Karl Marx, wars were waged solely in the interest of the monopoly capitalists.

In an influential tract titled *Imperialism: The Highest Stage of Capitalism*, Lenin advanced the Marxist thesis that Western imperialism—the late-nineteenth-century scramble for colonial territories—was an unmistakable sign that capitalism was teetering on the brink of extinction. Imperialism, according to Lenin, was a logical outgrowth of the cutthroat competition characteristic of monopoly capitalism. In their ceaseless struggle for profits, Lenin theorized, the capitalists eventually had to seek foreign markets where they could make profitable investments and dump their industrial surpluses. Thus monopoly capitalists, through their control of the machinery of the state, push their societies into war for their own selfish purposes. In Lenin's own words:

> When the colonies of the European powers in Africa, for instance, comprised only one-tenth of that territory (as was the case in 1876), colonial policy was able to develop by methods other than those of monopoly—by the "free grabbing" of territories, so to speak. But when nine-tenths of Africa had been seized (approximately by 1900), when the whole world had been divided up, there was inevitably ushered in a period of colonial monopoly and, consequently, a period of particularly intense struggle for the division and the redivision of the world.[16]

In sum, Lenin held that because war is good business for the capitalists of the world, capitalists make it their business to promote war.

This analysis of the causes of war seems far removed from the Wilsonian thesis that tyranny leads inevitably to international conflicts, and yet the two views coincide at one crucial point. Lenin and Wilson both believed that the nation-state—or, more precisely, a key element of some or most nation-states—produced wars. Such an approach presents a generally optimistic picture of the problem of war. Lenin and Wilson, no less than Rousseau and the opponents of nationalism, suggested that if only some glaring defect that corrupts nations could be eradicated, lasting world peace would ensue. Change is the key: Change the offending part of the nation-state, and human beings can live together in peace and harmony.

The Environment

Not all thinkers believe that political society or even human nature cause war. Other theorists maintain a third perspective—that war is often caused by perceived or real scarcity. This opinion can be traced at least as far back as to the philosopher John Locke.

The Lockean Perspective In his *Second Treatise on Civil Government* (1690), Locke argued forcefully that wars reflect conditions inherent in nature rather than defects in human nature or in human society. Simply stated, his proposition was that environmental circumstances beyond human control frequently place human beings in "do or die" situations that make conflict inevitable. Like Hobbes before him, Locke was not blind to the imperfections in human beings. Locke's examination of the state of nature led him to agree with Hobbes that self-preservation was the most basic human instinct. At this point, however, the two thinkers diverged. In the words of one authority:

> Locke's state of nature is *not* as violent as Hobbes's. If, as it seems, force will commonly be used without right in Locke's state of nature, it is not because most men are vicious

or savage and bloodthirsty; Locke does not, as Hobbes does, speak of every man as the potential murderer of every other man. The main threat to the preservation of life in the state of nature lies not in the murderous tendencies of men but rather . . . in the poverty and hardship of their natural condition.[17]

Why did Locke believe that humanity lived in poverty and hardship in the state of nature? Because enormous effort and a great amount of labor were required simply to provide for each individual's day-to-day survival. Furthermore, even after one assured oneself of ample food, one's property was still threatened by the aggression of hungry and impoverished neighbors. Thus Locke emphasized external circumstances, rather than internal character flaws, as the principal cause of human conflict.

Locke's views on human beings, society, and nature have a great bearing on the issue of war and peace. If the origins of war lie within human beings, as Hobbes believed, the eradication of war can come about only by changing the "inner self." If the problem lies in society rather than in human beings, as Rousseau and Lenin contended, the solution is to reconstitute society (or the state) to remove the particular defects thought to give rise to aggressive behavior. If, however, the problem lies neither in humans nor in society but in nature, the solution must be to transform nature.

Interestingly enough, the transformation of nature was precisely how Locke proposed to end human conflict in domestic society. Civil government, he asserted, must create the conditions to encourage the process of economic development. Through economic development, a major cause of social tension—the natural "penury" of the human condition—would be greatly mitigated. At the same time, when the uncertainties of nature were replaced with the formal rules of organized society, the need for every human being to be constantly on the defensive against the depredations of others would be lessened greatly. Human beings would thus finally leave the state of nature, with all its anarchy and danger.

Ironically, however, in leaving one state of nature, humanity ultimately found itself inhabiting another—the often brutal world of international politics. Although Locke did not apply his theory of politics to the realm of international relations, his reasoning lends itself readily to such an application. Before the invention of government, human beings lived in domestic anarchy; likewise, in the absence of an effective world government, nations exist in international anarchy. In this sense, the relationships among nation-states differ little from relations among individuals before the formation of civil society. The international state of nature, no less than the original state of nature, is perpetually a *potential* state of war. In other words, each nation-state behaves according to the dictates of self-preservation in an environment of hostility and insecurity, just as each individual presumably did in the state of nature.

One of the most common and valued "prizes" of war is, of course, territory. And judging from all appearances, the desire for more land and resources—property, in the Lockean sense—is also one of the most common *objectives* of war. Then, too, as we have already noted, Lenin attributed the European scramble for colonial territories toward the end of the nineteenth century to the search for new markets, cheap labor, and raw materials—that is, property. Significantly, Lenin held that the propensity for capital accumulation (property and money) described by Locke was directly responsible for the phenomenon of imperialism, which Lenin predicted would lead inevitably to war. Although many students of politics and history would reject Lenin's radical views on this subject, most would no doubt agree that territoriality has been prominently associated with war in virtually every age.

Locke wrote at a time when there was still plenty of land in the world that remained "unclaimed" (by Europeans) and uncultivated. Locke noted that even in the state of nature, human relations were probably fairly harmonious, so long as no one crowded anyone else. It stands to reason that as growing populations begin to place ever-greater pressures on easily available resources, however, the drawing of property lines becomes progressively more important. If, as Locke's analysis suggests, prehistoric people felt threatened by the pressures of finite resources, imagine how much greater those pressures have become in modern times!

Nature's Scarcity: War in the Making   Many contemporary writers have elaborated on the theme of resource scarcity propounded by Locke and, later, by Thomas Malthus (1766–1834) in his *Essay on the Principle of Population* (1798). Richard Falk, for example, has identified "four dimensions of planetary danger," including the "war system," population pressures, resource scarcities, and "environmental overload."[18] These four dimensions of danger, according to Falk, are interrelated aspects of a single problem and hence must be treated as a group.

Falk's assumptions about the causes of international conflict are obviously consistent with Locke's political philosophy, as Falk himself implicitly recognizes: "International society is, of course, an extreme example of a war system. Conflicts abound. Vital interests are constantly at stake. Inequalities of resources and power create incentives to acquire what a neighboring state possesses."[19] Just as humans were constantly vulnerable to the depredations of others in the state of nature, so nation-states are continually threatened by predatory neighbors. Throughout history, then, violence has played a vital role in the conduct of foreign affairs because, Falk argues, conditions beyond the control of individual nation-states compel them to regard their own security as being directly proportionate to their neighbors' distress. Hence, even after the unprecedented destruction wrought by World Wars I and II, "many efforts were made, often with success, to moderate the scope and barbarism of war, but no serious assault was mounted to remove the conditions that cause war."[20]

What exactly are these conditions? Professor Falk argues that access to food and water supplies had a great bearing on the earliest wars. And these considerations, moreover, have not lost their relevance in the modern world:

> Given the present situation of mass undernourishment (more than two-thirds of the world population), it is worth taking account of the ancient link between war and control of food surplus, as well as the age-old human practice of protecting positions of political and economic privilege by military means.[21]

Even more basic than the question of adequate food and water supplies, Falk points out, is the need to control the population explosion. In many ways, population pressure underlies the entire crisis of planetary organization. Under such conditions, it is understandable that no nation in the world, no matter how powerful, feels terribly secure in our times. The oil crisis served as a dramatic reminder of the vulnerability of even the richest and most powerful countries. Not only oil but also many other raw materials such as bauxite, copper, and tin are maldistributed and in short supply. At the same time, the poorest countries continue to experience shortages in the most basic of all raw materials, food.

Many researchers in the 1980s and early 1990s were predicting a decline in the reserves of a majority of the earth's essential nonrenewable mineral resources—notably, petroleum and natural gas, as well as such nonfuel minerals as tungsten, nickel, zinc, lead, silver, tin, and platinum. No less disturbing were the findings of Lester Brown, director of the Worldwatch Institute in Washington, D.C., who published a study showing that the supply of the earth's principal *renewable* resources also declined steadily during the 1970s.[22] These trends seem especially ominous when set against the backdrop of a steadily growing world population. In the near future, raw materials shortages may become increasingly severe and competition for such resources increasingly intense. Under these circumstances, the "inconveniences" Locke saw in the state of nature may become less theoretical as nations vie for access to the earth's dwindling stocks of food, fiber, and fuel. Then only a scientific miracle that would once and for all end material scarcity could prevent nations from fighting for their "fair share" of the earth's limited resources.

THEORIES OF WAR: A CRITIQUE

The three general views on the ultimate causes of war examined in this chapter are based on one of the most fundamental concepts in Western political philosophy—the triad of humanity, society, and nature. All three theories have some measure of validity. Together, they explain the origins of war in general. Individually or in combination, they explain why particular wars are undertaken.

The answer to the question "Why war?" would thus seem to lie in some mix of human psychology, society, and nature. Such a comprehensive formulation would encompass the views of both those who believe human nature to be the root cause of war and those who believe that the fault lies within the international system. To those who subscribe to Hobbes's way of thinking, the international system simply mirrors humanity's egocentric nature. By contrast, those who embrace Locke's view of the state of nature hold that people act egotistically because of the fears and anxieties engendered by a legitimate concern for self-preservation in a world of inaccessible, maldistributed, or insufficient resources. Supporters of each of these two theories would agree that human beings caught up in the whirlpool of competitive politics act in a self-interested way; they would disagree most fundamentally about the reasons why this is so. But this philosophical disagreement, though theoretically significant, does not have to be settled to draw meaningful conclusions about the causes of war.

Those who, like Lenin and Wilson, believe that certain structural aspects of the nation-state itself lead to war would not be pleased with this comprehensive formulation of the causes of war. Lenin and Wilson both believed that wars were caused by a single overriding factor, although they disagreed radically on what that factor was. Other observers have singled out still other aspects of society as the "true" causes of war. The eighteenth-century revolutionary Thomas Paine, for example, argued that hereditary monarchies were at fault; yet the age of kings ended long ago, and wars continue. In modern times, many inhabitants of the Western democracies have insisted that communism is the major cause of war in the world. Yet as we have already observed, many other contemporary commentators (and not only representatives of Communist countries) have maintained that capitalism is the root cause of war.

It is significant that those who attribute war to a single cause generally believe that if only that characteristic could be eliminated, people could live in peace and harmony forever. Such an interpretation offers hope to a war-weary world. Unfortunately, there is no conclusive evidence that one particular kind of nation or society is chiefly responsible for war.

Beyond Politics

Although it is widely believed that certain types of nations are more prone than others to go to war, it is no easy task to verify this belief; there are simply too many variables. For example, earlier we observed that some thinkers blamed war on politics in general, nationalism in particular. Although it seems reasonable to assume that all else being equal, nations exhibiting intense nationalism are more warlike than are politically apathetic nations, all else is seldom equal. Political leadership in particular nations and international circumstances are also profoundly important in this regard. If intense nationalism can lead directly to war, it can also be manipulated by power-hungry leaders or serve as a legitimate response to international events. Each specific situation must be judged individually.

The same criticism can be leveled against the Kantian/Wilsonian view that a nation's politics makes the difference between warlike and peaceable behavior and that tyranny is the primary cause of warfare. The relationship between dictatorial and belligerent or aggressive behavior has been stressed by many political writers. Aristotle, for instance, maintained that tyrants are "warmongers" who plunge their nations into war "with the object of keeping their subjects constantly occupied and continually in need of a leader."[23] Some modern political writers, such as Hannah Arendt, argue that totalitarian governments are inherently aggressive.[24] In the twentieth century, two of the most destructive conflicts (World War II and the Korean War) were initiated by totalitarian dictatorships. Nor can we ignore the role played by the conservative monarchies (especially Austria-Hungary and Germany) in the outbreak of World War I. Finally, the mass murders ordered by Stalin in the 1930s, by Hitler in the 1940s, and by

Pol Pot between 1975 and 1979 can only reinforce the view that totalitarian rulers have a special affinity for bloodshed.

There are also more objective reasons for asserting that dictatorships are naturally warlike. Dictators exercise absolute control over the armed forces and propaganda networks of their states. Then, too, they have often themselves been war heroes who rode to power on the wings of military victory—and successful soldiers rarely become squeamish about the use of force once they take the reins of government. For such rulers, war can provide a popular diversion from the tedium and rigors of everyday life; it can act as an outlet for pent-up domestic hostilities that might otherwise be directed at the dictator himself; it can help unify society and justify a crackdown on dissidents; or, finally, it can be used by the dictator to rejuvenate a stagnant economy or an uninspired citizenry.

But these observations, however suggestive, do not add up to conclusive proof that despotism and war *necessarily* go hand in hand. Before Woodrow Wilson's theory can be accepted, several objections must be addressed. In the first place, Wilson's analysis is not simple to apply, as an analysis of the Vietnam War illustrates. The Kennedy, Johnson, and Nixon administrations blamed that war on communist aggression. Critics of United States foreign policy, however, blamed much of the problem on misguided or provocative American actions in Southeast Asia. Thus depending on the evidence one regards as most valid, the Vietnam War can be used to "prove" either that dictatorships are more prone to war than democracies or that democracies are no more immune to crusading militarism than dictatorships.

In general, representative democracies have not been notably more successful than dictatorships at avoiding war. In this century, for example, India, the world's largest democracy, has waged several bloody wars against Pakistan, and the United States has remained anything but aloof from warfare, as the U.S.-led military action against Iraq in 1991 reminds us. Nor have democratic nations always been simply unwilling participants in war. As much as we might like to forget it, the United States did not go out of its way to avoid fighting the Spanish-American War of 1898. And it is difficult to overlook U.S. intervention in the Mexican Revolution in 1914, when President Wilson surprisingly ordered American Marines to seize the Mexican port of Veracruz and later sent a punitive expedition into Mexico against the forces of Pancho Villa.

In addition, scholarly studies of warfare simply do not support the conclusion that democratic nations are less warlike than either authoritarian or totalitarian states. As a rule, these analyses have been quite inconclusive,[25] and what conclusions they have drawn have been modest at best.

Some scholarly studies have suggested that different types of government are more apt to fight each other than are similar types. Such findings support Woodrow Wilson's conclusion that dictatorial regimes are the natural enemies of democracies, as well as Lenin's view that capitalist and communist nations are inevitable enemies. One study of Latin American politics concluded that "the more similar two nations are in economic development, political orientation, Catholic culture, and density, the more aligned their voting in the UN and the less conflictful their interaction will be." By the same token, "the more dissimilar two nations are in economic development and size and the greater their joint technological capability to span geographic distance is, the more overt conflict they have with each other." The study also concluded that "racial distance is the most important characteristic distinguishing between peace and conflict in international systems."[26]

If methodological studies do not support the often-stated assumption that democracies are less warlike than dictatorial states, does that mean that Wilson was *totally* wrong? Not necessarily. Quantitative studies, useful though they may be, have certain significant limitations. Generally, they deal with the frequency of state involvement in foreign conflict and establish correlations between numbers and kinds of conflicts on the one hand and a variety of social attributes on the other. Therefore, if it can be shown that *all* states, irrespective of form of government, fight wars, researchers are likely to conclude that form of government is not a significant causal factor in explaining why wars occur. But the statistics fail to take into account the issue of who launched the first aggressive salvo against whom. Further studies may address this issue and thereby enable us to pinpoint more precisely the relationship between politics and war.

Beyond Economics

If politics does not decisively influence a nation's tendency to go to war, what about Lenin's theory that wars are generally caused by economic concerns—specifically, by capitalism? From the historical evidence, it appears that Lenin's theory is even less persuasive than Wilson's. Although a few wars can be related to comprehensive economic motives such as imperialism, most cannot.[27]

This is not to say that economics is completely unrelated to the incidence of war. For instance, the U.S.-led coalition against Iraq in the 1991 Persian Gulf War *was* driven by clear economic motives: to protect the vast oil fields of Arabia and to keep the vital lifelines linking the Middle East with Europe, Asia, and North America from being controlled by Saddam Hussein. More generally, it may not be nations' form of economic organization that matters as much as the level of economic development. Between 1945 and 1967, according to one study, there were 82 armed conflicts involving regular forces or units of national armies: 26 of them international and 56 internecine.[28] Virtually all these wars were fought in Asia, Africa, and Latin America. On the face of it, this would seem to prove that less developed countries have been more predisposed to war than industrially advanced countries (or that they have had fewer incentives *not* to go to war). One expert has commented that

> the leaders of underdeveloped countries . . . often seem to be better able to overcome domestic strife and inertia by citing the hostility of the external environment than by stressing the need for hard work and patience at home. . . . They attempt to solve domestic issues by redefining them as falling in the foreign policy areas.[29]

Yet there are problems with this theory as well. For one thing, although many twentieth-century wars may have been fought on the territory of underdeveloped nations, the examples of Suez, Algeria, the Congo, Vietnam, Angola, Afghanistan, and the Falkland Islands demonstrate that industrially developed countries have been involved, directly or indirectly, in many Third World conflicts since 1945. And at least two recent studies report no significant correlation between levels of economic development and the frequency of military engagement.[30] In fact, other studies suggest that richer, more developed nations may be more war-prone than many poor nations.[31]

Another thesis linking economics and war holds that nations experiencing economic difficulties are more apt to go to war. To test this hypothesis, several in-depth statistical studies have been done on stress factors related to economic conditions—unemployment rates, population density, urbanization, pace of industrialization, and the like.[32] These studies demonstrate that stresses within society apparently correlate with deviant behavior at the personal level and foreign conflict at the national level. The precise relationships between these factors are complex, however, and the conclusions drawn by researchers have been either too general or too specific to be useful.

All members of the U.S.-led coalition forces in the 1991 Persian Gulf War feared that Saddam Hussein's intention was to establish Iraqi domination over the Arabian peninsula (and possibly beyond); in short, Saddam posed a perceived threat to the existing balance of power in the Middle East. (AP/Wide World Photos)

The Danger of Oversimplification

Simplistic theories abound, attributing the origins of war to some particular aspect of the nation-state. One theory, for example, holds that large states are more prone to war than small states. In the words of one writer:

> Historically, the major powers have used organized force, or have been involved in wars, far out of proportion to their numbers in the international system. To put it another way, the great powers are vastly more war-prone than are small states. The history of war is largely the story of great-power activity. Large states (defined as those with a population over 30 million) are also initiators of more conflict acts, aside from the use of force, than are small states.[33]

It may well be, then, that a nation's size is an important indicator of its propensity to go to war. And large, nationalistic, dictatorial states probably go to war more readily than small, commercial democracies. But it seems almost impossible to make more precise statements that can be verified. No one form of internal political or economic organization absolutely immunizes a state against the proclivity to go to war. And while certain internal characteristics *apparently* encourage a greater or lesser tendency to go to war, specifying those characteristics and determining their relative importance makes for heated controversy.

People who agree that the general cause of war is embedded somewhere in society (for example, Wilson and Lenin) disagree emphatically on the particular location or identity of the fatal flaw. As a result, accepting Wilson's, Lenin's, or someone else's interpretation of the exact cause means rejecting all other interpretations. For example, someone who believes that wars come about because of capitalist systems must reject not only theories that hold that wars grow out of a self-interested human nature or an anarchic international system but also all theories that blame war on other characteristics of nation-states, such as nationalism, totalitarianism, or religious fanaticism.

However, if there are many causes of war, we must recognize that doing away with any one cause will not do away with warfare. In fact, any attempt to eliminate a single cause of war may actually worsen the situation by *increasing* the possibility of war. As European history from 1919 to 1939 illustrates, concentrating solely on rearranging the international system while ignoring the role of human nature may actually encourage the ruthless to resort to war by removing impediments in the path of self-interested and ambitious rulers.[34] Had American, French, and British leaders in the 1930s not underestimated the role of the Nazis' ultranationalistic ideology or Hitler's pathological personality, it is possible that World War II could have been averted or at least contained.

A clear understanding of the causes of war, then, may help to effect at least modest improvements in the international system of "conflict management" by dispelling illusions about the prospects for peace. In such grave matters, simple solutions can be worse than no solutions at all: Many of the foremost political simplifiers in history have also been among the foremost contributors to war.

WARS NOBODY WANTS

So far, we have assumed that nations engage in warfare for specific purposes. They usually do. But sometimes a war can be caused by accident. In such instances, nations do not intend either the specific conflicts or the kinds of conflicts that result. And therefore, they may not be responsible or may be only partly responsible for the consequences. With the passing of the Cold War and a worldwide reduction of nations' stockpiling of vast quantities of sophisticated weapons systems, such unintentional conflict is less likely than it was even a decade ago. Yet, the possibility of such conflicts cannot be ignored.

War by misperception—war resulting from the misreading of real or supposed enemies' intentions or policies—is the most common kind of war nobody wants. Such wars have occurred all too often in the past. Sometimes a nation's leaders simply interpret political events in a rational way that nonetheless proves to be mistaken. At other times, a nation may declare war because its leaders misread political reality. On still other occasions, one nation may bully another, hoping to gain certain concessions but not intending to provoke an armed conflict. In these examples, nations may be culpable to different degrees. Yet none of them specifically intended to make war. Although misperception in politics may be impossible to eliminate, the potential that misperception may lead to war in this nuclear age is particularly worrisome.

Historically, *accidental war* has always been a possibility. An incorrect translation, a message not delivered, a diplomatic signal missed or misinterpreted—these and similar accidents precipitated unintended wars well before the advent of space-age weapons systems. In a technological era dominated by nuclear weapons, ballistic missiles, and computerized early-warning and guidance systems, however, the danger of war by accident has increased dramatically.

A *war of escalation* is not necessarily intended, but much of its violence is. Such a war could begin as a limited (and presumably localized) conflict between two nations. Whatever the immediate cause of war, neither side originally intended to use its most destructive weapons. But as emotions run high, casualties mount, and battlefield reverses occur, one side may be tempted to up the ante by introducing more powerful weapons, which the other side would have little choice but to match. If either side possesses nuclear weapons, the dynamics of such a situation could move the antagonists toward nuclear war. Thus what had started out as a limited, conventional war could move step by step up the weapons ladder until the conflict turned into an all-out nuclear confrontation.

Catalytic war can also generate violence and destruction well beyond any nation's intention. Historically, such wars usually occur because of alliances: Nations agree that an attack on one member will be treated as an attack on all members. In the present-day international scheme, a catalytic war might originate as a localized conflict between, say, two Third World countries that happen to have powerful allies. Local wars have always had the potential to turn into regional wars.

Nuclear War by Accident?

ALTHOUGH THE "SOVIET THREAT" no longer exists, Russia still possesses thousands of nuclear warheads, and the demise of the Soviet Union has brought into being two new nuclear powers—Ukraine and Kazakhstan. The possibility of nuclear war persists.

An accidental nuclear war might begin in many ways. Here is one chilling account of a near-miss:

> At 11:00 A.M. on June 3, 1980, the Air Force officers monitoring the early warning system deep underground inside Cheyenne Mountain, Colorado, were struck with terror. The fluorescent display screens connected to the Nova Data General computer were flashing a warning: The Soviet Union had launched a large attack from its land-based missiles and strategic submarines. The submarines had launched their missiles from positions close to the coast of the United States; the missiles would reach their targets in less than ten minutes.[35]

The alert was immediately fed into a computer network, and the U.S. strategic forces instantly began to mobilize. Fortunately, the "nuclear wheels" that had been set in motion were stopped before it was too late. A computer error, it turned out, had set off a false alarm—one of three such computer failures within eight months. According to a report prepared by the Senate Armed Services Committee, there were 3,703 alarms in the 18-month period from January 1979 to June 1980; of these incidents, 147 were sufficiently serious to require urgent evaluation.

Because the warning time available to government and military decision makers is being continually shortened by advances in weapons technology, effective and fail-safe systems of command, control, and communications (C_3) are absolutely vital today. Unfortunately, as we have just seen, these computerized systems are not error-free. And this situation has only been exacerbated by the development of counterforce weapons—those aimed at an adversary's strategic missile forces rather than population and industrial centers. With warning time reduced to as little as six minutes, counterforce missiles theoretically capable of disarming an unsuspecting enemy could make it necessary for nuclear powers to adopt "launch on warning" policies rather than absorbing the initial blows and then retaliating as prescribed by current strategic doctrines. Under "launch on warning," a country's nuclear forces are launched as soon as incoming enemy missiles or airplanes are detected, to prevent the destruction of those forces by counterforce weapons. The very existence of counterforce weapons, then, has apparently enhanced the danger of accidental nuclear war by simultaneously decreasing the time and increasing the urgency for a decision to "push the nuclear button" in a crisis.

Another danger: additional Third World states may soon acquire nuclear weapons and ballistic missiles. Nuclear proliferation is a threat because it increases the danger of nuclear war either by accident or by design.

The foregoing list of scenarios is by no means exhaustive; wars can begin in a number of other equally plausible ways. For example, a saboteur or a madman might manage somehow to "pull the nuclear trigger." What is important about all such scenarios—whether they involve sabotage, misperception, accident, escalation, or catalytic conflict—is not simply that they demonstrate how wars might begin; more important, they show how war may be the climax of an encounter in which none of the principal parties has any premeditated intent to commit armed aggression. Under such circumstances, it is very difficult to assign moral responsibility. Unintended wars are doubly tragic because they involve calamitous events that no one willed, planned, or desired.

IS WAR EVER MORALLY JUSTIFIED?

So far, we have considered war primarily from the standpoint of the perpetrators of aggression. But what about the victims? Few observers would dispute that nations have the right to resist armed aggression. When national survival is at stake, and all good-faith attempts to find an honorable way out of an impending confrontation have failed, it would seem that self-defense, even if it means widespread suffering and death, is morally justified. So despite Benjamin Franklin's assertion that "there was never a good war or a bad peace," some wars may be both necessary and proper.

The Just War Doctrine

The venerable doctrine of the *just war* holds that under certain circumstances, a war can be "good"—not in the sense of being pleasant or intrinsically desirable but rather in the sense of serving the welfare of a nation and the cause of justice. Thus the just war is a *justified* conflict, a necessary evil. This concept was advanced initially by early Christian theologians such as Saint Augustine and later refined by medieval philosophers. In the modern age, it has been reformulated by natural-law theorists and international scholars, most notably Hugo Grotius (1583–1645).

Among those who favor the concept of the just war, there has been unanimous agreement that defensive wars are justified. If a nation is the victim of an unprovoked attack, it is justified in waging war against its assailant. Some theorists expand this doctrine to give third-party nations the right to interfere on behalf of hapless victims of military aggression. The 1991 Persian Gulf War, which was preceded by Iraq's invasion and occupation of Kuwait, is an obvious case in point.

Most modern theorists limit the just war doctrine to defensive wars, but earlier writers did not always recognize such boundaries. Saint Augustine, for example, abhorred war in all its guises but found it necessary to justify even aggressive wars under some circumstances, as when a state "has failed either to make reparation for an injurious action committed by its citizens or to return what has been appropriated."[36] Another early Christian theologian, Saint Ambrose (A.D. 340?–397), argued that nations had a moral obligation, not simply a right, to wage aggressive war for the sake of higher principle. "Man has a moral duty," he wrote, "to employ force to resist active wickedness, for to refrain from hindering evil when possible is tantamount to promoting it."[37] Ambrose was aware of the need for limitations on this kind of war. Aggressive wars, he declared, should be fought only for a clearly just cause.

The just war doctrine finds expression in five distinct postulates. First, war must be the last resort available to a legitimate government; there must be no other effective political alternatives available. Second, the cause of the conflict must be just; a war should be fought only for the purpose of deterring or repelling aggression or righting a wrong. Third, the war cannot be futile; there must be some probability that the nation undertaking the conflict can succeed. Fourth,

Beyond all the theories about causes and factors, the agony of war often falls on innocent victims. Following the coalition victory over Iraq, Iraqi Kurds, fearing reprisals from Saddam Hussein, fled to northern Iraq and nearby Turkey and Iran. Many chose to stay in refugee camps that were established by coalition forces. Within a year, nearly 200,000 Kurds had been annihilated by Hussein's henchmen. (AP/Wide World Photos)

there must be proportionality of both ends and means; that is, the war's purpose must justify the cost of the war in money and lives, and the means employed in conducting the war must be appropriate to the reason why the war is fought. Finally, a just war must be waged in a manner that minimizes injury and death to civilians. If all of these conditions are met, a war can be considered justified.

The doctrine of the just war is rooted in a notion of justice that transcends immediate national interests. In contrast to the simplistic nationalism represented by such slogans as "My country right or wrong," the just war concept suggests a standard for measuring moral responsibility that transcends narrow national interest. The early Christian theologians based their notions of justice on Christian theological doctrines and scriptural teachings. More modern versions of the just war doctrine are grounded in a natural-law philosophy holding that there are self-evident truths concerning human welfare—truths that are obvious to rational human beings everywhere and that, taken together, point toward the true meaning of the ideal of "justice for all."

Criticisms of the Just War Doctrine

Of the various criticisms that have been leveled against the just war doctrine, we will focus on three of the most substantial: that the doctrine is guilty of *moral relativism,* that it embodies an *ethnocentric bias,* and that it is politically unrealistic.

Moral Relativism Some critics contend that the concept of the just war is based on highly subjective, and hence unprovable, value judgments. Because there is generally much room for disagreement about who was to blame for starting a particular war, it is argued, any attempt to assign moral responsibility is bound to reflect the opinions of the observer more than the often uncertain facts of the situation. The only way to avoid this type of moral relativism is to confine oneself to describing what happened before and during wars, sticking to accurate and verifiable facts.

Ethnocentric or Nationalistic Bias Similarly, it is charged that Western just war theorists tend to ignore justifications for war advanced by other cultures or ideologies. For instance, the traditional Islamic concept of a *jihad* ("holy war") against nonbelievers offers a moral rationale for aggressive war that has rarely been cited by Western proponents of the just war doctrine. Just war theorists also were similarly criticized for rejecting an interpretation that was advanced until recently by the former Soviet Union, namely that just wars advanced the interests of the Soviet state or of world communism (in Soviet theory, the two concerns tended to merge into one). Under this theory, just wars are wars waged by the working class against their oppressors, wars of "national liberation" fought by colonized peoples of the Third World against Western "imperialists," and wars waged to prevent the overthrow of socialist governments in eastern Europe and elsewhere.

Political Naiveté Finally, several opponents of the just war doctrine raise the practical objection that even if it were possible to arrive at a firm, unbiased, and universally accepted standard governing just and unjust wars, the resulting doctrine would be extremely difficult to apply fairly. Just as individuals are not good judges in their own cases, it is argued, so nations are not competent to pass judgment on controversies involving their own interests and well-being. Only a third party—an effective world court, a form of world government, or an impartial mediator of some kind—could possibly render fair judgments in such matters. Without an impartial referee, critics contend, the just war doctrine remains a sham advanced by aggressor nations to justify their self-serving policies and activities.

Defense of the Just War Doctrine

Defenders of the just war doctrine point out that moral judgments concerning the conduct of wars have long been thought both natural and necessary: natural in the sense that "for as long as men and women have talked about war, they have talked about it in terms of right and wrong,"[38] and necessary because without them, all wars would have to be considered equally objectionable (or praiseworthy). Admittedly, it cannot be proved scientifically that aggressive wars are more blameworthy than preemptive or preventive wars, but in a very real sense, no such proof should be required. Such a position should be no more controversial than the view that coldblooded murder is more reprehensible than a killing committed in self-defense—a distinction supported by both criminal law and common sense.

As to the charge of ethnocentrism, it has been argued that most approaches to the just war doctrine work to the advantage of the people who develop them. Such approaches aim at self-interest, not true justice. In defining a just war, it is essential to formulate its rules as neutral principles. (Neutral principles are rules that when unopposed by other like principles, are universally true and in the abstract work to the advantage of no one. Thus they would be willingly accepted by all nations or individuals were it not for divergent self-interests.) For example, this could be one such principle: It is unjust for any nation to attack another nation without provocation. If an imaginary "veil of ignorance" could induce temporary amnesia and all the world's leaders would momentarily forget which nations they governed, all would likely agree to this principle of nonaggression. The formulation of neutral principles presupposes that nations and individuals can overcome cultural and political prejudice. Such an objective approach makes value judgments on the morality of war both necessary and possible.

The realists' reservations about the just war doctrine hold a great deal of truth. At present, this concept has precious little efficacy in world politics. By itself, it provides no universally accepted, enforceable standard for constraining the behavior of nation-states. In our world, heads of state at times engage in moral talk and immoral behavior.

Despite this, the just war concept still remains valuable, if not as a means of controlling behavior, then as a method of evaluating it. Rigorously constructed, such a standard may help us to assign degrees of moral responsibility for war. Within countries where public debate precedes important policy decisions, such a doctrine may occasionally have some influence.

THE NUREMBERG WAR TRIALS

Following World War II, in what is history's most famous attempt to apply moral standards to wartime conduct, the Nazi leaders were charged in Nuremberg, Germany, with several types of crimes. First, they were accused of *crimes against peace* because they had waged aggressive war in violation of international treaties and obligations. Second, they were charged with *war crimes,* which encompassed such violations of the accepted rules of war as brutality toward prisoners of war, wanton destruction of towns, and mistreatment of civilians in conquered lands. Third, they were accused of *crimes against humanity,* including the persecution and mass murder of huge numbers of noncombatants.

Whereas crimes against peace and war crimes were concepts widely accepted under the just war doctrine, crimes against humanity represented a conceptual innovation designed to deal with crimes of unprecedented and staggering proportions. Although the Nazis had not succeeded in eliminating the Jewish people from the face of the earth, they had come very close. The decision to punish Nazi leaders for the wholesale slaughter of European Jewry was prompted by an understandable desire for retribution. Contrary to the well-known cliché, all is *not* fair in love and war. German actions could not be justified by the exigencies of war (which, of course, Hitler had started). Furthermore, the scope of the atrocities committed by the Nazi state had surpassed anything previously known in world history. Moral indifference seemed singularly inappropriate under these extraordinary circumstances.

The crimes against humanity concept provided firm support for the just war doctrine (and vice versa). The moral principle violated by the Nazis (that the needless suffering and death of innocent people is to be avoided) was so clear and the violation of it so flagrant that the Nazi actions were, beyond the slightest doubt, morally indefensible. The morality or immorality of many unfortunate actions in times of war may be problematical. Not so with the Holocaust, which is an unambiguous instance of criminal activity as defined under the just war doctrine.

Although the trials held at Nuremberg were justifiable, war crimes trials raise serious concerns. It is no simple task to apply the "crimes against peace," "war crimes," and "crimes against humanity" labels to concrete and often unique situations. The concentration camps clearly violate all standards of law, justice, and decency. But what about the Allied firebombing of Dresden? Or the brutalities against German civilians tolerated (if not encouraged) by the Soviet army? Or the utter devastation visited on Hiroshima and Nagasaki?

The nature of international politics in the modern age makes the question of morality in war highly ambiguous. In the case of the Nuremberg trials, however, the violation of moral and legal standards was so flagrant that all ambiguity vanished. The complicated relationship between war and morality is often more difficult to disentangle—but that is no reason not to make the attempt. Unfortunately, serious attempts to sort out relative degrees of moral responsibility are all too often drowned out by the clamor of public opinion or the clash of opposing armies.

Summary

Avoiding war is not always an objective of state policy. Some leaders—for example, Italy's fascist dictator Mussolini—have actually glorified it.

Many attempts have been made to identify the causes of war. The resulting theories can be divided into three categories: Some see human nature as the cause; others blame society; and still others believe that environmental factors hold the key. Thomas Hobbes thought that war was a product of human perversity; Jean-Jacques Rousseau maintained that human beings are basically good but society corrupts them; John Locke attributed human aggression to scarcities in nature (that is, circumstances beyond human control). Scarcities in nature encompass a wide variety of impersonal forces that impinge on nation-states, including uncertainty and accident.

All single-factor explanations fall short in analyzing the causes of war. Wars stem from a variety of factors—social, political, economic, and psychological. Indeed, the stress related to global and regional arms races can spark the outbreak of war. Under conditions of high tension, war may occur even if none of the principals wants it. Such unintended wars may erupt because of misperception, misunderstanding, accident, escalation, or a catalytic reaction.

The possibility of unintended war illustrates the potential difficulty in assigning moral responsibility. Often when war occurs, it is not clear who or what actually caused it.

Using war as an instrument of state policy violates international law and morality, but not all wars are equally objectionable. The just war doctrine holds that self-defense and the defense of universal principles are legitimate reasons for going to war. This doctrine, however, is frequently criticized on the grounds of moral relativism, cultural ethnocentrism, and political realism.

The Nuremberg war trials assigned guilt for criminal acts performed while waging a war of aggression. International lawyers developed a new category of war crimes—crimes against humanity—at Nuremberg. Although the Nuremberg trials were justified, such proceedings contain inherent pitfalls and must be approached with extreme caution.

Key Terms

state of nature	war of escalation	ethnocentric bias
national self-determination	catalytic war	crimes against peace
war by misperception	just war	war crimes
accidental war	moral relativism	crimes against humanity

Review Questions

1. Into what general categories do most explanations of the ultimate causes of war fall?

2. According to Thomas Hobbes, what is the root cause of all wars? What arguments did Hobbes offer in defense of his thesis?

3. What did Rousseau believe to be the root cause of war? How did his views differ from Hobbes's? What arguments did Rousseau advance to support his thesis?

4. Among those who believe that society is the ultimate cause of war, differences of opinion exist about precisely what aspect of society is most respon-

sible for the belligerency of nation-states. What are the four alternative theories presented in the text?

5. How did John Locke explain the phenomenon of war? How did his view differ from those of Hobbes and Rousseau? What arguments did he offer in support of his thesis?

6. Which explanation of the causes of war is correct? Explain your answer.

7. Why is it difficult simply to condemn the guilty party or parties whenever war breaks out?

8. In a world in which the technology of warfare is advancing by leaps and bounds, it becomes increasingly probable that a war will start even though nobody intends to start one. In what ways might this happen?

9. Are all wars equally objectionable from a moral standpoint? Explain.

10. Are the arguments, pro and con, concerning the validity of the just war doctrine equally balanced? Explain.

11. What prompted the Nuremberg trials? What are crimes against humanity? How does the just war doctrine fit into the picture?

12. Should (or could) Nuremberg-type trials be conducted after every war?

Recommended Reading

ARENDT, HANNAH. *Eichmann in Jerusalem: A Report on the Banality of Evil* (rev. ed.). New York: Penguin, 1977. A provocative study of the Israeli trial of Adolf Eichmann that raises a number of philosophical problems.

ARON, RAYMOND. *The Century of Total War.* Lanham, Md.: University Press of America, 1985. One of this century's most influential thinkers examines the causes and conditions of war in our age.

ARON, RAYMOND. *The Great Debate: Theories of Nuclear Strategy,* trans. Ernst Pawel. Lanham, Md.: University Press of America, 1985. A lucid analysis of strategic alternatives available to the Western alliance. First published in the early 1960s, it is still worth reading.

BARNETT, RICHARD. *Roots of War.* New York: Penguin, 1973. Barnett blames society in general and economically advanced societies in particular.

BROWN, SEYOM. *The Causes and Prevention of War.* New York: St. Martin's Press, 1987. A multidisciplinary overview of human aggression and violence by a widely recognized authority on the politics of war and peace; concludes with an integrated strategy for peace.

CARR, EDWARD HALLETT. *The Twenty Years' Crisis, 1919–1939.* New York: Harper & Row, 1981. An excellent case study of the influences and forces that led to World War II, written in 1939.

COHEN, MARSHALL, THOMAS NAGEL, AND THOMAS SCANLON (eds.). *War and Moral Responsibility*. Princeton, N.J.: Princeton University Press, 1974. A useful collection of essays on many of the central issues relating to war and morality.

COX, ARTHUR MACY. *Russian Roulette: The Superpower Game*. New York: Times Books, 1982. The danger of accidental war is highlighted in this study.

GOLDWIN, ROBERTS, AND TONY PEARCE (eds.). *Readings in World Politics*. New York: Oxford University Press, 1970. An excellent collection of classic writings on war and other aspects of international politics; the Butterfield, Clauswitz, Einstein, and Mead articles are particularly insightful.

HAUSNER, GIDEON. *Justice in Jerusalem*. New York: Herzl Press, 1978. Another view of the Eichmann trial, written by the Israeli prosecutor.

KNORR, KLAUS. *On the Uses of Military Power in the Nuclear Age*. Princeton, N.J.: Princeton University Press, 1966. An excellent study of the diminished usefulness of military power in the nuclear age. The author assesses the implications of this paradox for the postwar international system.

RICHARDSON, LEWIS. *Statistics of Deadly Quarrels*. Chicago: Boxwood, 1960. A frequently cited quantitative study of war.

SEABURY, PAUL, AND ANGELO M. CODEVILLA. *War: Ends and Means*. New York: Basic Books, 1990. A sober discussion of war as a permanent part of the human condition.

SCHELLING, THOMAS. *The Strategy of Conflict*. Cambridge, Mass.: Harvard University Press, 1960. A strategic examination of the role of war in the international system.

STOESSINGER, JOHN. *Why Nations Go to War* (5th ed.). New York: St. Martin's Press, 1989. An attempt to explain the causes of war.

WALTZ, KENNETH N. *Man, the State and War: A Theoretical Analysis*. New York: Columbia University Press, 1959. An extraordinarily lucid account of the origins of war, emphasizing the importance of human nature, the state, and the international political system.

WALZER, MICHAEL. *Just and Unjust Wars*. New York: Basic Books, 1979. A comprehensive effort to develop a just war theory and apply it to modern conflicts.

WRIGHT, QUINCY. *A Study of War* (abridged ed.). Chicago: University of Chicago Press, 1983. This is probably the most famous study of war in the English language.

Notes

1. Paul Seabury and Angelo M. Codevilla, *War: Ends and Means* (New York: Basic Books, 1990), p. 6.

2. G. W. F. Hegel, *Philosophy of Right*, trans. T. M. Knox, in *Great Books of the Western World*, ed. R. Hutchins (Chicago: Encyclopaedia Britannica, 1952), vol. 46, p. 149.

3. Benito Mussolini, ''The Doctrine of Fascism,'' trans. M. Oakeshott, in William Ebenstein, *Great Political Thinkers* (New York: Holt, 1965), p. 621.

4. The quotation is from Sir Norman Angell's *Neutrality and Collective Security,* cited in Edward Hallett Carr, *The Twenty Years' Crisis, 1919–1939* (New York: Harper & Row, 1964), p. 39.

5. Thomas Hobbes, *The Leviathan* (London: Everyman's Library, 1965), p. 64.

6. Carr, *Twenty Years' Crisis.*

7. Hans J. Morgenthau, *Politics among Nations: The Struggle for Power and Peace,* 5th rev. ed. (New York: Knopf, 1978), pp. 3–4.

8. Ibid., p. 29.

9. Jean-Jacques Rousseau, *First and Second Discourses,* trans. Roger and Judith Masters, ed. Roger Masters (New York: St. Martin's Press, 1964), p. 197. The quotation is from Rousseau's *Notes, Second Discourse.*

10. Ibid., pp. 195–196.

11. Ibid., *Second Discourse,* pp. 141–142.

12. Ibid., p. 161.

13. Frederick Hartmann, *The Relations of Nations* (New York: Macmillan, 1978), p. 32.

14. William Galston, *Kant and the Problem of History* (Chicago: University of Chicago Press, 1975), pp. 26–27.

15. Immanuel Kant, "Eternal Peace," in *Immanuel Kant's Moral and Political Writings,* ed. Carl Friedrich (New York: Modern Library, 1949), p. 438.

16. V. I. Lenin, *Imperialism: The Highest Stage of Capitalism* (New York: International Publishers, 1939), p. 124.

17. Robert Goldwin, "John Locke," in *History of Political Philosophy,* ed. L. Strauss and J. Cropsey (Skokie, Ill.: Rand McNally, 1963), p. 442.

18. The quotations in the following three paragraphs can be found in Richard Falk, *This Endangered Planet: Prospects and Proposals for Human Survival* (New York: Vintage Books, 1972), pp. 106–107.

19. Ibid., p. 107.

20. Ibid., p. 113.

21. Ibid., p. 155.

22. Bayard Webster, "Studies Warn of Declining Resources," *Minneapolis Tribune,* February 10, 1980, p. 70. For a more optimistic view, see Julian Simon, *The Ultimate Resource* (Princeton, N.J.: Princeton University Press, 1982). Also see *The Global 2000 Report to the President: Entering the 21st Century,* vol. 1 (New York: Penguin, 1982).

23. Aristotle, *The Politics,* trans. and ed. Ernest Barker (New York: Oxford University Press, 1962), p. 245.

24. Hannah Arendt, *Totalitarianism* (New York: Harcourt, 1951), pp. 113–114.

25. Quincy Wright, *A Study of War,* abridged ed. (Chicago: University of Chicago Press, 1964), pp. 161–163; see also R. Barry Furrell, "Foreign Politics of Open and Closed

Societies," *Approaches to Comparative and International Politics* (Evanston, Ill.: Northwestern University Press, 1966).

26. Rudolph Rummel, "Some Empirical Findings," *World Politics* 21 (1969), pp. 238–239.

27. Morgenthau, *Politics among Nations,* pp. 51–57.

28. David Wood, *Conflict in the Twentieth Century,* Adelphi Paper no. 48 (London: Institute of Strategic Studies, 1968), as cited in K. J. Holsti, *International Politics: A Framework for Analysis* (Englewood Cliffs, N.J.: Prentice Hall, 1979), pp. 306–307.

29. James Rosenau, ed., *Domestic Sources of Foreign Policy* (New York: Free Press, 1967), p. 25.

30. James Rosenau and Charles Herman, "Final Report of the National Science Foundation on Grant Gs-3117" (mimeo, n.d.), p. 19, as cited in Holsti, *International Politics,* p. 391.

31. Dina Zinnes, "Some Evidence Relevant to the Man-Milieu Hypothesis," in *The Analysis of International Politics,* ed. J. Rosenau et al. (New York: Free Press, 1972).

32. See Ralph Pettman, *Human Behavior and World Politics: An Introduction to International Relations* (New York: St. Martin's Press, 1976), pp. 250–252.

33. Holsti, *International Politics,* pp. 390 and 456. Also note Quincy Wright's comment: "There seems to have been a positive correlation between the warlikeness of a state and its relative power. The 'great powers' in all periods of history have been the most frequently at war and the small states have been the most peaceful." Wright, *A Study of War,* p. 168.

34. Kenneth N. Waltz, *Man, the State and War: A Theoretical Analysis* (New York: Columbia University Press, 1959), p. 233. Waltz's discussion of war is somewhat similar to ours. We acknowledge our debt to his scholarship.

35. Arthur Macy Cox, *Russian Roulette: The Superpower Game* (New York: Times Books, 1982), p. 3.

36. Quoted in Lee McDonald, *Western Political Theory: From Its Origins to the Present* (Orlando, Fla.: Harcourt Brace Jovanovich, 1968), p. 127.

37. Cited in James E. Dougherty and Robert L. Pfaltzgraff, Jr., *Contending Theories of International Relations* (Philadelphia: Lippincott, 1971), p. 151, n. 24.

38. Michael Walzer, *Just and Unjust Wars* (New York: Basic Books, 1968), p. 1.

CHAPTER 19

INTERNATIONAL RELATIONS

THE STRUGGLE FOR POWER

CHAPTER OUTLINE

IN "THE MELIAN CONFERENCES," the Greek historian Thucydides related the following episode in the Peloponnesian War (431–404 B.C.) between Athens and Sparta.[1] In 416 B.C., Athens sent ships and troops against the island of Melos, a colony of Sparta that had remained neutral and wanted no part of the war. Negotiating from a position of overwhelming strength, the Athenians insisted on unconditional surrender, bluntly telling the Melians, "You know as well as we do that right, as the world goes, is only in question between equals in power, while the strong do what they can and the weak suffer what they must." The Melians responded by asking, "And how, pray, could it turn out as good for us to serve as for you to rule?" "Because," the Athenians answered, "you would have the advantage of submitting before suffering the worst, and we should gain by not destroying you."

Undaunted, the Melians persisted in trying to persuade the Athenians that the interest of all would be enhanced by peaceful relations between the two states. The Athenians would have no part of this logic. With ruthless disregard for questions of justice, they reasoned that if Melos were permitted to remain independent, the Melians and others would take it as a sign of Athenian weakness. "[By] extending our empire," the Athenians pointed out, "we should gain in security by your subjection; the fact that you are islanders and weaker than others rendering all the more important that you should not succeed in baffling the masters of the sea." Thus the Melian state was doomed by the cold calculus of power politics.

Athenian intransigence was met by Melian resolve. Maintaining their position to the end, the Melians repeated that above all they desired neutrality; failing that, they vowed to put their trust in the gods and the Spartans. The Athenians proceeded to besiege the island, and the Melians counterattacked. The Spartans came but did not stay. Then disaster struck:

> Reinforcements afterwards arriving from Athens in consequence, under the command of Philocrates, son of Demeas, the siege was now pressed vigorously; and some treachery taking place inside, the Melians surrendered at discretion to the Athenians, who put to death all the grown men whom they took, and sold the women and children for slaves, and subsequently sent out five hundred colonists and inhabited the place themselves.

INTERNATIONAL POWER POLITICS: MACHIAVELLI'S LEGACY

Thucydides's account of the Melian tragedy is chilling. Resolved to defend their homeland and their honor, the Melians found themselves unable to ensure either, simply because they were in the wrong place at the wrong time. Through no fault of their own, they fell victim to military aggression. Such grave uncertainties have always attended politics among nations; like individuals in the state of nature, nations are not bound by the dictates of any kind of sovereign organization. They are free, in other words, to follow their own instincts and interests in choosing the measures they deem necessary for their own survival. Consequently, nations often pursue power the way a miser hoards money—avidly and relentlessly. Power provides insurance against the unpredictable winds of fortune; the more power a nation amasses, the more secure it feels.

No one understood this principle better than Niccolò Machiavelli, the sixteenth-century Italian political philosopher. In his masterwork, *The Prince* (1532), he advised rulers to diminish the importance of these forces in every possible way, observing (before sexism was an issue) that "fortune is a woman, and it is necessary, if you wish to master her, to conquer her by force."[2] Machiavelli's message was clear: For political success, rulers must constantly seek maximum control over resources and events.

In Machiavelli's view, rulers had an obligation to conquer chance, and therefore they could not be held to the same moral standards as private citizens. In other words, he denied that conventional morality could or should be practiced in external affairs. Individuals, he argued, may be free to seek moral self-fulfillment, but the ruler of the state must seek power. In short, Machiavelli believed that in politics, anything that enhances state power is good and anything that erodes state power is bad.

Under Machiavelli's assumptions, *virtue* becomes synonymous with *victory*, and *vice* becomes indistinguishable from *defeat*. Most of us have been taught from childhood that it is not whether we win or lose that counts but how we play the game. The wise ruler, Machiavelli taught, must always play to win, for "how we live is so far removed from how we ought to live, that he who abandons what is done for what ought to be done, will rather learn to bring about his own ruin than his preservation."[3]

The prudent ruler, he argued, recognizes what must be done to preserve and enlarge his dominions and does not allow moral qualms to cloud his judgment. For example, rulers should keep their promises (in his words, "keep faith") only when it suits their purposes to do so:

> A prudent ruler ought not to keep faith when by doing so it would be against his interest, and when the reasons which made him bind himself no longer exist. . . . If men were all good, this precept would not be a good one; but as they are bad, and would not observe their faith with you, so you are not bound to keep faith with them.[4]

The teachings of Machiavelli, together with the fate of the Melians, suggest that morality plays a much less significant role in politics between nations than it does in politics within nations. As long as international politics continues to resemble the state of nature, tensions between nations will persist, and chance will from time to time reduce a nation's alternatives to a question of survival. And when survival is at stake, necessity is often a remorseless tyrant.

POLITICAL REALISM

The theory that under almost all circumstances, nations will naturally pursue their own self-interest is commonly known as *political realism*. This theory of international relations is most closely associated with political scientist Hans

Political realists stress that the best way to ensure survival is to enhance the nation's power, both political and military. As Machiavelli put it: "Since love and fear can hardly exist together, . . . it is far safer to be feared than loved." (Regis Bossul/Sygma)

Morgenthau (1904–1980), who systematically explained its basic principles. Morgenthau and his followers assert that political realism can often be used to predict how nations will act. If you can discern the goals and objectives that serve a given state's **national interests** and can ascertain how accurately that nation's leaders understand those interests, you can calculate to a high degree of probability the future actions of that nation. Following Machiavelli's rationale, this school of thought displays relatively little concern for the way nations *ought* to act. Because other nations inevitably *will* act in a self-interested fashion, it is argued, one's own nation must also pursue such a course. Survival is the basic goal of national policy, and the best way to ensure survival is to enhance the nation's power.

Political realists stress that success in international politics, even when confrontation is absent, ultimately depends on maintaining political power. According to Morgenthau, power is "man's control over the minds and actions of other men."[5] Military force is the most important aspect of power in international politics. Accordingly, political realists tend to favor a tough-minded approach to national defense (more is generally better than less), nuclear arms control (to be pursued cautiously), and participation in international organizations (of limited utility and not the hope of the future). Yet military force and political power can never be considered synonymous. Other factors, including geopolitical, economic, and social concerns, contribute to a nation's power as well. Even the personal charisma or competence of a political leader or the effectiveness of a nation's political institutions can make the crucial difference. Neglect of a factor such as charisma

> accounts in good measure for the neglect of prestige as an independent element in international politics. Yet without taking into account the charisma of a man, such as Napoleon or Hitler, or of an institution, such as the Government or the United States Constitution, evoking trust and love . . . it is impossible to understand certain

phenomena of international politics which have been particularly prominent in modern times.[6]

Optimizing and balancing a nation's vital interests requires political prudence. According to Morgenthau, "Realism considers prudence—the weighing of the consequences of political action—to be the supreme virtue in politics."[7] Properly interpreted and applied, such prudence, Morgenthau argued, will correctly guide the affairs of a nation. A foreign policy based on a realistic appraisal of the national interest will avoid not only the dangers of hazardous timidity but also "the blindness of crusading frenzy [that] destroys nations and civilizations—in the name of moral principle, ideal, or God himself."[8] As Morgenthau saw it, then, the concept of the national interest is an antidote for the excesses and follies of misguided moralists. Obviously, what constitutes the national interest varies from country to country and even from year to year, although some interests are permanent and others temporary, some primary and others secondary, some general and others specific.

To the political realist, the successful statesman is one who masters the art of balancing national interests and objectives against national capabilities (or power). Prudence demands that a statesman, like a budget-conscious shopper in the supermarket, distinguish between items that are necessary and those that are merely desirable. According to this view of international politics, the essence of statesmanship lies in bringing the expectations and desires of a nation into line with the capabilities of the state and correctly differentiating between vital and expendable interests.

Political realism places a premium on flexibility and sobriety in the conduct of foreign policy. Thus the political realist would say that in international politics there are no permanent allies, only permanent interests. However appalling such Machiavellian precepts may seem to idealists, Morgenthau concluded, statesmen cannot afford to operate on any other basis.

FOREIGN POLICY GOALS: DETERMINING THE NATIONAL INTEREST

Distinguishing clearly between foreign policy ends and means is critical in the analysis of international politics. By foreign policy ends, we mean the overarching objectives or goals that animate and motivate nations. By foreign policy means, we refer to the strategies or policies that nations adopt to pursue their goals. Goals or objectives are by nature long-range, deeply rooted, and slow to change. Strategies or policies, in turn—which are usually pragmatic, short-lived, and tactical—are largely dictated by the goals that nations set. Strategies can vary from time to time and can be continental, regional, or local in scope.

Maintenance versus Enhancement

Two important and recurring types of goal orientation are seen in international politics: *power maintenance goals* and *power enhancement goals*. Nations that wish to increase their power and influence seek to do so at other nations' expense.

By contrast, nations seeking to maintain their power position relative to other nations—and power is always relative—choose a foreign policy strategy designed to prevent other nations from improving their relative position. Thus if no rival nation is engaging in an arms buildup, power maintenance nations are content to keep their own arsenals at existing levels. But if rival nations are increasing their military capabilities, those wishing merely to maintain their relative position feel compelled to increase their own capabilities as well.

Thus to the casual observer, it may sometimes appear as though there is no difference between the behavior of power maintenance and power enhancement nations, but in fact their motives and goals are quite different. Nations seeking to enhance their power want to change existing power relationships, often at the direct expense of nations wishing to maintain these relationships. Power enhancement nations are dissatisfied with their international power position. For this reason, they frequently provoke wars, initiate arms races, promote revolutions abroad, and seek generally to destabilize the international system. Such actions create a strong moral pressure against these nations, although each case must be evaluated individually.

There are a few exceptions to this generalization. Some nations balk at the stark choice between power maintenance and power enhancement; a few opt out of power politics altogether. Still others (like Great Britain, which after World War II shed its colonial empire) are forced by circumstances beyond their control to choose other, less common foreign policy objectives such as power reduction or, in extreme cases, self-liquidation. Nor are foreign policy goals always easy to distinguish, as we shall see.

The Ambiguities of Foreign Policy: The Arab-Israeli Conflict

To illustrate the complex and ambiguous nature of foreign policy goals in international relations, we need look no further than the prolonged conflict between Israel and the Arab world. Of particular importance is the 31-year period from 1948 to 1979. That interval remains crucial not only for its profoundly important historical importance (the contemporary Middle East situation cannot be understood except in light of it) but as a case study illustrating the occasional complexity of determining the foreign policy goals of particular nations. After World War II, Jewish nationalists, or *Zionists*, waged a successful war against the British and the Arabs for a homeland in Palestine. In defense of their actions, they cited historical, biblical, and legal authority and argued that in the aftermath of the Holocaust, Jews could live in security only in a Jewish homeland. The war they fought, however, was not without its innocent victims. Palestinian Arab refugees, hundreds of thousands of whom had fled their homes rather than live in a Jewish state, regarded the Israelis as imperialists. Arab nationalists everywhere took up the cause, declaring a holy war against Zionism and vowing to destroy the newborn state of Israel. Not surprisingly, Arab nations in the region refused to recognize Israel's right to exist as a sovereign state.

Subsequently, radical Palestinian groups directed acts of terrorism against the Israeli population with the complicity of several Arab governments, notably

Like the Arabs, Israel, too, has occasionally acted to alter the local and regional balance of power by permitting the establishment of Jewish settlements on land seized from the Arabs. Here, three Israeli soldiers guard four married Jewish couples from possible Palestinian retaliation. (Leonard Freed/Magnum)

Egypt. In 1956, Egypt seized the Suez Canal from Great Britain and France, which nations actively backed Israel in the ensuing war with Egypt over which nation would control access to the canal. This episode only strengthened the Arab belief that Zionism and Western imperialism were conspiring to dominate the Muslim nations of the Middle East.

After more than a decade of smoldering hostilities, another war erupted. In 1967, reacting to bellicose Egyptian threats and to intelligence reports suggesting that Egypt was on the verge of an attack, Israel launched a preemptive military operation that resulted in the so-called *Six-Day War*. After less than a week of fighting, the Israelis had routed their enemies and occupied large tracts of Arab territory, including the Sinai peninsula and Gaza Strip in Egypt, the Golan Heights in Syria, and the West Bank of the Jordan River in Jordan. The hitherto partitioned city of Jerusalem fell under complete Israeli control. Humiliated by this abject defeat, Egypt and Syria prepared for yet another round of fighting. In 1973, they attempted to revise the post-1967 status quo by attacking Israeli-held territories. The Israelis were again equal to the challenge, but this time they suffered a setback in the early going. With the United States acting as mediator, the Egyptians eventually regained the Sinai desert by agreeing to a peace treaty with Israel in 1979 (the Camp David accords), but the other Arab nations charged Egypt with selling out to Zionism and "imperialism."

Which nations have pursued a foreign policy goal of power enhancement? Since the founding of Israel in 1948, each side has accused the other of harboring imperialistic designs. From an objective standpoint, we can say that the Arab states (along with the Palestine Liberation Organization) that have repeatedly avowed their intention to destroy Israel have rejected the status quo in the Middle East. But Israel, too, has occasionally acted to alter the local and regional balance of power by permitting the establishment of Jewish settlements on land seized from the Arabs. Do the actions of one or both sides constitute a pervasive and hostile foreign policy designed to gain power and influence at the expense of the other? Considerable controversy characterizes this debate. Interestingly enough, each side has sought to justify its position on the ground that it was merely maintaining its power: Arab critics claim the moral high ground by asserting that they are simply defending the Palestinians' right to self-determination, while the Israelis cite the moral obligation to safeguard their right to exist as a sovereign nation.

Similar ambiguities crop up all the time in international politics. Fortunately, competing claims do not preclude judgments about nations' foreign policy goals. They merely make such judgments more difficult to reach.

FOREIGN POLICY STRATEGIES: PURSUING THE NATIONAL INTEREST

Nations implement their foreign policy goals by means of various strategies and policies. Surprisingly, the range of foreign policy strategies is quite restricted in international politics. Nations generally choose from among only four basic strategies. States pursuing *expansionism* seek to enlarge their territory or influence. By contrast, a nation that follows a *status quo strategy* seeks to preserve and continue a particular power relationship. By choosing a policy of *accommodation*, states intend to preserve or promote peace, sometimes at the expense of their power. A fourth option, *altruism*, is rarely exercised, although when it is, this strategy reveals both the prevalence and the limits of the pursuit of national self-interest in international politics.

We must recognize the important distinction between a nation's long-term goal and its more pragmatic strategies. The gap between goals and strategies raises three key points. First, regardless of whether a nation pursues power maintenance or power enhancement, it will simultaneously carry out different strategies to confront varying political problems. For example, a nation may seek to preserve the status quo by signing a peace treaty with one nation to launch an expansionistic attack on another: Nazi Germany (a nation actively pursuing the goal of power enhancement) signed a nonaggression treaty with the Soviet Union in August 1939 for strategic advantage in conquering eastern Europe. Or a nation seeking power maintenance may not confine its strategies to defense of the status quo and accommodation. Such a nation might even choose a strategy of expansionism when it believes that striking first and occupying a potential enemy's territory are necessary to ensure its survival.

These illustrations emphasize the second point: that power strategies are flexible; they change with circumstances and can be applied and altered whenever the nation's ruling leadership deems it appropriate. Thus less than two years after Hitler signed his peace treaty with Stalin, he invaded the Soviet Union.

This leads to a third key point: The same strategy pursued by different nations may have radically different implications, depending on each nation's overall goals. A nonaggression pact between two nations whose goal is merely to preserve their power may differ significantly from that same treaty signed by one of these nations and a third nation intent on expanding its power. In international politics, the meaning of any strategy usually turns on the motives of the leaders who implement it and their long-term policy goals. Because motives are not easily discerned and because foreign policy goals are rarely self-evident, determining such motives and goals can be the most difficult and most important tasks undertaken by the serious student of international relations.

Expansionism

A state that pursues a strategy of increasing its power and influence by changing the established international order—usually in accord with its foreign policy objective—naturally pursues an expansionist foreign policy. Historical examples of expansionism include the U.S. assertion of control over Cuba, Hawaii, and the Philippines following the Spanish-American War of 1898; the German annexation of Austria and seizure of Czechoslovakia in the late 1930s; the Vietnamese takeover of Kampuchea (Cambodia) in 1979; the Soviet invasion of Afghanistan that same year; and the Iraqi seizure of Kuwait in 1990. These are clear-cut examples of expansionist policies in action.

To understand the strategy of expansionism, one must also understand what it is not. Not every state with a territorial claim against another state or a desire for change in the global distribution of power and wealth is expansionist. The nature of the changes advocated—as well as the motives and methods of the state advocating them—must be carefully considered. For example, a border dispute does not in itself constitute evidence that either contending country has an appetite for empire. Nor does the demand of many Third World nations for a "new international economic order," meaning a redistribution of global wealth. Although the poor nations—using international forums like the United Nations—have challenged the status quo, it would be quite erroneous to accuse them of expansionism.

In addition, violent methods do not always denote a strategy of expansionism. Defenders of the status quo routinely associate insurgency with aggression and aggression with expansionism. It is logical, therefore, to link insurgency with expansionism (the ultimate challenge to the status quo). However, defenders of the status quo, including the United States, may also sponsor insurgencies.

Calling them "freedom fighters," the Reagan administration aided a variety of anticommunist insurgents around the world in the 1980s, including groups in Central America (the Contras in Nicaragua), Asia (the Mujaheddin rebels in Afghanistan), and Africa (UNITA guerrillas in Angola).

These examples demonstrate the importance (and difficulty) of moral objectivity in foreign policy analysis. A strategy aimed at changing the existing distribution of power and wealth is not necessarily a sign of imperialism or immorality. Thus the only way that *any* foreign policy can be evaluated on moral or ethical grounds is by reference to its particular historical context, the means employed, and above all, the ends sought.

Motives for Expansionism   Nations that pursue expansionist policies to enhance their political power are the most dangerous threats to the world order. Their leaders have a burning desire for change; they are dissatisfied and impatient. Frequently, such leaders display a thirst for glory and grandeur; sometimes, by arousing nationalistic fervor, a demagogue like Hitler or Mussolini taps hidden reserves of popular energy and willpower. As the most radical challengers of the status quo, such states actively seek to overthrow the existing balance of power, by armed force if necessary. For this reason, such nations disrupt the international order in the same way that revolutionaries undermine a nation's internal order.

Nations pursue expansionist strategies in a variety of circumstances. In the aftermath of a war, for example, the victorious state may choose to dismember or otherwise disable its vanquished adversary to guard against a reopening of hostilities. After defeating Carthage in 146 B.C., Rome utterly destroyed the city (the ancient equivalent of a modern state). Although this kind of "Carthaginian peace" has been outlawed by the rules of modern warfare, victorious powers still seek to weaken their fallen enemies. After World War I, for example, the United States and its allies demanded that Germany sign a treaty containing a "war guilt" clause, insisted that Germany pay huge reparations to neighboring states for war damages, and dictated Germany's form of government (the ill-fated Weimar Republic).

Defeat in war can furnish an equally powerful incitement to a nation's expansionist strategies and power enhancement objectives. What might be termed wars of national atonement sometimes erupt from the deep sense of humiliation felt by war's losers. After World War I, for example, many Germans felt that the honor of their country had been trampled underfoot by the peace treaty imposed on them by the victorious Allies. Beyond a doubt, one of the reasons for Hitler's rocketlike rise to power in the 1930s was his demagogic appeal to the ordinary German's wounded sense of pride in this regard. Whatever Hitler's twisted personal motives, the loss of World War I was clearly a major factor in making the German people receptive to his ultranationalistic strategies and objectives. Accordingly, Hitler was able to justify his military adventures on the ground that they were aimed at redressing the "unjust" status quo established by the Treaty of Versailles (1919).

The temporary weakness of neighboring states can also induce expansionism. It is axiomatic in international politics that power moves swiftly into a vacuum. The United States found the temptation to "win the West" in the nineteenth century irresistible in large part because of the weakness of both the native inhabitants and Mexico, which also laid claim to the lands beyond the Mississippi River. Had Mexico been a nineteenth-century military power on a par with Russia, Prussia, France, or even Spain, the oil wells of Texas might never have produced domestic gasoline for American cars.

States sometimes commit aggressive acts for defensive reasons: If a state is able to protect its territorial integrity against its neighbors but those neighbors are not able to protect themselves, the secure state may seek to forestall an attack on (or a revolt within) its weaker neighbors by taking preemptive military action against them. When this happens, the real target is not the hapless adjoining states but some other, more formidable foe that might pose a direct threat at some time in the future. The Soviet attack on Finland in the winter of 1940, for instance, was aimed at preventing Nazi Germany from using that country as a staging area for military action against the USSR.

Status Quo

Although all nations pursue a status quo strategy from time to time, nations opposed to changes affecting the regional or global balance of power pursue it most avidly. Such states normally assume a defensive posture in external affairs; finding the existing balance of power to their advantage, they seek stability and order. Examples abound: the U.S. invasion of Grenada in 1983 to prevent a radical Cuban-backed Marxist government from taking power there; Egypt's opposition to Libyan meddling in the internal affairs of neighboring North African states; South Africa's armed intervention against insurgents in Namibia; Saudi Arabia's support for Iraq as a bulwark against the spread of Iran's revolutionary Islamic fundamentalism onto the Arabian peninsula; Thailand's diplomatic efforts to dissuade Vietnam from occupying neighboring Kampuchea (Cambodia); the U.S.-led coalition's intervention against Iraq in 1991. In this last case, all members of the coalition feared that Saddam Hussein's intention was to establish Iraqi domination over the Arabian peninsula (and possibly beyond)—that is, Saddam posed a perceived threat to the existing balance of power in the Middle East.

Status quo strategies are essentially conservative. Nations adopting such a strategy aim to uphold the existing balance of power, and they cherish stability, peaceful intercourse among nations, and above all, legitimacy. Status quo states generally seek to use instruments such as international law, multilateral arrangements, and global authorities (such as the League of Nations and the United Nations) to legitimize the existing distribution of power and prestige in the world. Frequently, they refuse to recognize revolutionary governments on the grounds that such governments seized power unlawfully or pose a threat to the stability of the regional or global balance or that to reward violence and lawlessness with international acceptance would be to undermine respect for law and order everywhere.

As we have noted, few states consistently follow status quo strategies on all fronts. Sometimes the political posture of a particular nation shifts between, say, expansionism and pursuit of the status quo. The diplomatic history of the United States vividly illustrates this tendency. Although at various times it has practiced a policy of continental and even extracontinental expansion, the United States has for much of its history followed a strategy of maintaining the regional and international status quo. Two examples of this policy were the Monroe Doctrine and the post–World War II effort to contain what was perceived as Soviet aggression.

The Monroe Doctrine: A Regional Status Quo Policy   The *Monroe Doctrine* was promulgated by President James Monroe in his annual message to Congress on December 2, 1823. In this address, he pledged that the United States would respect strictly the existing political configurations in the Western Hemisphere. "With the existing colonies or dependencies of any European power we have not interfered and shall not interfere," Monroe observed. But as for

> the governments who have declared their Independence, and maintain it . . . we could not view any interposition for the purpose of oppressing them, or controlling in any other manner their destiny, by an European power, in any other light than as the manifestation of an unfriendly disposition towards the United States.[9]

With this declaration, the United States undertook to resist any attempt by an outside power to upset the hemispheric balance of power. In effect, the Monroe Doctrine allowed the United States to maintain preeminence in a part of the world believed to be vital to its security and well-being.

Containment: A Global Status Quo Policy   The second great example of American status quo policy originated in the late 1940s and remained in force until 1991 when the Soviet Union first faltered and then disintegrated. World War II had drastically altered the European (and thus global) balance of power and, in the aftermath of the war, the United States was thrust for the first time into the role of paramount world leader—a role challenged by a formidable adversary. Under the redoubtable leadership of Josef Stalin, the Soviet Union appeared to present a grave new threat to the security of the United States. At the time, it seemed as if Alexis de Tocqueville's century-old prophecy that the United States and Russia had each been "marked out by the will of Heaven to sway the destinies of half the globe"[10] was about to be fulfilled.

American policymakers eventually decided to deal with the perceived Soviet threat through a policy of *containment,* the main outlines of which were delineated in a celebrated article published in the prestigious journal *Foreign Affairs* in July 1947. The anonymous author, "Mr. X," turned out to be George F. Kennan, at the time the influential director of the State Department's Policy Planning Staff and later ambassador to the USSR. "It is clear," Kennan wrote, that the main element of any United States policy toward the Soviet Union must be that of a long-term, patient but firm and vigilant containment of Russian expansive tendencies. . . . Soviet pressure against the free institutions of the Western world is something that can be contained by the adroit and vigilant application of counter-force at a series of constantly shifting geographical and political points.[11]

Kennan went on to predict that if a policy of containment were applied consistently for a decade or so, the Soviet challenge would diminish significantly. He also suggested (prophetically, it can now be said) that if containment proved successful, the totalitarian Soviet state would ultimately fall victim to severe internal pressures.

This "new" doctrine of containment was actually nothing more (or less) than the age-old status quo policy applied to Europe. Its apparent novelty stemmed mainly from the specific adaptation of status quo initiatives to the unique set of circumstances that prevailed after World War II.

The first major test of containment came in 1947, when it appeared that Greece was about to fall victim to a Communist insurgency. After Great Britain, which had historically played the role of guarantor of the status quo in the eastern Mediterranean, declared that it could no longer afford to underwrite the legitimate government of Greece, the United States stepped in. In an urgent message to Congress requesting authority to provide foreign aid to the embattled governments of Greece and Turkey, President Harry Truman enunciated the containment principle that came to be known as the **Truman Doctrine:** "I believe that it must be the policy of the United States to support free peoples who are resisting attempted subjugation by armed minorities or by outside pressures."[12] When Congress approved the president's request, containment became the official policy of the United States government.

After a Communist government gained power in Czechoslovakia in February 1948, the United States countered with the **Marshall Plan,** a $16.5 billion program aimed at the reconstruction of the war-torn economies of western Europe. This program was designed to promote the recovery of western Europe not only economically but spiritually and politically as well. At the time, it was feared that communism might come in "through the back door"—that is, that the powerful Communist parties of France and Italy might be able to capitalize on the demoralization of the general populace and, with the covert backing of Moscow, gain control of their respective governments. Thus the Marshall Plan formed an integral part of the overall United States effort to preserve the status quo after World War II.

In 1949, the United States broke a tradition that dated back to its founding by sponsoring a peacetime military alliance, the North Atlantic Treaty Organization (**NATO**), comprising several western European countries plus Canada and the United States. NATO represented the logical extension of containment from the economic realm (foreign aid to Greece and Turkey, the Marshall Plan) to the military realm.

The fall of mainland China to the Communists in 1949 provoked another great wave of anxiety throughout the United States. When, in 1950, fighting broke out in Korea between the Communist regime in the north and the non-communist one in the south, the United States decided to apply containment as vigorously on the Asian perimeter as it had on the European. Although technically fought under the flag of the United Nations, the Korean War was actually waged in the main by the United States in pursuit of its own national interest, the preservation of the postwar status quo, this time in Asia.

During the 1960s, what had started out as a policy designed to prevent the spread of communism, first in Europe and then in Asia, turned into a firefighting strategy of anticommunist interventionism in the Third World. Military equipment, economic aid, diplomatic support, and the American nuclear umbrella were all extended to specific nations deemed to be under threat of Communist subversion or insurgency. Military intervention was considered an appropriate response under certain circumstances. This strategy of military containment reached its high-water mark when hundreds of thousands of U.S. troops were sent to South Vietnam, between 1964 and 1972, to help that nation in its battle against Communist guerrillas and North Vietnamese forces. After the Vietnam War, the United States placed much less reliance on large-scale military intervention to maintain the international status quo, although the main thrust of U.S. foreign policy did not change.

By the early 1990s, the United States' policy of containment had lost its *raison d'être*. The Soviet Union's decision to grant autonomy to its former eastern European satellite nations, its backing for the U.S.-led coalition against Iraq in 1991, and its disintegration later that year made it obvious that the American policy of containment had served its purpose. The breakup of the Soviet Union at the end of 1991 provided the last measure of convincing evidence that the Soviet threat could no longer be treated as the cornerstone of American foreign policy, thus making the American policy of containment obsolete.

Accommodation

A nation that chooses a strategy of accommodation acts in one of two ways: It may seek, as a matter of general policy, to promote the peaceful resolution of international disputes, or it may sacrifice values of great importance to its own well-being. A few nations, such as Finland, Sweden, Austria, and Switzerland, practice a *general policy* of accommodation. In defining their national interest, they give the highest priority to avoiding conflict or even the appearance of taking sides in present or future confrontations. A few so-called nonaligned states have also carefully cultivated a foreign policy of accommodation, but most are nonaligned in name only.

In cases where accommodation involves direct self-sacrifice, the nation usually submits to pressure (often in the form of direct military threats) rather than risk a war it knows it would lose. (Even when this type of blackmail is less apparent, nations may choose accommodation rather than face economic or political sanctions or the loss of potential benefits.) The Melian case mentioned at the beginning of the chapter is instructive in this regard. Confronted with the demands of an expansionist Athens, the Melians had to choose between resistance or accommodation, neither a satisfactory alternative. In the end, they chose the noble (if futile) course of resistance. Overmatched as they were, however, the Melians may have been better off giving in to the Athenian demands (that is, accommodation may have been in their national interest). Thus, like expansionist and status quo strategies, accommodation is intrinsically neither good nor bad.

Sometimes third-party nations are adversely affected by a nation's attempts at accommodation. On several occasions over the past quarter century, for example, various Arab nations have successfully used economic pressure (in the form of threats to withhold vital oil supplies) to persuade France not to sell replacement and spare parts to Israel for French-made airplanes and weapons. In this case, although it was France that practiced accommodation by violating a previous arms agreement with Israel, it was Israel that suffered the immediate consequence of diminished military power. In other words, the effects of French accommodation were felt in the Middle East, not in France.

Appeasement   The best-known example of accommodation in the twentieth century was the policy of *appeasement* undertaken by British Prime Minister Neville Chamberlain in 1937 and 1938. Chamberlain's strategy for dealing with the aggressive actions of Nazi Germany was grounded in the belief that German interests in Europe were limited to regaining land "unfairly" taken from Germany under the Treaty of Versailles. In Chamberlain's view, no irreconcilable differences marked the relationship between Great Britain and Germany, and hence the two nations could easily coexist without threatening or endangering each other's vital interests. In fact, he appears to have thought that nearly all international questions could and should be resolved by compromise. Such compromises were to be struck for the sake of peace. The establishment of a lasting worldwide peace was the central aim of his policy of appeasement, and his single-minded effort to secure that peace eventually proved to be his undoing.

To understand Chamberlain's policy, it is necessary first to understand what it was not. Obviously, Chamberlain's appeasement of Hitler was not a strict status quo policy. Under Chamberlain's guidance, Great Britain did little or nothing while an imperialistic Germany swallowed up Austria and annexed the Sudetenland (a largely German-speaking region of Czechoslovakia). Chamberlain did not try to preserve the local status quo; rather, he accepted the changes demanded by Germany in order to maintain a status quo on the Continent, reassuring himself that Hitler's actions amounted to a limited program of territorial expansion and believing that to intervene would make Great Britain (and not Germany) the instigator of a new world war.

In the final analysis, Chamberlain's appeasement proved unwise and myopic. Chamberlain should have known better. In reference to Hitler's prewar diplomacy, a noted British military historian writes, "Never has a man of such immense ambition so clearly disclosed beforehand both the general process and particular methods by which he was seeking to fulfill it."[13] Another British scholar observes that although there is surely a place for nations that pursue a benign foreign policy, Chamberlain never understood the proper place or limits of such a strategy. Applied to Hitler, making unilateral concessions as a foreign policy approach was unrealistic, for Hitler's record did not merit Chamberlain's trust. The German leader had demonstrated time and again that whatever concessions were offered him, he "preferred the path of unilateral action, surprise and threat of violence, vituperative language and overt brutality."[14]

Ever since Great Britain, under Chamberlain's leadership, reacted to German pressure by refusing to aid nations endangered by German expansionism, the word *appeasement* has been a term of opprobrium in international politics. At times, conciliation—a strategy to gain time, procure the most favorable arrangements possible under the circumstances, or minimize potential casualties—may represent the most prudent course of action. Unfortunately for Great Britain, as well as for the world as a whole, 1938 was the wrong time and a German-threatened Europe the wrong place for such a policy. Neville Chamberlain was an honorable but sadly misguided man. He believed he was courageously upholding, not sacrificing, his principles by placating Hitler. As it turned out, however, Adolf Hitler was incapable of distinguishing between conciliation and cowardice.

ALTRUISM: THE LIMITS OF POWER

When nations act for the sake of moral principle, with little regard for their self-interest (and sometimes in spite of it), they act altruistically. Altruism exists in international politics, although its scope and influence are quite limited. Unlike individual citizens, whose altruistic instincts can be reinforced by an impartially administered legal system that encourages them to act decently and justly, a nation's desire to act altruistically or benevolently must come solely from within; it cannot be imposed from without. For example, if a democratic nation aids regimes that respect human rights, and chooses not to help nations that flagrantly violate human rights (or if it aids democratic nations and, all else being equal, opposes nondemocratic nations), the nation's leaders are pursuing such policies because they are right and are dictated by the nation's fundamental political principles. A nation does *not* act in this manner because it is told to do so by another nation or by an international organization like the United Nations.

Examples of International Altruism

Sometimes nations can afford to act altruistically—usually when they are operating from a position of strength and when altruistic actions do not immediately threaten the fundamental well-being of their citizens. For example, nations with food surpluses often send supplies to famine-stricken parts of the world to forestall mass starvation. Another type of altruism is exercised by governments that offer asylum to refugees who flee political persecution, economic disaster, or war's devastation. A noted British historian points out that between the two world wars, Great Britain's leaders tried to alleviate the oppressive conditions imposed on Germany by the Treaty of Versailles. Presumably, they followed such a course because they believed it was right and because they felt that

Germany had been made to suffer disproportionately for its role in provoking World War I. Because it was pursued from a position of strength (until the late 1930s), this British policy was, according to this historian, "a noble idea, rooted in Christianity, courage, and common sense."[15] By the same token, British policymakers were probably also influenced by the (correct) warnings of J. M. Keynes and others that the economic consequences of the treaty would wreak havoc on the world economy.

Nations rarely practice undiluted altruism; benevolent policies almost always coincide with a nation's national interests. The Marshall Plan, initiated by the United States in the late 1940s, was a classic example of altruism mixed with self-interest. Without a doubt, the Marshall Plan was motivated partly by a humanitarian concern with rebuilding devastated European economies in the wake of World War II; Winston Churchill called this program the "most unsordid act in history."[16] Yet if the Marshall Plan had altruistic overtones, it was also highly consistent with the national interest of the United States. As we have observed, the U.S. national interest favored a post–World War II status quo. That objective, policymakers believed, could be achieved only by reestablishing a stable western European community able to resist armed aggression from without and organized subversion from within.

The collapse of communism in eastern Europe, the dissolution of the Warsaw Pact, and the disintegration of the Soviet empire left America's allies ascendant on the Continent—a vindication of the Marshall Plan and subsequent efforts to institutionalize supranational political, economic, and military ties through the North Atlantic Treaty Organization (NATO), the European Economic Community (EC), and other multilateral arrangements. But the dislocations that resulted from the dismantling of the centrally planned economies in the former Soviet bloc—and especially the Russian Republic—prompted a call for massive foreign aid (in effect, a new Marshall Plan for eastern Europe) from some quarters in the West. The Bush administration rejected the idea of a new Marshall Plan but did extend hundreds of millions of dollars in humanitarian and technical assistance. While the amounts involved pale by comparison with Germany's huge billion-dollar outlays, American food and medical supplies were not inconsequential in helping Russia get through the harsh winter of 1991–1992.

Was the United States motivated by pure altruism? Probably not. Turmoil in Russia and in other parts of the former Soviet Union was widely viewed as a danger to the stability of Europe as a whole. Any spillover into Poland, Czechoslovakia, and other neighboring states would have likely ramifications for the entire Continent—e.g., massive population movements resulting in a sudden influx of refugees into Germany and other prosperous European countries. Such influxes could prove highly disruptive, costly, and even destabilizing for the host societies. Other dangers posed by unrest in Russia involved nuclear weapons. With the country in dire straits, might not elements in the former Soviet Union—either the government or the armed forces—be tempted to sell advanced armaments to the highest bidder? What if Iraq, Iran, or Libya offered large sums for nuclear bombs, ballistic missiles, and other sophisticated weapons systems? This concern is clearly what motivated the United States to give Moscow $400 million to pay for the destruction of various nuclear arms the Russians now considered redundant (or at least expendable). Thus, even the Bush administration's "kinder and gentler" foreign policy toward Russia in the early 1990s was hardly far removed from old-fashioned *realpolitik*.

Theoretically, nations could act altruistically even at the expense of their own citizens' well-being. In reality, however, very few nations put themselves at risk for altruistic goals and survive. One authority points to an exception—the example of "little Denmark, [who,] too weak to seek self-preservation through power, limited its foreign policy largely to humanitarian causes and yet in the end survived Hitler's conquest."[17] Denmark's humanitarian resolve was indeed remarkable. Although an occupied country, Denmark had been granted a unique degree of political autonomy by the German government, whose principal concern was the Danish nation's small and uninfluential Jewish population. In an effort to protect its Jewish citizens (and other refugees as well), the Danish government and citizens endangered their very existence by openly defying German edicts aimed at isolating the Jews from the general population. Through acts of uncommon moral courage, the Danes were responsible for "an extraordinary obstacle which arose in the path of the German destruction machine: an uncooperative Danish administration and a local population unanimous in its resolve to save its Jews."[18]

Altruism and Political Realities

Altruistic actions such as those undertaken by Denmark in World War II should not obscure the fact that harsh realities normally govern international relations.[19] Governments seldom undertake policies that entail great sacrifices to their own citizens without dire necessity or some highly prized objective to be gained. Indeed, policies involving national self-sacrifice are almost always justified in pragmatic as well as altruistic terms. Churchill, for example, explained his decision to ally Great Britain with Stalinist Russia by citing the adage "The enemy of my enemy is my friend."

Churchill had no difficulty making a moral judgment in the face of a clear military threat posed by Nazi Germany. Often, however, the situations in which leaders and governments are called on to make moral judgments are anything but clear. Consider the question of whether the United States should provide economic aid to a moderately friendly yet somewhat ruthless and unsavory dictator. One's answer to this question would depend on whether one believed a more humanitarian (even if less friendly) successor would emerge if the present dictator were overthrown. Add past promises, strategic considerations, and other variables to the equation, and one's choice of the correct "moral" course becomes very difficult indeed.

Most of the time, the self-interested intentions of nation-states are checked not by benevolence or altruism but by the policies of other nations that, seeking to maximize their power, follow strategies they deem to be in their own self-interest. Out of the seeming chaos of international politics, a more or less stable pattern of relations, based on some sort of balance of power, can normally be discerned. Sometimes this pattern works to limit the danger to weaker nations. But the possibility that a nation may perish, exemplified by the fate of the Melians at the hands of the Athenians, always exists. Nor is the danger confined to the weak: All nations, large and small, live under the threat of war and destruction. All nations, therefore, have a vested interest in achieving some semblance of order, however limited, in their mutual relationships.

Summary

The workings of international politics differ significantly from those of national or domestic politics due to the absence of an overriding sovereign government. The Melian episode illustrates the preeminent role of military might in the international arena. The struggle for power, inherent in the nature of the international system, is designed to advance national interests. The concept of the national interest is not without ambiguity, however; it encompasses anything that a nation's leaders perceive as promoting the long-term security and well-being of the state.

Students of international politics must distinguish between foreign policy ends and means. Nations choose a variety of ends, but these are almost always overshadowed by one ultimate aim, the nation's "power goal." Some nations are satisfied with existing power relationships, seeking merely to maintain their power; others are dissatisfied and push to enhance their power. A few nations, however, avoid choosing between power maintenance and power enhancement; they tend to reject power politics altogether. Occasionally, nations are forced to opt for power reduction.

Nations may pursue four basic foreign policy strategies: expansionism, status quo preservation, accommodation, and altruism. Policies aimed at fundamental change in the global or regional balance of power are called expansionist. Expansionism can assume a number of forms. It is often unclear whether a particular nation is pursuing an expansionist strategy or merely trying to defend itself by momentarily going on the offensive.

Nations that oppose fundamental changes in the existing international distribution of power and wealth are said to pursue a status quo policy. The United States has been a status quo power (although at times it has practiced expansionism). The Monroe Doctrine was designed to perpetuate the regional status quo in the Western Hemisphere, and the containment of the perceived Soviet threat was a global status quo strategy adopted by the United States after World War II.

For some nations, avoiding conflict becomes the paramount political value. Such a stance leads to a strategy of accommodation, whereby concessions are made for the sake of peace. The most famous case of a nation opting for this strategy was Great Britain under the leadership of Neville Chamberlain, whose policy of appeasement toward Nazi Germany contributed to the calamity of World War II.

Sometimes nations act out of altruism. Such acts are usually isolated occurrences, however, rather than a concerted foreign policy strategy. Purely altruistic acts are rare because of the almost universal preoccupation with power in international politics.

Key Terms

political realism	expansionism	containment
national interests	status quo strategy	Truman Doctrine
power maintenance goals	accommodation	Marshall Plan
power enhancement goals	altruism	NATO
Zionists	Monroe Doctrine	appeasement

Review Questions

1. What does Thucydides's account of the confrontation between the Melians and the Athenians reveal about the nature of international politics?

2. What does a "Machiavellian" approach to politics entail? What sort of world view does this approach embrace?

3. What is the meaning of the term *national interest*? How do political realists use this term?

4. What are the two basic goals of foreign policy available to nation-states?

5. What foreign policy strategies are open to nation-states? Do they usually pursue one strategy at a time? Explain.

6. What is a policy of appeasement? What example of this type of policy was presented in the text? Are *accommodation* and *appeasement* synonymous? Explain.

7. Do nation-states ever practice altruism? If so, provide some examples of this type of policy. Is altruism usually pure, or is it commonly mixed with other motives? Does morality play any role in international politics, or is power the only factor that matters?

Recommended Reading

CARR, EDWARD HALLETT. *The Twenty Years' Crisis, 1919–1939*. New York: Harper & Row, 1981. An excellent discussion of the relationship between power and morality in international politics, written in 1939. The author shows how the principles of international politics contributed to the tragedy of World War II.

DOUGHERTY, JAMES E., AND ROBERT L. PFALTZGRAFF, JR. *Contending Theories of International Relations: A Comprehensive Study*, 3rd ed. New York: HarperCollins, 1989. An intelligent and comprehensive explanation of all aspects of the discipline.

HARTMANN, FREDERICK H. *The Relations of Nations*, 6th ed. New York: Macmillan, 1983. A basic textbook with insightful discussions of key concepts. Comprehensive in coverage.

KENNAN, GEORGE F. *American Diplomacy, 1900–1950*. Chicago: University of Chicago Press, 1985. An elegantly written interpretative history of American foreign policy during the first half of the twentieth century.

MACHIAVELLI, NICCOLÒ. *The Prince*. New York: Mentor Books, 1952. This book has been "required reading" for students and practitioners of diplomacy for several centuries.

MORGENTHAU, HANS J. *Politics among Nations: The Struggle for Power and Peace*, 5th rev. ed. New York: Knopf, 1978. This is the classic English-language international politics textbook, written by a leading theorist of political realism.

THOMPSON, KENNETH. *Morality and Foreign Policy*. Baton Rouge: Louisiana State University Press, 1980. An illuminating discussion of the relationship of political power, moral considerations, and the national interest in formulating and carrying out foreign policy.

WOLFERS, ARNOLD. *Discord and Collaboration: Essays on International Politics*. Baltimore: Johns Hopkins University Press, 1962. A superb compilation of scholarly essays dealing with key concepts and issues in international relations.

Notes

1. The quotations in this discussion can be found in Thucydides, "The Melian Conference," in *Readings in World Politics*, 2nd ed., ed. Robert Goldwin and Tony Pearce (New York: Oxford University Press, 1970), pp. 472–478.

2. Niccolò Machiavelli, *The Prince*, in *The Prince and the Discourses* (New York: Modern Library, 1952), p. 94.

3. Ibid., p. 56.

4. Ibid., p. 64.

5. Hans J. Morgenthau, *Politics among Nations: The Struggle for Power and Peace*, 5th rev. ed. (New York: Knopf, 1978), p. 11.

6. Ibid., pp. 22–23.

7. Ibid., p. 11.

8. Ibid.

9. Quoted in Alexander de Conde, *A History of American Foreign Policy: Growth to World Power*, 3rd ed. (New York: Scribner, 1978), vol. 1, p. 130.

10. Alexis de Tocqueville, *Democracy in America* (New York: Schocken Books, 1961), vol. 1, p. 522.

11. George F. Kennan, "Sources of Soviet Conduct," in *Caging the Bear: Containment and the Cold War*, ed. Charles Gati (Indianapolis: Bobbs-Merrill, 1974), p. 18.

12. *Congressional Record*, 80 Cong., 1st sess., p. 1981 (March 1947).

13. B. H. Liddell Hart, *Strategy* (New York: Praeger, 1967), p. 223.

14. Martin Gilbert, *The Roots of Appeasement* (New York: New American Library, 1966), pp. 184–185.

15. Ibid., p. xi.

16. Quoted in Marvin Jones, *The Fifteen Weeks* (New York: Harbinger, 1955), p. 256.

17. Arnold Wolfers, *Discord and Collaboration: Essays on International Politics* (Baltimore: Johns Hopkins University Press, 1962), p. 93.

18. Raul Hilberg, *The Destruction of the European Jews* (New York: Harper & Row, 1961), pp. 358–359.

19. An interesting example of altruism took place in 1920–1921, when a terrible famine occurred in the Soviet Union. Despite the Soviet government's avowed support of anticapitalist revolutions in the West, a relief organization (known as the Hoover Commission) was created by the U.S. government. Millions of dollars in food supplies were sent, and many lives were saved in the severely stricken Volga region. At the time, an official Soviet journal observed that "of all the capitalist countries, only America showed us major and real help." Quoted in Adam Ulam, *Expansion and Coexistence: Soviet Foreign Policy, 1917–1973*, 2nd ed. (New York: Praeger, 1974), p. 148. Also see John Lewis Gaddis, *Russia, the Soviet Union, and the United States: An Interpretive History* (New York: Wiley, 1978), pp. 99–101.

A New International Order

Patterns and Trends

(Tom Stoddart/Woodfin Camp)

INTERNATIONAL POLITICS IS politics without government: Sovereign nations, not independent individuals, act on the international stage. In most cases, these nations' goals and interests determine their actions. Because there is no all-powerful government to restrain the world's nations, the international arena has frequently been compared to a global state of nature where nations do whatever they can get away with. As we observed in Chapter 19, this is sometimes the case. Despite this, a kind of international system does exist in the absence of any overriding world government.

Most students of world politics agree that an international system in some form exists at most times (except during periods of general war, which represent the breakdown of the system). Any system—biological, mechanical, or political—must exhibit at least two key characteristics: a discernible structure and regular patterns of interaction among its component parts. This description fits international politics reasonably well. As one political scientist points out, "Because states constrain and limit each other, international politics can be viewed in rudimentary organizational terms."[1] Historically speaking, a system called the *balance of power* has been the principal mechanism of order in politics among nations (see Figure 20-1). Balance-of-power theorists view the maintenance of an equilibrium based on relative parity—especially of military power—among participating states or coalitions of states as the key to peace, order, and stability. It follows that the system is placed in jeopardy whenever any state or coalition becomes powerful enough to attack or threaten other states without fear of the punitive reprisals that normally make military aggression unprofitable.

THE TRADITIONAL EUROPEAN SYSTEM

The classical balance-of-power system began with the signing of the Treaty of Westphalia in 1648 and ended with the outbreak of World War I. With the short-lived exception of Napoleon's France, no state was able to establish hegemony on the Continent during this 266-year period—a remarkable achievement for any era.

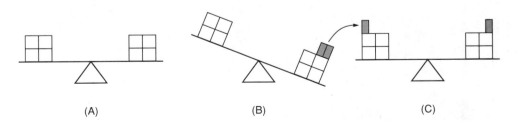

(A) (B) (C)

Equilibrium (A) is upset by adding a new participant (B); it is restored (C) by the transfer of one state from one alliance to another.

FIGURE 20-1   Adjusting the Balance of Power
SOURCE: Edward V. Gulick, *Europe's Classical Balance of Power* (New York: Norton, 1967).

Systemic Prerequisites

During this extended period, the international system functioned effectively because one nation—Great Britain—repeatedly threw its political and military weight behind the weaker alliance during times of crisis and conflict. Great Britain, acting as *keeper of the balance*, was ideally suited to play this role because of its geographic detachment and military (especially naval) prowess. An island power in close proximity to the Continent, Britain could cast a relatively dispassionate eye on international disputes and rivalries across the English Channel. A major British concern, historically, was which power controlled the Lowlands (modern-day Belgium and Holland) just across the Channel, which at its narrowest point is a mere 22 miles wide. In a larger sense, Britain was an impregnable fortress as long as no single power succeeded in conquering the Continent. Finally, Britain's unchallenged naval supremacy and economic vitality made it a powerful ally or a formidable foe, while its lack of a large standing army removed any threat of British domination on the Continent.

Another important factor undergirding the traditional European system was a basic moral consensus—a common outlook held by nations all sharing a single civilization. Historians Edward Gibbon and Arnold Toynbee, as well as the philosophers Emerich de Vattel and Jean-Jacques Rousseau, have stressed the paramount importance of the cultural and religious traditions that pervaded European society and transcended national boundaries during the heyday of the balance-of-power system.[2]

Under these extraordinary conditions, "international politics became indeed an aristocratic pastime, a sport for princes, all recognizing the same rules of the game and playing for the same limited stakes."[3] Limiting the stakes meant that even when war broke out, the belligerents did not seek to annihilate each other. For the most part, Europe's rulers, imbued with the rationalistic outlook of the eighteenth-century Enlightenment, adopted a pragmatic approach to governing that viewed any kind of fanaticism as absurd and dangerous. Not only the stakes but also economic and military capabilities were limited: Few countries could afford to squander the national wealth on high-risk adventures, and military action was constrained by the absence of modern technology.

Another fortuitous aspect of this pan-European culture was the absence of ideology. Realignments occurred as circumstances changed, adding to the smooth functioning of the system. Structural rigidity would have impeded the balancing process and made an all-out war more likely.

The Demise of the European Consensus

What happened to upset the relatively stable international order that had prevailed for over 2½ centuries in Europe? First, Napoleon's nearly successful attempt in the early nineteenth century to conquer Europe—creating the first mass-conscription, popular army in modern history—heralded the rise of modern nationalism. Although France's bid for hegemony ultimately failed, it was a harbinger of things to come and demonstrated the power of a nation united in a common cause. The cause itself was rooted in the explosive idea of human equality enshrined in both the American and French revolutions of the late eighteenth century. Between the Napoleonic wars and World War I, ideas like national self-determination and universal rights changed fundamental assumptions about politics and, in so doing, undermined the old aristocratic order.

In the nineteenth century, the Industrial Revolution also ushered in economic and technological changes that transformed the art of warfare. For example, Prussia used railroads to move troops in victorious military campaigns against Austria (1866) and France (1870). New instruments of war were not far off either—military applications of the internal combustion engine, for example, included self-propelled field artillery and, by World War I, even combat aircraft.

A final factor that helped to undermine the European system was the rigidity of military alliances. Toward the end of the nineteenth century, coalitions were becoming fixed and hardened while nations were steadily accumulating military power. Unprecedented peacetime outlays for military research and development, the creation of relatively large, standing armies, and a spiraling arms race reflected and reinforced the increasing division of Europe into two opposing alliances. This development set the stage for World War I, which signaled the beginning of the end of the classical balance-of-power system. It would take another world war to finish the job.

THE POST–WORLD WAR II SYSTEM

World War II produced a new configuration that has shaped world politics to the present day. Replacing the European system was a global one dominated by two preeminent powers. In this new *bipolar system*, both sides diverted huge sums toward development of total war capabilities, and each regarded the other as its ideological nemesis. The Cold War between the United States and the Soviet Union after 1945 lasted nearly half a century. It is appropriate, therefore, to discuss the structural characteristics of world politics during the heyday of this Soviet–American rivalry before turning our attention to the contemporary global system.

The End of Eurocentrism

One of the most pronounced changes in international politics since World War II was the reduced influence of the European nations, which had since the seventeenth century been the fulcrum of the international balance of power. Actually, Europe's decline was foreshadowed by the increasing prominence of two non-European powers, the United States and Japan, evident already in the late nineteenth century. But it was not until World War II had physically shattered Europe that the traditional great powers, Great Britain, France, and Germany, became second-rank states. Britain was forced to abandon a worldwide empire; France was preoccupied with the reconstruction of its economy, society, and government after the Nazi occupation; Germany was defeated, occupied, and partitioned into zones from which two new states—the Federal Republic of Germany (West Germany) and the German Democratic Republic (East Germany)—would emerge. The Soviet Union, which had suffered the heaviest war losses of all, rose miraculously from the ashes more powerful than ever.

The colonial empires of Britain, France, Portugal, Spain, Belgium, and the Netherlands disintegrated rapidly after World War II. From these former colonial territories emerged scores of new nations, which turned to the two industrial power blocs for economic and military aid. The Third World thus became one arena where the bipolar power struggle was played out. The hallmark of this struggle was the Cold War.

The Advent of Bipolarity

Although the transition from a European to a global international system had begun before World War II, the war greatly accelerated the process—in part by removing the European states as primary actors on the world stage. In place of the former great powers, of which there were seven at the outbreak of the war, were two "superpowers"—the United States and the Soviet Union. The United States formed a kind of protectorate over the western half of war-torn Europe, and the Soviet Union created a "satellite" empire in the eastern half.

The United States, which was the first to develop and use the atomic bomb, enjoyed a short-lived nuclear monopoly after World War II. The Soviet Union, to the surprise and dismay of Western observers, successfully tested an atomic device in 1949—serving notice that it, too, had the right stuff to become a full-fledged superpower.

In terms of military might, global reach, and economic resources, the United States and the Soviet Union dwarfed all other nations in the 1950s. However, the ideological chasm dividing them precluded collaboration of any kind.

The Primacy of Ideology

The two superpowers on opposite sides of the globe dominated the international scene, making them natural rivals. And because one was capitalist and democratic and the other communist and dictatorial, the rivalry turned especially dangerous and acrimonious. At the conclusion of World War II, Allied mistrust of Josef Stalin, the Soviet dictator, was greatly heightened by his nation's permanent occupation of eastern Europe, which the Red Army had liberated from the Germans, and by Stalin's attempt to force the Western powers to abandon West Berlin. No less alarming to the United States and its allies was the Soviet atomic bomb test in 1949.

The Soviets, meanwhile, charged that U.S. foreign policy actions (the cutoff of lend-lease aid, the refusal to grant large loans, and the launching of the Marshall Plan) were proof that "American imperialism" was plotting the destruction of the "world socialist system." Stalin's chief ideologue, Andrei Zhdanov, declared at a Communist party conference in 1947 that the world had been divided into two camps. This two-camp doctrine had its counterpart in the Western notion of a "world Communist conspiracy," which posited that a secret Soviet blueprint aimed to subvert democratic societies everywhere. Although these mirror images may seem exaggerated in retrospect, extreme rhetoric on both sides—fueled by the clash of ideologies—lent credibility to this interpretation.

The Soviet Union countered American containment, epitomized by NATO, with a military alliance of its own, the Warsaw Treaty Organization (commonly known as the *Warsaw Pact*, linking Moscow and eastern Europe. The aura of confrontation that permeated the two alliance systems left little room for compromise or conciliation.

At its inception, then, the Cold War was waged by two extraordinarily powerful nations whose aims, interests, and values seemed utterly incompatible. At the very least, each sought to block the ambitions of the other; at worst, each sought to bring about the other's collapse. In this respect, the postwar system contrasted sharply with the traditional European system it had replaced: The ends of war and diplomacy were no longer limited to such finite objectives as the acquisition of territorial tidbits or the assertion of royal entitlements.

The Threat of Nuclear Extinction

When the European balance of power held sway, nations observed certain rules that limited war aims. Limitations on available means of warfare also checked the ambitions of adventurous nations. Two technological breakthroughs in the twentieth century, however, greatly expanded the destructive potential of military weaponry. First came the development of airborne bombers and, later, missile delivery systems whose capabilities would have staggered the imagination a century earlier. Second, advances in nuclear physics led to the invention of fission (atomic) and fusion (hydrogen) bombs capable of leveling entire cities.

From these scientific and technological advances grew the formidable U.S. and Soviet arsenals of increasingly accurate land- and sea-based missiles, armed with multiple nuclear warheads. The two nations commanded a vast overkill capacity: Each side deployed enough nuclear weapons to destroy the other many times over. Under such circumstances, all-out war would have amounted to mutual suicide. This realization, as we shall see, played a major role in promoting a new international security scheme intended to ensure human survival in a world threatened with almost instantaneous destruction.

Mutual Deterrence

At the heart of the post–World War II balance-of-power system was deterrence. Deterrence began not as an abstract idea but as a historical necessity. The United States lost its nuclear monopoly shortly after World War II but continued to enjoy a measure of nuclear superiority until the mid-1970s. But in 1957, the Soviet Union put the first artificial satellite (*Sputnik*) into orbit. The Soviet space shot demonstrated to the world that the USSR had the technology to build long-range rockets—that is, the capability to launch offensive weapons from Soviet soil, aimed directly at U.S. targets.

By the late 1960s, the era of invulnerability was over for the United States: The Soviets had built a land-based missile force against which there was no adequate defense. Now both sides stared into the nuclear abyss. Deterrence became the new watchword in a "great debate" over military strategy and an integral part of the post–World War II balance of power.

According to deterrence theory, nuclear weapons are built so that they will never have to be used. Their purpose is to dissuade nations that might otherwise be tempted to use them from ever doing so. In this sense, public expenditure for such weapons is markedly different from money appropriated for such projects as building schools, libraries, and parks. If these facilities were *not* used, it would represent a serious domestic policy failure. By contrast, if nuclear weapons ever *were* used, it would constitute a far more serious foreign policy failure—one that could jeopardize the very survival of the human race.

Thus deterrence is fundamentally psychological. As such, it incorporates some of the elements of a high-stakes poker game. Like poker, deterrence involves a contest of wills based on a certain reality. Because survival hangs in the balance, players must minimize risks. Bluffing is part of the process. But if Country A successfully uses military power to keep Country B from pursuing its desired foreign policy objective, Country B's prestige is damaged and Country A gains a psychological edge. Thus nuclear deterrence depends not only on the realities of power but also on the perceptions each side has of the other's will, intentions, and resolve in the face of grave danger.

What assumptions underlie nuclear deterrence theory? First, deterrence holds that nations have communicated to potential adversaries their will to use weapons of mass destruction if attacked. Second, despite the resulting mutual distrust, decision makers on both sides are rational, and therefore neither side will launch a nuclear strike unless it can protect itself from a counterattack. Third, each side possesses a "second strike" nuclear capability, meaning that enough of the attacked nation's nuclear capabilities would survive a surprise attack (first strike) to make possible a retaliatory blow—or second strike—adequate to inflict unacceptable damage on the attacker.

To ensure the survivability of its nuclear forces, the United States built three separate but interrelated nuclear weapon delivery systems after World War II. This so-called *triad* consisted of land-based intercontinental ballistic missiles (*ICBMs*), submarine-launched ballistic missiles (*SLBMs*), and manned bombers (known as the Strategic Air Command, or SAC), some of which were always aloft. The Soviet Union also had a three-pronged deterrence system that depended heavily on land-based missiles and warheads, which it possessed in larger numbers than the United States. The United States' sea-based deterrent was more powerful than the Soviet Union's.

An important effect of the post–World War II system of deterrence has been to blur the usual distinction between offense and defense. Classifying nuclear weapons and their delivery systems depends on the varying uses to which they can be put. Thus *counterforce weapons* (weapons aimed at destroying other weapons) may be regarded as defensive; indeed, this rationale was used to justify building them. But the same weapons can also be part of an offensive strategy called "counterforce attack with reserves." (Under this scenario, one nation with a sizable nuclear advantage attacks another nation's weapons, threatening to destroy that nation's population centers if the attacked nation retaliates.)

How Much Deterrence Is Enough?

CONTROVERSY REGARDING THE proper level of weaponry and defense expenditures comprised a conspicuous and continuing part of deterrence strategy during the Cold War. Because nuclear weapons were not used for fighting wars, there was no need for numerical superiority or even parity, according to some nuclear weapons experts. In other words, the smallest nuclear strike force needed to deter is quite adequate. This view is known as *minimum deterrence*. Some observers believe that the ability to drop one nuclear bomb on a city is sufficient; others argue that while the number of nuclear weapons needed is finite, it takes more than a few to make deterrence work.

As secretary of defense in the mid-1960s, Robert McNamara calculated that the United States would need 400 warheads to inflict "unacceptable damage" on the Soviet Union. (Of course, it is difficult to say what level of damage

a potential adversary will find unacceptable, but McNamara estimated it to be the destruction of 20 to 25 percent of the population and 50 percent of industrial capacity.) If 400 warheads were actually needed, however, the U.S. arsenal would have to be considerably larger to allow for technical failures, weapons missing the target, defensive measures by the other side, and possibly even a massive first strike against our long-range missiles and bombers. This concept, known as the doctrine of *assured destruction*, was the centerpiece of McNamara's strategy. McNamara's critics argued that his idea of "finite deterrence" was not finite enough!

Most advocates of finite deterrence saw it as a two-way street. If both sides follow the same policy, they argue, the result will be a stable nuclear balance based on **mutual assured destruction (MAD)**. Opponents of this view found the name appropriate.

Another example of the blurring of offense and defense emerged from the debate over President Reagan's **Strategic Defense Initiative** project, an elaborate space-based AMB system that critics dubbed "Star Wars." The cost and feasibility of the Strategic Defense Initiative (SDI) provoked much controversy. Although the Reagan administration viewed SDI as purely defensive, the Soviet Union insisted that such a system, though while defensive in appearance, was inherently destabilizing because the nation deploying it might be tempted to launch a first strike and use that ABM capability to shield itself from a retaliatory assault.

Deterrence and the arms race went hand in hand for decades after World War II. Influencing the direction and pace of that arms race were a number of factors. First, each nation had specific goals and priorities that placed varying limits on expenditures for armaments. Second, each superpower had been swayed by its perception of what the other was doing. Thus an accelerated Soviet weapons buildup in the 1970s prompted the United States to launch a major rearmament program. One corollary of this effort is that a stable balance is not possible when one nation (particularly a nation practicing an expansionistic foreign policy) possesses a clear advantage in number and strength of nuclear weapons. Finally, technology exerted its own pernicious influence. On the one hand, technological knowledge cannot be unlearned, making nations wary of disarmament proposals; on the other, the possibility that another nation may achieve a technological breakthrough has proved to be an incentive to continuing high levels of weapons research and development.

Nuclear deterrence worked well for decades, but it was fraught with tension and danger. Although both superpowers consistently reassured the world that they did not intend to use their nuclear weapons, the nuclear arsenals themselves often exacerbated the fear and mistrust that led to their creation in the first place.

THE EMERGING INTERNATIONAL ORDER

The political collapse of the Soviet Union marked the end of the post–World War II balance of power. Presently, a new international order is materializing. Understanding its emerging outline is essential to any coherent view of international politics.

Before exploring the specific configuration of this new international order, three observations need to be emphasized. First, contemporary international politics does *not* constitute a balance-of-power arrangement whereby nations, through a system of conflicting interests and roughly equal power, help to ensure world peace. Such a scheme is simply not operative in the world today. Second, the emerging international order is marked by contradictory trends. Thus we will note the movement toward (European) integration, which transcends the traditional state boundaries, and the simultaneous rise of a sense of religious and ethnic particularism *within* existing nations that has caused the breakup of two multinational states in Europe (the Soviet Union and Yugoslavia) and threatens the existence of others (e.g., Czechoslovakia). Finally, we would argue that the present state of international relations is almost certainly temporary and transitional and will in time yield to some sort of still undefined balance-of-power arrangement.[4]

A Unipolar World

The crumbling of the Soviet empire and the demonstration of United States military prowess in the war against Iraq made clear that in the early 1990s, the United States prevailed as the world's sole remaining superpower. This conclusion was reinforced by the striking contrast between the robust, if sluggish, U.S. economy and the former Soviet economic disarray, by the juxtaposition of domestic stability in the United States and the upheaval in various parts of the former Soviet Union, and by the vitality of the Western alliance system even after the Warsaw Pact ceased to exist.

Although there is no universally recognized definition of *superpower,* most analysts agree that a superpower must meet a three-part test. First, it must have a full range of power capabilities, including not only military muscle but also economic, political, diplomatic, and even moral clout. Second, it must have global reach, defined as the capacity to project power to all parts of the world. Third, it must be willing to assert its leadership role in the international arena. By this test, only the United States qualifies as a superpower. Japan and Germany are primarily economic powers. Britain and France have substantial diplomatic power and considerable military capability but are not regarded as economic powers. The Russian Republic possesses formidable strategic nuclear capabilities and some diplomatic clout but is currently preoccupied with its own internal problems. China, a regional power, lacks global capabilities and is politically and diplomatically isolated as a result of its reputation for persistent human-rights violations.

One immediate consequence of a unipolar world is the significant reduction of major political tensions. The great power questions of war and peace that perpetuated the Cold War simply no longer exist. Furthermore, this reduction in friction is accompanied by the eclipse of the ideological conflict (capitalism and democracy versus socialism and communism) that defined the post–World War II world. This "deideologization" does not mean that the world today is free of reigning political ideas—as we will see, the ideas of national self-determination and political pluralism are very much alive. It only means that the way Americans have thought about the world for over four decades is suddenly subject to soul-searching revision.

Another consequence of a unipolar world is that there are few restraints on the world's chief superpower, the United States. What restraints will keep this world-class power in line? Although no nation is entirely free to do what it wishes (especially in a world where many nations have nuclear weapons), the chief restraints on the United States today are self-imposed ones. These can be economic (what can it afford to do?), political (how much foreign involvement will the electorate support?), or even moral (what kinds of actions ought a democratic nation committed to the protection of human rights undertake?).

The Rise of International Economics

With the reduction of political conflicts among the world's most powerful nations, international economics assumes increasing importance. This is only natural, for the more that problems of national survival and of war and peace appear to recede, the more nations and leaders can turn to the next order of business, ensuring national and international prosperity. There is no doubt that the world economies today are far more interdependent than at any time in human history. The question becomes, What does this mean? The short answer is that economic interdependence promises greater levels of both international cooperation and international competition.

Some problems necessitate international cooperation, including environmental issues (global warming, acid rain), international debt repayment and relief concerns, and the coordination of economic policies during times of crisis. A particularly important question that invites international cooperation is the issue of financial aid to eastern European nations and the republics of the former Soviet Union. Generally, it is believed that economic aid can considerably enhance the prospects for democracy in these nations. The problem is that virtually all of the world's wealthiest nations are encountering budgetary problems that inhibit their capacity to pledge capital to other nations. Hence there exists the need for international planning and cooperation.

Yet in the face of such cooperative efforts, economic competition among nations is also on the rise. Often governments attempt to benefit their citizens by subsidizing domestic industries or agriculture, by invoking tariffs on imports, or by erecting other trade barriers. Such protectionist practices inhibit free trade and can lead to international tensions, even among allies. A good example of such stress can be seen in the ongoing (and not always pleasant) trade negotiations between the United States and Japan. Occasionally, American and Japanese relations have been strained over the issue of the Japanese government's policy of protectionism. On the other side of the globe, trade talks between the United States and its European allies has become particularly acrimonious over the issue of governmental subsidization of agriculture. Such examples serve as a reminder that competition as well as cooperation continue to exist in the increasingly important world of international economics and trade.

The Regionalization of Economic Power

Increasingly, the world's wealthiest nations are forming geographic economic blocs. Often, these blocs transcend the narrowest economic interests of individual nation-states and promise great financial rewards. Cooperation among Western nations is especially noteworthy, especially in the realm of economics and trade. Thus the European Community (EC), scheduled to become an economically united Europe in 1992, envisions itself a single western European economic association with a single currency and genuinely free trade within its borders (see Figure 20-2). This economic collaboration among European nations has been evolutionary and grew out of years of prior economic (Common Market) and military (NATO) cooperation. Most impressively, this cooperative relationship has overcome centuries of rivalry and mistrust between France and Germany. This European economic unification was scheduled to occur only a year after the United States negotiated a full free-trade agreement with Mexico (similar to the one it had already signed with Canada). The eventual implementation of such agreements anticipates a potential North American bloc, not as integrated as the EC, but nonetheless possessing powerful economic clout. Finally, economically robust Japan has strengthened economic ties with other Pacific Basin nations, and it seems "that in the 1990s, Japan and the NICs of Asia [South Korea, Singapore, Hong Kong, and Taiwan] might form a powerful new economic bloc linked by trade, investment, and aid relationships."[5]

What will emerge from this tripartite concentration of economic power? Of course, within these economic blocs there will be extended cooperation. Some see within these cooperative efforts a scenario for a future political integration that transcends the boundaries of the nation-state. Many observers, for instance, see the emergence of a United States of Europe growing out of European economic cooperation. Any similar result in the Americas or in Asia appears far more distant.

A even more difficult question asks how these three geoeconomic blocs will coexist. Competition among them is inevitable, but given compatible (democratic) political systems, so is the potential for extensive political and economic cooperation. Finally, it is likely that nations in all three blocs will benefit greatly from their associations, very likely increasing the economic distance between themselves and the world's many developing nations.

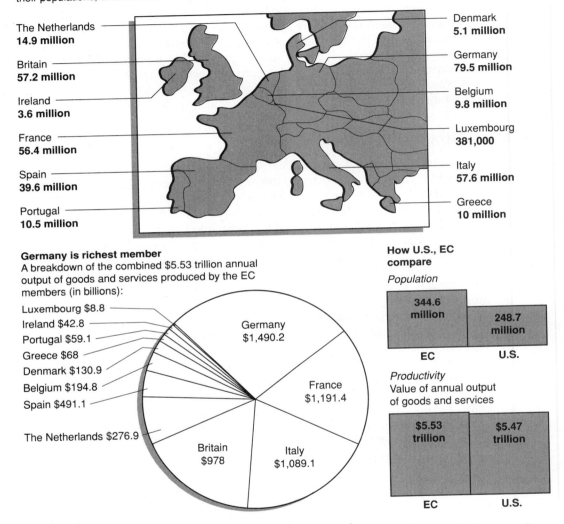

The dream of the European Community (EC) envisions a barrier-free market of more than 340 million people and more than $5 trillion in economic clout. Here are the members, their populations, and how their economic muscle is distributed:

The Netherlands
14.9 million

Britain
57.2 million

Ireland
3.6 million

France
56.4 million

Spain
39.6 million

Portugal
10.5 million

Denmark
5.1 million

Germany
79.5 million

Belgium
9.8 million

Luxembourg
381,000

Italy
57.6 million

Greece
10 million

Germany is richest member
A breakdown of the combined $5.53 trillion annual output of goods and services produced by the EC members (in billions):

Luxembourg $8.8
Ireland $42.8
Portugal $59.1
Greece $68
Denmark $130.9
Belgium $194.8
Spain $491.1

The Netherlands $276.9

Germany
$1,490.2

France
$1,191.4

Britain
$978

Italy
$1,089.1

How U.S., EC compare

Population

344.6 million — EC

248.7 million — U.S.

Productivity
Value of annual output of goods and services

$5.53 trillion — EC

$5.47 trillion — U.S.

FIGURE 20-2   Forging an Economic Power: The European Economic Community
SOURCE: Copyright 1991, *USA Today.* Reprinted with permission.

The Increasing Importance of Nationalism

When the United Nations was founded in 1945, it contained 51 nations. Of these charter members, approximately one-third were economically advanced countries, and the great majority were either European or (North and South) American states. Forty-one years later, however, there were no fewer than 159 UN members of which only about one-fifth were economically advanced and a clear majority (about three-fifths) were African or Asian. At the same time, nearly three-fourths of the world's population lived in developing countries.

This dramatic increase in UN membership and in world population represents a global revolution of sorts. It reflected the fact that, in the first part of the twentieth century, the originally European concept of **nationalism** took hold throughout the world, especially in the vast European empires that dominated Asia and Africa. Referring to the shared feelings of identity, loyalty, and shared values that unite a people, rising nationalism helped bring about a worldwide revolution. In the words of one authority:

> Everywhere in these areas nationalism became the rallying cry of the people. With the end of World War II these pressures mounted and new states appeared by dozens. Where 815 million of the world's 2.1 billion population prior to World War II were under colonial rule, by 1955 (with the world population estimated at 2.5 billion) some 750 million of the former colonial peoples were living in newly established states, and only 170 million were still under colonial administration. Colonial rule today barely exists.[6]

The existence of many new developing nations, pushed by nationalism toward independence and the exertion of local or regional political power at the expense of hostile or indifferent neighbors, has had a profound effect upon post–World War II international politics. Recently, a related version of impassioned nationalism has come to the fore. This nationalism has little to do with any reaction against old-style European colonialism. Rather, it is the outgrowth of demands made by ethnic, religious, or geographic minorities *within* independent nation-states. Usually, a key part of these nationalistic demands is the idea of peoplehood, and the belief that peoplehood and statehood should coincide. Thus, at the heart of this nationalism often rests the notion of self-determination—the belief that various minority peoples within nation-states deserve their own state and political autonomy. Historically, before the founding of Israel in 1948, such a feeling was most closely identified with Zionism, which was the Jewish people's desire for their own independent state. More recently, the Palestinian movement for a separate state within Israeli-occupied territories has been motivated by similar nationalistic sentiments.

Unlike Zionism, or the Palestinians' desire for political independence from Israel, nationalistic demands which recently have become so prominent have been advocated by various groups of citizens against their own government. Examples abound and include the Sikhs and some Moslems in India, the Volga Tatars in the Russian Republic, the South Ossetians in Georgia, the French-speaking Quebecois in Canada, the Slovaks in Czechoslovakia, the Kurds in Iraq and Turkey, the Tigris-Eritreans in Ethiopia, the Tamils in Sri Lanka, and the Timorese in Indonesia. Sometimes, the nationalistic feelings expressed by such groups can cross conventional political borders. Other times, there can (in any one country) exist a variety of intense nationalistic sentiments by competing and politically incompatible groups. Some countries, such as Yugoslavia, have not survived such conflicts (the most intense and destructive battles there were between Serbs and Croats). The Yugoslav example raises an important point. Although the nationalistic sentiments advanced by peoples within nation-states are usually made in the name of justice (advocating the belief that they are entitled to their own nation), it is worth noting that such claims are almost always associated with political instability or violence.

The Proliferation of Mass-Destruction Weapons

National instability and regional conflicts are made more dangerous by the spread of mass-destruction weapons systems. Increasingly, developing nations are intent on acquiring such weapons.

Nowadays, nuclear technology is easily understood, and the means of making nuclear weapons is relatively easy to obtain (see Table 20-1). Furthermore, by the year 2000, there will likely be two dozen developing nations with ballistic missiles, 30 with chemical weapons, and 10 with biological weapons.[7] Because such weapons are thought to be key elements in the exercise of national power and influence, it is not surprising that there appears to be no slackening in the desire of developing nations to obtain such weapons systems. An additional danger occurs when a nuclear power disintegrates, as happened with the Soviet Union, whose demise immediately created five nuclear powers.

The Future

What kind of world will be brought about by the new international order? Will it be safer than the one wrought by the post–World War II balance of power?

On the one hand, the absence of superpower rivalry and the increasing tendency toward economic integration probably bodes well for world peace.

TABLE 20-1
Proliferation of Nuclear Weapons

Have Nuclear Weapons Now	May Have Nuclear Weapons Now	Could Have Nuclear Weapons Soon
China	Canada	Argentina
France	Germany	Australia
India	Italy	Austria
Israel	Japan	Belgium
Kazakhstan	Pakistan	Brazil
Russia	South Africa	Egypt
Ukraine	Sweden	Finland
United Kingdom	Switzerland	Libya
United States		Netherlands
		Norway
		South Korea
		Spain

Seldom in world history has there been such a coincidence of political agreement and economic interests. On the other hand, the emergence of virulent nationalism and the continuing spread of lethal weapons systems throughout the world present serious dangers that cannot readily be managed.

One unique advantage of the new political and economic world order is sometimes asserted. When any one nation threatens the peace and economic well-being of the world, some experts believe that united diplomatic, economic, or even military action to meet the threat will be possible and should be employed. The joint Allied effort against Iraq in the Gulf War is held up as a model of world cooperation in successful peacekeeping efforts against aggressors. Yet, it is by no means obvious that the Gulf War will furnish any such model of a successful future regional or international security system. The fact that Iraq's invasion of Kuwait and potential invasion of Saudi Arabia threatened so many industrialized nations, and the fact that decisive American air power were already pre-positioned (and rendered Iraqi ground forces extremely vulnerable) alone comprise factors which likely will not be repeated. The present world order may feature a greatly diminished degree of political rivalry, but this lessening of political tensions by no means guarantees a continued high level of unopposed military cooperation among nations indefinitely into the future.

Summary

The traditional balance-of-power system that formally came into being in Europe in 1648 was limited in size and scope. One advantage of the Eurocentric system was that all members shared certain common values and beliefs. Also, Great Britain acted as the keeper of the balance. The European system worked because means and ends were limited, alliances were flexible, and there was a singular absence of crusading zeal. Changes in these conditions during the nineteenth century presaged the collapse of the system.

After World War II, a bipolar system emerged in place of the old multipolar European system. Broader in geographic scope than its predecessor, this bipolar system featured a bitter rivalry between two superpowers, the United States and the Soviet Union. Their rivalry was characterized by deep ideological differences and the overriding danger of a nuclear holocaust. By the late 1960s, a strategic stalemate based on mutual deterrence made war between these two titans equally irrational for both.

With the end of the Cold War, a new international order has emerged. Significantly, this is not a balance-of-power system. It is marked by contradictory tendencies, and there is good reason to believe that it is a temporary and transitional state of affairs.

The present international order is unipolar, headed by the United States. It is increasingly dominated by cooperation and competition over economics. Furthermore, economic power is becoming concentrated in three regions centered in western Europe, the United States, and Japan. The main threats to world peace arise from increasing instances and varieties of nationalism and from the proliferation of dangerous weapons systems among developing nations. Yet, as the Persian Gulf War demonstrated, worldwide cooperation may be capable of countering such threats under favorable circumstances in the future.

Key Terms

balance of power
keeper of the balance
bipolar system
Warsaw Pact
triad
ICBMs

SLBMs
counterforce weapons
Strategic Defense Initiative
mutual assured destruction (MAD)
nationalism

Review Questions

1. What is a balance of power? How did the traditional European balance-of-power system work? What were its chief characteristics? Why did it function more or less successfully for more than 260 years?

2. What brought about the decline and fall of the classical European balance-of-power system?

3. How did the post–World War II international system differ from its predecessors?

4. Is there a present-day balance of power?

5. What constitutes today's greatest threat to world peace?

Recommended Reading

BROWN, SEYOM. *New Forces in World Politics.* Washington, D.C.: Brookings Institution, 1974. An analysis of the impact of economic and social forces on the contemporary international system.

KEGLEY, CHARLES W., JR., and EUGENE R. WITTKOPF. *World Politics: Trend and Transformation* (2nd ed.). New York: St. Martin's Press, 1989. An introductory textbook that emphasizes interdependence in a changing global system.

MCCLELLAND, CHARLES A. *Theory and the International System.* New York: Macmillan, 1966. A theoretical examination of the applicability of systems analysis and behavioral methods to political science.

ROSECRANCE, RICHARD N. *Action and Reaction in World Politics: International Systems in Perspective.* Westport, Conn.: Greenwood Press, 1977. An imaginative attempt to put the history of international politics in the Western world into a systems perspective.

SPANIER, JOHN. *Games Nations Play,* 7th ed. Washington, D.C.: Congressional Quarterly, 1990. A well-written and popular text that has withstood the test of time.

WALTZ, KENNETH N. *Theory of International Politics.* New York: McGraw-Hill, 1979. This study examines theories of international politics and presents the author's own theory. Waltz cogently argues that a bipolar system is actually more compatible with a stable balance of power and effective conflict management than a multipolar system.

ZEIGLER, DAVID W. *War, Peace, and International Politics,* 5th ed. Glenview, Ill.: Scott, Foresman, 1990. A good basic text focusing on war as the age-old problem of international politics.

Notes

1. Kenneth Waby, *Theory of International Relations* (Reading, Mass.: Addison-Wesley, 1979), p. 100.

2. Hans J. Morgenthau, *Politics among Nations: The Struggle for Power and Peace,* 5th rev. ed. (New York: Knopf, 1978), pp. 221–223.

3. Ibid., p. 27.

4. Particularly helpful is Charles Krauthammer, "The Lonely Superpower," *New Republic,* July 29, 1991, pp. 23–27. Our discussion follows Krauthammer in several important respects.

5. Joan Edelman Spero, *The Politics of International Economic Relations* (New York: St. Martin's Press, 1990), p. 229.

6. Frederick H. Hartmann, *The Relations of Nations,* 6th ed. (New York: Macmillan, 1985), p. 28.

7. Krauthammer, "Lonely Superpower," p. 27.

CHAPTER 21

INTERNATIONAL LAW AND ORGANIZATIONS

COLLECTIVE SECURITY AND THE PURSUIT OF PEACE

(Sergio Larrain/Magnum)

THE STUDY OF history leads some observers to conclude that war will always be with us and that at best, the frequency of war can be reduced through a conscientious policy of military preparedness. Other observers, however, argue that war may indeed become less prevalent in the future, but not because of deliberate changes in the foreign policy of nation-states. Rather, in a world where

> the price of gasoline at American service stations is now determined by people meeting in foreign capitals . . . the availability of color televisions to the American consumer is governed not simply by internal market forces but also by agreements between Washington, on the one hand, and Tokyo, Tai-pei, and Seoul, on the other . . . decisions reached in the Kremlin influence the level at which Americans are taxed and how the revenues generated will be spent . . . supplies determine welfare everywhere—indeed, where everything appears to be connected to everything else—[in this kind of world] new ways of thinking and new conceptual modes are needed.[1]

As this quotation emphasizes, the well-being of any one nation today increasingly depends on the actions of other nations. This circumstance was foreseen and welcomed by the statesmen and political scientists who, after World War II, argued that effective international organizations would promote worldwide cooperation and that cooperation would in turn create shared economic interests, promote international understanding, and decrease world tensions and hostilities. The school of thought that embraced this view was called *functionalism*. Its proponents believed that through the evolutionary process of international cooperation, national leaders would eventually abandon their narrow concern for the welfare of a particular nation-state in favor of a higher level of concern for the good of all nations.

Contemporary political scientists often point to the increasingly intricate web of close ties among nations and postulate that heightened *interdependence* (mutual dependence) among nations is transforming the very foundations of the international order. In particular, the steady growth and development of the world economy has given rise to supranational structures to ensure proper regulation and to remove artificial impediments (such as tariffs and trade quotas). Growing regional trade ties and movement toward regional economic integration are evident in the decision of the European Community to create a unified economy in 1992, as well as in the emergence of new regional organizations such as the Asian Pacific Economic Council (APEC) and the South Asian Association for Regional Cooperation (SAARC). Increased cooperation and diminished competition among nations will, in this view, be the likely long-term result. Eventually, rational self-interest will prompt all nations to recognize that cooperation in trade and commerce, and even in solving the age-old problem of war, benefits everyone.

But has the rise of nonstate actors, heralded first by the functionalists and now by interdependence theorists, really advanced the prospect for increased national cooperation and peace? And has the creation of global and regional organizations, including a universal international organization (such as the United Nations), and the drafting and implementation of international law, truly promoted such cooperation? To answer these questions, we must first examine the various types of nonstate organizations in the world today.

NONSTATE ACTORS

International cooperation has been aided by entities other than nation-states. International organizations, multinational corporations, and economic pacts have each played an important role in world politics.

International Organizations

The number of international organizations has grown phenomenally over the past two centuries. This is true of both organizations of which governments are members, known as *international governmental organizations (IGOs)*, and those made up of private individuals and groups, *international nongovernmental organizations (INGOs)*. The first general-purpose international organization in the modern era, the Holy Alliance, came into being after the defeat of Napoleon in 1815. Between World Wars I and II, there was a proliferation of international organizations directly or indirectly associated with the newly formed League of Nations, which was the first truly universal (worldwide) IGO in history. By 1940, more than 80 IGOs and nearly 500 INGOs were in existence; following World War II, both types of organizations mushroomed (see Tables 21-1 and 21-2). It is projected that by the year 2000, there will be more than 850 IGOs and 9,600 INGOs in the world, compared to only 200 nation-states.[2]

This vast array of transnational associations has created what one writer has called "networks of interdependence."[3] The specific purposes of the IGOs range

---

TABLE 21-1
Some Representative International Nongovernmental Organizations (INGOs)

Afro-Asian Peoples' Solidarity Organization	International Federation of Air Line Pilots Associations
Amnesty International	International Handball Federation
Arab Lawyers Union	International Olympic Committee
European Broadcasting Union	International Political Science Association
European Federation of the Plywood Industry	International Union Against the Venereal Diseases and the Treponematoses
Federation of Asian Women's Association	International Union of Local Authorities
International Air Transport Association	Latin American Shipowners Association
International Alliance of Women	Nordic Association of Advertising Agencies
International Chamber of Commerce	Rotary International
International Committee of the Red Cross	Salvation Army
International Confederation of Accordionists	Save the Children
International Confederation of Arab Trade Unions	World Council of Churches
International Confederation of Free Trade Unions	World Federation of Jewish Journalists
International Council Against Bullfighting	World Federation of Master Tailors
International Council of Scientific Unions	World Federation of United Nations Associations
International Criminal Police Organization	

SOURCE: *Yearbook of International Organizations*, Volume 3.

TABLE 21-2
Some Representative International Governmental Organizations (IGOs)

African Development Bank	International Labor Organization
African Groundnut Council	International Olive Oil Council
Arab Postal Union	International Red Locust Control Organization
Asian Development Bank	for Central and Southern Africa
Asian Pacific Economic Council	International Telecommunications Satellite
Association of Southeast Asian Nations	Organization
Central American Common Market	International Whaling Commission
Conference on Security and Cooperation in Europe	Latin American Free Trade Association
Council for Mutual Economic Assistance	North Atlantic Treaty Organization
European Economic Community	Organization of African Unity
European Space Agency	Organization of American States
Food and Agriculture Organization	Organization of Petroleum Exporting Countries
Gulf Cooperation Council	Union of Banana Exporting Countries
Inter-American Tropical Tuna Commission	UN Educational, Scientific, and Cultural
International Bank for Reconstruction and	Organization
Development (World Bank)	United Nations
International Civil Aviation Organization	Universal Postal Union
International Coffee Organization	World Health Organization

SOURCE: *Yearbook of International Organizations*, Volume 3.

from the political and economic to the social, cultural, educational, and technical. Included in their ranks are such disparate groups as the Organization of American States, the International North Pacific Fisheries Commission, the International Labor Organization, the League of Arab States, and the International Olive Oil Council. Even more diversified are INGOs, which include such diverse associations as the World Confederation of Labor, the International Commission of Jurists, the International Planned Parenthood Federation, the International Air Transport Association, and the International Confederation of Catholic Charities.

Some observers attribute major political importance to the multiplication and diversification of IGOs and INGOs, which by their very nature cut across national boundaries and foster mutual dependence. However, most IGOs are narrowly defined, single-purpose organizations whose membership rolls are closed to many nations. One study found that of the nearly 300 IGOs in existence in 1980, fully 97 percent were limited-purpose organizations, and two-thirds were also limited-membership organizations.[4] And while some observers stress the interdependence and the increased likelihood of international cooperation resulting from the growing number of such organizations, others suggest that IGOs and INGOs reflect little more than the great number of routine concerns that must be addressed in an age of advanced technology and widespread international trade and travel.

Multinational Corporations

The *multinational corporation (MNC)*, also known as transnational corporations (TNCs), is the most prominent type of international nongovernmental organization. A multinational corporation may be defined as "a firm with foreign subsidiaries which extend the production and marketing of the firm beyond the boundaries of any one country."[5] Examples of U.S.-based MNCs are General Motors, International Telephone and Telegraph (ITT), Exxon, and Coca-Cola. Significantly, the number of U.S.-based foreign subsidiaries has increased almost exponentially since 1950.[6]

The emergence of MNCs as major economic actors on the world stage is a phenomenon not confined to the United States. Global conglomerates located in many countries now dominate the world market: If current trends continue, at least half of the world's total industrial production will be generated by a relatively small number of MNCs by the year 2000.[7] Indeed, some 200 MNCs accounted for about one-fifth of the nonsocialist world's gross domestic product in the late 1980s. The total sales of each of the top 20 MNCs, with a combined annual turnover of over $30 billion, exceeds the gross domestic product of more than half the world's nations, "and the very largest corporations can match dollar-for-dollar the economic strength of all but the very largest national economies."[8]

Direct foreign investment in the United States was more than $300 billion in 1988, some 3.5 times greater than the total in 1980 (but still about $30 billion less than the 1988 total for U.S. direct investment abroad).[9] There were no fewer than 2,500 businesses owned by some 1,600 foreign firms operating in the United States at the end of the 1980s.[10] Although the relative importance of direct foreign investment in the U.S. economy has grown rapidly in recent years (18.5 percent during 1987 alone!), foreign investors control businesses employing only about 5 percent of the U.S. civilian work force.[11]

The rapid growth of MNCs can be explained by a combination of improved technology and changing economic circumstances. Modern computers and communications and transportation technology have created the possibility for corporate expansion, integration, and personal mobility. The recent emergence of new market economies and the lowering of trade barriers have also aided this process. Furthermore, the process has snowballed as increasing numbers of corporations have expanded overseas to obtain comparative advantages either in terms of markets or in terms of lowered labor costs.[12]

Multinational corporations are here to stay. Some economists applaud them, arguing that they enhance worldwide competition, improve economic efficiency, and promote technology. Yet the rise of the multinational corporation has generated alarm in many quarters. Critics contend that MNCs too often pursue their own profit-making interests with little regard for the damage they might do to host countries in the process, that they have engaged in illicit interference in the internal affairs of host countries (the most notorious case being the involvement of ITT in the overthrow of the Chilean government in the early 1970s), and that because they operate outside the legal control of any one national government, they pose a challenge to the international system and a threat to the territorial nation-state itself.

Whatever the validity of these specific criticisms, there can be little doubt that MNCs collectively represent a potent force that may be changing the face of world politics. In the words of one well-known political scientist:

Multinational firms that coordinate production on a global scale and distribute their output throughout the world are one of the most striking recent manifestations of global interdependence. As such they put into question the value of models of world politics that proceed from the assumptions of national self-sufficiency and of the exceptional character of cross-boundary relationships. . . . According to one view, they are the international counterpart of the nineteenth-century industrial revolution; according to another, they may be the skeleton of the world economy of the future.[13]

Multinational Banks   Nations, like individuals, often find it useful or necessary to borrow money from outside sources. For this reason, the World Bank and the International Monetary Fund, both associated with the United Nations, have assumed great importance in the international system. In addition, American, European, and Japanese commercial banks have in recent years played an increasingly prominent role in the international monetary system. Many of these banks have become multinational, maintaining branches and offices throughout the world.

Commercial banks have attempted to stabilize the world's financial system during unsettled times. In the winter of 1973–1974, when the price of oil increased fourfold, and again in 1979–1980, when it more than doubled, great disparities in national wealth were created overnight, especially among developing countries. In these turbulent periods, the international banking system provided stability by lending money invested by oil-rich nations to countries that were short on cash because of the high price of oil (or that could no longer afford to import necessary foodstuffs). It was estimated that Third World countries in 1988 owed more than $1 trillion to foreign banks. (See Table 21-3.)

TABLE 21-3
Leading Debtor Nations in the Third World, 1988 (U.S. $, billions)

Rank	Nation	Debt
1	Brazil	120.1
2	Mexico	107.4
3	Argentina	59.6
4	Venezuela	35.0
5	Nigeria	30.5
6	Philippines	30.2
7	Yugoslavia	22.1
8	Morocco	22.0
9	Chile	20.8
10	Peru	19.0

SOURCE: World Bank.

Such huge debts represent a potentially serious problem for the international banking system. When oil prices fell in early 1983, it seemed likely for a time that some nations (such as Mexico) that had counted on steady or rising oil prices to repay their debts would be forced to default on their loans. Some observers even feared that if oil prices fell too quickly and too far, the leading creditors might be tempted to call in their loans and demand immediate repayment. Such actions could have sparked an international banking crisis and possibly a worldwide depression.

The key stabilizing role played by financial institutions in the oil crises of the 1970s and early 1980s was duplicated later in the 1980s when American multinational banks renegotiated multiyear rescheduling agreements (MYRAs) with nations that undertook concerted efforts to improve their economies and their international debt situation. These agreements grew out of close cooperation among the banks, the government of the United States, and a variety of foreign governments. In these agreements, the close cooperation between multinational banks and national governments reflects an interest in world financial stability that crosses national boundaries.

Economic Pacts

Many of the most significant international agreements of the post–World War II period have been trade treaties. The great majority of such compacts are bilateral treaties—ones that involve only two countries. In addition to bilateral agreements, five forms of multilateral (many-member) economic pacts have played varying roles in promoting some degree of economic integration among the member states.

Preferential Trade Arrangements   In these pacts, several states agree to grant each other exclusive trade preferences. Specifically, tariffs and other trade barriers are reduced on a mutual or reciprocal basis for the signatories of the agreement, who thus gain what is commonly referred to as *most-favored-nation status* within the orbit of the agreement. Perhaps the best-known preferential system is the British Commonwealth of Nations, made up of Great Britain and many of its former colonies.

Nondiscriminatory Trade Organizations   The prototype of nondiscriminatory trade organizations, whose membership rolls are open to all nations, is the General Agreement on Tariffs and Trade (GATT), forged in 1947 to promote closer trade relations on a global scale. From its inception, GATT has sought to block commonwealth-type preferential trading systems and to discourage increases in tariffs, duties, and other barriers to free trade. In the 1979 Tokyo Round negotiations, GATT members agreed to a 33 percent reciprocal reduction in tariffs. These reductions were beneficial chiefly to the industrial countries; most Third World countries refused to sign this agreement, charging that GATT had not responded to their need for more liberalized trade in primary commodities and processed goods. GATT's effectiveness has been limited because approximately one-third of the world's trading nations, including most of the communist countries and many Third World nations, have not joined. Even so, it has grown from the original 23 participants to more than 100 full and associate members who together carry on more than four-fifths of all international trade. Other similar organizations confined to specific regions include the Association of South East Asian Nations (ASEAN), the Asian Pacific Economic Council (APEC), and the South Asian Association for Regional Cooperation (SAARC).

Free-Trade Areas   Free-trade areas go beyond preferential systems in completely eliminating trade barriers among member states. Governments wishing to join a free-trade area must surrender their sovereign right to determine trade policy with other member states. At the same time, they retain total freedom to set their own *national* trade policies with nonmember states. Examples of free-trade areas include the European Free Trade Association (EFTA), founded in 1959, and the Latin American Free Trade Association (LAFTA), founded in 1960. In 1988, the United States and Canada negotiated a free-trade agreement. In the ensuing years, the United States and Mexico moved in the same direction.

Customs Unions   These economic pacts are based on free trade among the members *and* a common external tariff for all trade with nonmembers. As such, they represent a step above free-trade areas on the ladder of economic integration. An example is the Benelux Customs Union (encompassing Belgium, the Netherlands, and Luxembourg), established in 1948. Customs unions have occasionally proved to be the forerunners of political federations, as in the case of Germany in the nineteenth century.

Economic Unions   The European Community (EC), originally a customs union known as the Common Market, has grown into an economic union that provides for the free flow of goods and services, labor and capital, technology, and tourists within its vastly expanded borders. It also sets common external tariffs and adjusts taxes and subsidies that affect trade within the community. Among its other avowed aims are establishing common fiscal and monetary policies among member states and promoting greater economic specialization and cooperative ventures among members. Economic integration within the EC framework has been so successful that in the late 1980s, the member states agreed to complete economic unification by 1992. Where would this trend eventually lead? One glimpse of a possible future came in May 1991, when German Chancellor Helmut Kohl called for the creation of a United States of Europe.

The original European Economic Community (EEC), founded in 1956, consisted of six countries (Belgium, France, West Germany, Italy, Luxembourg, and the Netherlands); in the decades thereafter, Great Britain, Denmark, Greece, Ireland, Spain, and Portugal became members as well. In addition to economic institutions, the European Community has created political institutions that fulfill many of the functions of a supranational government. These institutions include the Council of Ministers, the Commission, the European Parliament, and the Court of Justice. The Council of Ministers and the Commission function as a dual executive, with the former directly representing the views of the member governments and the latter speaking for the interests of the EC as a whole. Important decisions must have the unanimous approval of the Council. The European Parliament is a deliberative body that advises and oversees but does not legislate. Since 1979, its members have been elected by direct universal suffrage. The Court of Justice interprets and applies EC treaties and adjudicates disputes between member states and the EC bodies. The European Community encompasses the European Coal and Steel Community (ECSC), established in 1952; the European Atomic Energy Community (Euratom), founded in 1958; and the European Investment Bank (EIB), also chartered in 1958.

THE UNITED NATIONS

Impressive as the modern network of international organizations and economic pacts may seem on the surface, it has not even come close to ridding the international community of quarrels and national rivalries. Many scholars and statesmen, in fact, have argued that peace and interdependence could best be promoted by one overriding organization rather than by many small international organizations. The supreme effort to found such an organization culminated in the creation of the United Nations.

Historical Background

To understand the United Nations, we must place it in historical context. Beginning in the nineteenth century, several international peacekeeping federations were founded, usually in the aftermath of increasingly destructive wars. The Holy Alliance, formed in 1815, in the wake of the Napoleonic wars, represented an attempt by Europe's major powers to control international events by means of meetings and conferences. A more elaborate organization was the League of Nations, set up in 1919, following World War I.

The League of Nations   It was with great hope and high expectations that the Covenant of the League of Nations was sealed in 1919. The actual machinery of the League of Nations included the Assembly, the Council, and the Permanent Secretariat. The Assembly was a deliberative body made up of representatives from each member state. Each representative in the Assembly cast one vote, and all votes carried equal weight. Motions on the floor of the Assembly required unanimous approval for passage, meaning that virtually every member state, no matter how tiny, enjoyed veto power over nearly every decision. The much smaller Council was made up of four permanent and four nonpermanent members. The role of the Council was to investigate and report on threats to the peace and to make proposals or recommend appropriate action to the Assembly. The two bodies were coordinated and supervised by the Permanent Secretariat, the administrative arm of the League.

In addition to building world understanding and cooperation, the League of Nations was charged with maintaining international peace and punishing aggressor nations. In this respect, the League became the institutional embodiment of President Woodrow Wilson's desire to replace the traditional balance of power with "a single overwhelming, powerful group of nations who shall be trustees of the peace of the world."[14] It was intended that the concentrated power of the League of Nations—the *collective security* it represented—would be so formidable that no single challenger would stand a chance against it. The military forces of all law-abiding nations were to be ranged against any state that violated international peace. In the view of the League's founders, the very existence of such an overwhelming force would make it unnecessary actually to use it, so cowed would potential aggressors be.

Despite President Wilson's advocacy, the United States initially refused to join the League of Nations, dooming it from the beginning. By the early 1930s, it was apparent that the League was fatally torn by conflicting national interests and bitter rivalries.

The Founding of the UN

The vast destruction, immense casualty count, and terrifying new weapons of World War II sparked renewed efforts to ensure world peace through the establishment of a powerful international organization. The founders of the UN recognized that if the new organization were to have any chance of succeeding, it would have to represent an organizational improvement over the League of Nations. It was widely believed that the League's structure had had at least two fatal flaws. First, its members were all treated as equals, irrespective of the realities of national power. In the Assembly, every member state had one vote, and every negative vote constituted a veto. And even in the Council, of which the Great Powers were permanent members, the nonpermanent members exercised veto power. Consequently, critics of the League argued, the lesser powers had too much clout and the Great Powers too little. The other great weakness of the League was its incompleteness. The scope of the League's peace aims may have been worldwide, but its membership was limited. The absence of several great powers—particularly the United States—meant that the League's mandate was universal in theory but circumscribed in practice.

The conferees who founded the United Nations in 1945 were intent on rectifying these defects in the League's collective security system. A major effort was made to ensure that no potential member state would be excluded from the new organization (see Figure 21-1). The General Assembly was designed as a deliberative body in which all UN members would have an equal voice and an equal vote. More important, the UN Charter created a Security Council entrusted with "primary responsibility for the maintenance of international peace and security." The charter specified that this body was to be made up of five permanent members (the United States, the Soviet Union [recently replaced by the Russian Republic], the United Kingdom, France, and China) and six nonpermanent members. Unlike their predecessors in the League, the so-called Big Five alone were given the right to veto proposed peacekeeping measures. In this manner, the UN Charter sought to correct the anomaly of legal equality in the

PRINCIPAL ORGANS OF THE UNITED NATIONS

INTERNATIONAL COURT OF JUSTICE	GENERAL ASSEMBLY	ECONOMIC AND SOCIAL COUNCIL	SECURITY COUNCIL	SECRETARIAT	TRUSTEESHIP COUNCIL

- Military Staff Committee
- Standing committees and ad hoc bodies

- Main and other sessional committees
- Standing committees and ad hoc bodies
- Other subsidiary organs and related bodies

Peace-keeping operations

▶ **MINURSO**
United Nations Mission for the Referendum in Western Sahara

▶ **ONUSAL**
United Nations Observer Mission in El Salvador

▶ **UNAVEM II**
United Nations Angola Verification Mission II

▶ **UNDOF**
United Nations Disengagement Observer Force

▶ **UNFICYP**
United Nations Peace-keeping Force in Cyprus

▶ **UNIFIL**
United Nations Interim Force in Lebanon

▶ **UNIKOM**
United Nations Iraq-Kuwait Observer Mission

▶ **UNMOGIP**
United Nations Military Observer Group in India and Pakistan

▶ **UNPROFOR**
United Nations Protection Force

▶ **UNTAC**
United Nations Transitional Authority in Cambodia

▶ **UNTSO**
United Nations Truce Supervision Organization

▶ **UNRWA**
United Nations Relief and Works Agency for Palestine Refugees in the Near East

■ **IAEA**
International Atomic Energy Agency

▶ **INSTRAW**
International Research and Training Institute for the Advancement of Women

▶ **UNCHS**
United Nations Centre for Human Settlements (Habitat)

▶ **UNCTAD**
United Nations Conference on Trade and Development

▶ **UNDP**
United Nations Development Programme

▶ **UNEP**
United Nations Environment Programme

▶ **UNFPA**
United Nations Population Fund

▶ **UNHCR**
Office of the United Nations High Commissioner for Refugees

▶ **UNICEF**
United Nations Children's Fund

▶ **UNITAR**
United Nations Institute for Training and Research

▶ **UNU**
United Nations University

▶ **WFC**
World Food Council

▶ **WFP**
World Food Programme

▶ **ITC**
International Trade Centre UNCTAD/GATT

● **FUNCTIONAL COMMISSIONS**
Commission for Social Development
Commission on Human Rights
Commission on Narcotic Drugs
Commission on the Status of Women
Population Commission
Statistical Commission

● **REGIONAL COMMISSIONS**
Economic Commission for Africa (ECA)
Economic Commission for Europe (ECE)
Economic Commission for Latin America and the Caribbean (ECLAC)
Economic and Social Commission for Asia and the Pacific (ESCAP)
Economic and Social Commission for Western Asia (ESCWA)

● **SESSIONAL AND STANDING COMMITTEES**

● **EXPERT, AD HOC AND RELATED BODIES**

■ **ILO**
International Labour Organisation

■ **FAO**
Food and Agriculture Organization of the United Nations

■ **UNESCO**
United Nations Educational, Scientific and Cultural Organization

■ **WHO**
World Health Organization

World Bank Group

■ **IBRD**
International Bank for Reconstruction and Development (World Bank)

■ **IDA**
International Development Association

■ **IFC**
International Finance Corporation

■ **IMF**
International Monetary Fund

■ **ICAO**
International Civil Aviation Organization

■ **UPU**
Universal Postal Union

■ **ITU**
International Telecommunication Union

■ **WMO**
World Meteorological Organization

■ **IMO**
International Maritime Organization

■ **WIPO**
World Intellectual Property Organization

■ **IFAD**
International Fund for Agricultural Development

■ **UNIDO**
United Nations Industrial Development Organization

■ **GATT**
General Agreement on Tariffs and Trade

▶ United Nations programmes and organs (representative list only)

■ Specialized agencies and other autonomous organizations within the system

● Other commissions, committees and ad hoc and related bodies

UNITED NATIONS
April 1992

FIGURE 21-1 The United Nations System
SOURCE: United Nations Office of Public Information.

midst of political inequality. In the UN, the most powerful nations would have responsibilities commensurate with their capabilities.

Key Points in the UN Charter   Precisely how these responsibilities were conceptualized was spelled out in Chapter 7 of the UN Charter, titled "Action with Respect to Threats to the Peace, Breaches of the Peace, and Acts of Aggression." Article 39 of this chapter specifies that "the Security Council shall determine the existence of any threat to the peace, breach of the peace, or act of aggression and shall make recommendations, or decide what measure shall be taken in accordance with Articles 40 and 42, to maintain or restore international peace and security." Subsequent articles spell out how the Security Council was expected to discharge its obligations. Article 41 deals with economic sanctions, including "complete or partial interruption of economic relations and of rail, sea, air, postal, telegraphic, radio, and other means of communication, and the severance of diplomatic relations." Article 42 contemplates situations in which economic sanctions may be inadequate; in such cases, the Security Council "may take action by air, sea, or land forces as may be necessary to maintain or restore international peace and security. Such action may include demonstrations, blockades, and other operations by air, sea, or land forces of Members of the United Nations." Other articles in Chapter 7 deal with organizing the military components of a full-fledged collective security system, including the establishment of the Military Staff Committee (Article 47).

The machinery of international peacekeeping outlined by these articles far surpassed the comparable machinery of the League of Nations. Moreover, the UN was intended to go well beyond merely maintaining peace and security, as the establishment of its so-called specialized agencies revealed. Through these agencies, the UN plays an important role in worldwide disaster relief, resettlement of refugees, technical assistance in the areas of food and agriculture, health concerns, and many other areas. In addition, the world body actively promotes a higher world standard of living through agencies such as the Economic and Social Council (ECOSOC) and the United Nations International Children's Emergency Fund (UNICEF). Finally, financial and developmental assistance has been extended to economically troubled states through the World Bank, the International Monetary Fund (IMF), and the United Nations Conference on Trade and Development (UNCTAD). The plethora of specialized agencies makes it clear that the UN was committed from the outset to promoting world welfare as well as preventing world war.

However, the UN Charter was not designed as a blueprint for a world government. Article 2, paragraph 7, of the charter makes it clear that matters "essentially within the domestic jurisdiction of any state" are beyond the purview of UN authority. In addition, Article 2 states unequivocally that the United Nations "is based on the principle of sovereign equality of all its members"—and the equality of sovereign states is a defining characteristic of *leagues*, not of *governments*.

Nevertheless, the declared equality of all members of the United Nations is undercut by other provisions of the charter that give greater weight within the

The United Nations buildings in New York City: inconsistencies and compromises are tolerated in the present in order to pave the way for the future. (United Nations)

organization to the most powerful or most prominent member states. The most obvious reason for these provisions was the need to guarantee the participation of the major states. But there was another, more subtle reason: Some of the UN's original supporters viewed the new international association not just as an organization of sovereign states but also as the forerunner of a world government. And if the UN's great potential were ever to be realized fully, it was evident that the larger states would have to play a greater role than the smaller, less powerful states. The seeming inconsistencies in the charter, accordingly, represented compromises made to pave the way for the future.

Stumbling Blocks and Limited Success

Unfortunately, the United Nations never fulfilled its early promise: It could not escape the same problems that had destroyed the League of Nations. Individual nations were simply not ready to commit themselves to the extent that the organization's proper functioning required.

On the one hand, the charter at several points obligates member states to act in accordance with the rule of law and empowers the Security Council to punish them when they do not; on the other hand, it provides a number of loopholes and escape clauses for states that wish to evade or ignore their obligations. Article 51, for example, states that "nothing in the present Charter shall impair the inherent right of individual or collective self-defense." As long as "self-defense" is a lawful justification to resort to force, and as long as individual states are free to define self-defense broadly enough to cover virtually any action they deem to be in their national interest, such a provision invites aggression. The dilemma is obvious: Without escape clauses such as Article 51, the UN Charter would not have been acceptable; with them, it may not be enforceable.

An additional problem plaguing the world body until recently was the persistent state of tension between the United States and the Soviet Union, which had seriously hampered the working of the United Nations since its inception. Because each superpower maintained a coalition of allies, followers, and admirers that at one time or another held the majority in the General Assembly, deadlock rather than decisive action became the hallmark of most UN deliberations. The high degree of consensus necessary to promote peace through collective security was for the most part lacking throughout the UN's history. Even when consensus was reached, one or another of the permanent members of the Security Council was able to block any significant action with a veto.

The waning of the Cold War after 1989, however, brought about a new dynamic for the UN and created new possibilities for an active UN role in resolving regional conflict and dealing with other global problems, as the UN-sponsored action against Iraq in 1990–1991 clearly demonstrated. The UN's active role in obtaining the release of the hostages in the Middle East and in establishing a stable government in Kampuchea (Cambodia) also proved to be successful.

In truth, the limited conflict-management functions of the United Nations were not always unsuccessful. At various times since its founding, the UN has contributed to peace by sending special mediators, truce supervision teams, or quasi-military forces to various parts of the world, including Cyprus, the Middle East, and the Congo. (The UN also provided the legal basis for U.S. collective security actions against Iraq in 1990 and 1991, in actions quite distinct from the peacekeeping function.) These efforts, though typically limited in scope and success, have been valuable exercises in peacekeeping (see Figure 21-2). Significantly, however, the more ambitious the peacekeeping operation, the more controversial the results have been. The UN's ongoing peacekeeping efforts in the Middle East are a case in point.

The UN and the Middle East   Following the Arab-Israeli struggle for control of Palestine shortly after World War II, the United Nations set up the Truce Supervision Organization (UNTSO) to observe and report on compliance with the armistice agreement between Israel and neighboring Arab states. In 1956, the *Suez Crisis* erupted into a second Arab-Israeli war, and again the United Nations was called on to calm the situation—this time by establishing a peacekeeping force known as the *United Nations Emergency Force (UNEF)*, the first of its kind. At its peak, UNEF consisted of roughly 6,000 troops drawn from ten countries. Its mandate was to supervise the 1956 ceasefire and the withdrawal of British, French, and Israeli forces; to patrol the border between Israel and Egypt (and the entrance to the Gulf of Aqaba at Sharm el-Sheik); and to oversee compliance with the armistice.

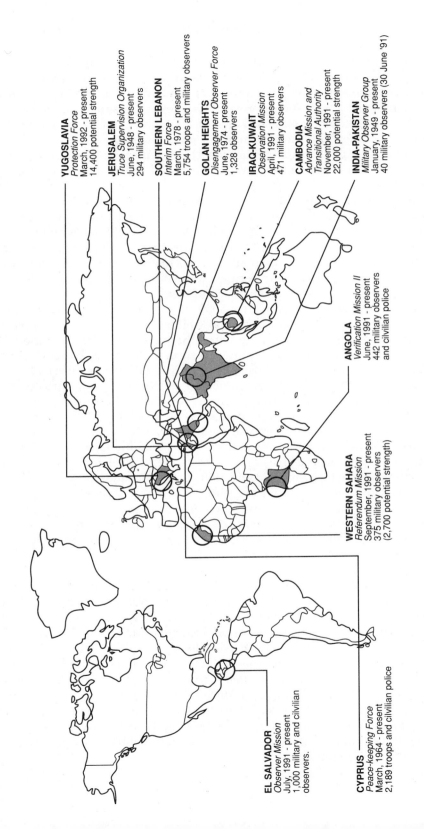

YUGOSLAVIA
Protection Force
March, 1992 - present
14,400 potential strength

JERUSALEM
Truce Supervision Organization
June, 1948 - present
294 military observers

SOUTHERN LEBANON
Interim Force
March, 1978 - present
5,754 troops and military observers

GOLAN HEIGHTS
Disengagement Observer Force
June, 1974 - present
1,328 observers

IRAQ-KUWAIT
Observation Mission
April, 1991 - present
471 military observers

CAMBODIA
*Advance Mission and
Transitional Authority*
November, 1991 - present
22,000 potential strength

INDIA-PAKISTAN
Military Observer Group
January, 1949 - present
40 military observers (30 June '91)

ANGOLA
Verification Mission II
June, 1991 - present
442 military observers
and civilian police

WESTERN SAHARA
Referendum Mission
September, 1991 - present
375 military observers
(2,700 potential strength)

EL SALVADOR
Observer Mission
July, 1991 - present
1,000 military and cilvilian
observers.

CYPRUS
Peace-keeping Force
March, 1964 - present
2,189 troops and cilivilian police

FIGURE 21-2   United Nations Peacekeeping Forces and Observer Missions

The UN peacekeeping force helped to prevent a renewal of hostilities for a decade, but in 1967, the force withdrew at the request of Egyptian President Nasser. The third Arab-Israeli war (known as the *Six-Day War*) erupted shortly thereafter. When the smoke cleared, Israel had crushed Egypt and occupied the Sinai peninsula (formerly Egyptian territory), the Golan Heights (formerly Syrian land), and the West Bank (formerly under Jordanian control), as well as East Jerusalem. In 1973, Egypt and Syria attacked Israel, sparking the *Yom Kippur War*—the fourth major conflict in the Middle East in 25 years. Israel counterattacked, driving the Syrians back and pursuing the retreating Egyptian forces across the Suez Canal. U.S. Secretary of State Henry Kissinger, practicing what the media dubbed "shuttle diplomacy," flew back and forth between Egypt and Israel in an attempt to work out new ceasefire and armistice arrangements. Sending in a new UN peacekeeping force (UNEF II) was one of the first steps.

A tense peace lasted through the 1970s, highlighted by the *Camp David accords*, under which Israel gave the Sinai back to Egypt and, in return, Egypt extended diplomatic recognition to Israel. Most other Arab states, however, denounced the Egypt-Israel peace treaty, accusing Cairo of selling out to the "imperialists" and "Zionists."

In 1982, still another war broke out when Israel reacted to repeated provocations by the Lebanon-based *Palestine Liberation Organization (PLO)* by bombing the PLO's strongholds across the Lebanese border and later, in a coordinated land, sea, and air attack, reinvading Lebanon. (Israel had invaded southern Lebanon for the first time in 1978 in retaliation against PLO cross-border terrorist raids.) Israeli and Syrian forces engaged briefly in the Bekaa Valley but quickly agreed to a truce. The Israeli army surrounded Beirut, and after a concerted bombing of PLO positions inside the city, Israel forced the PLO guerrillas, including their leader Yasir Arafat, to flee.

Unfortunately, Lebanon's troubles were far from over. In September 1982, Lebanon's newly elected president was assassinated and Israeli troops entered West Beirut to prevent extremist factions, backed by Syria and Iran, from taking over the city.

Where was the United Nations when Lebanon was being turned into the new Middle East battleground? After 1978, a peacekeeping force was stationed there—the *United Nations Interim Force in Lebanon (UNIFL)*. Like its UNEF predecessor, this force consisted of about 6,000 troops drawn from various UN member states, 15 in all. On paper, it looked impressive enough. And UNIFL's mandate was clear: to facilitate the withdrawal of Israeli troops from southern Lebanon, to restore Lebanese security, and to ensure the return of sovereignty to the Lebanese government. Unfortunately, despite the presence of UN "peacekeepers," the violence and terrorism in Lebanon continued for the rest of the decade. Only in the early 1990s were there faint signs of hope for a stable Lebanon, increasingly under the influence and control of Syria. This change did not result so much from the UN's moral influence as from the new realities of political power in the Middle East—the ascendancy of U.S. influence and the concomitant decline in Soviet influence in that part of the world.

The UN after the Cold War: Rebirth of Collective Security?

As we have seen, Woodrow Wilson's dream of a world free from the scourge of war and a League of Nations to guarantee perpetual peace was predicated on the concept of collective security. Wilson conceived of the League as an alternative to the balance of power, which in his view invited arms races and encouraged emphasizing military force in world politics without providing any effective deterrents to its use. But collective security—and the League of Nations—failed to prevent German or Japanese aggression in the 1930s; by the same token, a reformed collective security system failed to prevent repeated (though smaller-scale) acts of aggression by a variety of states after World War II. In June 1950, when North Korea invaded South Korea, the United Nations responded with military force. But even that instance of collective security was problematical: The Soviet Union did not participate and in fact objected strenuously to the use of the UN as a legal pretext for, in Moscow's view, an American military intervention in defense of a future client state, South Korea. Although the UN flag was raised, it was in truth a war fought by the United States against North Korea and, later, the People's Republic of China. The supreme commander, General Douglas MacArthur, was responsible to the president of the United States, not the secretary general of the United Nations.

It would be another four decades before the UN was again used in building an international coalition against an aggressor; the Cold War precluded any such effort—both superpowers used the veto to block enforcement actions proposed by the other.

But as we have noted initially, the decline and the collapse of the Soviet Union ended the Cold War. No longer should the Soviets automatically seek to obstruct efforts by the United States to resolve regional conflicts through the mechanism of the Security Council. Iraq's unprovoked invasion of Kuwait in August 1990 set the stage for the first major test of this proposition. The outcome of that crisis—and particularly the key role played by the United Nations—indicated that a new day could be dawning for collective security.

What exactly did the United Nations do? The Security Council became a forum for the major powers to meet and consult on how to respond to the Iraqi action. Additionally, the United States gained the Security Council's support for resolutions condemning Iraq, establishing tough economic sanctions, and ultimately approving the use of force to expel the Iraqi army from Kuwait. These actions were taken to win the general support of the USSR and the noninterference of the People's Republic of China.

What the United Nations did not do is equally important to note, however. The war against Iraq was predominantly an American effort. The United Nations did not provide any forces of its own. The secretary general had no control over how the coalition forces were deployed or employed. There was no United Nations general staff, nor did the United Nations coordinate the military or diplomatic operations undertaken by coalition members (principally the United States and Great Britain). The United Nations did not provide any funding either. In fact, the war was financed in large part by contributions from America's

Iraq's unprovoked invasion of Kuwait in August 1990 set the stage for the first major test of the United Nations Security Council to resolve regional conflicts. Iraqi troops were ultimately forced from Kuwait City only after they had inflicted horrific environmental damage to the region by dumping tons of oil into the gulf and setting wells afire. (Peter Menzel/Stock, Boston)

richest allies, including Japan, Germany, Kuwait, and Saudi Arabia. So it is an exaggeration to call the war against Iraq a United Nations enforcement action. It would also be an exaggeration to call it an exercise in collective security. To be precise, it was a broad-based coalition forged by the United States with the imprimatur of the United Nations. The United States provided most of the forces and firepower, with Great Britain in a strong supporting role and the Soviet Union providing no forces whatsoever.

Several conclusions can be drawn. First, the most important role played by the United Nations in this conflict was that of stigmatizing Iraq and legitimizing military action by the United States, Great Britain, and its allies. Second, this meant that the United Nations did not act as a truly independent force for world peace so much as a forum for coalition-building in support of American and British foreign and military policy. Although there existed broad political support for that policy, it is important to recognize that political power was concentrated in the Security Council generally and with the United States and Great Britain specifically.

Finally, although the precedent of UN sponsorship has become a new element of deterrence in international politics, it is also crucial to recognize that Iraq's invasion was particularly suitable for the application of the UN's collective security provisions. Iraq's act of unprovoked aggression threatened the interests of other Arab neighbors, Europe, Japan, and even developing countries that stood to suffer from disruption of oil supplies or a sharp rise in oil prices. It is too early to say if there will be equally appropriate opportunities for similar international cooperation or whether the United Nations will now blossom into an international organization capable of deterring and preventing future wars or punishing aggressors. Yet, given the long history of international conflict and the endemic clash of interests that characterizes politics on all levels, it does seem highly unlikely that the vision of a new world order based on a revitalized United Nations will ever be fully realized.

Restructuring the United Nations: Proposals for Reform

The success of collective security in punishing Iraq's aggression spawned renewed interest in the United Nations and prompted various proposals for restructuring and reforming that body. Perhaps the most widely publicized proposal was one called the Stockholm Initiative on Global Governance and Security put forward by an independent group of world statesmen. This prestigious group was led by former West German Chancellor Willy Brandt and included the

---

Swords into Plowshares?

SO POPULAR ARE United Nations peacekeepers these days that the world body can hardly keep pace with the demand.

All those troops, police, and civilians now heading for Cambodia and Yugoslavia will bring the global ranks of UN peacekeepers to an all-time high of about 50,000, a four fold jump since the start of the year. Somalia and Azerbaijan's Nagorno-Karabakh could be next.

The scope of peacekeeping in the newly energized United Nations is also broadening. The soldier wearing the UN blue beret is no longer just a monitor of a cease-fire. The peacekeeping operation in Cambodia will attempt the broadest array of tasks ever—from administering the country and organizing 1993 elections to helping repatriate refugees and promote human rights.

Peacekeeping is nowhere to be found in the UN charter. Undersecretary-General Marrack Goulding says that omission gives peacekeeping a rare flexibility. The only limits to the concept, he says, are what the parties to a conflict are ready to accept, what the Security Council will authorize, and what the General Assembly will finance.

The geographical spread of those supplying troops, police, civilian workers, and equipment to UN peacekeeping missions is also growing. Though most troops still come from a handful of countries long viewed as neutral, about one-third of the UN's membership, 58 nations, now make some materiel contribution. Since the end of the cold war, the permanent five members of the Security Council, often involved as brokers in past conflicts, have been encouraged to contribute, too. French and Russian troops are part of the UN Yugoslavian mission.

"Ideally, every member state should participate so that it feels a part of this high-profile activity," insists Mr. Goulding, the UN's top peacekeeping official.

Yet some governments are more willing to take part in such operations and to applaud their goals and gains than to actually pay for them. At the start of 1992 the UN was still owed $375 million in peacekeeping dues—about half of the operations' annual bill.

The Yugoslav and Cambodian ventures are expected to push the yearly cost to more than $3 billion. A number of US lawmakers say the 30 percent US share of dues is too high. The permanent five—China, France, Russia, the United Kingdom, and the United States—are assessed 57 percent of total peacekeeping costs. Many say Germany and Japan, barred constitutionally from contributing troops, should pay more than they do. Japan will pay more than its 12.5 percent share of the UN Cambodian mission's costs.

Members of UN peacekeeping battalions remain in national units and wear their own uniforms, but work together under one UN commander. Guns, not carried at all on observer missions, are to be used only in self-defense.

Though the UN supplies training guidelines, all troops are trained nationally. The Nordic nations for years have had a strong cooperative arrangement with national specializations such as Denmark's training of all military police. "We realized that we are small countries and had to organize our efforts; it's worked very well," says Col. Sigurd Friis, a military adviser with Norway's mission to the UN. Other regions have been urged by UN officials to emulate the pattern.

Each morning at the UN headquarters in New York, Undersecretary Goulding and his small military staff confer on daily situation reports from each of the UN's 11 peacekeeping operations. Frequent on-site visits provide guidance and support to commanders, who often have no previous experience with the UN.

Goulding made several trips to Yugoslavia this year to help pave the way for peacekeepers there. Shortly after Israel bulldozed a roadblock last month put up by the UN Interim Force in Lebanon (UNIFIL) and crossfire developed in which seven UN troops were wounded and one killed, Goulding made a quick trip to southern Lebanon and toured several sites during a blizzard. He cautioned both sides against further action. More recently, while visiting the UN Observer Mission in El Salvador, he spent 35 hours talking with government and guerrilla leaders to clear impediments on land and disarmament aspects of the recent cease-fire.

Though peacekeeping is not war, the job obviously can be dangerous. Over the years, some 784 UN peacekeepers have been killed. The tiny island nation of Fiji, long one of the most stalwart contributors of UN troops, has lost 25 soldiers just in UNIFIL operations, long considered the UN's most controversial and dangerous peacekeeping mission. Still, Isikia Rabici Savua, commander in charge of peacekeeping at Fiji's UN Mission, says, "We have never run out of volunteers who want to go."

To get a peacekeeping team up and going and paid for, however, is usually a long, slow process requiring numerous approvals. Several nations have earmarked standby troops, a practice encouraged by the UN, so they are ready when a UN call for help comes. The UN is also trying to speed action by surveying each UN mission in advance on the kind of equipment and personnel it could supply.

Goulding says one of the major remaining problems is in the UN headquarters itself. "When I say that the management capacity . . . is strained to the breaking point, I'm not criticizing my colleagues, who work incredibly long hours. But the resources of the Secretariat are finite. . . . We are very stretched."

Most of the 24 UN peacekeeping operations launched since 1948 have been disbanded. Many, such as the operation monitoring the withdrawal of Soviet troops from Afghanistan, are viewed as successful. But a number of others, particularly in the Middle East and Cyprus, have dragged on for years with no political settlement.

Some argue that such operations even inhibit solutions by removing a sense of urgency.

Marrack Goulding doesn't see it that way. "If you withdraw the forces in Cyprus, you might have a very nasty little war very quickly," he says. "Keeping the two sides apart is valuable. There are cases where keeping a peacekeeping operation in place for a long time may be the least bad option available."

prime ministers of Sweden and Norway and former prime ministers of Pakistan, Tanzania, and the United Kingdom. It also included former United States President Jimmy Carter, former Soviet Prime Minister Eduard Shevardnadze, and Czechoslovakian President Vaclav Havel.

The Stockholm Initiative recommended that the UN secretary general be given more authority to coordinate the work of UN agencies and to initiate action in crisis situations; that the Security Council veto be reviewed; that Security Council membership be expanded; and that a wider definition of security, including developmental and environmental issues, be embraced. The proposals called for creation of yet another independent commission to pick up where the Stockholm Initiative left off and also urged that a global summit be held by 1995—the fiftieth anniversary of the founding of the United Nations.

Skeptics pointed out that the permanent members are not likely to give up their veto power and that enlarging the Security Council very much would make it unwieldy. Others argued that it would be reasonable to create seats for Germany and Japan; however, opening the door too much might lead to pressures to throw it wide open. A Security Council with, say, twice as many members would probably be less effective than the present one. Moreover, those who advocate abolishing the veto would do well to remember its original rationale: The experience of the League of Nations demonstrated that unless the major powers can agree on a course of action, the measures adopted by any international organization are doomed to failure. When the Security Council cannot act for lack of unanimity, the problem is not procedural but political. Unless the political preconditions for major-power collaboration are present, streamlined voting procedures may do more harm than good by underscoring the fact that the United Nations has no independent power to enforce the resolutions it adopts.

Finally, one potential problem involving a permanent seat on the Security Council arose when the Soviet Union self-destructed at the end of 1991. The problem was quickly solved when the Security Council voted unanimously to transfer the former USSR's status as a permanent member to the Russian Republic. This ability to solve potentially controversial problems within the UN's existing framework reflects the remarkable changes in the climate of international politics that occurred in the late 1980s and early 1990s.

Problems Underlying Comprehensive International Organizations

Despite its successes, the United Nations has obviously not lived up to the highest expectations of its founders. Although its architects sought to solve the procedural problems associated with the League of Nations—such as the unanimity rule that prevented the League's Assembly from acting unless all its members could agree—the UN has not been free of procedural problems. And problems of procedure in international organizations invariably conceal more deep-seated difficulties. These must be faced by any comprehensive international organization.

The Problem of Universality   For an international body to be successful, all nations of significant size or consequence must be persuaded to join and remain part of the organization. As a minimum condition for success, all major powers must be members. The experience of the League of Nations clearly demonstrated the problems that arise when some nations are excluded or refuse to join. The history of the United Nations also illustrates the importance of including all potential member states—especially those with the capacity to disrupt world peace. (The difficulties caused by the absence of the People's Republic of China, which was excluded from the UN for two decades, was an obvious case in point.) Yet ensuring this universality of membership in a pluralistic world has proved to be problematic. In recent years, for example, some important nations (such as South Africa) have been stripped of full membership privileges, and others (including Israel) have been threatened with expulsion.

The Problem of Inequality   Smaller nations inevitably insist on the principle of formal equality. Anything less, they contend, would be an affront to their sovereignty. By the same token, powerful nations insist that their superior strength be reflected in special procedural arrangements (such as the veto power of the permanent members of the UN Security Council). Anything less, they argue, would represent a diminution of their real importance in the world. Moreover, as the relative strengths of member states fluctuate, the original formula governing such matters needs to be revised. Some nations that were formerly considered great powers have to be demoted to make room for newcomers whose stars are rising. This is more than merely a "technical" problem. No international organization can remain viable unless it resolves the problem of inequality while remaining flexible enough to change with changing circumstances.

The Problem of Competence   Organizations of this kind, by their very nature, are powerless to do any more than their least cooperative members are willing to countenance. As a result, international organizations tend to lack the competence to deal with a wide range of problems normally thought to fall within the realm of governmental action. The best they can do, as a rule, is deal with specific cases arising in general areas of common concern (for example, peacekeeping).

The Problem of Unity   In the past, the most successful international organizations have been alliances based on confronting a common enemy. The Holy Alliance, inspired by the fear of a resurgent France, was a case in point. The present-day Arab League is another: Without the unifying effect of facing a common enemy (Israel), the Arab states undoubtedly would have engaged in far more internecine squabbling over the past 50 years. Similarly, without the perceived threat of communist expansion in the late 1940s and early 1950s, the North Atlantic Treaty Organization would never have been founded. Finally, the high point of UN unity came in 1990–1991, when most nations of the world joined the United States in opposing a common enemy, Iraq. When the original threat fades, however, the bonds of alliance tend to disintegrate. Disunity, or the absence of any real sense of community in the international arena, is a major obstacle to all forms of international organization, from the simplest to the most complex and comprehensive.

The Problem of Sovereignty   Underlying all four problems just mentioned is the problem of sovereignty—the supreme power a state exercises within its boundaries. In the final analysis, sovereignty is indivisible: Either a nation has the last word in its own affairs or it does not. A nation can no more be partially sovereign, the nineteenth-century U.S. political leader John C. Calhoun once noted, than a woman can be partially pregnant. It follows that the creation of an effective world government would be possible only if individual governments could be persuaded to surrender not just part of their sovereignty but all of it—a prospect that has been regarded by most nations as entirely too dangerous in a world governed by mutual fear and mistrust.

INTERNATIONAL LAW

Considering that the United Nations has failed to secure world peace and that the organization's principal underlying problem centers on national sovereignty, we reach one key conclusion: The goals of world peace and international interdependence can be advanced only within the context of the present nation-state system. The framework of existing international law, in other words, may help to promote a safer and more secure world.

For roughly 350 years, the international system has been regulated to some degree by an ever-expanding body of *international law*. At the core of this legal code are basic and widely accepted rules defining the rights and obligations of states in relation to one another. These rules have been freely adopted by sovereign governments and have generally assumed the form of signed agreements (treaties, pacts, and the like). Other widely recognized sources of international law include long-standing custom; general legal principles based on such ideas as justice, equity, and morality; and the judicial decisions and teachings of eminent legal authorities.

The most famous codification of international law remains Hugo Grotius's *On the Law of War and Peace*, published in 1625—just 23 years before the formal establishment of the nation-state system in the Treaty of Westphalia. It was no accident that the rise of the modern international system coincided with the emergence of a set of rules governing the mutual relations of nations; on the contrary, the first development necessitated the second, and the second served to validate the first. In the $3\frac{1}{2}$ centuries since the Treaty of Westphalia, international law has become a vital part of what we might call diplomatic business as usual in the arena of world politics.

Usefulness

Consider for a moment the vast range of practical questions that could not be answered with any assurance apart from the rules and conventions of international law. How would territorial boundaries on land and sea be determined? If a river formed the boundary between two states, for instance, who would decide (1) whether the boundary should be drawn along the riverbed, along the river banks, or down the exact center of the river; (2) whether the river should be open to navigation for one state, both states, or neither state; or (3) whether upstream states have the right to build dams, reservoirs, and hydroelectric power plants on rivers that wend their way into the territory of the downstream states? What if the river changes course? Questions of this kind would crop up in many other areas of international relations. What would guarantee the safety of diplomatic representatives accredited to this or that foreign government? How would traffic on the high seas be regulated? Who would decide whether neutral states should have the right to carry on normal commercial relations with belligerents in times of war? These are only a few of the vital issues that would be extremely difficult to resolve in the absence of a preexisting body of international law.

Compliance and Enforcement

Surprisingly, international law has generally been observed or respected by the states it is designed to constrain. One authority notes:

> During the four hundred years of its existence international law has in most instances been scrupulously observed. When one of its rules was violated, it was, however, not always enforced and, when action to enforce it was actually taken, it was not always effective. Yet to deny that international law exists at all as a system of binding legal rules flies in the face of all evidence.[15]

The enforcement of international law has always posed unique difficulties. Under almost all national governments, the punishment for a crime committed by an individual is carried out by arrest, trial, and possible imprisonment. But obviously, no world government rules in the international sphere (certainly not the UN), and just as obviously, governments cannot be arrested, placed on trial, or thrown in prison. Nonetheless, they can be punished. The functional equivalent of government in the realm of international politics is the balance of power. In other words, states perceived as "lawbreakers" can be subjected to diplomatic censure or economic embargo or blockade by other governments. In extreme cases, they can even be overrun, despoiled, and occupied.

Clearly, there is little truth in the often-heard allegations that international law has no muscle behind it and that nation-states are never constrained to obey its dictates. Rather, the real difference between international and national law has to do with constancy: Whereas ordinary citizens generally expect to be punished if they break the law, governments can more often break the law and get away with it. Even so, political pressures to conform to the requirements of international law are real and meaningful. In this regard, it seems no exaggeration to say that the balance of power is "an indispensable condition of the very existence of International Law."[16]

Fear of political repercussions is not the only reason most governments play by the rules most of the time. As we saw earlier, every country has much to gain from the existence of a uniform body of international rules and regulations. Without such rules, international trade, travel, and tourism would be greatly impeded, and international financial transactions, foreign investments, technological transfers, and postal and telecommunications links would hardly be possible. And without the elaborate and widely respected rules of diplomatic immunity, few governments would send diplomatic representatives to foreign capitals. Under the circumstances, it is doubtful whether any government can afford to treat international law cavalierly for long. Faced with the discouraging prospects of diplomatic isolation, economic disruption, and military retaliation, governments have usually violated treaties, conventions, and common rules of good conduct only under the most extraordinary, extreme, or extenuating circumstances.

International Law in the Modern Era

Prior to World War II, the Hague and Geneva conventions set forth the rules of warfare. Since 1945, international law has advanced in several important areas—most notably, in arms control and the transnational environment. Agreements in these areas represent some of the most noteworthy examples of the workings of international law in the past century.

The Hague and Geneva Conventions   Until the middle of the nineteenth century, the rules of warfare were governed by custom. In 1856, several of the Great Powers endorsed the first of a series of multilateral international conventions—the Declaration of Paris, which limited war at sea by outlawing privateering and specifying that a naval blockade had to be effective to be legally binding. More important was the *Geneva Convention* of 1864 (revised in 1906), which laid down rules for the humane treatment of the wounded on the battlefield. Of still greater importance was the *Hague Convention* of 1899, which codified for the first time many of the accepted practices of land warfare. A second Hague convention, in 1907, revised the 1899 codes with regard to the rights and duties of belligerents and of neutral states and persons; it also prescribed rules concerning the use of new weapons such as dumdum bullets, poison gas, and gas-filled balloons for bombing.

Three later additions to this body of war rules deserve mention: (1) the Geneva Conventions of 1929, requiring decent treatment for prisoners of war as well as the sick and wounded; (2) the London Protocol of 1936, protecting merchant ships against submarine attack; and (3) the Geneva Convention of 1949, which revised the rules on the treatment of prisoners of war and the sick and wounded and the rules on protecting civilians. These conventions, like their predecessors, were aimed at reducing the cruelty and suffering associated with international conflict. (Note that these conventions made no attempt to abolish war itself, only to minimize its inhumane effects.)

Arms Control Treaties   In addition to the bilateral strategic arms limitation (SALT) accords negotiated by the United States and the Soviet Union in the 1970s, several multilateral arms control measures have been concluded under the auspices of the United Nations, beginning with the *Antarctic Treaty* of 1959. Signed originally by 12 countries including the two superpowers in 1961, this agreement prohibited all military activity on the Antarctic continent and accorded each signatory the right of aerial surveillance. Other provisions included a ban on nuclear explosions and the dumping of radioactive wastes; the right to on-site inspection of each other's installations; nonrecognition of existing territorial claims and agreement not to assert new claims; and a pledge to settle disputes peacefully and to cooperate in scientific investigations.

In October 1967, the *Outer Space Treaty* was put into force, and this time no fewer than 84 nations signed.[17] This treaty bans nuclear weapons from outer space, prohibits military bases and maneuvers on the moon and other planets, and bars claims of national sovereignty in outer space. In addition, the treaty calls for activities in outer space to be undertaken for the benefit of all countries and encourages international cooperation in space exploration and the exchange of scientific information. Unfortunately, the treaty contained no inspection clause; consequently, it did little to dispel mutual distrust between the superpowers, and military competition in outer space continued.

One year later, the Treaty on the Nonproliferation of Nuclear Weapons, more commonly known as the *Nonproliferation Treaty* (NPT), went into effect. This agreement obligated each nuclear weapons signatory "not to transfer . . . assist, encourage, or induce any non-nuclear weapon State to manufacture or otherwise acquire nuclear weapons." Each nonnuclear state further agreed "not to receive, . . . manufacture or otherwise acquire nuclear weapons." The United States, Great Britain, and the Soviet Union, along with most of the nonnuclear states, signed, but France and the People's Republic of China—together with several other potential nuclear powers such as Argentina, Brazil, Israel, Pakistan, and South Africa—refused to do so.

The NPT, like the two other treaties mentioned, was negotiated within the framework of the United Nations, underscoring its authors' intent to apply its provisions on a global scale. The treaty's significance, however, goes beyond the realm of international law. Politically, it focuses attention on the problem of nuclear proliferation. Morally, it places a stigma on the acquisition of nuclear weapons, adding a disincentive to threshold states that might otherwise be tempted to "go nuclear."

In 1970, the *Seabed Treaty*, banning nuclear weapons from the bottom of the world's oceans outside each state's 12-mile territorial limit, was endorsed by the General Assembly of the United Nations. Most UN members initially signed it; France and the People's Republic of China did not.

In a related development, a series of Law of the Sea conferences started in 1973 and continued over the next decade. These conferences resulted in general agreement in three important areas: (1) national jurisdiction over a 12-mile territorial sea (the strip of water immediately adjacent to a state's coast over which the state exercises sovereignty); (2) coastal-state rights (to exploit marine resources in a designated area along a state's coastline) over a 200-mile exclusive economic zone; and (3) unimpeded transit through, over, and under straits used for international navigation. The *Law of the Sea Treaty (LOST)*, which has been signed by most of the world's nations, calls for the creation of the United Nations International Seabed Authority to act as regulator of deep-sea resource exploration and mining beyond the 200-mile national economic zones. Fearing that this type of agreement would establish an unwise precedent and interfere with free enterprise, the United States in 1982 announced it would not support the LOST.

The problems that have arisen with respect to the Outer Space Treaty and the Law of the Sea Treaty reflect a key problem: Although governments have generally upheld the international pacts they have signed, there are limits to what such pacts can be expected to accomplish. Governments usually do not sign agreements that pledge them to act contrary to how they would act in the absence of such agreements. For example, both the United States and the Soviet Union signed the Nonproliferation Treaty, but neither country had any intention of supplying nuclear weapons to nonnuclear states. Where a proposed agreement on international rules of conduct has required the negotiating parties to give up something important to them, international law has generally not fared so well.

A New Era for Arms Control?   The waning of the Cold War in the late 1980s was accompanied by significant steps on arms control. In December 1988, at a Gorbachev-Reagan summit in Washington, the two nuclear superpowers agreed to dismantle all existing intermediate-range missiles (those with a range of 300 to 3,400 miles). This *Intermediate Nuclear Force (INF) treaty* was unprecedented—never before had the two Cold War rivals agreed to scrap a whole category of weapons. For the Soviets, this treaty meant eliminating hundreds of mobile SS-20s with multiple warheads; for the United States, it meant getting rid of Pershing II and cruise missiles stationed in western Europe (primarily western Germany).

Intense negotiations on the *Strategic Arms Reduction Treaty (START)* and the *Conventional Forces in Europe (CFE) treaty* followed the INF breakthrough. The United States and Soviet Union concluded a CFE treaty in 1990, but it soon hit a snag when Moscow tried to exempt some forces originally included under the terms of the agreement. (The matter was subsequently resolved, and the treaty went into effect.) The START treaty stalled in 1990 after internal turmoil in the Soviet Union forced President Mikhail Gorbachev to defer to military leaders who were skeptical of arms control in general and of Gorbachev's motives in particular. But Gorbachev restarted START in May 1991, and the two sides at long last agreed to deep reductions in strategic nuclear weapons.

The collapse of Soviet power after August 1991 convinced President George Bush that political events no longer required the same state of American military preparedness. In September 1991, he announced unilateral military reductions, including the elimination of all ground-launched short-range nuclear weapons and the withdrawal of all tactical nuclear weapons from submarines and surface ships. Bush also ordered the removal of all U.S. strategic bombers from day-to-day alert status and ordered their weapons to be stored. President Bush's reductions anticipated similar weapons reductions from the Soviet Union. Motivated by a recognition that political circumstances had changed dramatically, the American announcement (which eliminated several thousand nuclear warheads) sought to create a nuclear-free Europe, destroying weapons that might someday fall into the hands of small, politically unstable nations, and achieving long-term economic savings. Within a week, President Gorbachev responded to President Bush's offer by pledging to disarm all Soviet tactical nuclear weapons and to eliminate countless other nuclear ballistic missiles. Later, in his State-of-the-Union address in January 1992, Bush announced further defense reductions. Within a day, Russian Republic President Yeltsin countered with further reductions—sure signs of military de-escalation in a world no longer divided by a Cold War.

The Limitations of International Law

Treaties intended to outlaw war (such as the unsuccessful Kellogg-Briand Pact of 1928, eventually ratified by 64 nations) and fundamental agreements designed to promote peace and international understanding (such as the United Nations Charter) have never stood the test of time or the pressures of national ambition. Even modest "friendship" pacts solemnly signed by neighboring nations have been breached over the centuries. On balance, it appears that the failures of international law have been more conspicuous than its successes—we must keep in mind that the successes of international law are often taken for granted. Indisputably, the international system, as it currently exists, cannot provide the kind of framework that would make international law meaningful in instances when nations choose to ignore its requirements.

The contemporary international system lacks three practical prerequisites necessary to maintain the rule of law. To begin with, there is currently no single source of international legislative authority beyond the General Assembly of the United Nations, whose powers are negligible. Similarly, no international executive office possesses the power to initiate or enforce international law. (Symbolically, the secretary general of the United Nations could lay claim to this duty; but here again, the office commands no real power.) Finally, there exists no satisfactory way of adjudicating disputes among nations. The *World Court* does provide a framework for such action, but it, too, has proved to be ineffective (as we shall soon see).

Without these authorities, international law lacks the legislative, executive, and judicial powers that give other bodies of law their clout. Enforcement must be left to individual nation-states, which too often enforce its decisions unreliably. As long as international law lacks the predictability and coherence that give the rule of law its unique value, it will remain more of a convenience for governments than a constraint on them.

The World Court   The lack of compulsory enforcement of international law is reflected most clearly in the working (or nonworking) of the World Court. The World Court itself is a somewhat obscure institution—some would say justly so. The Court (more properly known as the International Court of Justice), one of six principal organs established by the charter of the United Nations, is a fully constituted judicial body, complete with judges, procedural rules, and all the solemn trappings of a dignified tribunal. All it lacks is a clearly defined jurisdiction.

The Peace Palace in the Hague, home of the World Court: complete with judges, procedural rules, and all the trappings of a dignified tribunal, the only thing it lacks is a clearly defined, compulsory jurisdiction.
(Reuters/Bettmann)

The World Court is one of the few courts in the Western world that does not have a backlog of cases; in fact, much of the time, it has no cases at all. Obviously, this paucity of work does not stem from an absence of international disputes. Rather, it is due to the fact that the Court's jurisdiction depends on the will of the parties involved.

For the Court to gain jurisdiction over an international dispute, the nations involved must confer jurisdiction on it in accordance with Article 36 of the Statute of the International Court of Justice. Article 36 specifically stipulates:

> Parties to the present Statute *may* at any time declare that they recognize as compulsory . . . *in relation to any other State accepting the same obligation,* the jurisdiction of the Court in all legal disputes concerning: (1) the interpretation of a treaty; (2) any question of international law; (3) the existence of any fact which, if established, would constitute a breach of an international obligation. (Italics added.)

In other words, the only time governments are legally obligated to abide by a decision of the International Court is when they have given their prior consent to the Court's adjudication of a case. They may make a declaration of intent to accept the Court's jurisdiction in advance, as Article 36 invites them to do, or they may simply choose to submit certain cases on an ad hoc basis.

In the first 20 years of the Court's existence, 42 governments declared their intent to accept the compulsory jurisdiction of the Court. This may seem like a large step in the direction of a law-based world order—but in international affairs, as in life in general, things are not always as they appear. The American "acceptance" of Article 36 is a case in point. Given its material affluence and attachment to the concept of due process of law, the United States might be expected to push hard for a stable and orderly world founded on respect for international law. Yet the declaration (made August 14, 1946) by which the United States ostensibly accepted the compulsory jurisdiction of the International

Court of Justice is a model of diplomatic sleight of hand. It states, in part:

> This declaration shall not apply to:
>
> **a.** disputes the solution of which the parties shall entrust to other tribunals by virtue of agreements already in existence or which may be concluded in the future; or
>
> **b.** disputes with regard to matters which are essentially within the domestic jurisdiction of the United States of America as determined by the United States of America; or
>
> **c.** disputes arising under a multinational treaty, unless (1) all parties to the treaty affected by the decision are also parties to the case before the Court, or (2) the United States of America especially agrees to jurisdiction.

Together, these qualifications lead to the inescapable conclusion that the government of the United States agreed to compulsory jurisdiction only on the condition that such agreement did not compel it to accept the Court's jurisdiction. Nor was Washington's qualified acceptance of compulsory jurisdiction unique. In truth, no government in the contemporary world has ever placed international law on such a high pedestal that it would agree unconditionally to commit itself to abide by the rulings of any world court.

The United States and the World Court   One might assert that if only the United States or some other country would take the lead, perhaps other nations would follow. What would prevent the United States and, say, Great Britain from setting a positive example by promising to submit all future disputes between them to the compulsory jurisdiction of the World Court? At least on the surface, nothing would appear to preclude this kind of contractual agreement between the two countries. But even if it were possible, why would it be necessary? For over a century, the United States and Great Britain have had very few disputes that have required protracted negotiations. And any disputes they might have in the foreseeable future are likely to be minor ones—close allies, almost by definition, seldom have the kind of differences that require adjudication. Obviously, the efficacy of compulsory jurisdiction cannot be gauged accurately when two governments are on such amicable terms that any differences that cannot be ironed out through normal diplomacy would be *voluntarily* turned over to the jurisdiction of an international tribunal anyway.

The confrontation between Nicaragua's former Marxist (Sandinista) regime and the Reagan administration offers a better test of the World Court's utility. In early 1985, Nicaragua filed suit against the United States in the World Court, charging Washington with aggression for mining the harbor at Corinto and supporting the Contra rebels. The State Department promptly announced that the United States government would boycott the proceedings and, as if to underscore the point, added that it was suspending bilateral talks with the Nicaraguan government. (President Reagan justified this action on the grounds that Nicaragua was using the Court for political and propaganda purposes.)

In June 1986, the World Court ruled decisively against the United States in

Ending ideological rivalries between the world's most powerful states is a significant step toward a safer, saner world and has given rise to new opportunities for building order as nations pursue their own self-interests, but it is, regrettably, no guarantee of perpetual peace. (Derek Hudson/Sygma)

this case. At Nicaragua's initiative, the Security Council voted on whether to support the World Court's decision. The vote went against the United States 11 to 1 (it would have been approved overwhelmingly, with the United Kingdom, France, and Thailand abstaining, except for the U.S. veto). Unfortunately, as this controversial case illustrates, the problem with compulsory jurisdiction, as with international law in general, is that it is least effective where it is most necessary.

International Law Evaluated

If international law works, but works imperfectly, we must evaluate precisely what its deficiencies are. Clearly, the fundamental problem is that not all the precepts of international law are observed universally. All nations place vital interests ahead of a blind devotion to international law. Of course, nations differ on this matter. Some nations break the precepts of international law infrequently; others may not care at all about such rules and obey them only as a matter of expedience. In either case, however, the fact that nations *can* refuse to be bound by it means that international law will be uniformly followed only when and if it is in the national interest of all governments to be bound by it. In other words, respect for international law ultimately depends on national self-interest, and not vice versa.

This is not to say that principles of justice are unimportant in international politics; on the contrary, they are of great value in understanding and evaluating political action. But the first principle of international political life is national self-preservation, and most lesser national interests follow from this principle. Whenever international law best serves the interests of the individual nation, therefore, national interest and legal principle become virtually indistinguishable in the implementation of international law. When this happy coincidence does not occur, however, the reality of national self-preservation always takes precedence over international cooperation.

THE CONTINUING QUEST FOR PEACE

In contemporary international politics, two key facts loom large: Nations pursue their own self-interest, and nuclear deterrence acts as the primary method of ensuring world peace. Nations seek to avoid all-out warfare by threatening to use weapons of mass destruction. This approach promotes peace—not by emphasizing human compassion, concern, or idealism but by playing on fear. Although balance-of-power politics and nuclear deterrence forged a relatively stable system of order after 1945, the sharply diminished rivalry between the United States and the Soviet Union and its successors in recent years has given rise not only to new opportunities for order building but also to new dangers and new sources of instability. Whether or not the proliferation of new international organizations—and the maturation of old ones—will prove to be potent enough sources of order to counterbalance the ever-present forces of disorder remains to be seen.

It would appear that none of the elements of international order and organization discussed in this chapter, significant as they are, can replace the age-old instruments of diplomacy and limited war (or the threat of war) as the usual means by which nation-states resolve disputes. Nor is respect for international law or the sanctity of treaties likely to increase enough so that countervailing force is no longer our chief means of preventing or limiting war. To the casual observer, it may seem that there ought to be a better solution to the persistent problem of war and peace. Indeed, the existence of nuclear weapons makes the search for other solutions more urgent than ever. But if history is any guide, we must acknowledge that international conflict—which appears to stem from the absence of international order—cannot be resolved by international organizations alone.

Nor is there any quick fix. No single act or event, no matter how momentous, can usher in a world without war. Ending the ideological rivalry between the world's most powerful states is a significant step toward a safer and saner world, but it is, regrettably, no guarantee of perpetual peace.

So the search continues. Even though world peace remains elusive, the need to avoid another world war is so compelling that people everywhere have a common interest in learning to manage conflict.

Is conflict management good enough? Should we not strive to end conflict once and for all? It has been said that politics is the art of the possible, or the best possible. Unfortunately, putting an end to conflict is not possible. Learning to cope with conflict more successfully, however, *may* be possible.

Summary

To what extent have international organizations and international law contributed to a more peaceful world? The removal of national barriers to trade, travel, and transfers of all kinds is reflected by the great increase in nonstate actors in the modern world, including international governmental organizations, international nongovernmental organizations, and multinational corporations and banks. Multinational economic pacts have also furthered the progress of interdependence.

This impressive network of international organizations and international pacts has not been free of national rivalries, however. And comprehensive international organizations have proved to be no more successful in bringing long-lasting peace and stability to the international arena. In the twentieth century, the League of Nations was torn apart by conflicting national interests. The United Nations has also encountered many obstacles, although it has enjoyed some limited success as a peacekeeping institution. The continuing crisis in the Middle East has severely tested the limits of the UN's effectiveness as a peacekeeper. In 1991, the UN-led coalition against Iraq gave the appearance of reviving the idea of collective security, although this was not truly an example of collective action.

International law facilitates and regulates relations among sovereign and independent states whose interactions might otherwise be chaotic. Like the United Nations, international law in general has had a checkered history. Modern-day examples of international law include the Geneva and Hague conventions, which set rules for warfare, and the multilateral arms limitation treaties of the 1960s and 1970s. The limitations of international law are starkly apparent in the difficulties encountered by the World Court. The limitations of the United Nations and international law derive from their inability to prevail over the divisive influence of national interests.

Key Terms

functionalism
interdependence
international governmental
   organizations (IGOs)
international nongovernmental
   organizations (INGOs)
multinational corporation (MNC)
most-favored-nation status
collective security
Suez Crisis

United Nations Emergency Force
   (UNEF)
Six-Day War
Yom Kippur War
Camp David accords
Palestine Liberation Organization
   (PLO)
United Nations Interim Force in
   Lebanon (UNIFL)
international law

Geneva Convention
Hague Convention
Antarctic Treaty
Outer Space Treaty
Nonproliferation Treaty
Seabed Treaty
Law of the Sea Treaty (LOST)

Intermediate Nuclear Force (INF)
    treaty
Strategic Arms Reduction Treaty
    (START)
Conventional Forces in Europe (CFE)
    treaty
World Court

Review Questions

1.   Name the most important nonstate actors in international politics. What impact have they had on the international system?

2.   What prompted the founding of the United Nations? How successful have the peacekeeping operations of the UN been?

3.   Does international law serve a useful purpose in contemporary international relations? If not, why not? If so, in what ways?

4.   What are the limitations of international law? How effectively has the World Court functioned? What suggestions for improvement are presented in the text?

Recommended Reading

AKEHURST, MICHAEL. *A Modern Introduction to International Law* (6th ed.). London: Hyman & Unwin, 1987. A good introductory textbook on international law.

BENNETT, LE ROY A. *International Organizations: Principles and Issues* (5th ed.). Englewood Cliffs, N.J.: Prentice Hall, 1990. A good basic introduction.

BRIERLY, J. L. *The Law of Nations* (6th ed.). New York: Oxford University Press, 1978. A classic.

CLAUDE, INIS L., JR. *Swords into Plowshares: The Problems and Progress of International Organization* (6th ed.). New York: McGraw-Hill, 1984. A classic introduction to international organizations, focusing on the theoretical and practical problems of the League of Nations and the United Nations. The author presents an incisive analysis of the difficulties international organizations have encountered in trying to carry out peacekeeping efforts.

HENKIN, LOUIS. *How Nations Behave: Law and Foreign Policy* (2nd ed.). New York: Columbia University Press, 1979. An incisive analysis that uses case studies and concrete examples to show how international law is interwoven into the foreign policy process.

HINSLEY, F. H. *Power and the Pursuit of Peace: Theory and Practice in the History of Relations between States.* Cambridge: Cambridge University Press, 1967. A scholarly historical study of proposals and schemes for the international management of conflict from the Middle Ages to the modern age.

JACOBSON, HAROLD K. *Networks of Interdependence: International Organizations and the Global Political System* (2nd ed.). New York: McGraw-Hill, 1984. The most detailed study of public and private international organizations available.

KEOHANE, ROBERT O., AND JOSEPH S. NYE. *Power and Interdependence: World Politics in Transition* (2nd ed.). Glenview, Ill.: Scott, Foresman, 1989. A groundbreaking work that not only challenges the realist theory of international relations but also attempts to construct an alternative theory based on the concept of interdependence.

STOESSINGER, JOHN G. *The United Nations and the Superpowers: China, Russia, and America* (4th ed.). New York: McGraw-Hill, 1977. A useful, well-written little volume that focuses on the performance and interaction of the United States and the Soviet Union at the United Nations.

Notes

1. Charles W. Kegley, Jr., and Eugene R. Wittkopf, *American Foreign Policy: Pattern and Process*, 2nd ed. (New York: St. Martin's Press, 1987), pp. 149–150.

2. Frederic S. Pearson and J. Marion Rochester, *International Relations in the Late Twentieth Century* (Reading, Mass.: Addison-Wesley, 1984), p. 318.

3. Harold K. Jacobson, *Networks of Interdependence: International Organizations and the Global Political System* (New York: Knopf, 1979).

4. Ibid., p. 52. See also Charles W. Kegley, Jr., and Eugene R. Wittkopf, *World Politics: Trend and Transformation* (New York: St. Martin's Press, 1985), p. 119.

5. Joan Edelman Spero, *The Politics of Economic Relations*, 4th ed. (New York: St. Martin's Press, 1990), p. 89.

6. Kegley and Wittkopf, *World Politics*, p. 129.

7. Robert Heilbroner, "The Multinational Corporation and the Nation-State." In *At Issue: Politics in the World Arena*, 2nd ed., ed. S. Spiegel (New York: St. Martin's Press, 1977), pp. 338–352.

8. Ankie Hoogvelt, *Multinational Enterprise: An Encyclopedic Dictionary of Concepts and Terms* (East Brunswick, N.J.: Nichols Publishing Co., 1987), p. ix.

9. Jeffrey S. Arpan, David A. Ricks, and Virginia M. Mason, *Directory of Foreign Manufacturers in the United States*, 4th ed. (Atlanta: Georgia State University Business Press, 1990), p. vii.

10. *Directory of Foreign Firms Operating in the United States*, 6th ed. (New York: Uniworld Business Publications, 1989), p. v.

11. Jeffrey S. Arpan, David A. Ricks, and Virginia M. Mason, *Directory of Foreign Manufacturers in the United States*, 4th ed. (Atlanta: Georgia State University Business Press, 1990), p. vii.

12. See Spero, *Politics of Economic Relations*, pp. 112–113.

13. George Modelski, ed., *Transnational Corporations and World Order* (New York: Freeman, 1979), p. 3.

14. Cited in Inis L. Claude, Jr., *Power and International Relations* (New York: Random House, 1962), p. 97.

15. Hans J. Morgenthau, *Politics among Nations: The Struggle for Power and Peace,* 5th rev. ed. (New York: Knopf, 1978), p. 281.

16. Lassa Francis Oppenheim, *International Law: A Treatise,* 2nd ed. (London: Longman, 1912), vol. 1, p. 93.

17. A similar treaty making Latin America a nuclear-free zone was signed in Mexico City in 1967 and subsequently ratified by most countries of the region.

CAREERS FOR POLITICAL SCIENCE MAJORS

PURSUING A MAJOR in political science is not intended to constitute career training. Rather, like literature, history, philosophy, mathematics, and many other disciplines, political science was originally part of the liberal arts tradition in higher education. In that tradition, education is an end in itself rather than a means to some other, more practical goal (such as getting a job and making a lot of money). Toward that end, the development of general skills—writing, speaking, critical thinking, and so on—is stressed. These skills are often manifested in leadership abilities, which in turn may account for the impressive percentage of political science graduates who perform key administrative and decision-making roles in government, business, journalism, and education

In this sense, an undergraduate major in political science is no more or less valuable than most other undergraduate majors. For students willing to continue studies at the graduate level, however, political science and its various branches can lead to fulfilling careers. Usually, an M.A. degree or its equivalent is required; the Ph.D. degree, with the notable exception of university teaching, is generally not necessary. Master's programs typically take two years to complete and entail the writing of a fairly lengthy thesis (requirements vary from one institution to another). Before deciding whether to pursue a career in political science, each student should seek professional advice from faculty members and practitioners in the fields of interest.

What questions should an undergraduate who is considering a career in political science ask? To begin with, you must decide which specific field to pursue. The most general course of study at the graduate level leads to a master's degree in political science. But even with this general degree, you will most likely need to choose a subfield (such as political theory, American government, comparative politics, international relations, or public administration).

Many universities have created special graduate programs designed to prepare students for careers related to political science. These programs cover such fields as public administration, public policy, international business, and international affairs. Often these fields have their own, more specialized areas. For example, a public administration program may emphasize state and local government, judicial administration, or even health administration. In addition, it is possible to pursue an M.B.A. (master's in business administration) or a graduate degree in management after earning an undergraduate degree in political science. Students interested in this possibility should consider getting a minor in economics or business administration and should take courses in mathematics, accounting, statistics, and computer science. It is even possible to combine business and government. Georgetown University, for example, has a special program in international business diplomacy, which focuses on this emerging subfield.

Jobseekers with a graduate degree in international studies may choose among several career possibilities. A public service career in foreign affairs is perhaps the most obvious choice, and in may people's minds synonymous with the foreign service. The number of career diplomats assigned to U.S. embassies and consulates around the world has fluctuated in recent times, but given the global reach of U.S. power and the proliferation of newly independent states (for example, 15 in the former Soviet Union in 1992, and several more in the former Yugoslavia), it is not surprising that America's diplomatic core numbers in the thousands. Nor is it surprising that the foreign service exam is quite rigorous. In a typical year there will be thousands of applicants competing for a few hundred openings. The failure rate for first-time test takers is always high, but applicants may take the test as often as they wish.

The foreign service, however, is not the only government entity involved in international relations. In fact, more than 40 federal departments and agencies conduct overseas programs—among them, the Departments of Agriculture, Commerce, Defense, and Treasury, as well as the United States Information Agency, Central Intelligence Agency, and Drug Enforcement Agency. Only about 25 percent of all the federal civilian employees assigned to U.S. embassies are foreign service officers. To cite one example, the United States Information Agency (USIA) alone employed over 8,700 people in the late 1980s (however, about half of USIA's workers are foreign nationals). At any given embassy or consulate, foreign service officers represent a minority—in some cases, no more than 15 to 20 percent of the civilian employees.

Frequently, political science majors choose to go on to law school. Careers in law are closely linked to government and public affairs in countless ways. Largely for this reason, prelaw programs at many colleges and universities are formally lodged in political science departments.

The layperson's idea that lawyers generally "practice law" is something of a misconception. Many legal professionals do, of course, have private practices or work in law firms. But lawyers also frequently take jobs as salaried employees in both the public and the private sectors. Most large corporations have legal departments, and labor unions and trade associations also employ lawyers on their permanent staffs. Finally, the legal profession is prominently represented in all three branches of the federal government as well as at the state and local levels.

Law graduates today may have difficulty finding desirable jobs, given the large numbers of young people entering the legal profession. As employment opportunities have become less abundant, class rank and the prestige of the graduate's law school have assumed greater importance. Even so, a legal education remains one of the most prestigious and lucrative types of professional training; and even though a law degree no longer carries a guarantee of a high-paying job right out of school, it should continue to be marketable for a long time to come.

Two other career fields related to political science are journalism and precollegiate education. A career in journalism does not necessarily require a graduate degree. Students interested in either print or broadcast journalism should take courses in politics, economics, history, English, and speech. Within the field of political science, courses in American government, party politics, state and local government, constitutional law, American foreign policy, and international politics would prove especially useful. Education at the primary and secondary levels in the United States does not normally break social studies down into separate disciplines. Thus political science (sometimes called civics) shares a place in the social science curriculum with history, geography, sociology, and economics. Someone who wishes to teach social studies at the secondary level will need to take certain basic education courses required for teacher certification in every state. (The supply of social studies teachers has generally exceeded demand of late. Sometimes having a special skill—for example, the ability to coach debate teams or direct plays—can be useful in obtaining a social science teaching position.) There are also opportunities for political science majors in educational administration and curriculum development, but these careers require individual initiative more than any specific form of graduate or undergraduate training.

This brief description of career opportunities is far from exhaustive, but it should help you to think about careers related to political science. The following suggestions may also help.

1 Research Your Field   Obtain information about your future profession as well as about the kind of education it entails. Undergraduates should acquaint themselves with as many career opportunities as possible. Fortunately, there are a number of publications available, including these:

Careers and the Study of Political Science: A Guide for Undergraduates (4th ed.), edited by Mary H. Crusan (American Political Science Association, 1527 New Hampshire Avenue, N.W., Washington, DC 20036).

Guide to Careers in World Affairs (Foreign Policy Association, 729 Seventh Avenue, New York, NY 10019; 1992).

Careers in International Affairs, revised edition edited by Pinto Carland and Daniel H. Spatz, Jr. (Edmund A. Walsh School of Foreign Service, Georgetown University, Washington, DC 20052; 1991).

International Jobs: Where They Are, How to Get Them, Eric Kocher (Addison-Wesley Publishing Company, Reading, Mass; 1989).

If you are thinking about law school, the following publications should prove useful:

The Official Guide to U.S. Law Schools (Law School Admission Services, Box 2400,

Newtown, PA 18940-0040. This official publication of the Association of American Law Schools contains information about specific admissions policies and describes the legal profession generally. The service also has publications titled *Financing Your Law School Education* and *The Right Law School for You.* The service will also send past copies of the Law School Admission Test, as well as special test preparation materials.

So You Want to Go to Law School, by John Dobbyn (St. Paul, Minn.: West Publishing Company).

2 Interview Professionals   Talk to people about your future profession. See if alumni from your college or university who are practicing in professions that interest you can be of any help. Also talk to other professionals in the field. Ask them about their jobs and careers. What did they expect? What are the advantages and disadvantages of their positions? Compare their comments with what your professors have told you. Perspectives sometimes differ.

3 Get Experience   Whenever possible, supplement your formal education with practical, hands-on experience. One of the best ways for students to learn what lawyers, administrators, planners, policy analysts, and civil servants actually do is to serve as an intern in a government agency, law office, or private, nonprofit organization. Internships have become a standard component of many political science curricula in recent years. The federal government makes extensive use of student interns in all three branches and in virtually every department and agency.

A good source of information about internships in the nation's capital is *Storming Washington: An Intern's Guide to National Government,* by Stephen E. Frantzich, which may be obtained from the American Political Science Association. Another useful source is the *Directory of Washington Internships* (National Center for Public Service Internship Programs, 1735 I Street, N.W., Suite 601, Washington, DC 20036). This directory gives specific information about internships and application procedures and also outlines summer programs.

Interested students might also consult a government publication titled *Summer Jobs in Federal Agencies* (Federal Job Information Center, 1900 E Street, N.W., Room 1416, Washington, DC 20415). This guide describes summer jobs throughout the federal government. Note that students seeking certain summer jobs may be required to take the Professional and Administrative Career Examination (PACE), the standard civil service exam. Individuals may get a PACE application by writing to the nearest Civil Service Commission office.

Interning can be a valuable aid in career planning, and in some cases it can lead directly to full-time employment. Even where immediate employment is not an option, internships can be indirectly helpful by showing a prospective employer that a job applicant has the practical and interpersonal skills needed to perform well in a bureaucratic setting. Finally, many internships are worthwhile learning experiences in their own right.

4 Plan Your Education   Once you have made up your mind what you want to study, you must decide *where* to study. Factors such as the general reputation of the institution, cost, and geographic location are all worth considering. More important, however, is the reputation of the program, the quality of the faculty, the admissions policy (and level of competition for available places), the availability of financial assistance, and the program's record for placing its graduates in suitable jobs.

In applying to graduate schools, one of the most important considerations is the prestige of the program. Because graduate degrees in political science provide less assurance of a satisfactory job upon graduation than law degrees do, it is extremely important to select a program with an established reputation and a good placement record. The American Political Science Association publishes the valuable *Guide to Graduate Study in Political Science,* which lists all political science departments fielding either M.A. or Ph.D. programs, along with information about faculty, admissions requirements, and curriculum.

Generally speaking, the level of competition for entering law school is higher than for entering graduate school. Law schools vary considerably in terms of admission standards, curricula, rigor, and reputation. The most important thing to consider at the outset is whether a particular program is accredited by the American Bar Association. Another question is what *kind* of law you wish to practice or what kind of law-related job you eventually hope to secure. Also give some thought to what state you wish to live and work in. Because the bar exam must be taken and passed before you can practice in any state, it is advantageous (though not essential) to attend law school where you plan to practice.

Find out all you can about the school and the program you are interested in, whether it be graduate school or law school. Talk to graduates from your college or university who have attended the program in which you are interested. Ask questions. How good is the instruction? Does the school make an active effort to place its students? Read the college's catalog and talk to a representative at the graduate or professional school you are considering. Better yet, visit the school, sit in on classes, and talk to students on campus. Look at facilities, including the library. This is a very important decision, so do not hesitate to ask questions.

Throughout the process of choosing a school, do not lose sight of practical details. For instance, it is essential to know admissions procedures and deadlines. Learning about the content of and appropriate dates for the tests required for advanced study is also necessary. Other details matter too. For example, it is significant that the LSAT (Law School Admission Test) generally plays a more important role in school admissions than the GRE (Graduate Record Examination) does in determining who will be admitted to graduate school. Finally, you may need to know details that do not even occur to you. For instance, state law schools may give preference to residents of that state; thus admission statistics may exaggerate your chance of being accepted. For these reasons, it is important that you discuss your career plans with your school's prelaw or pre-graduate-school adviser.

Finally, do not become discouraged. Keep in mind that some doubt will always exist when making such an important decision as choosing a school or a career. If you examine carefully the variety of materials available, discuss your concerns with a number of qualified people, and keep an open mind, things should turn out well. Although careful thought and preparation are no guarantee of success, they are its most important preconditions.

THREE FORMS OF GOVERNMENT

IN HIS LITTLE BOOK titled *Basic Forms of Government: A Sketch and a Model* (London: Macmillan, 1980), political scientist Bernard Crick develops a schematic comparison of autocratic (authoritarian), republican (constitutional democratic), and totalitarian governments.* This three-part classification is broken down into 11 separate categories, including: (1) the role of the inhabitants, (2) the official doctrine, (3) typical social structure, (4) elite group, (5) typical institution of government, (6) the economy, (7) theories of property, (8) attitude toward law, (9) attitudes toward knowledge, (10) attitudes toward the diffusion of information, and (11) attitudes toward politics. In this appendix, we have condensed the relevant portion of Crick's Chapter 13 ("The Three Patterns").

Crick's definitions are as follows:

An *autocracy* is a "form of government which attempts to solve the basic problem of the adjustment of order to diversity by the authoritative enforcement of one of the diverse interests (whether seen as material or moral—almost always, in fact, both) as an officially sponsored and static ideology." A *republic* is a form of government that attempts "to solve the basic problem of the adjustment to diversity by conciliating differing interests by letting them share in the government or in the competitive choosing of the government." Finally, a *totalitarian tyranny* is a form of government that attempts "to solve the basic problem of the adjustment of order to diversity by creating a completely new society such that conflict would no longer arise: it attempts to do this by means of guidance and enforcement of a revolutionary ideology which claims to be scientific, thus comprehensive and necessary, both for knowledge and allegiance."

Here is a schematic comparison of the three basic patterns:

1 The role of the inhabitants

   a *Autocratic:* passive obedience and social deference

   b *Republican:* voluntary and individual participation (conditional loyalty)

   c *Totalitarian:* mass participation and compulsory explicit enthusiasm

2 The official doctrine

   a *Autocratic:* allegiance is a religious duty and government is part of the divine order (only open disbelief is punished)

---

* In this book, we have designated "autocratic" states as *authoritarian* and "republican" states as *constitutional democracies* (see Chapters 4 and 5). *Totalitarian* states are discussed in Chapter 3.

b *Republican:* allegiance is demanded and given on utilitarian and secular grounds

c *Totalitarian:* allegiance is ideological (inner reservations are as subversive as open dissent)

3 Typical social structure

a *Autocratic:* a highly stratified caste or class structure

b *Republican:* a large middle class or bourgeoisie

c *Totalitarian:* egalitarian in aspiration

4 Elite group

a *Autocratic:* self-perpetuating and exclusive

b *Republican:* a stable political class enjoying social prestige

c *Totalitarian:* in theory, a meritocracy based on perfect social mobility

5 Typical institution of government

a *Autocratic:* the court or the palace

b *Republican:* a parliament, assembly, or congress

c *Totalitarian:* the single party (with an ideology as its shield)

6 The economy

a *Autocratic:* agrarian

b *Republican:* originally a market or capitalist economy, finally a "mixed economy"

c *Totalitarian:* the war economy, or planned and *rapid* industrialization

7 Theories of property

a *Autocratic:* the visible mark of status, hence land, treasure, and arms are all God-given to the rulers, and it is for no man to question their incidence

b *Republican:* the visible mark of worthiness—originally moral and economic endeavors are not clearly distinguished

c *Totalitarian:* no personal property (in theory) except the minimum of furniture, apparel, and cleaning materials; personal property is the mark of class differentiation

8 Attitude toward law

a *Autocratic:* customary and God-given

b *Republican:* both custom and tradition

c *Totalitarian:* laws of history

9 Attitudes toward knowledge

a *Autocratic:* all knowledge is seen as one and as part of the hidden "mystery of power" or inexplicable "reason of state"

b *Republican:* knowledge is fragmented, most moral truths become seen as relative, and all moral truths become open to some form of public questioning c *Totalitarian:* all knowledge is seen as one and is ideological: the censorship is general, but it is also positive: propaganda becomes a state institution

10 Attitudes toward the diffusion of information

a *Autocratic:* proclamations, but no regular news, hence rumor and gossip as institutions

b *Republican:* newspapers and a free press

c *Totalitarian:* mass communications controlled completely by the state

11 Attitudes toward politics

a *Autocratic:* either above politics, or politics is limited to the secrecy of the palace or the court

b *Republican:* politics is always tolerated

c *Totalitarian:* politics and opposition are seen as inherently subversive

GLOSSARY

accidental war In the modern age, the unintentional launching of a nuclear attack because of a mistake or miscalculation.

accommodation A national policy of adjustment to or acceptance of demands made by another state, usually in the face of superior military, economic, or political power. Accommodation is often seen as the lesser of two evils, chosen when the costs of resistance are deemed too great.

administrative decentralization The transfer of governmental powers from a central seat of power to local bureaucracies.

advisory referendum A vote by which citizens make clear their policy preferences regarding a specific issue. It is not binding.

affirmative action Giving preferential treatment to a socially or economically disadvantaged group in compensation for opportunities denied by past discrimination.

agrarian-bureaucratic states Nations characterized by an agriculture-based economy, a small and powerful landowning class, and a centralized, bureaucratic government. Such states may have a higher potential for revolution.

alienation The feeling on the part of the ordinary citizen that normal political participation is of no consequence or that he or she is barred from effective participation.

altruism A national policy pursued primarily because it is viewed as the morally right thing to do, even when there is no direct benefit to the nation.

anarchism A system that opposes in principle the existence of any form of government, often through violence and lawlessness.

Antarctic Treaty An international agreement that prohibits all military activity on the Antarctic continent and allows for inspection of all nations' facilities there. It also nullifies all territorial claims to Antarctic land and pledges the signatories to peaceful cooperation in exploration and research.

appeasement In general, a national policy of making concessions to an aggressor nation in order to prolong peace. The term was born in the policies of British Prime Minister Neville Chamberlain, who agreed to Hitler's territorial claims in central Europe before World War II.

ascriptive society A society wherein an individual's status and position are ascribed by society on the basis of religion, gender, age, or some other attribute.

autarky A form of government that aims at economic self-sufficiency and political isolation.

authoritarian governments Governments in which all legitimate power rests in one person (dictatorship) or a small group of persons (oligarchy), individual rights are subordinate to the wishes of the state, and all means necessary are used to maintain political power.

authority Command of the obedience of society's members by a government.

autocracy Unchecked political power exercised by a single ruler.

backyard steel furnaces Small-scale industrial enterprises that became a symbol of Mao Zedong's plan to decentralize all industrial production during the Great Leap Forward.

balance of power A classic theory of international relations that holds that nations of approximately equal strength will seek to maintain the status quo by preventing any one from gaining superiority over the others. In a balance-of-power setup, participating nations form alliances and fight limited wars, with one nation acting as a "keeper of the balance," alternately supporting rival blocs to prevent a power imbalance.

barrister In Great Britain, an attorney who can plead cases in court and be appointed to the bench.

Basic Law The West German constitution, adopted in 1949.

behavioral engineering The carefully programmed use of rewards and punishments to instill desired patterns of behavior in an individual or an animal.

behavioral political scientists Theorists whose study of politics is based on fact-based evaluations of action.

behavioral psychology A school of psychological thought that holds that the way people (and all animals) act is determined by the stimuli they receive from the environment and from other persons and that human or animal behavior can be manipulated by carefully structuring the environment to provide positive stimuli for desired behavior and negative stimuli for unwanted behavior.

bicameralism Division of the legislature into two houses.

bill of attainder A legislative decree that declares a person guilty and prescribes punishment without any judicial process.

bipolar system The breakdown of the traditional European balance-of-power system into two rival factions headed by the United States and the Soviet Union, each with overwhelming economic and military superiority over any other nation or group of nations and each unalterably opposed to the politics and ideology of the other.

blat Influence used to gain favors in the Soviet Union.

bourgeoisie In Marxist ideology, the capitalist class.

Brezhnev Doctrine The assertion, first made by Soviet leader Leonid Brezhnev, that the Soviet Union and other satellite states have the right to intervene in the internal affairs of another Soviet bloc country when a threat to the socialist system is perceived.

Bundesrat The upper house in the German federal system; its members, who are appointed directly by the *Länder* (states), exercise mostly informal influence in the legislative process.

Bundestag The lower house in the German federal system; most legislative activity occurs in this house.

bureaucracy Nonelected officials responsible for the administration of public policy.

Camp David accords Egyptian-Israeli peace treaty signed in 1978.

capitalism An economic system in which individuals own the means of production and reap the rewards or suffer the failures of their own efforts. Capitalist theory holds that government should not impose any restrictions on economic activity and that supply and demand should control the economy.

catalytic war A conflict that begins as a localized and limited encounter but grows into a general war after other parties are drawn into the conflict through the activation of military alliances.

cells Small, tightly knit organizational units at the grass-roots level of V. I. Lenin's Bolshevik party.

Central Committee The group that directed the Soviet Communist party between party congresses. Its members were chosen by the party leadership.

centralized unitary systems Government systems that guard their powers and prerogatives against encroachment by local governments.

charismatic leader A political leader who gains legitimacy largely through the adoration of the populace. Such adoration may spring from past heroic feats (real or imagined) or from personal oratorical skills and political writings. (See also *cult of personality*.)

checks and balances Constitutional tools that enable branches of government to resist any illegitimate expansion of power by other branches.

Christian Democratic Union The more conservative of the two major political parties in Germany.

citizen-leader An individual who can influence the government decisively without holding an official position.

citizenship The right and the obligation to participate constructively in the ongoing enterprise of self-government.

civic education The process of inculcating in potential citizens the fundamental values and beliefs of the established order.

civil disobedience Violation of the law in a nonviolent and open manner to call attention to a legal, political, or social injustice.

coalition government In a multiparty parliamentary system, the political situation in which no single party has a majority and the largest party allies itself loosely with other, smaller parties to control a majority of the legislative seats.

cohabitation In France, the uneasy toleration of a divided executive.

Cold War A high level of tension between two adversaries, in which diplomatic maneuvering, hostile propaganda, economic sanctions, and military buildups are used as weapons in a struggle for dominance.

collective security In international relations, the aim of an agreement among several nations to establish a single powerful bloc that will be turned on any nation that commits an act of aggression; because no single nation could ever overpower the collective force, aggression would be futile.

collectivism The belief that the public good is best served by common (as opposed to individual) ownership of a political community's means of production and distribution.

collectivization The takeover of all lands and other means of production by the state.

commando units Specially trained strike forces used to combat terrorism.

common law In Great Britain, laws derived from consistent precedents found in judges' rulings and decisions, as opposed to those enacted by Parliament. In the United States, the part of the common law that was in force at the time of the Revolution and not nullified by the Constitution or any subsequent statute.

Commonwealth of Independent States (CIS) A loose federation of newly sovereign nations created after the collapse of the Soviet Union. It consisted of almost all the republics that previously had comprised the USSR.

community Any association of individuals who share a common identity based on geography, ethical values, religious beliefs, or ethnic origins.

concurrent powers Joint federal and state control.

Congress of People's Deputies This 2,250-person legislative body comprised the institutional centerpiece of President Mikhail Gorbachev's program of political reform. Remarkable for its time, election to the Congress was (to a limited extent) determined by free, contested elections.

conservatism A political philosophy that emphasizes prosperity, security, and tradition above other values.

constitution Delineation of the basic organization and operation of government.

constitutional democracy A system of limited government, based on majority rule, in which political power is scattered among many factions and interest groups and governmental actions and institutions must conform to rules defined by a constitution.

constitutionalism See *rule of law.*

constitutional means The checks and balances purposely built into the U.S. Constitution to enable every department or branch of government to resist erosion of its powers by another branch.

containment The global status quo policy followed by the United States after World War II; the term stems from the U.S. policy of containing attempts by the Soviet Union to extend its sphere of control to other states as it had done in eastern Europe. NATO, the Marshall Plan, and the Korean and Vietnam wars grew out of this policy.

Conventional Forces in Europe (CFE) treaty A treaty between the United States and the former Soviet Union where each nation agreed to significantly reduce their respective number of ground troops in Europe.

conventional participation Engaging in the most common and least demanding of political activities, including voting, following political issues in the media, and attending political rallies.

convergence theory In international politics, the theory that the United States and the Soviet Union were moving toward similar political, social, and economic structures from opposite directions.

Council of Ministers The heads of the Soviet state bureaucracy, who directed all governmental and economic activities.

counterforce weapons Weapons designed primarily to destroy an enemy's strategic nuclear weapons before they can be used.

counterterrorism Methods used to combat terrorism.

coup d'état The attempted seizure of governmental power by an alternate power group (often the military) that seeks to gain control of vital government institutions without any fundamental alteration in the form of government or society.

crimes against humanity Category of crime, first introduced at the Nuremberg trials of Nazi war criminals, covering the wanton, brutal extermination of millions of innocent civilians.

crimes against peace A Nuremberg war crimes category, covering the violation of international peace by waging an unjustified, aggressive war.

cult of personality The political situation in which a ruler derives most of his or her power and authority from adoration by the general population and personally sets the major policies of the nation. (see also *charismatic leader*.)

delegate theory of representation Theory that elected officials should reflect the views of their constituencies.

demagogue A person who uses leadership skills to gain public office through appeals to popular fears and prejudices, then abuses that power for personal gain.

Democracy Wall A wall located in the heart of Beijing on which public criticism of the regime was permitted to be displayed in 1978.

democratic correlates Those conditions or circumstances thought to relate positively to the creation and maintenance of democracy within a nation.

democratic socialism A form of government based on popular elections, public ownership and control of the main sectors of the economy, and broad welfare programs in health and education to benefit citizens.

demokratizatsiia Mikhail Gorbachev's policy of encouraging democratic reforms within the former Soviet Union, including increased electoral competition within the Communist party.

de-Stalinization The relaxation of repressive domestic policies and activities on the part of any totalitarian regime. The term was coined when Soviet Premier Nikita Khrushchev assumed control after Josef Stalin's death and repudiated many of the latter's most repressive policies.

deterrence In criminal justice theory, punishing a criminal for the purpose of discouraging others from committing a similar crime. In international relations, the theory that aggressive wars can be prevented if potential victims maintain a military force sufficient to inflict unacceptable punishment on any possible aggressor.

development An ongoing process that depends on and promotes scientific discoveries, new technologies, and new patterns of social and economic interaction within a given society.

dialectical materialism Karl Marx's theory of historical progression, according to which economic classes struggle with one another, producing an evolving series of economic systems that will lead, ultimately, to a classless society.

dictatorship of the proletariat In Marxist theory, the political stage immediately following the workers' revolution, during which the Communist party controls the state and defends it against a capitalist resurgence or counterrevolution; the dictatorship of the proletariat leads into pure communism and the classless society.

diplomacy The normal and nonviolent process of negotiation, trade, and cultural interaction between sovereign nations.

direct democracy A form of government in which political decisions are made directly by the citizens, rather than by their representatives.

disciplined parties In a parliamentary system, the tendency of legislators to vote consistently as a bloc with fellow party members in support of the party's platform.

divided executive Situation in French government when the president and the prime minister differ in political party or outlook.

Dr. Bonham's case English court case (1610), in which Chief Justice Edward Coke propounded the principle that legislative acts contrary to the rule of law are null and void.

dual executive In a parliamentary system, the division of the functions of head of state and chief executive officer between two persons; the prime minister serves as chief executive, and some other elected (or royal) figure serves as ceremonial head of state.

due process of law A guarantee of fair legal procedure; it is found in the Fifth and Fourteenth amendments of the United States Constitution.

dysutopia A society whose creators set out to build the perfect political order only to discover that they cannot remain in power except through coercion and by maintaining a ruthless monopoly over the means of communication.

elitist theories of democracy In political thought, the theories that a small clique of individuals (a "power elite") at the highest levels of government, industry, and other institutions actually exercise political power for their own interests; according to elitist theories, ordinary citizens have almost no real influence on governmental policy.

establishment clause The clause in the First Amendment that prohibits the national government from founding a church or, by implication, directly supporting religion.

Estates-General The legislature of France before 1789, in which each of the three estates (clergy, nobility, and commoners) was represented.

ethnocentric bias The inability of nations to be reasonably objective when judging their own acts because of ideology or nationalism.

eugenics The science of controlling the hereditary traits in a species, usually by selective mating, in an attempt to improve the species.

Eurocommunism In western Europe, a modification of traditional Soviet communist theory that renounces violent revolution and dictatorship in favor of control of the existing governmental structure through elections.

exclusionary rule In judicial proceedings, the rule that evidence obtained in violation of constitutional guidelines cannot be used in court against the accused.

expansionism A strategy by which a nation seeks to enlarge its territory or influence.

ex post facto law A law that retroactively criminalizes acts that were legal at the time they were committed.

fascism A totalitarian political system that is headed by a popular charismatic leader in which a single political party and carefully controlled violence form the bases of complete social and political control. Fascism differs from communism in that the economic structure, although controlled by the state, is privately owned.

federalism A system of limited government based on the division of authority between the central government and smaller regional governments.

first stage of communism In Marxist theory, the period immediately following the overthrow of capitalism during which the proletariat establishes a dictatorship to prevent counter-revolution and seeks to create a socialist economic system.

First World The industrialized democracies.

Free Democratic party A minor political party in Germany that often exercises significant political influence through coalition with either of the two major parties.

functionalism In political thought, the theory that the gradual transfer of economic and social functions to international cooperative agencies (for example, specialized United Nations agencies such as UNESCO) will eventually lead to a transfer of actual authority and integration of political activities on the international level.

fusion of powers In a parliamentary system, the concentration of all governmental authority in the legislature.

Gaullism Philosophy of Charles de Gaulle designed to remedy France's previous constitutional crises.

gender gap This term refers to the difference in voting which occurs between men and women in the United States. This disparity is most obvious in political issues and elections which raise the appropriateness of governmental force.

gender norming A manner of scoring standardized tests, usually utilized for hiring purposes, which produces a result based both on the number of questions answered correctly and a person's gender. The purpose of gender norming is to help assure that equal numbers of men and women are hired for specific positions.

Geneva Convention A body of international law dealing with the treatment of the wounded, prisoners of war, and civilians in a war zone.

Gestapo In Nazi Germany, the secret state police—Adolf Hitler's instrument for spreading mass terror among Jews and political opponents.

glasnost Literally "openness," this term refers to Mikhail Gorbachev's curtailment of censorship and encouragement of political discussion and dissent within the former Soviet Union.

glasnot-**first model** A theory of development which argues that liberalizing political reforms should precede economic reforms.

Gleichschaltung Adolf Hitler's technique of using Nazi-controlled associations, clubs, and organizations to coordinate his revolutionary activities.

government The persons and institutions that carry out the political process in a community.

gradualism The belief that major changes in society should take place slowly, through reform, rather than suddenly, through revolution.

Great Leap Forward Mao Zedong's attempt, in the late 1950s and early 1960s, to transform and modernize China's economic structure through mass mobilization of the entire population into self-sufficient communes in which everything was done in groups.

Great Proletarian Cultural Revolution A chaotic period beginning in 1966 when the youth of China (the Red Guards), at Mao Zedong's direction, attacked all bureaucratic and military officials on the pretext that a reemergence of capitalist and materialist tendencies was taking place. The offending officials were sent to forced labor camps to be "reeducated."

green revolution A dramatic rise in agriculture output, resulting from modern irrigation systems and synthetic fertilizers, characteristic of modern India, Mexico, Taiwan, and the Philippines.

guerrilla warfare The tactics used by loosely organized military forces grouped into small, mobile squads that carry out acts of terrorism and sabotage, then melt back into the civilian population.

gulag archipelago Metaphorical name for the network of slave labor camps established in the USSR by Josef Stalin and maintained by his secret police, to which nonconformists and politically undesirable persons were sent.

Habeas Corpus Act An act, passed by the English Parliament in 1679, that strengthened the rights of English citizens to the protection of law.

Hague Convention A widely accepted set of rules governing conduct in land wars, the use of new weapons, and the rights and duties of both neutral and warring parties.

Hare plan In parliamentary democracies, an electoral procedure whereby candidates compete for a set number of seats and those who receive a certain quota of votes are elected. Voters vote only once and indicate both a first and a second choice.

human nature The characteristics that human beings have in common and that influence how they react to their surroundings and fellow humans.

Hundred Flowers campaign A brief period in China (1956) when Mao Zedong directed that freedom of expression and individualism be allowed. It was quashed when violent criticism of the regime erupted.

ICBMs Intercontinental ballistic missiles.

ideological terrorism Terrorist activity, usually Marxist in outlook, aimed at overthrowing the government.

ideology Any set of fixed, predictable ideas held by politicians and citizens on how to serve the public good.

illegal participation Political activity that is against the laws of the state.

incarceration The isolation of criminals in an effort to protect society and to prevent lawbreakers from committing more crimes.

individualism According to Alexis de Tocqueville, the direction of one's feelings toward onself and one's immediate situation; a self-centered detachment from the broader concerns of society as a whole. According to John Stuart Mill, the qualities of human character that separate humans from animals and give them uniqueness and dignity.

initiative A vote by which citizens directly repeal an action of the legislature.

institutional participation Engaging in the least common and most demanding political activities, such as participation through a paid political position or elective office.

interdependence In political thought, the theory that no nation can afford to isolate itself completely from the political, economic, and cultural activities of other nations and that as a result, a growing body of international organizations whose interests transcend national concerns has arisen.

interest group An association of individuals that attempt to influence policy and legislation in a confined area of special interest, often through lobbying, campaign contributions, and bloc voting.

Intermediate Nuclear Force (INF) treaty An agreement negotiated between the United States and the former Soviet Union in which the two countries agreed to significant arms reductions, especially regarding dismantling all intermediate ballistic missiles.

international governmental organizations (IGOs) International organizations of which governments are members.

international law The body of customs, treaties, and generally accepted rules that regulate the rights and obligations of nations when dealing with one another.

international nongovernmental organizations (INGOs) International organizations made up of private individuals and groups.

international terrorism Terrorist activity waged by one country against the government of another.

Iron Law of Oligarchy The elitist theory that because of the administrative necessities involved in managing any large organization, access to and control of information and communication become concentrated in a few bureaucrats, who then wield true power in the organization.

"islands of separateness" Family, church, or other social organizations through which internal resistance to the prevailing totalitarian regime can persist.

Jacobins During the French Revolution, a group of radicals, led by Maximilien Robespierre, who wanted to reshape French society into a virtuous and egalitarian utopia.

Jim Crow laws In U.S. history, the name for laws passed after the Civil War that perpetuated both private and public racial segregation; such laws were legitimized by the Supreme Court in the late nineteenth century but were overturned following the Court's landmark decision in *Brown v. Board of Education* (1954).

judicial review The power of a court to declare acts by the government unconstitutional and hence void.

junta A ruling oligarchy, especially one made up of military officers.

justice Fairness; the distribution of rewards and burdens in society in accordance with what is deserved.

just war A war fought in self-defense or because it is the only way a nation can do what is right.

keeper of the balance The nation in a balance-of-power system that functions as an arbiter in disputes, taking sides to preserve the political equilibrium.

koenkai In Japan, factions within the Liberal Democratic Party; *koenkai* are characterized by a form of patron-client relationship between a leader who relies on his followers for support and in turn uses his political influence to benefit them.

Ku Klux Klan A U.S. political organization whose ideology is racist, anti-Semitic, and anti-Catholic.

kulaks A class of well-to-do landowners in Russian society that was purged by Josef Stalin because it resisted his drive to establish huge collective farms under state control.

Kuomintang The Chinese Nationalist party, led by Chiang Kai-shek, defeated by Mao Zedong in 1949.

Länder German political units that function as states in the federal system and implement the laws enacted by the national government.

laissez-faire capitalism Capitalism that operates under the idea that the marketplace, unfettered by central state planning, is the best regulator of the economic life of a society.

law of capitalist accumulation According to Karl Marx, the invariable rule that stronger capitalists, motivated solely by greed, will gradually eliminate weaker competitors and gain increasing control of the market.

law of pauperization In Karl Marx's view, the rule that capitalism has a built-in tendency toward recession and unemployment, and thus workers inevitably become surplus labor.

Law of the Sea Treaty (LOST) An international pact intended to establish the United Nations Seabed Authority to regulate economic development of the oceans beyond the 200-mile economic limit. The United States rejected the treaty out of fear that it would impede exploitation of the oceans.

left-wing dictatorship A regime that is generally anti-Western (anticapitalist), pushed socialist economic reforms, and controls the population through mass movements, propaganda, and ideology backed by police force.

legitimacy The exercise of political power in a community in a way that is voluntarily accepted by the members of that community.

Liberal Democratic party The dominant political party in Japan since a parliamentary system was established at the end of World War II; it has a broad base of interest groups and coalitions.

liberal education Education that stresses the development of critical thinking through the study of literature, philosophy, history, and science.

liberalism A political philosophy that emphasizes individualism, equality, and civil rights above all other values.

liberalization In the Soviet Union, the term for relaxation of repressive internal policies. Periods of liberalization and repression alternated throughout Soviet history.

libertarianism A system based on the belief that government is a necessary evil that should interfere with individual freedom and privacy as little as possible; also known as *minimalism.*

limited government The concept that government cannot undertake an action, no matter how many people desire it, that conflicts with an overriding principle (such as justice) embodied in the constitution.

list system Method of proportional representation by which candidates are ranked on the ballot by their party and are chosen according to rank.

lobbyists People who attempt to influence governmental policy in favor of some special interest.

loyal opposition The belief, which originated in England, that the out-of-power party has a responsibility to formulate alternative policies and programs; such a party is sometimes called the loyal opposition.

Magna Carta A list of political concessions granted in 1215 by King John to his barons that became the basis for the rule of law in England.

majority rule The principle that any candidate or program that receives at least half of all votes plus one prevails.

Marshall Plan A post–World War II program of massive economic assistance to western Europe, inspired by the fear that those war-devastated countries were ripe for communist-backed revolutions.

mass line Mao Zedong's belief that any problem could be solved by instilling individuals with ideological fervor, thereby inspiring and mobilizing the masses to action.

mass movement Any large group of followers dedicated to a leader and/or ideology and prepared to make any sacrifice demanded of them for the sake of the movement.

Meiji Restoration The end of Japan's feudal era, in 1868, when a small group of powerful individuals crowned a symbolic emperor, embarked on an economic modernization program, and established a modern governmental bureaucracy.

mixed economy An economic system that combines both publicly and privately owned enterprises.

mixed regime A nation in which the various branches of government represent social classes.

modernization Synonymous with the idea of national development, it is thought that a nation's ability to modernize correlates positively with its ability to establish and maintain democracy.

monarchism A system based on the belief that political power should be concentrated in one person (for example, a king) who rules by decree.

Monroe Doctrine A status quo international policy laid down by U.S. President James Monroe, who pledged the United States to resist any attempts by outside powers to alter the balance of power in the American hemisphere.

moral relativism The idea that all moral judgments are inherently subjective and therefore not valid for anybody but oneself; the belief that no single opinion on morality is any better than another.

mosaic society A society characterized by a large degree of sociocultural diversity (often found in African and Latin American nations) that can pose significant barriers to the nation's development.

most-favored-nation status Nondiscriminatory tariff treatment to all states participating in an international system of reciprocal trade agreements.

MP In Great Britain, a member of Parliament.

multinational corporation (MNC) A company that conducts substantial business in several nations.

mutual assured destruction (MAD) Theory that equal numbers of nuclear weapons on opposing sides will deter either side's use of them.

National assembly Focal point of France's bicameral legislative branch that must approve all laws.

national interest The aims of policies that help a nation to maintain or increase its power and prestige.

nationalism The collective feelings of identity, loyalty, and shared values held by the citizens of a nation-state; nationalism manifests itself in patriotic sentiment, a willingness to sacrifice for the national interest, and support of national policies.

national security Protection of a country from external and internal enemies.

national self-determination The right of a nation to choose its own government.

nation-building The process by which inhabitants of a given territory—irrespective of ethnic, religious, or linguistic differences—come to identify with symbols and institutions of their nation state.

nation-state A geographically defined community administered by a government.

NATO The North Atlantic Treaty Organization, a military alliance (founded in 1949) consisting of the United States, Great Britain, Canada, Germany, France, Italy, Greece, Turkey, Portugal, Norway, Belgium, Denmark, the Netherlands, Iceland, and Luxembourg; its principal aim has been to prevent Soviet aggression in Europe.

Nazism A totalitarian political order characterized by racism, militarism, and ruthless use of police terror to achieve its goals.

new science of politics The eighteenth-century concept that political institutions could be arranged to produce competent government while preventing tyranny from developing out of an overconcentration of power.

no-confidence vote In parliamentary governments, a legislative vote that the sitting government must win in order to remain in power.

nomenklatura The Soviet Communist party's system of controlling all important administrative appointments, thereby ensuring the support and loyalty of those who managed day-to-day affairs.

Nonproliferation Treaty An international agreement, drafted in 1968, not to aid nonnuclear nations in acquiring nuclear weapons; it was not signed by France, China, and other nations actively seeking to build these weapons.

oligarchy A form of authoritarian government in which a small group of powerful individuals wields absolute power.

OPEC The Organization of Petroleum Exporting Countries—a cartel established in 1961 that since 1973 has successfully manipulated the worldwide supply of and price for oil, with far-reaching consequences for the world economy and political structure.

Outer Space Treaty An international agreement, signed by the United States and the Soviet Union, that bans the introduction of military weapons into outer space, prohibits the extension of national sovereignty in space, and encourages cooperation and sharing of information about space research.

Palestine Liberation Organization (PLO) Umbrella organization for Arab groups dedicated to the establishment of a Palestinian state on land recovered from Israel.

Pamyat An ultra-national, fascist, anti-Semitic political organization within Russia.

parliamentary system A system of democratic government in which authority is concentrated in the legislative branch, which selects a prime minister and cabinet officers who serve as long as they have majority support in the parliament.

partiinost The spirit of sacrifice, enthusiasm, and unquestioning devotion required of Communist party members.

Party Congress The highest Soviet political body, which met every five years. It supposedly represented the party membership but actually served to legitimize the policies of the ruling elite.

patron-client relations A form of political participation, most often found in developing countries, in which a hierarchical system of influential persons obtain benefits in return for votes, payoffs, or political power bases.

peer group A group of people who are similar in age and characteristics.

perestroika Term given to Mikhail Gorbachev's various attempts to restructure the Soviet economy while not completely sacrificing its socialist character.

perestroika-**first model** A theory of national development that emphasizes that liberalizing, market-oriented reforms should be undertaken before political reforms are attempted.

personal motives Any person's ambition, pride, and self-interest, which in a political context can be used to provide a personal stake in preventing other officeholders from upsetting the balance of power.

Petition of Right An act, passed by the English Parliament in 1628, that established due process of law and strictly limited the monarch's powers of taxation.

philosopher-kings Wise philosophers who govern Plato's ideal city in *The Republic*.

plebiscite A vote by an entire community on some specific issue of public policy.

pluralists Theorists who believe that in any large democracy, the political system is decentralized and institutionally fragmented and that therefore control of the power structure is possible only by single-issue coalitions in confined areas of special interest.

police powers Powers of states to maintain the internal peace and order, provide for education, and generally safeguard the people's health, safety, and welfare.

Politburo A small clique that formed the supreme decision-making body in the Soviet Union. Its members often belonged to the Secretariat and were ministers of key governmental departments as well.

political action committees (PACs) Groups organized to raise campaign funds in support of or in opposition to specific candidates.

political apathy Lack of interest in political participation.

political correctness controversy A debate regarding the correctness of radical egalitarian theory which dominated American academic life during the early 1990s.

political efficacy The ability to participate meaningfully in political activities, usually because of one's education, social background, and sense of self-esteem.

political party Any group of individuals who agree on some or all aspects of public policy and organize to place their members in control of the national government.

political penetration Promotion of economic development through road and bridge construction and telephone line installation in order to create a more integrated national economy.

political realism The philosophy that power is the key variable in all political relationships and should be used pragmatically and prudently to advance the national interest; policies are judged good or bad on the basis of their effect on national interests, not on their morality.

political socialization The process by which members of a community are taught the basic values of their society and prepared for the duties of citizenship.

politico A legislator who follows the will of constituents on issues that are most important to them and exercises personal judgment in areas that are less important to constituents or are fundamentally important to the national welfare.

politics The process by which a community selects rulers and empowers them to make decisions, takes action to attain common goals, and reconciles conflicts within the community.

power The capacity to influence or control the behavior of persons and institutions, whether by persuasion or by coercion.

power enhancement goals A foreign policy aimed at increasing power relative to other states.

power maintenance goals A foreign policy aimed at preventing other nations from increasing relative power.

prefects In France, the heads of major governmental agencies.

presidential system A democratic form of government in which the chief executive is chosen by separate election, serves a fixed term, and has powers carefully separated from those of the other branches of government.

prior restraint The legal doctrine that the government does not have the power to restrain the media from publication except in cases of dire national emergency.

private interest groups Groups organized to advance the self-interest of their members.

privatization An economic policy by which a government ends state ownership of an industry or industries, allowing them to become privately owned, competitive enterprises.

professional participation Engaging in the least common and most demanding political activities, such as a paid political position or elective office.

proletariat In Marxist theory, the working class.

propaganda The use of mass media to create whatever impression is desired among the general population and to influence thoughts and activities toward desired ends.

proportional representation Any political structure under which seats in the legislature are allocated to each party based on the percentage of the popular vote each receives.

public good The shared beliefs of a political community as to what goals government ought to attain (for example, to achieve the fullest possible measure of security, prosperity, equality, liberty, or justice for all citizens).

public interest groups Groups that promote causes they believe will benefit society as a whole.

public opinion A view held by citizens that influences the decisions and policies of government officials.

public opinion polling Canvassing citizens for their views.

purge The elimination of all rivals to power through mass arrests, imprisonment, exile, and murder, often directed at former associates and their followers who have (or are imagined to have) enough influence to be a threat to the ruling elite.

race norming A manner of scoring standardized tests, usually utilized for hiring purposes, which produces a result based both on the number of questions answered correctly and a person's race. Its purpose is to help assure that persons of different race are guaranteed equal and fair results.

random selection Polling method that involves canvassing people at random from the population.

recall Direct voting to remove an elected official from office.

rectification In Maoist China, the elimination of all purported capitalist traits, such as materialism and individualism.

referendum A vote through which citizens may directly repeal an action taken by the legislature.

rehabilitation Education, training, and social conditioning aimed at encouraging imprisoned criminals to become normal productive members of society when they are released.

Reign of Terror In the French Revolution, the mass executions, ordered by Maximilien Robespierre and his Committee of Public Safety, of all persons whose political outlook differed from their utopian ideal.

retribution The punishment of criminals on the ground that they have done wrong and deserve to suffer.

revolution A fundamental change in the political and social institutions of a society, often accompanied by violence, cultural upheaval, and civil war.

revolution of rising expectations A revolution achieved through development that Third World nations experience as they emulate First and Second World successes.

revolutionary communism The ideology that the capitalist system must be smashed by a violent uprising by the working class and replaced with public ownership and a government-controlled economic system.

right to revolution John Locke's theory that when governmental actions undermine the essential rights of life, liberty, and property, citizens have a right to revolt and replace the government with one that will rule correctly.

right-wing dictatorship An authoritarian regime, commonly military, that resists social reforms and maintains the current distribution of wealth and power. Such regimes tend to be pro-Western and anticommunist and to rely on secret police or military force to stay in control.

rule of law The concept that the power and discretion of government and its officials ought to be restrained by a supreme set of neutral rules that prevent arbitrary and unfair action by government.

"salami tactics" The methods used by V. I. Lenin to divide his opponents into small groups that could be turned against one another and easily overwhelmed.

Seabed Treaty An international agreement that forbids the establishment of nuclear weapons on the ocean floor beyond the 12-mile territorial limit.

second stage of communism In Marxist theory, a utopian classless society in which individual fulfillment and social cooperation and harmony are achieved and from which war has been entirely eliminated.

Second World The Communist states.

Secretariat The main decision-making body of the Soviet Communist party, second only to the Politburo in power, which exercise complete control over the entire party organization.

sedition The fomenting of revolution.

separation of powers The organization of government into distinct areas of legislative, executive, and judicial functions, each responsible to different constituencies with their own powers and responsibilities.

simple majority The largest bloc of voters in an election.

Six-Day War 1967 war between Arab states (Syria, Jordan, and Egypt) and Israel.

SLBMs Submarine-launched ballistic missiles.

Social Democratic party The more liberal of the two major political parties in Germany.

socialism An ideology favoring collective and government ownership over individual or private ownership.

solicitor In Great Britain, an attorney who can prepare court cases and draw up contracts and other legal documents but cannot plead cases or become a judge.

sovereignty A government's capacity to assert supreme power successfully in a political state.

spoils system In politics, the granting of government jobs to supporters, friends, and associates of the political figures in power.

Star Chamber Historically, a British court whose jurisdiction was extended to allow the king arbitrarily to punish anyone who disobeyed a royal decree.

state-building The creation of political institutions capable of exercising authority and allocating resources effectively within a nation.

state of nature The condition of human beings before the creation of a social code of behavior and collective techniques to control normal human impulses.

statesman A politician in a position of authority who possesses exceptional political skills, practical wisdom, and concern for the public good and whose leadership has a significant positive effect on society.

state-sponsored terrorism Terrorism supported by governments.

state terrorism Usually violent methods used by a government's own security forces to intimidate and coerce its own people.

status quo strategy A national policy of maintaining the existing balance of power through collective security agreements, diplomacy, and negotiation, as well as through "legitimizing instruments" such as international law and international organizations.

Strategic Arms Reduction Treaty (START) A treaty negotiated between the United States and the former Soviet Union which limited strategic nuclear weapons.

Strategic Defense Initiative A space-based antiballistic missile system.

stratified sampling A manner of polling in which participants are chosen on the basis of age, income, socioeconomic backbround, and the like so that the sample mirrors the larger population; the opposite of random selection.

subversion The attempt to undermine a government, often using outside assistance.

subversive terrorism Terrorism that originates within society and is directed against the state; usually separatist or ideological.

Suez Crisis In 1956, Israel, having been denied passage through the canal since 1950 and having suffered repeated border raids from Egypt, invaded Egypt. Intervention by the UN emergency force brought an armistice.

Supreme Soviet The legislative branch of the government of the former Soviet Union.

terms of trade Economic elements such as prices of industrial goods and agricultural products that determine the success or failure of a developing country's import and export capacities.

terrorism Political activity that relies on violence or the threat of violence to achieve its ends.

theocracy A government based on religion and dominated by the clergy.

Third World Collectively, the developing nations of Asia, Africa, and Latin America, most of which were once European colonies; Third World nations tend to be poor and densely populated.

Tiananmen Square massacre A student-led, pro-democracy protest that took place in China in spring 1989. The protest was violently crushed by the anti-democratic Chinese government.

totalitarianism A political system in which every facet of the society, the economy, and the government is tightly controlled by the ruling elite. Secret police terrorism and a radical ideology implemented through mass mobilization and propaganda are hallmarks of the totalitarian state's methods and goals.

tracking polls Repeated sampling of voters to assess shifts in attitudes or behavior over time.

traditional political scientists Theorists whose study of politics is based on examining fundamental and enduring questions.

traditional society A society that depends heavily on tradition for guidance in daily living; often characteristic of developing nations in the Third World.

true believer A person who is totally committed to the revolutionary movement and fanatical in his or her devotion to, and self-sacrifice for, the cause.

Truman Doctrine President Harry Truman's pledge of U.S. support for any free people threatened with revolution by an internal armed minority or with outside aggression.

trustee theory of representation The theory that elected officials should be leaders, making informed choices in the interest of their constituencies.

tutelage The system of central bureaucratic supervision of all local decisions found in a unitary system of government (for example, France).

tyranny of the majority The political situation in which a dominant group uses its control of the government to abuse the rights of minority groups.

unconventional participation Political activity that is legal but considered inappropriate by a majority of citizens.

Union Treaty An agreement proposed by President Mikhail Gorbachev during his last months in power that would have given the republics more political power at the expense of the central government. It was rendered moot by the collapse of the Soviet Union.

unitary system System in which the government may choose to delegate affairs to local government.

United Nations Emergency Force (UNEF) Multinational peacekeeping force established by the UN in 1956.

United Nations Interim Force in Lebanon (UNIFL) The multinational peacekeeping force established by the UN in 1978 to facilitate the withdrawal of Israeli troops from southern Lebanon, restore Lebanese security, and ensure the return of sovereignty to the Lebanese government.

utopia Any visionary system embodying perfect political and social order.

utopian socialists Individuals who believed that public ownership of property could be effectively accomplished and could solve most important political problems.

war by misperception Armed conflict that results when two nations fail to perceive each other's true intentions accurately.

war crimes Crimes committed during warfare that constitute gross violations of the generally accepted rules of war.

war of escalation In an armed conflict, the movement from fighting on a relatively local and limited scale to all-out warfare, usually initiated when the underdog of the moment choses to increase its military forces, rather than lose, until both sides have committed their total capabilities.

Warsaw Pact A military alliance between the Soviet Union and its satellite states, created in 1955, that established a unified military command and allowed the Soviet army to maintain large garrisons within the satellite states, ostensibly to defend them from outside attack.

watchdog role The power of the legislature periodically to review executive branch compliance with legislative actions. In the United

States, congressional committees carry out this function; in Great Britain, the "question hour" in Parliament serves this function.

Weimar Republic the constitutional democracy founded in Germany at the end of World War I by a constitutional convention convened in 1919 at the city of Weimar; associated with a period of political and economic turmoil, it ended when Adolf Hitler came to power in 1933.

welfare state A state whose government is concerned with providing for the social welfare of its citizens and does so usually with specific public policies such as health insurance, minimum wages, and housing subsidies.

winner-take-all system System under which the candidate receiving the most votes wins.

workers' councils In Yugoslavia, groups popularly elected by the workers that exercise control over profits, plant management, and other economic and labor issues.

World Court Also known as the International Court of Justice (ICJ), the principal judicial organ of the United Nations; the Court is competent to hear any case brought before it by parties who voluntarily accept its jurisdiction.

Yom Kippur War The 1973 war that pitted Egypt and Syria against Israel.

Zionists Persons desirous of establishing and maintaining a Jewish national homeland in the biblical land of Palestine.

INDEX

589